D1594389

Fighting for the Speakership

PRINCETON STUDIES IN AMERICAN POLITICS

HISTORICAL, INTERNATIONAL, AND COMPARATIVE PERSPECTIVES

Ira Katznelson, Martin Shefter, and Theda Skocpol, Series Editors

A list of titles in this series appears at the back of the book.

Fighting for the Speakership

THE HOUSE AND THE RISE OF
PARTY GOVERNMENT

JEFFERY A. JENKINS
CHARLES STEWART III

PRINCETON UNIVERSITY PRESS
PRINCETON AND OXFORD

Copyright © 2013 by Princeton University Press

Published by Princeton University Press, 41 William Street, Princeton,
New Jersey 08540
In the United Kingdom: Princeton University Press, 6 Oxford Street,
Woodstock, Oxfordshire OX20 1TW
press.princeton.edu

All Rights Reserved

Library of Congress Cataloging-in-Publication Data

Jenkins, Jeffery A.
Fighting for the speakership : the House and the rise of party
government / Jeffery A. Jenkins, Charles Stewart III.
p. cm. — (Princeton studies in American politics : historical,
international, and comparative perspectives)
Includes bibliographical references and index.
ISBN 978-0-691-11812-3 (hardback) — ISBN 978-0-691-15644-6 (pbk.)
1. United States. Congress. House—Speakers—
History.   2. Political parties—United States—History.
I. Stewart, Charles Haines.   II. Title.
JK1411.J45 2012
328.73'0762—dc23   2012010959

British Library Cataloging-in-Publication Data is available

This book has been composed in Sabon

1 3 5 7 9 10 8 6 4 2

CONTENTS

ILLUSTRATIONS

❧

TABLES

❦

ABBREVIATIONS

Frequently cited congressional publications and newspapers are abbreviated in the text as follows:

AA	*Albany Argus*
Annals	*Annals of Congress*
ASP	*American State Papers*
BG	*Boston Globe*
CG	*Congressional Globe*
CR	*Congressional Record*
CT	*Chicago Tribune*
HJ	*House Journal*
LAT	*Los Angeles Times*
NYEP	*New York Evening Post*
NYH	*New York Herald*
NYJC	*New York Journal of Commerce*
NYT	*New York Times*
NYTrib	*New York Tribune*
RE	*Richmond Enquirer*
Register	*Register of Debates*
WP	*Washington Post*

PREFACE

❧

This book both tells a story and uses that story to explore an institutional feature of legislatures that has heretofore gone unappreciated in political science: the organizational cartel. The story is about how the election of the Speaker of the House of Representatives has evolved over the past two centuries from an ad hoc proceeding devoid of partisan structure to a ritualized proceeding that seals near-monopoly control over the tools of lawmaking by the majority party. Stated in terms of a single question, the story asks, how did we get from the world of the first Speaker, Frederick Muhlenberg, to the world of the current Speaker, John Boehner?

This story forms the structure on which a larger, more abstract argument is made: that the history of how speakership elections developed was propelled forward by a desire to establish an *organizational cartel* in the House. An organizational cartel is a device through which the majority party asserts exclusive control over the speakership and other top offices in order to achieve three goals: to control House patronage, distribute authority among important factions of the majority party, and influence the agenda-setting apparatus of the House. This last goal suggests both theoretical and empirical affinity with the *procedural cartel* championed by Gary Cox and Mathew McCubbins (1993, 2005). Needless to say, we have not chosen our label randomly.

As our families, colleagues, and editor have often reminded us, this book has been more than a dozen years in the making, if we trace its origins to the first working papers that went into it. What took us so long? Part of an honest answer is that we were sometimes distracted by other projects, but those distractions probably only added a few months, maybe a year, to the book's gestation period. The real answer is that the book project itself transmogrified after we had signed our contract with Princeton University Press in 2002 and began to write the book in earnest.

Once we shifted gears from writing a series of related papers and articles to writing a book with a unified argument, it became obvious that our original ideas about how antebellum speakership fights fit together needed revision. What originally drew our attention to speakership elections was the spectacle of speakership battles that stretched over days, weeks, and even months. Modern political scientists long for a "hung" presidential nominating convention. We had a topic that was almost as good: a series of hung speakership elections. Very little has been written about these episodes by employing the tools of modern social science; this seemed to be fertile ground to till.

Because these hung speakership contests, upon first glance, seemed to share some of the structure of modern parliamentary politics, it was natural to jump in, armed with modern theories of social science, to explain their dynamics. At the very least, they seemed like classic examples of chaotic decision making under pure majority rule, which was the setting in which they occurred. It also seemed likely that these episodes should share qualities with bargaining over portfolios in parliamentary systems, and thus would be ripe to explain in light of work by Michael Laver and Kenneth Shepsle (1990, 1994, 1996).

However, as we delved deeper into the stories of speakership battles, we discovered other things. Some were even more interesting than the speakership battles that had initially drawn us to the project. But even within the confines of telling how Speakers were elected before the Civil War, it became obvious that we would also have to understand how elections for other House officers, such as the Clerk and the Printer, proceeded during the same era. One reason is that in trying to understand why the House moved from voting for Speakers by using a secret ballot to using *viva voce* (public) voting in 1839, we had to first understand parallel fights that erupted over electing the Printer. That was our first indication that the antebellum speakership was just part of an intricate puzzle related to the organization of the House. We could not tell the story of electing Speakers without also telling the intertwining story of electing Clerks and Printers.

We later came to realize that the larger puzzle of officer elections was interesting because party leaders used these elections in the service of party building. Therefore, we concluded that in order to frame these antebellum elections, we had to expand our conceptual reach and move beyond the inward-looking theories of legislative coalition building in order to incorporate more outward-looking theories about the construction of mass political parties.

In time we discovered that the antebellum speakership was part of a *matryoshka* nesting doll. As conceived by Martin Van Buren and other architects of the Second Party System, the Speaker, Printer, and Clerk should nest inside a larger congressional party apparatus, with committees nesting inside the Speaker. In addition, the congressional party apparatus should nest within a larger national party organization. The outermost doll should be the president of the United States.

Thus, this project first expanded because it had to link the internal organizational politics of the House with the nationwide political ambitions of party leaders. However, once we had gained some control over the antebellum organizational politics of the House, we then discovered that ending the story at the Civil War was like washing your face after a week of hiking the Appalachian Trail and not taking a shower—something seemed incomplete.

The incompleteness came in recognizing that the organization of the House during the Civil War Congresses marked an inflection point in the history of the chamber. That is, with the election of Schuyler Colfax as Speaker in 1865, the House settled into a pattern of electing House officers that was essentially the same as today. As a result of this recognition, we anticipated dashing off a final chapter that quickly dealt with organizational politics of the House from then to the present. However, we quickly encountered two roadblocks to the swift completion of this task.

First, after reading newspaper accounts of the caucus meetings that nominated Speaker candidates after 1865, we came to realize that protracted struggles over the speakership did not end in 1865—they were only relocated to the caucuses. So this only pushed our antebellum research into a new location. The story was not over. Second, as we started to account for nomination politics after the Civil War, we recognized that our story intersected in profound ways with the advent of the "Reed Rules" and with the model of legislative organization that Cox and McCubbins have used to demonstrate the logic and power of Reed's system. It was clear to us that the question of "why Reed and not an earlier Speaker" could best be answered by saying, "earlier Speakers could not count on controlling the floor and the committees, which is necessary for his system to work." This, in turn, required us to consider, what was this thing that Reed relied on?

Our answer, the organizational cartel, became the conceptual framework upon which it was logical to hang the complete narrative. This required a return to the complete narrative, so that the story that progresses from Muhlenberg to Boehner can be told in light of this new framing device.

Despite the fact that this book has taken more than a decade to complete, we could have spent an equal amount of time exploring the questions that our analysis raises about the Senate, the American party system, state legislatures, parliaments in a comparative context, and, indeed, all legislatures in general. We have put down some markers about these topics in chapter 10, but for the sake of everyone involved, we have decided to declare victory and withdraw. Those other questions will occupy some of our time in the future. We especially hope it will occupy the time of many other scholars in the future, including those who believe our framing device is nonsense. Our legacy, we hope, will be that scholars and other observers of legislative politics will no longer take the organization of the House of Representatives— nor of any other legislature at any level of government—for granted.

A project this big accumulates debts along the way. It is traditional to acknowledge these debts in the preface. We do so here with trepidation that we have left someone out. Among the research assistants who have contributed to this effort are Deborah Dryer, Donald Gordon, and Stephen Douglas Windsor. This project has been aided by funding from the Dirksen Center; the Dean of Humanities, Arts, and Social Sciences at MIT; the Workshop in Politics, Economics, and Law at the University of Virginia; and the Kenan

Sahin Distinguished Professorship fund. Craig Goodman, Greg Koger, Eric Schickler, Randy Strahan, and Greg Wawro provided critical feedback on early chapters as the project got off the ground. Ira Katznelson offered sage advice about the structure of the manuscript and the integration of historical and statistical analyses. And, of course, Chuck Myers, our editor at Princeton University Press, provided considerable encouragement (and showed colossal patience!) as the manuscript took and changed shape.

As our writing was drawing to a close, eight individuals provided invaluable feedback that helped us further focus the manuscript and see the bigger picture. John Aldrich, Richard Bensel, Charles Kromkowski, and Nolan Mc-Carty graciously agreed to meet with us for two days in Charlottesville, Virginia, in the summer of 2009, to help tear apart the first completed manuscript. We benefited immeasurably from their counsel, although they will recognize that we did not always take their advice. (We did take a lot of it, however.) Shortly thereafter, Michael Holt and David Mayhew furnished us with extensive comments that, among other things, helped us get the history right at various points in our narrative. Finally, once the manuscript was 99.44 percent complete, two anonymous reviewers provided us with a set of detailed, thoughtful comments that forced us to sharpen our theoretical argument and better emphasize the role of the organizational cartel in the House's political development.

We wish we could say that with the completion of this volume, we are now able to devote more time to our patient families, who have had to put up with our late nights of working on this manuscript. Alas, as with most rewarding research projects, we find there is now more to do, not less. Still, we could not have completed this book without the support and forbearance of our spouses, Lisa Milligan and Kathy Hess. We thank them from the bottom of our hearts.

Introduction

The U.S. House of Representatives is organized by whichever political party holds a majority of its seats. This fact has consequences. Controlling the organization of the House means that the majority party decides who will preside over its deliberations, who will set the policy agenda, and who will dominate the workhorses of the chamber: the standing committees. Organizing the House does not mean the majority party will win all battles, but it does give the party a leg up in virtually any question that gets considered by that body.

There is nothing in the Constitution that rests the organization of the House in the hands of the majority party. The practice has evolved over the past two centuries to the point that party organization of the House has become routinized. Ahead of each election, the two parties announce that they will meet in caucus on a certain date, just after the election, to choose not just their own leaders but also their nominees for the leadership positions of the *chamber*, notably the Speaker, as well as other officers, such as the Clerk. The party caucuses also select the committee slates, including the chairs. When the new House finally convenes, the decisions determined in the caucus are presented to the full House by the caucus leaders, where they are ratified either by party-line votes (as in the case of the speakership election) or by unanimous consent (as in the case of committee slates, including the chairs).

It was not always this way. For the first half century after the nation's founding, it would be a stretch to say that parties controlled the organization of the House at all; it would be a lie to say that the organization of the House was routine. Although the Speaker and other officers who were chosen to lead the first several Congresses were known by contemporaries to be dedicated Federalists and Republicans, they were not nominated by Federalist or Republican caucuses. When caucuses arrived on the scene in the 1840s, their record was spotty. They sometimes settled on a nominee, sometimes not. Even when they did, the nomination often exhibited little weight on the final outcome. For example, anyone who was not physically present at the caucus meeting was under no obligation to support the nominee and was free to carry the fight onto the House floor. Thus, party caucuses *might* settle organizational matters, but they could also just be the first round of a fight that would spill out into the entire chamber.

Before the Civil War, struggle, contention, and deadlock over the organization of the House were common. Nearly one-third of all speakership contests from the founding of the Republic until the outbreak of the Civil War (13 of 41) took more than one ballot to resolve. At least twice, the minority party actually saw one of their own elected Speaker. Even the selection of subordinate officers could be contentious. During the same antebellum period, the House required multiple ballots to select its Clerk nine times and its Printer four times.

If the majority party did not routinely control the top officers of the House, why would we expect them to control the committees? Even though party caucuses and leaders had a role in determining committee lists, the composition of important congressional committees frequently favored the minority party well into the nineteenth century (Canon and Stewart 1995, 2001; Canon, Nelson, and Stewart 2002).

The first Speaker, Frederick Muhlenberg, was selected through an informal process that lacked any trappings of formal party politics, and he initially lacked the authority to appoint committees. Modern Speakers, such as Newt Gingrich, Dennis Hastert, and John Boehner, are recognized primarily as partisan agents who are expected (normatively and empirically) to use the formal levers of power in the House to further their parties' legislative goals. The standing committees are constructed by party-based "committees on committees" that have increasingly used party loyalty as a major criterion in the distribution of prime committee assignments and chairmanships (Cox and McCubbins 1993; Dodd and Oppenheimer 2001; Aldrich and Rohde 2005; Sinclair 2005, 2006).

How did we move from the world of Muhlenberg to the world of Boehner? What difference did this evolution make for internal House politics, policy making, and the course of American political development? These are the questions that animate this book. At the empirical core is our account of how the majority party, formally constituted as the caucus sitting as a decision-making body, came to own the chief House officers, but especially the Speaker.[1] The empirical core of the book goes hand in hand with the theoretical core, which is to note that this "ownership" of the speakership

---

[1] We emphasize here, and throughout the book, the caucus as a formal decision-making body. In doing so, we remind the reader that scholars and legislators often use the term "caucus" in ways that may cause confusion. The first way is as an umbrella term for all who consider themselves to be members of the same "party in the legislature." In this sense, it is a synonym of "membership." The second way the term "caucus" is used is as an assembly of party members that has officers (even if elected only for one occasion) and that takes votes that are binding on its members. (For the moment, we leave unspecified the domain of issues over which votes are taken and the mechanism by which members are bound by those votes.) The latter sense of the term "caucus" is more formal and institutionalized than the former. Unless the context clearly indicates otherwise, when we discuss the caucus in this book, we have in mind the more institutionalized usage. The Republican preference for the term "conference" comes from the desire to distance themselves from the binding aspect of caucus practice. As our nar-

and other top offices was the focal point of an *organizational cartel* in which the House offices were used in the furtherance of majority party goals. These goals were of three types:

> first, to claim the patronage benefits that flowed from controlling the top House offices for the general benefit of the majority party, ultimately for the electoral advantage of the party;
> second, to garner favor with the various factions within the majority party, so that they had more to gain by supporting the party's leaders (who had been determined through a majority vote of the caucus) than by challenging those leaders in the larger arena of the House floor; and
> third, to bend the agenda-setting apparatus of the House in the direction of the majority party's policy aims.

This third goal suggests an overlap between the organizational cartel and the *procedural cartel* that Cox and McCubbins (1993, 2005) have identified as being at the heart of partisan power in the House. That is no accident. As Cox and McCubbins note, the existence of a procedural cartel—a coalition that controls agenda-setting power in the House—relies on an intraparty agreement about the election of the Speaker and the distribution of committee assignments. Our theoretical contribution is in showing that the organizational cartel on which the procedural cartel rests is itself endogenous. That is, an organizational cartel—a coalition that controls the selection of key House officers, including the Speaker, with certainty—did not emerge spontaneously; rather, it had to be *built*. Our empirical contribution is in showing how difficult it was for the majority party in the House to coordinate and become such an organizational cartel. While political entrepreneurs envisioned the construction of such an organizational cartel in the decades before the Civil War, a host of political forces delayed the majority party's ability to consistently organize the chamber until the latter part of the nineteenth century.

Our larger theoretical agenda aside, the fact remains that political scientists and historians have shown little attention to how the Democratic and Republican Parties reached the point that they both now rely on self-contained, routinized procedures to manage—wholly within the caucuses —the struggle over who will be elected Speaker. Therefore, we proceed inductively by first asking about the series of battles that helped establish the caucus as the stage on which the fight for the speakership was conducted.

Party caucuses first arose in the mid-1790s in an attempt to bind party members on the critical organizational votes that are the first order of busi-

---

rative in chapters 8 and 9 demonstrate, for all practical purposes, this is a distinction without a difference.

ness when a new Congress convenes (Harlow 1917; Risjord 1992).[2] Yet they were only sporadically employed in the earliest years of the Republic and largely fell into disuse in the early years of the nineteenth century.

The role of the majority party caucus in the formal organization of the House reentered regular practice later in the nineteenth century. The grip of the majority party caucus on organizational matters tightened twice, at moments when the political stakes were high and party leaders saw control of the Speaker and other senior House officers as central to achieving their political goals. The first instance was during the early years of the Second Party System, when Martin Van Buren and his followers recognized that the formal leadership of the House possessed valuable resources for the creation of effective mass political parties in the United States. The second instance was during the Civil War, when efforts to effect a cross-party organization in the prior Congress nearly backfired for the majority Republicans.

These were two critical moments in the history of the House's organization that resulted in the majority party caucus claiming an enhanced role in determining who would sit in the chair and who would dominate the committees. However, the influence of party on the House's organization did not grow monotonically. Rather, from the 1830s to the 1860s, the House often fought bitterly over who the Speaker and other officers would be, with the party caucus playing a variable role in determining the final outcome. The primary reason why the majority party failed to guarantee its predominance in organizing the House after the 1830s is that Van Buren and his followers also unwittingly created a visible platform on which anti- and proslavery forces could test their strength in national politics. This platform was constructed by a House rules change in 1838 that for the first time made the ballot for Speaker public. (Previously, the balloting for all House officers, including Speaker, had been secret.) The rules change was instituted to give party leaders reliable information about who had supported the party nominee for Speaker and other officers. Before long, it was transformed into a mechanism for the *ultras* on both sides of the slavery debate to observe who was voting for nominees considered to be on the "right" side of the issue—not at all what the Van Burenites had in mind.

The modern Republican Party, starting with the second Civil War Congress, established the party caucus once and for all as the only legitimate venue for the resolution of intraparty divisions over who would be Speaker. The utility of settling internecine disputes in caucus and then presenting a united front on the floor was quickly recognized by the minority Democrats, who followed suit by settling on their Speaker nominee in caucus, too.

[2] At the same time, congressional caucuses (made up of party members of *both* the House and Senate) were major players in determining presidential nominations. These congressional nominating caucuses were a staple of the First Party System and lasted through 1824.

The Civil War Congresses were unique in American history because of the exclusion of the South from the body. The majority Republicans were a purely regional party by construction and highly cohesive. The minority Democrats were also Northern, but not by construction. After the South returned to the House and Reconstruction came to an end, the two parties became more evenly matched numerically. They also became more ideologically diverse. These two factors—narrow party margins and ideologically divided parties—had been the primary ingredients that fueled the intense battles over the speakership before the Civil War. And yet, unlike the antebellum era, the parties after the Civil War managed to keep their fights to themselves and prevent their ideological divisions from spilling out onto the House floor. As a consequence, when Thomas Brackett Reed (R-Maine) became Speaker in 1889, the common understanding in the House, bolstered by more than two decades of experience, was that the party caucuses were cohesive on organizational matters.[3] The imposition of the Reed Rules in 1890 supported the development of tools to help the majority party control the legislative agenda and guide the course of policy making in the House. The regime set in place by the Reed Rules—which transformed the majority party into a procedural cartel and established the "modern structure of agenda power in the House" (Cox and McCubbins 2005, 50)—was nearly a century in the making.

The centrality of the party caucus for the organization of the House was demonstrated in the two most important challenges to majority party authority in the twentieth century. The first was the revolt against Speaker Joseph Cannon (R-Ill.) in 1909. In that case, the insurgent faction in the majority Republican Party refused the offer by Cannon to knock him out of the Speaker's chair, which was an important recognition that when it came to personnel matters, the caucus was still king. The second was the revolt by progressive Republicans at the opening of the 68th Congress (1923), when, in a dispute over the rules, 20 progressives refused to vote for Frederick Gillett (R-Mass.) for Speaker. In the ensuing three-day standoff, there was never any doubt about whether the insurgents might join with the Democrats to organize the chamber—all the negotiating was internal to the Republican Party and centered on the majority leader, Nicholas Longworth (R-Ohio).

Finally, it is significant that in the middle part of the twentieth century, when the most dominant interparty *policy* coalition ever to walk the halls of Capitol Hill—the Conservative Coalition—was at the height of its power, disputes over who would be Speaker were always settled within the confines of the two party caucuses.

---

[3] Our primary source for the partisan affiliation of House members across time is Martis (1989). At times, we will supplement the Martis party codes with other party data, notably that of Dubin (1998).

Thus, the modern Speaker sits at the top of two powerful institutions: the House of Representatives *and* the legislative party of which she or he is the leader. The former flows directly from the latter. The core narrative of this book explains how this happened and explores why the role of Speaker-as-party-leader is an institution that took as long to build as a small cathedral.

THE WIDER IMPLICATIONS OF SPEAKER-AS-PARTY-LEADER

The first contribution to scholarship this book makes is providing a comprehensive accounting of how Speakers have been elected in the U.S. House of Representatives from 1789 to the present. In our view, the fights over how the House would be organized, especially the fights before the Civil War, are among the most consequential turning points in American political history. They should be better known by students of Congress, parties, American history, and American political development. Therefore, telling the history of these conflicts fills a serious hole in our understanding of how Congress evolved into the institution it is today. We hope that by laying out these conflicts and suggesting how they fit into the larger politics of the age, we will entice others to pick up where we have left off.

Yet the history we recount in this book does more than plug an important empirical gap in our understanding of how Congress evolved. Studying how organizational politics developed in the House allows us to encounter more general themes about Congress and its role in the American political system. Here we mention two that particularly stand out: (1) the construction of mass political parties in the early nineteenth century and (2) the role that political parties play in guiding the agenda of Congress today.

The House and the building of mass political parties

In its early years, the American polity was an elite game by design. In time, mass politics came to dominate American politics at the national level. The circumvention of the original elite polity owes its initial success to Martin Van Buren, who was the brains behind the rise of Andrew Jackson and his transformation of American political life. It is an oft-told tale of how Jackson, denied the presidency in 1824, even though he won the most popular votes, connected with the Little Magician, who masterminded a plan that altered the American electoral landscape. This occurred when a network of pro-Jackson forces gained control of a critical set of state legislatures, which in turn changed the laws that governed how presidential electors were selected. Electors were now to be chosen directly, through the popular vote of a state's electorate, rather than indirectly, through the vote of the state legislatures. This reform shifted the electoral terrain onto ground that Jackson's followers were more adept at holding. This, in turn, led to a rapid democratization of American politics, as voters gladly took to the polls when they knew their votes would have a direct impact on choosing the next president.[4]

An important part of this story of early party building is often overlooked. The biggest obstacle that Van Buren faced in establishing a new interregional party was not the political elites who dominated the choice of presidential electors in the states, but the threat posed by the introduction of slavery into national politics, which was highlighted by the proposal to admit Missouri to the Union in 1820 (Silbey 2002, 41–42).[5] Dealing with the threat represented by virulent regionalism was *the* major project of the party builders during the Jacksonian era, even bigger than electing Jackson to the White House. This was a threat that just would not go away, as antislavery advocates had a knack for introducing slavery into national politics at the popular level, even as mainstream political elites were trying to mold institutions, especially parties, into transregional alliances.

Consequently, the Jacksonians faced two great organizational obstacles. The first was to create a robust political network, truly national in scope, that could deliver the votes on a regular basis. The second was to do this in a way that suppressed regional sentiments, especially those excited by slavery. How these two organizational problems were addressed already constitutes two well-trodden paths of American political history. The national partisan network was established by Van Buren and other Jacksonian leaders by a democratization and professionalization of the political process.[6] Parties became organizations that were open to all and were not driven by individual personalities or cliques. Success in the form of "spoils" of office— patronage-based positions emanating from control of the executive and the legislature—would be shared and distributed based on loyalty to the party (often to those who mobilized voters on Election Day) rather than on some form of elite-based social status. Moreover, the party would permeate the everyday life of citizens and build allegiances not only by direct spoils but also by the creation of various social institutions like clubs, festivals, parades, and barbecues.

To suppress slavery and other regional animosities, Van Buren and other party builders developed a set of complementary political institutions that would serve as circuit breakers to prevent problems from arising that might threaten the interregional arrangement.[7] A constant voicing of "party over

[4] On Van Buren's role in salvaging the political career of Andrew Jackson by masterminding the effort to revitalize the flagging organizational strength of what became the Democratic Party, see Remini (1959), Hofstadter (1969), and Aldrich (1995).

[5] For a general overview of the congressional politicking over Missouri, see Moore (1953) and Richards (2000, 52–82).

[6] See Hofstadter (1969) and Silbey (1992) for a more extensive overview.

[7] See Aldrich (1995, 127–35) for a more extensive overview.

its men" would be undergirded by sops to the South in the forms of a tacit "balance rule" for the joint admission of free and slave states (thereby providing the South with an effective veto in the Senate), a regional balancing of candidates on the presidential/vice presidential tickets, and a two-thirds rule for nominations in the newly created Democratic National Convention.[8]

Thus, the Jacksonian party system contained and channeled, but did not destroy, the material basis that created the deep regional animosities in the first place. The North and South developed in parallel as different (though linked) economic and political nations (Sellers 1991). The North developed into a vibrant, diversified economy that was increasingly integrated with Europe and Asia through a healthy international shipping trade. The South developed into a less vibrant, less diversified economy and was dependent on the North (and Europe, to some degree) for capital and markets for its agricultural commodities. While there was certainly trade and economic interdependence between the two regions, net wealth tended to flow North; when waves of immigrants voluntarily came to the United States, they almost always settled in the more promising cities of the North, even if they eventually set out on paths further west—to the *North*west.

And, of course, there was slavery, which introduced a host of economic, social, and political tensions between citizens of the two regions. There were always individuals in both regions who had pangs of conscience over chattel slavery, but it was long before these pangs became sufficient to ignite large-scale, mass political movements. At the level of popular sentiments, it was probably the economic advantage held by the South in menial labor that most rankled voters in the North.[9] As more economically rooted tensions grew and conscience-based opposition to slavery found its voice in the North, attempts to suppress the rights of Northern whites on issues related to slavery raised the temperature considerably (Freehling 1990, 287–352; Miller 1996; Jenkins and Stewart 2003a). To top things off politically, attentive citizens could not help but notice that the three-fifths apportionment clause in the Constitution required the (white) population of the North to grow significantly faster than that of the South, just for it to maintain its political influence in the House and in the Electoral College.[10]

The mounting and tangled regional tensions that slavery exacerbated eventually made the interregional bargains that underlay the two major national parties untenable. The bigger meltdown occurred within the Whig

---

[8] This two-thirds rule would come back to haunt Van Buren. In 1844, he sought the Democratic nomination for president but could only muster a bare majority in the convention. His opposition to an aggressive Texas annexation policy drew the ire of Southern Democrats, and eventually, after an extensive battle, James K. Polk (Tenn.), a fervent supporter of Texas annexation and former Speaker of the House, was nominated. See Silbey (2002, 2005).

[9] This argument is made most forcefully by Foner (1970).

[10] See Freehling (1990) and Richards (2000) for a discussion and analysis of the distorting effects of the three-fifths clause.

Party, which split into distinct regional blocs over the issue of slavery extension in the territories and, as a result, disintegrated nationally by the mid-1850s. This provided an opening for a wholly Northern party, the Republicans, to emerge, which ushered in the Third Party System.[11] The Republicans would increase their electoral showings throughout the late 1850s and eventually win the presidency in 1860 amid a delayed regional meltdown in the Democratic Party. These events will be described in detail later in the book.

Missing from most accounts of antebellum party building is a serious understanding of the role played by Congress, particularly the House of Representatives, in the fate of the party system. During the Jacksonian era, the congressional activities that have caught the eye of historians have largely involved the senators who were the most vocal on regional issues, whether they were for slavery or preservation of the Union.[12] In the series of events charting the transition from the Second to the Third Party Systems, the focus has been on conflicts in the West (such as "Bleeding Kansas"), physical violence in the halls of Congress (such as the caning of Charles Sumner), the ineptitude of President James Buchanan, the *Dred Scott* case, the election of Lincoln, and the secession crisis. Scholars have not entirely left Congress out of the story (e.g., Potter 1976; Morrison 1997), but by and large the Jacksonian party-building story and its eclipse by the Republican system has been one that is firmly situated within the "presidential synthesis" of American political history, and leaves Congress with a supporting role at most.

Antebellum party building cannot be fully understood without a close examination of House organization. Party development during the Second and Third Party Systems required two things: (1) achieving policy outputs and (2) securing patronage. In the Van Burenite conception of party government, key positions in the House's governing structure—chiefly the Speaker, but also the Clerk and Printer—played major roles in both regards. The Speaker staffed the standing committees and ruled on points of order in the chamber, actions that played a major role in determining the House's policy agenda. The Clerk and Printer controlled significant financial resources that could be used to underwrite important national partisan activities, such as the creation of partisan business and information networks.[13] Antebellum party leaders understood the value of controlling the House organization,

---

[11] The history of the mid-1850s was more complicated than this simplified story. For example, nativism became a significant issue and took the political system by storm, competing with slavery for the attention of both voters and political leaders. As a result, the nativist American Party emerged during this time to vie with the Republicans for the right to succeed the Whigs as the nation's second major party. See chapters 6 and 7 for a detailed discussion.

[12] Mayhew (2000) provides a thorough accounting of noticeable congressional actions throughout its history. The observations made here are based on an independent analysis of the database that forms the basis of much of Mayhew's book.

[13] The Clerk was also the de facto chamber leader at the opening of each new Congress (prior to the election of the Speaker). This will be an important factor in our subsequent analysis.

and a number of bitter fights over the various officer positions were waged. These battles, and the sense of what was at stake, form the bulk of this book. A thorough examination of these battles provides a new and interesting lens through which to view the dynamics of antebellum party building.

The Jackson/Van Buren party model was only moderately successful in the House. The Democratic membership was often poorly disciplined due to sectional distrust rooted in the slavery issue. These regional tensions invariably surfaced at the biennial organization of Congress, and, as a result, the important, subordinate, patronage-based officers (Clerk and Printer) occasionally fell into the hands of the opposition.

The unwillingness of the House rank and file to act consistently according to script was a critical sign—the canary in the coal mine—for those looking for signs of whether the clashing Northern and Southern factions could, in fact, coexist. The first major rift in the Van Buren/Jackson project occurred in the 34th Congress (1855–57) during the organization of the House when Northern antislavery representatives eventually banded together to elect Nathaniel Banks as Speaker—an act that was arguably the first formal success of the Republican Party and the beginning of the Third Party System.

The Civil War dramatically changed the hold that party caucuses had on the organization of the House and brought to fruition Martin Van Buren's view that the influence of political parties in legislatures should have an institutional grounding rather than being based on loyalty to individuals or sections. Certainly, by 1865, the transition was complete. Since then, even though party factions have tested the boundaries of the majority party caucus's ability to dictate how the House will be organized, victories by insurgents have been rare.

Stated another way, a strong party caucus, capable of unifying its members around the organization of the chamber as the first step in controlling policy, was a central element of Martin Van Buren's system of strong party government. An important question that emerges is why this aspect of Van Buren's system was so difficult to install. Related to this question is the observation that the modern parties in Congress seem to be the full embodiment of what Van Buren had in mind. If they are, then does the world led by Speakers Gingrich, Hastert, and Boehner represent the apotheosis of legislative party organization in the United States?

Party strength in Congress

A major theme in American political development is the ambivalent view American citizens have of political parties. Textbooks are full of ritual references to the Founders' worries about the "mischiefs of faction" (Federalist No. 10) and "the baneful effects of the spirit of party" (Washington's Farewell Address). In the modern day, parties fare no better. In the 2008 American National Election Study, for example, respondents were asked to rate 30 politically relevant groups (working-class people, big business, etc.) and institutions (Congress, the military, etc.), plus the two political parties, by using an instrument called a "feeling thermometer." (Like it sounds, a feeling thermometer asks respondents to report how much they like particular groups based on a 0–100 scale, with 0 being the most "cold" and 100 being the most "warm.") The average of the rating for the two parties on this 100-point scale (52.5) was below that of 24 of the groups and institutions and above only 6. The parties were more warmly regarded than Congress (52.1), Muslims (50.3), gay men and lesbians (49.4), the federal government in Washington (48.7), atheists (41.0), and illegal immigrants (39.4).[14] And yet the political party remains the single most important cue in guiding how citizens vote, evaluate new policies, and interpret the political world (e.g., Green, Palmquist, and Schickler 2002).

The prominence of political parties in the life of Congress has spawned the most contentious line of research within legislative studies over the past two decades. Party resurgence has been the talk of congressional scholars since the mid-1980s (e.g., Schlesinger 1985; Rohde 1989, 1991; Cox and McCubbins 1993; Aldrich 1995).[15] To these scholars, the clearest sign of partisan resurgence has been a steady rise in various objective measures of intraparty agreement and interparty disagreement on roll call votes since the late 1970s. To the public at large, the signs of resurgence have been the rise of party-based campaign operations; a renewed tendency to choose as party leaders individuals with a more ideological, less conciliatory approach to politics; and a willingness to impose a party-loyalty test in choosing the leaders of its committees (Dodd and Oppenheimer 2001; Aldrich and Rohde 2005; Sinclair 2005, 2006; Stewart 2011).

Explaining *why* parties seem so active has caused most of the current scholarly contention. Are parties more cohesive and "powerful" nowadays because their leaders are more likely to exercise the party whip? Or are leaders and party-based organs more prominent because party members are more likely to come from similar circumstances than in the past, and thus are more willing to be cohesive without a party whip?[16]

---

[14] The complete set of averages is as follows: working-class people (82.7), the military (79.6), Christians (77.1), middle-class people (76.4), whites (73.1), poor people (72.1), southerners (69.8), blacks (68.8), Catholics (67.4), Hispanics (65.3), Asian Americans (65.1), Jews (65.0), environmentalists (64.7), Israel (61.2), the U.S. Supreme Court (60.5) conservatives (60.3), rich people (57.3), feminists (56.6), Christian fundamentalists (56.3), labor unions (55.7), Hindus (55.3), liberals (54.7), people on welfare (54.4), big business (53.3), Congress (52.1), Muslims (50.3), gay men and lesbians (49.4), federal government in Washington (48.7), atheists (41.0), and illegal immigrants (39.4).

[15] An entire literature on "party decline" emerged in the 1970s and 1980s with a subsequent literature on the aforementioned "party resurgence" developing in the mid-1980s. For a short overview and analysis of these literatures, see Aldrich (1995, 14–18).

[16] These questions have sparked a flood of research over the last decade. See Krehbiel (1993) for the first direct explication of the competing perspectives. See Cox and McCubbins (2005) and Smith (2007) for a review of the relevant literature.

Two complementary literatures have dominated how contemporary scholars think about formal party influence in Congress—especially in the House of Representatives. The first, the "cartel" view of parties, has been articulated most fully by Gary Cox and Mathew McCubbins (1993, 2005). This theory starts with the premise that majority party members in the House recognize that the success of the party's legislative record is an important contributor to their reelection prospects. Legislative success is, in turn, a team effort. Thus, majority party members delegate to their party leaders, and other agents like committee chairs, the responsibility for charting a legislative agenda that results in policy outcomes consistent with the party's "brand name." Majority party leaders achieve these policy results not by "bossing" the rank and file in a brute way but by controlling and using the mechanisms of agenda control—that is, by "cartelizing" the agenda—to produce majority party–favored outcomes in a majority-rule institution.

Relevant to our argument, Cox and McCubbins discuss the internal operation of the party-based legislative cartel this way: "In the United States, the cartel ensures a near-monopoly on agenda-setting offices to the extent that it can control the relevant votes on the floor (on election of the speaker and the appointment of committees). To aid in controlling these floor votes, the cartel establishes an intracartel procedure to decide on the nominee for speaker and on a slate of committee appointments" (2005, 24n9). That "intracartel procedure" that allows the majority to secure the House organization, which Cox and McCubbins (1994) discuss at length elsewhere, is the party caucus.[17]

A second theory, termed the "conditional party government" (CPG) approach, was coined by David Rohde (1989, 1991). The idea behind CPG is that party power in the House is *conditional*—party caucuses will delegate to leaders greater latitude to achieve caucus goals only if party members' preferences are cohesive and polarized from those of the other party. Thus, at times like the present or the late nineteenth century—when the parties have relatively few internal divisions, are ideologically distinct, and are closely balanced numerically—majority party leaders will be given more authority by the majority rank and file. When the parties are divided—as they were in the mid-twentieth century (especially the Democrats)—the rank and file will withhold autonomous authority from leaders, which results in policy making in which the distinctive flavor of the majority party is less obvious.

Cox and McCubbins stress the relatively constant operation of party mechanisms across time, while Rohde stresses the variable latitude given to the formal components of partisan power. But each takes as given the im-

[17] Notably, Cox and McCubbins say, "[t]o the extent that membership in the majority party's caucus is valuable, it constitutes a bond, the posting of which stabilizes key features of the structure of the House and hence key features of the policy decisions made in the House" (1994, 218).

portance of putting formal party organizations at the center of explaining congressional behavior, which is in contrast to rival approaches that start with a deep skepticism about whether parties as formal institutions can have an independent influence on policy making (Krehbiel 1991, 1993, 1998). Both the cartel and CPG approaches take for granted the post–Reed Rules reality of the House of Representatives, in which the Rules Committee plays a potent role in structuring legislative outcomes and the caucuses operate as permanent institutions whose members ultimately decide how much agenda-setting authority is given to the current set of party leaders.

By focusing most of our attention in this book on how the House chose to elect its leaders before the Reed Rules, we are able to draw greater attention to the prior conditions that are necessary for institutionally based theories of party power to make sense in the U.S. Congress. Coordination among partisans does not just happen. The institutions of cooperation must be built. Party members must be comfortable that they know how the mechanisms will operate before they delegate significant authority to key partisan and institutional leaders. The majority's ability to act as an organizational cartel is a necessary condition for its development into a procedural cartel.

A Chronological Road Map

The remainder of the book presents a chronological account of organizational politics in the House from 1789 to the present. In this section we provide a brief overview of that account and highlight the important signposts that appear along the way.

It is convenient to divide the history we cover into five eras that empirically correspond to periods when organizational politics presented a common set of themes. Those periods are (roughly) 1789–1811, 1811–39, 1839–65, 1865–91, and 1891 to the present.

The first period, 1789–1811, represents the least institutionalized period of organizational politics. Although some historical accounts remark on the appearance of partisan caucuses in the 1790s and comment on the partisan flavor injected into the two speakerships during John Adams's administration (Jonathan Dayton [F-N.J.] and Theodore Sedgwick [F-Mass.]), Speakers gave relatively little weight to party (however construed) in overseeing the House, and the basic authority given to the Speaker to control debate and appoint committees was rarely used to programmatic ends. Consequently, the speakership was regarded as a somewhat minor prize among the rank and file and by those who might rise to the office. Four Speaker elections during the first 11 Congresses were multiballot affairs, not because the House was riven with deep partisan divisions but because politicking for the post was haphazard and personal factions and nascent party organizations were too weak to winnow down the field prior to the actual convening of the House. The lack of intense and lasting animosities over the choice of Speaker is evident in how none of the multiballot affairs went beyond three ballots. Thus, the repercussions of organizational jockeying tended to be minor.

We mark the beginning of the second period, 1811–39, with the appearance of Henry Clay (R-Ky.) in the House and his transformation of the speakership into an important national office worth fighting over. Clay's dominance of House politics is well known. He served as Speaker over three nonconsecutive terms—1811 to 1814, 1815 to 1820, and 1823 to 1825—and is credited with using the formal tools of the speakership, such as the right of recognition and the appointment of committees, to turn the House into a more effective legislative body.[18]

Less well known is how Clay ushered in a period in which organizational politics was ratcheted up to a new level. First, during the 1811–39 period when Clay was *not* Speaker, the fights were intense and often protracted. When Clay resigned in the middle of the 16th Congress (1820) to attend to business back home, his successor, John W. Taylor (R-N.Y.), was chosen in a four-day, 22-ballot affair. At the convening of the following Congress (17th) in 1821, Philip Barbour's (R-Va.) election took 12 ballots to resolve. When Taylor was elected at the start of the 19th Congress (1825), again replacing Clay, it took two ballots. Toward the end of this period John Bell (Jack.-Tenn.) was elected in a 10-ballot contest.

Second, not only were Speaker battles messy but elections for Clerk and Printer also became nasty. The increased competition over all the chamber offices was due to party leaders—and sometimes factional leaders within parties—realizing the value of these offices for larger political goals. Why the Speaker was important is obvious. Why the Clerk and Printer were important is less obvious to modern readers, until we understand the roles that these subordinate offices played in the nineteenth-century House. Deferring a detailed discussion of these offices to chapter 2, suffice it to say that party and factional leaders attempted to control these offices to their advantage, one consequence being that contention for these positions became volatile and often unpredictable.

Third, as a result, this period ends in 1839 with the House changing the rules about how House officers were elected: a secret ballot was replaced by a public roll call termed *viva voce* voting. Viva voce voting was first used to fill the vacant Clerk's position in the middle of the 25th Congress (1838) and was then made a permanent part of the rules in time to govern the convening of the 26th Congress (1839). The switch to a public roll call was fa-

[18] Much has been written about Clay and his role in the institutionalization of the House, both by augmenting the Speaker's role in guiding debate and in developing the standing committee system. See particularly Gamm and Shepsle (1989), Jenkins (1998), Stewart (2007), Strahan et al. (2000), and Strahan (2007).

vored by the leaders of the majority Democrats as a tool to enforce party regularity in the election of House officers, with the assumption that if House members could be observed voting for officers, they would be less likely to enter into cross-party coalitions in these elections.

The introduction of viva voce voting ushered in the third era of organizational politics, which lasted from 1839 to 1865. The viva voce mechanism worked as predicted for a few Congresses, but in the end it became one of the best examples of the Law of Unintended Consequences in the history of the House. If party leaders could now observe how the rank and file voted, so, too, could constituents and activists who cared more about slavery—the most pressing social issue of the day—than about the smooth functioning of a spoils-based party system.

This is the period of the greatest internal political strife in American history, much of which ended up being played out on the House floor as Speakers were elected. Four pitched battles occurred over the election of the Speaker—in 1839 (26th Congress), 1849 (31st Congress), 1855–56 (34th Congress), and 1859–60 (36th Congress), with a smaller skirmish in 1847 (30th Congress). Twice, in 1849 and 1855–56, divisions ran so deep that it proved impossible to form a majority to organize the House, which led the membership to adopt a *plurality rule* to elect the Speaker. At one point, the House seriously considered just adjourning Congress to wait for new elections to break the deadlock.

We find this 1839–65 period interesting because it provides an example of a powerful social issue competing head-to-head with the material economic issues around which leaders typically try to organize parties. As is often the case in this type of competition, the presence of a compelling social issue often frustrated the ability of party leaders to negotiate the division of power within the family. What made this period especially vexing is that the most valuable resources that leaders could mete out were either economic (e.g., pork) or institutional (e.g., plum committee assignments), while social activists could determine reelection. Without reelection, the leaders' inducements were worthless; without material gains from serving in office, the office might not be worth election. No wonder members found it so difficult to reach agreement during this period.[19]

From the perspective of the organizational politics of the House, the Civil War was a bit of a deus ex machina in two senses. First, the war itself placed a premium on national unity and thus dampened divisions over organizing the House just as the conflict began. Second, the war resulted in the exclusion of much of the Democratic Party's geographic base from the House for about a decade, which gave the Republican Party the opportunity to explore

---

[19] It is probably because of this incompatible tug of party and constituency that attempts to seek reelection declined during the decades immediately preceding the Civil War, which reversed the steady rise of careerism in the House that had occurred during the first decades of the nineteenth century (Fiorina, Rohde, and Wissel 1975).

16

CHAPTER 1

ways of organizing the chamber without worrying so much about losing
control to the Democrats on a floor vote.

The transition to this fourth period, 1865–91, was bumpier than the previous paragraph suggests, as it included an episode in which the Clerk, who
had Southern sympathies, attempted to manipulate the call of the House at
the start of the 38th Congress (1863) to exclude the majority Republicans
from claiming the speakership. However, that quasi-coup was put down,
and in the ensuing years, the caucus became established as the sole legitimate venue for settling intraparty conflicts over chamber leadership. The
opening of the 39th Congress (1865) represented the first time that *both
parties* presented formal nominees for Speaker at the convening of a new
Congress, a practice that continues (virtually) unbroken to this day. More
important, during the quarter century covered by this period, both parties
actively worked to keep conflict over the organization of the House confined
solely to the caucuses, even in circumstances that prior to the Civil War
would have resulted in chaos and gridlock.

The caucus became such a predictable venue for settling leadership fights
that some even tried to push its influence further by binding members on
policy votes as well. That innovation failed to take hold. However, by the
time that Thomas Brackett Reed (R-Maine) became Speaker in 1889 (51st
Congress), he could count on the support of his party's caucus in organizational matters. Resting on the binding party caucus on organizational matters, which had been built and perfected for a quarter century (with the help
of explicitly sanctioning the occasional disloyalist), Reed's parliamentary
innovations made it possible for modern political scientists to speak in terms
of "party cartels" and "conditional party government."

The final period runs from the rise of the Reed Rules to the present. This
period has seen authority in the House ebb and flow between party leaders
(especially the Speaker) and the rank and file, but rarely has the organization of the House been anything other than a *party* affair. The only two
serious challenges to this regime, in 1909 and 1923, involved progressive-
conservative rifts within the Republican Party that drifted out to the floor.
These episodes revealed that the reach of the caucus in the organization of
the House did not yet extend to the passage of the House rules, but they did
reinforce the observation that the caucus now owned the most important
personnel decisions made at the start of the Congress. Owning these decisions, members of the majority party can count on receiving a positive hand-
icap when virtually any important question of policy reaches the House.

A NOTE ABOUT DATA AND METHODS

Empirical research into parliamentary fights over the organization of the
antebellum House has been spotty and anecdotal. The purpose of the fol-

lowing chapters is to comprehensively explore this history by using a two-pronged approach that builds a series of narrative accounts alongside more systematic, quantitative analysis.[20]

In exploring this history, it is important to understand the paucity of hard data on which to rest an account of struggles over organizing the antebellum House. Two important data problems loom large. First, the House elected the Speaker via secret ballot for the first half century of its history. Until the onset of viva voce balloting for Speaker (and other House officers, such as Clerk and Printer) in 1839, the House left no direct evidence about who supported whom at any step in the process. What is more, until the 26th Congress, the House *Journal* did not regularly record even the aggregate vote returns for the various speakership candidates, which means we had to rely on occasionally conflicting and incomplete newspaper accounts in order to analyze the aggregate results. Second, even after the inception of public balloting for Speaker, the standard electronic versions of House roll call votes omit the balloting for House officers (see Inter-University Consortium for Political and Social Research [ICPSR] roll call study no. 0004). Even when speakership ballots are included in the electronic files, only the votes received by the leading candidates are typically recorded, which seriously limits our ability to analyze razor-thin elections in which the ballots of pivotal voters are often recorded in the catchall category of "scattering."

To overcome this lack of basic data concerning the election of House officers, appendix 1 summarizes the balloting for Speaker, Clerk, and Printer from the First through the 112th Congresses using the best data sources available—usually the *House Journal* and *Congressional Record*, but occasionally newspapers from the earliest years.

With these data—aggregate results for virtually all elections and individual-level ballots beginning in the late 1830s—we can provide two summary measures of the rise of party as an influence in House organization. The first measure uses the aggregate results and constructs a simple ratio: the number of votes received by the top vote-getter from the majority (or plurality) party on the first ballot for Speaker divided by the number of seats held by the majority (or plurality) party in each Congress. We can do the same for the main minority party. Those ratios are plotted in figure 1.1. The second measure starts in 1839 and represents the degree of party loyalty on the first ballot for Speaker in each Congress. This measure is constructed by recording the percentage of major-party House members who voted for

[20] Lientz's (1978) essay is the most extensive research devoted specifically to the topic of this book. Jenkins and Nokken's (1997, 2000) research on the speakership contest of 1855–56 is the first analysis of multiballot speakership contests to use modern social scientific theories and measurement techniques. Other notable original research and secondary accounts can be found in Follett (1896), Fuller (1909), House (1965), Young (1966), Peters (1997), Strahan et al. (2000), Strahan, Gunning, and Vining (2006), Strahan (2007), and Green (2010).

their party's top candidate for Speaker at the beginning of a Congress. After 1865, this "top candidate" is, by definition, the candidate nominated by the caucus; before 1865, this "top candidate" is identified as the individual who received the most votes by members of the party. This time series is plotted in figure 1.2.

Looking first at figure 1.1, prior to 1861 the number of votes received by the top candidates of the two major parties was rarely equal to the size of the party delegations. With only a couple of exceptions, the ratio was considerably less than 1.0, which suggests that there was a significant amount of party defection. (The few times when the ratio was greater than 1.0 suggests a few cases of cross-party voting.) The ratio began approaching 1.0 in the 1860s and has continued there—dipping slightly below on occasion—ever since.

The deficiency of figure 1.1 is that it does not examine individual-level roll call votes, which is what figure 1.2 does, once we have the roll call data starting in 1839.[21] Here, too, we see that prior to 1860, the degree of party loyalty in the individual roll call record was highly variable in the election of Speakers. In some years, such as those between 1839 and 1845, both major parties were very unified in voting for Speaker—nearly as unified as in recent Congresses. However, starting in 1845 and running until 1861, at least one of the parties had loyalty levels below 80 percent, and in some, such as 1847 and 1851, at least one of the parties was near or below 50 percent. In the 1860s the loyalty levels began to rise. Since 1871, party loyalty levels in the election of Speaker have fallen below 95 percent only three times for the majority party (Republicans in 1909 and 1923, Democrats in 1945) and six times for the minority (1873 and 1953 for the Democrats, 1911, 1913, 1945, and 1949 for the Republicans).

We will examine these voting patterns in more detail by using a multi-pronged approach. Along with traditional techniques that draw on primary and secondary historical sources, we will also employ various quantitative approaches that include statistical methods (such as regression analysis) and applied formal theory (primarily spatial models). A quantitative measure that will play a major role in our various analyses is the NOMINATE score—developed by Poole and Rosenthal (1991, 1997, 2001, 2007)—which has become ubiquitous in the literature on Congress over the last two decades. Because of its ubiquity, we will only broadly describe the measure here

[21] One other difference between figures 1.1 and 1.2 bears mentioning. In figure 1.1, the ratio is calculated using the size of the party contingents as reported by Martis (1989) as the denominator. Figure 1.2, on the other hand, is based only on House members who are present and voting. Thus, there is no distinction made in figure 1.1 between abstaining (although present) and being absent from the House when the roll was called. Because the number of abstainers and absentee members was relatively small, this difference does not affect the overall point these two figures make together, which is that the degree of party regularity in structuring balloting for the Speaker increased markedly in the decade of the 1860s.

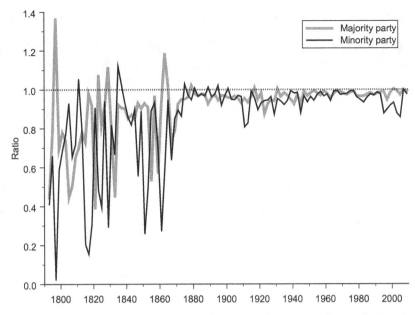

FIGURE 1.1. Ratio of the number of votes for principal recipient of votes for Speaker to the size of the party contingent, 1789–2011. *Sources*: *House Journal* and newspapers described in appendix 2; Martis (1989).

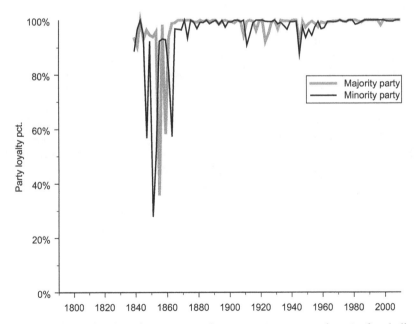

FIGURE 1.2. Party loyalty of majority and minority House members in first-ballot voting for Speaker, 1839–2011. *Source*: *House Journal*, various years.

and encourage readers unfamiliar with NOMINATE to examine the Poole-Rosenthal citations above.

As a general class of estimates, NOMINATE scores represent a way to compare the behaviors of different members of Congress. They represent the output of a multidimensional unfolding technique (derived from the psychometrics literature) that is applied to a set of roll call votes. More generally, the NOMINATE estimation technique generates "scores" for members of Congress based on how they vote on a set of roll calls. NOMINATE scores generally range from -1 (most liberal) to 1 (most conservative), and members who vote more alike will have scores that are more similar.[22] The scores themselves are often ascribed different meanings. Some scholars refer to them as measures of "spatial ideology," others as measures of "revealed preferences." Generally, they can be viewed as members' central tendencies on the underlying issue dimension(s) of consequence.

Poole and Rosenthal find that much of what occurs in Congress (in terms of roll call voting) across American history can be explained quite well by a single NOMINATE dimension, which typically is interpreted as a left-right dimension that separates members of the two major parties on economic issues.[23] At times, a second NOMINATE dimension, which takes on different substantive interpretations depending on the context, is also important in explaining individual-level vote choice. For the period we examine in this book, the most common second dimension dealt with issues related to slavery. Thus, using members' second-dimension NOMINATE scores will, in fact, be critical to a number of our analyses.

Several variants of NOMINATE scores exist. Some, such as DW-NOMINATE scores, are dynamic in that they are estimated across a set of Congresses and allow explicit intrachamber comparisons over time, while others, such as W-NOMINATE scores, are more static, in that they are estimated on a Congress-by-Congress basis and are thus limited to intrachamber comparisons at a single point in time. Both the DW-NOMINATE and W-NOMINATE estimation techniques, however, generate unique scores for individual members by Congress. Another variant, the "common space" W-NOMINATE (or CSW-NOMINATE) estimation technique, produces a *single* set of scores for a *set* of Congresses.[24] These CSW-NOMINATE scores will be useful when we study the multiballot speakership elections of the 1850s (see chapters 6 and 7). Because a winning speakership candidate typi-

[22] See Poole and Rosenthal (1997) and Poole (2005) for a more technical description of this multidimensional, unfolding technique.

[23] For a brief period, from the early 1850s through the Reconstruction era, the content of the first NOMINATE dimension shifted from economic issues to slavery/racial issues. See Poole and Rosenthal (1997, 5, 41, 95–100).

[24] Moreover, CSW-NOMINATE scores allow interchamber (i.e., House-Senate) comparisons as well. We do not take advantage of this feature in our subsequent analyses.

cally did not vote in Congress after becoming Speaker, a method of determining his revealed preference in that specific Congress is needed. CSW-NOMINATE scores fill that need. While all of the NOMINATE variants are highly correlated, we will take care to discuss which set of NOMINATE scores we are using at various points.

OUTLINE OF THE BOOK

Before delving into the cases of extended speakership (and general House officer) battles in the antebellum period, in chapter 2 we first detail what the stakes actually were by discussing each of the major House officer positions—mainly the Speaker, but also the Clerk and Printer—and what sorts of power and resources these positions had at their disposal. We trace how the Speaker, Clerk, and Printer positions could bestow significant policy and patronage to the parties that controlled them. At a time when the mass party system was still developing, these House positions could be pivotal in giving one party a significant edge in building partisan attachments and electoral advantages throughout the nation.

In chapter 3, we provide a brief accounting of organizational politics in the earliest years of the Republic. This was a period characterized by a mix of factors surrounding the selection of House officers, beginning with region and personality, but quickly becoming partisan. These fights were thinly documented in the press and in the proceedings of Congress, hence the ability to do systematic analysis of speakership battles before 1837 (when the chapter ends) is limited. However, the contrast with subsequent cases is striking, which suggests that later efforts to institutionalize leadership selection—especially by making it part of the roll call record—heightened partisan factors in the selection of House officers.

In chapter 4, we examine an institutional change that raised the stakes in speakership elections (and all officer elections more generally): the decision to make voting public (or viva voce). Prior to 1838, such elections were conducted by secret ballot, which provided a suitable context for politicians to select strong leaders while sidestepping potentially divisive issues that might affect coalition building. It also provided a context for majority party dissidents to bolt the party's chosen speakership candidate and enter into intrigues with minority party members. The move to viva voce voting was intended to bring these dissidents "out in the open" and thus stymie the development of cross-party coalitions. However, it also allowed *constituents* to observe how their representatives voted in speakership elections, just as slavery was once again becoming a major political issue. This would prove to be a critical blunder. Deals that could have been cut within the majority party in the secret ballot days no longer worked in the viva voce voting days, as members were afraid of losing their constituents' trust by voting for a candidate from the other region. This would greatly destabilize the House organization in the latter part of the antebellum period, and on several occasions led to lengthy multiballot speakership contests.

In chapter 5, we focus on the first two extended speakership battles after the passage of the viva voce voting rule. These were the speakership elections of 1839 (to the 26th Congress) and 1847 (to the 30th Congress). Each would highlight the conflicting impulses of party and region at a time when national party leaders were striving for greater organization over House affairs. In 1839, the dangers of sectionalism emerged in full force, as Southern Democrats close to John C. Calhoun bucked the caucus bond and elected a Whig (who was more in keeping with their ideological tastes) to the speakership after an 11-ballot affair. In 1847, sectionalism was a critical factor again, but disaster was avoided, as two Northern antislavery Whigs delayed—but did not prevent—the election of a proslavery ("Cotton") Whig to the speakership after a three-ballot contest. Party stalwarts hoped the 1847 outcome was a positive sign, as it represented the third consecutive speakership election that ratified the nomination made by the majority party caucus. Under the surface, however, sectionalism continued to build in intensity—and was preparing to burst forth in short order.

In chapter 6, we examine the two lengthiest speakership battles in American history: the 1849 speakership election (to the 31st Congress), which covered 63 ballots and three weeks, and the 1855–56 speakership election (to the 34th Congress), which required 133 ballots and extended over two months. In both cases, third parties emerged—the Free-Soilers in the late 1840s and the Americans in the mid-1850s—to threaten the two-party equilibrium that had developed in speakership elections up to that point. In 1849, this resulted in a multidimensional speakership contest, while in 1855–56, this led to a three-party battle along a single dimension. In addition, divisions within the major parties on slavery made preventing defections difficult; as a result, major party leaders found it that much harder to negotiate with the minor parties. In both elections, a plurality rule was eventually adopted to choose a Speaker in the face of the reality that no candidate could ever win a majority vote in the House. These two speakership elections signaled the intensifying rift within the nation on the issue of slavery and foreshadowed the growing separation that would eventually end in Civil War.

Chapter 7 picks up where chapter 6 leaves off: the nascent Republicans had just captured the speakership in the 34th Congress, but could they now successfully organize the House? We discover that they achieved some success by winning the clerkship and organizing the committees around antislavery tenets, but they were unable to win the printership. The latter defeat was especially vexing, as the House Printer could have been put to use advertising and promoting the new party. The Republicans lost control of the chamber to the Democrats in the 35th Congress, but reemerged as the plurality party in the 36th Congress. This time, the party was more internally organized; it held firm and weathered another extended speakership race (44 ballots) in 1859–60 before winning all major House officer positions. In effect, the Republican Party was built as an institutional party and made initial strides in the 34th Congress before wholly emerging in the 36th Congress; the House officer positions were used as devices (and signals) for the construction of the electoral component of the party.

In chapter 8, we examine why the tumultuous period of extended speakership balloting suddenly (and nearly completely) came to an end. Our argument centers on the congressional party caucus and its emergence as an institutional solution to the instability on the House floor. Beginning in the Civil War, decisions were made in caucus on officer nominees, and members were bound to support the caucus decisions on the floor. To cement the deal, party members who lost in caucus were rewarded with committee assignments by the Speaker to soften the blow. Thus, a system was established whereby power was explicitly shared within the party, and thus "out" factions would be compensated in exchange for their continued loyalty and support of the majority's decisions. This caucus-Speaker-committees arrangement—in effect, the culmination of Van Buren's master plan—institutionalized quickly, as both parties adopted the setup. The result was the creation of an organizational cartel, as the majority party routinely (and without incident) controlled the election of the Speaker (and other House officers), as well as the more general makeup of the chamber. This organizational certainty provided the necessary condition for the imposition of the Reed Rules in 1890.

Chapter 9 covers leadership selection after the Reed Rules and the persistence of the organizational cartel, and focuses particularly on the only episode in the twentieth century when the party monopoly over the House's makeup was challenged—in 1923, due to a rift between progressive and conservative elements in the Republican Party. That episode is the exception that has most recently proved the rule. Although divisions within the Grand Old Party were deep, and progressive Republicans could have readily walked over and voted with the Democrats to organize the House, they chose to keep the dispute a family affair, finally settling it within the caucus.

We conclude in chapter 10 by considering the larger questions of organizational control, party building, and party strength, which the events chronicled in this book inform. We start by recapping our idea of the organizational cartel and its relationship with the procedural cartel, which is identified with the work of Cox and McCubbins. Next, we consider the applicability of the organizational cartel mechanism in other legislatures, most notably the U.S. Senate, American state legislatures, and parliaments around the world. Then we revisit the view of political parties advocated by Martin Van Buren, both to suggest ways that bringing Congress into the equation enriches our understanding of Van Buren's efforts at party building, while at the same time noting ways in which tensions within the modern organizational cartel carry flavors of the tensions that Van Buren and his contemporaries wrestled with.

The Evolving Roles and Responsibilities of House Officers in the Antebellum Era

Why would antebellum House members fight over who should wield the gavel? While to us the answer seems trivial, that is only because we live at a time and place in which the House has endowed the speakership with significant authority. Other legislative presiding officers, by comparison, lack such authority. For example, the U.S. Senate's presiding officer in the absence of the vice president, the president pro tempore, is purely honorary and bestowed as a function of seniority. The Speaker of the British House of Commons is also endowed with little authority; little of consequence rests on who holds the position.

One answer to this question is found by examining the resources controlled by the Speaker and how they have been used. From the start, the Speaker recognized members in debate and ruled on points of order, and it was only a short time after the first convening of the House that the Speaker also received the authority to appoint committees.

Yet an inductive examination of the aforementioned resources and authority quickly reveals that the Speaker's role has varied over time, and that the speakership was not the only House office worth fighting for. This was particularly true before the Civil War, when the Clerk and Printer were often equally contested. The Clerk presided over a sizable patronage empire and gaveled the House to order at the opening of each new Congress. The Printer controlled the dominant party's propaganda machine and possessed considerable patronage capacities as well. In a world where it was better to have more power than less, it was better to be in the coalition that controlled the House's legislative apparatus than to be outside of it.

By considering the organization of the House from 1789 to the present, we see that the portfolio of valuable positions has changed across time. In the present day, power is concentrated in the speakership and other party offices (like majority leader and majority whip), along with important committee chairs. These are the positions that members jockey for and expend considerable energy trying to attain. In the antebellum period, the Clerk and Printer were politically valuable positions, too; important national leaders, including members of the House, worked hard to elect their candidate. (This was also true of subsidiary House officer positions, like the Sergeant at

Arms, Doorkeeper, and Postmaster, but considerably less so, as they were not nearly as politically valuable; thus, while they will enter our narrative occasionally, the lion's share of the non-Speaker attention will be devoted to the Clerk and Printer.) And, of course, before the Civil War, there *were* no formal party positions to fight over.

We assume that the reader of this book is familiar with the array of important positions in the contemporary House, why those positions are considered important, and how they are contested. We also assume that most will be unfamiliar with how these positions acquired their importance; we particularly assume that few will be familiar with the role that the Clerk and Printer played in the early House. Therefore, in this chapter, we take a step back to try to understand, at a higher level of historical and theoretical abstraction, just what antebellum House members were fighting for when they struggled over electing their officers. This general understanding rests on a discussion of the evolving roles and responsibilities of these officers. We will detail in specific terms how the Speaker, Clerk, and Printer were valuable power nodes that could be used for the benefit of whichever party controlled the chamber.

The Speakership before the Civil War

Article I, Section 2 of the Constitution states that the presiding officer of the House shall be a Speaker of its own choosing. Like so much of the Constitution, this is just a starting point. After all, the Constitution also designates the vice president as the Senate's presiding officer—a designation so meaningless in practice that Woodrow Wilson was prompted to issue the biggest putdown in the history of legislative studies: "The chief embarrassment in discussing [the vice president as president of the Senate] is, that in explaining how little there is to be said about it, one has evidently said all there is to say" (Wilson [1885] 1973, 162). The rise of the House Speaker as both the formal and de facto leader of the House therefore needs to be explained, or at least described.

To appreciate the evolution of the Speaker as the effective head of the House, one need only consider the speakerships of two individuals who currently serve as bookends: Frederick Muhlenberg (F-Pa.), the first Speaker, and John Boehner (R-Ohio), the current Speaker as these pages are being written.

Frederick Muhlenberg was elected Speaker on April 1, 1789, the first day the new House achieved a quorum. He had arrived in New York City, the seat of the new government, on March 3, and joined in a caucus of the Pennsylvania delegation over the choice of House leaders. That meeting eventually pledged to push for his election as Speaker (Peters 1997, 24–28).

Why Muhlenberg? Most likely because he had already served three terms as Speaker of the Pennsylvania House of Representatives, had held many other positions in Pennsylvania, had been a member of the Confederation Congress, and was a devoted champion of the new Constitution. Why Pennsylvania? In the earliest days of the Republic, political leaders were keenly aware of the regional distribution of power; by the time Congress assembled in New York City, all of the other large states had a lock on leadership in the different branches of government—the presidency and vice presidency were held by citizens of Virginia and Massachusetts, and the chief justiceship was about to go to a New Yorker. The House speakership was the only leadership position left.

Once elected, Muhlenberg exercised his formal duties with a light hand, appointing committees, maintaining decorum, and representing the House in ceremonial occasions in all his physically imposing glory. Muhlenberg's only obvious policy intervention was when he broke a tie that allowed Germantown, Pennsylvania, to remain in the running for the new capital (*House Journal* [hereafter abbreviated as *HJ*], 1-1, 9/28/1789, 127; *Annals of Congress* [hereafter abbreviated as *Annals*], 1-1, 9/28/1789, 962). He was replaced by Jonathan Trumbull (F-Conn.) as Speaker in the Second Congress. Historians agree that the replacement of Muhlenberg by Trumbull represented an early triumph of the principle of rotation in office rather than a partisan judgment about Muhlenberg's continued suitability in the chair (Hildreth 1856, 290; Fuller 1909, 25). Yet as political parties began to congeal in the Second Congress, rotation gave way to more partisan concerns, which resulted in Muhlenberg's return to the speakership in the Third Congress. His reascendance to the chair represented a concerted effort among Jeffersonians to oust Trumbull, who had become aligned with the Federalist forces (Lientz 1974, 1978). Still, even in his second, more partisan incarnation as House Speaker, Muhlenberg continued to turn to Federalists to populate important committees, to lead debate, and often to prevail in policy matters. Muhlenberg became a partisan politician, but his partisan actions were largely confined to his activities out of doors. When indoors, he was the institution's man.

This contrasts considerably with the John Boehner story. Boehner was elected Speaker at the start of the 112th Congress (2011), when the Republicans ousted the Democrats as the majority party following a landslide midterm election. Boehner, who represents the most conservative district in rural western Ohio, is an exception to the maxim that one does not get a second chance in American politics. He was first elected to the House in 1990 and quickly rose in prominence among Republican Party councils. He became a lieutenant of Newt Gingrich (R-Ga.) and helped draft the *Contract with America*, which set the agenda for the Republican takeover of the House in the 1994 midterm elections. Boehner was elected chair of the Republican Conference in 1994, but was deposed in 1998 when it was rumored that he was part of a cabal to unseat Speaker Gingrich. He then turned his attention to committee work and served as chair of the Education Committee, where he was regarded as a serious legislator. He returned to the leadership in February 2006, when Tom DeLay (R-Tex.) stepped down as majority leader due to a corruption scandal. Boehner's upset election surprised even him and was viewed as a sign that the Republican caucus was looking for a relatively fresh face that was unassociated with the tainted incumbent House leadership (Weisman 2006). He served as minority leader when the Republican Party was cast into the role of minority following the 2006 midterms, and was then elevated to Speaker following the 2010 elections.

Boehner took the reins of a House that had become polarized through a line of Speakers running back to Nancy Pelosi (D-Calif.), Dennis Hastert (R-Ill.), and Gingrich. Pelosi presided over a highly partisan House, just as her predecessor, Hastert (R-Ill.), did before her. As Speaker, Hastert inherited the partisan organizing principles of Gingrich (R-Ga.), who was elected Speaker in 1995, when the Republicans gained control of the House for the first time in a generation. Under Gingrich's leadership, the new Republican majority ended the practice of relying solely on seniority as the informal rule in choosing committee chairs, which opened up the committee chairmanship selection process to a new set of partisan criteria (Aldrich and Rohde 2005). Under Hastert's speakership, these criteria reached full flower, so that committee chairs were chosen based on their fealty to party leaders, orthodoxy in ideological matters, and success in raising funds for party candidates (Sinclair 2005, 2006).

The Democrats chafed bitterly at the partisan yoke imposed on them by the Republicans, but when they regained majority control in 2007, with Pelosi in the Speaker's chair, they continued to lead the House in a partisan style. This pattern has continued under Boehner, even as he has sought to placate the conservative Tea Party faction within the Republican Party.[1]

Muhlenberg and Boehner were Speakers in different eras, and their differences reflect how the office of Speaker has changed. In the earliest Congresses, House members had emergent partisan affiliations and strong opinions, but party was only one factor among many that influenced the organization of the House. In the earliest years of the Republic, there were no permanent party organizations in Congress, so the path to the speakership could not be trod along a series of partisan stepping-stones. The Boehner story illustrates how the speakership has become the apex of a pyramid of increasingly important party offices. Leaders generally (though not always) acquire higher party offices in the House by performing well in lower

---

[1] A major subtheme in the debt ceiling negotiations that dominated national politics in the summer of 2011 was the difference in partisan intensity displayed by Boehner and the majority leader, Eric Cantor (R-Va.). That Cantor is seen by some as being a partisan bulldog to Boehner's conciliator is more evidence of Cantor's ambitions and the polarization of congressional politics than it is evidence that Boehner is less of a partisan player than his immediate predecessors. It may also reflect a difference in preferred leadership styles. On the stylistic differences between Boehner and Cantor, see Stanton (2011) and Ferraro (2011).

party offices. In the days of Muhlenberg, the speakership was not *fundamentally* a partisan office. In the contemporary Congress, the organization of the chamber is *fundamentally* partisan, and the Speaker is chosen precisely because of her or his relationship to the party organization.[2]

Muhlenberg was not fundamentally a partisan Speaker, yet Boehner is, and if Muhlenberg's and Boehner's behaviors are different because the nature of the House's organization and the role of the Speaker have changed, when did that change occur? We will see in the chapters that follow that concerted efforts were made in the 1820s to transform the House's organization into something far more partisan, but the biggest shift from nonpartisan to partisan organization occurred later in the antebellum period (beginning in the late 1830s), before being fully consummated in the Civil War and Reconstruction Congresses. Since that time, party leaders have been more or less strong, but no serious challenge has ever been mounted against the notion that the majority party, as a party, organizes the House.[3]

In the period that is the focus of this book, the fundamental nature of the House organization was buffeted between two poles, partisan and majoritarian,[4] and the fundamental nature of the Speaker's role was likewise buffeted between two poles: party leader and chamber leader. The major forces that beset the chamber as it struggled to organize for business were

[2] This is not to say that this relationship is always simple, nor that the Speaker is always a type of political boss. Hastert, for instance, was a protégé of former minority leader Robert Michel (Ill.), and had been appointed chief deputy whip—the top appointed party position for House Republicans—by Michel. Many accounts record that Tom DeLay (Tex.), who was the majority whip during the fiasco that attended the replacement of Newt Gingrich as Speaker between the 106th and 107th Congresses, was the natural next candidate for the speakership when Robert Livingston (La.) withdrew. However, DeLay himself withdrew from consideration because he believed that he was too polarizing a figure to be an effective Speaker. In the eyes of some, Hastert began his speakership as the "kinder and gentler" face of DeLay. Regardless, what is significant is the fact that the list of possible Speakers in 1999, when Hastert was chosen, was limited to a small set of individuals who were known quantities within the House Republican conference.

[3] The one possible exception was the progressive challenge to the election of a Republican Speaker at the start of the 68th Congress. However, as we discuss in chapter 9, the purpose of the progressive revolt was to force certain changes *within the Republican caucus*, not challenge the principle that the majority party would eventually unite around a single candidate for Speaker.

[4] In the jargon of contemporary legislative studies, a "majoritarian" organization is one that is controlled by the median member of the chamber, whereas a "partisan" organization is one that is controlled by the median member of the majority party. If parties are arrayed ideologically (i.e., in one substantive dimension) and all members of one party are "to the left" of all members of the other party, the median member of the chamber will be a member of the majority party. Thus, in operational terms we can think of these competing views of chamber organization as disputing over which member of the majority party is most consequential in the organization of the House—one who is often sympathetic to the minority party (e.g., a conservative Democrat or a liberal Republican) or one who is typical of the majority party (e.g., a liberal Democrat or a conservative Republican).

(1) the designs of party builders, like Martin Van Buren, who endeavored to build party structures that transcended personalities and (2) regional pressures, notably the desire of the Southern planters to protect and extend slavery, and the contrasting visions of economic development held by Northerners and Southerners more generally.

For most of the antebellum period, Speakers were both political and parliamentary leaders of the House, but their degree of domination over events was far from steady. The political leadership provided by Speakers before the Civil War was ad hoc; Speakers themselves had few levers with which to exercise independent political control (Follett 1896, 96–97; Young 1966, 131–34; Peters 1997, 50). In thinking about the "strength" of Speakers, we can take a cue from scholars of the American presidency who note a break with Woodrow Wilson in delineating periods of strong and weak presidents. The break in the House came half a century before Wilson's presidency, with the Civil War and the speakerships of Galusha Grow (R-Pa., 1861–63) and Schuyler Colfax (R-Ind., 1863–69).[5] Before then, only a few Speakers (Banks, Clay, Cobb, Polk, and Winthrop) combined sufficient political and personal strength to be considered substantial political leaders. After that, Speakers were normally strong leaders who put their own stamps on the House's proceedings. The exceptions, such as J. Warren Keifer (R-Ohio, Speaker, 1881–83), are easier to list because they were so atypical.

If we use modern language, the antebellum Speaker often possessed partisan ambitions but was still highly constrained by the majoritarian politics of the chamber. Thus, even when party leaders successfully orchestrated the election of a Speaker, it would be a stretch to claim that this represented the operation of a partisan *cartel* of the sort described by Cox and McCubbins (1993, 2005).

In attempting to structure proceedings to the advantage of those who elected him, a Speaker had two primary formal levers at his disposal: committees and floor debate. It is to these features of the House's formal organization that we now turn our attention.

COMMITTEES IN THE ANTEBELLUM HOUSE

When the House of Representatives first met in 1789, it adopted a set of rules that delineated a simple set of expectations for the Speaker to follow

---

[5] At the risk of wading into historical psychoanalysis, it is perhaps not surprising that many of the characteristics that bothered Wilson in his classic book *Congressional Government* took off during these Civil War speakerships. According to Lippmann, Radical Reconstruction had a profound influence on Wilson's worldview because he was a native of Virginia (Lippmann [1885] 1973). One does not have to buy the psychoanalytical approach to understanding Wilson's presidency, which was so popular during the 1970s, to recognize that one reads *Congressional Government* in a different way when one knows about Wilson's formative years.

in exercising his duties and for the full body to follow in deliberating on legislation (*HJ*, 1-1, 4/7/1789, 8–11).[6] Very little was written in the original House rules about committees, except that Speakers would appoint small ones (with three or fewer members) and the whole body would ballot to appoint larger ones. No standing committees were mentioned. An additional set of rules was appended less than a week later. The first of these allowed "any member [to] excuse himself from serving on any committee, at the time of his appointment, if he is then a member of two other committees" (*HJ*, 1-1, 4/13/1789, 13). Another provided for a standing committee on elections, whose duty it was to judge the credentials of newly elected members. Shortly after the second session of the First Congress convened, the provision for appointing large committees by ballot was rescinded, with the duty of appointing these committees given over to the Speaker (*HJ*, 1-2, 1/13/1790, 140).

Rather than rely on standing committees, which eventually came to dominate the congressional landscape, the House routinely appointed ad hoc committees to consider every piece of legislation that came before the body. This led to the appointment of 220 select committees in the First Congress (Canon and Stewart 1995, table 1).[7] These 220 select committees contained 209 unique combinations of members, so these truly were ad hoc in name and in fact.

Fast-forwarding to the eve of the Civil War, we see that the prominence of committees within the House rules was quite different. By the 35th Congress (1857–59), six pages of the Standing Rules and Order were devoted to committees, most of which dealt with the chamber's 34 standing committees (*HJ*, 35-1, 1157–62). Virtually every House member was appointed to several standing committees; it was exceedingly rare for an individual to be appointed to none, unless he was infirm or arrived on the scene close to adjournment. Select committees were now used infrequently. The House appointed select committees only 23 times in the 35th Congress, almost all of which were investigatory.

Between the First Congress and the Civil War, the transformation from a committee system dominated by ad hoc committees to one dominated by standing committees was fairly steady (Canon and Stewart 2001). A significant acceleration occurred in the 1810s, beginning around the 12th Congress (1811–13), when the House started regularly appointing a series of select committees and charging them with taking under consideration broad subjects contained in the president's annual message. These committees "on the president's message" were eventually reappointed at the beginning of each session. Starting with the 14th Congress, they were authorized to re-

---

[6] Portions of the following subsection are based on Jenkins and Stewart (2002).

[7] For committee membership data throughout this book, we rely on the work of Canon, Nelson, and Stewart (2002).

port by bill (*Annals*, 14-1, 12/6/1815, 376–77; Cooper [1962] 1988, 58). In the 17th Congress (1821–23), these committees were officially made standing (Jenkins and Stewart 2002), and in short order the vast majority of the House's business was handled by standing committees (Gamm and Shepsle 1989; Jenkins 1998). It was also during the decade of the 1820s that membership on standing committees became universal in the House.

How does one think about House committees, standing and select, in the antebellum period? Over the past quarter century, students of Congress have developed an approach to committee behavior that is rooted in rational choice theory. This modern approach has embedded committees in a spatial model of legislative deliberation. Within this spatial model, like any spatial model of decision making, the overarching goal has been to identify why legislatures reach closure, or equilibrium, in their deliberations. As a general matter, if we rely on the preferences of legislators alone, they will not reach closure—there is no "preference-induced equilibrium" (PIE) in the argot of the approach. However, a set of institutional constraints that look a lot like a committee system can induce stability in legislative decision making, which rational choice scholars term a "structure-induced equilibrium" (SIE) (Shepsle 1979; Shepsle and Weingast 1981).

The SIE model rests on top of a simple spatial model of legislative voting. In its most direct manifestation, we can think of a complicated, multidimensional world in which each policy dimension is associated with a different committee and each member is assigned to a committee that has certain special authority with respect to its own dimension. Usually we think of the committees as being composed of members who are "high demanders" with respect to policies that the committee oversees—farmers predominate on agriculture committees, members from money-center cities predominate on banking and urban affairs committees, and so on (Weingast and Marshall 1988; cf. Krehbiel 1991). Finally, we also assume that committees possess at least "negative agenda control," and sometimes "positive agenda control." (Negative agenda control, or gatekeeping authority, means that once a matter is referred to a committee, the committee can decide whether to return the bill to the floor for further consideration—"opening the gates" or not to policy change. Positive agenda control means that the committee has the right to decide what new proposals look like on the policy dimension for which they are responsible; thus, the committee's bill is protected against amendment on the floor.)

In a world in which the jurisdictional allocations are clear and respected, in which committee members and nonmembers of a particular committee are strategic in their thinking, and in which committees have special rights at protecting their proposals, we should observe committee recommendations that generally pass unscathed on the floor (Shepsle and Weingast 1987). In other words, committees should rarely "get rolled" on the floor.

There are plenty of examples of committees getting rolled on the floor of the antebellum House of Representatives, even though it is also clear that members of Congress and the attentive public intuited a rudimentary SIE model of committee politics in those days. Few were indifferent about the composition of the committees, and committee makeup was frequently a subject of speculation during extended speakership contests. As we will see later in the book, the 31st Congress (1849–51) was tied into knots over the issue of how the committees would be composed.

As congressional scholars have only begun applying modern tools of legislative analysis to the study of congressional politics during the antebellum period, whether committees actually enjoyed the authority ascribed to them by contemporary observers or modern SIE political scientists is still very much an open question. We do know that although select and standing committees were typically obliged to report back on legislation for ultimate disposition by the chamber, they in fact usually just sat on legislation that was referred to them, which allowed bills to die by inaction. Antebellum committees thus exercised negative agenda control, though precisely how often and with what effects is still subject to speculation (Canon and Stewart 2001).

Southerners generally dominated the standing committee system for almost the entire antebellum period (Canon and Stewart 2001). We can illustrate this by showing the percentage of seats on the more desirable committees that were held by slave state members and compare that to the overall share of slave state seats in the House. To do this we must first identify the "desirable committees" in the House during the antebellum period, which we have done for the period from the 17th Congress (1821–23) to the 38th Congress (1863–65) using the "Grosewart" method of estimating the value of service on House committees (Groseclose and Stewart 1998; Stewart and Groseclose 1999). This method, which relies on members' committee transfer patterns to establish a committee hierarchy, identified 10 House committees during this period that were the most highly desirable: Claims, Commerce, Foreign Affairs, Indian Affairs, Judiciary, Military Affairs, Naval Affairs, Public Lands, Territories, and Ways and Means.

Throughout this period, as illustrated in figure 2.1, the fraction of House seats held by slave state members steadily declined, from 43 percent in the 1820s to 37 percent in the 1850s. By contrast, slave states held considerably more seats on the desirable House committees, claiming roughly half of the seats with only a couple of exceptions. The pattern broke with the speakership of Nathaniel Banks in the 34th Congress (1855–57). The two exceptions prior to Banks were the 29th and 30th Congresses (1845–49), during the speakerships of John W. Davis (D-Ind.) and Robert Winthrop (W-Mass.). Perhaps not surprisingly, both Davis and Winthrop faced Southern suspicions during their tenures.

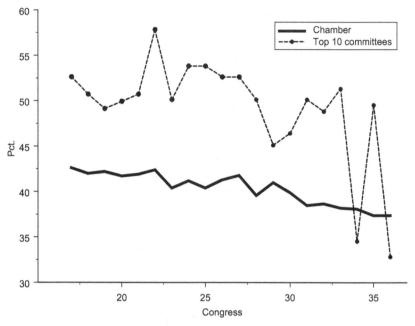

FIGURE 2.1. Percentage of seats held by slave state representatives in the whole House and in the 10 most desirable standing committees, 17th–36th Congresses. *Source*: Canon, Nelson, and Stewart (2002).

A similar pattern is evident if we look at regional membership patterns on two House committees that often drew much attention because of their key roles in slavery controversies: Territories and the District of Columbia. Figure 2.2 graphs these time series. The District of Columbia Committee, which had a major role in the controversy over slavery in the District, almost always had a healthy representation from the slave states. Of course, that was helped by the practice of regularly assigning members from the surrounding slave states of Maryland and Virginia to the committee; together, these two states held only 12 percent of the House seats, but 34 percent of the committee assignments during this period. Still, the two other overrepresented states on the committee were the slave states located far from the District—Mississippi and Tennessee—while the most underrepresented states were in the North: Illinois, Massachusetts, New York, and Pennsylvania.

The Territories Committee in the earliest Congresses tended to closely parallel the regional composition of the whole House, with the exception of the 22nd Congress (1831–33) during the second speakership term of Andrew Stevenson (Jack.-Va.). However, beginning with the speakership of John White (W-Ky.) in the 27th Congress (1841–43), regional patterns of

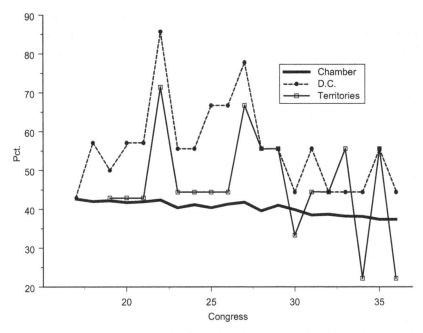

FIGURE 2.2. Percentage of seats held on the District of Columbia and Territories Committees by slave state members, 17th–36th Congresses. *Source*: Canon, Nelson, and Stewart (2002).

membership on the committee became much more volatile. This was the period when the House was embroiled in the controversy over the "gag rule" and extension of slavery into the territories (Jenkins and Stewart 2003a). Three speakers in a row who were from the midsection of the country—White, John W. Jones (D-Va.), and John W. Davis (D-Ind.)—appointed Territories Committees with clear slave state majorities. They were followed by Robert Winthrop (Mass.), the Cotton Whig who was nonetheless distrusted by many Southerners, and who appointed the first Territories Committee with a disproportionate number of free state members. From then on, the composition of the Territories Committee followed the outcome of the speakership battles, with the Democratic Speakers Cobb (Ga.), Boyd (Ky.), and Orr (S.C.) favoring Southerners and the (proto-)Republican Speakers Banks (Mass.) and Pennington (N.J.) disfavoring them.

These patterns suggest that committee compositions were not randomly distributed by region and are consistent with a view that committee seats were intensely contested and determined by the outcome of speakership contests. What they do not show is whether the committees used their agenda control authority to bottle up major legislation or extract rents from the rank and file.

Evidence on this point is spotty and anecdotal. Henry Clay's inability as Speaker to translate his personal popularity into policy triumphs during the Era of Good Feelings was largely due to his failure to protect committees from getting rolled on the floor (Young 1966, 131–34; Stewart 2007). Beyond studying Clay's hapless attempts at stacking committees in order to push legislation in directions he desired, little systematic scholarship has studied the success of committees in molding policy outcomes in a manner consistent with the SIE model. Without a centralized institution such as the modern Rules Committee to fashion mechanisms to protect committee bills on the House floor—thus providing the means to exercise positive agenda control—it is unsurprising that stacking committees was insufficient to deliver outcomes consistent with a legislative cartel.

Before the Civil War, committee seats were very important symbolically; they were the currency through which the various interests kept score in congressional politics. Yet there were limits to what a committee could do if it was stacked against a determined House majority. For that reason, we should not simply assume that the most rabid commentators of the time were correct when they ascribed dictatorial powers to committees or to the Speakers who appointed them. Nonetheless, such views were powerful, and were capable at times of rallying political forces.

Another important question about committee composition concerns *party control* of committees. In the modern House, the majority party holds a majority of seats on all the standing committees, with possible rare exceptions, such as the current practice of appointing an equal number of Democrats and Republicans to the House Committee on Ethics.[8] The best illustration that committee seats are considered to be party property is that the House routinely passes separate resolutions to name majority and minority committee members.

Looking at the historical endpoints, we see that Speakers had effective control over committee appointments from (virtually) the very beginning, and that the parties currently have control. When did the shift in authority from the Speaker to the parties occur, and to what effect?

The shift to party control of committee assignments is typically said to coincide with the adoption of House Rule X in 1911, which specified that committees would be elected rather than appointed. Nothing in the rule initially specified that *parties* would take the lead in shaping how these elections would proceed. However, immediately upon adoption of Rule X, the Democrats devolved practical authority over making assignments to the Democratic contingent of the Ways and Means Committee, which gave the minority leader the authority to make Republican appointments (Alexander

---

[8] Other exceptions may occur when third party members are appointed to small, minor standing committees, which leaves the majority party per se with only a plurality of members of a particular committee.

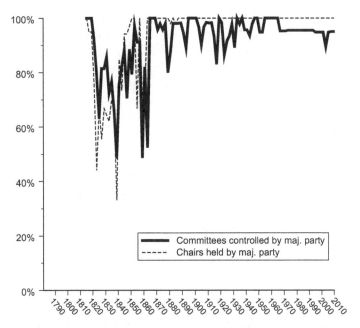

FIGURE 2.3. Percentage of House committees with majorities from the chamber's majority party and percentage of House committees with a chair from the majority party. *Source*: Canon, Nelson, and Stewart (2002); Nelson (1994); Nelson and Stewart (2010).

1916, 81–82). More recently, Rule X has been written to make explicit the fact that the majority party names the chair of each committee, and that the resolutions appointing committees come from the two caucuses.

The *practice* of the majority party claiming the lion's share of committee assignments arose after the Civil War. This is illustrated in figure 2.3, which shows the percentage of House standing committees in which the majority party held a majority of the seats, as well as the percentage of standing committees in which a member of the majority party was the chair. Before the Civil War, the majority party typically controlled *most* committees, but often a bare majority. The practice of the majority party claiming nearly all committees and all committee chairs dates from 1865 (39th Congress), which is also the first Congress in which both caucuses officially presented dueling nominees for Speaker.[9]

[9] The few exceptions to uniform control of committees by the majority party since 1865 are easily explained. The nonmajority committee chairs since 1865 have all been senior minor party members who tended to support the majority party. The committees in which the majority party did not have a majority of seats were all either the House ethics committees, with an even number of members from each party, or minor committees with a contingent of minor party members who voted with the majority party on organizational matters.

Thus, while party was certainly an important factor in the composition of committees before the Civil War, it was not the same looming factor as it was afterward. This suggests that the idea that committees would be agents of the majority party, rather than ad hoc majorities that might form around the election of the Speaker, was late in developing. However, once the party Committee on Committees became institutionalized in the 1910s, the House had already been organized around norms that advantaged the majority party in the formation of committees.

The Rules and Floor Proceedings in the Antebellum House

When we observe the House actually considering legislation in the antebellum period, we see that committee recommendations were frequently under savage attack and often eviscerated; the floor was a more obvious venue for real work than in the present-day Congress. Woodrow Wilson's famous aphorism, that "Congress in session is Congress on display, but Congress in committee is Congress at work," was much more characteristic of the postbellum House than the antebellum House. Indeed, the strengthened party grip on the chamber that arose during the Civil War laid the foundation for the institution that Wilson described, and which in certain fundamental respects still characterizes the House. In the period before the war, committee work was much more provisional; issues that were fought out in committee were just as likely to be fought out again on the floor. In such an environment, the rules that shaped floor consideration of legislation were the most important formal element of the House. Since the Speaker's hand in presiding over the House made him the keeper of those rules, understanding their evolution in the antebellum period helps to clarify what was at stake in selecting the Speaker.

It has frequently been remarked that Article I, Section 5 of the Constitution, which gives each chamber of Congress the authority to "determine the rules of its proceedings," was a significant tool for allowing chamber majorities to take control of the policy-making apparatus of the federal government—in stark contrast to the state of affairs under the Articles of Confederation, in which the ability of Congress to impose any rules on its members was always in question (Jillson and Wilson 1994; Stewart 2005). Yet even though the Constitution gave congressional majorities the right to shape the institution to their liking, in practice the rules had little influence on House proceedings. This fact stemmed from a conception of representation, such that no set of constituents should be unduly privileged at the expense of another. Joseph Cooper (1970; cf. Harlow 1917) identifies this belief as deriving from a set of "Jeffersonian" attitudes about the source of law and the authority of individual legislators to develop it. Because of these attitudes, rules that restricted debate or allowed committees to set legislative agendas were considered illegitimate.

These Jeffersonian attitudes had two major consequences for the development of the House rules before the Civil War. The first was a constant tension between the rush to get legislative business passed in the limited time that Congress met and the desire to keep the House highly participatory. This tension was evident in the earliest days of the House's history, when it voted in its first session to choose all committees by ballot, and then voted in the second session to allow the Speaker to appoint committees; if Congress was only going to meet for a few months a year, House members wanted to spend their time actually working rather than figuring out who would do the work. Another moment in which this tension was evident occurred during the decade-long controversy over the gag rule, when the House changed its rules about the introduction of petitions and allowed them to be handed to the Clerk rather than introduced from the floor by members (*HJ*, 27-2, 3/29/1842, 609)—this streamlining rules change was proposed by John Quincy Adams, who was a master in using the old rule to his political advantage.

A second-order consequence of the tension between expediency and participation was a constant tinkering with the rules, which caused them to grow more numerous and complex. Ironically enough, the House's efforts to remove routine business from the floor often backfired, since these efforts also caused the rules to grow in length and complexity. This in turn led to more opportunities for the Speaker to adjudicate among contradictory provisions and precedents, and thus more opportunities to appeal from the decision of the chair.

Minority delay was a major consequence of the Jeffersonian ethos. Not only were the rules often cumbersome under the best of circumstances, but they also provided minorities who were intent on obstructing the intentions of the majority with numerous opportunities to slow down the congressional proceedings.

Balancing between the ambitions of the majority and the rights of the minority thus became an important theme in the development of the House rules before the Civil War. Keep in mind that the modern practice of expediting the consideration of legislation on the House floor through the use of "rules" was a postbellum development (Alexander 1916; Cooper and Young 1989). Before then, it was common for opponents of legislation to employ delaying tactics like the filibuster, dilatory motions (e.g., endless motions to adjourn and appeals from the decision of the chair), and disappearing quorums (i.e., refusing to answer a roll call even when physically present in the chamber).

The apotheosis of delay occurred on May 11, 1854, when a resolution was brought to the House floor that limited debate in the Committee of the Whole on the Kansas-Nebraska Act. By the end of the day, the House had endured roll call votes on 110 motions, including 41 to adjourn, 16 to set the time of the next meeting of the House, 11 to order a call of the House, and 7 to excuse members from voting.[10] Of the 110 roll calls taken that day, only 16 prevailed.

In recent years two major works by political scientists have explored the ebbing and flowing of minority rights, and the ability of House minorities to obstruct the will of a majority (Binder 1997; Dion 1997). A couple of points from this scholarship are especially relevant here. The first reminds us that from the perspective of Anglo-American men of affairs in the late eighteenth and early nineteenth centuries, delay and obstruction were highly valued legislative functions—at least as important as legislating itself. Notions of "efficiency in government" gained their greatest currency in the *late* nineteenth century after parties secured their hold on House organization. Thus, in the antebellum era, even frustrated House majorities were often loath to cut off the means of obstruction, and the most vociferous of obstructors typically viewed their actions as something more than mere tactics. Episodes such as John Quincy Adams's protests against the gag rule were not *purely* for show.

The second point, nonetheless, is that obstruction was tactical much of the time, and that attempts to override minority obstruction were also tactical. The correlation of institutional and substantive preferences skyrocketed with the onset of the "partisan era" in the 1830s, and with it, the willingness of minorities and majorities to actively use procedural maneuvers.

As we focus on struggles over electing Speakers, two other points in this literature on the evolution of minority procedural rights should be highlighted. The first is that the notion of "a majority" should always be regarded as a little suspect, especially when it is operationalized as a partisan majority. The parties were often rent with factions, and those divisions were often most evident when the party margins were close. Even at the height of the partisan era, Speakers had to manage the factionalism within their own parties. This observation was made by John Quincy Adams in his diary, when he reported that newly elected Speaker James K. Polk (D-Tenn.) "made a clumsy address to the House, in which he said it would be impossible for him to keep order unless supported by the House—which was true enough as an appeal to the party majority; but he promised impartiality, which if he does practise [*sic*] at all, will be only between the two sides of his own party" (Adams 1876, vol. 9, 9/4/1837, 366).

The second is that the role of the Speaker in implementing restrictive rules cannot be underestimated. The willingness of Speakers to use the tools at their discretion, or their ability to use them, mattered significantly. The cases of two speakers, Henry Clay and James K. Polk, are illustrative here. In Clay's case, his success in restricting the obstructive tactics of opponents

---

[10] ICPSR study no. 9822, file 33.dtl.

of war against England in the 12th Congress (1811–13) has led many to believe that Clay actually created the previous question motion to cut off debate. In fact, the previous question rule that Clay used so effectively in his first term as Speaker had been adopted in the *prior* Congress (*Annals*, 11-3, 2/27/1811, 1092). What was significant was Clay's *willingness* to use any tools at his disposal, including the previous question rule, to stifle the obstreperous John Randolph (R-Va.).[11]

In Polk's case, while in the Speaker's chair, he faced a vigorous campaign of parliamentary harassment that was led by his archrival and speakership predecessor, John Bell (Anti-Jack. [Tenn.]). To prosecute this harassment, the number of appeals from the decision of the chair increased by an order of magnitude compared to the immediate past, and attempts to adjourn the chamber in the midst of debate doubled.[12]

By their actions, Clay and Polk each launched eras that re-formed expectations about how much delay the Speaker, and the chamber he led, would tolerate. When Clay first claimed the Speaker's chair in 1811, the previous decade had witnessed a new level of minority obstruction that was ushered in by the Jeffersonian juggernaut in the Seventh Congress (1801–3). Obstructive tactics had risen sharply under Speaker Varnum in the 10th and 11th Congresses (1807–11). Clay put a stop to it. His influence was such that even as sectional tensions rose, the Speakers who immediately followed him—Taylor, Barbour, Stevenson, and Bell—faced relatively few challenges on the floor. Bell's guerilla warfare against Polk in the 24th Congress (1835–37) reintroduced the House to the power of determined minority obstruction. Polk was much less successful than Clay in responding to such dilatory behavior—to the detriment of the nation's peace and tranquillity.

It was this later era that witnessed so much contention over the selection of the Speaker. Obstruction by minorities was honed to a sharp point beginning in the 1830s and came to an end with the cementing of the Reed Rules more than a half century later.[13] In subsequent chapters we will encounter

[11] On several occasions, Clay interpreted the previous question rule to eliminate all debate *and* amendments on the main question. Used strategically, this had the effect of privileging a committee bill and forcing an up-or-down vote on the floor—and can be interpreted as a brute-force "closed rule" of sorts. Stevenson would also use Clay's interpretation of the previous question rule on several occasions during his speakership. The House would restrict future Speakers from pursuing this strategy by altering the previous question rule in 1840, wherein a successful vote on a previous question motion would immediately require the House to vote on pending amendments. See Alexander (1916, 189–90) and Binder (1997, 92–93).

[12] Here are the comparative statistics: Andrew Stevenson faced eight challenges to his rulings in the 22nd Congress (1831–33) and Bell faced four in the 23rd Congress (1833–35). Polk faced 62 challenges in the 24th Congress (1835–37) and 16 in the 25th Congress (1837–39). Furthermore there were 39 motions to adjourn in the 22nd Congress, 40 in the 23rd, 53 in the 24th, and 90 in the 25th.

[13] Cox and McCubbins (2005, 55–56) argue that minority obstruction had gotten so bad in the 1870s and 1880s, thanks to antiquated techniques for conducting business and a plethora of minority-friendly House procedures, that both the majority and minority parties had an ef-

episodes when the House balloted for days, weeks, and even months, with no resolution to the problem of organizing itself for business. In visiting these episodes, it will be natural to ask whether significant numbers of House members *really* wished to grind Congress to a complete standstill, and the answer will often be "yes." The same Congresses that endured endless balloting for Speaker (and subsidiary officers) also endured endless motions to adjourn and challenges to the Speaker's rulings. To some, a Congress that did precisely nothing was the best Congress of all.

THE HOUSE CLERK IN THE ANTEBELLUM ERA

Of all the House officers, the main political player by far was the Speaker. But the subsidiary House officers also played important institutional and political roles in the antebellum period—certainly more so than in the modern era. Even before the Jacksonian party system had entrenched the idea that "to the victor belong the spoils," these officers were not only political, they were partisan. Although the House Printer was the most visible of these politically connected subsidiary officers, the Clerk was formally at the top of the heap.[14]

The first House Clerk (John Beckley) was elected immediately after the election of the first House Speaker on April 1, 1789 (*HJ*, 1-1, 4/1/1789, 6). The Clerk's formal role for the first several Congresses was largely administrative. He was responsible for initiating the call of the House; reading bills and motions; attesting and affixing the seal of the House to all writs, warrants, and subpoenas issued by order of the House; certifying the passage of all bills and joint resolutions; and printing and distributing the *Journal* to the president and all state legislatures (*HJ*, 3-2, 227–31). Additional administrative tasks, such as noting all questions of order (and subsequent decisions) and providing House members with copies of the *Journal*, eventually followed (*HJ*, 12-1, 530; 22–21, 899).[15]

A casual observer might take note of these administrative duties and believe the House Clerk to be little more than a secretary, or as John S. Millson (D-Va.) once remarked, simply a "mouthpiece" (*Congressional Globe* [hereafter abbreviated as *CG*], 36-1, 12/8/1859, 66). This characterization would significantly underestimate the office's authority and prerogatives. First, the Clerk controlled a number of resources. For example, the Clerk was allowed to employ a staff in order to carry out his litany of administrative duties. Initially, such appropriations were modest. In the Second Congress (1791–

---

fective veto over the legislative agenda. They refer to this institutional context as a "dual veto system."

[14] Much of this section is drawn from Jenkins and Stewart (2004).

[15] In 1819, the House created the office of Printer to handle printing and distributing the *Journal*, among other duties.

93), the Clerk was provided with funds for three assistant clerks (*American State Papers* [hereafter abbreviated as *ASP*], 2-2, 59). By the 14th Congress (1815–17), the Clerk supervised five assistant clerks, in addition to a messenger and a librarian (*ASP*, 14-2, 311). This broadening of the Clerk's sphere of influence continued steadily over time. Table 2.1 tracks the size of the Clerk's Office from 1823 to 1870.[16] The number of full-time positions grew slowly, with an explosion of part-time positions through 1835.[17] Beginning in the late 1850s, appropriations for full-time positions expanded, and by the mid- to late 1860s, the Clerk supervised approximately 50 full-time employees at combined annual wages in excess of $80,000 (or as much as $119 million in 2010 dollars).[18]

Not to be overlooked was that the House Clerk was relatively well paid. In the First Congress, the Clerk's pay was set at $1,500 per year, plus a $2 per diem for every day Congress was in session. Congress set its own compensation at $6 per diem (plus travel). Assuming an average of 150 days per year in session, this set the Clerk's annual pay at $1,800 and a rank-and-file member's pay at $900. By 1860, things were not quite as rosy for the Clerk, but he was still paid $3,600, compared to $6,000 for rank-and-file House members and $12,000 for the Speaker. In 1802, the position of Librarian of Congress was created, and the practice emerged of appointing the House Clerk to that position. This gave the Clerk an additional $2 per diem, or roughly $300 per year, plus control over a larger empire. This practice continued until Patrick Magruder's disgrace during the War of 1812, when the Capitol was burned. Magruder left town without first securing various texts and records, which were lost forever when the library was destroyed (Gordon 1975). After that, the Librarian of Congress became a patronage position that was controlled by the president and allocated to his political supporters.

The Clerk also controlled the House's contingent fund, which was used for the day-to-day operations of the chamber and the general upkeep of the

---

[16] The number of employees in the Clerk's Office was reported sporadically until a joint resolution was passed in March 1823 that required the Clerk to provide an accounting on an annual basis.

[17] Many of these part-time workers were pages. Their steady increase did not go unnoticed by House leaders. On March 31, 1838, the Committee on Accounts submitted a report investigating the duties of various officers of the House. The committee resolved that the Clerk should employ no more than 12 pages, and that this number should be reduced whenever possible (*House Report* 750 [25-2], 335). The House took up the report on April 4, 1838, and the resolution was amended, with the power of page appointment taken from the Clerk and given to the Doorkeeper (*CG*, 25-2, 4/3/1838, 281).

[18] Here we use 1865 as our base year and the "relative share of GDP" as our deflator. This is the most appropriate deflator to use in this case, as it measures "how economically 'powerful' that person [in this case, the Clerk] would be" today. See Samuel H. Williamson, "Seven Ways to Compute the Relative Value of the U.S. Dollar Amount, 1774 to the Present," Measuring Wealth, http://www.measuringworth.com/uscompare.

TABLE 2.1.
Resources under the Clerk's control, 1823–1870

Year	Congress-session	Full-time employees	Part-time employees	Contingent fund appropriations
1823	18-1	7	9	25,000
1824	18-2	7	12	60,000
1825	19-1	7	11	50,000
1826	19-2	8	13	72,500
1827	20-1	8	13	92,235
1828	20-2	8	13	80,000
1829	21-1	8	15	85,000
1830	21-2	8	19	85,000
1831	22-1	8	19	80,000
1832	22-2	8	22	155,000
1833	23-1	8	22	100,000
1834	23-2	8	32	213,089
1835	24-1	8	36	200,000
1836	24-2	***	***	200,000
1837	25-2	***	***	200,000
1838	25-3	***	***	225,000
1839	26-1	***	***	200,000
1840	26-2	***	***	200,000
1841	27-2	***	***	160,836
1842	27-3	12	6	175,000
1843	28-1	9	5	125,000
1844	28-2	9	5	175,000
1845	29-1	9	5	75,000
1846	29-2	10	5	170,000
1847	30-1	10	5	216,703
1848	30-2	10	5	200,000
1849	31-1	***	***	167,757
1850	31-2	***	***	312,000
1851	32-1	11	5	197,749
1852	32-2	13	4	209,971
1853	33-1	14	3	456,610
1854	33-2	13	5	288,344
1855	34-1	16	3	323,796
1856	34-3	25	7	593,658
1857	35-1	20	0	548,495
1858	35-2	20	0	581,305
1859	36-1	32	11	434,065
1860	36-2	24	0	557,125
1861	37-1	***	***	365,200
1862	37-2	***	***	432,000
1863	38-1	***	***	189,200
1864	38-2	47	2	290,033
1865	39-1	50	2	243,592

TABLE 2.1. (*Cont.*)

Year	Congress session	Full-time employees	Part-time employees	Contingent fund appropriations
1866	39-2	49	6	291,250
1867	40-2	52	9	308,622
1868	40-3	51	0	495,865
1869	41-2	44	8	534,435
1870	41-3	51	0	301,783

Source: Various House documents, House miscellaneous documents, and *Statutes at Large* volumes.
*** Indicates that employee rosters were not made available.

facilities and grounds. Expenses ranged from the purchase of newspapers, journals, stationary, and writing materials for member use; to the purchase of fuel, furniture, horses, Capitol police, and maps for continuing chamber operations; to the hiring of carpenters, painters, bricklayers, blacksmiths, chimney sweeps, and general laborers, as well as the purchase of materials for general physical plant upkeep. As a result, the Clerk was responsible for entering into any number of contractual agreements with few programmatic guidelines;[19] he also had little institutional monitoring.[20] Moreover, the an-

[19] Certain stipulations did affect the congressional printing, however, with various efforts to secure low-cost bids and establish per-page cost ceilings (Smith 1977). Few other expenses were monitored closely. One exception was the purchase of stationary, which was typically a significant expense on a per-Congress basis. This exception had a political origin. In 1842, during the 27th Congress, the House investigated the contracts of Hugh Garland, the House Clerk in the 25th and 26th Congresses. The Committee on Public Expenditures reported that Garland purchased stationary at inflated prices, in effect paying nearly 40 percent more than in previous years, when lower-cost bidders had also vied for the House contract (*House Report* 880 [27-2], 410). Several reasons for this overpricing were suggested, all of which involved fraud. In particular, patronage-based partisanship and indirect embezzlement, via kickbacks, were strongly intimated. Garland vociferously denied the fraud charge, as well as any other wrongdoing, in a lengthy memorial complete with detailed itemizations (*House Document* 275 [27-2], 405). Note that Garland had also been at the heart of the highly partisan battle over organizing the 26th House (see chapter 5), which infuriated the Whig Party. The Whigs controlled the House and the Committee on Public Expenditures in the 27th Congress, so partisan payback could have been the motivation for the investigation and the potential trumped-up fraud charge. Nevertheless, the implications of the investigation led the House to require the Clerk to begin soliciting and reporting bids for stationary contracts (*Statutes at Large*, 27-2, 526–27).

[20] The Clerk's control of the contingent fund was unquestioned prior to March 1, 1823, when Congress passed a joint resolution that required the House Clerk and Senate Secretary to publish an annual statement detailing the expenses from the contingent fund of their respective chambers (*Statutes at Large*, 17-2, 789). Yet, the guidelines for reporting the expenses were broad, and Clerks typically responded with summary totals rather than specific itemizations. On August 26, 1842, this changed, as the Whig-controlled Congress adopted a new resolution requiring the House Clerk and Senate Secretary to provide more precise statements of their

nual sums underlying these contracts became substantial over time. As the right-most column of table 2.1 indicates, beginning in the early 1830s, the Clerk controlled a contingent-fund purse routinely in excess of $100,000. In some years, the Clerk would have nearly $600,000 at his disposal (or more than $2.1 billion in current dollars).[21] This led a correspondent for the *National Era* to remark that "[i]t is easy to see that the man who has such a fund at his disposal must be a personage of influence" (11/20/1856, 186).

Thus, the partisan implications of controlling the Clerk's Office were significant. The Clerk was in a position to dole out patronage, both directly, via positions of employment, and indirectly, via supply and labor contracts with outside agents.

In addition to the financial resources and patronage powers that came with the office, the House Clerk also played a role in the internal organization of the chamber as a whole. Specifically, the Clerk of the *previous* Congress served as the interim presiding officer of each *new* Congress. This decision that the Clerk "carry over" to the start of the next Congress was made in the First Congress (*HJ*, 1-3, 3/1/1791, 396) and hearkened back to an ordinance adopted in 1785 in the Continental Congress (Alexander 1916, 12). As interim presiding officer, the Clerk called the roll of members-elect, thereby formally determining the House membership for organizational purposes. Once the membership was determined, a new Speaker would then be elected, after which a new Clerk would be chosen.

For the first few decades of the Republic, the House Clerk prepared the roll in consultation with the Committee on Elections, which possessed the authority to validate members' credentials (*HJ*, 1-1, 4/17/1789, 16). By the 1830s, however, the Committee on Elections neglected its credential-validating duty, which left the Clerk to construct the roll completely on his own (*Hinds' Precedents*, chap. 2 § 18).[22] This afforded the Clerk a good deal of institutional power. In effect, he became the sole arbiter of the House membership when the chamber initially convened, as the lack of strict certi-

---

contingent-fund expenses (*Statutes at Large*, 27-2, 527). Specifically, the resolution required the Clerk to provide "the names of every person to whom any portion [of the contingent fund] has been paid; and if for any thing furnished, the quantity and price; and if for any services rendered, the nature of such service, and the time employed, and the particular occasion or cause, in brief, that rendered such service necessary; and the amount of all appropriations in each case on hand, either in the Treasury or in the hands of any disbursing officer or agent." The Whigs' adoption of this more stringent accounting system may have been partially related to the investigation of Hugh Garland, but it was also part of a more general pattern of retrenchment in response to the prolonged economic depression of the early 1840s.

[21] The $593,658 at the Clerk's disposal in 1856 is worth $2.15 billion in 2010 dollars, using the "relative share of GDP" as our deflator. See Samuel H. Williamson, "Seven Ways to Compute the Relative Value of the U.S. Dollar Amount, 1774 to the Present," Measuring Wealth, http://www.measuringworth.com/uscompare.

[22] On two separate occasions during this period, on February 19, 1838, and January 28, 1839, John Quincy Adams proposed resolutions that would have required members-elect to submit election-certification credentials to the House Clerk (*CG*, 25-2, 2/19/1838, 190; 25-3, 1/28/1839, 143). Both resolutions were postponed and never subsequently acted upon.

fication rules provided him with substantial discretion in making out the roll. Alexander, writing in the early twentieth century, noted the potential repercussions: "This opens the door to great temptation, for . . . [the Clerk] may omit from the list the name of any member, the regularity of whose election he questions. In other words, he can, if so disposed, refuse to recognize a sufficient number of credentials because of technical errors or spurious contests to give his party a majority of those privileged to participate in the election of a Speaker" (1916, 93).

Such partisanship would become an issue at the opening of the 26th Congress (1839), when the House Clerk, Hugh Garland, passed over five Whig members-elect from New Jersey in his call of the roll because their seats were being contested by five Democrats. Garland's decision gave numerical control of the chamber to the Democrats, which was the immediate cause of the first extended speakership battle of the viva voce era. We explore Garland's actions in more detail in chapter 5.

In 1861, a series of cases established that the House could correct the Clerk's roll of the members-elect by either adding or striking a member (*CG*, 37-1, 7/4/1861, 7–9; 7/5/1861, 13–16). However, this was merely a second-order alteration, in that it did not restrict the Clerk's ability to influence the initial partisan makeup of the chamber. That is, the House could only correct the Clerk's roll *after* the membership of the chamber was first determined by the Clerk. Thus, the Clerk still maintained the ability to tilt majority control of the chamber when partisan margins were close.

On March 3, 1863, the last day of the 37th Congress, the Clerk's ability to certify the election credentials for members-elect, which had simply been a norm since the 1830s, was codified (*Statutes at Large*, 37-3, 804). This action was spurred by Republican leaders' concern that midterm losses could jeopardize the party's control of the House in the next Congress. The codification tailored the law in such a way as to direct the Clerk to recognize the election certificates of "loyal" members-elect from former Confederate states but to bar those who would oppose the Republican agenda. Used strategically, the 1863 law could bias the roll in favor of the Republicans. In reality, the House Clerk, Emerson Etheridge (Tenn.), attempted to use the 1863 law *against* the Republicans in a failed intrigue over the composition and organization of the 38th Congress (1863). While Etheridge's attempt failed, it helped solidify in the minds of Republican leaders the need for a regular party caucus to nominate officers prior to the convening of a new Congress. Etheridge's replacement as Clerk, Edward McPherson (Pa.), also used his discretion to manipulate the initial House roll, but this time as a part of the Republican juggernaut, so his actions have been less subject to historical scrutiny and approbation. We cover Etheridge's and McPherson's actions in more detail in chapter 8.

On February 21, 1867, the 1863 law was revised to include a provision directing the Clerk to place on his roll only those members-elect from states represented in the preceding Congress (*Statutes at Large*, 39-2, 397). By this time, the Radicals were firmly in control of the Republican Party and were waging a war with President Andrew Johnson over the course of Reconstruction policy. The passage of the 1867 law helped to secure a "Radical Reconstruction" of the South by eliminating the possibility that the Clerk— should another Etheridge-type control the office—could recognize pro-Johnson governments prior to congressional organization.

The 1867 law proved to be the last major alteration of the Clerk's institutional position in the nineteenth century. To this day, the House Clerk has the authority to determine the membership roll based on state election certificates (*Deschler's Precedents*, chap. 2 § 8).

The House Printer in the Antebellum Era

Below the Clerk in the House hierarchy was the Printer, who was responsible for printing and distributing House documents, including not only the *Journals* and other official publications (like committee reports), but also politically important texts, such as member speeches and executive messages.[23] The contracts to print for both chambers—which included all official publications of government—were more valuable than most executive branch printing contracts (except for the post office) and were also more politically freighted. Reporting the debates of Congress was another matter and was handled entirely by the private sector until the *Congressional Record* was established in the 1870s.[24]

Even prior to the rise of Jackson, members of Congress and their political hangers-on had grasped the political significance of the Printer's position. The printing contract itself was one of the largest business deals transacted between the federal government and a single contractor. In an era devoid of mass communication and with few diversions, word from Washington about the people's business was eagerly awaited, distributed hand-to-hand, and discussed among neighbors just like episodes of *Dancing with the Stars* are today. The accuracy and attractiveness of congressional publications were important factors, as was the relative speed with which they could be distributed to the hinterland.

In addition, official printing contracts provided a secure financial base for

[23] Much of this section is drawn from Jenkins and Stewart (2003b), with additional background information on early governmental printing coming from Cook (1998), Mott (1941), Schmeckebier (1925), Smith (1977), and White (1954).

[24] Providing for the verbatim reporting of debates was separate from, but related to, official printing. Several of the characters who emerge as official Printers of Congress were involved at some time in private efforts to report the verbatim deliberations of Congress, which were then distributed among paid subscribers. These were Joseph Gales Jr. and William Winston Seaton, who published the *Annals of Congress* (1789–1824) and the *Register of Debates* (1824–37), and Francis Preston Blair and John C. Rives, who published the *Congressional Globe* (1833–73). These private efforts were largely underwritten by the excess moneys that these individuals received as Printers of Congress.

publishers whose primary business was producing partisan communications. The Jacksonian democratization of electoral politics also brought with it an elevation of the politically connected Printer and the explosion of the party organ as a mode of informing and rallying the troops. When prominent state politicians were elected to a federal position, they often brought the local press to Washington in an effort to better integrate state and local politics. It is not surprising, for instance, that three of the five members of Andrew Jackson's Kitchen Cabinet were newspaper publishers.[25]

Table 2.2 reports the identity of the Printers of the House and Senate from 1819 to 1860, along with amounts paid to these Printers under the congressional contracts. Table 2.3 reports major publishers during this period and their relationship to major political figures. A series of congressional investigations over time, along with scholarly research, has suggested that more than half the amounts paid to the congressional printers in the antebellum period were pure profit. Much of these profits did not go to the Printer himself but rather were skimmed for political purposes, notably to benefit the interests of the Printer's party (Smith 1977). The Printer used these excess moneys in a variety of ways; underwriting party press organs throughout the country was typically the major goal,[26] but he also contributed to congressional election campaigns and distributed funds to lobbyists and congressmen.[27]

---

[25] Amos Kendall (*Argus of Western America* [Kentucky]), Isaac Hill (*New Hampshire Patriot*), William B. Lewis, Andrew J. Donelson, and Duff Green (*St. Louis Enquirer; United States Telegraph*).

[26] These funds, distributed by the House and Senate Printers, were the chief source of congressional patronage for party newspapers. The executive branch had its own source of patronage, wherein the secretary of state would select two newspapers in each state to publish the laws of the nation. Newspapers selected by the secretary of state would receive a subsidy and, in many cases, the editor of the paper would receive a postmastership (which came with a generous stipend). Over time, a norm was established in which members of Congress would select the newspapers in their given states, and the secretary of state would accommodate their requests. Nevertheless, the congressional funds provided by the Printers ensured that the congressional party's perspective—when different from the president's perspective—would also receive a fair hearing in the news coverage. See Fowler (1943) and Smith (1977) for additional details.

[27] Many of these shady activities came to light during the Republican investigation of the Buchanan administration in 1860. Three different House committees were appointed at various points to look into a range of fraud and corruption charges leveled against Buchanan and Democratic Party leaders, the chief committee being a select one chaired by John Covode (R-Pa.). Among the witnesses called before the Covode Committee was Cornelius Wendell, House Printer in the 34th Congress (1855–57). In two sets of testimony, Wendell outlined the various activities that he conducted for the Democratic Party by using the excess funds that he received from the congressional printing. In addition to subsidizing various Democratic newspapers, Wendell also paid Democratic operatives in several congressional campaigns and attempted to "buy" the votes of select members of Congress on the Kansas issue. Thanks in part to Wendell's testimony, Congress eliminated the Printer positions in both chambers and established the Government Printing Office to handle subsequent congressional printing. See Bruns (1975) and Smith (1977, 206–32) for more detailed accounts.

TABLE 2.2.
Congressional Printers, 1819–1860

Cong.	Years	House			Senate		
		Party control	Printer	Amt. Paid	Party control	Printer	Amt. Paid
16	1819–21	Rep.	Gales & Seaton	$228,837	Rep.	Gales & Seaton	$91,857
17	1821–23	Rep.	Gales & Seaton		Rep.	Gales & Seaton	
18	1823–25	—	Gales & Seaton		—	Gales & Seaton	
19	1825–27	Adams	Gales & Seaton			Gales & Seaton	
20	1827–29	Jack.	Gales & Seaton	$62,154	Jack.	Duff Green	$32,249
21	1829–31	Jack.	Duff Green	$66,050	Jack.	Duff Green	$28,247
22	1831–33	Jack.	Duff Green	$108,566	Tie.	Duff Green	$34,152
23	1833–35	Jack.	Gales & Seaton	$144,092	Anti-J.	Duff Green	$92,244
24	1835–37	Jack.	Blair & Rives	$128,291	Tie	Gales & Seaton	$40,035
25	1837–39	Dem.	Thomas Allen	$192,078	Dem.	Blair & Rives	$88,588
26	1839–41	Dem.[a]	Blair & Rives	$111,078	Dem.	Blair & Rives	$76,601
27	1841–43	Whig	Gales & Seaton	$259,920	Whig	Thomas Allen	$40,791
28	1843–45	Dem.	Blair & Rives	$169,486	Whig	Gales & Seaton	$182,737
29	1845–47	Dem.	Ritchie & Heiss	$185,407	Dem.	Ritchie & Heiss	$82,940
30[b]	1847–49	Whig	--------	----	Dem.	----	----
31[b]	1849–51	Dem.			Dem.		
32	1851–53	Dem.	Robert Armstrong	$54,081	Dem.	Robert Armstrong	$51,220
33	1853–55	Dem.	Armstrong &A.O.P. Nicholson	$188,237	Dem.	Beverly Tucker	$148,354
34	1855–57	Opp.	Cornelius Wendell	$257,497	Dem.	A.O.P. Nicholson	$164,425
35	1857–59	Dem.	James Steedman	$179,230	Dem.	William A. Harris	$94,652
36	1859–61	Rep.	Thomas A. Ford	c	Dem.	George Bowman	c

Source: Smith (1977), 250–52. Party control taken from Martis (1989).

[a] Although Democrats nominally controlled the House, a Whig was elected Speaker.

[b] Printers were not elected in these two Congresses; instead, Congress adopted a low-cost bidding system and established five classes of printing contracts. Payments not reported.

c Payments not reported. The Printer position was dissolved in 1860 with the creation of the GPO.

TABLE 2.3.
Major publishers and their relationships to newspapers and political officials, 1819–1860

Publisher/printer	Newspaper	Founded	Partisan affiliation	Congressional Printer	
				House	Senate
Joseph Gales & William W. Seaton	National Intelligencer	1800	Official organ of the Jefferson, Madison, and Monroe administrations; moved toward the Whigs (esp. Webster) under Jackson; official organ of Harrison and Fillmore administrations	1819–29, 1831–35, 1841–43	1819–27, 1835–37, 1843–45
Peter Force	National Journal	1823	Official organ of J. Q. Adams administration	—	—
Duff Green	United States Telegraph	1826	Official organ of Jackson administration; transferred support to Calhoun in 1831	1829–1833	1827–1835
Frances Preston Blair & John C. Rives	Globe	1830	Official organ of Jackson and Van Buren administrations	1835–37, 1839–41, 1843–45	1837–41
Thomas Allen	Madisonian	1837	Official organ of Tyler administration	1837–39	1841–43
Thomas Ritchie & John P. Heiss; Robert Armstrong; A.O.P. Nicholson; Cornelius Wendell; William A. Harris[a]	Union	1845[b]	Official organ of Polk, Pierce, and Buchanan administrations	1845–47; 1851–54; 1854–55; 1855–57	1845–47; 1851–53; 1855–57; 1857–59
George Bowman	Constitution	1859[c]	Official organ of Buchanan administration		1859–61

Source: Smith (1977), 249–52.
[a] The Union changed editors/publishers several times during this period.
[b] The Globe was sold in 1845 and renamed the Union.
[c] The Union was sold in 1859 and renamed the Constitution.

Consequently, the Printer was in a position not only to shape public opinion for his party—through his own newspaper and the various party newspapers he kept afloat—but also to affect congressional elections and policy outputs in Congress. In helping shape public opinion for the party, the Printer also served as a whip of sorts. When individual party members broke with the president or the majority of his party, the Printer would transmit this information through his columns, which would be reprinted throughout the nation. Thus, individual members could be "called out" by the Printer via his ability to go public and communicate directly to the members' constituents. This also served as a deterrent to party members when controversial issues arose. The Printer was thus the "voice" of the party and, at least at times, also the party's chief bagman.

The turnover in the printership described in table 2.2 provides a foretaste of the politics we will examine in the following chapters. Here we comment on two general features of this turnover pattern. First, throughout this period, both the House and the Senate went through several phases in how they chose the Printer. From 1800 to 1819, the House Clerk and the Secretary of the Senate selected Printers on a purely lowest-bid basis. A combination of factors, such as dissatisfaction with the quality of the printing under this system and a desire to benefit more politically connected Printers, led the House and Senate to pass a joint resolution in 1819 on the final day of the 15th Congress (1817–19) that established a new system (*Statutes at Large*, 15-2, 538). Under this system, the House and Senate would set fixed amounts for printing, and then each chamber would separately elect a printer by (secret) ballot.

Ames (1972, 110–11) contends that the bill to establish elected Printer positions was pushed through by Henry Clay. Looking ahead to the presidential election of 1824, Clay sought a power structure to help him vie with John Quincy Adams, John Calhoun, and William Crawford—all of whom held cabinet positions and thus possessed a patronage-based staff that could be used for electioneering—for the presidential nomination. By creating congressional printerships, he hoped to establish his own base of patronage. The Printers would be tied to press organs, which Clay hoped would produce favorable public opinion for his candidacy. His favored editors, Gales and Seaton of the *National Intelligencer*, would go on to win the first set of Printer positions. In describing the overall scenario, Ames argues that "Clay had put together one of the richest patronage schemes the country yet had seen" (111).

Aside from a six-year window in which low-cost bidding was resuscitated, Congress continued electing Printers in this way until the Government Printing Office was established in 1860, at which time all congressional printing became the business of the federal government itself.

The six-year hiatus occurred from 1846 to 1852. The push for reform in congressional printing began in 1842 during the unified Whig Congress.

Calling for "retrenchment in government," and noting abuses in congressional printing practices, many Whigs sought to eliminate the House and Senate Printer positions and create a government-run printing operation. After an initial failure, a coalition of Whigs and Democrats eventually formed and established a system of low-cost bidding on August 3, 1846. This system turned out to be a practical failure, so Congress changed course and readopted the prior system of elected Printers in each chamber on August 26, 1852. We discuss the onset of the low-cost bidding regime and its demise in more detail in chapter 5.

The second general feature of the turnover pattern in table 2.2 was the increased politicization of the choice of Printer, which resulted from the influx of Jacksonians into Washington in the late 1820s. The first explicit example of this came in the 20th Congress (1827–29), when Jackson's supporters wrested control of the chamber from Adams's supporters. Martin Van Buren, Jackson's chief lieutenant and party builder, understood the importance of a vital party press in promoting the interests of the party (Remini 1959, 10). In New York, Van Buren had helped establish the *Albany Argus*, which served as the press organ of his Albany Regency. Stories and editorials in the *Argus* would be reprinted throughout the state, which created a vast information network for the party. And, like the congressional printers, the editors of the *Argus* were subsidized by government contracts to print local laws (Silbey 2002, 25).

Spurred on by Van Buren, Jackson's supporters launched an attack on Gales and Seaton, the House Printers who were tied more closely to the Adams wing of the Republican Party. A committee on retrenchment, controlled by Jacksonians, began an investigation into Gales and Seaton's printing practices based on "suspicions" that they were overinflating costs (Ames 1972, 158–61). While the committee uncovered no meaningful evidence and brought no real charges, the die was cast—the Printer would thereafter be a hotly contested position in the partisan wars. The churning of Printers reported in table 2.2 was a reflection of this new reality.

In general, the Printers who were elected in the years comprising the Second Party System reflected the political sentiments of the majority party. However, political intrigue sometimes entered the picture and resulted in the election of some Printers through a combination of support from the minority party and dissident majority party members. The intrigue came from two directions. First, dissident Democratic factions were sometimes willing to ally with Jackson's (and Van Buren's) opponents in selecting the Printer. (The dissidents could be either Calhounite Nullifiers or pro-Bank Democrats.) Second, intrigue *within the two major parties* resulted in a flurry of behind-the-scenes activity, as prominent political operatives created new publishing ventures in an effort to win the congressional contract. The timing of the choice of Printer is an important detail in what follows.

54

When the federal government retired to Washington in 1800, members of Congress found themselves in a village with little publishing capacity. In response to this situation, a law was passed that allowed the *expiring* Congress to provide for the printing needs of the *next* Congress. Under this arrangement, the House Clerk and the Secretary of the Senate were allowed to advertise for bids for the printing needs of the following Congress nine months in advance of the new Congress convening, so as to allow a Printer (or Printers) sufficient time to assemble the needed equipment and personnel.

The justification for this administrative quirk eventually disappeared, as Washington became a major publishing center, but the timing of the choice of congressional printers persisted. The resolution of 1819, which provided for the election of Printers by the two chambers, required the Printer to be elected by the *prior* Congress during the lame-duck session.

Needless to say, this provision of the law became quite controversial as the political importance of congressional printers increased and the Jacksonian/Democratic grip on Congress loosened. In some cases, opponents of this arrangement could simply force the issue by drawing out the end-of-Congress balloting, which pushed the Printer election into the following Congress. Some members of Congress took a more direct route by agitating for a change in the rule about when the Printer would be elected. Finally, beginning in the 24th Congress (1835–37), the choice of House Printer for a given Congress would be made at the opening of *that* Congress.[28]

In sum, in the third decade of the nineteenth century, the House Printer (along with his Senate counterpart) emerged as a valuable player in party leaders' efforts to build and expand their mass party organizations. The Printer was the chief propaganda organ of the governing party and possessed significant patronage abilities that could be used to spread the party "gospel" throughout the nation as well as to influence elections and policy decisions in Congress. As such, the Printer was an institutional actor to be reckoned with in chamber politics. Smith captures this sentiment and the general political context well, stating:

> The publishers as printers to Congress and their papers as party or administration organs had become a functional part of the government without benefit of specific Constitutional sanction. . . . The value of these publishers and their papers to the political parties or factions of the period is suggested by the incredible amount of time consumed in debates by the two houses on the choice of printer. (1977, 161–62)

[28] The Senate would not adopt such an arrangement for election of its Printer until the 27th Congress (1841–43). Here, the Whigs entered the Senate as the majority party and rescinded the decision of the *previous* Congress (controlled by Democrats) to elect Blair and Rives as Senate Printer for the next Congress (27th). Thomas Allen, editor of the *Madisonian*, would then be elected Senate Printer *in* the 27th Congress *for* the 27th Congress to replace Blair and Rives. See Smith (1977, 159–61).

Conclusion

As we embark upon an exploration of how members of the House of Representatives have fought over control of the chamber, the purpose of this chapter has been to (re)acquaint us with the principal elements of House organization—the top House offices, the rules of procedure, and the committee system—before the Civil War.

Most modern students of American politics are familiar with these elements for the period *following* the Civil War, especially how they have been configured since the onset of the Reed Rules in the 1890s. Three things are striking in considering these elements in the antebellum era. The first is that all were regularly viewed as political resources. The second is that party leaders saw the potential of these resources for helping to cement the edifice of a party-centered legislative institution. The third is that party was just one claimant, and not always the dominant one at that.

Looking forward to the rest of the argument in this book, gaining control over the elements of institutional power required a mechanism through which party divisions could be negotiated and in which leaders could be chosen who would satisfy all elements of the party. This required a strong party caucus that could observe the behavior of its members and credibly sanction them if they defected from the agreed-upon strategy of the caucus. The difficulties we will observe arose from the deep regional divisions that pervaded the nation throughout most of the nineteenth century. Ironically (or, perhaps, inevitably) enough, it would be the first uniregional party, the Republicans, that provided the "proof of concept" of the party caucus as the focal point of strong parties.

We now turn our attention to these early struggles to forge the institutional mechanisms of party government.

CHAPTER 3

Organizational Politics under the Secret Ballot

❧

As it became clear that officers like the Speaker and Clerk could be politically valuable, conflict over organizing the House took on an increasingly partisan cast in the early Republic. Yet it would be a mistake to leap from the observation that House members viewed officer votes through the lens of nascent partisanship to an inference that this was part of an organized, formal manifestation of party activity, much less the first budding of an organizational cartel. At first, there were no formal party organizations at the national level, including the House.

Organizational politics during the earliest years remain mysterious, not only because the national media, diarists, and the like wrote little about it, but also because House rules helped to submerge the politics of organization. Although the Constitution requires that the two chambers "shall keep a Journal of its Proceedings, and from time to time publish the same, . . . and the Yeas and Nays of the Members of either House on any question shall, at the Desire of one fifth of those Present, be entered on the Journal," the House did not regard the votes they cast for officers to be "Yeas and Nays," and instead adopted a secret ballot to govern these elections. As a result, for the first half century of the nation's history, we do not know how individual House members voted for Speaker or other officers. To the extent that the House kept records, only aggregate results were reported.

Nevertheless, these battles left traces on the public record—increasingly so, as the House officers became more prominent on the national stage. In this chapter, we lay the groundwork for later analysis by examining speakership and other officer contests during the period when elections were held by secret ballot—ending in 1837.

HOUSE ORGANIZATION IN AN ERA OF WEAK PARTIES, 1789–1811

In the years preceding the War of 1812, the election of Speaker and other House officers occurred in a chamber whose internal institutions were in flux. Party identification among the rank and file was loose, even as some polarization was evident around the personalities and policies of Thomas Jefferson and Alexander Hamilton.

During the First Congress (1789–91), a set of norms emerged wherein all matters of policy and procedure were first discussed by the entire chamber. "First principles" would be established in the Committee of the Whole (COW), a procedural entity composed of all House members, so that the deliberative process could produce the most democratically informed outcome. If additional, specialized information was required, or if a detailed policy initiative needed to be created, then the matter would be sent to a select or standing committee based on the relevant jurisdiction. This was the House's typical modus operandi for dealing with legislative business for the first two Congresses (Cooper 1970).

As a result, the Speaker was something of a minor figure in institutional proceedings. Because the COW was the primary repository of House business, the Speaker's role in the chamber was somewhat limited. But it was not entirely inconsequential. The Speaker ruled on parliamentary points of order, determined assignments on select and standing committees, and broke legislative ties. Thus, early on, the Speaker could be best characterized as part traffic cop, part chamber manager.

The transformation of the speakership into a partisan office followed the evolution of the chamber itself. The first Speaker, Frederick A. C. Muhlenberg (Pa.), was a policy moderate who did not aspire to use his position in a distinctly partisan manner. This was in keeping with the fluidity in the House, as partisan sorting was still in its infancy. By the Second Congress (1791–93), as institutional parties began forming, Jonathan Trumbull Jr. (Conn.) was elected Speaker to replace Muhlenberg. Trumbull's election was due in part to shared norms of rotation and regional balancing of the speakership, but it was also a reaction to the policy stances of the candidates. Trumbull was a strong backer of the Hamiltonian agenda and became an active member of the Federalist Party. While he was Speaker, Trumbull cast the tie-breaking vote against James Jackson, an ardent opponent of the Washington administration, in his Georgia contested election case, thus vacating the House seat (*Annals*, 2-1, 3/21/1792, 479).

The Third Congress (1793–95) saw the forces of Madison and Jefferson, the Republicans, hold a slim advantage over the Federalists in the distribution of House members. They were unable to leverage their numerical majority in the speakership election, however, as their attendance when Congress convened was lacking.[1]

This would prove to be the first multiballot speakership election in U.S. history. On the first ballot, three major candidates emerged: Theodore Sedg-

---

[1] Tardiness on the part of Republicans was an issue on more than one occasion in these early Congresses. Risjord (1992, 630) notes that Republicans represented districts from the South and West, which made it more difficult for them (in an age before mass transportation) to arrive on time for the start of the congressional session. He also suggests that the Federalists might have been more "motivated" to arrive promptly, as they had a clear partisan mission in Congress, while the Republicans eschewed parties and factions and thus had little incentive to travel with due haste. The former explanation strikes us as more plausible.

wick (Mass.), an active Federalist; Abraham Baldwin (Ga.), a moderate Republican; and ex-Speaker Muhlenberg, a weak Federalist. Sedgwick garnered 24 votes to 21 for Muhlenberg and 14 for Baldwin, with 7 votes scattering. On the second vote, Baldwin's support vanished, as Muhlenberg took the lead with 33 votes to Sedgwick's 29. On the third ballot, Muhlenberg emerged victorious, garnering 37 votes to Sedgwick's 27 (*Philadelphia General Advertiser*, 12/3/1793, 3).[2]

The increasing partisanship in both House politics and speakership elections overlapped with changing norms of doing business in the chamber. By the Third Congress, it became clear that determining first principles on all issues within the COW was unrealistic; in attempting to do so, the House found itself quickly overextended (Cooper 1970, 9). Thus, the House began bypassing the COW on a fairly routine basis, and instead referred more and more legislative business directly to select and standing committees.

This increasing reliance on the committee system altered the dynamics of House decision making. Whereas select and standing committees were established initially to fact-find and determine specific policy details, they now were given considerably wider discretion. In effect, committees became *policy proposers*, constructing bills in accordance with the conception and preferences of their members (Cooper 1970, 15–16). Committees, therefore, became a key node of power within the House and a critical stake in the emerging institutional squabbling between Federalists and Republicans. Leaders on both sides came to realize that policy making in the House was increasingly driven by the committee system, and that the Speaker, as distributor of committee assignments, was thus an officer of some importance.

A first sign of this committee autonomy appeared in the Third Congress. In response to concerns regarding the nation's internal and external safety and protection, which were raised by the president in his Annual Message, Speaker Muhlenburg established four select committees that would have a significant effect on chamber business during the session. As Risjord (1992, 639–40) notes, "Established to consider matters of public policy, they governed the legislative agenda . . . Dominated by Federalists, each committee drafted highly partisan measures that generated weeks of debate." Further, the role of the Ways and Means Committee, now elevated to standing committee status, shifted in a direction advocated by Madison as a way to stem Hamilton's influence within the chamber (White 1948, 71–73; Furlong 1967). But before long, Madison realized that the committee would be a Federalist conduit, and found that it was "composed of a majority infected by the fiscal errors which threaten so ignominious and vexatious a system to our country."[3] As a result, Madison and Jefferson acknowledged that "they

---

[2] On the second and third ballots, in addition to the votes for Muhlenberg and Sedgwick, there were "some" and "a few" scattered votes, respectively.

[3] Letter from Madison to Jefferson, April 14, 1794. Reprinted in Stagg (1989, 306–7).

had been thwarted by the appointive power of the Speaker" (Risjord 1992, 641).

The speakership election in the Fourth Congress (1795–97) saw Jonathan Dayton (N.J.) defeat Muhlenberg by a 46–31 vote on the first ballot. While Muhlenburg's committee appointments had appeared to help the Federalists in the prior Congress, there was a growing sense that his leanings were shifting toward the Republicans. As a result, the Federalists threw their support to Dayton, a centrist within the party ranks (Lientz 1978, 65).

Once in the Speaker's chair, Dayton delivered by appointing Federalist chairs and majorities to two new standing committees—Ways and Means (elevated from select status) and Commerce and Manufactures—which were critical to the party's economic agenda. He also took a leading role in the appropriation of funds to implement the Jay Treaty—a source of strong disagreement between the two parties—and actively lobbied Federalist members to support the underwriting of the accord with Britain (Charles 1955, 604–5; Risjord 1992, 645–46).

Dayton was easily reelected Speaker in the Fifth Congress (1797–99) and continued to behave in a strict partisan fashion. In particular, his committee assignments, both in terms of standing committees like Ways and Means and select committees that were responsible for handling important policy matters—like military and naval affairs, as well as the Alien and Sedition Acts—betrayed a strong Federalist bias (Risjord 1992, 647). Moreover, Dayton voiced his partisan preferences openly in House debate. For example, after relinquishing his position briefly due to illness—at which point a Speaker pro tempore, George Dent (F-Md.), was elected—Dayton appeared on the House floor and "conducted himself so violently in partisan debate ... that he was called to order by the temporary occupant of the chair" (Hinds 1909, 157). As a result of his partisan behavior, Dayton drew the ire of many Republicans in the chamber, which is clearly seen in the 40–22 vote to "thank him" for his service prior to the adjournment of the session—a roll call that was customarily unanimous (Dauer 1953, 232–33).[4]

The speakership election to the Sixth Congress (1799–1801) witnessed a brief internal rift within the Federalist ranks. While the Federalists held a small numerical advantage over the Republicans, regional factions within the party pushed for one of their own for Speaker. Northern Federalists backed Theodore Sedgwick (Mass.), while Southern Federalists supported John Rutledge Jr. (S.C.). The Republicans hoped to take advantage of the Federalists' sectional division by pushing Nathaniel Macon (Va.), a moderate Southern partisan, as a way of drawing in Rutledge's Southern supporters. After an informal Federalist caucus suggested that a party split might

---

[4] In response, Dayton responded, "As in all public bodies, there have ever been found men whose approbation must be considered by the meritorious as censure, so in this body, there are, unhappily, some whose censure must be regarded by all whose esteem I value, as the highest testimony of merit" (*Annals*, 5-3, 3/3/1799, 3055).

occur, Rutledge concluded his chances of winning were slight and, not wishing to help Macon, urged his supporters to back Sedgwick (Furlong 1967). This conciliatory action helped heal the party's sectional division. On the first speakership ballot, Sedgwick fell one vote shy of a majority, garnering 42 votes to 27 for Macon, 13 for George Dent, and 3 scattering. On the next ballot, Dent's supporters moved to Macon, but Sedgwick gained 2 votes, bringing his total to 44, enough for a bare majority (*Annals*, 6-1, 12/2/1799, 185–86).

Sedgwick proved to be the most partisan Speaker to date. While not actively participating in House debates, as Dayton had done, Sedgwick controlled chamber politics from the Speaker's chair. Of the eight most important House committees in the Sixth Congress—five standing and three select —Sedgwick appointed clear Federalist majorities to each, and indicated that his appointments were made explicitly to push a Federalist agenda (Welch 1965, 206–7; Risjord 1992, 649). He also used his procedural authority in a distinctly partisan way, as he "displayed little tolerance for parliamentary maneuvering and dilatory tactics" (Kennon 1986, 25).[5] He was also the pivotal voter on six roll calls in his capacity as presiding officer, two on particularly important policy matters—first, to create a uniform bankruptcy system throughout the United States, and second, to maintain the Sedition Act (*Annals*, 6-1, 2/21/1800, 534; 6-2, 2/19/1801, 1038–39). Another of Sedgwick's pivotal votes supported a motion to bar two reporters from the *National Intelligencer* (a Republican newspaper that had been critical of the Federalists and the Speaker in particular) from the House floor (*Annals*, 6-2, 12/9/1800, 816). This move created a Republican uproar over censorship and denial of free speech that lasted for months (Welch 1965, 207; Ames 1972, 23–26).

The combination of Sedgwick's partisan committee assignments and procedural parochialism led to a narrow 40–35 vote of "thanks" to him at the end of the session. The roll call broke down strictly along partisan lines, as all participating Republicans voted against Sedgwick (*Annals*, 6-2, 3/3/1801, 1079–80).

The elections of 1800 swept the Federalists from power, where they would languish in the minority until their demise two decades later. Nevertheless, the Federalists left behind a legacy by establishing the structure by which the majority party, through the Speaker and committees, could influence the policy-making process in the House. The initial system of hashing out policy and procedural details in the COW was gradually shunted aside as Federalist Party leaders learned that committees under the direct control

---

[5] Sedgwick also worked behind the scenes as a partisan leader. Evidence suggests that he conferred with other Federalist leaders on procedural tactics. He also appears to have personally tailored legislation on a national road bill, but passed it on to Henry Lee (F-Va.) to steer through the legislative process rather than present it himself. See Risjord (1992, 649), which cites letters from Sedgwick to Peter Van Schaack (Feb. 4 and 9, 1800).

of the Speaker could more efficiently generate policy that was suited to the majority party as a whole.

Still, committees possessed only a limited degree of agenda control. Although a Speaker could appoint a partisan committee, refer bills to it, and recognize committee members who wished to report bills to the floor, once a piece of legislation was before the House, there was no procedural way to expedite its passage or protect it against amendment. The "special rules" that are commonplace in today's House were still almost a century away; although a previous question rule was part of the House rules from the First Congress, it was largely ineffectual.[6] That the Federalists experienced some success in enacting legislation was due mostly to the inability of the Republicans to organize effectively so that they *could* obstruct (Harlow 1917, 163–64). Within a decade, however, the majority party would alter House rules so that the Speaker-committee arrangement of policy making would work more efficiently, and thus the majority would not have to rely on the ineptitude of the minority to work its will.

The Seventh Congress (1801–3) saw the Republicans with a substantial majority, which translated to a quick speakership victory, as Nathaniel Macon (R-N.C.) defeated James A. Bayard (F-Del.) on a 53 to 26 vote (*New York Commercial Advertiser*, 12/12/1801, 3). With all levers of national power in their hands, the Jeffersonians worked to coordinate their efforts. And Macon was a willing participant, as he used his appointment power as Speaker to replace the Federalist majorities on the five House standing committees with Jeffersonian majorities (Cunningham 1978, 230–31).[7] Yet Macon was distinctly less partisan than Sedgwick had been in the Speaker's chair, to the point that "some members of his party resented [his] impartiality to the opposition" (Kennon 1986, 30).

Macon was easily reelected Speaker in the Eighth Congress (1803–5),[8] and continued his relatively evenhanded work on behalf of the party. His relationship with Jefferson became strained, however, due to his close friendship with John Randolph (Va.), the chairman of Ways and Means and leader of the Quid faction of the Republican Party. A rift between Randolph and Jefferson had developed in 1805, first around various claims on land in western Georgia (the Yazoo land transfer) and later on the desirability of acquiring Florida from Spain (Carson 1986). As a result, Macon was increasingly viewed as a liability by the Jeffersonians, and he faced stiff competition in the speakership election to the Ninth Congress (1805–7). None-

---

[6] As Alexander states, "Although it cut off debate on the main question, [the previous question rule] permitted each member to speak at least once on the expediency of ordering it" (1916, 184). Thus, the previous question itself could be filibustered.

[7] Two of the five standing committees—Claims and Revisal and Unfinished Business—were chaired by Federalists: John Cotton Smith (Conn.) and John Davenport (Conn.), respectively.

[8] Lientz (1978, 67) notes that Macon's election was so uncontroversial that the newspapers of the time offered little coverage and no final tally.

theless, he survived, winning reelection after three closely contested ballots (*Richmond Enquirer* [hereafter abbreviated as *RE*], 12/6/1805, 3).

The division within the party remained, however, as battles between the Randolph and Jefferson factions continued throughout the session. Eventually Macon was targeted for retribution—this occurred on the first day of the second session, when Willis Alston (N.C.), a supporter of Jefferson's, moved that standing committee assignments be determined by ballot rather than by the Speaker. Joseph Clay (Pa.) responded by moving to strike out the words "by ballot," and his motion carried by a slim 44–42 voice vote (*Annals*, 9-2, 12/1/1806, 111). Macon had (barely) retained his authority, but the message was clear: the party regulars were unhappy with his performance as Speaker and had him in their sights.

Macon's luck would run out in the speakership election to the 10th Congress (1807–9), when Joseph Varnum (R-Mass.), the Jeffersonian candidate, was elected by a bare majority on the first ballot (*Annals*, 10-1, 10/26/1807, 782). Varnum quickly made his presence known by reconfiguring the standing committees to better suit the preferences of the Jeffersonians. He also supported Jefferson's desires to resist a standing army and the construction of a navy, and later backed the president's embargo against Great Britain.

And yet, while Varnum would be reelected Speaker in the 11th Congress (1809–11) in a two-ballot affair (*Annals*, 11-1, 5/22/1809, 54–56), all was not well. As Peters notes, "[i]n Varnum, the House had a leader who . . . wished to avoid conflict" (1997, 33). In particular, he struggled in vain to rein in the Randolph wing of party, and was the target of increased dilatory tactics by both Quids and Federalists.

Varnum's inability to eliminate obstructionist behavior led the Jeffersonians to enhance the majority's procedural authority (and restrict minority rights) by strengthening the House's previous question rule. The new interpretation of the rule, which was ratified on a 66–13 vote (*Annals*, 11-3, 2/27/1811, 1092), was a significant alteration, as "approval of the previous question was now considered to suppress debate and to bring the pending matter to a vote" (Binder 1997, 50).[9] Thus, a simple majority, if cohesive, now possessed a procedural mechanism to ward off minority obstructionism. This new previous question rule would be codified in the House rules at the beginning of the 12th Congress (1811), just in time for the appearance on the scene of an ambitious new Speaker: Henry Clay.

---

[9] In 1807, Speaker Varnum sought to interpret approval of the motion in just this way—that all debate would be cut off and the House would proceed to an immediate vote on the pending business (Binder 1997, 50). But the House was unwilling at that point (not yet having had their fill of John Randolph, apparently) to restrict minority rights, and the membership overruled Varnum, 103–14 (*Annals*, 10-1, 12/15/1807, 1784). In the 11th Congress, Varnum interpreted the rule as he believed the House wanted it interpreted—treating debate as sacrosanct—but the membership (now having had enough of Randolph's antics) reversed itself and expressed a new openness to curtailing debate. Thus, in providing a majority with the ability to bring debate to a close, the House in fact overruled Varnum.

The evolution of the House Clerk during this period can be examined by tracking the career path of one individual, John Beckley, who held the office for most of this time. Beckley was a political lifer who had worked his way up through the ranks in Virginia by serving in clerical roles during the Revolution and afterward. His various positions put him in contact with the state's political notables, and he secured recommendations from Edmund Randolph and James Madison in his quest to become the first Clerk of the U.S. House.[10] Beckley's "campaigning" was ultimately successful, as he was elected House Clerk of the First Congress on the second ballot, the first ballot having ended in a tie (*HJ*, 1-1, 4/1/1789, 6; Berkeley and Berkeley 1975, 85).

Beckley had the option to bury himself in the clerical duties that comprised his position, but he was not content simply to be an observer to the House's political drama. He soon realized that being Clerk provided distinct opportunities to support the Jeffersonian cause to which he was dedicated. Taking advantage of his privileged administrative position, Beckley passed on sensitive information on a range of topics to Jefferson and his lieutenants, Madison and James Monroe. This information was often used strategically to give Jefferson and his party an advantage in the framing of public opinion, as well as in congressional debates and roll call votes (Martin 1949–50). Beckley also performed behind the scenes as a protowhip, "using his position to organize the [Jeffersonian] congressmen and, through them, the party membership" (Jahoda 1960, 254).

Despite his efforts on behalf of Jefferson, Beckley was reelected Clerk in the Second Congress, which still had a majority of pro-administration (Federalist) members (*HJ*, 2-1, 10/24/1791, 434). He was also reelected in the Third and Fourth Congresses, which had anti-administration (Republican) majorities (*HJ*, 3-1, 12/2/1793, 4; 4-1, 12/7/1795, 365). The lack of an ironclad tie between electoral and institutional partisanship is illustrated here, in that his election in the Third Congress was by acclamation. In the Fourth Congress, he received more votes for Clerk than the number of Republicans in the House.

However, Beckley's activities during the Fourth Congress elevated and highlighted his partisan role, which led him and the clerkship to be regarded in a new light. The main event was the debate over the Jay Treaty during the winter of 1795–96. Beckley opposed diplomatic treaties generally, but as a devoted Francophile, he especially opposed them with the British. He used his influence and all of the information at his disposal to organize the Jeffersonians in the House against the treaty, but fell short in the end, as it passed on a 51–48 roll call (*HJ*, 4-1, 4/30/1796, 531).

Now clearly identified as an active partisan, Beckley focused his efforts on getting Jefferson elected president in 1796. In this capacity, he became

[10] For coverage of Beckley's long and dynamic political life, see Marsh (1948), Martin (1949–50), Cunningham (1956), Jahoda (1960), Berkeley and Berkeley (1962, 1973, 1975), Gawalt (1995), Pasley (1996), and Jenkins and Stewart (2004).

known as one of the nation's first party managers. Beckley targeted his adopted home state of Pennsylvania and began a determined electoral campaign, which included the production and distribution of thousands of handwritten ballots and political handbills (Martin 1949–50; Cunningham 1956). Beckley won the battle, chalking up 14 of Pennsylvania's 15 electoral votes for Jefferson, but lost the war, as Adams secured an Electoral College majority nationwide.

Beckley's high-profile activities involving the Jay Treaty and the election of 1796 alerted Federalists to the value of the Clerk's office as a partisan post. If nothing else, supporters of President Adams had no interest in subsidizing Beckley's political activities by continuing his tenure as House Clerk. Having gained control of the House in the Fifth Congress, the Federalists targeted him for removal, and they managed to oust him by a single vote, 41–40, in favor of Federalist James W. Condy (*Annals*, 5-1, 5/15/1797, 52).[11]

After his downfall, Beckley managed to eke out a living as an essayist.[12] When Republicans rode to triumph on Jefferson's coattails in the House elections of 1800–1801, Beckley was rewarded again with the House clerkship in the Seventh Congress, which he subsequently reclaimed in the Eighth and Ninth Congresses. In the midst of this tenure, in 1802, he was also elected the first Librarian of Congress, a position he held until his death in 1807. And, as Jahoda notes, "Even as a librarian Beckley was political. His conception of duty on the job was simple; he tried to keep Federalists from seeing documents which would give them useful information" (1960, 257).

HOUSE ORGANIZATION IN AN ERA OF INSTITUTIONAL DEVELOPMENT, 1811–1837

From a modern perspective, the House during the first 11 Congresses was underdeveloped. As the speakerships of Jonathan Dayton and Theodore Sedgwick and the life of John Beckley show, however, it was possible for the leadership positions in the House to be put to partisan use. Still, in an era where a "Jeffersonian ethos" (Cooper 1970; cf. Risjord 1992) characterized the House culture, there were no loud and persistent voices that argued that the organization of the chamber should be constructed self-consciously with partisan ends in mind. The House as a formal institution was underfunded and underorganized. As a consequence, any role that the incumbent of a House office might play in policy or partisan intrigues was ad hoc and far from institutionalized.

[11] Like so many House Clerks, with the exception of a few like Beckley, Condy has left no trace upon the historical record other than his tenure as House Clerk in the Fifth and Sixth Congresses.

[12] Beckley is the one who persuaded James Thomas Callender to publish the infamous charges of adultery against Alexander Hamilton (Berkeley and Berkeley 1975, 89).

That began to change around the time Henry Clay became Speaker in the 12th Congress (1811–13). From Clay's first speakership until the time when the House began to ballot for its Speakers publicly in the 26th Congress (1839–41), the formal structure of the House became more complex, the role of political parties was transformed, and the value of House offices, including positions like the Printer and Clerk, was much enhanced.

What makes the 12th Congress a logical break in considering the House organization was the demonstration by Clay that the speakership could be used to the programmatic advantage of the faction that controlled it, whether that faction be personality-driven or partisan. Clay's own dynamic leadership in the run-up to the War of 1812 demonstrated that it was possible for the House to take an active, leading role in momentous policy decisions. Clay skillfully used new parliamentary tools, like the beefed-up previous question rule that had been adopted in the prior Congress to cut off floor debate (Binder 1997, 49–50; Stewart 1998, 2007). The 1810s also were the time when both chambers of Congress shifted from select committees to standing committees to process most legislation (Gamm and Shepsle 1989; Jenkins 1998). Although the power and capacity of these standing committees was still in the formative stages, it was the Speaker who appointed them. Thus, the Speaker was beginning to acquire parliamentary tools that could make this office the most influential policy post in the nation.

This was also a transitional period for the party as well. From the 12th to the 24th Congresses (1811–37), the Republicans (later Democrats) were formally the dominant party. Throughout this quarter century, the partisan heirs of Thomas Jefferson always held a majority of House seats. Yet it would be a mistake to characterize this as a period of one-party domination, as party affiliations were quite fluid in the electorate and in government.

The early part of this period was dominated by the War of 1812 and its immediate aftermath. As such, the formal rise of the Republicans to numerical dominance was as much a consequence of the Federalists being considered disloyal (due to their participation at the Hartford Convention) as anything else.[13] Being a Federalist became the electoral kiss of death, so many intellectual heirs of Hamilton reluctantly took up the Republican mantle. Following the war, during the so-called Era of Good Feelings, national politics lacked the polarization that accompanied the debates over whether to align with England or France. This led to the Republicans becoming a catchall party.[14]

[13] As the War of 1812 was winding down, the Federalists met in Hartford, Connecticut, to discuss the possibility of a peace accord with the British. Their efforts, reported in the press on the heels of General Andrew Jackson's victory at New Orleans, appeared to border on treasonous. Already institutionally weak, the Federalists could not survive this negative portrayal, and by the middle part of the decade they had disappeared as a viable national party.

[14] President James Monroe also pushed for an end to partisanship and attempted to subsume the remaining set of Federalists under the Republican banner. Hofstadter (1969) argues that this "amalgamation" program under Monroe eliminated legitimate opposition in the na-

The lack of a viable partisan foil and the resulting lack of a polarizing pull in national politics created regional divisions within the Republican Party, as members began to focus on parochial interests, which often brought them into conflict with copartisans from other regions. These battles over regional issues made legislating problematic, as party mechanisms that had been created to coordinate shared interests broke down. As a result, voting became fluid and highly unstable, which is illustrated in Poole and Rosenthal's (1997) historical analysis of congressional roll call voting. They find that the period from 1815 to 1825 is the one prolonged stretch in American history when congressional voting amounted to "spatial chaos" (31, 38–39).[15]

Thus, for the first half of this quarter century, political leaders jockeyed for new advantages based on personal appeals. As a result, politics became localized, with regional fissures emerging within the Republican coalition. In the second half, however, Martin Van Buren and his political allies made strides toward shrinking the Republicans' big tent in order to create a more potent and politically valuable institution known as the Democratic Party. Personal appeals that invoked region were out; partisan appeals in a national vein were in—or at least in theory. Try as they might, Van Buren and his organizational heirs could never secure their dream of a strong interregional party, devoid of competing personal or regional tugs, into a neat package. Nonetheless, that was the goal, and it transformed how everyone in national politics viewed the formal positions of leadership in the House.

The portfolio that Van Buren assembled in the interest of creating a national party was diversified. Certainly, the core of this portfolio was executive patronage, so that the victors could claim the spoils. But this system also rested on building an enduring network of propaganda and political operatives, and for that project, the House (and Senate) possessed valuable assets. During this period, federal patronage of local newspapers grew; a major goal of that patronage was the creation of a network of local partisan newspapers that could reprint the reports that originated in Washington (Smith 1977). The most important node of these partisan newspaper networks was the "party organ"—a newspaper supported by national leaders and published in the nation's capital. Private investment was one way to maintain these mouthpieces, but national party leaders figured out another way: funnel money through the congressional printers who were elected in each chamber.

In the earliest days of the Republic, the House and Senate Printers were chosen simply on a low-bid basis. In the House, the choice was made by the Clerk. (In a detail that will become important later on, the choice was made

tion and led to a factionalization of the political system around key personalities—principally those who had their sights set on the presidency in 1824 (John Quincy Adams, William Crawford, John Calhoun, Henry Clay, and, later, Andrew Jackson).

[15] Another shorter period of "chaos" occurred in the early 1850s amid the rapid deterioration of the Whig Party (Poole and Rosenthal 1997, 31, 52).

before the new Congress convened. Thus, the House Printer was chosen by the House Clerk who had held the position in the *previous* Congress.) The independent political significance of the congressional printers was marked by the passage of a joint resolution on the last day of the 15th Congress (March 3, 1819) that provided for the election of the Printer by (secret) ballot in each chamber (3 *Stat.* 538; *Annals*, 15-2, 3/3/1819, 247–49, 281). In keeping with the prior practice, each chamber's Printer would be elected by one Congress, to take office in the next.

During the quarter century that we focus on here, contention over the House organization grew gradually, as party leaders sought to capture the major House offices to be used for distinctly partisan goals. Amid their efforts, they were hounded by persistent minority regional factions and third parties that were bent on undermining their goals.

In the initial organization of the 12th–16th Congresses (1811–21), the personal dominance of Henry Clay was so great that the festering political divisions below the surface were hardly in evidence. Clay himself was easily elected and then reelected Speaker at the start of each of these Congresses— in the last two by virtual acclamation. The clerkship and printership contests were similarly muted. Patrick Magruder, who was first elected Clerk at the start of the 10th Congress (1807) in a four-ballot affair, consolidated his hold on the office and was easily reelected at the start of the next three Congresses. When Magruder was discredited over his actions during the British burning of the Capitol, he resigned in the middle of the 13th Congress; his successor, Thomas Dougherty, claimed the office in a brief two-ballot contest. Dougherty was then reelected unanimously (or virtually so) in each of the next four Congresses. In the first official Printer election on the final day of the 15th Congress, Joseph Gales Jr. and William Seaton were the uncontested choice (*Annals*, 15-2, 3/3/1819, 1441). Their *National Intelligencer* had been publishing in Washington since 1800 as the unofficial Jeffersonian mouthpiece; Gales, later joined by Seaton, had been the editor and publisher since 1801.[16] Once in control of the House printership, Gales and Seaton held it firmly, winning first-ballot reelections in each of the next four Congresses.

Clay's reelection as Speaker at the start of the 16th Congress (1819–21) marked the end of the House's own era of good feelings in the selection of its officers. Of the next nine speakership elections—two of which were replacement elections—four required multiple ballots to resolve. While the choice of Clerk remained relatively uneventful, controversy over the Printer increasingly roiled the waters as well.

Clay relinquished his speakership between the first and second sessions of the 16th Congress to attend to his deteriorating financial circumstances

---

[16] Gales and Seaton had been taking shorthand notes of debates in both chambers for a decade and printing the transcribed debates in the *National Intelligencer*, to a national audience. Even though they did this reporting in an informal capacity, each was awarded a coveted seat on the floor of each chamber to facilitate their note taking (Ames 1972, 113).

back home (Peterson 1987, 66–68). The first session of the 16th Congress is known for the battle to admit Missouri to the Union, a battle that turned on the resolution of various amendments barring slavery in the new state. The result of the battle was the so-called Missouri Compromise, which provided for the admission of Maine and the drafting of a constitution by the residents of Missouri. A lightning rod in the struggle over Missouri was the "Taylor amendment," which was proposed by Republican John W. Taylor (N.Y.) to prohibit slavery west of the Mississippi.[17] The Taylor amendment did not appear in the final compromise, but Taylor's dogged fight on its behalf, which included some deft parliamentary maneuvers, marked him as a legislative leader to be reckoned with.

When the second session convened, Taylor naturally emerged as the chief candidate of Northern antislavery forces to succeed Clay.[18] Taylor's campaign was complicated, however, by political divisions in his native New York, which pitted supporters of Governor DeWitt Clinton (the "Clintonites") against supporters of Martin Van Buren (the "Bucktails"). It took 22 ballots spread over three days before Taylor could bring along enough Bucktails to win the speakership (Spann 1960; Lientz 1978).

Although Taylor attempted to be conciliatory in his appointment of committees, the House was immediately thrown back into a further row over the extension of slavery. Taylor's speakership would be hamstrung by the deadlock that emerged over accepting Missouri's constitution, and he eventually became so associated with the forces that wanted to restrict slavery in the new state that he had to turn to Clay, who remained a frequently absent member of the House, to provide a way out of the Missouri quagmire (Brown 1926, 35–43, 65; Peterson 1987, 62–66).

Even though the resulting "second Missouri Compromise" was considered to be a slight victory for proslavery advocates, Southern House members distrusted Taylor and vowed to elect one of their own to the speakership in the next Congress (Brown 1926, 67; Spann 1960). Furthermore, the Bucktail forces in the House found themselves battling with Taylor over economic development issues. Consequently, Van Buren himself took an interest in the speakership election that led off the 17th Congress and vowed to defeat Taylor and install a Speaker who would help cement the New York–Virginia axis he was working to construct.

Van Buren was successful, though it took him two days and 12 ballots to depose Taylor. Van Buren's success came when he reached out to John C.

[17] Taylor's amendment was the successor to the "Tallmadge amendment" that had been proposed in the second session of the 15th Congress, which began the controversy in the first place. See Richards (2000, 52–82) for a lengthy treatment.

[18] It also appears that Clay supported Taylor, even though they had fought over the resolution of Missouri. Clay's support came from his estimation that the Missouri question was now behind the House and that a question even dearer to Clay, protective tariffs, was next on the agenda. Clay and Taylor agreed on tariff matters, and thus Clay hoped that Taylor's parliamentary skills would be put to good use on this matter (Spann 1957, 224).

Calhoun to arrange the election of Philip P. Barbour (R-Va.), who was a well-known ultra on slavery. At the same time, regional moderation was achieved, as Barbour proceeded to staff the various standing committees in an evenhanded manner. This constituted one of Van Buren's first material successes in his strategy to build a transregional party (Jenkins and Stewart 2002).

During the recess between the first and second sessions of the 17th Congress, the incumbent House Clerk, Thomas Dougherty, died. The subsequent replacement election was hotly contested—more than a dozen candidates received votes at various points—and required 11 ballots over two days before Matthew St. Clair Clarke was chosen.[19] Once in office, Clarke consolidated his hold on the clerkship and won reelection in the next five Congresses—all but one by unanimous resolution.

After Barbour's speakership victory in the 17th Congress, subsequent speakership contests for the next two decades always proceeded with the implied threat that regional divisions might dominate. More often than not, however, the spirit of the deal brokered between Calhoun and Van Buren at the start of the 17th Congress prevailed. Clay accepted the speakership one last time, in the 18th Congress, when he garnered support from more than three-quarters of the body. Taylor would reemerge to win the speakership in a two-ballot affair in the 19th Congress, despite significant resistance, thanks to his close relationship with John Quincy Adams and Henry Clay, to whom a majority of House members were linked.[20]

The convening of the 20th Congress (1827–29), though, marked a sea change in national politics that would eventually bring Andrew Jackson to the White House. The midterm elections of 1826–27 produced a strong anti-(Adams) administration House, and the chamber decisively elected Andrew Stevenson (Jack.-Va.), a supporter of Andrew Jackson and former speaker of the Virginia House of Delegates, as Speaker of the House (Wayland 1949). Stevenson would be reelected to the speakership in the next three Congresses. Critical to his success was his relationship with Jackson, and the two worked together to further Jackson's legislative agenda in Congress (Follett 1896, 84–85). Jackson would subsequently repay Stevenson

---

[19] Clarke, who holds the record for length of tenure among House Clerks, is a political enigma. Although Charles Lanman claims he "was quite famous as a politician" (1887, 97), his life has eluded biographers. Based solely on available information, he appears to have begun his political career as a moderate Republican; as factions in the party emerged, Clarke was probably best characterized as a nominal Jacksonian, a loyal party member who in fact displayed more Whiggish tendencies. Over time, his ideological preferences moved him into the Whig column, as the Whig Party became a viable foil to the Democrats. On the whole, though, Clarke probably sat at the cut point between the Democrats and Whigs, which made him a suitable compromise candidate in the event of a deadlocked or extended election. Such a scenario developed at the beginning of the 27th Congress (1841), which we detail in chapter 5.

[20] Beginning in the 19th Congress, Martis (1989) breaks the chamber into "Adams" and "Jackson" factions, depending on whom members were more closely associated with. The Adams group comprised a majority in this Congress.

for his loyalty by appointing him ambassador to England in 1834, after Martin Van Buren had been rejected by the Senate for the same post.

A small drama enveloped the clerkship at the start of the 23rd Congress, as Clarke was defeated for reelection by Walter S. Franklin in a three-ballot affair. In describing the Clarke-Franklin contest, Lientz contends, "In an effort to build party unity, the Democrats made selection of House clerk a partisan matter for the first time in ten years" (1978, 74). Clarke's gradual move over time into the Anti-Jacksonian camp was too much for the Jacksonian majority, and they chose to oust him.[21] In addition, the selection of Franklin, a Pennsylvanian, was intended to shore up party support in the Pennsylvania delegation (Lientz 1974, 39; 1978, 74).[22] Franklin would go on to win reelection easily in the next two Congresses.

Stevenson's departure from the speakership midway through the 23rd Congress thrust the House into a succession crisis. The Jacksonians failed to settle on a single candidate, even though (or perhaps because) they held a considerable majority in the chamber. A complicating factor was the ongoing assault by Jackson on the Bank of the United States, a move that did not sit well with conservative elements in the party. When voting for Speaker commenced, 10 ballots would be necessary to replace Stevenson. Six Jacksonians received more than 10 votes for Speaker on the first ballot, including 4—Richard H. Wilde (Ga.), James K. Polk (Tenn.), Joel Sutherland (Pa.), and John Bell (Tenn.)—who received more than 30. The contest eventually reduced to a race between Polk and Bell; Bell emerged triumphant by appealing directly to Anti-Jacksonians (soon to be called Whigs) who were willing to join in coalition with pro-Bank Democrats (Sellers 1957, 234–66). Bell, in turn, favored Anti-Jacksonians in making his committee assignments and eventually took on the Anti-Jacksonian (Whig) label himself.

Bell's actions as Speaker galvanized supporters of the president, who rallied behind Polk at the opening of the 24th Congress and elected him easily on the first ballot (Parks 1950, 58–162; Sellers 1957, 292–97). Two years later, at the opening of the 25th Congress, Polk would be reelected Speaker, again on the first ballot, but this time by a slimmer margin.

The arc of the battles over the speakership during these years is broadly consistent with the contours of the rise and then travails of the Jacksonian party system more generally. Van Buren's efforts at creating a transregional party that was committed to a relatively small and inactive federal govern-

[21] In his diary, John Quincy Adams described Clarke's ouster as an "act of heartless cruelty . . . a dark foreboding of what is to follow during the session" (Adams 1876, vol. 9, 12/2/1833, 43).

[22] Pennsylvania Jacksonians had groused over Stevenson's continued hold on the speakership and wanted a greater say in organizational matters. As Lientz notes, "Pennsylvania's Jacksonian leaders had claimed that Pennsylvania should receive some of the national offices, and made desperate efforts to elect a Pennsylvanian Vice President in 1832" (1974, 38). Thus, "the clerkship was used to buy back [their] support and friendship" (39).

ment were more successful than not. As a result, Republicans with a more favorable view toward industrialization and capital (and political mechanisms like protective tariffs, federal internal improvement programs, and a national bank), such as Adams, Clay, and Daniel Webster, coalesced around the label "National Republicans." This group would join briefly with other third parties under the broad Anti-Jackson label before forming the core of a new national party—the Whigs. In (rhetorical) response, the followers of Jackson would adopt the label Democratic-Republicans, to differentiate themselves from their more elite opponents, before settling on the simpler label of Democrats (Watson 2006).

As this development proceeded, the congressional printers, Gales and Seaton, found themselves increasingly on the side of Jackson's opponents. At the same time, Jackson's rise to the presidency was abetted by the efforts of a cadre of activists (his Kitchen Cabinet) that was dominated by western editors. One of these editors was Duff Green.[23] (The remainder of this section on House Printers is discussed in more detail in chapter 4.)

Duff Green emerged as a confidant of Jackson in his run-up to the election of 1828. By then, Gales and Seaton's *National Intelligencer* had become the organ of the Adams administration, which left the Jacksonians in need of a mouthpiece. To that end, supporters of Jackson purchased the financially woebegone *Washington Gazette* in 1826 and changed its name to the *United States Telegraph*. Scouting around for a zealous and capable editor for the *Telegraph*, the paper's new backers quickly settled on Green, who as editor of the *St. Louis Enquirer* had vigorously championed Jackson's presidential ambitions.

Installed as the new chief propagandist for Jacksonian Democracy, Green would defeat Gales and Seaton for Senate Printer in the 20th Congress (1827–29, elected at the end of the 19th Congress) and House Printer in the 21st Congress (1829–31, elected at the end of the 20th Congress). His position now secure, Green would easily win reelection in both chambers at the end of the 21st Congress (for service in the 22nd, 1831–33).

In time, Green's role within the Democratic Party would become controversial, as divisions formed over who would be the party's presidential nominee in 1832, with one faction loyal to Jackson (or Secretary of State Van Buren, should Jackson not seek reelection) and another to Calhoun. Green found himself in a host of controversies over loyalties and patronage, the sum of which identified his sentiments as lying closer to Calhoun's than to Jackson's. This led loyalists of Jackson and Van Buren to form a new publishing venture, led by Francis Preston Blair, named the *Globe*, which started in December 1830.

The rifts between Green and Jackson and between Calhoun and Jackson all had consequences for the election of House Printers in the 22nd, 23rd,

---

[23] The following account draws heavily on Smith (1977, 61–64, 150–62).

and 24th Congresses. In the 22nd Congress (which elected the Printer who would serve in the 23rd Congress), these rifts were exploited by the Anti-Jacksonians to yield the election of Gales and Seaton as the House Printer after a bruising two-day, 14-ballot affair. And, in fact, the election of Gales and Seaton in the House was part of a larger logroll between the Anti-Jacksonians and pro-Calhoun Democrats that led to the election of Duff Green as the Senate Printer. Thus, the Jacksonians were dealt a serious blow by having to endure congressional printers hostile to their agenda.

With the politics of choosing congressional printers now pushed to a new level of acrimony, the 23rd Congress was unable to elect the Printer for the 24th House owing to a filibuster that benefited the Jacksonian opposition.[24] When the 24th Congress finally convened, the Jacksonians closed ranks, and Blair and his new partner, John C. Rives, were easily chosen.

The Jacksonian victory in the 24th Congress did not endure, however, as the selection of the Printer in the 25th Congress would hit a snag. Joining the teams of Blair and Rives and Gales and Seaton in the contest was Thomas Allen, editor of the *Madisonian*. Allen was a newspaperman (with no printing press) who enjoyed the support of conservative (pro-Bank) Democrats. Unbeknownst to administration supporters (see chapter 4), Van Buren refused to intervene in support of Blair and Rives, as he hoped that the sacrifice of the House printing contract to a conservative Democrat-Whig coalition would save the administration's subtreasury bill in the Senate. After three days and 12 ballots, House Whigs united with conservative Democrats to defeat Blair and Rives and award the House printing contract to Allen—who then turned around and subcontracted the bulk of the work to Gales and Seaton. To supporters of the administration who were not privy to Van Buren's ploy, this was yet another case of failed party building.

If we take the convening of the 17th Congress (1821–23) as the beginning of the Jacksonian era in the House, then we see in miniature the party-building struggles experienced by Van Buren. On the one hand, Van Buren succeeded in raising the House offices, especially the speakership and the printership, to the level of valued partisan prizes. Speaker Stevenson was indispensable for Jackson's legislative success, and control of the congressional printing operation was indispensable for rallying the troops in far-off hamlets. On the other hand, Van Buren's designs were not embraced by everyone, even those nominally within the Jacksonian coalition. There were weak points to be exploited. Particularly nettlesome was the person of John C. Calhoun, who could always command the loyalty of a dedicated group of Southerners whose partisan labels were chosen for short-term expediency. Calhoun and his supporters twice played direct roles in undermining

---

[24] The delay occurred as the House sorted through two issues: whether any Congress had the right to bind a future Congress in the choice of officers and whether voting for the Printer should be by viva voce balloting (see chapter 4).

the Van Burenite project by helping to elect John Bell Speaker in the second session of the 23rd Congress and by preventing the anointed mouthpiece of the Jackson/Van Buren administration from securing either congressional printing contract in the previous Congress.

Thus the mode of party building imagined by Van Buren was imperfect in execution. In the minds of party strategists, one of those flaws was the ease with which backroom intrigues in Washington could undermine the party-building work being done throughout the country. Their solution to this problem was to make the selection of House officers more transparent by replacing the secret ballot with a public ballot. Making this change produced unintended consequences, however, as new political forces were unleashed that undermined the stability not only of the parties but of the Union itself.

CONCLUSION

As the cases discussed in this section indicate, prior to the use of public roll call votes for House officer elections, organizational politics unfolded around a collection of factors that included party, personality, and region. Unfortunately, because we do not have individual voting records to examine the importance of these factors in any particular organizational struggle, we cannot precisely determine the relative influence of each. By looking at aggregate voting patterns, however, we can gain some insight into the relatively weak pull of party during this period.

We undertake such an aggregate analysis by relying on the party labels of Kenneth Martis (1989), and particularly the percentage of House seats held by the "majority" party in each Congress according to his classification. If party were the primary factor in determining the outcome of organizational votes, such as that for the Speaker, then the fraction of the votes received by the winning candidate would approximate the fraction of seats held by the majority party.

Figure 3.1 shows the fraction of votes received by the winning candidate in each speakership election before the Civil War (y-axis) graphed against the percentage of seats held by the majority party (x-axis). The figure is divided into two parts: figure 3.1a illustrates the relationship through 1837, when balloting for Speaker was secret; figure 3.1b illustrates the relationship after 1837, when balloting for Speaker became public (or viva voce).

Prior to the use of public roll calls—during the period covered by this chapter—the correlation between majority party strength and winning vote for the Speaker was weak ($r = .14$); after the adoption of viva voce (public) voting, the correlation between majority party strength and winning vote for the Speaker was very strong ($r = .92$). Of course, this is aggregate analysis, but the overall weak correlation in the secret-ballot era is consistent with the

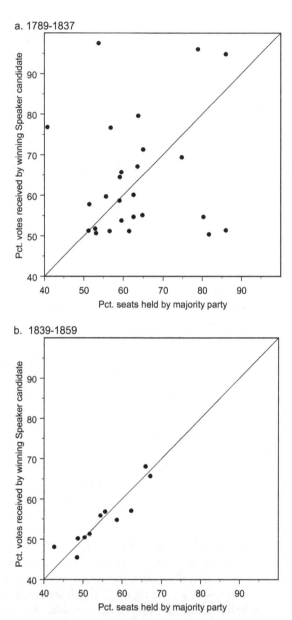

FIGURE 3.1. Percentage of votes received by winning speakership candidate plotted against percentage of seats held by majority party, 1789–1859.

view that party was only emerging as a formal presence in national politics through the early nineteenth century. As we have already seen, by the end of this period a number of important national leaders sought to enhance the strength of formal party organizations at the national level. The first step was to create a mechanism that would allow leaders to observe whether the rank and file contributed their votes to the organizational efforts of leaders. That mechanism, the viva voce vote for House officers, is the focus of chapter 4.

CHAPTER 4

Bringing the Selection of
House Officers into the Open

In the two decades that preceded the Civil War, the conflicting impulses of region and party were often pitted against each other in Congress, with House politics frequently degenerating into a free-for-all fight over the organization of the chamber.[1] Three of the chapters that follow focus on those fights, how they were resolved, and the consequences of these resolutions for American politics. But for a fight to happen, there needs to be an arena; for a public fight, there needs to be a public arena. The geographic arena of these antebellum speakership fights was the chamber of the House of Representatives, as well as the cloakrooms and rooming houses of the city and newspapers of the country. The bricks-and-mortar arena in which most of the fights occurred was first occupied in 1807.[2] The parliamentary arena was constructed much later, in 1839, when the House decided to elect all of its officers in a public, or viva voce, roll call vote.

That the House before 1839 chose its officers by secret ballot was not unusual; many state legislatures also selected their officers by secret ballot and would continue to do so for decades to come (Cushing 1856, 36–37).[3] Bringing the vote into the open was still relatively unusual for the time, and was not easily achieved in the House. Although moving to a viva voce vote for House Speaker helped inaugurate an era of contentious fights over the speakership, the precipitating events that prompted the change pertained

---

[1] Portions of this chapter are based on Jenkins and Stewart (2003b).

[2] The old chamber of the House of Representatives, now termed Statuary Hall, was occupied by the House in 1807 and used as the body's chamber until 1857, at which time the current hall of the House was occupied (Allen 2001).

[3] For instance, the Massachusetts House of Representatives continued to ballot in secret for its Speaker until 1911. The abandonment of secret balloting for Speaker in Massachusetts is very similar in basic structure to its abandonment in the U.S. House, even though the partisan identities of the protagonists were reversed. The election of 1910 threatened to end Republican dominance of the Massachusetts House, which they had held since the Civil War. Fearing he would be vulnerable to a Democrat-Progressive-Republican fusion, incumbent Speaker Joseph Walker (R) advocated an "open ballot" for Speaker at the start of the 1911 legislative session. Martin Lomasney, the Democratic leader, led the troops in opposing an open ballot. After protracted parliamentary wrangling, the open ballot motion passed and Walker was reelected Speaker ("Walker is Speaker," *Boston Daily Globe*, 1/5/1911, 1; Hennessy 1935, 148–50).

more to the printership and, to some degree, the clerkship. Thus, opening the choice of House officers to public scrutiny bore a significance that went beyond the narrow organization of the chamber itself and penetrated into the broader project of building national political parties.

Then, as now, election to the speakership required a majority vote of all House members present.[4] If no candidate received a majority, balloting continued until a majority winner was achieved.[5] Of the 28 speakership elections prior to 1839, eight (28.6 percent) required more than one ballot to elect a Speaker. Of the 11 speakership elections that occurred from 1839 to 1859 under viva voce voting, five (45.5 percent) required more than one ballot. (See appendix 1 for a breakdown.)

As regional tensions mounted over time, these viva voce speakership battles became centerpieces of the ongoing struggle for control of the federal government by pro- and antislavery forces. The choice to use viva voce voting for speakership elections may thus have been the most important change to the House rules for the course of early American history. The immediate political effect was certainly great. As Lientz commented, "Constituents would now know whom their representative had supported, and congressmen would have to stop and think before backing a party candidate whose opinions were objectionable to the home folk. Party leaders would know exactly who had deserted. Congressmen pledged to back a candidate could no longer secretly break that pledge" (1978, 76).

As important as this rules change was, few political scientists and historians have taken note of it. Understanding why the change was made is the goal of this chapter. Understanding the consequences of the change is the goal of chapters to come.

The answer for why the change occurred can be summarized as follows: The decision to institute viva voce voting in speakership elections was an

---

[4] There has been some dispute about this. The *House Manual* (§ 27) states that the Speaker "is elected by a majority of Members-elect voting by surname, a quorum being present." During the organization of the 46th Congress, on March 18, 1879, Samuel Randall appeared to receive 143 votes out of 282 cast (*CR*, 46-1, 3/18/1879, 5). This was a majority of votes cast but not a majority of all members-elect—287 at the time (Dubin 1998, 249). The Clerk stated that all that was required was a majority of a quorum voting to elect a Speaker. His ruling turned out to be moot, as a 283rd member, Daniel O'Reilly (D-N.Y.), arrived at the last moment and cast his ballot for Randall—giving him 144 votes, a (bare) majority of members-elect (*NYT*, 3/19/1879, 7). Nonetheless, the Clerk's ruling on the election requirement stood without challenge. (We discuss this episode in more detail in chapter 8.) At the organization of the 68th Congress, Frederick Gillett was eventually elected Speaker with 215 votes out of 414 cast—a majority of votes cast, but not a majority of all members-elect (435) (*CR*, 68-1, 12/5/1923, 16). These two precedents were cited by House Clerk Robin H. Carle on January 7, 1997, when Newt Gingrich was elected Speaker with 216 votes out of 425 total votes cast (*CR*, 105-1, 1/7/1997, 117)—less than "a majority of all the members."

[5] The exceptions were in the 31st Congress (1849) and the 34th Congress (1855–56), when the House could not produce a majority winner after three weeks and two months, respectively. In each case, a plurality rule was adopted to decide the election. We cover these contests in chapter 6.

inadvertent consequence of party-building activities of the 1830s, in which the elections of other officers were as consequential as the Speaker. To House members acting *at the time*, the issue was not the speakership but rather the printership and the clerkship. The former would determine who would get the nation's largest printing contract and thus which party press organs would be publicly subsidized, while the latter would determine which party would gain the upper hand in resolving election disputes that arose in the initial organization of the House.

In the short term, the effect of instituting viva voce voting in House officer elections was to cement party ties. Making officer elections transparent allowed party leaders to crack down on defections within their ranks, which was a constant problem during the secret-ballot era, and provided the necessary ingredient (in theory) for the creation of a strong party caucus system that would generate officer nominations and bind members to those choices on the House floor. In the long term, however, viva voce voting in House officer elections helped to undermine party ties by highlighting nonpartisan—that is, regional—considerations in the choice of House leaders. A public ballot allowed citizens, as well as party leaders, to observe vote choices; as the slavery issue grew in importance and the nation polarized along North-South lines, some members chose to break with their party— and *not* support a party candidate from the *other* region—rather than risk losing the trust of their constituents back home.

To reach these conclusions, we first establish the political context by describing how national political leaders sought to build a new type of political party in the 1830s. We then examine efforts to change the election rules affecting House officers by focusing on three important moments: a failed attempt to institute viva voce voting in the 23rd Congress (1833–35); two attempts to change the rule in the 25th Congress (1837–39), the second one successful; and the last gasp of viva voce opposition in the 26th and 27th Congresses (1839–43). In detailing these moments, we provide evidence that support for viva voce voting was tied to party-building efforts among Democrats and Whigs. We close by offering more detailed thoughts about the effects of this new way of electing Speakers, which sets the stage for the analysis of particular speakership contests in subsequent chapters.

The Search for Party Discipline

The most lasting effect of the War of 1812 was the destruction of the First Party System, in which Federalists and Republicans had vied for power. In the aftermath of the war, American national politics devolved into a shifting landscape of issues and personalities that has received the ironic title of the Era of Good Feelings. However, this period also witnessed the first significant injection of slavery into national politics, which raised the specter of Southern secession.

With the dangers of regional polarization palpable, prominent political heirs of Thomas Jefferson worked to create a political party that knit together North and South by suppressing the slavery issue and emphasizing a list of less regionally charged issues. The mastermind of this party building was Martin Van Buren, who seized the opportunity presented by Andrew Jackson's widespread personal appeal to construct a national political party that was built around political ambition, patronage, and weak allegiances to policy goals.[6]

By the time Van Buren himself was elected president in 1836, the Democratic Party had developed into a sophisticated electoral machine dedicated to the electoral success of its members. Van Buren and his disciples also succeeded in creating an ethos among party followers that elevated organizational loyalty over loyalty to individual candidates. This transformation was so great that the loosely organized opposition to the Jacksonian juggernaut eventually abandoned their allegiances to their particular brands of political belief (National Republican, Anti-Mason, etc.) to coalesce as a single political party: the Whigs.

To be sure, the Democratic and Whig Parties that emerged in the 1830s each embodied a core set of political beliefs and goals to which most adherents subscribed.[7] The Democratic Party grew up around Jeffersonian Republican principles that were manifested by a distaste for centralized economic power, which was represented, for example, by the Bank of the United States. The Whigs sprang up in support of a more activist commercial role for the federal government, which recalled the principles of Alexander Hamilton. Still, both parties were big tents that were willing to endure internal strife, as long as the organization could deliver the votes.

This brings us to that organization. First the Democrats, then the Whigs, created institutions dedicated to coordinating electoral strategies to win elections up and down the ticket. This organization went far beyond convincing party members to swallow hard and support the party candidate at all costs; it also tapped public officials, elected and appointed, to fill campaign coffers (Ferguson 1983). Money was shifted in national elections to races that were competitive. The parties also created campaign literature to instruct candidates on the party line and to educate followers on the sterling qualities of the parties' nominees and the nefarious character of the opposition. Out of this activity came an enduring structure to national politics that had been missing for decades. As a result, the multidimensional spatial chaos that had plagued congressional roll call voting after the fall of the First Party

[6] This account of Van Buren's party-building activities relies on Schlesinger (1947), Remini (1959, 1963, 1972), McCormick (1960, 1966), Hofstadter (1969), Chambers and Davis (1978), Aldrich (1995), and Silbey (2002).

[7] A host of books examine in great detail the internal logics of the Democrats and Whigs. For some recent treatments, see Gerring (1998), Holt (1999), Wilentz (2005), Watson (2006), and Howe (2007).

System was replaced by a remarkably sturdy and unidimensional partisan politics (Poole and Rosenthal 1997).

As organizational capacity within the parties increased, the electorate expanded and congressional elections became more competitive. The number of voters in congressional elections grew by more than 60 percent between the elections of 1830–31 (to the 22nd Congress) and 1838–39 (to the 26th Congress). Simultaneously, the number of party labels under which candidates ran was reduced substantially; as a result, multiparty competition in much of the country gave way to two-party competition almost everywhere.[8] Finally, partisan margins shrank. When the decade of the 1830s began, the Jacksonians enjoyed a 10 percentage point advantage in the national congressional vote over the National Republicans. As the decade ended, the Democrats and Whigs were running neck and neck.[9]

Of course, this tightening of electoral fortunes was not due solely to the growth of the Whig electoral machinery to match that of the Democrats. Whig electoral fortunes were helped at the end of the decade by the Panic of 1837, which precipitated the longest economic contraction in American history. The Panic of 1837 has been blamed on a host of financial actions that were taken in the closing months of the second Jackson administration. Most prominent of these was the so-called Specie Circular, which announced that the federal government would only accept gold or silver in payment of obligations to it (Watson 2006, 207–8). This caused the market for federal lands to collapse, which brought down a host of overextended state banks and, eventually, money-center financial houses.

Although the Specie Circular was issued in mid-1836, its disastrous consequences were not fully felt until the spring of 1837, after Van Buren had been inaugurated to succeed Jackson. With the New Orleans cotton market collapsing, mobs taking to the street in New York to raid warehouses, and eastern banks suspending the payment of specie, the electorate was primed to punish the Democrats as the party responsible for the Panic.

Democrats took a beating in the congressional elections in the summer of 1837.[10] Compared to 1835, when they held their own against the Whigs with 46.5 percent of the vote, the Democrats only received 40.5 percent of the summer 1837 vote. The end result was devastating for the Democrats,

---

[8] Aldrich (1995, 307–8n12) notes that during this period the number of states using winner-take-all systems to allocate electoral votes increased, which, by the operation of Duverger's Law, would encourage a drive toward two parties competing for presidential votes at the state level. It is likely, though not demonstrated, that the migration to two parties competing for congressional seats was an extension of Duverger's logic down the ballot.

[9] Turnout, electoral party label, and voting data are taken from Dubin (1998) and Rusk (2001).

[10] A large number of congressional elections were held in odd-numbered years well into the nineteenth century (Dubin 1998). For a discussion of the timing of congressional elections and the effect that bringing congressional elections into sync with presidential elections had on the presidential coattails phenomenon, see Engstrom and Kernell (2005).

who had supposedly created a political machine dedicated to the electoral longevity of its members.

The immediate consequence of the decline in Democratic popular vote totals was a tightening of the majority enjoyed by House Democrats. The Party of Jackson had started the decade with a 39-seat advantage over their opponents in the 22nd Congress (1831–33). When the 25th Congress (1837–39) convened, that margin had shrunk by nearly two-thirds. Moreover, internal divisions over banking and finance were such that it was not until James K. Polk was reelected Speaker at the start of the 25th Congress that the Democrats were assured of even nominal control over the chamber.

Therefore, the question of how the House would elect its officers emerged in the midst of the first major political crisis for the Democrats in the Second Party System. While efforts to enforce party regularity had been attempted at the state level, efforts to impose the party's whip at the national level had been mostly subterranean. By proposing that they bring the choice of House officers into the open, the Democratic Party was moving one step closer to being an actual machine that exerted party discipline publicly. Yet, as we will also see, shining a light on officer elections was a tactic whose utility rose and fell in the fluid give-and-take of politics. Once the idea was broached on the House floor by a cadre of Democrats, it would take several years before the leadership would embrace the tactic wholeheartedly.

The Viva Voce Question

The question of how House officers would be elected arose on several occasions in the 1830s and 1840s. Although the resolution of this question would yield a significant change in how the Speaker was elected, the issue itself first emerged in debates about electing the Printer and was eventually resolved in debates about electing the Clerk. Much of the narrative and the statistical analyses that follow focus heavily on the politics of congressional printing. (To help in keeping the partisan sentiments of Printers straight, the reader may wish to refer back to table 2.3.)

We focus here on the four Congresses when the issue of how to elect House officers was contested on the floor: the 23rd Congress (1835), the 25th Congress (1839), the 26th Congress (1839), and the 27th Congress (1841).

The 23rd Congress: Francis Blair calls foul

The Jacksonian tidal wave that washed over Washington in the late 1820s brought with it an explicit tie between political publishing and congressional printing. Duff Green, one of Jackson's trusted advisors and publisher of the *United States Telegraph*, would serve as Senate Printer in the 20th Congress (1827–29, elected at the end of the 19th Congress), and as House Printer in the 21st Congress (1829–31, elected at the end of the 20th Congress). In installing Green, the Jacksonians ousted Joseph Gales Jr. and William Winston Seaton, publishers of the *National Intelligencer*, who were tied more closely to the forces of John Quincy Adams and Henry Clay.[11] Green had no problem gaining reelection as Printer in both chambers at the end of the 21st Congress (for service in the 22nd, 1831–33). However, soon after his reelection, Green was involved in the publication of a series of letters that marked the public break between Calhoun and Jackson—an episode that also revealed Green to have shifted loyalties away from Jackson and toward Calhoun (Niven 1988, 175–76).

In turn, this break led loyalists of Jackson and his new vice president, Martin Van Buren, to form a new publishing venture, led by Francis Preston Blair, named the *Globe*. As the 22nd Congress drew to a close, attention turned to the choice of Printers for the next Congress. Friends of the administration were naturally eager to depose Green as congressional printer in favor of Blair. In the end, balloting for House Printer, which was held in secret, came down to a race between the three major publishers in town: Green (pro-Calhoun), Blair (pro-Jackson), and Gales and Seaton (pro-Adams/Clay).

On the first day of balloting, February 14, 1833, no majority winner emerged. (For a breakdown of the balloting, see appendix 4.) The tenth and final ballot of the day found Jackson's candidate Blair eight votes short of a majority, although on one ballot (the eighth) he had received precisely half the votes (*Register of Debates* [hereafter abbreviated as *Register*], 22-2, 2/14/1833, 1725). Overnight, Calhoun supporters of Green met with the small handful of Anti-Masons in Congress and cut a deal: the Calhounites agreed to join with the Anti-Masons in support of Gales and Seaton for House Printer,[12] while in return, the Anti-Masons (along with Clay's National Republicans) would join with the Calhounites and support Green for Senate Printer (Smith 1977, 151–52). As a result, Gales and Seaton started the next day's balloting with the lead for the first time. On the 4th ballot of the day and 14th overall, they achieved a bare majority and were elected (*Register*, 22-2, 2/15/1833, 1726). Green was subsequently elected Senate Printer to complete the deal.

The Jacksonites were politically devastated because they knew that they would start their second term with congressional printers who were hostile to administration plans, even though both chambers were nominally made up of administration supporters. Blair himself was financially devastated, as

---

[11] In time, Gales and Seaton would become the most prominent printers backing the Whig Party.

[12] The Anti-Masons had split their votes after initially supporting Thurlow Weed.

he had been induced to start a publishing enterprise that was now bereft of the assumed congressional subsidy to support it.[13]

Blair canvassed his political allies in the House to inquire how they had voted. He eventually convinced himself that he had been rightfully elected House Printer by a majority of at least one and charged that the election had been stolen from him through fraudulent miscounting of the ballots (Smith 1977, 153; Smith 1980, 79). Blair's behavior may have been un-seemly, even a bit pathetic, but the balloting saga demonstrated how the secret ballot for electing officers presented problems for Democrats if they intended to use the organization of the House as a party-building tool in national politics.

Blair's supporters would bide their time and press their revenge indirectly. As the 23rd Congress (1833–35) was drawing to a close, attention began to focus on the choice of a House Printer for the following Congress. On De-cember 24, 1834, John Reynolds (Jack.-Ill.) moved that, "hereafter, in all elections made by the House of Representatives for officers, the votes shall be given *viva voce*, each member, in his place, naming aloud the person for whom he votes" (*HJ*, 23-2, 12/24/1834, 129). This represented the first pro-posal to elect House officers via public ballot and signaled the Democrats' willingness to pursue an institutional remedy for their intraparty discipline problem. The viva voce resolution was tabled, however, and not taken up again until January 14, 1835, when Reynolds moved to suspend the rules so that his resolution could be reconsidered. Reynolds received a majority in favor of his motion (93–87), but it was less than the two-thirds required for suspension (*HJ*, 23-2, 1/14/1835, 215–17).

Less than two weeks later, on January 24, 1835, Reynolds moved his resolution yet again, with debate stretching over two days. By this time, the intent of the resolution was common knowledge in the House, as John Quincy Adams stated in his diary that evening:

> This is a party measure. The object is to secure the public printing for the next House of Representatives to the publishers of the *Globe* newspaper. The *Globe* is openly devoted to the Vice-President, Van Buren, as a candidate for the succession to the Presidency. There is a part of the Jackson party in the House opposed to Van Buren, and who, if the vote for printers should be by [secret] ballot, would vote against the publishers of the *Globe*; if they are called to vote *viva voce*, it is supposed they will not dare to vote against them, for fear of the brand of opposition to the Administration. (1876, vol. 9, 1/25/1835, 201)

---

[13] Blair and John C. Rives began the *Congressional Globe*, a (roughly) verbatim report of the debates of Congress at the start of the 23rd Congress, in part to financially support the enterprise until an official congressional contract could be secured (Smith 1977, 153).

TABLE 4.1.
Voting to consider the Reynolds resolution under suspension of the rules and to table Reynolds resolution, 23rd Congress

	Suspend rules and consider Reynolds resolution[a]			Table Reynolds resolution[b]		
	Yes	No	Total	Yes	No	Total
Anti-Masons	3	19	22	19	1	20
Anti-Jacksonians	6	46	52	58	2	60
Jacksonians	84	17	101	17	110	127
Nullifiers	0	5	5	8	0	8
Total	93	87	180	102	113	215

[a]ICPSR Study No. 9822, 23rd Congress, roll call number 251.
[b]ICPSR Study No. 9822, 23rd Congress, roll call number 264.

Opponents of voice voting temporized to the point of threatening other House business. Even though one parliamentary test vote—a motion to table made by Davy Crockett (Anti-Jack.-Tenn.), which was defeated 102–113 (*HJ*, 23-2, 1/24/1835, 270–71)—revealed that the viva voce forces had a narrow majority, its advocates dropped the matter in the face of relentless dilatory behavior by the opposition.

We explore the partisan and factional divisions that lay behind the selection of House officers in general, and the Printer in particular, through the analysis of two roll call votes taken during this attempt to consider the viva voce procedure. Table 4.1 shows the cross tabulation of party membership and voting to consider the Reynolds resolution under suspension of the rules (January 14) and later to table it when it was considered under the regular order (January 24). In the first vote, a "yea" is pro–viva voce; in the second vote, a "nay" is pro–viva voce. Note particularly that on the motion to table, the vote was largely along party lines, with the three non-Jacksonian "parties" strongly in favor of tabling and the Jacksonians strongly against. Still, there were some splits in the ranks, especially among the Jacksonians.

What explains this Jacksonian rift? In table 4.2 we analyze Jacksonian voting on these two roll calls as a function of the two W-NOMINATE dimensions.[14] The voting patterns are entirely consistent with the standard story that has been associated with this episode. The nominal Jacksonians who were the most susceptible to defecting were those prone to one of two

---

[14] In the 23rd House the first dimension strongly distinguished Jacksonians on the "left," Anti-Jacksonians and Anti-Masons on the "right," and Nullifiers in the center. The second dimension placed the Nullifiers on one end of the dimension ("up"), the Anti-Masons at the other ("down"), and the larger Jacksonians and Anti-Jacksonians in the middle. Thus, dimension 1 can be thought of as a nascent partisan dimension that splits members along economic preferences; dimension 2 can be thought of as defining dedication to states' rights and the Union.

TABLE 4.2.
Voting on the Reynolds resolution among Jacksonians, 23rd Congress (robust standard errors in parentheses)

	Consider Reynolds resolution[a]	Table Reynolds resolution[b]
W-NOMINATE first dimension	-0.44	1.39**
	(0.50)	(0.53)
W-NOMINATE second dimension	-1.45***	1.95***
	(0.45)	(0.48)
Constant	1.12**	-1.37*
	(0.30)	(0.28)
N	101	127
χ^2	14.49***	31.14***
LLF	-35.65	-30.24
Pseudo R^2	0.22	0.40

$*p < .05$; $**p < .01$; $***p < .001$.

[a]Dependent variable is ICPSR Study No. 9822, 23rd Congress, roll call number 251, probit coefficients.

[b]Dependent variable is ICPSR Study No. 9822, 23rd Congress, roll call number 264, probit coefficients.

different impulses—those with pro-business feelings (toward the right of the issue space) and those in sympathy with Calhoun's nullification theories (toward the top of the space). Of these two threats to Jacksonian regularity, nullification was a bigger problem than pro-business sympathies in these votes.

Overall, voting on the Reynolds resolution was an exercise in self-interest. The Jackson loyalists were transparent in their desire to install the party's official printer as the House Printer. To that end, as Adams had alluded to in his earlier diary entry, they favored a public vote for all House officers, so that potential defectors could be compelled more easily to toe the party line. The Calhounites and pro-business Jacksonians, on the other hand, were the most likely to be involved in partisan intrigue to deny the Jacksonian mainstream their desires. The conflicted Jacksonians were the most likely to defect on issues of party building, and thus had the strongest reasons to want to hide their votes on the organization of the House. They overwhelmingly supported keeping the balloting for House officers secret to facilitate such intrigue.

While unsuccessful in their initial viva voce attempt, the Jacksonian regulars would try again less than three weeks later. The issue of electing a Printer via public ballot resurfaced on February 9, 1835, when John McKinley (Jack.-Ala.) moved that, three days hence, the House would proceed to vote for a Printer, which was amended by Joel Sutherland (Jack.-Pa.) to be viva voce. The hour allotted to debating McKinley's motion having passed, consideration of McKinley's resolution was renewed on February 25. The Speaker ruled that the resolution would take a two-thirds vote to pass; when the roll call was taken, it failed to even gain a majority and lost 103–110 (*HJ*, 23-2, 2/25/1835, 448–49).

On the vote to proceed to the election of a Printer viva voce, the anti-Jacksonian forces were united in voting "nay" 4–85, while the Jacksonians were split in favor, 99–25. As with previous votes in this Congress, the Jacksonian split reflected factional divisions, with the Calhounites and pro-business Jacksonians voting to put off the election.[15]

The 25th Congress: Viva voce is brought to the threshhold

Because of the extended debate over viva voce voting at the end of the 23rd Congress, the business of electing a House Printer for the 24th Congress (1835–37) was left unfinished when Congress adjourned sine die. Thus, for the first time in nearly two decades, an incoming House had the opportunity to select its own Printer. This was especially important, as the Jacksonians had scored a convincing victory in the House elections to the 24th Congress. As a result, James K. Polk was elected Speaker and Blair and his partner John C. Rives were chosen as House Printer at the start of the 24th Congress, both by large margins on the first ballot (*CG*, 24-1, 12/7/1835, 3).

The large pro-Jackson majority in the 24th Congress probably explains why the effort to introduce viva voce election of the Speaker, brought by John Patton (D-Va.), was brushed aside when the House convened (*CG*, 24-1, 12/7/1835, 2–3). After the opening roll of the House was taken, Patton challenged the Clerk's announcement that the balloting for Speaker would be by secret ballot. In the brief skirmish that ensued, a host of Democrats and Whigs rose to state the positions that were becoming associated with the two parties on the matter.[16] However, after expressing their general support for public voting for House officers, several Democrats urged Patton to put his motion aside for the moment, arguing that a debate on the method

---

[15] Given the fact that the House was aware that the 24th Congress would be friendlier toward the administration, the delay in electing a Printer only postponed the inevitable—the election of a pro-administration Printer in the 24th Congress, which we discuss in the next section.

[16] To this point, relying on Martis (1989), we have been using protoparty labels like "Jacksonian" and "Anti-Jacksonian." From this point forward, we will use the more straightforward "Democrat" and "Whig" labels. In general, ascertaining the exact transition from Jacksonian to Democrat and Anti-Jacksonian to Whig is practically impossible, given the fluidity of party labels by state and locality during this period. For example, whereas Martis starts using "Democrats" and "Whigs" for members in the 25th Congress, Dubin (1998, 114n24) states that "[t]he Anti-Masons and the National Republicans merged in most states into the Whig Party, effective with [elections to the 24th Congress]."

of election would only delay the organization of the House late into the night without affecting the outcome. The motion was unceremoniously laid on the table after Patton was unable to even rally the one-fifth of the House necessary to demand a roll call.

Danger was just around the corner, however, as the Democrats lost a handful of seats throughout the country in the summer-fall congressional elections of 1836, which were led by a Whig sweep in New Jersey. When Congress reconvened for the lame-duck session on December 5, 1836, the rising Whig electoral tide prompted House Whigs to throw up roadblocks when the matter of electing a Printer for the following Congress was proposed. These roadblocks were successful, meaning that a new Printer would not be chosen before the conclusion of the session. Looking ahead to the 25th Congress (1837–39), it was apparent to all that the Democrats would have a difficult time organizing the House and that Blair and Rives would struggle to secure reelection.

The Democrats' fears were confirmed on the first day of the 25th Congress, when Polk was narrowly reelected House Speaker over John Bell (W-Tenn.) on the first ballot, 116–103 with five votes scattering (CG, 25-1, 9/4/1837, 3). On the following day, September 5, 1837, when the balloting for Printer commenced, three leading candidates emerged. The veteran combatants, Blair and Rives and Gales and Seaton, were joined by a new entrant, Thomas Allen, a 24-year-old lawyer from New York City and editor of the *Madisonian*.

Allen was an avowed Democrat, albeit a proponent of "soft money" and centralized banking, a position that was termed "conservative." Allen's *Madisonian* had emerged to compete with the *Globe* for Democratic support. He was often seen in the company of Senators Nathaniel P. Tallmadge (N.Y.) and William C. Rives (Va.), two members of Jackson's conservative Democratic opposition; rumors abounded as to their role in the *Madisonian*'s funding (Smith 1977, 156–57).[17]

The election for Printer proceeded as one would expect, given the narrow Democratic majority and the presence of a third candidate who was appealing to the pivotal faction. On September 5, 1837, five ballots were taken, with Blair and Rives running neck and neck with Gales and Seaton, each duo falling about 10 to 15 votes short of victory (see appendix 4 for a breakdown of the balloting). Allen ran a distant third but garnered enough support to prevent either of the two other candidate duos from winning. Late in the afternoon, with trench warfare looming, adjournment was agreed to on a narrow 108–102 vote (CG, 25-1, 9/5/1837, 11).[18]

[17] Tallmadge and Rives would jump to the Whig Party in the next Congress (26th).
[18] The adjournment vote was taken by tellers, so there is no firm evidence to indicate which forces were the most eager at this point to adjourn and regroup. The motion was made by George W. Owens (D-Ga.), who had been a loyal Jacksonian in the 24th Congress, and so it

88   CHAPTER 4

The following day was even more contentious. The session opened with
several proposals—one to suspend balloting for Printer until the third week
in September, one to award printing contracts to the lowest bidder, and one
to split printing duties between the *National Intelligencer* (Gales and Seaton)
and the *Madisonian* (Allen) until the Printer election was resolved. Each of
these proposals produced impassioned debate before being laid on the
table.[19]

The House then resumed balloting for Printer. Three additional ballots
were taken without producing a majority winner (*CG*, 25-1, 9/6/1837, 13).
A pattern was developing, however, as Gales and Seaton's vote total gradually declined while Allen's gradually rose.

Preparations for further balloting had begun when proceedings digressed
once again. Initially, the digression seemed harmless enough, as adjournment was moved unsuccessfully and a proposal to install Blair and Rives as
Printer until a victor emerged was offered and failed. Then Ratliff Boon (D-
Ind.) jolted the chamber to attention by offering a resolution that "the vote
of the members" in the election of the Printer "shall be given *viva voce*"
(*CG*, 25-1, 9/6/1837, 13). John Patton (D-Va.), who had interjected the viva
voce issue into the opening moments of the 24th Congress, responded by
declaring that the principle of viva voce voting should be extended to the
elections of *all* House officers and announced that he was preparing an
amendment to Boon's resolution to that effect.

Before Patton could follow through, however, Horace Everett (W-Vt.)
moved to table Boon's resolution. Everett's tabling resolution failed 91–131,
as a group of conservative Democrats unsuccessfully joined with the Whigs
to oppose the Democratic leadership, largely as the previous votes had gone
(*HJ*, 25-1, 9/6/1837, 38–39).[20] Inexplicably, 16 Whigs who had previously
remained loyal to their party on procedural matters defected, which provided the anti-tabling forces a larger margin than they needed to keep the
viva voce motion alive.

Patton then pushed forward with his amendment to subject all officers to
viva voce election, and a vigorous debate commenced. Patton and James
Bouldin (D-Va.) argued for viva voce voting in *all* cases in response to "the
right of constituents to know all the public acts of their representative" (*RE*,
9/12/1837, 2). George Briggs (W-Mass.) considered the resolution "entirely

---

appears that adjournment was favored by Polk and the Democratic leadership; the Whigs
wished to press on.

[19] These are roll calls numbered 12 to 15 in ICPSR data set 9822. As a general matter, these
roll call votes found a consistent coalition of Whigs and conservative Democrats joining in
unsuccessful efforts to delay the election of a printer and to deny the contract to Blair and
Rives.

[20] The vote is incorrectly reported as 88–132 in the *Congressional Globe* (25-1, 9/6/1837,
13).

unnecessary, and expressed his unfeigned astonishment at the introduction of such a measure, after [the House] had been going on with the [secret] ballot for two days." And, in response to the arguments of Patton and Bouldin, Briggs stated that if "constituents could not trust [members] to act in a case like this, the days of the republic were indeed numbered" (CG, 25-1, 9/6/1837, 13). William Dawson (W-Ga.) reiterated Briggs's sentiments and believed that the amendment's only purpose was to "place in the harness gentlemen who were a little chafed, and seemed unwilling to draw in the old yoke" (RE, 9/12/1837, 2). After a lengthy debate by an assortment of members, the House agreed to postpone consideration of the resolution until the following day.

On September 7, the action started again. Boon resubmitted his resolution, now with Patton's amendment incorporated into it. However, the momentum from the previous day had turned. Unbeknownst to Boon, Democratic congressional leaders had convened the prior evening and decided to postpone consideration of viva voce voting for the time being. John Clark (D-N.Y.) took to the floor and announced that while he supported viva voce voting and felt "no desire to disguise [his vote choices] from the House, or from his constituents," he "thought it better to take some other opportunity to consider it" (CG, 25-1, 9/7/1837, 15). Clark then moved to lay the resolution and amendment on the table, to which the House, refusing the yeas and nays, agreed.

Voting for Printer commenced once again by secret ballot. Although the ninth ballot proved inconclusive, Gales and Seaton continued to lose ground to Allen. The next two ballots saw this trend continue, until, on the fourth ballot of the day (and the 12th overall), Allen was elected Printer by a bare majority (CG, 25-1, 9/7/1837, 15–16).[21]

Why did Democratic leaders back away from the viva voce juggernaut at the start of the final day of voting? Why did they allow the upstart Allen to claim the printership to the detriment of the administration's loyal propagandist? The answer is: for strategic reasons tangentially related to the printership itself.

As the struggle for the House Printer was reaching its climax, the Van Buren administration was fighting over the details of a new subtreasury bill in the Senate. From the time that the Panic of 1837 had begun to unfold, the

[21] Although Allen had secured the lucrative House printing contract, he did not have the printing equipment necessary to fulfill the duties of the position. The Madisonian had begun operations only three weeks prior to the opening of the special session of Congress and was at the time only published semiweekly. As a result, Allen entered into an agreement with Gales and Seaton to use the National Intelligencer's printing press until he could acquire the requisite machinery to perform the job himself (National Intelligencer, 9/8/1837, 3). Smith posits that "presumably this plan was considered and agreed upon before the final ballot in the House and could have given the Whigs an incentive to vote for Allen" (1977, 157–58).

administration Democrats had been working to resolve the schism in their ranks over banking and financial issues. During the course of the Senate debate, John Calhoun (D-S.C.) had offered an amendment to the bill that would have tilted it considerably toward the hard-moneyed interests of the Democratic Party. Van Buren felt that accepting the amendment was the best course of action, as it would appease a majority of the core Jacksonian coalition. He also knew, however, that concessions would have to be made to the soft-moneyed conservative Democrats in the House, lest the amended bill fail.

Thus, the House Printer became a bargaining chip in this seemingly separate issue.[22] Because of its value in securing an even greater policy gain, Democratic leaders decided to moderate the intensity of their efforts to claim the House printership this one time.

Van Buren instructed his House deputies to sacrifice Blair and Rives and permit the Printer election to proceed, which allowed the coalition of conservative Democrats and Whigs to form unimpeded around Allen and the *Madisonian*.[23] The House Printer, therefore, would serve as a sop to the conservative Democrats.

Van Buren hoped that the gift of the public printing, along with pressure applied by Speaker Polk and Churchill Cambreleng (D-N.Y.), chairman of Ways and Means, would line up enough conservative Democrats to pass Calhoun's bill once it reached the House.[24] Presumably, rank-and-file members like Boon, Patton, and Bouldin had not been privy to Van Buren's plotting when they pushed for viva voce voting on September 6. Overnight, the backbenchers were informed of the behind-the-scenes details and put up no resistance as the Democratic majority allowed the viva voce resolution to be tabled quickly and quietly. Supporters of bringing the selection of House officers into the open would have to wait to fight another day. Unbeknownst to them at the time, they would not have to wait long.

[22] See Wilson (1959, 544–73) and Niven (1988, 230–31) for a description of this intrigue.

[23] Niven (1983, 421–22) tells a somewhat different story, claiming that Van Buren first entered into an arrangement with the conservatives to elect Polk Speaker because he was concerned that John Bell might beat Polk otherwise. Niven claims that Van Buren promised the conservatives top committee positions and the printership, but then Polk reneged by withholding the committee spots when he distributed the assignments. Van Buren, however, kept to his original bargain and gave the Printer to the conservatives. The problem with this story is that Polk made his committee assignments *after* all the officers were elected, including the Clerk. Thus, Niven's account is faulty. Five years later, Niven (1988, 230–31) revisited the drama, but this time dropped the whole Polk-Speaker-committee angle and focused on an explicit side-payments story—the conservatives would get the Printer in exchange for their support on the subtreasury bill (which they eventually withheld).

[24] Dion (1997, 82–84) presents a different version of events by building an account around Polk (and his parliamentary strategies as Speaker) while leaving Van Buren and the subtreasury story out of the drama entirely. Moreover, he characterizes the Printer election as a minor affair.

The 25th Congress: Second attempt

The viva voce voting matter was taken up again unexpectedly at the convening of the third session of the 25th Congress, on December 3, 1838, owing to the death of House Clerk Walter S. Franklin. Franklin's death made election of his successor the first order of business when the House reconvened.

This particular clerkship election was a choice more fraught with significance than typical, because the third session was the lame-duck session, held after the Democrats' disastrous showings in the summer-fall congressional elections of 1838. The Democratic edge in the House had been reduced by four seats (Dubin 1998, 120–22), and a major election dispute—affecting five additional seats—was gathering steam in New Jersey. The individual chosen to replace Franklin as House Clerk would have the authority to make provisional judgments about the initial disposition of disputed electoral credentials when the next Congress convened and thus could determine which party would organize the 26th Congress. Given their already tenuous majority status, the administration Democrats in the House were now poised to revisit viva voce voting and squelch the conservative movement within their ranks.

Immediately after Speaker Polk formally notified the House of Franklin's death on the opening day of the session, John Milligan (W-Del.) followed precedent by moving a resolution to proceed directly to the election of a new Clerk. Breaking with precedent, George Dromgoole (D-Va.) then moved an amendment to provide that the election be viva voce. After some initial confusion as to whether Dromgoole's motion was in order, the House passed the amendment, 119–91, with Democrats voting 98–5 in favor and opposition party members (mostly Whigs) voting 21–86 against. The House then proceeded to the election of a Clerk by viva voce, selecting Hugh Garland, a Virginia Democrat, on the third ballot (CG, 25-3, 12/3/1838, 2). Garland would in fact play a raw partisan role when the 26th Congress convened. (We defer the full accounting of this episode until chapter 5.)

Fresh from victory and feeling their oats, the administration Democrats set their sights higher. Dromgoole rose again three days later and submitted an amendment to the House rules that stated that "in all cases of election by the House the vote shall be taken *viva voce*" (CG, 25-3, 12/6/1838, 17), in effect revisiting the Reynolds amendment from the 23rd Congress. On December 10, Dromgoole's amendment was considered, and a heated debate arose. Henry Wise (W-Va.) declared that he "considered this resolution a direct attack upon the independence of the House and the freedom of its elections, as it would have the effect of applying the screws to doubtful members, so that they might sometimes be made to vote for party against their own convictions or predilections" (*Niles' National Register*, 12/15/1838, 249). Dromgoole responded that he had offered the amendment because he believed it "in accordance with the fundamental law of his own state, and as an essential accompaniment of the democratic principle of accountability to the constituent body" (ibid.). Moreover, he hoped that "no Representative would oppose it because he wished to vote in secret and skulk away from accountability, or because he desired to conceal his conduct from his constituents" (CG, 25-3, 12/10/1838, 20).

Francis Pickens (Nullifier-S.C.) agreed with Dromgoole's general notion of representation, but argued that "there was a wide distinction between the responsibility [members] owed to their constituents for the exercise of lawmaking power and that of choosing their mere ministerial officers" (CG, 25-3, 12/10/1838, 20). He went on to state, "let a man here dare to express the convictions of his heart, separate from party ties and party allegiance, and what would be the consequence? He trembles under it with more fear than any of the voters of France in the worst days of Jacobin rule." James Pearce (W-Md.) followed by claiming that "the people desired no such accountability as that asked for [by Dromgoole] in unimportant matters of this kind" and argued that if the resolution were adopted, "I shall feel that it makes me the subject of a most exact and unscrupulous discipline, because I know that the power of party can condescend to the smallest, most unimportant, and contemptible matters." John Reed (W-Mass.) agreed with Wise, Pickens, and Pearce that the intent of those advocating viva voce voting was not to promote democracy, but "to rally party feeling, and concentrate and drill it, and bring it to bear in all its force in every election, however trivial" (all quotes from Niles' National Register, 12/15/1838, 250).

After additional debate, Edward Stanly (W-N.C.) moved to lay the whole subject on the table, which failed 81–125, with Democrats voting 5–98 against and Democratic opponents voting 76–28 in favor. Finally, the more general viva voce rule was considered and passed, 124–84, with Democrats voting 96–5 in favor and Democratic opponents voting 28–79 in opposition (CG, 25-3, 12/10/1838, 20). Voting in all House elections would henceforth be public.[25]

A more systematic analysis of the viva voce voting dynamics appears in table 4.3. The four major House roll calls from the 25th Congress are analyzed: the first tabling attempt from the first session, the extension of viva voce voting to the election for Clerk in the third session, the second tabling attempt, and the extension of viva voce voting to all House elections. As the results show, first-dimension W-NOMINATE scores are a significant predic-

---

[25] Dromgoole struck again later in the session. On January 14, 1839, he proposed a resolution to amend House rules by substituting viva voce voting in all cases in which the secret ballot had been standard (like committee elections, for example). Two days later, Dromgoole asked for a suspension of the rules so that his resolution could be considered, but the vote failed to obtain the two-thirds majority necessary for suspension (CG, 25-3, 12/14/1839 and 12/16/1839, 117, 121). Statistical analysis of this roll call (number 404) reveals patterns similar to the analysis of the other roll calls on viva voce voting in the 25th Congress. The primary difference is that this last vote was the most purely partisan in structuring.

TABLE 4.3.

Analysis of voting on viva voce voting legislation, 25th Congress (robust standard errors in parentheses)

	Table viva voce resolution first attempt[a]	Extend viva voce voting to election for Clerk[b]	Table viva voce resolution second attempt[c]	Extend viva voce voting to all House elections[d]
W-NOMINATE first	1.57***	-2.98***	2.76***	-3.31***
dimension	(0.45)	(0.66)	(0.66)	(0.82)
W-NOMINATE second	-0.35	0.37	-0.22	0.17
dimension	(0.29)	(0.34)	(0.28)	(0.30)
Party = Democrat	-1.32*	0.20	-0.12	-0.22
	(0.53)	(0.58)	(0.59)	(0.64)
Constant	0.33	0.36	-0.58	0.80
	(0.29)	(0.37)	(0.37)	(0.43)
N	221	209	207	208
χ^2	132.43***	72.76***	80.05***	67.31***
LLF	-57.67	-45.39	-54.25	-50.59
Pseudo R^2	0.61	0.68	0.61	0.64

$*p < .05; **p < .01; *** p < .001.$
[a]Dependent variable is ICPSR Study No. 9822, 25th Congress, roll call number 15, probit coefficients.
[b]Dependent variable is ICPSR Study No. 9822, 25th Congress, roll call number 341, probit coefficients.
[c]Dependent variable is ICPSR Study No. 9822, 25th Congress, roll call number 348, probit coefficients.
[d]Dependent variable is ICPSR Study No. 9822, 25th Congress, roll call number 349, probit coefficients.

tor of individual vote choices on all four roll calls. Unlike the previous viva voce analysis in the 23rd Congress, the second-dimension W-NOMINATE scores provide little additional explanatory power. We attribute this change to the transformation of partisan dynamics during the 1830s, and particularly to the reaction of incumbent House members to the unfolding congressional elections. Even conservative Democrats wanted the next House called to order by a Democratic Clerk.

We also included a control for party, equal to one if the member was a Democrat, zero otherwise. With the exception of the first motion to table, party is never a significant factor in explaining how members voted on these motions. Because Democrats who appear on the "left" of the first W-NOMINATE dimension were virtually unanimous in casting pro–viva voce votes, the lack of statistical significance of the party variable, along with the strong significance of the ideology variable, helps to explain the behavior of the Whigs, who were more conflicted in their votes. The analysis suggests that Whigs who were ideologically similar to Democrats in general also sided with the Democrats on these procedural votes.[26]

[26] We also find this if we confine our analysis in table 4.3 only to Whigs.

That the Democrats showed more internal discipline than the Whigs on this issue is consistent with the historical view of the two parties. The Democrats were a more cohesive organization than the Whigs, with older, more established connections between state, local, and national party units. The development of the Whig organization had been a "best response" by the disparate anti-Jacksonian groups of the early to mid-1830s, and thus lacked the ideological glue that held the Democratic organization together. As Watson (2006, 159) notes:

> the Whig Party in its infancy was an unstable compound of diverse elements. Clay and Webster stood at its head, but Calhoun also acted with them at first. Many Anti-Masons were inclined to join them, as were former Democrats who favored internal improvements, high tariffs, and of course the Bank of the United States. Other early Whigs were strict constructionists who deserted [Jackson] because they feared that he had stretched the Constitution even more than the outright supporters of broad construction. Initially, all they had in common was a resentment of the methods or the substance of Jackson's Bank policy.

Moreover, unlike the Democrats, who relied on the design of institutional commitments to achieve partisan success, it was, as Aldrich states, "more the personal commitment and leadership of moderates . . . that held the Whig alliance together" (1995, 135). Thus, those Whigs with more Democratic (i.e., states' rights) leanings did not feel compelled to vote with their party on the viva voce voting legislation, because, presumably, they feared an electoral backlash more than potential sanctions by party leaders.

The 26th Congress: Viva voce voting survives the first Whig assault

While the viva voce voting issue seemed to be resolved at the end of the 25th Congress, some additional fireworks lay ahead. The midterm elections of 1838–39 leveled the partisan playing field, as the gap between the Whigs and Democrats in the House narrowed considerably. Adding to the tensions, the aforementioned New Jersey election dispute threatened to determine majority control of the chamber, and delayed the organization of the House for several days (Rowell 1901, 109–12; Jenkins 2004). Once balloting commenced for Speaker in the 26th Congress, regional blocs in both parties proved unwilling to support moderate candidates from the other region. After 11 rounds of balloting over two days, this deadlock eventually led to a coalition of convenience, in which the Whigs settled on one of their own with Democratic leanings, Robert M. T. Hunter (Va.), who was able to draw enough support from Calhounites to eke out a six-vote victory. (This episode is fully explored in chapter 5.)

The Whigs had finally delivered a significant blow and, sensing the Democrats reeling, went for the knockout. On December 20, 1839, after more discussion of the election dispute in New Jersey, the House turned to the election of its remaining officers, at which point Josiah Hoffman (W-N.Y.) proposed that the standing rules of the previous House be adopted, *except* the rule that called for viva voce voting in all House elections. Robert Craig (D-Va.) responded by offering an amendment to Hoffman's resolution that would strike out the viva voce voting exception.

This produced yet another impassioned debate. At first, both Whigs and Democrats recapitulated the expected positions. Leverett Saltonstall (W-Mass.) argued that viva voce voting was objectionable "because it had the tendency to effect a party organization." Hiram Hunt (W-N.Y.) followed by contending that viva voce voting was introduced not for democratic reasons but "for the purpose of enabling the party in the majority to put upon gentlemen the party screws." John Bell (W-Tenn.) concurred, stating that the secret ballot was necessary "to protect [members] from the influence of the Executive." Jesse Bynum (D-N.C.) shot back that "the idea that we should not vote *viva voce*, through fear of Executive influence, is ridiculous," while John Weller (D-Ohio) stated that "he was not afraid to let his constituents be the judge of his conduct." Finally, David Petrikin (D-Pa.) wondered "if it is not disappointed ambition—the mortification of a defeated party, which powerfully influences those who now ask to destroy the *viva voce* principle" (all quotes from *CG*, 26-1, 12/21/1839, 69–73).

As the debate progressed, however, a number of Whigs reversed positions on viva voce voting. This new stance reflected a recognition of the party's electoral rise in recent years and, in turn, a growing sentiment among many Whigs in favor of greater party discipline. Thus, viva voce voting, which had been the Democrats' weapon to keep party members in line, now began to appeal to some Whigs as well. For example, Caleb Cushing (W-Mass.) contended that "the Whigs ought to go for the viva voce system, because that was the popular principle." Julius Alford (W-Ga.) followed by stating that he "had ever been taught to believe the viva voce mode of voting was the most Republican in principle, and was sorry to see his friends opposing it." Moreover, in response to the claims of his Whig colleague John Bell, Alford "thought that the Executive possessed as many charms as terrors, and preferred the open manly mode of voting *viva voce*" (all quotes from *CG*, 26-1, 12/21/1839, 74).

Once voting commenced, the Craig amendment passed 142–86, with Democrats voting 115–2 in favor and Whigs voting 25–78 in opposition (Anti-Masons and Conservatives voted 0–6 and 2–0, respectively), leaving the viva voce provision in place (*CG*, 26-1, 12/21/1839, 74–75). An analysis of the voting is presented in table 4.4. We present results with and without a control for being a Whig.

TABLE 4.4.
Voting on the Craig amendment, 26th Congress (robust standard errors in parentheses)

	$(1)^a$	$(2)^a$
W-NOMINATE first dimension	-3.07***	-5.95***
	(0.42)	(1.07)
W-NOMINATE second dimension	0.86**	0.59
	(0.33)	(0.36)
Party = Whig	—	3.07**
		(1.18)
Constant	1.04**	-0.18
	(0.26)	(0.60)
N	228	228
χ^2	56.35***	79.05***
LLF	-41.75	-36.84
Pseudo R^2	0.72	0.76

*$p < .05$; **$p < .01$; ***$p < .001$.
[a]Dependent variable is ICPSR Study No. 9822, 26th Congress, roll call number 50, probit coefficients.

The results in column 1 show that, as before, significant explanatory leverage comes from the first W-NOMINATE dimension, which reflects that viva voce voting fit squarely in the ideological division between the two parties. However, as column 2 shows, once we account for ideology *and* party, Whigs were *more* supportive of viva voce voting compared to ideologically similar Democrats. Although Whigs *overall* opposed viva voce voting, we see that some in the party were beginning to see the device as potentially helpful to their position in the House as well.[27]

The 27th Congress: Viva voce survives the Whig ascent

By 1840, the Panic of 1837 had steadily evolved into a full-blown depression, and the national electorate had pointed the finger of blame at the incumbent Democrats. As a result, the Democrats were swept out of national government in the elections of 1840–41. The Whigs captured the presidency, as well as both chambers of Congress, by wide margins: William Henry Harrison trounced Van Buren 234–60 in the Electoral College, while the Whigs picked up 7 seats in the Senate and 33 seats in the House (Martis 1989, 31).

[27] A Whig-only analysis confirms this. More generally, Whig support was drawn predominantly from the left-hand portion of the party's ideological distribution, that is, from those Whigs who were ideologically closer to the Democrats.

TABLE 4.5.
Voting on the Williams amendment, 27th Congress (robust standard errors in parentheses)

	(1)[a]	(2)[a]
W-NOMINATE first dimension	1.43***	1.08*
	(0.22)	(0.50)
W-NOMINATE second dimension	-0.10	-0.23
	(0.20)	(0.28)
Party = Whig	—	0.47
		(0.63)
Constant	-0.74***	-1.03*
	(0.12)	(0.60)
N	220	220
χ^2	43.69***	41.03***
LLF	-102.73	-102.40
Pseudo R^2	0.24	0.24

*$p < .05$; **$p < .01$; ***$p < .001$.
[a]Dependent variable is ICPSR Study No. 9822, 27th Congress, roll call number 11, probit coefficients.

As the 27th Congress assembled, the Whigs found themselves in an unfamiliar role. No longer relegated to obstruction, they were now the *initiators* of legislation. Suddenly the need for strict party discipline became a Whig priority for the first time and was the leading topic of conversation in the Whig caucus.

The degree of Whig party discipline would be challenged immediately in the new House. On May 31, 1841, the first day of the session, proceedings began harmlessly enough, as the Clerk called the roll, after which Hiram Hunt (W-N.Y.) moved that the House proceed to the election of a Speaker by viva voce. Lewis Williams (W-N.C.) then rose and moved to amend Hunt's resolution by striking out viva voce and inserting "by [secret] ballot" instead. Williams's amendment failed by a vote of 67–153, with majorities of *both* parties opposing—Democrats by a 4–80 margin and Whigs 63–72 (*HJ*, 27-1, 5/31/1841, 8–9).

As the result indicates, although there was far from a consensus within the Whig ranks, a majority of Whigs now preferred viva voce voting to the secret ballot as the method for electing House officers. With the Democrats' continued solid opposition to the secret ballot, viva voce voting remained the rule in speakership elections.

An analysis of the voting appears in table 4.5.[28] As in previous Congresses, the explanatory leverage stems from the ideological division be-

[28] The following analysis differs from our previous published analysis of this episode. See Jenkins and Stewart (2003b, 502–3).

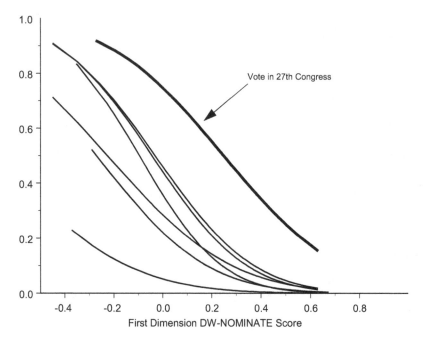

FIGURE 4.1. Predicted probability of voting in a pro–viva voce direction on all viva voce–related roll call votes, 23rd–27th Congresses, Whigs only (Anti-Masons and Anti-Jacksonians in 23rd Congress).

tween the two parties, as reflected by the first W-NOMINATE dimension. However, the shifting preferences of the Whig Party produced a poorer over-all model fit than in prior Congresses.

This shift in Whig sentiment can also be illustrated if we reexamine all of the roll calls on viva voce voting that occurred, starting with the 23rd Congress. This time we confine our analyses simply to the Whigs.[29] We conduct a probit analysis on each roll call vote as a function of the first dimension DW-NOMINATE score.[30] Because a "yea" vote in some cases was pro–viva voce and in other cases a "nay" vote was pro–viva voce, we have rescaled all of the votes so that a "yea" is pro–viva voce.

Figure 4.1 reports the predicted probabilities of voting in a pro–viva voce manner for all Whigs during these Congresses as a function of pro-Whig sentiment. Only one curve is labeled, which is the predicted probability of voting pro–viva voce in the 27th Congress. Notice that this curve is shifted

[29] For the 23rd Congress, we confine ourselves to the members identified by Martis (1989) as being anti-Jackson and anti-Mason.

[30] We use DW-NOMINATE scores in this case because we are explicitly comparing analyses across Congresses. The substance of what follows is not affected by the choice of NOMINATE scores, however, as a replication with W-NOMINATE scores reveals the same patterns.

significantly up compared to all of the other curves.[31] In substantive terms, this means that support for the viva voce procedure increased substantially for Whigs of all ideological persuasions in the 27th Congress. Almost overnight, mainstream Whigs had become supporters of the procedure after their party took control of the House.

If we are ignorant about the political history of this period, this Whig reversal might seem odd. The reason is that viva voce voting had previously been touted by loyal Democrats as a tool to ensure that pivotal party members would not defect and form a coalition with like-minded Whigs. The new Whig behavior makes it appear as if the bloc of Whigs who would be the most likely to form coalitions with like-minded Democrats in the organization of the House were making it *harder* for themselves to do just that— or at least to coalesce with moderate Democrats under the cloak of a secret ballot. However, policy was not the only thing at stake between the parties in the early 1840s. Also at stake was the nature of party organizations themselves and whether they would be haphazard or purposeful coalitions.

As noted earlier, the Whig Party first emerged in the 1830s as a loose confederation of individuals and political movements whose primary motivation was opposition to Andrew Jackson. These groups and individuals could more easily agree about what they were *against* than what they were *for.* If the new Party of Jackson was dedicated to building a strong political party that was willing to use coercive tactics to impose party discipline, the emergent Whigs would eschew those tactics as a consequence on principle. Therefore, the strategy of building a tight, formal party organization to oppose Jackson could best be described as "watchful waiting" during the 1830s.

All of that changed in the Tippecanoe election of 1840, the Whigs threw off their principled opposition to strong party organization in order to rally behind Harrison to defeat Van Buren (Holt 1985). Thus, the grudging willingness of a majority of Whigs to stand behind viva voce voting at the start of the 27th Congress was a continuation of the more general strategy of embracing party discipline measures first supported by the Democrats. This was still a transition, however, as not all Whigs jumped on the viva voce bandwagon. The sentiments of the old guard were reflected by the biting sarcasm of John Quincy Adams (W-Mass.) in a floor speech on June 1, 1841, when he rose to state that

> from the one vote given yesterday [on the secret ballot], he should apprehend that [the Whigs'] opposition to Executive power was beginning to melt away something like the ice in the dog days. If he might take that vote as a standard, he did not think that the Whigs would be so distinguished for their opposition to Executive power as they were

[31] Note that all the curves are relatively close together on the left side of the graph, but this is a region with few Whigs.

a year ago. It might probably, therefore, be convenient for them to take the name Democrats; and probably, in the change of things, the Democrats of last year would become the Whigs. So far at least as Executive power went, he thought that was likely to be the case. (*CG*, 27-1, 6/1/1841, 9)

The Effects of Viva Voce Voting

Once the viva voce procedure survived the onslaught from the Whigs in the 26th Congress, the election of Printer was fairly straightforward and occurred along party lines. Indeed, the election of Printer did not experience any of the cross-party intrigues that had affected the election of Speaker earlier in the Congress. The states' rights Democrats who threw the speakership election to the Whigs returned to the Democratic fold and supported the official party organ for Printer, even though it had been established because of a break between their patron Calhoun and Jackson. The election of House Clerk went the same way, and it was the Democrats, not the Whigs, who dominated floor politics for the rest of the Congress.

These short-term effects aside, the adoption of viva voce voting had longer-term effects on important elements in the national political system. Here we focus on two that will structure the remainder of the book: (1) House officer nominations and (2) speakership elections.

The effect of viva voce voting on House officer nominations

One immediate effect of viva voce voting was on how officer candidates would be selected by the two parties. In the secret-ballot era, the parties typically used informal politicking to coordinate support around candidates preferred by the leadership. Of course, such politicking, and promises of support made by party members, could be undone on the House floor, as members' vote choices were hidden from view. Now, with the public ballot governing all House elections, members' vote choices were *observable*— which provided a means to enforce preballot agreements and promises. As a result, ambitious party leaders had an incentive to eschew informal politicking and adopt a more formal institution for candidate selection. That institution was the *party nominating caucus*.

Caucuses themselves were not a new feature on the congressional landscape. They had a long history in congressional politics. Legislative party caucuses went back to the early Federalist era; the congressional nominating caucus dictated party selection of presidential nominees through 1824.[32] But

---

[32] On the rise and fall of the congressional nominating caucus, see Ostrogorski (1899) and Morgan (1969).

for the first four decades of our federal system, a regular party caucus to make officer nominations never took hold, perhaps due to the secret ballot (and resulting enforceability issues) that ultimately determined officer selection on the House floor.[33] Party nominating caucuses *did* exist in several state legislatures, however, the most notable example being New York.[34] There the caucus stood at the heart of an organization built in the early 1820s on the tenets of strict party discipline and unwavering party loyalty (Wallace 1968; Hofstadter 1969, 244–45).[35] At the helm of this New York party organization—the Albany Regency—was Martin Van Buren. Now, a decade and a half later, Van Buren was at the head of a different party organization, the national Democratic Party, as he sought to extend the Albany Regency's party blueprint to the congressional level.

The passage of viva voce voting would allow Van Buren and his supporters to adopt a party nominating caucus in the House, which would meet just prior to the start of a new Congress. Within the confines of the caucus, nominations for each of the major House officer positions would be made, after which elections would be held and choices determined. Minority factions—those members of the party who supported unsuccessful nominees—would eventually be placated, usually through committee assignments or promises of patronage, and in exchange they were expected to "be regular," that is, to support the caucus nominees on the House floor. Most important, though, unlike during the secret-ballot era, Democratic leaders could now identify whether party members followed through and voted for the caucus nominees on the floor. Dissidents could no longer defect and escape the notice of the leadership. Defectors could now be punished. The caucus thus had the potential to be *binding*.

Wasting no time, the Democrats organized a party nominating caucus prior to the opening of the 26th Congress. The Whigs made a halfhearted attempt to follow the Democrats' lead before actively adopting the same

[33] Follett (1896, 40) notes, "Although some concerted action must always have been necessary to produce a majority result, caucuses as we know them did not appear until towards the middle of the [nineteenth] century." Harlow (1917, 249–50) disagrees with Follett by noting newspaper evidence (reports in the *Columbian Centinel*) that caucuses formed in advance of the speakership elections of 1799 and 1814; from these cases, Harlow concludes that it is "fairly evident" that the Speaker had always been elected by a party caucus. To examine the issue further, we examined a range of newspapers from 1831 to 1837—covering the five speakership elections prior to the contest in the 26th Congress—and found *no* evidence that a party caucus was held in advance of the given election. From this, we feel confident in claiming that party nominating caucuses were not "regular" events prior to the 26th Congress.

[34] New Jersey was another prime case. See Levine (1977).

[35] The logic of the caucus system was recounted by Jabez D. Hammond, a former U.S. House member, New York state senator, and loyal foot soldier in the Albany Regency: "when political friends consent to go into caucus for the nomination of officers, every member of such caucus is bound by honor to support and carry into effect its determination. . . . unless you intend to carry into effect the wishes of the majority, however contrary to your own, you have no business at a caucus" (1850, 192–93).

caucus machinery prior to the opening in the 27th Congress (wherein they would enjoy majority control of the House). As a result, a caucus-directed system of House organization had begun.

The Van Burenites' goal of instituting Regency-level discipline and loyalty was not to be, however, which meant that a full-blown organizational cartel would remain an aspiration for decades to come. As we describe below (and in considerable detail in chapters 5 and 6), slavery would become an increasingly difficult issue for the interregional coalitions underlying the Second Party System, and would eventually trump partisanship in the mid-1850s and lead to a realignment later in the decade (which we cover in chapter 7).

But the Van Burenites' efforts were not entirely in vain. While initially unsuccessful, they laid the foundation for the pattern of seamless and consistent House organization that began in the mid-1860s—after slavery was no longer a wedge issue. The permanent emergence and institutionalization of a caucus-induced system of House organization will be examined fully in chapters 8 and 9.

The effect of viva voce voting on speakership elections

The ultimate motivation in investigating why the House adopted viva voce voting was not to understand how Printers and Clerks were elected in the 1830s but how Speakers were elected in the 1840s and 1850s. Viewed one way, making the election of Speaker public had precisely the effect that its supporters desired—it was impossible for House members to hide from their ballot choices, and therefore impossible for them to avoid partisan (caucus) pressure over the choice of Speaker. But, as the cases presented in the following chapters will show, the viva voce election of Speaker had exactly the opposite effect in the long term compared to what was desired. Democratic supporters of viva voce voting assumed that the partisan era they had ushered in was here to stay, in precisely the way that Van Buren had designed. Thus, they assumed that by making votes for officers like Speaker transparent, in combination with the discipline imposed by a party nominating caucus, party leaders could exert more effective command over the rank and file and more firmly control the reins of government.

What these supporters of viva voce voting did not count on was the power of the regional divisions that were simmering in the country. (It is telling that the battle over viva voce voting happened in parallel with the House battle over the gag rule.) In the end, the daylight that shone on speakership elections highlighted regional animosities just as much as partisanship, as constituents as well as party leaders could now observe members' speakership choices. As a result, it became more difficult to elect Speakers and organize the House than before the onset of viva voce voting.

Over the next 20 years, viva voce voting would be the most important strategic reality facing party leaders as they organized the House for business every two years. It induced both parties to choose "slavery moderates" as their caucus nominees for Speaker, whereas Speakers from the secret-ballot era had been chosen for their parliamentary skills, even if they possessed strong beliefs about slavery. Indeed, Speakers who were elected prior to viva voce voting—such as Taylor (N.Y.), Stevenson (Va.), Bell (Tenn.), and Polk (Tenn.)—held strong views on the slavery issue that reflected their home regions. Strong pro- or antislavery views did not interfere with their election, as long as they possessed the other leadership qualities needed to advance the majority party's shared agenda, including fairness in dealing with the party's factions and the ability to exercise firm control over the House floor.

In the era of secret ballots, Speakers with strong regional opinions were often elected with little drama. The atmospherics at least suggest that many of these candidates were elected with support among copartisans who disagreed with them on slavery. Even when the majority party could not initially agree on a single candidate, the disagreement could be worked out within a couple of ballots. This was because ideologically opposed copartisans could cut deals behind a veil of secrecy, secure in the knowledge that their constituents could not observe their vote choices.

The commencement of viva voce voting for Speaker changed things. Now, with one's vote for Speaker public knowledge, there was a greater premium put on the parties settling on an actual slavery moderate (not just a North/South geographic median), and by and large that is what happened.

This pattern can be illustrated by examining the spatial location of Speakers along the dimension(s) of preference most closely correlated with region—which we take to be a surrogate for attitudes about slavery—during the Second Party System, roughly the 19th (1825–27) through 34th (1855–57) Congresses. Using W-NOMINATE scores for this exercise, the first dimension was most strongly correlated with region for the 19th–21st (1825–31) and the 32nd–34th Congresses (1851–57); the second dimension was most strongly correlated with region for the 23rd–30th Congresses (1833–49); both the first and second dimensions were similarly correlated with region in the 22nd (1831–33) and 31st (1849–51) Congresses; and the third dimension was the most strongly correlated with region for the 32nd Congress (1851–53).[36]

---

[36] The Pearson correlation coefficients between the first two dimensional scores and a dummy variable indicating a Southern representative are as follows:

	Congress															
Dim:	19	20	21	22	23	24	25	26	27	28	29	30	31	32[a]	33	34
1st	-.70	-.65	-.62	-.53	.05	.19	-.02	-.04	-.31	-.30	-.37	-.35	-.62	-.31	-.57	-.77
2nd	.01	-.10	.14	.55	.66	.79	.84	.83	.80	.79	.82	.86	.70	.20	-.13	.04

[a]Third-dimension correlation = .52.

Because the W-NOMINATE algorithm imposes an assumption of orthogonality between the dimensions, we council caution in thinking about comparisons that involve dimensions

Keeping in mind that the Speaker rarely voted, in order to illustrate the pattern of regional moderation, we need to look back to the Congress preceding a Speaker's initial election to see where he stood on the regional issues of the day. Table 4.6 reports the Speaker's W-NOMINATE score along the regional dimension in the Congress preceding his initial election to the speakership, as well as the W-NOMINATE median and quartile cutoffs for the Speaker's party along the regional dimension.

As a general rule, when voting for Speaker was handled through a secret ballot (Speakers Taylor through Polk), the victorious candidate was a regional extremist (defined as being *outside* the party's interquartile range of W-NOMINATE scores). Also as a general rule, once balloting became viva voce, *all* of the victorious speakership candidates were regional moderates (defined as being *within* the party's interquartile range of W-NOMINATE scores).[37]

The one exception to the general pattern was the first Speaker who was elected via public ballot, Robert M. T. Hunter (W-Va.). But even here the exception proves the rule. Hunter, a House member with "confused party loyalties" (Lientz 1978, 77), was not the first choice for Speaker of either of the parties in 1839. Following the logic that had guided secret ballot contests, the Democrats and Whigs had settled on highly partisan candidates with strong Southern sentiments: John W. Jones (D-Va.) and John Bell (W-Tenn.). The strong regional opinions of both men were unpalatable to Unionist Southerners and to Northerners. The regional fracturing of the two parties gave an opening to Southern Whigs to rally around Hunter, as he possessed strong regional sentiments but was quite moderate (located near the House median) on the major commercial, ideological dimension (Stew-

---

higher than the first. Substantively, although the kernel of the first dimension during the Jacksonian era was a commercial one and the second dimension a racial one, political discourse at the time invoked federal power on both—a federal government powerful enough to actively develop an economy (dimension 1) would be strong enough to abolish slavery (dimension 2). Therefore, in practical terms, attitudes about the two issues were undoubtedly correlated at the time. Because the W-NOMINATE algorithm estimates the second dimension from what is left unexplained by the first, the "federal power" aspect of the second dimension is already accounted for by the first dimension, even though contemporaries understood federal power to be involved in both. As a consequence, our interpretation of the "regional" dimension is as a more purely moral issue that contemporaries would probably have recognized.

[37] The cases of Bell (23rd Congress, 1834) and Boyd (32nd Congress, 1851) are ambiguous, since they are "inliers" on one of the two dimensions and "outliers" on the other. In the case of Bell, the first dimension in the 22nd Congress is much more highly correlated with the regional dimensions on either side of the Congress, therefore it is likely that Bell was a regional outlier at the time of his election—a judgment shared by contemporaries. Likewise Boyd was an outlier on the first dimension in the 31st Congress, which was most highly correlated with the partisan (commercial) dimension in the 30th, so that it is also likely that Boyd was a regional moderate among Democrats—which is also a judgment shared by his contemporaries. (Boyd, like the Southern Speaker who preceded him, Howell Cobb, refused to sign Calhoun's "Southern Address," which alienated him from Southern fire-breathers.)

TABLE 4.6.
Spatial location of speakers on regional dimension, 19th–34th Congresses

Speaker (state)	Party	First Cong. (years) as Speaker	Dimension examined	W-NOMINATE score[a]				Speaker inside interquartile range
				Speaker	1st Q	Median	3rd Q	
Taylor (N.Y.)	Ad.	19 (1825–27)	1	.555	-.384	.192	.527	
Stevenson (Va.)	J	20 (1827–29)	1	-.413	-.256	-.004	.224	
Bell (Tenn.)	J	23 (1833–35)	1	-.738	-.655	-.381	-.065	
			2	.034	-.329	.051	.374	yes
Polk (Tenn.)	J	24 (1835–37)	2	-.491	-.439	.044	.286	
Hunter (Va.)	W	26 (1839–41)	2	-.889	-.493	.142	.457	
White (Ky.)	W	27 (1841–43)	2	-.195	-.196	.276	.399	yes
Jones (Va.)	D	28 (1843–45)	2	-.269	-.300	.012	.358	yes
Davis (Ind.)	D	29 (1845–47)	2	-.047	-.311	.104.	.487	yes
Winthrop (Mass.)	W	30 (1847–49)	2	-.041	-.232	.062	.189	yes
Cobb (Ga.)	D	31 (1849–51)	2	-.319	-.415	.127	.465	yes
Boyd (Ky.)	D	32 (1851–53)	1	-.544	-.463	-.253	-.09	
			2	-.111	-.294	.053	.410	yes
Banks (Mass.)	Am.	34 (1855–57)	1	.426	.062	.631	.812	yes

[a]This is the score along the dimension most strongly correlated with region (North/South) in the Congress preceding the Speaker's initial election. For Taylor, Stevenson, Bell, and Banks, this is the first dimension. For the remaining Speakers, this is the second dimension.

art 1999, 18–20). In the end, although the Democrats held a nominal majority in the 26th Congress, they lost hold of the speakership when Hunter was elected through a coalition of Whigs and a few Southern Democrats who were allies of Calhoun (this episode will be explored in greater detail in chapter 5).

The Hunter fiasco led the Democrats to understand the importance of settling regional differences within the caucus, lest the fight for the Speaker erupt on the floor. This realization guided speakership choice for the next decade, as the majority party generally nominated regional moderates and imposed that choice on the first ballot.

Even though the rise of viva voce voting for Speaker put a premium on finding a slavery moderate in caucus, and binding members to that caucus choice, defection still occurred on the House floor. The slavery issue, and the potential position-taking benefits and costs of speakership votes, led some members to eschew party in favor of regionally inspired constituency interests. This is illustrated in table 4.7, which reports the fraction of Northerners and Southerners who supported each party's principal speakership vote-getter in each Congress. When a Congress experienced multiple ballots to choose a Speaker, the first and last ballots were analyzed.

In most cases, one or both of the parties experienced a regional division in their voting for Speaker. One interesting detail in this pattern, which is not entirely surprising, is that when there were regional differences, Southerners were almost always more likely to defect—even when the party's candidate was a (moderate) Southerner.[38] Additionally, the Whigs were more regionally divided than the Democrats, with Southern Whigs more likely to rebel against their party's regular candidate.

Thus, in the long term, viva voce voting interacted in an interesting way with the two conflicting impulses that were identified at the opening of this chapter: region and party. When one of the parties had a comfortable margin in the House, no difficulties arose in organizing it—the most cross-pressured members of the majority could abandon their party in the speakership balloting without serious consequences, as a Speaker could still be elected. However, whenever the party division was close, as it was on several occasions, choosing a Speaker became nearly impossible—speakership elections often became deadlocked because the regional factions within the parties found it difficult to rally around a single candidate, yet were unwilling (because of the party principle) to reach across the aisle to form an interparty coalition comprised of members from the corresponding region. Viva voce voting helped to push the parties apart during the chamber's organization, since it made partisan defection easy to observe by party leaders. At the same time, viva voce voting also helped to push the regions apart in the

---

[38] The only notable exception was in the 34th Congress (1855–57), when the party system was in full collapse.

TABLE 4.7.
Support for major party speakership candidates by region, 26th–34th Congresses

Cong. (Years)	Main candidate	State	South	Non-South	χ^2	prob.
Democrats						
26 (1839–41) -first ballot-	Jones	Va.	82.6% (46)	100% (73)	13.6	.000
26 -last ballot-	Jones	Va.	51.5% (45)	42.5% (73)	0.83	.36
27 (1841–43)	Jones	Va.	90.3% (31)	100% (55)	5.52	.019
28 (1843–45)	Jones	Va.	100% (85)	100% (43)	—	—
29 (1845–47)	Davis	Ind.	82.7% (52)	100% (77)	14.33	.000
30 (1847–49) -first ballot-	Boyd	Ky.	67.4% (46)	48.3% (58)	3.82	.051
30 -last ballot-	Boyd	Ky.	53.3% (45)	65.5% (58)	1.57	.210
31 (1849–51) -first ballot-	Cobb	Ga.	96.2% (52)	92.9% (56)	.56	.455
31 -last ballot-	Cobb	Ga.	96.2% (53)	89.1% (55)	2.00	.157
32 (1851–53)	Boyd	Ky.	84.2% (38)	98.7% (76)	9.21	.002
33 (1853–55)	Boyd	Ky.	88.7% (53)	100% (89)	10.52	.001
34 (1855–57) -first ballot-	Richardson	Ill.	98.0% (51)	79.2% (24)	7.90	.005
34 -last ballot-	Aiken	S.C.	100% (50)	82.6% (23)	9.20	.002
Whigs/Opposition						
26 (1839–41) -first ballot-	Bell	Ky.	77.1% (48)	98.3% (58)	11.75	.001
26 -last ballot-	Hunter	Va.	97.9% (47)	100% (58)	1.25	.264
27 (1841–43)	White	Ky.	86.0% (50)	92.9% (84)	1.68	.195
28 (1843–45)	White	Ky.	100% (15)	100% (41)	—	
29 (1845–47)	Vinton	Ohio	87.0% (23)	98.1 (52)	3.91	.048
30 (1847–49) -first ballot-	Winthrop	Mass.	93.9% (33)	97.5% (79)	.84	.359
30 -last ballot-	Winthrop	Mass.	100% (32)	97.5% (79)	.825	.364

TABLE 4.7. (*Cont.*)

Cong. (Years)	Main candidate	State	South	Non-South	χ^2	prob.
31 (1849–51) -first ballot-	Winthrop	Mass.	76.0% (25)	97.4% (78)	12.14	.000
31 -last ballot-	Winthrop	Mass.	77.8% (27)	100% (76)	17.93	.000
32 (1851–53)	Stanly	N.C.	5.3% (19)	37.0% (54)	6.92	.009
33 (1853–55)	Chandler	Pa.	23.5% (17)	62.5% (30)	7.64	.006
34 (1855–57) -first ballot-	Campbell	Ohio	0% (26)	44.1% (118)	17.93	.000
34 -last ballot-	**Banks**	Mass.	0% (26)	87.6% (113)	79.16	.000

Note: Victorious candidates are in **bold** type. The χ^2 statistic tests whether support for the top vote-getter within each party was independent of region. (Numbers in parentheses indicate number of members.)

House, as the highly aggressive regional press that emerged in future years worked to make political life difficult for House members who stuck with their party's Speaker nominee, regardless of region.

Finally, the path of the viva voce election rule illustrates an interesting, recurring dynamic concerning rule changes in Congress. Narrowly considered, arguing over adopting the viva voce rule is an example of Riker's "heritability problem"—the tendency of procedural matters to "inherit" the substantive considerations that give rise to them (see Riker 1980). In this case, what motivated the viva voce voting controversy was not the simple principle of publicly declaring one's support for House leadership, but rather the principle of how strong parties would be.

At the same time, once the rule had been put into place, future House members, and other national political actors, began to consider a wider range of ramifications of the viva voce rule. As players on the national stage gained experience with life under viva voce voting, those motivated more by regional considerations than party principles recognized the potential that public votes for Speaker could have to excite regional passions and therefore (ironically enough) *undermine* the very partisan system that its original supporters desired. Thus, the larger story of viva voce voting is cautionary to students of institutional change. The original motivation behind institutional transformation may end up getting buried under the new, unanticipated possibility—or unintended consequence—that the transformation opens up.

CHAPTER 5

Shoring Up Partisan Control:
The Speakership Elections of 1839 and 1847

The House began to vote publicly to elect its Speakers and other House officers just as the country was entering a period of monumental, and ultimately cataclysmic, political change. Within a generation, 11 Southern states would secede from the Union and a bloody civil war would commence. In the late 1830s, however, the sectional tensions that would ultimately spell national doom were just coming to light—over the next decade, they would slowly but steadily ratchet up. While the viva voce voting procedure was introduced for partisan reasons, it quickly got caught up in those escalating sectional tensions.

Viva voce voting was used for the first time in a speakership election at a treacherous moment in congressional history: during the disputed organization of the 26th Congress (1839–41). Partisan sentiments were closely and bitterly divided in the House, and control of national political institutions was determined by the resolution of a disputed election in a single state (New Jersey).[1] Despite the Democrats' championing the device, viva voce voting could not bring them together, even though they held a narrow majority. The end result was one of the most politically confusing organizational outcomes the U.S. House has ever seen: a Whig was eventually elected Speaker, but Democrats were chosen as Clerk and Printer. The officer choices were dictated by a small group of nominal Democrats, the followers of John C. Calhoun, who placed regional interests (specifically, support of states' rights) over partisanship, the exact opposite of what Van Buren had been trying to foster with the construction of the public ballot and the party nominating caucus.

After the contentious 26th Congress, the next three Congresses were organized largely along the lines envisioned by Van Buren. House officer nominees were chosen in caucus and elected on the floor by public ballot.[2] Partisan margins in the House were sufficiently large during these years that majority party floor success could be achieved even with a nontrivial num-

---

[1] On the New Jersey election dispute, see Rowell (1901, 109–12), McCormick (1953), and Jenkins (2004).

[2] There was a small hiccup in 1841, when the Whigs' Clerk nominee was defeated.

ber of defections from the caucus agreement. These defections were tied to increasing sectional tensions, as the continuing struggle over the gag rule in the House and conflict over western expansion and the annexation of Texas led some members to question the wisdom of placing party over region. Finally, in the 30th Congress (1847–49), a narrower partisan margin created explicit difficulties, as three ballots were necessary before the majority Whigs could elect one of their own as Speaker. More disturbing, the outcome was achieved when a *non-Whig* cast the deciding vote, after several Whigs refused to support the caucus nominee on principle—with that principle being that the caucus candidate was not sufficiently antislavery at a time when war with Mexico raged and additional western land for slavery expansion was sought.

Thus, the intended consequence of viva voce voting (enhanced partisan cohesion on House officer votes) was increasingly met with an unintended consequence (enhanced electoral responsiveness and partisan defection, as members sought to stay true to their constituents' interests). While this tension created by the public ballot would cause some difficulties between 1839 and 1847, which is the subject of this chapter, the main conflictual drama was still to come.

PARTISAN DIVISION AND INSTITUTIONAL CHAOS: HOUSE ORGANIZATION IN THE 26TH CONGRESS

The organization of the 26th Congress (1839–41), of which the speakership election was just one in a sequence of events, was perhaps the most divisive in American history. To understand that divisiveness, we have to cast our sights back a full year before it convened, to the fall of 1838, when the election season for the 26th Congress was in high gear.

Democratic House candidates took a drubbing in the fall elections of 1838 over ongoing discontent fostered by the Panic of 1837. Election returns from the 14 states that had held elections in the fall showed a net shift of 16 seats to the Whigs, which put control of the House within their grasp.[3] The prospect of the Whig Party gaining control of the House for the first time in its history focused attention on New Jersey, where the election was closest and the stakes were highest.

The Garden State was pivotal because it continued to elect its six-member House delegation via a general ticket, that is, on an "at large" basis. Initial newspaper reports of the election returns showed that five of the top six vote-getters were Democrats, yet the margins were tiny.[4] The House candi-

---

[3] The worst electoral showings for Democrats in the fall elections of 1838 were in Georgia (net loss of 8 seats) and New York (net loss of 11 seats). See Dubin (1998, 115–25).

[4] The congressional election stretched over two days, October 9–10, 1838. The election returns reported here come from Dubin (1998, 121), which are based on accountings in the Trenton *Emporium & True American*, 11/9/1838.

date who received the most votes statewide, Peter D. Vroom (D), outpolled the last-place finisher, John B. Ayerigg (W), by only 197 votes.

The 1838 New Jersey House election is a prime instance of partisan officials using the mechanics of the electoral canvas to sway the outcome of an election. The opportunity for partisan shenanigans presented itself in the town of South Amboy, which had given the Democratic House slate an average majority of 252 votes. South Amboy's election returns were delivered to the Middlesex county clerk, a Whig, without a certification from the election inspectors and without the signature of the election clerk. The county clerk chose to ignore South Amboy's returns, claiming they were invalid. As a result, what had been a narrow statewide victory for five of the six Democratic candidates became an even narrower victory for the entire Whig slate.

The decision of the Middlesex county clerk cascaded through state politics in an episode that came to be known as the Broad Seal War. The Whig governor, William Pennington, and his council chose not to send for the missing South Amboy returns, declared all the Whig House candidates victorious, and issued official writs of election to all six under the "broad seal" of the state of New Jersey. The Democratic secretary of state, who was in receipt of all the election returns, including those from South Amboy, issued an irregular writ of his own to the candidates he deemed to be victorious, including the five Democrats who would have been elected if the South Amboy returns had been counted, along with John F. Randolph (W), whose inclusion among the victorious slate was never in dispute.

This local dispute over the membership of the 26th Congress was dominating the national news when the lame-duck session of the 25th Congress convened on December 3, 1838. As discussed in the previous chapter, the first order of business in the reconvened House was to fill the vacancy caused by the intersession death of the House Clerk, Walter S. Franklin. Due to vacancies and late arrivals, the House membership in the lame-duck session was equally balanced between Whigs and Democrats, which raised the possibility that the election of the Clerk could rest on the most arbitrary of contingencies. House members knew that if the New Jersey election was still under dispute when the 26th Congress convened a year later, the Clerk they were about to elect would preside over the organization of the next House in a highly charged partisan atmosphere. And, as described in chapter 4, after nearly a decade of arguing off and on about whether to subject the election of House officers to the light of day, the chamber decided, in a largely party-line vote, to select the Clerk viva voce. The balloting for Clerk then commenced. (For a breakdown of the balloting, see appendix 3.)

As neither party had settled on a single candidate for Clerk in advance of the House's formal convening, nine candidates received votes on the first ballot. The Democrats split their votes among Hugh A. Garland (Va., 48 votes), Edward Livingston (N.Y., 31 votes), Henry Buehler (Pa., 16 votes), John Bigler (Ohio, 8 votes), and Reuben M. Whitney (D.C., 2 votes); the Whigs divided their support among Matthew St. Clair Clarke (D.C., 55 votes), Samuel Shoch (Pa., 21 votes), Arnold Naudain (Del., 20 votes), and James H. Birch (Mo., 9 votes).

The split within the two major parties revealed different types of partisan cleavages and, perhaps, different ideas about how to build a majority to elect a Clerk in an environment in which the parties were closely matched. On the Democratic side, the primary cleavage was regional, with Southern Democrats uniting behind Garland and Northerners split among Garland, Livingston, and Buehler. Garland had served five years in the Virginia House of Delegates as a staunch Jacksonian, which probably accounts for his strong support among Southerners. He was also the administration's candidate, which undoubtedly accounts for his strong (though not unanimous) showing among Northerners.[5] Divisions among Northern Democrats arose over the continuing rift over the subtreasury plan, which had divided the party and threatened its control of the chamber (*Albany Argus* [hereafter abbreviated as *AA*], 12/6/1838, 2). This rift was largely orthogonal to the main partisan divide; support for each of the three major Democratic Clerk candidates was, in fact, spread across the board on the main party dimension, as measured by W-NOMINATE scores.

The division was quite different on the Whig side. Clarke, the main Whig vote-getter, had (as noted in chapter 3) served previously as the House Clerk from the mid-17th (1822–23) through the 22nd Congresses (1831–33), until he was defeated for reelection at the start of the 23rd Congress (1833). These were the transitional Congresses when the Republicans were a catch-all party and the primary loyalty of representatives was to personalities. Clarke's strongest support in those earlier Congresses came from the Adams-Clay faction, which explains his attractiveness as a Whig Clerk candidate in the 25th Congress. Among Clarke's Whig opponents, Naudain was a former senator from Delaware who drew support that was similar to Clarke's, across the ideological perspective and from both North and South, only in smaller numbers. Shoch's support was concentrated entirely in the North.

On the second ballot, the Whigs coalesced around Clarke, while the dueling factions of Northern Democrats continued to be polarized around Buehler and Livingston, leaving Garland, the leading Democratic candidate, without Northern support. At the end of this ballot, Clarke led Garland 87–59.[6]

---

[5] On the first ballot Garland received 25 of 26 votes cast by Deep South Democrats, but only 19 of the 79 votes from Democrats of other regions. Northern support was mostly split between Edward Livingston (N.Y.) and Henry Buehler (Pa.). This pattern persisted into the second ballot. In the third, Garland collected all but 7 of the 104 votes cast by Democrats. Six of those votes were cast for Clarke, the Whig candidate, all by Democrats whose W-NOMINATE scores suggest they were closer ideologically to the Whigs. News of Garland's partisan activities shows up several times in the letters contained in the papers of Martin Van Buren. See Library of Congress (1910, 693).

[6] The *House Journal* (25-3, 12/3/1838, 13) lists the total vote for Clarke at 88; however, only 87 names are recorded as having voted for Clarke (12). Here, as elsewhere in this book, we rely on the actual roll call, rather than the recapitulated vote.

Whig leaders were counting on conservative Democrats to eventually defect to Clarke, who in previous Congresses had won their support, but to no avail. Prior to the third ballot, the names of the minor candidates for Clerk were withdrawn. With nowhere to go and the clerkship on the line, the Northern Democratic holdouts threw their support to Garland, providing him with a narrow victory (106–104) on the third ballot. The viva voce procedure had fulfilled its intention: exposing individual members' votes for Clerk and forcing dissident conservatives to toe the party line or risk penalties.[7] Press accounts hailed Garland's election as a clear victory for Van Buren and his administration.[8]

The significance of Garland's victory became apparent a year later, when the 26th Congress convened and Garland found himself in the chair for the organization of the House. The partisan tide had eventually turned in the House elections of 1839, as the Democrats achieved a net gain of 5 seats, thus reducing some of the sting of the net loss of 16 seats they had endured in 1838.

Nonetheless, the congressional elections of 1838–39 were indecisive from the perspective of organizing the House for business. Unlike the present day, when partisan attachments of House candidates are universally understood, in the 1830s enough candidates were sufficiently cagey about their sympathies that no one was quite sure which was the majority party. Furthermore, with travel delays and the presence of several disputed elections, not just in New Jersey, we can understand why both parties entered the organizational struggle with a high degree of caution and an unwillingness to give ground. The *New York Evening Post* summarized the situation this way:

Parties are so nearly equally divided that the determination of the preliminary question as to the right of certain members to their seats, is looked forward to with the deepest interest. The House of Representatives, with the exception of four members, to be elected in the Franklin District of Massachusetts, the Potter District in Pennsylvania, and the state of Mississippi, is complete. The seats of eight members, of whom six are Whigs, five from New Jersey, one from Virginia, one from Pennsylvania, and one from Illinois, are disputed. If these members are al-

---

[7] A reporter for the *New Yorker* who was covering the House organization documented the effect of the viva voce procedure this way: "Whigs, Administration men, and Conservatives, prepare to show your colors: there will be no dodging allowed" (12/8/1838, 190).

[8] The *Albany Argus* put it this way: "[Garland's] election is a triumph to the friends of the administration, and a sore mortification to its opponents, who had confidently counted upon a different result. . . . The conservatives, who have not resolved to become part and parcel of the [Whig] party, supported Mr. Garland with cordiality" (12/6/1838, 2). The *Jeffersonian* emphasized the role played by the Calhounites: "The result is an Administration and still more a Southern triumph. No candidate North of the Potomac could have been elected by the Administration party. But the votes of Southern Conservatives and ultra 'States Rights' men have secured Mr. Garland's election. He is a strong 'States Rights' man of great respectability and weight of character" (12/15/1838, 346).

lowed to vote in the election of Speaker, the House will stand, democrats 119, whigs 122, showing a whig majority of three votes. But if
they are all excluded and the controverted questions are settled, the
democratic majority will be one. It is not certain, however, that all the
members will vote with the party to which they are nominally attached—Great doubt rests upon the course that may be pursued by
many who are called State Rights men, and both parties, it is to be
presumed, will make serious efforts in their nominations of candidates
for the office of Speaker, to make themselves acceptable to that portion
of the House. (11/23/1839, 3)

Within this confusion, the most important decision that needed to be
made regarding the complexion of the upcoming House was how to determine the rightful occupants of the New Jersey seats. The Clerk's role was
presumably not to decide the issue but to get the House organized and its
members sworn in so that *they* could decide. As Dempsey notes, under the
rules and precedents of the House, Garland's course of action should have
been obvious:

Five of the claimants (Whigs) carried certificates of election signed by
the Governor who was the legal authority empowered to issue such
certificates. They were unquestionably in valid form. Under the existing rules of the House, the Clerk had no alternative other than to accept the certificates, since they were *prima facie* evidence of the right
to the seats. On the basis of all precedents, the persons certified by the
Governor should have been seated, and contests brought later. (1956,
65)

However, Garland did not pursue the obvious.

On December 2, 1839, the 26th Congress convened, and Garland began
to call the roll of members-elect. When he reached New Jersey, Garland announced that conflicting evidence existed regarding the election of five members. He then stated that he would skip their names and finish calling the
roll, thus allowing the House to deliberate and sort out the specifics of the
New Jersey case afterward (*CG*, 26-1, 12/2/1839, 1).[9]

The chamber erupted. Over the next several days, debate was protracted
and vicious. The Whigs wanted Garland to follow the precedent that should
have governed his actions. The Democrats supported the Clerk's extraordi-
nary course.[10]

[9] Rumors that Garland might attempt such a maneuver abounded well in advance of the
vote. On November 23, a story in the *New Yorker* reported: "Some [rumors] indicate . . . that
the Clerk of the last House (who is *ex officio* of this until a new election) will take the responsibility of reading from a newspaper a list of the claimants from New Jersey, instead of the returned Members. We trust that better Councils will prevail" (153).

[10] John Quincy Adams kept a log of the politicking in his diary. To Adams, Garland's parliamentary maneuver was obvious: "This movement has been evidently prepared to exclude the

Garland's opening gambit of deferring the New Jersey question until after the House had organized itself quickly devolved into a parliamentary quagmire that threatened pure disorder. He disclaimed any authority to decide with finality the New Jersey election dispute, wielded the House gavel with the lightest hand, and asserted that only a presiding officer of the House, elected by members of the House, could channel debate and motions in any direction. The result was a tangled knot of motions, appeals, and protests that frustrated all sides.[11] Various resolutions were put forth so that the House could organize itself, some excluding the New Jersey members and some including them, but none carried (CG, 26-1, 12/2/1839, 1–11).

Out of desperation, John Quincy Adams was made "chairman" of the House on December 5, until the organization could be settled. Adams, of course, was probably the most divisive member of the House at the time, owing to his persistence in submitting antislavery petitions in the face of the gag rule. (Adams would face censure from the House in the next Congress over precisely this behavior.) Still, the concern over pure anarchy prevailing was so great that Adams's quasi-coup was greeted by nearly unanimous approbation within the chamber. After two additional days, and some unrecorded teller votes, Adams noted in his diary, somewhat presciently, that "it is apparent . . . that the choice of the Speaker will depend entirely upon the New Jersey vote" (1876, vol. 10, 12/7/1839, 150).

With Adams in the chair, the House endured several more days of debate. Eventually, on December 11, the House voted swiftly in turn to deny seats to the five New Jersey Whigs and then to complete the call of the roll, skipping over New Jersey (CG, 26-1, 12/11/1839, 40–41). Garland subsequently completed the task of calling the roll, sans the New Jersey members, the following day.

The Whigs had lost the battle of New Jersey but refused to surrender the war. On December 13, Henry Wise (W-Va.) moved to amend the roll, stating that the election credentials of the five New Jersey Whigs were sufficient to entitle them to their seats. The previous question was called and seconded, but lost on a tie (117–117) vote (CG, 26-1, 12/13/1839, 48). Wise had believed his amendment would pass, but he was undone by two would-be supporters who went missing: Thomas Kempshall (W-N.Y.), who had not yet arrived in Washington, and Richard Hawes (W-Ky.), who had taken ill.[12]

---

five members from New Jersey from voting for Speaker; and the Clerk had his lesson prepared for him" (1876, vol. 10, 12/2/1839, 143).

[11] Fuller was direct in his assessment of Garland: "The self-serving Garland, concealing unworthy motives behind the pleasing mask of modesty, had arbitrarily disfranchised a State which was entitled to vote in the constitution of the House—either by one set of delegates or the other—and had then effectually fortified his position by obstructing all business in an effort to compel that body to bow to his purpose" (1909, 75).

[12] This loss led Adams to claim: "There was therefore a vote of eight majority of the whole House affirming the right of the New Jersey members to their seats, which they lost by this tie" (1876, vol. 10, 12/13/1839, 161). Adams's math here included Kempshall and Hawes, plus one

Hawes's absence was especially frustrating, as he was known to be in Washington and a call had gone out requesting his presence. But he was evidently too sick to attend the vote (Adams 1876, vol. 10, 12/13/1839, 161).

Democratic leaders now looked to end the organizational standoff. Albert Smith (D-Maine) gained the floor and moved that the House proceed to the election of a Speaker. Smith's motion attracted a thicket of dilatory motions before passing, 118–110 (*HJ*, 26-1, 12/13/1839, 40–42). The speakership election commenced the following day, December 14, 1839, nearly two weeks after the House had first convened.[13]

Parallel with the politicking over organizing the House, the two parties' caucuses had been busy considering their leadership options and had settled on plans of battle for the speakership contest. Such plans were not easily determined, however, as clear divisions within each party caucus had emerged.[14]

The Democratic caucus had met on December 2 and began with the consideration of Francis W. Pickens (S.C.), a staunch ally of John C. Calhoun, for Speaker.[15] Pickens's candidacy was actively pushed by President Van Buren in an effort to reach out to the Calhounites and thus solidify the Democratic coalition. Pickens, however, was unwilling to make *ex ante* concessions concerning committee assignments and the moderation of his strong states' rights views, and so he withdrew. In Pickens's place, Dixon Lewis (Ala.) was offered as an alternative by those hoping to lock in support from the pivotal bloc of Calhounites. A group of Northern Democrats, guided by Senator Thomas Hart Benton (Mo.), proposed John W. Jones (Va.) instead and argued that Jones would appeal not only to Democrats but also to certain Conservatives and states' rights Whigs from his home state of Virginia.[16]

---

recently deceased Whig member from Massachusetts (James C. Alvord), along with the votes of the five excluded New Jersey members.

[13] Note that from Wise's motion on Dec. 13 to the final procedural motion in advance of the speakership balloting on Dec. 14, there were 24 roll call votes. On all of these roll calls, the side favored by the Democrats prevailed. The one exception was a vote on a procedural motion on whether to enter a set of propositions in the *Journal* regarding the election of the New Jersey delegates. Most of the motions were dilatory tactics that the Democrats opposed to divided Whig opposition. With the Democrats winning consistently, it was simply a matter of time until the Whigs would capitulate (or the Democrats would vote to proceed to vote for Speaker).

[14] Subsequent accounts of the two-party caucuses are taken from the *NYJC* (12/3/1839, 3); *NYEP* (12/6/1839, 3); *Madisonian* (12/4/1839, 3); *AA* (12/6/1839, 1; reprinted from the *NYEP*, 12/4/1839, 3); *Hartford Courant* (12/10/1839, 3); *Alexander Gazette* (reported in *Richmond Enquirer*, 11/19/39, 1); *New Hampshire Sentinel* (12/11/1839, 1); *Pittsfield Sun* (12/12/1839, 1; correspondence of the *NYEP*, 12/2/1839); the *Daily Atlas* (12/12/1839, 1; correspondence of the *NYEP*, 12/2/1839); and the *NYH* (12/19/1839, 1).

[15] Like many of his South Carolinian brethren, Pickens was classified as a "Nullifier" in the previous three Congresses in which he served (see Martis 1989, 92–94).

[16] Three such Virginia members were explicitly mentioned in the press: Conservatives James Garland and George W. Hopkins and Whig Robert M. T. Hunter.

In the caucus ballot for Speaker that ensued, Jones defeated Lewis by one vote, 50–49, which suggested the fragility of the Democratic coalition. Moreover, the legitimacy of the outcome was questioned, as the ballot was held when the entire South Carolina delegation was absent; had the ballot been delayed until the South Carolina members were present, "they would have doubtless voted for Mr. Lewis" (according to a *Saturday Evening Post* correspondent who covered the caucus proceedings, as reported in the *Pittsfield Sun*, 12/12/1839, 1). The Calhounites would further claim that Benton and his followers cheated Lewis out of the nomination by strategically scheduling the caucus vote when they knew the South Carolinians would be absent.

The politicking in the Democratic caucus thus revealed a serious cleavage in the ranks, as Bentonites and Calhounites vied for control of the party while Van Buren and his supporters worked feverishly to achieve unity. The caucus finally agreed to unite behind Jones in the early balloting for Speaker and to shift to Lewis if Jones proved unable to garner a majority on the floor. Van Buren and his allies worried that even this weak caucus agreement was tenuous, and feared that the Calhounites would readopt their independent habits and pursue their own selfish interests.

On the Whig side, former Speaker John Bell entered the caucus as the presumptive nominee, though there were rumors that the newer generation of Whigs preferred another candidate.[17] Part of their uneasiness with Bell stemmed from the 1839 elections in Tennessee, which turned on his very bitter personal rivalry with Speaker Polk, who was then running for governor. Polk got the better of the direct matchup back home, resulting not only in a personal victory but a general repudiation of Whig candidates statewide. Polk exhibited strong enough coattails to reverse national tides and produce a doubling (from three to six seats) of Tennessee's Democratic delegation to the U.S. House. Bell, the old Whig lion, was damaged goods.

The Whig caucus deliberated over several evenings while the New Jersey controversy was blazing during the day. Like the Democrats, the Whigs finally settled on a contingent strategy: they would support Bell in the early House balloting for Speaker, but would switch to William C. Dawson (Ga.), a strong states' rights advocate and supporter of Van Buren's subtreasury plan, should Bell falter.

Figure 5.1 illustrates in spatial terms the strategies employed by the two parties in their opening moves in the speakership contest. The scattering of points shows the spatial locations, using W-NOMINATE scores, of all members of the 26th Congress, with the locations of Jones, Lewis, Bell, and Dawson specifically indicated. Both parties chose Southerners who leaned toward a states' rights stance but who, importantly, were also not allies of

[17] In addition to the newspaper accounts cited in footnote 14, the account of Bell's role in the speakership contest relies heavily on Parks (1950, chap. 9).

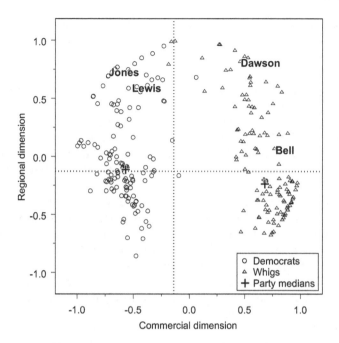

FIGURE 5.1. Spatial location, using W-NOMINATE scores, of major party speaker-ship candidates, initial ballots of the 26th Congress (1839). *Note*: Dashed lines indicate overall chamber medians.

Calhoun. Lewis and Dawson, the candidates both caucuses selected as their backups, were each shaded toward the other party ideologically along the main partisan dimension, but were also among the most fervent states' rights supporters in the chamber.

As the speakership balloting began on December 14, 1839, the Democrats seemed to possess a clear advantage. Thanks to the exclusion of the five Whig members from New Jersey, the Democrats counted 120 members to the Whigs' 114 and the Conservatives' 2 (with one vacancy, due to Whig James C. Alvord's death).[18] The Democrats thus constituted a majority of seated members; if they held together, they could elect a Speaker without any help from the opposition party members. But the Democrats were deeply divided, which led to a protracted speakership contest. Indeed, when all was said and done, the Democrats failed to elect one of their own.

The early speakership balloting illustrated the promise and limitations of the nomination strategies (see appendix 2 for a breakdown of the balloting).[19]

---

[18] See footnote 21 for a note on our partisan coding of several members.

[19] Individual votes on the speakership balloting appear in *CG*, 26-1, 12/14/1839, 52–54 (ballots 1–6), and 12/16/1839, 55–56 (ballots 7–11); and *HJ*, 26-1, 12/14/1839, 57–70 (ballots

On the first ballot, with 235 members voting, 113 Democrats united behind Jones while Bell received 102 votes from fellow Whigs. Jones was thus left five ballots short of election. While both parties' caucus agreements largely held, a small number of defections occurred, which in the Democrats' case proved decisive and led to prolonged balloting. Specifically, six Democrats (five from South Carolina) spurned Jones and voted for either Lewis (two votes) or Pickens (four votes).[20] As Van Buren had feared, the Calhounites had risen up and rejected the caucus bond.

The second ballot was substantially a repeat of the first, with one notable exception—Robert M. T. Hunter (W-Va.), who would eventually go on to win the contest, received his first vote from Charles Ogle (W-Pa.), who had supported Bell on the first ballot. What is significant about Ogle being the first to vote for Hunter is that Ogle, who served in the previous Congress as a member of the Anti-Mason Party, was strongly *anti*–states' rights.[21] This marked the beginning of an effort to rally Whigs around candidates irrespective of their views on nullification.

On the Whig side, party leaders observed that ten of their members rejected Bell on each of the first two ballots in favor of Dawson. Thus, they sought a new strategy. Plan B was rolled out on the third ballot, with Dawson as the party's new standard bearer. The Whig membership immediately shifted support en masse from Bell to Dawson, which resulted in Dawson receiving 103 votes, a pickup on the Whig side of four votes.[22] However, confounding this shift, Ogle managed to convince four of his Pennsylvania colleagues to move instead to Hunter. Furthermore, John Quincy Adams now picked up one protest vote (from Seth Gates, W-N.Y.) while Bell attracted the vote of Dawson. If we add together all the votes received by

---

1–6), 12/16/1839, 70–79 (ballots 7–11). Accounts of the speakership election appear in Benton (1856, 160–62); Jameson (1900, 436–37); Wiltse (1949, 405–7); and Niven (1988, 234–35).

[20] Jones himself voted for Lewis. During this period it was common for speakership candidates to refrain from voting for themselves. Jones would continue to vote for Lewis throughout the contest before switching to Francis Thomas (Md.) on the 11th and final ballot, while Bell voted for Dawson on each of the 11 ballots.

[21] Note that Martis (1989, 95) continues to list Ogle as a member of the Anti-Mason Party in the 26th Congress, along with five other members of the Pennsylvania delegation (Francis James, John Edwards, Edward Davies, Richard Biddle, and Thomas Henry). He notes, however, that "In the 1838 Pennsylvania congressional elections there was an Anti-Masonic/Whig coalition. . . . After the 1838 election . . . the Whig party gained dominance over the coalition as many Pennsylvania Anti-Masons joined the Whigs" (362). Given this explanation, and as Dubin (1998, 122) classifies these six individuals as Whigs in the 26th Congress, we consider them as Whigs in this analysis. Using DW-NOMINATE scores—which allow for cross-time comparisons of spatial ideology—we find that Ogle's location on the second dimension was -0.454 in the 25th Congress, compared to Hunter's at 0.898.

[22] Bell's vote total had slipped from 102 on the first ballot to 99 on the second ballot. In addition to Ogle switching to Hunter, Hiram Hunt (W-N.Y.) and William Cost Johnson (W-Md.) shifted their votes to Dawson.

Whig candidates, the total had fallen to 110, fewer than had been received by all the Whig candidates on the first two ballots.[23]

The Whig countermove on the third ballot was met with a standpat strategy by the Democrats, as they continued to rally behind Jones. But Jones slipped in this round to 110 votes and never recovered. The remaining votes went to Lewis and John Clark (D-N.Y.). The third ballot ended with the aforementioned Democratic candidates receiving 117 votes, the Whigs combining for 110 votes, and Pickens holding the balance with 7 votes.[24]

Believing they might be able to corral the stragglers, the Democrats entered the fourth ballot still formally wedded to Jones. However, Jones's support continued to sag, while support for Dawson on the Whig side began to collapse altogether. Sensing the pull of the Calhounites, elements of both parties migrated to even surer states' rights candidates. Jones lost 9 votes on the fourth ballot, only one of which failed to shift to Lewis. On the Whig side, Dawson lost a quarter of his support, to 77 votes, while Hunter surged from 5 votes on the third ballot to 29 on the fourth. However, none of this churning had any effect on the strength of the Calhounite bloc, as Pickens picked up yet another vote, raising his tally to 8.

At this point, Dawson, recognizing his inability to do any better than Bell had done in securing a Whig victory, withdrew his name from consideration, leaving the Whigs without a single candidate to rally behind (CG, 26-1, 12/14/39, 54). As a consequence, the fifth ballot saw Dawson's former vote split, with 19 former supporters returning to Bell, 36 flocking to Hunter, and 19 others scattering their votes among 8 other candidates. Meanwhile, resisting pressure from some Democrats to bow out of the race, Jones lost considerable support on the fifth ballot when 28 of his erstwhile supporters—mostly those with strong states' rights sentiments—defected to Lewis. As a consequence, the fifth ballot witnessed the most fractured voting pattern of the entire episode. The two front-runners were now Jones (71 votes) and Hunter (68 votes). A sizable number of Democrats (49) were now with Lewis, and a smaller but still significant number of Whigs (22) were with Bell. The Calhounites held firm behind Pickens (6 votes).

The sixth and final ballot of the day was held immediately after the fifth, with the voting proving to be nearly as fractured. Jones continued to lose votes to Lewis among the Democrats, as Jones dropped to 39 votes while Lewis surged to 79 votes. Also, Lewis garnered the support of four of the six Calhounites who withheld their support from Jones on the first ballot. This

[23] Richard Hawes (W-Ky.), who had been ill earlier in the Congress, voted for Bell on the first two ballots, but then failed to cast a vote for the remainder of the speakership contest. In addition, two Georgia Whigs, Walter T. Colquitt and Mark A. Cooper, who had voted for Dawson on the first ballot, switched to Lewis (and thereby crossed the partisan aisle) beginning on the second ballot.

[24] The seven votes for Pickens on this ballot consisted of six of the nine-member South Carolina delegation, plus Hunter.

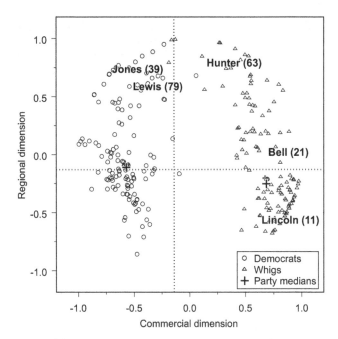

FIGURE 5.2. Spatial location, using W-NOMINATE scores, of major party speaker-ship candidates, end of balloting on the first day, 26th Congress (1839). *Note*: Dashed lines indicate overall chamber medians.

suggested to some that Lewis could command a majority of votes when the balloting resumed once again. On the Whig side, Hunter's support dipped to 63 votes, while Bell held steady with 21 votes. The only additional develop-ment worth noting was the appearance of Levi Lincoln (W-Mass.) as a fac-tor, with 11 votes. Lincoln, an "Adams Whig," provided the only glimmer of hope for a Northern candidacy during the entire proceedings, but faded away altogether once the balloting resumed the next day.

Figure 5.2 depicts the spatial situation as balloting came to a close at the end of Day One. What is amazing about this figure is that the two leading vote-getters were located far from the greatest number of votes in each of the respective parties. If we ignore Lincoln, who has never been mentioned as a serious factor in any historical account of this episode, and consider the spatial voting situation, Bell should have garnered the lion's share of Whig votes; likewise for Jones among the Democrats. And yet by this point, the voting for Speaker within party contingents had ceased being ideological, which explains why we see the leading candidates occupying the spatial hinterlands.

This decline in the ideological structuring of the balloting is illustrated in table 5.1, which shows simple probit analyses of voting for Speaker for Whigs (top panel) and Democrats (bottom panel) on the first and sixth bal-

TABLE 5.1.
Votes for Speaker, first and sixth ballots, 26th Congress, by party (probit
coefficients with robust standard errors in parentheses)

	1st ballot	6th ballot
a. Whigs only. Dependent variable = 1 if vote is for Bell, 0 otherwise.		
W-NOMINATE dimension 1	2.24*	1.43
	(0.95)	(0.90)
W-NOMINATE dimension 2	-1.54**	-0.08
	(0.52)	(0.45)
Intercept	0.53	-1.88
	(0.52)	(0.62)
N	113	108
χ^2	18.26***	4.76
LLF	-19.54	-51.07
Pseudo R^2	.46	.04
b. Democrats only. Dependent variable = 1 if vote is for Jones, 0 otherwise.		
W-NOMINATE dimension 1	-4.46**	-1.53*
	(1.81)	(0.72)
W-NOMINATE dimension 2	-2.39***	0.51
	(0.72)	(0.28)
Intercept	0.44	-1.38**
	(0.89)	(0.45)
N	120	118
χ^2	22.17***	6.74*
LLF	-12.46	-70.17
Pseudo R^2	.53	.05

*$p < .05$; ** $p < .01$; *** $p < .001$.

lots. For the Whigs, the dependent variable is equal to one if the member supported Bell on the ballot, zero otherwise. For the Democrats, the dependent variable is equal to one if the member supported Jones on the ballot, zero otherwise. On the first ballot, both W-NOMINATE dimensions are significant in each party regression, and model fit is good. Loyalty to each party candidate was strongest among the most ideologically extreme members and among those with weak states' rights sentiments. On the sixth ballot in both parties, the coefficient on the first W-NOMINATE dimension retains the same sign as before, but it has shrunk and is significant only for the Democrats (and, now, only at the $p < .05$ level). The coefficient on the second W-NOMINATE dimension also shrinks, changing signs for the Democrats, and fails to reach statistical significance in either case. In both sets of analyses, the overall model fit declines substantially.

Thus, what had started out as an episode organized around substantial party loyalty, undercut with small amounts of ideological noise on both sides, progressed to the point where members of both parties abandoned ideological purity in search of a party candidate who could win.

As the first round of voting occurred on a Saturday, the House took Sunday off and reconvened on Monday (December 16). Reports of party machinations over that weekend suggest that the Whigs were unable to agree on a clear strategy, while Democratic leaders were working to consolidate support behind Lewis (*Fayetteville Observer*, 12/18/1839, 1). Indeed, the Democrats' superior coordination led John Quincy Adams to note in his *Diary* on Monday that "When I went to the House this morning, it was with a firm conviction that Dixon H. Lewis, the Silenus of the House—a Falstaff without his wit or good humor—would be chosen Speaker, probably at the first trial" (vol. 10, 12/16/1839, 164).

After the House reconvened, Jones removed himself as a candidate for the speakership (*CG*, 26-1, 12/16/1839, 55); this left Lewis as the obvious Democratic choice. While the first ballot of the day (and seventh overall) was no more decisive than the six from Saturday, the parties seemed to be moving in opposite directions. The Democrats regrouped cohesively around Lewis, giving him 110 votes (five short of a majority), while the Whigs failed to consolidate around a single candidate. The bulk of the Whig votes (64) had returned to Bell, but Hunter retained 22 votes and Francis Granger (W-N.Y.) inherited Levi Lincoln's mantle as the recipient of protest votes (12 in all) from the most determined Northern Whigs. Statistical analysis of who voted for Hunter rather than Bell reveals only a weak ideological structuring of this ballot (and no regional structuring at all), which suggests that by now the Whig rank and file were rallying around the candidate they felt the most electable, rather than the one most congruent with their own policy desires.

The next ballot (eighth) saw Lewis extend to 113 votes, four short of election. There was a small amount of consolidation on the Whig side, as the Northern protest vote returned to Bell's side, raising his total to 80. Hunter hung tight at 16 votes.

Despite Lewis's gains on the seventh and eighth ballots, it had become clear that a small band of Democrats was absolutely resistant to electing a nullification sympathizer as Speaker. While Lewis had won over the bulk of the Democratic membership, and actually gained five votes from states' rights Whigs from Georgia, a set of 10 Democrats failed to support him and instead scattered their votes among several minor candidates.[25] These 10 Democrats had supported Jones throughout the early stages of the balloting, and appeared to be paying the Calhounites back for their earlier defec-

---

[25] The five Georgia Whigs who voted for Lewis were Edward J. Black, Walter T. Colquitt, Mark A. Cooper, Eugenius A. Nisbet, and Waddy Thompson. The 10 Democratic defectors were Julius W. Blackwell (Tenn.), Zadok Casey (Ill.), John Carr (Ind.), Henry W. Connor (N.C.), George C. Dromgoole (Va.), Cave Johnson (Tenn.), John Reynolds (Ill.), Francis Thomas (Md.), Philip F. Thomas (Md.), and Hopkins L. Turney (Tenn.). An 11th Democrat, John T. H. Worthington (Md.), defected on the seventh ballot but returned to the fold and voted for Lewis on the eighth and ninth ballots.

tion from the caucus agreement. If even half of these 10 Democratic defectors had voted for Lewis on either the seventh or eighth ballots, they would have pushed him over the top and given control of the speakership to the Democrats.

The eighth ballot proved to be Lewis's high-water mark, as his support on the ninth ballot sagged to 110 votes, six short of a majority. While Lewis managed to pick up a sixth Whig vote, he now faced 13 defectors within his own Democratic Party.[26] Lewis's problems aside, perhaps the most significant development on the ninth ballot was the continued churning of voting patterns among the Whigs, as support swung from Bell to Hunter. Bell saw his vote total fall from 80 to 33, while Hunter's tally grew from 16 to 59.

The momentum shifted decidedly toward Hunter on the 10th ballot. His support surged to 85 votes, now besting Lewis, whose support had shrunk to 73 votes. At this point, the Democrats became more confused as the Whigs consolidated. It was the Democrats whose members now began to desert their party's official candidate in favor of candidates with more purely regional appeal. Lewis realized his opportunity had passed and formally withdrew from the contest (CG, 26-1, 12/14/1839, 55).

On the 11th ballot, Hunter broke through and captured the speakership. He received 119 of 232 votes cast, a 3-vote majority, which he achieved by winning the support of every Whig who cast a vote (111 in all), along with one Conservative (George Hopkins, Va.) and seven Democrats—the Calhounites Sampson H. Butler, John Campbell, John K. Griffin, Isaac E. Holmes, Francis Pickens, and Thomas D. Sumter (all S.C.), and Charles Fisher (N.C.). Five of these seven Calhounites had voted against John W. Jones, the Democratic caucus nominee, on the first ballot, and in doing so had extended the contest. Now, in voting for the Whig Hunter, they went a step further and denied the Democrats the speakership.

In engineering the election of Hunter as Speaker, the Whigs elevated someone who was the most heterodox on the issue that divided the party at the time (banking) and the most extreme on the issue that almost everyone wanted to avoid (sectionalism). Hunter was raised in an environment that was steeped in traditional Jeffersonian politics, and his affiliation with the Whig Party was prompted almost entirely by his revulsion toward what he (and other Whigs) regarded as the dictatorial aggrandizement of power in the presidency under Andrew Jackson. He shared very few of the substantive ideas of the Whig leaders who were busy building a national party—"American System" ideas like the protective tariff, a national bank, and federal funding of internal improvements—and in fact had gained notoriety by

[26] The sixth Whig vote was Sherrod Williams (Ky.). The three new Democratic defectors (all of whom had supported Lewis on the previous two ballots) were Linn Banks (Va.), Thomas Robinson (Del.), and Lewis Steenrod (Va.). Francis Rives (D-Va.), who had supported Lewis on the previous two ballots, did not cast a vote on the ninth ballot.

favoring Van Buren's subtreasury plan, which was anathema to mainstream Whigs.[27]

If Hunter had any enduring sentiments on national matters, it was on the issue of states' rights. He engaged in an active correspondence with John C. Calhoun and regarded him as a mentor.[28] Hunter stood by his beliefs in the speakership balloting, snubbing his Whig brethren and voting for Calhounite Francis Pickens throughout.[29] Calhoun was clearly pleased by Hunter's election, which he communicated in a letter to a family friend: "I have great confidence in his good sense and discretion, and, if he should act as well as I think he will, it will do much to advance our [states' rights] principles and doctrines."[30]

In sum, Hunter was apt to espouse "principles over party" in public and seemed to revel in his perceived independence. He enunciated these feelings in his acceptance address to the House after winning the speakership: "Called as I have been to his high station, not so much from any merits of my own as from the independence of my position, I shall feel it especially due from me to you to preside as the Speaker, not of a party, but of the House" (*CG*, 26-1, 12/17/1839, 56).

Given all of this, what were the Whigs (and Whig leaders who coordinated votes on the floor) thinking when they elected Hunter? Clearly he was outside of mainstream Whig thinking. But, as the minority in the chamber, the Whigs were constrained in their ability to influence the outcome. A successful Whig candidate had to appeal to some pivotal bloc of non-Whig members. In this case, it was the Calhounites, which meant advocating policy stances at odds with orthodox Whiggery. As the *Rhode Island Republican* reported, "In giving their suffrages to Mr. Hunter, the whigs did but choose the least of the evils that beset their path" (12/25/1839, 2).

Yet, selecting the "least bad" candidate was not all Whig leaders expected to gain by electing Hunter. They were, after all, selecting a *Whig*, which they hoped would translate into tangible benefits for the party. As a correspondent for the *New Hampshire Gazette* stated:

> The whigs doubtless thought that if elected by their votes, he would
> ... favor them somewhat in appointing committees, and in the general
> exercise of powers, as far as he could safely, without compromising the
> great principles upon which he stands pledged to his constituents and
> the country at large. And they knew the administration candidates

---

[27] For background on Hunter's political career and policy preferences, see Hunter (1903), Simms (1935), and Fisher (1968, 1973).

[28] An 1843 biography of Calhoun, published anonymously, is thought to have been written by Hunter. See Anderson and Hemphill (1972).

[29] Hunter voted for Pickens on the 1st–5th and 9th–10th ballots. He did not cast a vote on the 6th–8th and 11th ballots.

[30] Letter to Mrs. T. G. Clemson, Dec. 18, 1839; published in Jameson (1900, 436–37).

would not give them one inch beyond their just rights as a minority.
(12/31/1839, 1)[31]

Whether Hunter would behave in a fashion consistent with this was
unclear.

More generally, Hunter's election was met with crowing on behalf of
House Whigs, who taunted the Democrats for failing to coordinate and
elect one of their own. However, the Whig press received Hunter frostily,
given his anti–American System policy positions, while the Democratic
press gave appraisals that were remarkably subdued considering partisan
fears that had run rampant only days before. The hope among Democratic
editors was that Hunter would be more "states' rights" than "Whig" as
presiding officer.

Less than a week later, Hunter released his committee assignments (*HJ*,
26-1, 12/27/1839, 136–38), which only reinforced the equivocal reaction to
his election.[32] The partisan composition of committees (chairs and majorities) appears in table 5.2. At first glance, Hunter seemed to favor his Whig
brethren—at least to some extent—as exactly two-thirds (22 of 33) of committee chairs were given to Whigs, and nearly half of all committees (14 of
33) were fully controlled (i.e., Whig chairs and Whig majorities) by the
party. Yet, his independent streak was also apparent, as nine committees
exhibited divided control (i.e., chair of one party versus committee majority
of the other) while 11 others were fully controlled by the Democrats.[33]
Moreover, the four most important committees during this era—Foreign
Affairs, Military Affairs, Naval Affairs, and Ways and Means—were comprised of Democratic chairs and Democratic majorities. And the Elections
Committee, which would investigate the disputed New Jersey election and
thus have an important organizational role in the 26th Congress, was also
fully controlled by the Democrats. Thus, although the Whigs no doubt
would have been worse off under a Democratic Speaker, Hunter did them
no favors in his committee assignments.[34]

---

[31] The correspondence was dated Dec. 19, 1839, but did not appear in print until Dec. 31,
1839.

[32] Note that a discrepancy exists between the *House Journal* and the *Congressional Globe*,
as the latter reports that Hunter released his committee assignments on Monday, Dec. 30, not
Friday, Dec. 27. See *CG*, 26-1, 12/30/1839, 88–89.

[33] In total, the Democrats were the majority on 19 of 33 committees.

[34] In his diary, John Quincy Adams took an especially dim view of Hunter's committee assignments: "John W. Jones, Chairman of the Ways and Means, Francis W. Pickens of the Foreign Affairs, and the whole organization as subservient to the Executive administration as if the
appointments had been made in the President's Cabinet. So much for Mr. Robert M. T. Hunter's
independent positions" (1876, vol. 10, 12/30/1839, 179). A year later, Adams wrote that
Hunter was "an amiable, good-hearted, weak-headed young man, prematurely hoisted into a
place for which he is not fit, precisely for his Virginian quiddities. I sat and conversed an hour
with him, but could make absolutely nothing of him" (12/20/1840, 379).

TABLE 5.2.
House committee assignments, 26th Congress

Committee	Chair (party-state)	Members	Dem.	Whigs
Commerce	Edward Curtis (W-N.Y.)	9	4	5
Public Lands	Thomas Corwin (W-Ohio)	9	5	3
Claims	William C. Dawson (W-Ga.)	9	5	4
Post Office and Post Roads	James I. McKay (D-N.C.)	9	5	3
District of Columbia	William C. Johnson (W-Md.)	9	3	6
Judiciary	John Sergeant (W-Pa.)	9	3	6
Revolutionary Claims	Robert Craig (D-Va.)	9	6	3
Territories	John Pope (W-Ky.)	9	4	5
Revolutionary Pensions	John Taliaferro (W-Va.)	9	5	4
Invalid Pensions	Sherrod Williams (W-Ky.)	9	3	6
Roads and Canals	Charles Ogle (W-Pa.)	9	4	5
Patents	Isaac Fletcher (D-Vt.)	5	5	0
Public Buildings and Grounds	Levi Lincoln (W-Mass.)	5	4	1
Revisal and Unfin. Business	Luther C. Peck (W-N.Y.)	5	3	2
Accounts	Joseph Johnson (D-Va.)	5	3	2
Manufactures	John Quincy Adams (W-Mass.)	9	4	5
Agriculture	Edmund Deberry (W-N.C.)	9	7	2
Indian Affairs	John Bell (W-Tenn.)	9	4	5
Mileage	Thomas W. Williams (W-Conn.)	5	3	2
Exp. in the State Dept.	Joseph R. Underwood (W-Ky.)	5	2	3
Exp. in the Treasury Dept.	George Evans (W-Maine)	5	2	3
Exp. in the War Dept.	Rice Garland (W-La.)	5	3	2
Exp. in the Navy Dept.	Leverett Saltonstall (W-Mass.)	5	2	3
Exp. in the Post Office Dept.	Richard P. Marvin (W-N.Y.)	5	2	3
Exp. on the Public Buildings	Edward Stanly (W-N.C.)	5	2	3
Foreign Affairs	Francis W. Pickens (D-S.C.)	9	5	4
Naval Affairs	Francis Thomas (D-Md.)	9	5	4
Private Land Claims	Zadok Casey (D-Ill.)	9	4	5
Military Affairs	Cave Johnson (D-Tenn.)	9	5	4
Militia	George M. Keim (D-Pa.)	9	5	4
Elections	John Campbell (D-S.C.)	9	5	4
Public Expenditures	George N. Briggs (W-Mass.)	9	4	5
Ways and Means	John W. Jones (D-Va.)	9	5	4

Note: Conservatives James Garland (Va.) and George Hopkins (Va.) served on Public Lands and Post Office and Post Roads, respectively.

While the Democrats scuffled badly in their pursuit of the speakership, they quickly righted the ship and, in general, ruled the 26th Congress. The two other major House officer votes quickly went the Democrats' way. Hugh Garland was reelected House Clerk on the first ballot, receiving 118 votes to 105 for Matthew St. Clair Clarke and 8 for Richard C. Mason (HJ, 26-1, 12/21/1839, 97–99). Garland received every Democratic vote cast, including those of the seven Calhounites who defected (in favor of Hunter) on the final speakership ballot.[35] The House then spent a month debating the printership generally, as resolutions to adopt an open-bid system (to replace the elective system) and to divorce the public printing from the newspaper presses were offered (and defeated) before proceeding to the election of a Printer.[36] And, on the first ballot, Francis Blair and John C. Rives were elected with 110 votes—capturing every Democratic vote cast—to 92 for Joseph Gales and William W. Seaton, and 5 votes scattering (*HJ*, 26-1, 1/30/1840, 261–63).[37] Blair and Rives served as the administration Printer, and thus signified another victory for the Democrats.

After completing the officer elections, the House turned to the New Jersey election dispute, which had been tabled at the start of the session. On a pure party-line vote, with 110 Democrats opposing 81 Whigs, the case was resolved in favor of seating the Democratic slate, which was consistent with the recommendation of the democratically controlled Elections Committee (*HJ*, 26-1, 3/10/1840, 576–77).[38] Later in the summer of 1840, President Van Buren's subtreasury plan finally came to fruition. The bill that would become the Independent Treasury Act passed 123–107 in the House on a largely party-line vote, with Democrats voting 120–3 in favor and Whigs voting 3–103 against (*HJ*, 26-1, 6/30/1840, 1175–77).[39] This act completed the drama (at least temporarily) that had begun when Andrew Jackson pulled federal deposits from the Bank of the United States in 1836.

[35] Garland ran unopposed in the Democratic caucus, while the Whigs made no Clerk nomination (see *Pittsfield Sun*, 12/12/1839, 1; printed correspondence of the *NYEP*, 12/2/1839).

[36] In considering the Printer election, recall that the House was still bound by the 1819 law that established the practice of electing the Printer at the expiration of one Congress to take effect in the following Congress. Spurred on by the prospect that they might win control of the chamber in the 26th Congress, Whigs at the end of the 25th Congress managed to delay the choice of Printer. Thus, the House Printer election in the 26th Congress was *for* the 26th Congress.

[37] The Democratic caucus made no Printer nomination, although Blair and Rives were considered the "strongest" option, while the Whig caucus nominated Gales and Seaton (see *Pittsfield Sun*, 12/12/1839, 1; printed correspondence of the *NYEP*, 12/2/1839).

[38] McCormick (1953) notes that the dispute that centered on the South Amboy election returns also involved the election to the state legislature, which had already considered the dispute resolved. It is significant that when the disputed election was referred to the Whig-dominated committee on elections, it took the unusual step of going behind the returns to investigate charges of widespread fraud due to noncitizens voting for both Whigs and Democrats. Once the committee on elections was finished with its work, it concluded that the *Democratic* slate was entitled to be seated. Members of the U.S. House undoubtedly were aware of the proceedings in the New Jersey state legislature, which probably explains why Whigs in the national legislature opposed sending the matter to a committee that might also go behind the returns. Also see Rowell (1901, 109–12) and Jenkins (2004) for a summary of proceedings in the House on the election dispute.

[39] Conservatives were split 1–1 on the House vote. In the Senate, the Independent Treasury bill passed on a 24–18 vote, with Democrats voting 24–4 in favor and Whigs voting 0–14 against (*Senate Journal*, 26-1, 1/23/1840, 131).

A PERIOD OF RELATIVE PEACE: HOUSE ORGANIZATION IN THE 27TH–29TH CONGRESSES

The next three congressional elections were routs, first for the Whigs (1840–41) and then for the Democrats (1842–43 and 1844–45). Because the majority party in each of these Congresses enjoyed a comfortable margin in the House, the organizational dynamics were quite different from the 26th Congress. The Whigs took full advantage of the nationwide economic depression and the public's ire toward the ruling Democrats in the elections of 1840 and 1841. Unified behind a single presidential candidate and riding the coattails of William Henry Harrison, the Whigs won majority control of both the House and Senate in the 27th Congress. In the House, they picked up a net total of 27 seats, which gave them a 142–98 advantage over the Democrats (Martis 1989, 96).[40]

When the first unified Whig Congress in American history convened on May 31, 1841, Tippecanoe had been dead for nearly two months.[41] In his place sat John Tyler, whose Whig loyalties had always been suspect, and who immediately communicated that he would not accept the full economic agenda proposed by the congressional leadership. In fact, Tyler's ideological proclivities were almost precisely those of outgoing Speaker Hunter; both men had arisen from a Virginia planter context that was nearly identical (Holt 1999, 128).[42] In his presidential message, delivered at the opening of the extra congressional session, Tyler declared that he would embrace parts of the Whig agenda, such as repealing the Independent Treasury Act, but strongly oppose others, such as raising tariffs significantly (CG, 27-1, 6/1/1841, 5–8).

When the Whigs assembled in caucus on May 29 to settle on House officer nominations, they experienced divisions by region (North vs. South) and ideology (nationalist vs. states' rights). Tensions over slavery had escalated in recent years, thanks to the growing antislavery movement in the country, the resulting gag rule debates in Congress, and the *Amistad* case,

---

[40] In calculating these net gains, we again count the six Anti-Masons in the 26th Congress as Whigs. See footnote 21.

[41] The Senate met in a special session from March 4–15, 1841, before the official convening of the full Congress (in an extra session, called by President Harrison via proclamation before his death) at the end of May.

[42] Both Tyler and Hunter served in the House and the Senate, but not contemporaneously. Therefore, we cannot directly compare their roll call voting records. However, for the years when Hunter was in the Senate, he was always in the top 10 among those with extreme values on the second (regional) W-NOMINATE dimension; Tyler was always in the top 3. Both were solid states' rights legislators. Tyler's scores on the first (partisan/ideological) W-NOMINATE dimension were always much more centrist than Hunter's, which suggests that Tyler was truly more conflicted over economic issues than Hunter, who was never far from Jeffersonian principles.

which was argued before the Supreme Court in early 1841. As a result, Whig Party cohesion was weak, and four caucus ballots were needed before a speakership nomination was decided.

The choice was John White (Ky.), a protégé of Henry Clay, who garnered 72 of the 105 Whig votes on the final ballot (*New York Herald* [hereafter abbreviated as *NYH*], 5/31/1841, 2).[43] Clay was active in rallying House Whigs behind White and built on loyalists from Kentucky and New England, who provided the strongest support in White's favor. White had a solid reputation as an active and skilled debater, was an untiring advocate of a national bank, and possessed a safe (but not ultra) stance on states' rights.

For the Clerk nomination, the two leading Whig candidates were Francis Ormand Jonathan ("Fog") Smith (Maine) and Matthew St. Clair Clarke (D.C.). Smith, who was Clay's handpicked candidate, had previously served three terms in the House as a conservative Democrat. In Clay's mind, a ticket of White and Smith would cement the interregional coalition that he was trying to build, one that united Whigs with conservative Northern Democrats. With the substantial pressure applied by Clay and his House lieutenants, Smith won a bare majority on the first nomination ballot (*NYH*, 6/1/1841, 3). Yet Clay's gambit was viewed as excessively heavy-handed and alienated a significant portion of the Whig caucus, which broke up the meeting "in high dudgeon" (*AA*, 6/2/1841, 2, reprinting a *New York Evening Post* [hereafter abbreviated as *NYEP*] story; *New York Commercial Advertiser*, 6/2/1841, 2). Concerns were expressed that should the Democrats decide to support Clarke, the ex-Republican and former House Clerk who received the lion's share of Whig votes in the two previous clerkship elections, some portion of the disgruntled Whigs would bolt the caucus and back Clarke as well.

Once the House convened, White was elected Speaker on the first ballot, capturing 121 of the 221 votes cast (*HJ*, 27-1, 5/31/1841, 10–11). The Whig majority was substantial enough that White easily endured six defections among Southerners, who supported Henry Wise (W-Va.), five defections among Northerners, who supported Joseph Lawrence (W-Pa.), and two scatters.[44] The Democrats unified behind their candidate from the previous

---

[43] For additional background on Whig politicking over the House organization, see *Richmond Enquirer*, 5/14/1841, 3; *NYH*, 6/1/1841, 3; *AA*, 6/2/1841, 2; *NYEP*, 5/31/1841, 2; and *New Hampshire Patriot and State Gazette* (reprinting a correspondence from the *New York Commercial Advertiser*), 6/11/1841, 3.

[44] The six Wise defectors were Julius C. Alford (Ga.), Meredith P. Gentry (Tenn.), Thomas W. Gilmer (Va.), William L. Goggin (Va.), Francis Mallory (Va.), and John Taliaferro (Va.); the five Lawrence defectors were John Quincy Adams (Mass.), Seth M. Gates (N.Y.), Joshua R. Giddings (Ohio), John Mattocks (Vt.), and William Slade (Vt.); and the two scatters were Nathaniel B. Borden (Mass.), who voted for George N. Briggs (W-Mass.), and Wise (Va.), who voted for William Cost Johnson (W-Md.). Adams's description of White in his moment of triumph is priceless: "White was sworn by Lewis Williams, took the chair, and made a namby-pamby speech about his incompetency and impartiality" (1876, vol. 10, 5/31/1841, 470).

Congress, John W. Jones. Robert M. T. Hunter (elected to the 27th Congress as an Independent) voted for Jones, not White, which marked his formal break with the Whig Party that had elected him Speaker only two years before.

The Whig defections on the speakership ballot were an omen. While a number of Southern Whigs had threatened to bolt and support their own candidate for Speaker—viewing White as too moderate on the slavery issue—in the end they largely stayed loyal and supported the caucus nominee. The rebellion occurred instead on the vote for Clerk.

On the first clerkship ballot, the Whigs split between Smith (89 votes), Clarke (39), and Richard C. Mason (8), while Democrats rallied once more behind Garland. Those Whigs who defected from Smith were significantly closer to the Democrats on the main ideological dimension that divided the parties, as measured by first-dimension W-NOMINATE scores. On the second ballot, some Democrats saw an opportunity and broke ranks, redistributing their votes to Clarke and Mason. The third ballot saw an even greater defection of Democrats to Clarke, but now 10 Whigs also broke in his favor. The fourth and final ballot saw further consolidation of Clarke's position, as he won with a coalition that was essentially half Democrat (63 votes) and half Whig (64 votes).

In the words of the Whig-backed *New York Commercial Advertiser*, "The locos [Democrats] wished to help the southern Whigs to kill off a conservative and, at the same time, to foment jealousies in the Whig ranks" (6/2/1841, 2). In helping to elect Clarke, and thus defeat Smith, the Democrats did just that. While Whig leaders were upset that Smith, the caucus nominee, was not supported by the full Whig membership on the floor, they could at least take comfort in the ouster of the despised Hugh Garland, who saw his Democratic base evaporate in the process.[45] Moreover, the Printer election went the Whigs' way, quickly and easily, as Gales and Seaton won a first-ballot victory, receiving 134 votes to 75 for Blair and Rives, and 6 for

---

[45] In fact, defeating Garland was simply the first step in the Whigs' ultimate plan for him. During the 27th Congress, the Whig-controlled House proceeded to dish out some "payback" by examining his behavior as Clerk. The Committee on Public Expenditures, controlled by a Whig majority, conducted an investigation and claimed that Garland had been involved in fraudulent activities while serving as Clerk, most notably in overcharging suppliers and receiving kickbacks (see footnote 19 in chapter 2 for more details). Garland denied committing fraud and countered each of the committee's specific charges in detail (*House Document 275* [27-2], 405). Moreover, he endeavored to explain his reasons for not calling the names of the five Whig members from New Jersey during the organization of the 26th House, citing various British parliamentary procedures from the seventeenth century (*House Document* 106 [28-1], 442).

Yet, in the end, Garland's efforts to explain his actions and clear his name were to no avail. His reputation was tarnished, and he faded into political obscurity. His final legacy was to be known as the House Clerk who perhaps most influenced the course of congressional proceedings.

Peter Force (*HJ*, 27-1, 6/11/1841, 88–89).[46] Unlike the Clerk balloting, Whig coordination was not a problem, as only one Whig (Thomas Gilmer [Va.]) defected from Gales and Seaton.

In constructing his standing committees, White behaved quite differently than Hunter, stacking all the important ones with Whig majorities and giving Democrats the chairs of only five trivial committees, such as Mileage (*HJ*, 27-1, 6/8/1841, 49–52). From this position of institutional strength, the Whig Congress acted swiftly, repealing the Independent Treasury Act before it could even be implemented and passing a new Bankruptcy Act. As a general matter, however, the Whig majority in Congress was met with a series of Tyler vetoes. Twice, for example, Tyler vetoed a new Bank of the United States bill and new protective tariff legislation.

The Whigs' electoral success in the 1840–41 elections turned out to be their undoing in the subsequent House elections of 1842 and 1843.[47] When the electoral dust had settled, the Whigs had lost nearly half the seats they had controlled in the 27th Congress, one of the most devastating losses by a majority party in American history. Historians have attributed this electoral skewering to several factors, ranging from the inability to govern effectively, to the Tyler fiasco, to reapportionment. With Tyler as president, rather than Harrison, the Whig economic recovery plan was stymied; casting around for policy alternatives made Whig leaders in Congress look incompetent. Tyler, drummed out of the Whig Party and embraced by the Democracy, used his patronage appointments in major cities to reinforce Democratic strength in mobilizing midterm voters. This is an oft-told story. Less well known is the bloodbath visited upon Whigs nationwide by a reapportionment act that reduced the size of the House (thus redistributing the number of seats in various states), mandated single-member districts, and touched off one of the most substantial redistricting exercises in American history through the agency of a passel of largely Democratic state legislatures. As a consequence, the Whigs experienced a small dip in the national vote in the midterm House elections (3.5 percent point drop), but saw their share of seats in the House decline significantly (26.4 percent point drop).[48]

The House elections that were held in the shadow of the presidential election of 1844 left the Democrats and Whigs where they had been at midterm. The principal issue in the 1844 election was Texas annexation, which yet again forced slavery and regional politics onto the national stage and resulted in large surges in turnout, North and South, in response to the issue. Democrats were associated with pro-annexation sentiment while Whigs

[46] We could find no record as to whether the Whig caucus made an explicit Printer nomination.

[47] The accounts of these congressional elections draw heavily on Holt (1999, 151–61).

[48] The Whigs totaled 142 of 242 (58.7%) seats in the 27th Congress, and 72 of 223 (32.3%) seats in the 28th Congress (see Martis 1989, 96–97).

were anti-annexation (Morrison 1997; Silbey 2002). On net, the regional equation largely balanced out, with Democrats picking up a handful of seats in the South and Whigs picking up a few seats in the North. As a result, Democrats held healthy majorities in the 28th and 29th Congresses, and in both cases the organization of the House was settled in the Democratic caucus.

Prior to the opening of the 28th Congress, after Calhoun supporters pushed through a two-thirds rule for all caucus nominations, the Democrats chose John W. Jones (Va.) for Speaker once again, along with Caleb J. Mc-Nulty (Ohio) for Clerk and Blair and Rives for Printer.[49] All were considered "Van Buren men," and all were elected easily on the floor: Jones 128–59 over John White on a strict party-line vote (*HJ*, 28-1, 12/4/1843, 8–9); Mc-Nulty 124–66 over Matthew St. Clair Clarke, with only two Democratic defections (*HJ*, 28-1, 12/6/1843, 29–30); and Blair and Rives 124–62 over Gales and Seaton, with only one Democratic defection (*HJ*, 28-1, 12/7/1843, 35–37).[50]

Prior to the opening of the 29th Congress, after repealing the two-thirds nomination rule adopted two years earlier, the Democrats chose John W. Davis (Ind.) for Speaker,[51] along with Benjamin B. French (N.H.) for Clerk[52]

[49] Jones won a first-ballot victory in caucus, with 78 votes to 15 for William Wilkins (Pa.), 9 for Dixon Lewis (Ala.), 7 for John W. Davis (Ind.), and 4 scattering (*Daily National Intelligencer*, 12/8/1843, 3; reprinting a 12/6 story in the *Richmond Enquirer*), while McNulty required three ballots to emerge victorious, winning 101 of 118 votes on the third (*Ohio Statesman*, 12/12/1843, 3). No vote totals were discovered in Blair and Rives's victory, although it was reported that it occurred only "after a sharp struggle" (*Southern Patriot*, 12/9/1843, 2). No information about Whig caucus nominations was found. For more on the caucus nominations, see *Farmer's Cabinet*, 12/1/1843, 2; *NYH*, 12/4/1843, 2; *Madisonian*, 12/4/1843, 3; *Daily Atlas*, 12/11/1843, 2; *Southern Patriot*, 12/6/1843, 2, and 12/7/1843, 2; *Sun*, 12/5/1843, 4, and 12/7/1843, 4; and the *Emancipator and Free American*, 12/14/1843, 130.

[50] The two Democratic defectors on the Clerk vote were Edward Cross (Ark.) and ex-Whig Henry A. Wise (Va.), both of whom voted for Clarke. The single Democratic defector on the Printer vote was Thomas Gilmer (Va.), who voted for Jacob Gideon (the only vote he received).

Several Democrats from Southern states (South Carolina and Virginia, for example) did not vote in the Printer election, but did vote in the Sergeant at Arms and Doorkeeper elections, which occurred *immediately* afterward. Blair and Rives had issues with some House members (and this was reciprocated); thus, these abstentions may have been strategic. Rather than break the caucus agreement, these members simply abstained, knowing the Democrats had plenty of votes to spare.

[51] John W. Jones did not run for reelection to the 29th Congress, so he was not an option for the speakership.

[52] Note that French replaced McNulty as Clerk in the 28th Congress. McNulty was dismissed by the House on a 196–0 vote after a report presented by the Committee on Accounts charged him with embezzling as much as $60,000 from the House's contingent fund (*HJ*, 28-2, 1/18/1845, 230–31; for a description of the report, see *CG*, 28-2, 1/17/1845, 147). French, who was at that time first assistant to McNulty, was then elected House Clerk unanimously by resolution (*CG*, 28-2, 1/18/1845, 153–54).

and Thomas Ritchie and John P. Heiss (editors of the *Union*) for Printer.[53] The overwhelming Democratic majority allowed Davis, a proslavery moderate who supported western expansion, to prevail over Samuel Vinton (W-Ohio) in a cakewalk, 120–71 with 19 votes scattering (*HJ*, 29-1, 12/1/1845, 7–9). But the defection of nine Calhounite Democrats to Moses Norris (D-N.H.) was evidence of lingering regional animosities within the Democratic caucus.[54] The Calhounites were unhappy with the repeal of the two-thirds nomination rule and, more important, were suspicious of Davis's states' rights credentials (*Georgia Telegraph*, 12/16/1845, 2).[55] The other officer elections proceeded without a hitch, however, as French was unanimously elected by resolution (*HJ*, 29-1, 12/2/1845, 13), while Ritchie and Heiss won handily over Jesse E. Dow and Theophilus Fisk (editors of the *U.S. Journal*) 123–69 with 6 votes scattering and only one Democratic defection (*HJ*, 29-1, 12/3/1845, 46–47).[56] Both Jones and Davis appointed committees that heavily favored the Democrats and assigned Whig majorities or chairs to only a few minor committees that were far removed from the hot political issues of the time, such as Texas annexation and the Mexican War.[57]

By the 29th Congress the organizational system that the Van Burenites had devised in the late 1830s was beginning to come together. After an initial failure in 1839, the party nominating caucus, combined with viva voce voting, had generated the majority party's desired results three consecutive times. This successful run (especially with regard to the speakership) was noticed in contemporary press accounts. For example, the *Georgia Telegraph* reported that "Mr. Davis is the third Speaker who has been elected by

[53] Davis won a second ballot victory in caucus, with 77 votes out of 153 Democratic members present (*NYH*, 12/3/1845, 2). French won a first-ballot victory, besting ex-House member John B. Weller (Ohio) 78–26, while Ritchie and Heiss, who bought the *Globe* from Blair and Rives and changed its name to the *Union*, were elected unanimously (*Sun*, 12/3/1845, 4). For more on the caucus nominations, see *Southern Patriot*, 12/1/1845, 2, and 12/2/1845, 2; *Farmer's Cabinet*, 12/4/1845, 2; *Daily Ohio Statesman*, 12/1/1845, 2, and 12/5/1845, 2; *NYH*, 12/7/1845, 3; *Constitution*, 12/10/1845, 2; and *Georgia Telegraph*, 12/16/1845, 2.

[54] The defectors were Armistead Burt (S.C.), John H. Harmanson (La.), Isaac E. Holmes (S.C.), Robert Barnwell Rhett (S.C.), James A. Seddon (Va.), Richard F. Simpson (S.C.), Alexander D. Sims (S.C.), Joseph A. Woodward (S.C.), and William Lowndes Yancey (Ala.).

[55] According to the *Telegraph*, while Davis voted to maintain House Rule 25—the gag rule that prevented antislavery petitions from being read on the House floor—as a member of the 28th Congress, he voted to abolish Rule 25 *within* the Rules Committee (where he was a member).

[56] The one defector was Armistead Burt (S.C.), who voted for the Whig-nominated team of Dow and Fisk.

[57] In the 28th Congress, Jones allowed Whig majorities on four of the Expenditures committees, plus Manufactures and Public Buildings and Grounds; he appointed Whig chairs to four of the Expenditures committees, plus Manufactures, Agriculture, Patents, and Claims. In the 29th Congress, Davis allowed Whig majorities on the Committee on Expenditures in the War Department, Public Expenditures, Revolutionary Claims, and Roads and Canals; he appointed Whig chairs to Manufactures and to Claims (Canon, Nelson, and Stewart 2002).

caucus. Mr. White was the first by the Whigs; Mr. Jones, the Speaker of the last Congress, was the second" (12/16/1845, 2). This organizational good fortune would soon be tested, however, as simmering regional tensions threatened continued interregional partisan harmony.

One final point about House organizational politics in the 29th Congress deserves mentioning.[58] Thanks to a joint resolution, which became law on August 3, 1846, the House Printer (and its Senate counterpart) as an *elective* position was abolished. In its place, a somewhat elaborate bidding system was established in which the lowest bidder would receive the printing contract. Arguments for reforming the congressional printing had begun in the early 1840s, when separate House and Senate committees recommended placing the job in the government's hands—a change the committees felt would significantly reduce printing costs as well as enhance professionalism and impartiality. In 1845, the Whigs made a strong push for change that was led by Garret Davis (W-Ky.), who argued that the current patronage-based printing system was fraught with corruption. In pushing their case, the Whigs benefited from the actions of the current House Printer, Thomas Ritchie, who had taken several policy stances after ascending to the printership—specifically, supporting President Polk's handling of the war with Mexico, supporting the Walker Tariff of 1846, and opposing the British position on the Oregon border question—that proved unpopular with many Democrats, Calhounites and Bentonites alike.[59] While other Democrats, like Stephen Douglas (D-Ill.), argued that the Whigs' advocacy of reform was simply a case of the minority playing politics (as they were cut out of the congressional printing in both chambers in the 29th Congress), momentum for change had been building, and in July 1846 both chambers passed a joint resolution that put the low-bid system into operation.[60]

This low-bid system would prove to be a failure, and a return to an elective Printer position would occur in 1852. But for the next two Congresses, the 30th (1847–49) and 31st (1849–51), the House Printer would not exist as a patronage plum to fight over.

---

[58] This section relies heavily on Ambler (1913, 251–65) and Smith (1977, 206–10). See also the *Boston Daily Atlas*, 7/25/1846, 2 and 8/5/1846, 2; *North American*, 7/28/1846, 1; *Pittsfield Sun*, 7/30/1846, 2; and *Southern Patriot*, 8/3/1846, 2.

[59] In adopting these positions, Ritchie was actively supporting the views of President Polk. His *Union* newspaper was the official organ of the Polk administration, and over time he became Polk's scapegoat.

[60] The House roll call was 134–26, with Whigs voting 55–0 and Democrats voting 75–26 (*CG*, 29-1, 7/22/1846, 1129–30), while the Senate roll call was 38–13, with Whigs voting 23–0 and Democrats voting 14–13 (*CG*, 29-1, 7/30/1846, 1167). In explaining why the Democrats supported the low-bid system, a correspondent for the *Boston Daily Atlas* noted, "At first it was proposed to disgrace [Ritchie], by expelling him, by a public vote, from the office of Printer; but, upon reflection, Col. Benton, who was the prime mover in the affair, thought it best to take the equally effectual method of passing the joint Resolution to let the printing be by contract; knowing full well that the Organ could hardly exist beyond the next session" (8/5/1846, 2).

THE CALM BEFORE THE STORM: HOUSE ORGANIZATION IN THE 30TH CONGRESS

While unified Democratic control of the national government during the 29th Congress was viewed initially as a setback for the Whigs, domestic and foreign policy decisions would turn the situation to the party's advantage. War with Mexico began in 1846, and the Whigs (with some effort) were able to frame the conflict as a case of unprovoked aggression perpetrated by President Polk. Their contention was that "Mr. Polk's War" was conducted solely to acquire territory in the West, so as to provide for the expansion of slavery and thus appease the "Slave Power" in the Southern states. The Whig slogan of "No Territory" was used to knit together both Southern and Northern wings of the party while sidestepping the more controversial Wilmot Proviso, which separated both parties by region (Morrison 1997, 78–82; Holt 1999, 252–57).[61] In addition, the Whigs capitalized on new Democratic policies—like the Walker Tariff of 1846, which reduced tariff rates, and a new Independent Treasury Act—to spread fear of an impending economic downturn for the country.

As a result, the elections of 1846–47 went the Whigs' way and returned them to majority status in the House, but just barely. The Whigs controlled 116 of the 228 seats at the opening of the 30th Congress, with Democrats controlling 108 seats and four third-party candidates filling out the remainder.[62] Thus, the Whigs had just a bit of wiggle room in their pursuit of the House organization; party cohesion would be critical if they hoped to secure the important House officer positions.

The Whigs held a caucus on the evening of December 4, 1847, to settle on officer nominations.[63] Samuel Vinton (Ohio), the Whig speakership candidate in the 29th Congress, emerged as the caucus choice for Speaker on the

---

[61] The Wilmot Proviso, first offered by David Wilmot (D-Pa.) in 1846 and by others in subsequent years, would have prohibited slavery in any new western territories taken from Mexico. The Proviso split both parties into Northern and Southern contingents; for the Whigs, Southern representatives could not support such a measure, not because they necessarily disagreed with its provisions, but because it was viewed as disrespectful of the South. Opposition to territorial annexation could be supported by both Northern and Southern Whigs, however, as "honorable" justifications could be provided by region. That is, the "No Territory" slogan was more malleable and could be styled to members' particular electoral goals. For example, Northern Whigs could frame "No Territory" as limiting the further extension of slavery, while Southern Whigs could claim that western lands were not suitable for slavery, and, thus, that any new states carved out of that land would organize themselves as free states.

[62] Wisconsin would enter the Union in May 1848 and receive two House seats in the 30th Congress, bringing the chamber total to 230.

[63] Details on caucus proceedings and nominations are taken from the *North American and United States Gazette*, 12/2/1847, 2, 12/6/1847, 2, and 12/7/1847, 2; *Boston Daily Globe*, 12/6/1847, 2 and 12/8/1847, 2; *Morning News*, 12/7/1847, 2; *Farmer's Cabinet*, 12/9/1847, 2; and the *New Hampshire Patriot and State Gazette*, 12/9/1847, 2.

first ballot, but he declined the nomination due to poor health. Robert C. Winthrop (Mass.) was then chosen on the following ballot.[64] For Clerk, the Whigs chose Thomas J. Campbell (Tenn.), a former House member in the 27th Congress. The Democrats also met in caucus, but produced no nominations.

Two hundred twenty-one members were present when the Clerk called the roll on December 6 to convene the 30th Congress. Three Whigs and four Democrats were absent, which maintained the narrow Whig majority in the chamber that had resulted from the 1846–47 elections.[65] A sense of foreboding was in the air, however, as Whig leaders heard rumblings over the weekend from extreme elements within the party. At issue was Winthrop's slavery credentials. Southern firebrands were concerned that Winthrop could be a "Wilmot Proviso man," while Northern agitators believed Winthrop was not firm enough in opposing territorial expansion. In his home state of Massachusetts, Winthrop was a leader of the Cotton Whigs, party members who were principally concerned with commercial and manufacturing interests. This contrasted with the goals of the Conscience Whigs, party members who emphasized moral issues, notably opposition to slavery and slavery extension. The Cotton Whigs' economic focus often led them to de-emphasize slavery whenever possible so as to maintain positive and profitable relations with the Southern wing of the party.[66]

By all accounts, Winthrop was considered middle-of-the-road on the slavery issue. He had generally been against annexation of Texas and territorial expansion, but he also worked against extreme antislavery agitation, most recently by helping to defeat a strident antislavery plank in the 1847 Massachusetts state convention. Winthrop was a pragmatist at his core, which helped determine his performance in the speakership election.

Prior to the balloting, two Conscience Whigs, Joshua R. Giddings (Ohio) and John G. Palfrey (Mass.), contacted Winthrop via a note penned by Palfrey and asked whether he as Speaker would organize the standing committees around antislavery tenets (Giddings 1864; Gatell 1958).[67] Winthrop

[64] Vote totals on the Whig Speaker nominations are sketchy. The most thorough account was provided in the *Boston Daily Globe* (12/8/1847, 2), which characterized Vinton's nomination as "unanimous" while reporting that Winthrop received 59 out of 97 votes. However, in a diary entry, Winthrop claims that Vinton received 51 votes on the first ballot (with no mention of other votes cast), while he (Winthrop) received 57 votes (to 25 for Caleb B. Smith [Ind.]) on the subsequent ballot. Diary entry quoted in Gatell (1958, 222).

[65] Winthrop would not participate in the speakership balloting, so in effect the narrow Whig majority in the chamber resulting from the 1846–47 elections was *exactly* maintained.

[66] For more on the differences between Cotton Whigs and Conscience Whigs, see Gatell (1958) and Brauer (1967).

[67] In his *History of the Rebellion*, Giddings (1864, 261–63) would provide an overview of the speakership election of 1847 that emphasized Winthrop's shortcomings on various slavery-related issues and documented Winthrop's subsequent failings as Speaker. More than a decade later, Winthrop would read Giddings's account and take issue with many of his claims. Win-

responded by refusing to make any pledges and instead advised interested parties to search his public record for evidence of his issue positions.[68] Thus, Giddings and Palfrey (along with a third strongly antislavery member, Amos Tuck, an Independent [N.H.] with ties to the nascent Liberty Party) were left in a quandary—follow the caucus dictate or not?—as the balloting began.[69]

Winthrop received 108 of 220 votes that were cast on the first ballot, which left him only 3 votes shy of victory.[70] All 108 of his votes came from the Whig side of the aisle, while the Democrats revealed their disorganization by splitting their votes among Linn Boyd ([Ky.], 61 votes), Robert McClelland ([Mich.], 23), John A. McClernand ([Ill.], 11), and a host of others. In the end, four Whigs failed to support Winthrop, which proved to be his undoing. Giddings and Palfrey rejected the caucus dictate and voted instead for James Wilson (W-N.H.) and Charles Hudson (W-Mass.), respectively, and they were joined by John William Jones (Ga.), who voted for John P. Gaines (W-Ky.), and Patrick W. Tompkins (Miss.), who voted for John Gayle (W-Ala.). While disheartening for those whose aim was party unity, Winthrop's showing indicated that preballot concerns about sizable defections by extremist Whigs (both on the left and the right) were unfounded. The key now was for Winthrop and his allies to secure the few remaining votes needed for victory.

A second ballot was taken, and still no decision was made. But Winthrop inched closer by picking up Jones's vote to take his total to 109. Tompkins was also convinced to abstain on the vote, which brought the overall ballot tally to 219. Thus, Winthrop was now just one vote short of victory. He now had the complete support of the Southern Whigs (directly, or, in Tompkins's

---

throp considered Giddings's book "a mere attempt to justify a rash public career, & to make himself out the Hero of the whole Antislavery struggle." And of the man himself, Winthrop remarked, "Giddings always coveted martyrdom, & lost no opportunity, as his book shows, to magnify & intensify every indignity which could succeed in provoking the Hotspurs of the South to offer him." Quotes taken from an 1872 letter to Charles Deane, reprinted in Borome (1951, 291).

Giddings's account of the 1847 speakership election is flawed in at least two respects—he contends, first, that Winthrop's victory came on the *second* ballot rather than the third, and, second, that Winthrop's election was secured by the strategic abstention of *two* Southern Democrats. As Giddings wrote his *History* almost two decades after the speakership election, it appears that his memory of events was a bit faulty.

[68] Palfrey's letter to Winthrop, and Winthrop's letter of reply to Palfrey, are reprinted in the *Georgia Telegraph*, 1/4/1848, 3, and Winthrop (1897, 68–70).

[69] In discussions of the 1847 speakership election, Tuck is sometimes considered a Whig and grouped together with Giddings and Palfrey as an extreme, antislavery Northern Whig trio (see Winthrop 1897, 67). Tuck's partisan loyalties were quite fluid throughout his career. While he would later be elected on a Whig/Free-Soil fusion ticket to the 31st and 32nd Congresses, he was elected as an Independent to the 30th Congress in a runoff, after running under the Liberty Party label in the regular election (see Gatell 1958, 223n20; Dubin 1998, 148–49, 154, 161). Tuck would go on to vote against Winthrop for Speaker and Campbell for Clerk.

[70] For individual tallies on the speakership balloting, see *HJ*, 30-1, 12/6/1847, 8–14.

case, indirectly), but he could not fully consolidate the Northern wing of the party, as Giddings and Palfrey continued throwing their support to Wilson and Hudson, respectively. An assortment of Whig members, including John Quincy Adams, pleaded with Giddings and Palfrey to support Winthrop, and warned that persistent balloting and intraparty strife could swing the election to the Democrats—especially as they seemed to be coordinating more effectively around Boyd (82 votes). But Giddings and Palfrey rejected such entreaties and maintained that their principles must be upheld at any cost (Brauer 1967, 219–21).

On the third ballot, Winthrop broke through and won the election, as he captured 110 out of 218 votes cast. But his bare majority came without the assistance of Giddings and Palfrey, who continued to throw away their votes. In fact, the deciding 110th vote was cast *not* by a Whig but by the sole American Party member in the House, Lewis C. Levin (Pa.). Moreover, press reports suggested that Winthrop was actually stuck on 109 votes at the completion of the voting on the third ballot, at which point Levin switched his vote to Winthrop (and away, presumably, from Joseph R. Ingersoll [W-Pa.], for whom he had voted on the first two ballots) before the Clerk could assemble and announce the complete tabulation (see *National Era*, 12/9/1847, 3).

Thus, Winthrop had ascended to the Speaker's chair by the slimmest of margins.[71] While he and his supporters were elated, a dark cloud hung over the festivities—success was determined by the unexpected support from a minority party member, not by perfect adherence to the caucus agreement.

[71] In combing through the histories of the 1847 speakership election, a couple of small errors were discovered. These errors originate in a biography of Winthrop that was written by his son in 1897. First, Winthrop (1897, 70–71) argues that *three* Southern Whigs (Jones, Tompkins, and William M. Cocke [all Tenn.]) opposed Winthrop on the first ballot, and *two* of them (Tompkins and Cocke) abstained after the first ballot. This story has been repeated verbatim by Brauer (1967, 219–20) and in a slightly different form by Schroeder (1973, 147) and Howe (2007, 796.) In fact, only *two* Southern Whigs (Jones and Tompkins) opposed Winthrop on the first ballot, and only Tompkins subsequently abstained on the second and third ballots. Cocke was not eligible to vote in the speakership contest, as he was not sworn in by the Clerk until the following day, December 7 (*HJ*, 30-1, 12/7/1847, 15; *CG*, 30-1, 12/7/1847, 4). Second, Winthrop (1897, 71) contends that the abstention of Democrat Isaac Holmes (Miss.) on the third ballot, which reduced the overall vote total from 219 to 218, was *pivotal* to the outcome. This story has been repeated by Brauer (1967, 220), Gatell (1958, 223), and Schroeder (1973, 147). However, Holmes's abstention *by itself* meant little; if Holmes had voted for someone other than Winthrop, Levin's vote would have still provided Winthrop with a bare majority (110 out of *219* votes). Holmes's abstention only mattered in combination with Tompkins's continued abstention; if *both* had decided to vote for someone other than Winthrop on the third ballot, their *joint* decision would have been pivotal (leaving Winthrop with 110 out of 220 votes). This contingent requirement is rarely mentioned in the histories (but for an accurate press account, see *National Era*, 12/9/1847, 3); rather, Holmes's somewhat dramatic departure from the hall during the voting on the third ballot is typically described as a uniquely crucial factor. (Note that additional, separate errors are found in Giddings 1864, 261; see footnote 67. These errors have not been propagated in subsequent histories.)

The slavery issue, which had infiltrated prior speakership elections during the decade, but never before in a pivotal fashion, overrode party allegiance at a critical time. This would prove to be a harbinger of more partisan difficulties, as the war with Mexico was drawing to a close and the organization of the western territories (soon to be ceded by Mexico) would demand attention.

The following day, December 7, the House turned to the election of a Clerk. The Whig candidate, Thomas J. Campbell, faced off against Benjamin B. French, the incumbent House Clerk. Overnight, four additional members arrived in town—two Whigs and two Democrats—which left the party margins in the House at their previous level. On the first ballot of the morning, in which all 225 members in the chamber participated, Campbell eked out the narrowest of victories, winning by a bare majority with 113 votes to 109 for French and 3 votes scattering (*HJ*, 30-1, 12/7/1847, 15–17). Campbell survived two Whig defections: John Quincy Adams, who voted for French, and Joshua Giddings, who voted for Nathan Sargent (who would be elected Sergeant at Arms the following day).[72] Thus, working with a thin margin, and amid an ideologically charged environment, the Whigs were able to overcome partisan defections and elect their caucus nominees to the House's two most important posts.

Once in the Speaker's chair, Winthrop would walk a tightrope between regional elements in his party. The war with Mexico and slavery extension, and the rules by which it would be allowed or prevented, dominated the public consciousness, and members of Congress increasingly made the slavery issue a litmus test for assessing a man's ideological allegiance. ("Popular sovereignty"—a method for resolving the question of slavery extension in

---

[72] Adams's plan to vote for French was widely known (*Boston Daily Atlas*, 12/8/1847, 2). Adams noted in his diary that he had made French a promise "some months since" to vote for him, as did (according to Adams) several other Whigs, but they were "overpowered by the Caucus screw" (entry of 12/6/1847, Adams Family Papers, Massachusetts Historical Society). In his journal, French also hinted at receiving prior Whig promises, noting specifically that "[t]he evening previous to the election [Whig] Henry Nes, of Pennsylvania, held up his hand & swore before the God that made him, in presence of Mr. Levin, that he would vote for me, and then perjured himself by voting for Campbell! Let the unprincipled, perjured wretch answer to his conscience and his God for this crime! I despise him" (entry of Dec. 16, 1847, reprinted in French 1989, 197). As for Giddings, the *National Era* (12/9/1847, 3) claimed that his failure to support Campbell stemmed from an interaction they had when they were both members of the 27th Congress. At that time, Giddings faced censure in the House, due to resolutions he introduced concerning the natural rights of slaves, and Campbell voted in favor of censure. In a subsequent letter to the editor of the *Cleveland Herald* (1/5/1848, 3), Giddings confirmed the general thrust of the *National Era* story, but framed Campbell's vote of censure as a violation of the Constitution rather than a personal affront. Giddings would also claim that the Whig caucus was unaware of Campbell's prior censure vote, and "if it had been known he could not have received the nomination." Whether Giddings was correct in this assessment (or whether it was simply bluster) is impossible to know, but it seems clear that he was not the type to forgive and forget.

the West by letting the people in the territories decide the matter—became a household term and a moderate position during this period, and it would be a major factor in the presidential election of 1848.) Thus, Winthrop knew his construction of committees would be watched carefully, and he worked on the matter incessantly behind closed doors. Later, he confided to a friend: "the assignment of committees has been the hardest work I ever did in my life" (quoted in Winthrop 1897, 74).

Winthrop's committee assignments appear in table 5.3. Committee power was stacked heavily in the Whigs' favor. Winthrop distributed nearly all chairmanships to Whigs; the only exceptions were Accounts, which was given to his main speakership rival, Linn Boyd (D-Ky.), and Engraving, which was given to Lewis Levin (A-Pa.), who cast the deciding vote in his speakership victory. He also made sure that Whigs constituted majorities on most committees and on all major policy committees. Democrats held a majority on only a few minor committees, such as Mileage and Revolutionary Pensions. Thus, based on this evidence, few could claim that Winthrop was anything less than partisan in his construction of committees.

Perhaps the more important question was whether Winthrop was *ideological* in his construction of committees. As the slavery issue was gripping the nation and producing rifts within the parties, did Winthrop acquiesce to extremists (either on the pro- or antislavery side) and tilt important committees in a given ideological direction? To answer these questions, we incorporate second-dimension W-NOMINATE scores that tap slavery preferences in this Congress (Poole and Rosenthal 1997, 49). We then examine the ideological location of key actors (the chairman and the median member) on the nine most important House committees—Ways and Means, Commerce, Judiciary, Foreign Affairs, Territories, Agriculture, Military Affairs, Naval Affairs, and District of Columbia—in the 30th Congress.[73] These locations are illustrated in table 5.4.

As the table indicates, most of the key actors on these nine committees fell within the interquartile range on the second W-NOMINATE dimension, which represented the "moderate" range of policy positions. Only three of the nine committee chairmen—Botts on Military Affairs, King on Naval Affairs, and Chapman on the District of Columbia—were extreme proslavery advocates; none of the remaining chairs were extreme in the antislavery direction. In terms of committee medians, most were representative of the overall chamber, with only Agriculture *slightly* tilted in an antislavery direc-

[73] The first six committees—Ways and Means, Commerce, Judiciary, Foreign Affairs, Territories, and Agriculture—represent the overlap of Silbey's (1989, 12) "key" committees and Alexander's (1916, 399–410) "important" committees. The last three committees—Military Affairs, Naval Affairs, and District of Columbia—are considered "important" by Alexander but not "key" by Silbey; nonetheless, their composition was discussed in detail in newspapers of the time, as they had direct influence on issues related to the war with Mexico, slavery, and slavery extension.

TABLE 5.3.
House committee assignments, 30th Congress

Committee	Chair (party-state)	Members	Dem.	Whigs
Elections	Richard W. Thompson (W-Ind.)	9	4	5
Ways and Means	Samuel F. Vinton (W-Ohio)	9	3	6
Claims	John A. Rockwell (W-Conn.)	9	4	5
Commerce	Washington Hunt (W-N.Y.)	9	4	5
Public Lands	Jacob Collamer (W-Vt.)	9	4	5
Post Office and Post Roads	William L. Goggin (W-Va.)	9	4	5
District of Columbia	John G. Chapman (W-Md.)	9	4	5
Judiciary	Joseph R. Ingersoll (W-Pa.)	9	4	5
Revolutionary Claims	Daniel P. King (W-Mass.)	9	4	5
Public Expenditures	Thomas L. Clingman (W-N.C.)	9	4	5
Private Land Claims	John Gayle (W-Ala.)	9	4	5
Manufactures	Andrew Stewart (W-Pa.)	9	4	5
Agriculture	Hugh White (W-N.Y.)	9	4	5
Indian Affairs	Meredith P. Gentry (W-Tenn.)	9	4	5
Military Affairs	John M. Botts (W-Va.)	9	3	6
Militia	John B. Thompson (W-Ky.)	9	6	3
Naval Affairs	Thomas Butler King (W-Ga.)	9	3	4
Foreign Affairs	Truman Smith (W-Conn.)	9	3	6
Territories	Caleb B. Smith (W-Ind.)	9	4	5
Revolutionary Pensions	William M. Cocke (W-Tenn.)	9	5	4
Invalid Pensions	Henry Nes (W-Pa.)	9	4	4
Roads and Canals	Robert C. Schenck (W-Ohio)	9	3	5
Patents	John W. Farrelly (W-Pa.)	5	3	2
Public Buildings & Grounds	John W. Houston (W-Del.)	5	2	3
Revisal and Unfin. Business	John W. Hornbeck (W-Pa.)	5	3	2
Accounts	Linn Boyd (D-Ky.)	5	3	2
Mileage	Hiram Belcher (W-Maine)	5	3	2
Engraving	Lewis C. Levin (A-Pa.)	3	1	1
Library of Congress	John Quincy Adams (W-Mass.)	3	1	2
Exp. in State Dept.	Daniel M. Barringer (W-N.C.)	5	2	3
Exp. in Treasury Dept.	Joseph M. Root (W-Ohio)	5	2	3
Exp. in War Dept.	John H. Crozier (W-Tenn.)	5	2	3
Exp. in Navy Dept.	Patrick W. Tompkins (W-Miss.)	5	2	2
Exp. in Post Office Dept.	James Wilson (W-N.H.)	5	2	3
Exp. on Public Buildings	E. Carrington Cabell (W-Fla.)	5	2	3
Enrolled Bills	James G. Hampton (W-N.J.)	2	1	1

Note: American Lewis C. Levin (Pa.) served on Naval Affairs; Independent Amos Tuck (N.H.) served on Naval Affairs and Exp. in the Navy Dept.; Independent Democrat George Petrie (N.Y.) served on Invalid Pensions; and Independent Democrat Robert Smith (Ill.) served on Roads and Canals.

Table 5.4.
Ideological orientation of important House committees, 30th Congress

Committee	Chair	Median
Agriculture	-0.368	-0.397
Commerce	-0.370	-0.283
Territories	-0.191	-0.191
Foreign Affairs	-0.137	-0.137
Ways and Means	-0.100	-0.100
District of Columbia	0.744	-0.082
Judiciary	0.314	0.035
Military Affairs	0.820	0.204
Naval Affairs	0.731	0.347

Note: Entries represent second-dimension W-NOMINATE scores. Negative values indicate antislavery preferences; positive values indicate proslavery preferences. Intensity of preference increases as one moves toward -1 or 1.

Interquartile W-NOMINATE range: First Q = -0.439; Median = -0.082; and Third Q = 0.451.

tion and Naval Affairs *slightly* tilted in a proslavery direction. Thus, Winthrop did not construct disproportionately biased committees—and when he did grant chairmanships to extreme members, he made sure to balance them by ensuring that the pivotal committee members (the medians) were policy moderates.

The story that emerges from these committee data largely supports contentions in news reports of the time. Most complaints against Winthrop were levied by extreme antislavery advocates who were angry that he did not staff all major committees with those who would hold the line against the Slave Power. Southern interests, by contrast, were generally satisfied with his committee decisions.[74] In a sense, only liberal extremists were unhappy; conservative extremists were content with generally representative committees, as the moderate position in Congress (and the country more generally) was to maintain the status quo: continue the war with Mexico and be open to some form of slavery extension. The South had consistently won on slavery-related policy matters over time (see Richards 2000), and Southern leaders were confident that maintaining the current course would help them achieve their goals.

Still, as the slavery issue heated up over the course of his two-year tenure in the Speaker's chair, Winthrop ran afoul of Southern extremists within his party, notably Alexander Stephens (Ga.) and Robert Toombs (Ga.). A key moment occurred in 1849 during the lame-duck session of the 30th Con-

[74] See, for example, *Emancipator*, 12/22/1847, 2 and 1/26/1848, 1 (reprinting an article from the *Charleston Mercury*); *Farmer's Cabinet*, 12/23/1847, 2; *Semi-Weekly Natchez Courier*, 12/31/1847, 3; *New Hampshire Patriot and State Gazette*, 1/13/1848, 2; and the *Liberator*, 1/17/1848, 1. See, also, Giddings (1864, 263).

gress, when Stephens and Toombs wanted Winthrop to stack a general appropriations conference committee with proslavery advocates, so as to concur with the Senate and *oppose* the wishes of a House majority that favored a pro–Wilmot Proviso bill. Winthrop refused to do so, and later had to discipline Toombs on the House floor during debate on the bill (Winthrop 1897, 91–92).[75] These decisions would have consequences, as the 31st Congress and Winthrop's speakership reelection campaign loomed.

CONTROLLING THE SPEAKERSHIP AND CONTROLLING THE FLOOR

Thus far in this chapter we have described the dynamics of organizational roll calls once the House began electing Speakers and other officers through viva voce voting. Certainly the combatants believed that the speakership was valuable for policy reasons. However, given the occasional disconnects between the outcomes in voting for Speaker and voting for other House officers, plus the fact that the apparatus of party government was informal and weak at best, we can only somewhat be assured that the coalition that elected the Speaker actually controlled the legislative process once the actual work of the Congress got under way. How can we tell in a systematic way?

One way to tell whether the election of the Speaker had significant policy consequences in subsequent decision making is to cast the question in terms of the procedural cartel model associated with the work of Cox and McCubbins (1993, 2005). Recall from chapter 1 that a procedural cartel can be defined as a legislative majority—usually the majority party—that captures the internal legislative institutions for the purpose of structuring policy more to the liking of that majority. Such a procedural cartel is distinct from a chamber in which the ideological center (the median) rules, with roll call votes regularly pitting a centrist bipartisan coalition against first one partisan extreme and then the other. A procedural cartel typically operates through the control of agenda-setting rules. These rules, in turn, operate in such a way that roll call behavior is influenced in predictable ways.

One way in which the majority party might use the rules to encourage policy to march toward the majority party median, as distinct from the chamber median, is illustrated through the following spatial voting example. Begin with the standard unidimensional spatial model that operates under pure majority rule. Suppose the ideal points of members of a legislature are arrayed uniformly in a unidimensional space, as illustrated in figure

---

[75] Toombs would later complain about Winthrop's staffing of committees in the 30th Congress, focusing much of his attention on the slight antislavery majority on the District of Columbia Committee (Winthrop 1897, 75–76).

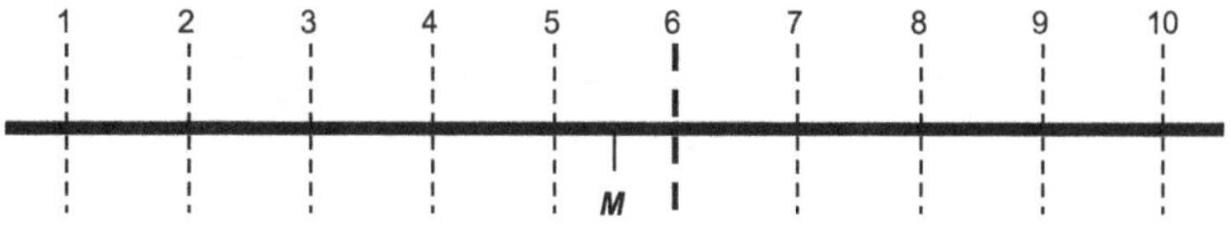

FIGURE 5.3. Winning and losing roll call voters under majority rule.

Vote	1	2	3	4	5	6	7	8	9	10
1	L	W	W	W	W	W	W	W	W	W	W
2	L	L	W	W	W	W	W	W	W	W	W
3	L	L	L	W	W	W	W	W	W	W	W
4	L	L	L	L	W	W	W	W	W	W	W
5	L	L	L	L	L	W	W	W	W	W	W
6	W	W	W	W	W	W	L	L	L	L	L
7	W	W	W	W	W	W	W	L	L	L	L
8	W	W	W	W	W	W	W	W	L	L	L
9	W	W	W	W	W	W	W	W	W	L	L
10	W	W	W	W	W	W	W	W	W	W	L
Win pct.	50	60	70	80	90	100	90	80	70	60	50

5.3. This legislature considers 10 roll call votes with "cut points" located as indicated in the figure.[76] In terms of roll call vote no. 1, with cut point no. 1, the rightward alternative prevails, since that is the side of the space that includes the chamber median. Thus, everyone to the left of the cut point is on the losing side of the roll call and everyone to the right is on the winning side. The Ls and the Ws in the figure indicate whether members of the separate ideological regions vote on the losing or winning sides of that roll call.

After all 10 roll calls are taken, all the legislators who lie between the fifth and sixth cut points—which includes the median—have been on the prevailing side on each roll call vote. Members lying farther away from this region prevail less often, in direct proportion to how far they are from the median.

Now, consider a legislative world that is ruled by a procedural cartel, and that operates as follows: First, for simplicity, assume that all members of the minority party lie to the left of all members of the majority party, as illustrated in figure 5.4. Second, assume that the majority party controls the agenda-setting mechanisms of the legislature, such that no votes are allowed

---

[76] A "cut point" in spatial voting theory is the point in a unidimensional model that separates those who vote *yea* from those who vote *nay*. In two dimensions, a cut point becomes a "cut line" (or "cutting line").

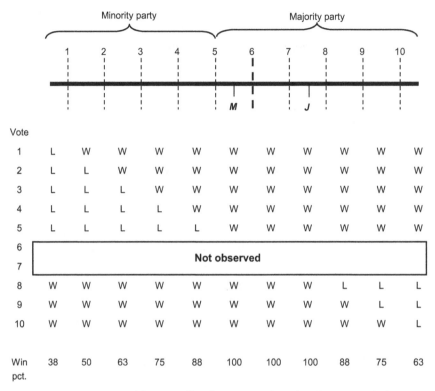

FIGURE 5.4. Winning and losing roll call voters under a legislative cartel that controls the agenda.

on the floor that would result in the median of the majority party (indicated by *J* in the figure) being on the losing side. In such a world, any roll call vote involving cut points 6 and 7 would be blocked, since *J* would lose the vote.[77] As a consequence of this agenda control, all members who lie in the regions between the one occupied by the chamber median and the one occupied by the majority party median prevail in all *observed roll calls*. Empirically, the ideological region of the "most frequent winners" of roll call votes has expanded, shifting toward the majority party median.

The frequency of being on the winning side of observed roll call votes under these two regimes—pure majority rule versus agenda-controlling procedural cartel—as a function of ideological location is summarized in figure 5.5. This figure illustrates an important implication that is likely to be associated with a party-based procedural cartel controlling the agenda: majority party members win more often than they would under pure majority

[77] Our characterization of agenda control here is akin to "negative agenda control," or gatekeeping (blocking) power.

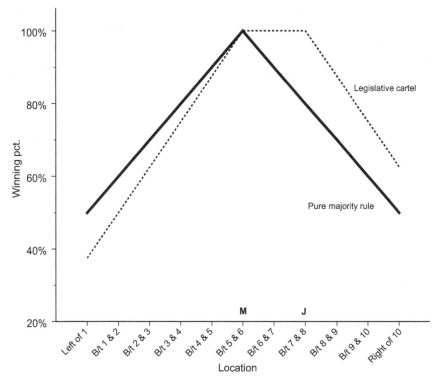

FIGURE 5.5. Frequency of being on the prevailing side of a roll call as a function of ideological location and decision-making agenda.

rule, and the members who win the most lie in the region between the floor median and the majority party median.[78] By keeping a set of votes off the floor that would split the majority party, policy moves away from the middle.

In applying this insight to roll call voting in the antebellum House, we need to make one important modification. Because parties did not uniformly unite behind a single candidate for Speaker, it is probably best to explore how frequently House members are on the winning side of roll calls with respect to the coalition that supported the victorious speakership candidate on the final ballot—what could be called the *organizing coalition*.[79]

[78] See Lawrence, Maltzman, and Smith (2006) and Smith (2007) for an examination of a similar model that uses a more modern set of roll call votes. Also see Cox and McCubbins (2002, 2005) for a parallel model that focuses on how often the majority *loses* (or is "rolled") on the floor.

[79] In coining the phrase *organizing coalition*, we remain agnostic for the moment about whether the coalition was anything more than simply an empirical phenomenon.

If agenda setting operates in a manner consistent with this example, then we should discover that the most frequent winner of roll call votes is not the median of the House but rather the median of the organizing coalition. Figure 5.6 graphs, separately for the 26th through 30th Congresses, the percentage of times that each House member was on the prevailing side of roll call votes against his spatial (ideological) location as measured by first-dimension W-NOMINATE scores.[80] Also indicated are the location of the floor median and the median of the organizing coalition. A third-degree polynomial has been fit through the data in each graph, via least squares regression, to help in identifying where the most frequent roll call winners are located in each Congress.[81]

Visual examination of figure 5.6 suggests a mixed bag with respect to the procedural cartel idea in the antebellum House. The most frequent winner of roll call votes was located away from the floor median in three of these five Congresses, so a centrist "pivotal politics" model hardly seems descriptive. However, in one of these cases (the 26th Congress), the organizing coalition could not reasonably be called a procedural cartel, since the most frequent policy winners were located *across* the policy space from the coalition that elected the Speaker. Recall that this was the Congress in which Robert M. T. Hunter was elected Speaker, despite the fact that he was heterodox within his Whig Party on its core economic issues and the last of the strongly pro-slavery Speakers. Hunter also gave significant committee assignments to Democrats, including majorities on most of the House's key policy committees, along with the committee that led the investigation of the disputed New Jersey election. Finally, despite the fact that the Whigs gained the speakership in the 26th Congress, they failed to claim the clerkship or printership. This is all consistent with a larger picture of the 26th Congress, in which the only thing "Whig" about it was its Speaker. Most important, it illustrates that the House had a long way to go before its members could assume that the coalition that determined the speakership would automatically control the chamber's agenda-setting apparatus.

This section has introduced a formal way to explore whether the coalition that elected Speakers in the early nineteenth century could in any way look like a governing coalition, or even a procedural cartel. Of course, the entirety of the evidence for these Congresses demonstrates that procedural

[80] Whereas other work (see footnote 78) tends to use only final-passage votes in calculating frequency of success/failure, we incorporate all roll call votes in our analyses.

[81] The choice of a third-degree polynomial is entirely a matter of empirical curve fitting. After some experimentation, the third-degree polynomial seems generally to be more conservative than a second-degree polynomial (from the perspective of the simple median voter model), since the global maximum of the curves it tends to fit are shifted toward the center of the issue space. Polynomials of a higher degree do fit the data better but produce only marginally different curves compared to the third-degree polynomials.

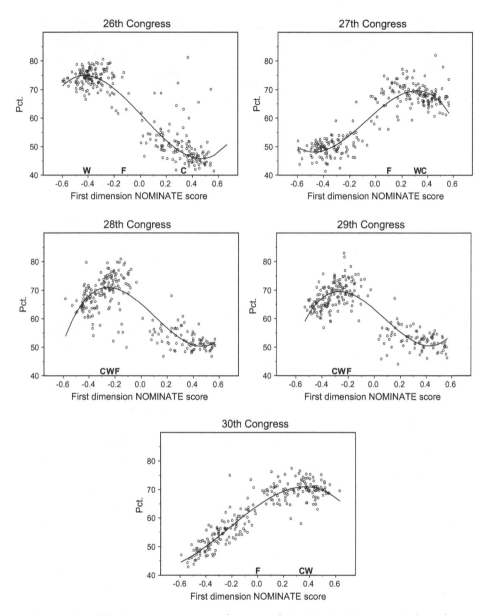

FIGURE 5.6. Winning percentage as a function of W-NOMINATE score 26th–30th Congresses. F = floor median; C = median of coalition that voted for winning Speaker candidate; W = estimated location of member most frequently on winning side of roll call votes.

cartels were never fully established, but some Congresses came closer to the ideal type than others. In chapter 7, we use this same analysis to examine the relationship between Speaker elections and floor control, and find that controlling the speakership was no guarantee of controlling the floor for the remainder of the antebellum period. We will revisit this technique one final time in chapter 9 as a way to illustrate the sequencing of the rise of the organizational and procedural cartels.

CONCLUSION

This chapter has examined the earliest Congresses when the House balloted in public for its officers. As irony would have it, the first time viva voce voting was applied to the speakership, the majority Democrats were unable to parlay it into a victory. Nonetheless, the Democrats were able to control the 26th Congress even without the speakership. In the subsequent four Congresses, a combination of factors conspired to make the election of Speakers more predictable, and having a public record of which party members failed to support the caucus candidate certainly was of use to party leadership.

Still, caucuses were advisory, not binding, and party leaders found it difficult to corral members whose political instincts were intensely regional. Sometimes this did not matter, as in the 27th, 28th, and 29th Congresses, when partisan margins were large enough that some defections could be tolerated. But at other times this *did* matter, as in the 30th Congress, when a narrow partisan majority was hamstrung by a few defections that threatened the organizational control of the chamber.

The events recounted in this chapter were preliminary, though, to the intensifying debate over the role of slavery in America and the grass-roots pressure that would be brought to bear on members of the House over the following decade and a half. In the immediate chapters that follow, we will find that organizational problems that arose in the 30th Congress were just the tip of the iceberg—party leaders would come to realize that the viva voce mechanism that was supposed to tighten up partisan commitments actually backfired. The public vote for Speaker provided information to proslavery and antislavery forces outside the chamber, which fanned the regional flames that had sprung up throughout the country. This would make the work of party leaders who were trying to instill caucus discipline nearly impossible.

Partisan Tumult on the Floor:
The Speakership Elections of 1849 and 1855–1856

❧

The patina of success that surrounded the caucus/public-ballot strategy of selecting House officers would be wiped away in 1849. The cross pressures between party and constituency that had been building throughout the decade, thanks to the growing importance of the slavery issue, could no longer be managed successfully within the existing structure of the interregional two-party system. The free-soil issue, set in motion by the Wilmot Proviso in the summer of 1846, exposed cracks in both the Democratic and Whig Parties, and placed more and more pressure on leaders to hold their regional blocs together. As we discussed in chapter 5, the growing tension associated with slavery extension influenced House officer choices in the 30th Congress (1847–49), when two pivotal Northern Whigs failed to support the party's caucus nominee for Speaker, Robert Winthrop, because his views were insufficiently antislavery. While the Whigs avoided protracted balloting, thanks to the timely support of a non-Whig in that instance, the 1847 speakership contest presaged darker events yet to come.

This chapter examines those darker events, the most difficult instances of officer selection in the history of the House of Representatives. The four speakership elections between 1849 and 1855—covering the 31st–34th Congresses, which are the focus of this chapter—derived their energy from sectional tensions that were building in the nation. The two speakership contests that bookend this period would be especially protracted and divisive. The 1849 election would require 63 ballots and three weeks to yield an outcome, while the 1855 contest would necessitate 133 ballots and two months, bleeding into 1856. In each case, the prior strategy of nominating a slavery moderate in caucus and electing him on the House floor broke down due to the heightened salience of slavery, which worked its way into the electorate and into the attention of the press. No party had a majority in either Congress; the balance of power in each was held by a party with an extreme view on slavery.

In each of these Congresses, increased public awareness of the speakership choice made it infeasible for numerically small minority elements of the two major party caucuses to support the regular party nominees, lest they invite the wrath of their constituents who cared most about slavery. At the same time, insurgent minor parties with intense single-issue mass support, and a desire to demonstrate they could challenge the established parties in the legislative arena, proved not only to be gadflies but to be unworkable coalition partners for the major parties. In the end, these factors made speakership choice practically impossible and prompted an alteration in the voting rule (in both 1849 and 1856) from majority rule to plurality rule before Speakers were elected.

During the Congresses under examination here, the Second Party System would weaken and eventually collapse as the slavery issue overwhelmed the interregional partisanship that had been in place for two decades. The Democrats would suffer a severe blow but survive, while the Whigs would be destroyed, torn apart along a North/South divide. New parties, the Americans and the Republicans, would emerge out of the Whigs' charred remains and compete for the right to settle alongside the Democrats in a new party system. The first institutional victory for the Republicans, a wholly sectional Northern party, would come in the speakership election of 1855–56, when a motley group of "anti-Democratic opposition" members would coalesce around antislavery tenets, elect a Speaker, and establish Republicanism over Americanism as the dominant party paradigm. This would serve as a first glimpse of what would become known as the Third Party System. In time, the Van Burenites' strategy of securing the House organization through the mechanism of a party nominating caucus in advance of a new Congress convening would eventually take hold as the Third Party System consolidated at the conclusion of a bloody civil war.

A SHORT DIGRESSION:
SOPHISTICATED BEHAVIOR AND SPEAKERSHIP ELECTIONS

Before proceeding to an analysis of the speakership contests in 1849 and 1855–56, a word on member intent is needed. The notion that politicians behave in a strategic or sophisticated manner has been a standard element of the rational-choice paradigm for quite some time. As the notion goes, because they are utility-maximizing actors, politicians will sometimes alter their voting behavior and manipulate voting agendas to increase the likelihood of achieving their most preferred outcomes.

Sophisticated voting refers to the way that actors (voters) react to a given binary voting agenda. A sophisticated voter is anticipatory, or forward-looking, in that he focuses on outcomes at the end of the game tree rather than alternatives at any intermediate stage in the agenda. As a result, sophisticated voters will often vote for alternatives early in the agenda that they do not immediately prefer in order to "follow the path" to their most preferred outcome (Farquharson 1969).

Sophisticated agenda setting refers to the manipulation of alternatives under consideration by the agenda setter prior to the voting stage. The placement of alternatives on the agenda—whether early or late, and in consideration against other alternatives in given stages—will have an impact on the outcome achieved *when voters vote sincerely*, that is, when voters select their most preferred alternative at each stage of the agenda. Moreover, the decision regarding which choices will be actual *alternatives* also falls within the rubric of agenda setting. An issue that could potentially beat all others is moot until it is actually placed on the agenda (Levine and Plott 1977).[1]

Speakership elections are generally determined by a form of sophisticated agenda control. During periods of two-party government, party institutions and the party leaders who manage them serve as effective agenda setters. Decisions regarding who the party's speakership candidate will be are traditionally made in caucus prior to the speakership election. Party members are allowed to fight it out behind closed doors until a candidate is selected, after which *all* members are expected to fall in line behind the given nominee on the floor. Thus, speakership elections usually boil down to a choice of two candidates along a basic partisan dimension,[2] with voters selecting their party's nominee and the winner emerging (rather deterministically) from the majority coalition on the first ballot.

Speakership elections during the Second Party System were a case in point. As discussed in chapter 4, passage of viva voce voting led the parties to rely more often on a formal nominating caucus to select candidates. In cases in which one party had a clear numerical advantage (as in 1841, 1843, and 1845), speakership elections were decided on the first ballot. One reason for the efficiency of the selection process had to do with the makeup of the two parties. Both the Whigs and Democrats were interregional coalitions; thus, an issue like slavery, which could drive a wedge between such sectional alliances, was a very real danger to the health of each party. In response to this danger, both Democratic and Whig Party leaders labored to prevent slavery from being a criterion in the selection of a speakership candidate by emphasizing the need to choose policy (slavery) moderates in caucus. Consequently, speakership elections would be decided along a basic partisan dimension. This was but one way in which parties served as solutions to various collective choice problems during the early to mid-nineteenth century.[3]

---

[1] See Ordeshook (1986) for a review of the literatures on agenda setting and sophisticated voting. Manipulation of the issue space itself may also be considered under the rubric of sophisticated agenda setting, although the term "heresthetics" tends to be applied to this practice (Riker 1986).

[2] This is similar to Poole and Rosenthal's (1997, 35, 46) explanation for the low-dimensionality results in congressional roll call voting. They argue that majority party leaders manipulate the voting agenda to include only those issues that separate their party members from the opposing party's members.

[3] See Aldrich (1995) for other examples.

At times, however, the speakership selection process did not run smoothly. This was the case in 1839 and 1847, but it was especially apparent in the latter part of the Second Party System, when the slavery issue exploded onto the national scene and altered partisan dynamics. Third parties emerged— first the Free-Soilers in the late 1840s, then the Americans and Republicans in the mid-1850s—to threaten the two-party equilibrium that had developed in speakership elections. Sometimes this was manifested as a multidimensional speakership race (in the 1849 election), and other times as a three-party battle along a single dimension (the 1855–56 election). Regardless of the details, the rise of viable third parties injected instability into the standard sophisticated agenda-setting process.

However, a question arises. Since the muddled dynamics of these multi-party periods were apparent to all, sophisticated behavior was still an option that could have been exercised to cut through the instability. For example, it is commonly observed that attempts at agenda manipulation can be overcome through sophisticated voting (Enelow and Koehler 1980; Enelow 1981). Given that so much was to be lost by not organizing with regard to both time and policy outputs, it seems odd that lengthy speakership races would be observed. And yet, two very lengthy speakership elections in 1849 and 1855–56 transpired. Were members unable to recognize the costs of a protracted speakership battle and thereby unable to evaluate the alternatives (i.e., candidates) in a sophisticated manner?

We think not. A number of accounts suggest that members of the nineteenth-century Congress were as rational as members are today (Stewart 1989; Jenkins and Sala 1998). A more likely explanation is that members were unable to behave in a sophisticated manner because of electoral considerations. This situation is described by Denzau, Riker, and Shepsle (1985, 1118):

> Result-oriented strategic calculation and sophisticated behavior in the legislative arena may require actions that run contrary to the nominal preferences of important constituents. Although helpful in producing a final result desired by constituents, a strategic vote . . . may nevertheless entail behaving in a manner that directly conflicts with the wishes of constituents. Such actions will need to be explained by the legislator. But can he explain those actions?[4]

This constituent-based explanation is especially relevant to the 1849 and 1855–56 speakership elections, contests that were quite salient and covered extensively in the press. Members of each major party, as well as members from the minor parties, understood that sophisticated voting would produce a much quicker outcome—but was it worth it? A majority-rule outcome in

---

[4] On the issue of members maintaining the trust of their constituents, also see Bianco (1994).

a three-party battle required that members from one of those parties choose a candidate of an opposing party. For members of minor parties (like the Free-Soilers in 1849) or burgeoning parties (like the Republicans and Americans in 1855–56), such a solution could mean partisan destruction. For members of major parties, such a solution could mean electoral fallout in the resulting congressional elections. Either way, *some* members would have had to run the risk of losing their constituents' trust.

Based on the evidence from the 1849 and 1855–56 elections, members felt that the position-taking benefits associated with "saving electoral face" exceeded the time and policy costs associated with an unorganized House. Inevitably, what was accomplished—voting "correctly" on an important issue (the speakership)—appears to have been more visible to constituents than what was not accomplished: an organized House and passage of policy outputs, because in 1849 and 1855–56, a majority never did agree on a speakership candidate. Both speakership elections were eventually decided by a change in the selection rule, from majority rule to plurality rule, which had the practical effect of forcing the third-highest-ranking candidate out of the race. Thus, the House was organized without any members having to incur a position-taking hit.

SECTIONALISM UNBOUND:
THE SPEAKERSHIP ELECTION OF 1849

The speakership battle of 1849 followed the election of 1848, the first national election in which slavery was a major theme. The offering of David Wilmot's (D-Pa.) proviso in August 1846 toward the end of the first session of the 29th Congress (1845–47) was the moment that framed subsequent events. The Wilmot Proviso put the House on record as opposing the expansion of slavery in territories acquired from Mexico. The conclusion of the war in February 1848 during the first session of the 30th Congress (1847–49) brought the matter of slavery expansion to a head, as the issue of organizing these lands began to be pressed upon Congress. Most urgently, the citizens of California were writing a Constitution that, in the end, would prohibit slavery. The admission of California, without a matching slave state to enter alongside it, promised to upset the "balance rule" (Weingast 1996, 1998) that had provided the South with an effective veto in the Senate over legislation that restricted slavery nationally.

The House found itself unable to resolve the slavery extension issue before the first session of the 30th Congress adjourned. Several compromise bills were offered, but a variety of roadblocks emerged (Potter 1976, 75–77). Hoping to regain the presidency, the Whig majority in the House was unwilling to help the Democrats achieve a harmonious ending to Mr. Polk's War. Northern House members in particular were reluctant to sign off on any bill that would allow slavery a foothold in the West for fear of upsetting the growing free-soil coalition in the Northern electorate.

Antislavery extension agitation grew throughout the summer and early fall of 1848, as both Democratic and Whig Party leaders labored to keep free-soil sentiment bottled up and citizens' attention on the traditional issues that divided the parties (Silbey 2009). Not content with working through the two major parties, antislavery advocates began organizing politically; in short order a new party, the Free-Soil Party, had emerged. Made up of disgruntled Conscience Whigs, "Barnburner" Democrats, and members of the abolitionist Liberty Party, the Free-Soil Party held a convention in August 1848 and chose Martin Van Buren as their presidential nominee. Van Buren, who had entered the national scene as the chief architect of the national Democratic Party, was a pariah by summer 1848. Over the previous four years, he had grown increasingly estranged from his old party—he was denied the Democratic presidential nomination in 1844 because Southerners considered his conservative view on Texas annexation to be unacceptable, and his Democratic Party faction in New York (the Barnburners) was increasingly passed over by President Polk when allocating patronage appointments (Silbey 2005). By 1848, Van Buren was willing to kill the national Democratic Party—or, rather, kill the Southern-capitulating leadership that was now controlling the party—in order to save it. Thus, he accepted the Free-Soil nomination and sought to raise the slavery extension issue to a point that would topple the existing interregional duopoly that comprised the Second Party System.

In the end, after great effort, the two parties managed to keep most of their Northern members from straying into the Free-Soil camp. Van Buren was only able to carry 10 percent of the national vote and captured no Electoral College votes. He did, however, receive roughly a quarter of the vote in New York, Massachusetts, and Wisconsin; his strong second-place showing in New York may have cost the Democratic nominee, Lewis Cass (Mich.), a plurality in the state, thus throwing the election to the Whig nominee, Zachary Taylor (La.).

Van Buren's showing not only affected the presidential election, but the congressional elections as well. In the elections of 1848–49, the share of the House vote won by minor parties was 12 percent, up from 6 percent in 1846–47.[5] Virtually all of this increase was directly attributable to the success of Free-Soil congressional candidates, nine of whom were elected to the 31st Congress (1849–51).[6] Moreover, these nine Free-Soilers would be piv-

---

[5] Election results taken from Dubin (1998). Recall that during this period there was no single national Election Day. Congressional elections were held over the course of nearly a year in the various states.

[6] Six of the Free-Soilers in the 31st Congress were rookies who replaced Whigs. Two members from Ohio, Joshua Giddings and Joseph Root, had served in the 30th Congress as Whigs; Amos Tuck, from Massachusetts, had served in the 30th Congress as an Independent.

otal in the chamber, as no party would hold a majority of House seats. The
Democrats would maintain plurality control of the chamber with 113 seats,
while the Whigs controlled 107 (with one American and one vacancy round-
ing things out).[7]

This lack of a majority party in the 31st Congress would prove to be key,
as the lame-duck session of the 30th Congress was unable to reach a resolution on the issue of slavery extension in the western territories. Thus, the
decision would fall to the members of the 31st Congress—which made the
organization of the House crucial to all sides involved.

In the meantime, agitation over the slavery issue continued to heat up. In
December 1848, John C. Calhoun led a caucus of congressional Southern
Whigs who were intent upon forming a Southern party. Ultimately the
movement broke down, but the caucus meetings led to Calhoun's original
"Address to the Southern People," which rehearsed Northern injustices visited upon Southern rights and slavery. The tone of the address implied that
any Southerner who failed to resist Northern aggression to the point of secession was a traitor (Holt 1999, chap. 12). On the other side of the issue,
Northern antislavery forces expressed frustration with the slavery-extension
stances of both parties, which continued to emphasize compromise in various "unionist" formulations.

Hopes for a speedy organization of the House were further dashed when
the parties caucused on the evening of December 1, 1849, to decide on their
nominees for Speaker.[8] First, after some speculation that the Free-Soilers
might caucus with one of the two major parties—especially those such as
Giddings who had strong major party ties—they decided to caucus separately and support Wilmot for Speaker.[9] Second, the Democrats caucused,

[7] These party labels come from Martis (1989, 103). (Later in the session, California would
enter the Union and two additional House seats—controlled by a Democrat and an Independent, respectively—would be added.) As there was fluidity in electoral politics during this era,
party labels of members of Congress were not always known with certainty. For example,
Dubin (1998, 156) counts only eight Free-Soilers at the opening of the 31st Congress, along
with 113 Democrats, 107 Whigs, 1 American, 1 Anti-Rent Whig, and 1 vacancy. The difference
in the Free-Soil count between Martis and Dubin is the coding of John W. Howe (Pa.), whom
Martis classifies as a Free-Soiler and Dubin classifies as a Whig.

[8] Accounts of the various opening caucus proceedings can be found in *NYJC* (12/3/1849, 2;
12/4/1849, 2); *NYEP* (12/4/1849, 2); *RE* (12/4/1849, 2; 12/7/1849, 1, 2); *AA* (12/3/1849, 2);
Daily National Intelligencer (12/3/1849, 3; 12/6/1849, 3); *North American and United States
Gazette* (12/4/1849, 2); and *Boston Courier* (12/6/1849, 2). On the speakership battle more
broadly, see Holt (1999, 461–72), Hamilton (1951, 243–53), and Smith (1988, 106–7).

[9] The *Richmond Enquirer* (12/7/1849, 2) reported that 12 to 15 Free-Soil sympathizers had
held three informal conversations at the National Hotel prior to the convening of the House. A
pledge by these members was made "of entire fidelity to the principle of opposition to the extension of slavery under our Constitution, [and] will in no contingency support any man for
Speaker of the House who will not pledge himself to cordial and effectual co-operation with
them on this principle." This pledge was subscribed to by Preston King (N.Y.), David Wilmot
(Pa.), Walter Booth (Conn.), and Charles Durkee (Wis.), who had previously been Democrats,
and by Amos Tuck (N.H.), Charles Allen (Mass.), Joshua Giddings (Ohio), Joseph Root (Ohio),

choosing Howell Cobb (Ga.) as their nominee.[10] More than 20 Democrats stayed away from the caucus, however, presumably to avoid being bound by its decision.[11]

When the Whigs caucused on the eve of the House's convening, informed speculation held that Winthrop would be easily re-endorsed by his party for Speaker. Therefore, most were shocked when Robert Toombs (Ga.) arose, after the initial organization of the caucus, to offer the resolution "[t]hat Congress ought not to pass any law prohibiting slavery in the territories of California or New Mexico, nor any law abolishing slavery in the District of Columbia" (*Trenton State Gazette*, 12/5/1849, 2).

Toombs's motion led to a heated debate within the caucus, with the preponderance of remarks from both North and South doubting the wisdom of endorsing any resolution that took a position on slavery in the territories.[12] (Recall that Toombs had locked horns with Winthrop in the 30th Congress over legislation with a free-soil provision, which led to Winthrop ordering Toombs to take his seat.) When the Toombs resolution was tabled, he led a walkout of Southern Whigs, later termed the "Impracticables," that was numbered at five or six by the press.[13] The caucus's subsequent endorsement of Winthrop by acclamation was anticlimactic and tarnished.[14]

John W. Howe (Pa.), and William Sprague (Mich.), who had previously been associated with the Whigs. Sprague later switched his allegiance back to Winthrop. The *New York Evening Post* (12/4/1849, 2) also claimed that George Washington Julian (Ind.) would act in concert with the Free-Soilers and that Chauncey Cleveland (Conn.) and Loren P. Waldo (Conn.) would oppose both Cobb and Winthrop.

[10] The *New York Evening Post* (12/4/1849, 2) reported that John L. Robinson (Ind.) nominated Cobb, Richard K. Meade (Va.) nominated W. A. Richardson (Ill.), Milo M. Dimmick (Pa.) nominated James Thompson (Ill.), and David K. Cartter (Ohio) nominated Emery D. Potter (Ohio). The results were as follows: Cobb (47), Richardson (14), Thompson (11), and Potter (7). If the *Richmond Enquirer*'s (12/4/1849, 2) claim that 87 Democrats were in attendance is true, then eight Democrats abstained from the nominating ballot. Because 113 Democrats were elected to the 31st House and almost all had arrived in Washington in time for the caucus, about two dozen Democrats did not attend the caucus meeting at all.

[11] The Democrats also nominated John W. Forney (Pa.) for Clerk, Newton Layne (Ky.) for Sergeant at Arms, and Benjamin F. Brown (Ohio) as Doorkeeper.

[12] The *Richmond Enquirer* (12/7/1849, 2) report, drawing from the *New York Express* correspondent (Horace Greeley), records the following as opposing the Toombs motion: Edward Stanly (N.C.), William Duer (N.Y.), Daniel Breck (Ky.), Alexander Evans (Md.), Edward D. Baker (Ill.), James G. King (N.J.), James Brooks (N.Y.), Thomas L. Clingman (N.C.), George Ashmun (Mass.), Robert C. Schenck (Ohio), and Charles M. Conrad (La.). Henry W. Hilliard (Ala.), Allen F. Owen (Ga.), and Alexander Stephens (Ga.) spoke in favor of passing the resolution.

[13] The *NYEP* (12/4/1849, 2), *Trenton State Gazette* (12/5/1849, 2), and *Boston Courier* (12/6/1849, 2) reported 6; the *Richmond Enquirer* (12/7/1849, 2) and the *Daily National Intelligencer* (12/6/1849, 3) reported "5 or 6." The *Courier* and *Gazette* identified the caucus bolters as Toombs, Alexander Stephens (Ga.), Allen F. Owen (Ga.), Henry W. Hilliard (Ala.), Edward C. Cabell (Fla.), and Jeremiah Morton (Va.).

[14] The Whig caucus was so consumed by the issue of opposition to the Wilmot Proviso that it did not get around to making nominations for Clerk and Sergeant at Arms.

TABLE 6.1.
First ballot for Speaker, 31st Congress (1849)

	Party				
	Dem.	Whigs	F.S.	Amer.	Total
Howell Cobb (Ga.)	102				102
Chauncey Cleveland (Conn.)	1				1
David Disney (Ohio)	1				1
James L. Orr (S.C.)	1				1
Joseph Root (Ohio)	1				1
James A. Seddon (Va.)	1				1
James Thompson (Pa.)	1				1
Robert Winthrop (Mass.)		95		1	96
Horace Mann (Mass.)		2			2
Meredith Gentry (Tenn.)		6			6
David Wilmot (Pa.)			8		8
Total	108	103	8	1	220

When the 31st Congress convened on Monday, December 3, divisions within the two major parties and the separate organization of the Free-Soil Party led to a badly split first ballot for Speaker, even though the Democrats and Whigs mostly held together. The first ballot is summarized in table 6.1. The vote results revealed the two major parties to be almost perfectly matched numerically, making the Free-Soil contingent the focus of attention on both sides.[15] However, subsequent events proved the Free-Soilers to be anything but pivotal in a technical sense. Because they themselves were made up of an equal number of erstwhile Democrats and Whigs, efforts to side with one or the other of the major parties proved internally divisive. And, as we will see, the migration of the Free-Soilers to any one candidate raised suspicions among Southerners of both parties, which made it nearly impossible to build a majority coalition that involved Free-Soil members.

The scattering vote of both parties is almost entirely explained by divisions over slavery. On the Whig side, the six Impracticables threw their votes to Meredith Gentry (W-Tenn.), who had not even arrived on the scene to protest their action. Two Northern Whigs with free-soil tendencies voted for Horace Mann (W-Mass.). On the other side of the House, the irregular Democrats also cast votes in line with their feelings on slavery, although they did not coordinate their voting to the same degree as the Impracticables. The ballots for Root, Cleveland, and Disney (table 6.1) were cast by

[15] The *Richmond Enquirer* (12/7/1849, 2) reported that on the first day of the session, five Whigs, two Democrats, and one Free-Soiler had not yet arrived in town. Adding these members to those actually in attendance on the opening day would have brought the partisan division even closer.

House members who had expressed support for the Wilmot Proviso (Wilmot himself, Thompson, and Doty); the ballots for Seddon and Orr were cast by South Carolinians.[16] An additional three ballots were held on December 3, still with no majority winner. While participants realized that further balloting could be protracted, few could have predicted that a full three weeks would be necessary to elect a Speaker.

Figure 6.1 helps to summarize the voting over the three weeks as the House searched for a way around this impasse. (For a breakdown of the balloting, see appendix 2.) For each ballot, we have plotted (a) the number of votes necessary to achieve a majority, (b) the total number of votes received by all of the Democratic and Whig candidates, and (c) the number of votes received by the top Democratic and Whig vote-getter. Letters indicate, for each ballot, which candidate was the top vote-getter. (The legend below the plots associates the letters with the candidates.) Finally, below the plots, we have indicated where the ballots fell with respect to the three weeks, and where caucuses were held, as reported in the press.

Until the middle of the second week of balloting, the Whigs remained firmly committed to Winthrop. His vote total grew glacially, as one Impracticable (Hilliard [Ala.]) came over to his side and a few other Whigs either arrived in town or abandoned their scattering of votes. The Democrats, however, sought out alternatives to Cobb more actively, as his support immediately began slipping after the first ballot. Leaders began looking to the West (trans-Appalachia) for alternatives, in the hopes that a non-Southerner might attract the support of either irregular Democrats or even the Free-Soil members themselves. Emery Potter (Ohio) and William Richardson (Ill.), who had challenged Cobb for the Democratic endorsement in the nominating caucus, were both identified as possibilities. Supporters of their candidacies broke from the caucus's endorsement of Cobb by the middle of the first week. The caucus formally endorsed Potter as the first week of balloting came to a close.[17]

On December 8, beginning with the 24th ballot, Potter became the top Democratic vote-getter. Even though Potter's vote totals rose ever upward, they peaked at a level (78) considerably below Winthrop's (102). Southern Democrats were particularly reluctant to support Potter, who was cagey on the issue of slavery extension. As a reporter for the *Vermont Watchman and State Journal* noted, "Many Southern men called upon Mr. Potter to ascertain his views [on the Wilmot Proviso]. He simply said he will be governed by no sectional ends" (12/13/1849, 2).

Informal politicking over the weekend failed to rally Southern Democrats around either Potter or Richardson. The Democrats then decided formally

---

[16] The *NYJC* (12/5/1849, 2) correspondent counted the party votes somewhat differently, claiming that 14 Free-Soilers had voted, along with 6 Impracticable Southern Whigs.

[17] Proceedings of the Democratic caucus that endorsed Potter can be found in *NYJC* (12/6/1849, 3; 12/10/1849, 3) and *NYEP* (12/6/1849, 2, 3).

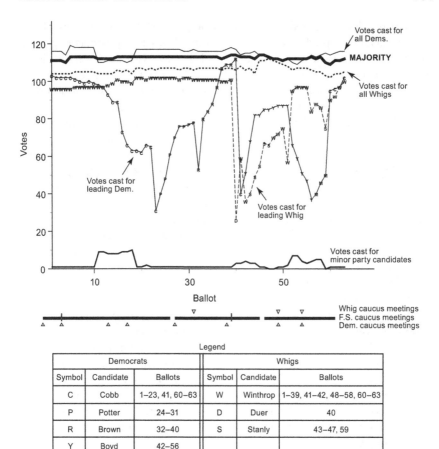

FIGURE 6.1. Summary of speakership balloting, 31st Congress. The dark solid lines below the graph indicate the three weeks during which balloting proceeded. (Week 1: Mon., Dec. 3, 1849 to Sat., Dec. 8, 1849; Week 2: Mon., Dec. 10, 1849 to Sat., Dec. 15, 1849; Week 4: Mon, Dec. 17, 1849 to Sat., Dec. 22, 1849.) The open triangles pointing downward indicate recorded Whig caucuses (Dec. 11, 18, and 19). The open triangles pointing upward indicate recorded Democratic caucuses (Dec. 3, 4, 6, 7, 10, 12, 18, and 19). The vertical lines indicate recorded Free-Soil caucuses (Dec. 4 and 13).

to abandon Potter, settling instead on William J. Brown (Ind.). After three ballots on December 10, Potter formally withdrew and Brown became the top Democratic vote-getter—on the 32nd ballot (and last of the day).

Brown was an inspired choice. Although "feeble in health" (*New York Journal of Commerce* [hereafter abbreviated as *NYJC*], 12/6/1849, 3 and 12/13/1849, 2), he was a westerner who could also appeal to Southerners.

He had previously served in the 28th Congress (1843–45), but his House service was interrupted when he was appointed assistant postmaster general in the Polk administration. Consequently, Brown was absent from the House when the principles involved in the Wilmot Proviso were first voted on.

In addition, in his role as assistant postmaster general, Brown had been responsible for overseeing patronage appointments. During the election of 1848, he had a direct hand in the sacking of local postmasters in western New York State who disagreed with the party's presidential nominee, Lewis Cass, on slavery. (Cass took a position he called "squatter sovereignty," which later became Stephen A. Douglas's "popular sovereignty.") Brown's efforts in New York ultimately came to naught, as Cass failed to carry the state. However, Brown endeared himself to Southern Unionists, who admired his actions in imposing party orthodoxy concerning slavery in Northern locales where free-soil sentiments were strong. Finally, although Indiana had pockets of free-soil sentiment, Brown's own central Indiana district was virtually devoid of it—of the 16,000 votes cast for president in 1848 from the Fifth District, Van Buren received only 600.

On the morning of December 11, Brown received 80 votes on the first ballot of the day (and 33rd ballot overall), garnering solid support from all regions. By the end of the day's seven ballots, Brown's total had risen to 109, more than Cobb had ever received, and five short of a majority. The election seemed in the bag. Winthrop, sensing his imminent defeat, withdrew his candidacy in an emotional speech from the floor (*CG*, 31-1, 12/11/1849, 17). Winthrop's impromptu exit took the Whig rank and file by surprise. Needing to regroup, the Whigs managed to tie up the House in parliamentary knots for the rest of the afternoon. The House eventually adjourned for the evening, without taking another ballot.

Balloting resumed the next day amid rumors that Brown had consummated a deal with Free-Soil members overnight. Great excitement was stirred when the third name was reached on the roll—Charles Allen, a Free-Soil member from Massachusetts. Allen had been dutifully casting his ballot for Wilmot for nearly two weeks. This time he answered with the name "Brown," thus confirming the rumor. Once this ballot was complete, six Free-Soil members had switched their support to Brown.

If Brown's previous support had held firm, he would have been elected Speaker. However, in the midst of the balloting, three Southern Democrats who had previously supported him—Thomas S. Bocock (Va.), James A. Seddon (Va.), and Daniel Wallace (S.C.)—threw away their votes, casting them instead for Linn Boyd (D-Ky.). As a result, Brown fell two votes short of a majority.

The motivations of Bocock, Seddon, and Wallace became clear when Edward Stanly (W-N.C.) gained the floor and confronted Brown directly as to whether he had made a deal with David Wilmot concerning the composition of the committees.[18] After Brown's supporters equivocated in his defense, Brown himself responded, confirming that he had indeed communicated with Wilmot about the organization of the House. Wilmot then took the floor and confirmed that he had conversed with Brown (*CG*, 31-1, 12/12/1849, 21).

The chamber erupted. After the Clerk successfully restored order in the hall, Brown read from a letter that he claimed to have sent to Wilmot, the substance of which was as follows:

> Should I [Brown] be elected Speaker of the House of Representatives, I will constitute the Committees on the District of Columbia, on Territories, and on the Judiciary, in such a manner as shall be satisfactory to yourself and your friends. I am a representative from a free state, and have always been opposed to the extension of slavery, and believe that the Federal Government should be relieved from the responsibility of slavery, where they have the constitutional power to abolish it. (*CG*, 31-1, 12/12/1849, 22)

Brown's Southern supporters sat ashen-faced as the letter was read. Pandemonium then followed, as Southern Democrats and Whigs denounced this devil's pact between the Democratic candidate for Speaker and the Free-Soil leader. The House adjourned without taking another ballot that day. A Democratic caucus held that night was inconclusive. The House reconvened the following day, December 13, "in a state of uncertainty, hesitation, and confusion" (*NYJC*, 12/15/1849, 3). The parties were in disarray, as evidenced by 30 men receiving at least one vote on the 41st ballot—and six receiving more than 10 votes.

Both parties struggled to coordinate for the remainder of the week. Most Democrats informally rallied behind Linn Boyd (Ky.), while most Whigs supported Edward Stanly (N.C.). Still, neither party could fall in line behind a single nominee, and voting took on a highly regional cast in both parties, which had not happened previously. Floor proceedings also took a highly regional and acrimonious turn. A confrontation between William Duer (W-N.Y.) and Richard Meade (D-Va.) ensued, as the two nearly came to blows on the floor.[19]

As balloting continued into a third week, a resolution to the contest seemed no closer. Boyd continued as the Democrats' leading candidate, while the Whigs swung their support back to Winthrop beginning on the 48th ballot. But rifts within each party left both candidates far from a ma-

---

[18] In addition to the official proceeding in the *Congressional Globe*, accounts of this episode appear in *NYEP* (12/13/1849, 2; 12/14/1849, 2, 3; 12/15/1849, 1, 3). Brown's explanation appears in *AA* (12/17/1849, 3) and *RE* (12/18/1849, 3).

[19] See *NYEP* (12/14/1849, 2, 3) and the (New York) *Weekly Herald* (12/15/1849, 396).

jority. As a result, unconventional proposals to settle the speakership battle became more common. Throughout the previous two weeks, motions had been made to settle the affair by lot, by successive elimination of low-ranking candidates, and by plurality. Each was tabled in turn. Now, however, members who preferred *any* organization of the House to continued stalemate became willing to compromise.

The opening came on the evening of December 19, when the Whig caucus adopted a resolution proposing that six Democrats join a committee of six Whigs to suggest "a mode of definitive organization of the House of Representatives, upon just and fair principles" (*NYJC*, 12/22/1849, 3). The Democrats accepted the Whig invitation and appointed six members of their own.[20]

By the time the "Conference Committee" met on the evening of December 20, the House had taken 59 ballots with no resolution in sight—the 59th ballot indicated the general disorder in the floor proceedings, as 21 different individuals received votes (*CG*, 31-1, 12/20/1849, 51). The committee reached no decision that evening, and it was agreed that balloting would be suspended on the following day while the committee assembled again. Eventually, a majority of the committee agreed to a plan in which the speakership battle would be settled by plurality. There would be three more ballots in an attempt to resolve the matter by majority vote. If no majority emerged, then a final ballot would be held in which the plurality winner would be declared Speaker. All of the Whigs on the committee supported the plan; the Democrats were split. The Whig caucus unanimously endorsed the proposal of the Conference Committee; the Democratic caucus was divided.

Just how divided the Democrats were is the source of some confusion, because newspaper accounts varied in how they reported the Democratic reception to the plan. The *New York Evening Post* (12/24/1849, 1) claimed that the proposal lost in caucus on a 50–30 vote, while the *Trenton State Gazette* (12/24/1849, 2) reported that the compromise "was rejected by a majority of ten or twelve." On the other hand, the *Boston Daily Atlas* (12/24/1849, 2) and *Albany Argus* (12/24/1849, 2) claimed that the caucus endorsed the plan "by a majority of twelve."

[20] Both parties' resolutions are reprinted in *CG*, 31-1, 12/20/1849, 49. The committee was composed as follows:

Whigs		Democrats	
Hugh White	N.Y.	James Thompson	Pa.
George Ashmun	Mass.	Frederick Stanton	Tenn.
Samuel Vinton	Ohio	John McClernand	Ill.
Daniel Breck	Ky.	Emery Potter	Ohio
Charles Conrad	La.	Sampson Harris	Ala.
Edward Stanly	N.C.	Thomas Bayly	Va.

TABLE 6.2.
Regional support for plurality election of Speaker, 31st Congress

	North	West	South	Total
Dem.	.40	.19	.16	.21
	(20)	(32)	(56)	(108)
Whig	1.00	.67	.69	.88
	(62)	(12)	(26)	(100)
Total	.85	.32	.33	.53
	(82)	(44)	(84)	(208)

Note: Entries are the fraction favoring plurality election (Ns in parentheses).

There was also confusion about the implied arrangement between the parties, if any, and the motivations behind the actors. The *Albany Argus* later reported:

> It is said that at least two of the whig committee, Mr. Ashmun and Mr. Vinton, had anticipated [the ultimate election of Cobb], making no mistake in their calculation as to every vote given. But they and the whigs generally were desirous of bringing the struggle to a close, and in fact, saw little chance of electing Mr. Winthrop. (12/28/1849, 3)

In addition, reports from the Whig caucus claimed that those in attendance assumed that the result would be the election of Cobb as Speaker in return for allowing Whigs to dominate the Finance and Foreign Affairs Committees. At the same time, reports from the Democratic caucus claimed that those in attendance *there* assumed exactly the opposite would happen— Winthrop would be Speaker, but Democrats would control the most important policy committees. In any event, it *is* known that the Democratic and Whig caucuses chose to regroup around Cobb and Winthrop, respectively. Lines were drawn for a final battle on the floor.

When the House reconvened on Saturday morning, December 22, Frederick P. Stanton (D-Tenn.) made the motion on behalf of the Conference Committee. After considerable parliamentary maneuvering, the motion carried, 113–105 (*CG*, 31-1, 12/22/1849, 65). Most Whigs favored it (88–12) and most Democrats opposed it (23–85), while all eight Free-Soilers voted nay. Voting also betrayed a regional structure, which is illustrated in table 6.2. All Northern Whigs and almost half of the Northern Democrats supported plurality rule, while only two-thirds of the remaining Whigs and less than one-fifth of the remaining Democrats supported it.

The structure of support for the plurality rule becomes more intriguing when we analyze the vote in a multivariate context. To do so, we estimated a probit regression in which support for the plurality rule resolution is the dependent variable and measures for region (South = 1); party irregularity

TABLE 6.3.
Vote on conducting ballot for Speaker under plurality rule, 1849 (robust standard errors in parentheses)[a]

	Party		
	All	Democrats	Whigs
South	-1.68***	-2.02***	-0.34
	(0.46)	(0.62)	(0.81)
Irregular	-1.17*	-0.55	-3.13***
	(0.53)	(0.68)	(0.63)
W-NOMINATE 1st dimension	2.02***	1.93	13.74***
(party)	(0.29)	(1.12)	(3.39)
W-NOMINATE 2nd dimension	1.47***	1.34**	4.97***
(slavery)	(0.33)	(0.50)	(1.27)
Election percentage	-1.63	-3.50*	5.15
	(0.86)	(1.64)	(2.98)
Constant	1.47**	2.74**	-6.46**
	(0.58)	(1.02)	(2.43)
N	206	97	100
χ^2	103.18	19.71	39.39
LLF	-71.45	-42.02	-11.11
Pseudo R^2	.50	.23	.71

*$p < .05$; **$p < .01$; ***$p < .001$.
[a]Dependent variable is ICPSR Study No. 9822, 31st Congress, roll call number 26, probit coefficients.

in the support of Speaker nominees (Irregular = 1), defined here as a majority party member who refused to vote for his party's Speaker nominee on the first ballot; ideology (as measured by the two W-NOMINATE dimensions); and vote margin in the last election (as measured by the percentage of the vote cast for the incumbent) are the independent variables. Table 6.3 reports the results of these regressions.

In the multivariate analysis, the South, once again, was less likely to support the plurality rule motion after controlling for other factors. Party irregularity also had a negative effect, especially among the Whigs, whose Impracticables had been key in preventing the House from organizing under the majority-vote rule. The most interesting effects, however, are the two ideological variables as measured by the first two dimensions of the W-NOMINATE scores. In this Congress, the first W-NOMINATE dimension, which "represents conflict over the role of government in the economy" (Poole and Rosenthal 1997, 35), was highly correlated with party (negative signs associated with Democrats), while the second W-NOMINATE dimension was highly correlated with slavery (positive signs associated with being proslavery). It is not surprising, given the marginals, that the first (party) dimension has a positive sign—strong Democratic partisans tended to oppose plurality the most. It *is* surprising that proslavery members also favored plurality. Given the role of the proslavery Impracticables in complicating the Whigs' nominating caucus, one would have supposed that proslavery members on the whole would have seen the plurality rule as a way around their objections.

Also intriguing is the effect of electoral margin on support for the plurality rule. The effect interacts with partisanship. Marginal Democrats supported the plurality rule more than safe Democrats, whereas safe Whigs were more likely to favor the rule. This is an interesting finding that deserves further analysis, since we expected electorally marginal members of *both parties* to be more inclined to hide behind the effect of the plurality rule than electorally safe members.

The adoption of the plurality resolution set the stage for the final rounds of voting. On December 22, the House met and moved toward a conclusion. On the 60th ballot—the first of three majority-rule ballots following the committee agreement—Cobb received 93 votes, Winthrop 88, Wilmot 9, and 26 votes scattered among 10 other candidates. On the 61st ballot, Cobb picked up 2 votes, Winthrop 4, and Wilmot held steady, leaving the margin at 95–92–9, with 23 scattering among 10 candidates. (Three former abstainers now entered.) On the 62nd ballot Winthrop picked up another 3 votes, leaving him tied with Cobb at 95, with 9 votes still for Wilmot and 21 scattering.

The end was at hand. The agreed-upon three majority-rule ballots failed to produce a majority winner. Thus, the 63rd ballot would be the *final* ballot, and it would be decided by plurality rule. When the balloting was completed and the Clerk had finished his tabulation, Winthrop picked up 4 new votes, but Cobb bested him with 6 new votes, which resulted in a final tally of 101 for Cobb, 99 for Winthrop, 8 for Wilmot, and 12 scattering (CG, 31-1, 12/22/1849, 66). Cobb had won the speakership.

Breaking down the final balloting results, Cobb's biggest problem came from Democrats with free-soil proclivities. Ultimately, some of these members, including three from Indiana (Joseph E. McDonald, Graham N. Fitch, and Andrew J. Harlan) and three from Ohio (John K. Miller, Joseph Cable, and David K. Cartter), came to Cobb's aid, which proved to be decisive. Winthrop had exactly the opposite problem as Cobb. When the last stage of balloting began on the 60th ballot, Winthrop faced two sets of defectors—the Impracticables and a set of more moderate Northerners. As the balloting progressed, Winthrop easily won the support of the moderate Whigs but picked up no appreciable support among the Impracticables.

A final postscript on the organizational politics of the 31st House raises two points worth noting. First, on the Monday following his election as Speaker (December 31), Cobb announced his committee assignments (CG, 31-1, 12/31/1849, 88–89). While there had been some concerns raised by Democrats prior to the conclusion of the speakership balloting—around the time the Conference Committee was formed—as to whether Cobb would stack committees (especially important ones) with Democratic members, these proved to be overblown. Cobb's assignments are reported in table 6.4. Like Winthrop, his Whig predecessor in the 30th Congress, Cobb proved to be quite partisan in his appointment of chairs and committee majorities.

Digging deeper, for the most important committees, Cobb tended to favor the appointment of *Southern* Democrats over *Northern* Democrats. However, he was also more willing to spread out committee appointments among all regional and partisan factions—much more so than Winthrop had done as Speaker in the previous Congress. This is illustrated in table 6.5, which compares Winthrop's and Cobb's appointments to three contentious committees—Judiciary, Territories, and District of Columbia. While Winthrop had constructed these committees to be ideologically moderate (see table 5.4), he did so without appointing regionally balanced Whig contingents. In fact, he chose *none* of his Southern copartisans to serve on Judiciary and Territories and instead favored Southern *Democrats* when he wished for regional diversity. (Winthrop's District of Columbia Committee was regionally balanced.) Cobb, on the other hand, spread his appointments fairly evenly among the various factions. Not only did Cobb ensure that Northerners and Southerners from both parties were appointed to all three committees, he even appointed a Free-Soil member (!) to these committees as well.

Second, the election for Clerk, which was the first order of business when the House reconvened in the New Year, inherited some of the contentiousness that plagued the speakership contest. More than a week and 20 ballots were needed before an outcome was achieved.[21] (See appendix 3 for a breakdown.) A hint that a quick resolution would not be forthcoming was suggested when 11 different names were placed in nomination before the balloting began (*CG*, 31-1, 1/3/1850, 95). Nonetheless, John W. Forney, the Democratic caucus nominee, was within striking distance of a majority on multiple ballots (coming as close as two votes shy on the second ballot) but could not break through. The Whigs did not produce a caucus nominee.[22] Instead, they informally coordinated on current Clerk Thomas J. Campbell (Tenn.) at the outset, before later turning to Solomon Foot (former House member from Vermont) on the 7th–15th ballots and Philander B. Prindle (N.Y.) on the 16th–17th ballots.[23] On the 18th ballot, the Whigs shifted

[21] The *Albany Argus* reported that the Democrats wanted to extend plurality voting to the other officers, but that the Whigs resisted, standing "for the old rule for a majority" (12/28/1849, 3).

[22] After failing to nominate a candidate for Clerk in early December, the Whigs met a second time in early January, but once again could not settle on a nominee. A correspondent for the *Boston Daily Atlas* reported that "The Whigs seem to think, if the present officers hold over under the law, they are well enough off, or as well as could be expected" (1/8/1850, 2).

[23] Note that Prindle's first name is identified as "Orlando" in the *Congressional Globe*. See, for example, *CG*, 31-1, 1/3/1850, 95.

TABLE 6.4.
House committee assignments, 31st Congress

Committee	Chair (party-state)	Members	Dem.	Whigs
Elections	William Strong (D-Pa.)	9	5	4
Ways and Means	Thomas H. Bayly (D-Va.)	9	5	4
Claims	John R. J. Daniel (D-N.C.)	9	5	3
Commerce	Robert M. McLane (D-Md.)	9	5	4
Public Lands	James B. Bowlin (D-Mo.)	9	5	4
Post Office and Post Roads	Emery D. Potter (D-Ohio)	9	5	3
District of Columbia	Albert G. Brown (D-Miss.)	9	4	4
Judiciary	James Thompson (D-Pa.)	9	5	3
Revolutionary Claims	Cullen Sawtelle (D-Maine)	9	5	4
Public Expenditures	Andrew Johnson (D-Tenn.)	9	4	4
Private Land Claims	Isaac E. Morse (D-La.)	9	5	4
Manufactures	Lucius B. Peck (D-Vt.)	9	5	4
Agriculture	Nathaniel S. Littlefield (D-Maine)	9	5	4
Indian Affairs	Robert W. Johnson (D-Ark.)	9	5	4
Military Affairs	Armistead Burt (D-S.C.)	9	5	4
Militia	Charles H. Peaslee (D-N.H.)	9	5	4
Naval Affairs	Frederick P. Stanton (D-Tenn.)	9	5	3
Foreign Affairs	John A. McClernand (D-Ill.)	9	5	4
Territories	Linn Boyd (D-Ky.)	9	5	3
Revolutionary Pensions	Loren P. Waldo (D-Conn.)	9	4	4
Invalid Pensions	Shepherd Leffler (D-Iowa)	9	5	4
Roads and Canals	John L. Robinson (D-Ind.)	9	5	3
Patents	Hiram Walden (D-N.Y.)	5	3	2
Public Buildings & Grounds	Franklin W. Bowdon (D-Ala.)	5	3	2
Revisal and Unfin. Business	Williamson R. W. Cobb (D-Ala.)	5	2	2
Accounts	Daniel P. King (W-Mass.)	5	3	2
Mileage	Graham N. Fitch (D-Ind.)	5	3	2
Engraving	Edward Hammond (D-Md.)	3	2	1
Rules	David S. Kaufman (D-Tex.)	9	5	4
Exp. in State Dept.	Kinsley S. Bingham (D-Mich.)	5	3	2
Exp. in Treasury Dept.	George A. Caldwell (D-Ky.)	5	3	2
Exp. in War Dept.	Milo M. Dimmick (D-Pa.)	5	3	2
Exp. in Navy Dept.	Alexander R. Holladay (D-Va.)	5	3	2
Exp. in Post Office Dept.	William Thompson (D-Iowa)	5	3	2
Exp. on Public Buildings	James M. H. Beale (D-Va.)	5	3	2

Note: The following Free-Soilers also served: Joseph M. Root (Ohio) on Claims; Charles Durkee (Wis.) on Post Office and Post Roads; Charles Allen (Mass.) on D.C.; Preston King (N.Y.) on Judiciary; Walter Booth (Conn.) on Public Expenditures; Joshua Giddings (Ohio) on Territories; Amos Tuck (N.H.) on Revolutionary Pensions; John W. Howe (Pa.) on Roads and Canals; and George W. Julian (Ind.) on Revisal and Unfinished Business. American Lewis C. Levin (Pa.) served on Naval Affairs.

TABLE 6.5.
Comparison of Winthrop's committee appointments (30th Congress) with Cobb's
(31st Congress)

	N. Whig	S. Whig	N. Dem.	S. Dem.	Free Soil
Winthrop					
Judiciary	5	0	2	2	
Territories	5	0	2	2	
D.C.	3	2	2	2	
Cobb					
Judiciary	2	1	2	3	1
Territories	2	1	2	3	1
D.C.	2	2	1	3	1

back to Campbell, and he took the lead from Forney. Campbell's vote total increased by seven votes on the 19th ballot, leaving him seven votes from election. And on the 20th ballot, Campbell gained nine additional votes, which provided him with a two-vote majority and the clerkship.

Thus, the Democratic caucus nominee for Clerk was defeated, and a Whig was installed.[24] The outcome was bad enough for the Democrats. But the *way* the drama unfolded was even worse. The last push that put Campbell over the top was accomplished through the efforts of Southern Democrats. Specifically, eight of Campbell's votes on the 20th ballot were cast by Democrats from the South.[25] One of the Southern Democrats in question, Abraham W. Venable (N.C.), justified his (and his comrades') actions by claiming that he had supported Forney through a majority of the ballots (which was true), but grew to believe that Forney could not win; he found Campbell to be "a gentleman and a competent officer," and felt that he owed it to his constituents to complete the organization and allow Congress to get down to business.[26]

[24] The minor House offices also gave the Democrats trouble. Their caucus nominee for Sergeant at Arms, Newton Lane (Ky.), was not able to win a quick victory, and had his name withdrawn after the fourth unsuccessful ballot. Eventually, the Democrats turned to Adam J. Glossbrenner (Pa.) and, with the help of four Free-Soilers, elected him on the eighth ballot. The election for Doorkeeper extended for 14 ballots without producing a majority winner. At that point, the House agreed to postpone further balloting for Doorkeeper *and* Postmaster until March 1, 1851 (two days before the end of the Congress). The House later postponed the elections indefinitely. This had the effect of allowing the Doorkeeper and Postmaster from the 30th Congress—Robert E. Horner (N.J.), a Whig, and John M. Johnson (Va.), a Democrat—to maintain their duties throughout the 31st Congress.

[25] These eight Southern Democrats were William F. Colcock (S.C.), Andrew Ewing (Tenn.), David Hubbard (Ala.), John McQueen (S.C.), Joseph A. Woodward (S.C.), James L. Orr (S.C.), Abraham W. Venable (N.C.), and Daniel Wallace (S.C.).

[26] Remarks by Venable published in the *Fayetteville Observer*, 1/22/1850, 3.

The pragmatism expressed by Venable was not shared by many in the press who were covering the drama. For them, the regional impulse had trumped party, and this was a critical moment that could not be glossed over. A correspondent for the *Baltimore Sun* reported, "The House has, at last, made a Clerk by overthrowing King Caucus. The power of caucuses is pretty well ended, in the House of Representatives" (1/11/1850, published in the *Greenville Mountaineer*, 1/25/1850, 1). An editorial in the *Bangor Daily Whig and Courier* further stated: "The Democrats are indignant at the defeat of Mr. Forney, and confidence in caucus nominations is pretty well shaken" (1/17/1850, 2). In the end, Southerners joined together to elect a Whig Clerk.[27]

Campbell would die in office just over three months later. Another multiballot affair would be necessary to select a replacement. After two days and nine ballots, Richard M. Young, a former Jacksonian senator from Illinois, was elected. Perhaps still smarting over the Campbell drama, the Democrats did not call a caucus for the purpose of choosing a party nominee.[28] Rather, an initial show of strength was conducted on the first ballot, with Young garnering more votes than any other Democratic candidate (including Forney, whose name was once again placed in nomination). Slowly, over the course of the balloting, additional votes moved his way, until he finally secured a two-vote majority on the ninth ballot. Despite his Northern affiliation, Young was deemed acceptable by Southern Democrats, because he was raised in Kentucky and was appointed commissioner of the General Land Office by President Polk. Thus, after much drama and intrapartisan wrangling, the Democrats would control the key House officer positions for much of the 31st Congress.

In stepping back and assessing the importance of the speakership election of 1849, we recognize it as the first of a series in which an important ritual that had cemented the Second Party System—the selection of regional moderates to preside over the House using the mechanism of the party nominating caucus—became politically untenable. Thus, the institutionalization of the arrangement sought by Van Buren, which we call the organizational cartel, was still a long way off.

In the Congresses that were organized in the early years of the viva voce regime, the parties were able to organize themselves around the principles that had given rise to the parties in the first place, that is, their divergent views about the proper road to economic development and the balance of power between the states and Washington. (The 26th Congress, of course, was the exception to this statement.) In the best of all worlds, whichever

[27] For additional editorial commentary on the resolution of the clerkship battle, see *North American and United States Gazette* (1/15/1850, 2), *Daily National Intelligencer* (1/16/1850, 3), and *Fayetteville Observer* (1/22/1850, 3).

[28] *Daily Ohio Statesman* (4/22/1850, 3).

party held the majority desired to choose a Speaker who would best help achieve these partisan aims. Because this individual could be a Northerner or a Southerner, and might also hold either moderate or extreme views on slavery, the partisans of both sides wished they could rally behind the best candidate, disregarding geography. Electoral politics prohibited that, however. Thus, a second-best strategy emerged: selecting the best Speaker among the set of slavery moderates.

As we have just seen, however, when slavery became a hot issue in the elections of 1848–49, even this second-best strategy was no longer a safe choice for many House members. Facing electoral agitation at home, a small number of members in both parties felt compelled to abandon their party. The close Democrat-Whig margin complicated matters further. The ensuing stalemate only drew more and more newspaper attention the House's way. The presence of the Free-Soilers as the swing bloc only heightened this attention.[29]

The looming presence of slavery behind the balloting for Speaker in the 31st Congress is illustrated in figure 6.2, which graphs the degree to which individual House members' support for slavery (measured by their second-dimension W-NOMINATE scores in the 31st Congress) was correlated with their chosen speakership candidates' support for slavery (measured by the *candidates'* second-dimension W-NOMINATE scores). Here we see that in early balloting the unified Democratic support for Cobb meant that the Democratic vote for Speaker was not determined by support for slavery. The Whig schism resulted in a greater correlation between members' preferences for slavery and the candidates they supported for Speaker. As the balloting progressed, the dissolving Democratic unity rapidly led to speakership balloting that was strongly structured along pro- and antislavery lines. The brief rush toward Brown caused the Democrats to submerge their pro- and antislavery tendencies. However, when Brown's candidacy disintegrated, members spent a week simply voting for candidates within their respective parties who agreed with them on the slavery issue. This was clearly not a time to submerge one's own preferences for the good of the party. It was a time to take a position! The imposition of the plurality rule lessened the impact that the slavery issue had in the process of choosing a Speaker. Still, the relatively minor role that support for pro- and antislavery positions played in the *final* ballot for Speaker hides the fact that some sort of extra-policy structure was needed to contain temptations to take positions.

The intrusion of slavery into the speakership election of 1849 was brought about by the actions of Robert Toombs of Georgia. Toombs was a puzzling character to lead the charge on the issue, since he was one of the Southerners who had earned Calhoun's ire only a year before when he had

---

[29] Typical of the partisan press of the day, newspaper accounts of the Speaker's power only added fuel to the flame. Although there was plenty of contemporary evidence that Speakers had very little power to "stack" committees and dictate the course of policy, most newspapers treated the Speaker as a dictator.

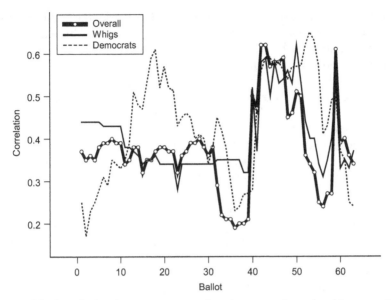

FIGURE 6.2. Correlation between support for slavery and speakership vote, 31st Congress.

refused to endorse Calhoun's Southern Address while supporting (in his district) a measured response to Northern outrages. Modern scholarship suggests the electoral context of Toombs's actions. Holt (1999, 466–72) documents that Toombs found himself in deep political trouble back in Georgia due to his failure to back Calhoun. Democratic gains in recent elections had made Georgia Whigs nervous, and local elites laid some of the blame at the feet of moderates like Toombs. Therefore, it is not unreasonable to conclude that Toombs's actions, and those of his Deep South followers, were intended for consumption back home.

Whether Toombs actually intended for his actions to lead to a stalemate will never be known. Once he had acted, however, the behavior of all Southerners came under close scrutiny, which made compromise impossible. The *New York Journal of Commerce* expressed the situation this way:

> More than one of the six Southern Whigs who are now voting for Gentry [the Impracticable candidate] has stated that there would have been less difficulty in electing Mr. Winthrop, had there been no caucus. The slavery question would not have been lugged into the election of Speaker had not the occasion been offered, by the caucus, for its introduction. Each of those Southern gentlemen, except, perhaps, Mr. Toombs, would have voted for Mr. Winthrop, but for this circumstance. (12/8/1849, 3)

Turning our attention to the other side of the aisle, the William Brown affair handed the Democrats a public relations disaster. Although Brown's later explanation of his actions is self-serving, it contains an unassailable core of Second Party System logic. Brown claimed that Wilmot never asked that Free-Soilers (or free-soilers) dominate the slavery-related committees. All he asked was that they be given representation on the committees, and that the members from the major parties also include Northern members with free-soil sympathies.

It is reasonable to conclude that it was not the agreement between Wilmot and Brown that killed Brown's chances at the speakership but the fact that it was written down—which provided hard evidence to the Southern press about Brown's perfidy. Evidence for this comes from the simple fact that Speaker Cobb implemented precisely the strategy that Brown and Wilmot had agreed to—Free-Soilers and Northern Whigs and Democrats *were* included on the relevant committees, and Northerners held majorities on the Judiciary and Territories committees. The partisan press in the North reacted with outrage about the domination of the *Democratic* contingents of these committees by Southerners, but there is no evidence that Southern newspapers viewed Cobb's appointment of Free-Soil members to these committees as being traitorous.

A Brief Lull: The Speakership Elections of 1851 and 1853

The inability to impose party regularity in the 31st Congress came about because unusual electoral pressures interacted with razor-thin partisan margins within the House. In the following two Congresses, the Democrats held more comfortable margins, which provided much-needed slack in the House organization process. The Compromise of 1850, which settled the slavery-extension issue in the western territories on the basis of "popular sovereignty," was exceedingly controversial and further eroded the stability of the Second Party System (Holt 1978). The Whig Party was hopelessly split by section, and Southern Whigs found it increasingly difficult to remain in partnership with a Northern wing that had become increasingly antislavery. Using this split to make gains in the South, Democrats captured some Whig districts and enticed other Whigs to switch to the Democratic Party.[30]

Prior to the convening of the 32nd Congress (1851–53), the Democratic caucus selected Linn Boyd (Ky.) for Speaker and John Forney (Pa.) for

---

[30] Georgians Alexander Stephens and Robert Toombs, two of the intellectual leaders of the Whig Party, switched to the Democratic Party in the 33rd Congress (after taking on the Unionist label in the 32nd Congress). See Martis (1989, 104–7).

Clerk,[31] while the Whigs, in considerable disarray and facing a significant Democratic majority, made no officer nominations.[32] Per the words of George W. Jones (D-Tenn.) during his nomination speech on the floor, Boyd was "a sound Democrat, and a tried and thorough compromise and Union man" (CG, 32-1, 12/1/1851, 5). Thus, Boyd fit the basic pattern in speaker-ship choice over the preceding decade—he was a Southerner and a regional moderate. Boyd suffered a handful of Democratic defections (primarily ul-tras from Georgia and South Carolina), but thanks to a comfortable Demo-cratic majority in the House (54.5 percent), he was able to win a first-ballot victory by securing 118 of 231 votes cast. Still, the breakdown of the vote was unnerving. With the Democrats still battling sectional tensions and the Whigs allowed to indulge in regional position-taking, 20 different men re-ceived at least one vote for Speaker. The Clerk election went considerably smoother, as Forney faced fewer Democratic defections and won a first-ballot victory with 129 of 208 votes cast.[33]

A final organizational matter had yet to be decided in the 32nd Congress. In late August 1852, the contract system in public printing that had been established in 1846 was repealed. Both chambers of Congress, therefore, would return to the previous system of electing printers. House Democrats wasted no time electing Robert Armstrong, the editor of the Union, to the printership. (Armstrong's Union newspaper would become the official organ of the Franklin Pierce administration in the following Congress.) Armstrong secured a first-ballot victory by capturing 107 of 187 votes cast (HJ, 32-1, 8/27/1852, 1096–97).[34] Thus, the Printer would once again be a valuable House officer position to vie over at the convening of a new Congress (and in the preceding caucuses).

Organizing the House in the 33rd Congress (1853–55) would be similar to the 32nd Congress, only easier. The Democrats now controlled two-thirds of the seats in the chamber, which made the possibility of regional position-taking defection within their ranks much easier to tolerate. A brief bout of factionalism entered the Democratic caucus nomination for Speaker, which resulted in Linn Boyd needing two ballots to achieve a majority, as the

[31] The New York Times (12/1/1851, 1) reported that Boyd and Forney were each nominated on the first ballot; Boyd received the votes of "two thirds of the whole caucus" while Forney bested Richard M. Young 92–19. Additional reports indicated that a number of members left the caucus in advance of the nomination balloting after a vote was taken on a resolution sus-taining the Compromise of 1850. Further reports of the Democratic caucus activity appear in the North American and United States Gazette (12/2/1851, 2) and the Trenton State Gazette (12/2/1851, 2).
[32] See Daily National Intelligencer (12/3/1851, 5) and Ohio Observer (12/3/1851, 3).
[33] The Democratic caucus nominees for Sergeant at Arms (Adam J. Glossbrenner [Pa.]), Postmaster (John M. Johnson [Va.]), and Doorkeeper (Zadock W. McKnew [D.C.]) were all elected unanimously on the House floor via resolution (CG, 32-1, 12/1/1851, 11).
[34] No evidence of caucus nominations was uncovered.

Northern antislavery wing and the Southern ultras also fielded candidates: David T. Disney (Ohio) and James L. Orr (S.C.), respectively.[35] Forney was nominated for Clerk on the first ballot with only minor opposition from Richard M. Young, and Robert Armstrong was nominated for Printer.[36] As in the previous Congress, there is no evidence that the Whigs made caucus nominations.

Boyd, Forney, and Armstrong all won easy first-ballot victories on the House floor. Boyd secured 143 of 217 votes cast, with the only Democratic defections being five ultras from South Carolina. Forney captured 122 of 200 votes cast, although some Southerners defected to Richard M. Young. Finally, Armstrong secured 126 of 218 votes cast, with some Northern Democrats (the "Hards") distributing their votes to Nathaniel Beverley Tucker.[37] The House organization was complete.[38]

Thanks mainly to the large Democratic majority, the regional impulse had been averted again. Union supporters in the press crowed about the victories and took fairly explicit digs at the sectional agitators who had emerged four years before. For example, a *New York Times* correspondent announced: "Congress has organized. The dread day is past; and all the hopes and predictions of those who prophesied the triumph of factions have proved idle as the wind. King Caucus still reigns and the cohesion of 'the Democracy' is not destroyed" (12/8/1853, 4).

The ease of these organizational victories may have emboldened Democrats to strike out in policy directions that, in hindsight, only hardened sectional attitudes and proved destructive to the future of the Union. Once the 33rd Congress began conducting business, the Democrats, spurred on by the Southern wing and accommodated by Northern "dough faces" like Stephen Douglas (D-Ill.), raised the slavery-extension issue yet again. With the settlement of the western territories only four years old, a move was made to open up the old Louisiana Purchase tract north of the 36° 30′ line to slavery. This land had been closed to slavery by the Missouri Compromise of 1820; now, Southerners wanted the ability to bring their property (i.e., slaves) anywhere in the Union that they pleased. After a desperate struggle, the Democrats were successful in repealing the 1820 compromise and replacing it with the Kansas-Nebraska Act of 1854. The former free areas of the Louisi-

---

[35] On the first caucus ballot, Boyd received 45 votes to 37 for Disney, 35 for Orr, and 1 for Thomas Bocock (Va.). On the second caucus ballot, Boyd received 63 votes to 31 for Disney and 23 for Orr. Reported in the *New York Times* (12/5/1853, 1) and the *Daily National Intelligencer* (12/5/1853, 3).

[36] The *Fayettesville Observer* (12/8/1853, 3) reported that Forney received 92 votes in caucus. No details about Armstrong's caucus nomination were uncovered.

[37] Armstrong would also vie for the Senate Printer position in the 33rd Congress, but lose the election to Tucker, thanks in part to the efforts of the Hards.

[38] The Democratic caucus nominees for Sergeant at Arms (Adam J. Glossbrenner [Pa.]), Postmaster (John M. Johnson [Va.]), and Doorkeeper (Zadock W. McKnew [D.C.]) were all elected unanimously on the House floor via resolution (*CG*, 33-1, 12/5/1853, 51).

ana Purchase would now be open to "popular sovereignty." This decision would frame the subsequent 1854–55 elections and the House organization in the 34th Congress (1855–57).

ORGANIZATION AMID PARTISAN CHAOS: THE SPEAKERSHIP ELECTION OF 1855–1856

The speakership battle of 1855–56 took place during a time that could best be characterized as "partisan instability."[39] The Second Party System was dealt a fatal blow by the Kansas-Nebraska Act. The Whig Party, critically wounded after the Compromise of 1850, finally expired after the act's passage revealed severe and irreparable regional rifts. The Democratic Party, while remaining intact, was also feeling the strains of the time, as antislavery members in the North openly rebelled against the leadership's proslavery agenda (Potter 1976; Sewell 1976). All of this adversity was felt in the legislative process: institutional party ties began breaking down, shifting coalitions became the norm, and voting in the 33rd Congress can best be characterized as "chaotic" (Poole and Rosenthal 1997, 30).

As a result of this partisan instability in Congress, along with the many partisan and sectional battles over the issue of slavery during the previous decade, a general antiparty mood arose in the mass public. This coincided with the emergence of a new, salient issue in 1854: nativism. A growing nativist movement spread throughout the nation in response to the large influx of immigrants (principally Catholics) from Ireland and Germany. This immigration wave altered the nation's demographic makeup significantly, as Anbinder states: "by 1855, immigrants outnumbered native-born citizens in Chicago, Detroit, and Milwaukee, and the immigrant population would soon surpass the native in New York, Brooklyn, Buffalo, Cleveland, and Cincinnati" (1992, 8). Native-born Protestants were appalled at the extensive connections that Catholic immigrants seemed to possess with members of local and state courts, as well as with their carousing on Sundays.[40] More to the point, the governing Protestant population feared that these new immigrant groups would turn their numerical majorities into electoral majorities, and thus sought to limit their political participation (Billington 1938).

Nativism and the general antiparty mood meshed with antislavery sentiment in the North to produce a dynamic and divisive electoral environment in 1854–55.[41] A new series of candidates emerged and campaigned on a combination of anti-immigrant, anti-Catholic, antiliquor, and antislavery positions. When the electoral dust had cleared, this new "opposition" or

[39] Portions of this section are based on Jenkins and Nokken (2000).
[40] Temperance activists were determined to destroy the "immigrant liquor interest" and succeeded in passing a number of state-level prohibition laws (Potter 1976; Tyrell 1979).
[41] A wholly nativist movement was also moderately successful in the South.

"anti-administration" group won a majority of seats to the 34th Congress, which reduced the Democrats to minority status. At first glance, a successful "antiparty revolution" seemed to have been completed.

The stability of this new anti-administration majority, however, was largely artificial. While most anti-administration candidates ran under fusion labels, thereby adopting a range of different issue platforms, most were wedded to *particular* issues. This new majority was composed of two types: Americans (or Know-Nothings) and Republicans (or Anti-Nebraskans).[42] The Americans were a mysterious, decentralized organization that claimed adherents in the both the North and the South. Their meetings were held in secret, and members of the order, when confronted, disclaimed knowledge of its existence. While they supported antislavery tenets in the North, Americans were concerned primarily with the issue of nativism (Anbinder 1992). The Republicans, on the other hand, were a sectional party composed of former Free-Soilers, free-soil Democrats, and Northern Whigs. While they were not beyond appealing to nativist sentiments in order to secure victory, Republicans were concerned first and foremost with the issue of slavery (Potter 1976; Sewell 1976; Gienapp 1987).

Prior to the opening of the 34th Congress (1855–57), neither the Republicans nor the Americans were well-organized coalitions. Each group, however, made attempts to unify. In June 1855, the Americans assembled in Philadelphia to establish a national party platform. The convention's platform committee drafted a 14-section creed to clarify and consolidate the group's positions on nativism and slavery. Few delegates objected to the first 11 sections, which dealt specifically with issues of nativism; however, a major dispute arose around the 12th section and its statement on slavery. The leadership's position was to "abide by and maintain the existing laws upon the subject of slavery, as a final and conclusive settlement of that subject," which meant it implicitly accepted the provisions of the Kansas-Nebraska Act.[43] Many Northern members, elected in part on antislavery rhetoric, rejected this plank. They called for the reestablishment of the Missouri Compromise, but they were outnumbered by Southern proslavery members and conservatives from the North (Anbinder 1992, 167–72). This rift on the slavery issue crippled attempts to nationalize the American organization, as many Northern antislavery delegates walked out of the convention rather than accept the proslavery plank (Harrington 1939, 188; Van

---

[42] The fusion movement, along with the secret nature of the Know-Nothing society, made it difficult to identify clear partisan attachments for new House members. The *Congressional Globe*, which traditionally listed party labels for members at the opening of each session, failed to do so for the 34th House, and historians' attempts at party identification have not produced a consistent view (see Martis 1989, 33–34). This muddled state of affairs is summarized nicely by Mayer: "When the votes were counted . . . the Democrats knew that they had lost, but nobody knew who had won" (1967, 30).

[43] Excerpt taken from the convention minutes, as quoted in Anbinder (1992, 167).

Horne 1967, 209). Additional attempts at reconciliation in the days prior to the convening of the 34th Congress proved elusive, as a general American caucus to discuss speakership candidates could not be organized. Instead, Northern and Southern factions met separately.[44]

The Republicans also had a difficult time organizing. This was true even though Republican leaders Horace Greeley and Joshua Giddings saw an opportunity to use the slavery issue to break up the national American coalition. They believed the House to be composed of a majority of anti-slavery representatives and worked to frame the upcoming speakership election as a ratification or rejection of the Slave Power, as expressed by the Kansas-Nebraska Act. To marshal the antislavery forces, Greeley and Giddings called for a party caucus to select a suitable Republican candidate, but their call went largely unanswered, as fewer than half of those members opposed to slavery extension showed up (Harrington 1939, 188–89; Hollcroft 1956, 445; Silbey 1989, 5–7). As a result, the Republican caucus made no nominations.

As the opening of the 34th Congress neared, informal politicking suggested that the two strongest Republican candidates were Lewis D. Campbell (Ohio), a former Whig and American who left the latter party after the adoption of "section 12," and Nathaniel Banks (Mass.), a former Democrat and American.[45] Despite the Republicans' failure to initially frame the speakership contest as a clear test of slavery sentiments in the House, slavery nonetheless became the major issue on which the election would be decided. Ironically, the *Democrats* organized their campaign for the speakership on the basis of slavery by selecting William A. Richardson (Ill.) as their caucus nominee.[46] The choice of Richardson continued the Democratic strategy of choosing a regional moderate as their speakership nominee. Richardson had also been the Democratic point man in the House on the Kansas-Nebraska legislation in 1854, and was thus viewed as an optimal choice by party leaders; he was a supporter of slavery extension, which appealed to Southern members, as well as a close associate of Stephen Douglas, and a friend to many Northern members (Harrington 1939, 190; Gienapp 1987, 244).

Yet the Democrats made a crucial blunder. Like Greeley and Giddings, Democratic leaders also viewed the splintering of the American coalition as a potential windfall and began conversing with Southern Americans several weeks prior to the caucus. Initial discussions seemed fruitful, and suggested

[44] *NYT* (11/29/1855, 1; 11/30/1855, 1; 12/1/1855, 4; 12/3/1855, 4).

[45] *NYT* (12/1/1855, 4; 12/3/1855, 4); *North American and United States Gazette* (12/3/1855, 2).

[46] *NYH* (12/2/1855, 1; 12/3/1855, 1–2); *Daily National Intelligencer* (12/3/1855, 3); *North American and United States Gazette* (12/3/1855, 2). The *Intelligencer* reported that all officer nominations (including the Speaker) were unanimous. The *Baltimore Sun* reported that "It is understood that the democrats have resolved to vote first and last for their caucus nominees, refusing all coalitions with other parties" (11/30/1855, 2).

to many political observers that a proslavery union on a speakership candidate was likely (Hollcroft 1956, 445). Prudent judgment gave way to arrogance, however, as Democratic leaders eventually tried to bully the Southern Americans into supporting Richardson. When their nominating caucus opened, the Democrats unanimously accepted a resolution that denounced the Know-Nothing organization,[47] and Democratic leaders privately informed Southern American leaders that "very frankly ... they had two choices, either to surrender, lock, stock, and barrel to the Democrats, or to the Republicans," and offered them nothing in return for their allegiance (Overdyke 1968, 164). The Southern Americans bristled at the Democrats' arm-twisting and vowed to remain united behind a candidate who was sympathetic to the nativist cause.

The speakership election formally commenced on December 3, 1855.[48] The first ballot indicated just how disorganized the new anti-Democratic coalition really was, as 17 different candidates received votes. Campbell was the leading Republican with 53 votes, followed by Banks with 21. The Americans split their votes between former Whigs Humphrey Marshall of Kentucky (30 votes) and Henry M. Fuller of Pennsylvania (17 votes), while the Democrats coalesced behind Richardson (74 votes). Yet all candidates fell far short of a majority (113 votes). Over the next day and a half, eight additional ballots were taken, with no meaningful difference in results.[49] (See appendix 2 for a breakdown of the balloting.)

Two days later, Marshall withdrew his name, which left the Southern Americans to eventually coalesce around Fuller—after first scattering their votes for several ballots—as the only major American candidate left in the race (Harrington 1939, 194; Lientz 1978, 84–85). This consolidation was no accident, as Fuller had met with Southern Americans and assured them of his support of the Kansas-Nebraska Act.[50] This had the countervailing effect of driving some additional antislavery Americans into the Republican camp. Still, Fuller's outreach to Southern Americans had the overall effect of slowly solidifying the bulk of the American coalition, Southerners and proslavery Northerners, behind one candidate.[51] Fuller's "popular sovereignty"

[47] *NYTrib* (12/3/1855, 5); *NYH* (12/3/1855, 2).

[48] Vote data for all speakership ballots used in this analysis are taken from the *Congressional Globe*, 34-1, 12/3/1855, 3–337.

[49] On the evening of Dec. 3, the Republicans met in caucus to discuss coordinating behind a single candidate, but an arrangement was not reached (*NYT*, 12/4/1855, 1).

[50] According to Horace Greeley, "Fuller is understood to have answered some questions put to him by the Missouri delegation respecting slavery in Kansas, in such a manner as to have secured their good will" (*NYTrib*, 12/6/1855, 5), while the *New York Times* reported that Fuller had declared that he was "in favor of the admission of Kansas into the Union either with or without Slavery" (12/6/1855, 1; see also *NYH*, 12/7/1855, 1). Others were less kind in their assessment of Fuller. Edwin Barber Morgan (R-N.Y.) referred to Fuller as "the most consummate [doughface] that has taken the stand in years" (Hollcroft 1956, 454).

[51] Many of Marshall's supporters would scatter their votes among a variety of Southern

stance also established him as a moderate on the slavery issue by placing him between the Republican and Democratic positions.

Campbell continued to be the top Republican vote-getter throughout the balloting on December 5 but failed to muster more than 81 votes. Yet, a change was not made. As the *New York Times* reported, "The present determination of the Republicans is to press Campbell's cause until he is elected, or until they are satisfied that he cannot be" (12/6/1855, 1). After six additional ballots on December 6, Campbell's vote total fell to 46, which spurred Republican leaders to act. That evening, an informal antislavery caucus was organized and members agreed that Campbell's candidacy was dead. They agreed to support him for two additional ballots the following day, after which they would settle on Banks as their sole candidate.[52] Campbell was informed of this decision so that he might withdraw gracefully at the observed time (Harrington 1939, 192–93; Hollcroft 1956, 449). As planned, on December 7, Republicans supported Campbell on the first two ballots (the 22nd and 23rd overall), which drove his vote total to 75, after which Campbell withdrew and members began to move to Banks.[53] Thus, four days and 27 ballots into the contest, only three viable candidates remained in the field: Richardson the Democrat, Banks the Republican, and Fuller the American.[54]

With Campbell out of the way, Banks made his move. Even before he had become the sole Republican candidate, Banks had begun to create a large lobbying network within Congress by cajoling members and making promises to them in return for their votes.[55] Given his new position as Republican top dog, these promises now seemed more credible, which showed in his vote totals. By the end of the balloting on December 8, Banks stood at 100

---

ex-Whigs for the next day and a half before moving to Fuller near the end of the balloting on December 7.

[52] Banks was chosen, rather than other potential candidates, "because of his eminent fitness, and in response to the necessity for recognition of the Democratic element in the Republican movement" (*NYT*, 12/6/1855, 1).

[53] Campbell's exit would not be graceful, however. As he announced his withdrawal, Campbell suggested that other antislavery candidates were less than devoted to the cause and willing to cut deals to achieve election (*CG*, 34-1, 12/7/1855, 11). Nor was his subsequent behavior less tempered. As Harrington states, "For the duration of the contest [Campbell] brooded on his defeat and frequently, quite obviously in spite, voted against his antislavery-extension colleagues" (1939, 193).

Some former Campbell supporters moved to Banks immediately, while others scattered their votes on the remaining four ballots taken on December 7. By the first ballot on December 8, however, all former Campbell voters had moved to Banks.

[54] That evening, the American members caucused, but little was achieved, as the slavery question continued to divide them. As a result, they adopted no new strategies and continued to support Fuller (*NYT*, 12/8/1855, 1).

[55] According to Harrington, "Banks representatives made offers of committee posts, and there was even talk of bribery. Banks had a slippery lobby agent, S. P. Hanscom, who did most effective work" (1939, 195).

votes, 12 short of a majority. Two days later (on the 38th ballot), Banks's total crept up to 107 votes, only 6 short of a majority, but could move no higher. This appeared to be the maximum that the Republican coalition could muster without further help from American members who had previously espoused antislavery beliefs. The Republicans were aware of this; as Edwin Barber Morgan (N.Y.) remarked:

> We are much excited at the course of the Know Nothings of our state who have had and now hold the power to elect a free Northern man for Speaker over Slave masters of the South. [Bayard] Clarke, [William] Valk, [Thomas] Whitney, [Solomon] Haven and [John] Wheeler have had it in their hands on Saturday and today and yet the rascals refuse. What can be said of them at home and what can the *free soil and honest Know Nothings* say of them? (Hollcroft 1956, 450; emphasis in original)[56]

Realizing that they held the election in the balance, some antislavery Americans offered to throw their support behind an antislavery (but pro-nativist) candidate other than Banks. Two names were suggested: former Democrat John Wheeler of New York and former Whig Alexander Pennington of New Jersey. Wheeler was never a serious candidate among Republicans,[57] but Pennington wielded a fair amount of support within the party,[58] and a move was made in caucus to support him in place of Banks. However, a sizable pro-Banks majority voted them down, and Banks continued to be the official nominee of the antislavery forces.[59]

As illustrated in figure 6.3, this Banks-Richardson-Fuller equilibrium proved to be quite robust, as little change occurred in the candidates' vote totals over the next six weeks. Moreover, a simple, one-dimensional spatial model, in which slavery represents the substantive dimension, explains a large percentage of the variance in voting. Specifically, using CSW-NOMINATE

[56] The *New York Times* (12/11/1855, 1) singled out these same five New York members, along with John Williams (N.Y.), Edward Ball (Ohio), John S. Harrison (Ohio), Oscar F. Moore (Ohio), George G. Dunn (Ind.), and Harvey D. Scott (Ind.), as individuals elected on antislavery platforms who promised, but subsequently refused, to vote for Banks. Several days later, a *New York Times* editorial was even more direct: "If John Wheeler, of this city, and ten or a dozen others from different States, could be convinced that they will not be Speaker in any event, the House would be organized without difficulty" (12/15/1855, 4).

[57] Edward Barber Morgan put it simply: "John Wheeler, poor dunce, has the maggot in his head that he can be Speaker. Of course no other man ever dreamed of it, and it makes an ass of him" (Hollcroft 1956, 450).

[58] While Pennington had supported Banks on previous ballots, his antislavery credentials were questioned by some. According to Edward Barber Morgan, "It is ascertained that many of the Southern National Know Nothings have only been waiting for us to run [Pennington] up, that they might jump on and elect him. A man is judged by the company he keeps" (Hollcroft 1956, 451).

[59] See *NYT* (12/15/1855, 1), *NYTrib* (12/15/1855, 4), and *NYH* (12/15/1855, 1). The *New York Times* reported that 62 of 69 members present agreed to continue supporting Banks.

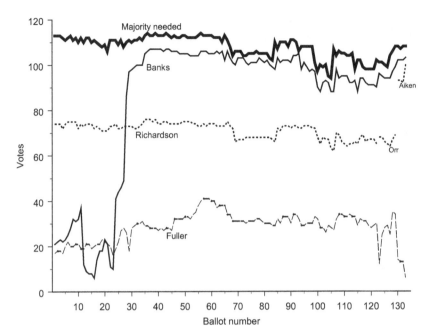

FIGURE 6.3. Summary of speakership balloting, 34th Congress.

scores, we are able to generate ideal points for all House members and the three speakership candidates on the primary dimension of choice, which Poole and Rosenthal (1997, 40) characterize as a slavery dimension.[60] A distribution of the House membership, along with the locations of Banks, Richardson, and Fuller, appears in figure 6.4. We then examine a typical ballot during this time. A good example is the 51st ballot on December 13, in which Banks, Richardson, and Fuller tallied 105, 75, and 33 votes, respectively (*CG*, 34-1, 12/13/1855, 24). We find that a one-dimensional spatial model correctly classifies 193 of the 213 individual vote choices, or 90.6

[60] CSW-NOMINATE scores were introduced in chapter 1. Common space scores are necessary because to conduct our analysis, we need an ideal point estimate for Nathaniel Banks, the eventual Speaker of the 34th House. Because speakers do not typically vote, the "regular" W-NOMINATE score for Banks is based only on a handful of votes. Rather than incorporate this "noisy" score, we use the common space technique to take advantage of Banks's voting record in the 33rd House, when he was a regular member.

The common space estimation we employ here incorporates votes from the 33rd through the 37th Congresses, the period in which the first W-NOMINATE dimension is characterized by slavery (Poole and Rosenthal 1997, 40, 95–100). Moreover, the CSW-NOMINATE scores have face validity, as they correlate at a very high rate with the regular W-NOMINATE scores: 0.98 across all five Congresses, and 0.982 in the 34th House, specifically. For a lengthier discussion of the common space estimation, its application to the 34th House, and additional diagnostics, see Jenkins and Nokken (2000, 106–8).

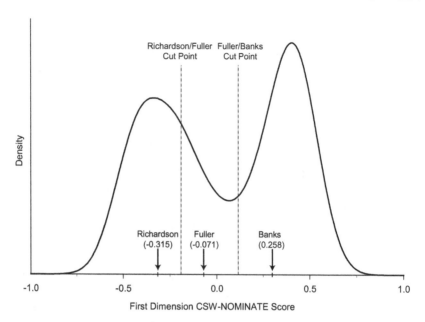

FIGURE 6.4. One-dimensional spatial distribution of House members and speaker-ship candidates, 34th Congress.

percent.[61] Of the 20 votes classified incorrectly, only *two* were inconsistent with spatial preferences, that is, either predicted-Banks voters selecting Richardson or predicted-Richardson voters selecting Banks. Rather, most of the errors fell near the two cut points between the three candidates—predicted-Fuller voters selecting Richardson, predicted-Richardson voters selecting Fuller, predicted-Fuller voters selecting Banks, or predicted-Banks voters selecting Fuller.

As nativism was instrumental to the electoral emergence of the Americans and partly responsible (through fusion) to the electoral emergence of the Republicans, we examine whether it also affected members' vote choices for Speaker by incorporating a second CSW-NOMINATE dimension. According to Poole and Rosenthal, the second NOMINATE dimension in the 34th House, while weak relative to the first dimension, "appears to capture the nativist sentiment of the time, because it tends to separate members of the American Party from the rest of the House" (1993, 21–22). In fact, we find that a two-dimensional spatial model, in which both slavery and nativism are accounted for, performs *less well* than a simple one-dimensional spatial model where slavery is the relevant dimension. Looking again at the

---

[61] This analysis ignores eleven members who scattered their votes.

51st ballot, a two-dimensional spatial model correctly classifies 184 of the 213 individual vote choices, or 86.4 percent, which is a 4.2 percent (or 9-vote) falloff from the one-dimensional model. Moreover, the two-dimensional model performs poorly in *precisely* the domain that we would have expected it to improve classification—with Fuller voters. Stated differently, the addition of a dimension to account for nativism should better explain votes cast for Fuller, the American candidate; yet, this is not the case. The two-dimensional model correctly classifies only 10 of the 33 votes cast for Fuller compared to 18 of 33 for the one-dimensional model. These results suggest that nativism had little or no effect on the speakership election, and that the slavery issue, by itself, was the driving force behind members' vote choices.

Thus, after several weeks of balloting, the parties' positions were fleshed out. Despite pressures to settle on a compromise candidate, both the Republicans and Americans strove to elect one of their own. In lieu of that outcome, both preferred to maintain the electoral gridlock and prevent the House from organizing—each party's continued existence was at stake, and a wholesale concession could have been fatal (Silbey 1989, 4–7).[62] Leaders on both sides also felt that the incumbent Democratic administration stood to lose more from an unorganized House; thus, each would gain in relative terms (Hollcroft 1956, 452). Moreover, if both Republicans and Americans believed that members of the other two parties would continue to vote sincerely, then each could continue casting ballots for their most preferred candidate and guarantee their second-best outcome (given that each group was pivotal).

The Democrats also wanted to elect one of their own, but felt pressure to avoid a lengthy deadlock. Since they controlled the presidency and the Senate, the Democrats were anxious to pursue a partisan agenda. If they could not capture the speakership, they preferred to have either a Republican- or American-controlled House rather than an unorganized one; from their established position, vote trades and compromises were better than no legislative outputs at all. The Democrats also felt, however, that the American and Republican organizations were shaky and could not hold out indefinitely. Thus, they were torn by conflicting pressures: settle now and guarantee a moderate stream of policy outputs or settle later and receive a lottery payoff (a possible unorganized House and no policy outputs, or a possible unified Democratic organization—after one of the other parties collapsed—and a large stream of policy outputs). Based on actual events, the Democrats ap-

---

[62] In letters and newspaper columns, Republicans vowed to oppose the Slave Power, even if it meant balloting until March 4, 1857, the end of the congressional term. See Harrington (1939, 196); Edward Barber Morgan to Henry and Richard Morgan, December 10, 1855, in Hollcroft (1956, 450, 452); Charles Sumner to Theodore Parker, January 20, 1856, in Palmer (1990, 441–42).

pear to have chosen the lottery, as they believed that the likelihood of an American or Republican collapse was high enough to warrant pursuing the risky strategy.

The Democrats underestimated their adversaries' resolve. The balloting continued through the rest of December 1855 and into January 1856, with little change in the relative positions of the candidates (see appendix 2 for a breakdown of the balloting).[63] Between ballots, several alternate methods of deciding the speakership contest were offered: proposals for continuous sessions, the resignation of all current candidates, the election of temporary speakers, the curtailment of debate, and, most notably, the substitution of a plurality rule in place of the standard majority rule (*CG*, 34-1, 34, 72, 139, 149, 235, and 241). All failed.

On January 24, 1856, prior to the 123rd ballot, the Democrats replaced Richardson as their speakership candidate with James Orr (S.C.), an unabashed opponent of nativism. But the difference proved to be negligible as far as resolving the contest was concerned. As the month was coming to a close, the Americans and Republicans were still holding fast, and the Democrats were at the end of their rope. President Franklin Pierce, once confident that an extended struggle would result in either the Americans or Republicans caving and a Democrat elected Speaker, was growing frustrated with the deadlock and believed that an unorganized House was becoming a distinct possibility (Harrington 1939, 197–200). Anxious to send his message to Congress and perceiving little expected payoff from further delay, he urged Democratic House leaders to bring the contest to a close.

Alexander Stephens (Ga.), a chief Democratic floor leader, would attempt to do Pierce's bidding. Moreover, he envisioned a way to end the contest *and* elect a Democrat via the passage of a plurality rule. To that point, the pro-Banks forces had repeatedly proposed a plurality rule, as they believed their man (as the top vote-getter) would be the logical beneficiary. The Democrats and Americans had generally opposed a plurality rule for these same reasons. However, as the contest moved into February 1856, Stephens now saw how a plurality rule could lead to a Democratic victory, and he began to fashion a plan.

Stephens recognized that should a plurality rule pass, a Democrat could only be elected with the assistance of the American coalition. But, after their organization was unanimously denounced by the Democratic caucus, the Americans had refused to support a Democratic candidate. Stephens's solution was simple—the Democrats would select a new candidate who had *not* participated in the caucus and thereby had *not* denounced the American organization. The selection was William Aiken (S.C.), an avowed

---

[63] A good deal of pairing occurred during this time, which suppressed the overall vote totals.

supporter of slavery who did not attend the Democratic caucus and had not committed himself on record against the Americans. Stephens felt that the ploy would be successful: "From my knowledge of the House, its present tone and temper, knowledge of Aiken and the estimation he was held in by several scatterers, I believed he would beat Banks ... I sounded out some of the Western Know Nothings—Marshall and others—and found that they could be brought into it."[64] Next, Stephens spoke to Fuller and his Northern supporters and reportedly effected an agreement (*New York Tribune* [hereafter abbreviated as *NYTrib*], 2/6/1856, 4). Finally, he persuaded several Democrats to switch their votes to support a plurality rule, thereby ensuring its passage. With that, all of Stephens's ducks appeared to be in a row.

Unfortunately for Stephens, on February 1, two Democrats—Williamson R. W. Cobb (Ala.) and John Kelly (N.Y.)—acted prematurely by moving that Aiken be declared Speaker *before* the plurality rule had been passed. Their motion failed 103 to 110 (*CG*, 34-1, 2/1/1856, 334–35), but, more important, it alerted the pro-Banks forces to Aiken's candidacy and thereby cost Stephens the element of surprise. The House adjourned shortly thereafter, allowing all parties to close ranks in anticipation of a conclusion. The Republicans, who had pushed for a plurality rule for many weeks, were now concerned—despite the failed motion to elect Aiken, he *still* managed 103 votes, which was many more than Richardson or Orr could muster. Aiken did this by drawing in a number of Americans who had been supporting Fuller, as well as some members who had been scattering their votes.

The following day, Samuel A. Smith (D-Tenn.) offered a plurality resolution of the 1849 form—three additional majority-rule ballots would be tried, and if no winner emerged, then a fourth plurality-rule ballot would be held—which passed on a 113–104 vote (*CG*, 34-1, 2/2/1856, 335). As arranged by Stephens, 12 Democrats had joined with the pro-Banks coalition to secure passage. Republican leaders sensed impending doom and tried first to rescind the plurality motion and then to force adjournment, but were voted down 102–116 and 84–133, respectively (*CG*, 34-1, 2/2/1856, 336).[65]

[64] Diary entry, Alexander H. Stephens, February 1, 1856, in Johnston and Brown (1878, 305–6).

[65] Additional attempts to rescind the plurality rule and to force adjournment (both of which failed) were made by *Southern Democrats* (*CG*, 34-1, 2/2/1856, 337). These Southerners might not have been privy to Stephens's plan, or perhaps Southerners generally saw the danger of anything less than a majority—and maybe even a supermajority—in deciding important questions of institutional design. In the 31st Congress, for example, the press emphasized the opposition of Southern Democrats to plurality voting. They were barely holding on to their peculiar institution, and if it became any easier for antislavery forces to prevail, it was all over, as far as they were concerned. Thus, even those Southerners who believed that they would win under plurality rule still opposed it on principle; that is, they were unwilling to support a voting

Stephens then introduced Aiken as the new Democratic candidate, which set the stage for an electoral showdown.

The first majority-rule ballot (the 130th overall) saw Banks capture 102 votes, Aiken 93, and Fuller 14, while 6 votes were scattered. Twenty of Fuller's prior supporters (from the 129th ballot) defected to Aiken; all 20 of these members were closer to Aiken than to Banks in a one-dimensional spatial analysis. This breakdown remained virtually the same on the next two majority-rule ballots (the 131st and 132nd overall), with Fuller and Aiken losing one vote apiece. Finally, the plurality-rule ballot was at hand. Prior to the start of this 133rd and final ballot, Fuller announced his withdrawal from the race (CG, 34-1, 2/2/1856, 337). Whether this was part of a larger deal negotiated earlier with Stephens is unclear. Regardless, all of the ingredients seemed to be in place for the remaining Fuller voters to move to Aiken.

But the plurality vote did not go as the Democrats had planned. When all of the votes were counted, Banks had defeated Aiken 103 to 100, with 11 votes scattering. Seven Southern Americans who had previously supported Fuller switched to Aiken, which provided him with his final tally. However, six Americans from the Mid-Atlantic region—Jacob Broom (Pa.), Bayard Clarke (N.Y.), Elisha D. Cullen (Del.), Henry Winter Davis (Md.), William Millward (Pa.), and Thomas R. Whitney (N.Y.)—continued to support Fuller on the plurality ballot.[66] Three of these six (Broom, Clarke, and Whitney) along with one other American who abstained on the plurality ballot (William Valk, N.Y.) had previously supported Aiken on the February 1 motion. Democrats were livid at this intransigence and first threatened, then begged, these Americans to reconsider (Harrington 1939, 202). But it was to no avail. Stephens's carefully arranged plan had failed.

Analyzing the final speakership ballot spatially, we find that members' preferences on the slavery issue (as measured by their first-dimension CSW-NOMINATE scores) predict their final votes for Speaker nearly perfectly. Focusing only on those members who voted for either Aiken or Banks, a one-dimensional spatial model correctly classifies 198 of the 203 votes, or 98.5 percent.[67] Only five errors are uncovered, and all are of the "predicted Banks but selecting Aiken" variety. (Four of these five errors represent members who had previously been supporting Fuller.) As in previous ballots, the

---

mechanism that would give them their man *in the short term*, if it would be detrimental to their interests in the long term.

[66] Each of these six sincerely preferred Fuller to either Aiken or Banks.

[67] Of the 11 scatters on the final vote, 6 were Fuller supporters, 4 cast votes for Lewis Campbell, and 1, John Hickman (D-Pa.), voted for Daniel Wells (D-Wis.). Our one-dimensional spatial model shows four of the six Fuller voters, all four of Campbell's voters, and Hickman to be closer to Banks than to Aiken. Thus, if these 11 members would have voted for one of the two major candidates, a sincere spatial voting model would not predict a change in the outcome; in fact, Banks would be predicted to win by a larger margin.

addition of a second dimension leads to a poorer spatial fit—only 170 of the 203 votes (83.7 percent) cast for Aiken or Banks are classified correctly.

To further evaluate our one-dimensional spatial model's performance, we compared it to a simple baseline: a regional model in which members from slave states vote for Aiken while members from free states vote for Banks. The regional model performs quite well, correctly predicting 185 of the 203 votes, or 91.1 percent. The one-dimensional spatial model, however, improves the fit considerably, as measured by the proportional reduction in error (PRE) between the two models (Poole and Rosenthal 1997, 29–30).[68] The PRE is (18-5)/18 = 0.722, which indicates that the spatial model provides a 72.2 percent improvement in fit over the regional (baseline) model. The use of ideology, then, substantially improves classification, because it picks up members from free states who supported slavery, a dynamic that is not captured by a regional model.[69]

Why did the six Americans stick with Fuller, even after he had dropped out of the race? Electoral considerations would be the obvious answer. Supporting a proslavery Southern Democrat might have been too difficult to explain to their Mid-Atlantic constituents. For example, according to Harrington (1939, 202), one of these six Fuller voters, when asked at the time of the vote to switch to Aiken to save the Union, replied, "I'll be —— if I do!" Horace Greeley made the same point in his *New York Tribune* column: "These [six Fuller voters] could not afford to elect Mr. Aiken—that, in dealing a blow to us 'black Republicans,' they would utterly demolish themselves and their National American party. So they held off and let Mr. Banks be elected" (reprinted in the *Mississippian*, 2/27/1856, 2). Thus, for these six members, continuing to position-take by supporting Fuller was a safer strategy.

In assessing the larger significance of the 1855–56 speakership contest, it helps to start by casting our gaze back to the speakership battle of 1849 that began this chapter. That battle signaled an end to the parties' ability to keep slavery off the agenda in speakership elections. A brief period of relative peace then followed for two reasons. First, oversized Democratic majorities in 1851 and 1853 allowed the party to choose moderate Speaker nominees without worrying about defections from slavery extremists on both sides of the issue. Second, the Whigs were so weak that they could not effectively exploit factional divisions among the Democrats. Thus, although the slavery issue replaced "general economics" as the primary dimension of conflict during the early 1850s, thus presenting a fundamental long-term challenge

---

[68] The PRE provides a measure of how a given model improves upon a simple baseline. The PRE = (Baseline Classification Errors – Ideological Model Classification Errors)/Baseline Classification Errors.

[69] All 18 of the regional model's classification errors were one-directional: members from free states who voted for Aiken. The list includes one from Maine, three from New York, one from New Jersey, one from Iowa, three from Pennsylvania, two from Indiana, three from Illinois, one from Michigan, one from Wisconsin, and two from California.

190

CHAPTER 6

to the viability of the nation's politics, it did not come into play in speakership selection because of the brief interlude of (essentially) one-party politics early in the 1850s.

Returning to the 1855–56 contest, with the rise of two new parties—the Americans and the Republicans—instability was once again at hand. Now that slavery had become the primary issue cleavage in national politics, the passions associated with the issue made it impossible to settle speakership contests by compromise or by adopting the Van Burenite strategy of simply ignoring it. Furthermore, the institutional imperatives of the emergent parties made compromise untenable. For instance, Americans could not simply agree to form what we would recognize as a "coalition government" with either the Republicans or Democrats because doing so would likely require them to suppress their agenda on nativism in return for positions of institutional power, such as committee assignments. Yet Americans and their followers were not interested in spoils of office; they were interested in policy. To enter into the organization of the House as a junior partner to one of the larger parties would risk breaking the electoral bond with voters back home. Furthermore, in the fluid environment of party politics, the American Party did not want to be anyone's junior partner—it was jockeying to become one of the two major parties. It was much more interested in utilizing its pivotal status to full advantage.

Thus, the American leadership decided to espouse a moderate slavery agenda, split the vote three ways, and hope that either the Republicans or Democrats would see them as the compromise solution. Passage of the plurality rule after two months of balloting was the undoing of this strategy. The plurality rule forced the third-place candidate, who in this case was Fuller, the American candidate, out of the running. With Fuller out, the American members were pushed toward one or the other of the two major camps. When forced to choose, most chose Aiken, the Democratic candidate, but a pivotal group of Americans abstained because they could not bring themselves to support a Democrat. This proved to be decisive, as Nathaniel Banks, the Republican candidate, eked out a narrow victory.

Once elected, Banks would work to organize the House around antislavery tenets. (This will be explored in detail in chapter 7.) While the American Party would remain in existence until the Civil War, its numbers slowly diminished as the Republicans rose to join the Democrats as one of the nation's two major parties.

CONCLUSION

Scholarship examining antebellum political institutions has emphasized the practices that sought to create a credible commitment to interregional coali-

tions. Most notable of these mechanisms has been the balance rule governing the admission of states and the selection of national tickets (Weingast
1996, 1998; Aldrich 1995). Another mechanism, which has gone largely
unappreciated until now, was the attempt to manage the slavery policy dimension of speakership choice by first hiding the speakership vote from
public view and then, once viva voce voting was instituted, selecting slavery
moderates as nominees in the party caucuses.

Probably because speakership selection was a biennial event driven by
the most popular of national political events—House elections—mechanisms that attempted to maintain the Second Party System within the chamber were inherently unstable. They were vulnerable to the electoral dynamics that produced congressional majorities in the first place.

This chapter has described, between 1849 and 1855, the tension between
"Farquharson and Fenno," a tension identified within political science by
Denzau, Riker, and Shepsle (1985). The rising popularity of new parties in
congressional elections (like the Liberty, Free-Soil, and American Parties)
made politicians in both major parties wary of drawing the ire of constituents who might be sympathetic to these insurgent messages. The narrow
margins in congressional races of this period made the appeals of the more
radical parties especially perilous.[70]

The goals of political entrepreneurs who attempted to leverage the un-
settled status of the party system also undercut the ability of congressional
actors to compromise over the organization of the House. To achieve their
goals, they had to somehow stay pure on policy while at the same time gain
influence over House decision making out of proportion to their numerical
strength. These goals could not be met by joining with the major parties,
especially the ones dedicated to keeping issues like slavery off the agenda, if
all that was to be gained was internal patronage.

One unappreciated factor that helped make compromise over the internal organization of the House nearly impossible was the dramatic expansion in the size of the congressional electorate during the period covered
by this chapter. During the 1850s, the number of voters in congressional

---

[70] One interesting detail that illustrates the electoral peril during this time comes about by
examining New England congressional elections. During most of the period covered here, the
states of Maine, Massachusetts, New Hampshire, and Vermont required congressional candidates to receive a *majority* of votes cast in order to be elected to Congress. Failure of any candidate to receive a majority would result in another election a few months later. There was no
formal process to eliminate minor candidates, so a series of runoff elections could, in theory,
continue forever. Of the 248 congressional elections held in New England from the 26th to the
36th Congress, 56 (23%) were decided in runoffs, requiring in one case eight ballots to finally
elect a House member. In virtually all of these affairs, the spoilers were antislavery candidates
who picked up a handful of votes—just enough to keep the top vote-getter from receiving a
majority.

elections grew by around 50 percent.[71] This expanding electorate also certainly increased the danger associated with making the "wrong" political decisions.

The electoral peril that parties in the Second Party System faced also provided opportunities. As the political universe was changing, new avenues for coalitional organization emerged, and the initial claimant in February 1856 was the new Republican Party. But was the speakership victory a fluke? Or could the new antislavery coalition hang together, organize the House, and aspire to be a major institutional and electoral party? If a purely sectional party like the Republicans could achieve major party status, could Van Buren's vision of rigid party discipline in House organizational matters be accomplished? That is, without the bugaboo of slavery affecting party-building activities, could organizational coordination become a reality? Chapters 7 and 8 take up these questions. Suffice it to say that on issues of party development and organizational decision making in the House, *much* would change in the next decade.

---

[71] Combining the on-year off-year surge-and-decline phenomenon with the admission of new states makes estimating the growth of the congressional electorate in the 1850s less than precise. Here are the raw numbers (Dubin 1998):

Election years	Congress	Total cong. votes	Election years	Congress	Total cong. votes
1840–41	27	2,272,094	1850–51	32	2,574,021
1842–43	28	2,222,260	1852–53	33	3,152,708
1844–45	29	2,732,222	1854–55	34	3,293,774
1846–47	30	2,406,131	1856–57	35	3,942,338
1848–49	31	2,766,883	1858–59	36	3,882,241

Between the off-year elections of 1850–51 to 1858–59, the total electorate grew by 50.8 percent. Between the on-year elections of 1848–49 to 1856–57, the total grew by 42.4 percent. Notice also the lack of a significant decline in turnout for the off-year elections of 1850–51 and 1854–55.

CHAPTER 7

The Speakership and the Rise
of the Republican Party

The election of Nathaniel Banks as House Speaker in the 34th Congress after two months of wrangling and 133 ballots marked the rise of the Republicans as the primary opposition party to the Democrats. Although multiple issues characterized the opposition movement immediately after the passage of the Kansas-Nebraska Act in 1854, slavery extension dominated all others by late 1855; it dictated speakership balloting and allowed the Republicans to seize control of the House's top position. But Banks's election was simply the first Northern victory—organizing the House and building a lasting coalition, two crucial steps in the Republican Party's development, still lay ahead.

Although a general anti-Nebraska sentiment tied them together, the Republicans were in fact a hodgepodge collection of members from defunct and scattered party backgrounds. An inspection of the coalition that elected Banks reveals an assortment of former Whigs, Democrats, Americans, Free-Soilers, and anti-Democratic newcomers. Banks himself was a former Democrat who was elected to the 34th Congress as an American. Thus, while a single issue allowed the Republicans to capture the speakership, an encompassing partisan identity was missing. To govern and maintain a national presence, Republican leaders would need to integrate members of these different groups and establish a clear partisan agenda.

In the end, the Republicans would exhibit some growing pains. The election of House officers and the distribution of committee assignments in the 34th Congress were successful by and large, even though the party's inability to elect a Printer was damaging in the short-term.

Policy making in the 34th Congress was helped along by persistent slavery politics, but the residual American Party presence hampered the Republicans' electoral fortunes in the elections of 1856–57, which cost them control of the House in the 35th Congress. Nonetheless, the Republican Party organization persevered. The burgeoning power of the slavery issue helped the party build and maintain internal unity. Controlling a plurality of House seats in the 36th Congress, the Republicans would have their resolve tested yet again in the speakership election of 1859, another lengthy multiballot affair. Emerging victorious, the Republicans would complete the chamber organization and lay claim to House control for the next decade and a half.

The Organization of the 34th House

After a rousing victory on the 133rd ballot, Nathaniel Banks found himself at the head of a burgeoning party organization.[1] Although some, like ex-Whig party boss Thurlow Weed, assumed Banks's election meant that "the Republican Party is now inaugurated . . . [and] can work with a will," there were still hurdles to be overcome.[2] Specifically, the remainder of the House organization would need to be completed—the additional officers would need to be elected and the standing committees would need to be assembled. Thus, with little time to savor their initial success, Banks's victorious coalition would quickly be put to the test.

The election of House officers

After Banks was sworn in on February 2, 1856, the House adjourned, reconvening two days later to elect a Clerk. William Valk (A-N.Y.) offered a resolution that William Cullom (Tenn.) be declared Clerk. Cullom was experienced in House politics, having served as a Whig in the 32nd and 33rd Congresses before running unsuccessfully for reelection to the 34th Congress as an American. As a result, Cullom became the American candidate for Clerk and was also tapped as the Republican choice, mainly due to his opposition to the Kansas-Nebraska legislation while a member of the 33rd Congress (*NYTrib*, 2/5/1856, 4; *Chicago Tribune* [hereafter abbreviated as *CT*], 2/6/1856, 2). James Orr (D-S.C.) offered a tabling motion that failed 101–113, thanks to a coalition of Americans and Republicans, following which the resolution electing Cullom was adopted on a 125–89 vote (*CG*, 34-1, 2/4/1856, 354). Cullom was then sworn in amid "manifestations of approval in the galleries" (*New York Times* [hereafter abbreviated as *NYT*], 2/5/1856, 4).

Cullom's election as Clerk was lauded by most Republican media outlets, and was spun in such a way as to emphasize the party's broadest possible appeal. For example, the *New York Times* reported: "The election of Mr. Cullom shows conclusively that this North is not sectional, but can seek merit south of Mason and Dixon's line, and give it substantial recognition when found. It shows, too, that the North is magnanimous, and not willing to retaliate the sectionalism of the South, but ready, on the contrary, to stand by the men of the South who are true to correct principles" (2/8/1856, 1).

---

[1] Portions of this section are based on Jenkins and Nokken (2000).

[2] Thurlow Weed to Banks, February 3, 1856. Quoted in Harrington (1939, 204–5).

More radical Republican media outlets were less pleased with Cullom's election. The *National Era* (2/14/1856, 26), for example, argued that despite his vote against the Kansas-Nebraska legislation while in Congress, Cullom had subsequently supported section 12 of the Philadelphia (American) Convention, which in effect meant that he had agreed to "abide by and maintain the existing laws upon the subject of slavery, as a final and conclusive settlement of that subject," and had thus implicitly accepted the provisions of the Kansas-Nebraska Act.[3] In effect, the *National Era* argued that Cullom was more American than Republican, and chafed at the Republicans' willingness to cooperate with the Americans.

The clerkship having been decided, next up was the election of a Sergeant at Arms. At this point, a problem surfaced. Mathias Nichols (R-Ohio), a Banks supporter and former free-soil Democrat, moved a resolution that Adam J. Glossbrenner, the incumbent Sergeant at Arms and a Democrat, be reelected. The Republicans quickly moved adjournment so that they might regroup, discuss nomination strategies, and settle on a slate of candidates for the remaining House officer positions. This motion passed 114–99 over Democratic opposition.

An anti-administration caucus of Republicans and Americans was called for that evening, with John Pettit (R-Ind.) serving as chairman and more than 90 members attending. By the end of the meeting, a set of caucus nominations was agreed to: French S. Evans (D.C.) for Sergeant at Arms; Nathan Darling (N.Y.) for Doorkeeper; Robert Morris (Pa.) for Postmaster; and Oran Follett, editor of the *Ohio State Journal*, for Printer (*NYT*, 2/5/1856, 4; *NYTrib*, 2/5/1856, 4; *National Era*, 2/7/1856, 22).

This slate suggested that the compromise movement between Republicans and Americans extended beyond Cullom's candidacy. Evans, Darling, and Morris were, or had been at one time, Americans, and Follett, while a Republican, was reported to have previously cooperated with the American movement in Ohio (*National Era*, 2/7/1856, 22; 2/14/1856, 26).

The following day, February 5, the House reconsidered Nichols's resolution to declare Glossbrenner Sergeant at Arms of the 34th Congress. Thomas Flagler (R-N.Y.) proposed tabling the resolution, but his motion was defeated 96–108, as several Republicans defected and voted with the Democrats. The main question (Nichols's resolution) was then considered and passed 103–98 (*CG*, 34-1, 2/5/1856, 358–59). Thus, Glossbrenner, the incumbent Democratic Sergeant at Arms, was reelected.

What of Evans, the anti-administration caucus nominee for Sergeant at Arms? Again, the evidence suggests that he was a compromise candidate who was pushed by the Americans and accepted by the Republicans. Yet, his nomination, as the *New York Times* suggested, "was of at least doubtful propriety" (2/8/1856, 1). While his American affiliation was clear, his broader

---

[3] Section excerpt taken from convention minutes, as presented in Anbinder (1992, 167).

background was sketchy. Some contended that he was firmly opposed to slavery extension, others that he supported the proslavery 12th section of the American national platform. This latter possibility induced many Republicans to ignore the caucus bond and either sit out the Sergeant at Arms votes or support Glossbrenner's candidacy on principle.

After Glossbrenner was sworn in, John Sherman (R-Ohio) offered a resolution that Nathan Darling be declared Doorkeeper. Humphrey Marshall (A-Ky.) moved to table the resolution, but his motion failed 87–118, thanks to a united coalition of Republicans and Northern Americans that was augmented by some Southern Americans. Sherman's resolution was then passed, 119–85, and Darling was thereby elected (CG, 34-1, 2/5/1856, 359).

James Campbell (R-Pa.) then offered a resolution that Robert Morris be declared Postmaster. John Phelps (D-Mo.) moved to table the resolution, which failed 105–108. Campbell's resolution then passed, 108–97, and Morris was thus elected and immediately sworn in (CG, 34-1, 2/5/1856, 359). The narrowness of Morris's victory was due in part to a split in the anti-administration caucus, as a number of Republicans had lobbied for the reappointment of the current Postmaster, John M. Johnson, who "while a decided Democrat of Virginia birth [had] heartily condemned the Nebraska bill" (NYTrib, 2/8/1856, 4).[4] Several Republicans subsequently defected from the caucus agreement and voted for Phelps's tabling motion, then abstained on Campbell's resolution.

Finally, after adopting the House rules of the previous Congress, at the request of Thomas Clingman (D-N.C.), the House considered the election of a Printer. John Bingham (R-Ohio) offered a resolution that Oran Follett be declared Printer of the House for the 34th Congress. After a brief confusion regarding points of order, the House adjourned, and Bingham offered his resolution again the following day (February 6). However, Clingman raised a point of order, noting that the House rules, which had only just been adopted, stipulated that officer elections, except those involving House members, must involve previous nominations, thereby disqualifying an election by simple resolution, such as that offered by Bingham. Speaker Banks pondered Clingman's argument, agreed with the logic, and ruled Bingham's resolution out of order (CG, 34-1, 2/6/1856, 372).[5] Clingman's rules-

---

[4] According to Horace Greeley, "Had [Johnson] not received the nomination of the [Democrats], I think that he may have obtained that of [the Republicans] and been triumphantly re-elected" (NYTrib, 2/8/1856, 4).

[5] Prior to Clingman gaining the floor, John Carlisle (A-Va.) raised a similar point of order—specifically, that the House could not declare a Printer by resolution—and cited a section of an Act of Congress from August 26, 1852: "And be it further enacted, That there shall be elected a public Printer for each House of Congress, to do the public printing for Congress for which he or they may be chosen" (emphasis in the original). Carlisle claimed that the word "elected" in the act required the House to conduct an actual vote. However, in this case, Speaker Banks ruled that this was a question not for the chair but for the House as a whole to decide. See CG, 34-1, 2/5/1856, 360.

adoption move the previous day was therefore strategic, done to preclude the subsequent Republican-American resolution to elect a Printer.[6]

In the blink of an eye, the Republicans had found themselves outflanked. As a result, nominations for Printer were made, seven in all, before voting commenced. (See appendix 4 for a breakdown of the balloting.) The first ballot resulted in no majority winner, as 12 different candidates split 195 votes, with Oran Follett the top candidate with 80. A second ballot was then taken, with similar results: 11 candidates split 191 votes, with Follett leading with 77. A third ballot followed suit: 10 candidates split 189 votes, with Follett on top with 74. Thomas Flagler (R-N.Y.) then moved adjournment, which passed by a 66–50 teller vote (*CG*, 34-1, 2/6/1856, 373–74).

A glance at these ballot results reveals a pattern similar to that of the speakership race. Once nominations for Printer were allowed, the anti-administration caucus nominee, Oran Follett, fell prey to partisan division, as Americans withdrew their support and rallied behind several candidates, principally Robert Farnham and Nathan Sargent. A reporter for the *New York Times* summarized the contest as follows: "The best judgment I can form tonight is that Follett cannot get above eighty votes, unless he can harmonize two opposing interests" (2/7/1856, 8).

The Printer election resumed the following day (February 7). Lewis Campbell (R-Ohio) opened by moving to reconsider the resolution involving the process of electing a Printer.[7] George Washington Jones (D-Tenn.)

---

[6] The Democrats had attempted twice before to adopt the rules of the previous House, but each time they were ruled out of order by Speaker Banks. The first attempt was made by John Millson (D-Va.) shortly after the Clerk's election (*CG*, 34-1, 2/4/1856, 354–55), while the second attempt was made by Clingman immediately before the Sergeant at Arms election (*CG*, 34-1, 2/5/1856, 358). Thus, it seems that once the Democrats observed the anti-administration strategy of election via simple resolution, they intended to split the Republican-American coalition on each officer election. Their inability to expedite the rules adoption, however, likely cost them the Doorkeeper and Postmaster positions.

[7] Campbell is vague on his intentions here, but his previous comments during the debate on February 6 may suggest that he envisioned altering the rules of the House so as to allow the selection of a Printer to proceed by resolution (see *CG*, 34-1, 2/6/1856, 372–73). In addition, Campbell was acting strangely during the course of the balloting; on more than one occasion he moved to postpone further votes until an appropriation to buy wood for the poor in the District of Columbia could be secured (see *CG*, 34-1, 2/7/1856, 381; 2/11/1856, 388–89). Van Horne (1966, 216, 218–19, 273n76) argues that Campbell's motion to reconsider and his discussion of relief for the poor were strategic, specifically that Campbell was attempting to slow the proceedings and thus postpone the election of the Printer until the following week, which would give Cornelius Wendell, the Democratic candidate, enough time to secure the necessary votes for election. Campbell's subsequent motion on February 7 to postpone matters until the following Monday is thus consistent with this argument. Regarding motives, Van Horne contends that Campbell blamed Follett for his speakership defeat; according to Campbell, while Follett had initially played the role of his "manager," by working to build a coalition around his candidacy, Follett came to realize that both a Speaker and a Printer could not emerge from the same region (in this case, the West). Thus, Follett undercut Campbell's candidacy and convinced him to withdraw, so that Banks, a candidate from the Northeast, could take the speaker-

responded by offering a tabling motion, which failed by an 82–95 vote. The question on the motion to reconsider was then taken, pending which Jones called for the question to be divided, specifically to inquire whether the election of Printer should be postponed. Amazingly, it passed 102–81, with most Republicans and Americans supporting postponement. The anti-administration coalition was clearly disorganized. Campbell then backpedaled and sought to postpone the matter until the following Monday, after which a lengthy and scattered argument ensued. Finally, adjournment was moved and passed 87–82, due mostly to Republican support (*CG*, 34-1, 2/7/1856, 381–86).

The confusion on the floor betrayed a Republican-American conflict. To that point, Republicans had compromised considerably with the Americans, supporting former or current Americans for the positions of Clerk, Sergeant at Arms, Doorkeeper, and Postmaster. Now, the Republicans were attempting to elect one of their own as Printer, apparently without offering sufficient considerations to the Americans.[8] As Horace Greeley stated, "it is to be hoped some satisfactory arrangement may be made by which the friends who have heretofore acted together may be kept united. The present division of strength is solely attributable to mismanagement at the outset, and to an attempt to disregard influences which are now found to be potential in determining the result" (*NYTrib*, 2/9/1856, 4). Greeley urged Republicans to compromise: "This patronage is too valuable to be engrossed by any single individual, and the system heretofore practiced by both parties, of conferring it upon a particular organ or party pet, will hardly be repeated again."

The battle was joined once more on February 11. Lewis Campbell again pushed for reconsideration of the initial decision on the Printer vote, but was ruled out of order by Speaker Banks. Balloting for Printer then proceeded (the fourth overall) with no resolution: 173 votes were cast for 12 candidates, with Follett the top contender with 68. A fifth ballot was then taken, again with no majority winner; however, on this occasion, the leading candidate was Cornelius Wendell, the Democratic nominee, with 74 votes. Warner Underwood (A-Ky.) then proposed a resolution that the Printer election be decided by plurality rule, but he was ruled out of order. A sixth ballot was then taken, again with no resolution: 167 votes were cast for 11 candidates, with Wendell leading with 71 votes (*CG*, 34-1, 2/11/1856, 388–90).

---

ship. This would allow Follett a greater chance of winning the printership and its accompanying six-figure profit. Follett, while not acknowledging much of Campbell's story, did blame Campbell for his defeat in an editorial in his newspaper, the *Ohio State Journal* (2/21/1856).

[8] The *National Era* provided some background on this Republican-American disagreement involving Follett from their coverage of the anti-administration caucus on February 4: "Mr. Follett, of Ohio, got the [anti-administration caucus] nomination by one majority, and . . . the opposition to him then bolted" (2/14/1856, 26).

Seeing the printership slowly slipping away, the Republicans sought to regroup, with Benjamin Stanton (R-Ohio) moving that further balloting be postponed until the following day. After a somewhat lengthy debate, postponement was defeated 81–87, with the Democrats combining with many Americans to stymie the Republicans. Samuel Galloway (R-Ohio) then moved adjournment, which was defeated 71–87 by a similar coalition of Democrats and Americans. Underwood then moved to suspend the rules, so that a plurality rule could be proposed, but the necessary two-thirds was not achieved. Finally, Alexander Stephens (D-Ga.) again moved adjournment, which passed without a recorded vote (*CG*, 34-1, 2/11/1856, 390–91).

Republicans were clearly frustrated by the course of events. Their attempt to elect a Republican Printer was failing, and Oran Follett, having just arrived in Washington, was adamantly opposed to bargaining for the votes of the Americans (*NYT*, 2/15/1856, 1). Horace Greeley opined, "In this contest everybody is out for himself, and what is called 'the cause' figures very subordinately to the pocket" (*NYTrib*, 2/13/1856, 5). Republicans met in an informal caucus that evening, but could not agree on a change of strategy. As the *New York Herald* reported, the Republicans "are determined not to yield. The Printer, by right, they say, belongs to them, and they will not withdraw Mr. Follett" (2/13/1856, 4).

The next day, February 12, the House returned to the Printer election. A seventh ballot was taken, with no resolution: 164 votes were cast for 10 candidates, with Wendell leading the way with 69. An eighth ballot was then tried, again with no majority winner: 163 votes were cast for nine candidates, with Wendell the top vote-getter with 65. A ninth ballot was attempted, again with no resolution: 162 votes were cast for 11 candidates, with Wendell leading with 62 (*CG*, 34-1, 2/12/1856, 396–97). The House then adjourned for the day.

That evening, stretching into Wednesday morning, the Republicans met and discussed various options (*NYT*, 2/13/1856, 1; *NYH*, 2/13/1856, 4 and Feb. 2/14/1856, 4; *NYTrib*, 2/14/1856, 4). Some members wanted to drop Follett, while others pledged to stand behind him to the end. Follett's vote total had declined steadily during the balloting, from a high of 80 on the first ballot to a low of 54 on the ninth and most recent ballot. As a result, he grew tired of the affair and asked his supporters to withdraw his name. In the end, no new caucus nominee was selected, although some members announced that they would attempt to coordinate behind a new candidate. The *New York Times* predicted a Wendell victory and bemoaned the events leading up to it: "This deplorable result will be in consequence of the strange folly of the Opposition working at cross purposes" (2/13/1856, 1).

When the House convened at noon, the first order of business was the Printer election. A 10th ballot was taken, still with no majority winner, as 160 votes were divided among 11 candidates. However, a resolution to the contest was closer, as Wendell captured 73 votes, 8 short of a majority. By contrast, Follett's vote total continued to dwindle to 36 overall, as some Republicans flocked to Joseph J. Coombs, a new candidate nominated by Aaron Harlan (R-Ohio) prior to the vote. Sensing defeat, Benjamin Stanton (R-Ohio) sought to postpone the Printer election until December but was ruled out of order by Speaker Banks. An 11th ballot was then taken, and when all votes were counted, Wendell was declared the winner with 91 of 160 votes cast. Speaker Banks then officially declared him House Printer for the 34th Congress, which "was greeted with applause from the galleries" (CG, 34-1, 2/13/1856, 410).[9]

How did Wendell capture the printership? According to Horace Greeley, the deed was accomplished via side payments: "somebody has made a 'good thing of it,' in Congressional parlance . . . a good many pockets have been lined" (NYTrib, 2/15/1856, 4).[10] The chief target of these accusations was the Southern Americans.[11] By the last ballot for Printer, 18 Americans who had supported Henry Fuller throughout much of the speakership balloting had joined Wendell's coalition, whereas at the outset of the balloting for Printer, *none* of these 18 supported Wendell but rather divided their votes among several American candidates. Accusations were also directed at Republicans in two regards. First, nine members who had supported Banks for Speaker voted for Wendell. Second, 38 other Banks supporters sat out the final vote for Printer, in effect lowering the threshold for a majority-rule victory. Summing up the loss of the Printer, Greeley stated succinctly, "the most important part of the patronage belonging to the House was voted away for the benefit of a few desperate adventurers and venal borers of Congress."

Thus, the election of House officers was complete for the 34th Congress. After capturing the speakership, the Republicans had mixed results in filling out the rest of the officer positions. Lacking a chamber majority, they combined with the Americans to nominate a set of compromise candidates. This anti-administration coalition was able to elect the Clerk, Doorkeeper, and Postmaster, but was rolled by the Democrats in the election of the Sergeant at Arms and the Printer. The latter defeat was devastating because of the Printer's influential position for mass party building. Without it, the Republicans were hindered in expanding and underwriting state and local party presses throughout the nation. In the end, the Republicans were unwilling to

[9] This enthusiasm was not shared by all. As the New York Herald reported, "Our army in Flanders never swore half so much as did some Republicans when it was announced that Wendell was elected printer" (2/14/1856, 4).

[10] For a similar perspective, see NYH, 2/14/1856, 4.

[11] In this regard, the American Organ, a Washington-based newspaper sympathetic to the American cause, stated: "It has been currently reported during the last few days that Mr. Wendell had promised a portion of the proceeds of the public printing to some Southern Americans, to be dispensed by them in the establishment of a press [in Washington], to sustain the notions and opinions of the Southern branch of the American party, and to keep up the other presses now advocating those opinions elsewhere" (excerpted in the NYH, 2/16/1856, 4).

share the Printer with the Americans; they preferred to control it completely or not at all.

The appointment of the standing committees

Having filled out the rest of the officer corp, the House then proceeded to the announcement of standing committee assignments. Here, then, was the Republicans' great opportunity: while their lack of a majority limited their influence in officer elections, only one person, the Speaker, controlled the appointment of standing committees. If the Republicans were to reap the benefits of controlling the speakership, it was up to Nathaniel Banks to make it happen by organizing the various standing committees in an ideological fashion around antislavery tenets.

To expedite the Republican agenda, Banks should have done two things when appointing committees. First, he should have awarded committee chairmanships to those members who supported his speakership election. Second, he should have stacked committees, especially important policy committees, with his supporters, thereby increasing the likelihood that an antislavery agenda would be advanced.

Examining members' votes on the final (133rd) speakership ballot, we find that Banks disproportionately appointed allies to committee chairs.[12] As table 7.1 indicates, 27 of 34 House committees were chaired by Banks voters, which implies that committees were quite reflective of Banks and the emerging Republican Party.[13] An examination based on CSW-NOMINATE scores supports these findings: in 23 of 34 cases, the chair's ideal point was actually *to the right* of Banks (0.258), which suggests that he *strongly* favored antislavery members. In all, 28 of 34 committee chairmanships went

---

[12] Our contentions conflict with those of Silbey (1989), who argues that Banks could not organize the House effectively because he had too many factions to placate; consequently, he was forced to balance competing interests, which prevented him from building an antislavery coalition. To support his thesis, Silbey claims that Banks appointed a significant number of non-Republicans to committee chairs. By Silbey's count, only 11 Republicans received chairmanships, while the other 26 chairs were divided among Whigs, Americans, Democrats, and various hybrids. Based on these figures, Silbey claims, "The final distribution of committee chairmanships . . . hardly reflected secure Republican hegemony" (1989, 11).

We base our claim on a different accounting of party labels, one we consider to be more informative for this analysis. As discussed previously, partisan-affiliation data for anti-administration House members during this period was far from reliable given the changing partisan dynamics and fluid nature of fusion-based electoral politics. Because we argue that the Republican Party began as an ideological coalition in the House—specifically, an antislavery coalition—that evolved into a partisan coalition during the 34th Congress, members' votes for speaker and their CSW-NOMINATE scores should be regarded as more reliable measures of partisanship. See Jenkins and Nokken (2000) for additional discussion.

[13] Aiken voters were given six chairs, while Jacob Broom, a Fuller voter, was given the remaining chair. Most of these committees were executive oversight or housekeeping committees, with no obvious connections to the slavery issue.

TABLE 7.1.
House committee chairmen, 34th Congress

Committee	Chairman (state)	CSW-NOMINATE score	Speaker vote	Banks supporter
Engraving	William Kelsey (N.Y.)	0.509	Banks	Yes
Patents	Edwin Morgan (N.Y.)	0.503	Banks	Yes
Judiciary	George Simmons (N.Y.)	0.483	Banks	Yes
Naval Affairs	Samuel Benson (Maine)	0.479	Banks	Yes
Expenditures in the War Dept.	Aaron Cragin (N.Y.)	0.479	Banks	Yes
Agriculture	David Holloway (Ind.)	0.473	Banks	Yes
Elections	Israel Washburn (Maine)	0.469	Banks	Yes
Revisal and Unfinished Business	Alvah Sabin (Vt.)	0.468	Banks	Yes
Manufactures	Ezra Clark (Conn.)	0.457	Banks	Yes
Public Expenditures	Sidney Dean (Conn.)	0.440	Banks	Yes
Indian Affairs	Benjamin Pringle (N.Y.)	0.438	Banks	Yes
Public Lands	Henry Bennett (N.Y.)	0.414	Banks	Yes
Commerce	Elihu Washburne (Ill.)	0.410	Banks	Yes
Foreign Affairs	Alexander Pennington (N.J.)	0.410	Banks	Yes
Roads and Canals	James Knox (Ill.)	0.394	Banks	Yes
Claims	Joshua Giddings (Ohio)	0.384	Banks	Yes
District of Columbia	James Meacham (Vt.)	0.384	Banks	Yes
Territories	Galusha Grow (Pa.)	0.380	Banks	Yes
Expenditures in the Treasury Dept.	Henry Waldron (Mich.)	0.376	Banks	Yes

Committee	Member	Speaker vote	Banks supporter	
Expenditures in the Post Office	John Pettit (Ind.)	0.342	Banks	Yes
Revolutionary Claims	David Ritchie (Pa.)	0.329	Banks	Yes
Ways and Means	Lewis Campbell (Ohio)	0.324	Banks	Yes
Public Buildings and Grounds	Edward Ball (Ohio)	0.322	Banks	Yes
Militia	John Kunkel (Pa.)	0.255	Banks	Yes
Accounts	Benjamin Thurston (R.I.)	0.241	Banks	Yes
Post Office and Post Roads	Daniel Mace (Ind.)	0.237	Banks	Yes
Invalid Pensions	Andrew Oliver (N.Y.)	0.212	Banks	Yes
Revolutionary Pensions	Jacob Broom (Pa.)	-0.030	Fuller	Yes
Private Land Claims	Gilchrist Porter (Mo.)	-0.119	Aiken	No
Expenditures in the Navy Dept.	Thomas Harris (Ill.)	-0.202	Aiken	No
Mileage	William Sneed (Tenn.)	-0.274	Aiken	No
Military Affairs	John Quitman (Miss.)	-0.377	Aiken	No
Expenditures in the State Dept.	Preston Brooks (S.C.)	-0.389	Aiken	No
Expenditures on the Public Bldgs.	Fayette McMullen (Va.)	-0.464	Aiken	No

Note: "Speaker vote" indicates the member's vote on the final (133rd) ballot for Speaker. "Banks supporter" indicates whether the member was ideologically closer to Nathaniel Banks (0.258) or William Aiken (-0.357).

to members who were ideologically closer to Banks than to Aiken (labeled "Banks supporter" in the table).

A glance at the various committee chairs also reveals Banks's attempt to recognize important members of the Republican Party. Lewis Campbell, an early party front-runner for Speaker, was given the chairmanship of Ways and Means, which established him as the prime Republican floor leader in the House. Ex-Whig Alexander Pennington, who at times garnered substantial support in the Republican caucus during the speakership balloting, was provided with the chairmanship of Foreign Affairs. Finally, Joshua Giddings, one of the intellectual leaders of the Republican Party and perhaps the prime mover in caucus, was given the chairmanship of Claims and the second position (behind ex-Free-Soil Democrat Galusha Grow) on Territories, the committee that would take the lead in all matters of slavery extension (or prohibition).[14]

An examination of the composition of House standing committees, illustrated in table 7.2, reveals a similar story. Relying again on CSW-NOMINATE scores, we find that Banks voters, while only constituting a plurality of the chamber (103 of 234 seats), controlled majorities on 18 of the 34 standing committees. Focusing on antislavery preferences more generally, we find that Banks supporters comprised majorities on 27 of the 34 standing committees.

We also examine the eight standing committees in the House that Silbey (1989, 12–13) identifies as the "key" policy committees in the 34th Congress: Ways and Means, Commerce, Public Lands, Judiciary, Manufactures, Agriculture, Foreign Affairs, and Territories. First, six of the eight committees were controlled by Banks voters, while all eight possessed pro-Banks (i.e., antislavery) ideological majorities.[15] Finally, all eight committees were chaired by Banks voters. Thus, Banks distributed his plurality coalition quite efficiently by staffing the most important House committees with antislavery advocates.

Taken as a whole, Banks's committee assignments were seen as a significant victory for the Republican Party. As the *New York Herald* reported: "The antislavery element is the governing power of the House committees" (2/15/1856, 4). The *Washington Union*, the main Democratic Party media organ, was more strident in its analysis: "Mr. Banks selects as the heads of those Committees to which are to be confided questions immediately material to the people of the South . . . the most offensive and the most reckless fanatics of the Free States" (reprinted in the *NYTrib*, 2/16/1856, 5).

---

[14] Horace Greeley suggested that Giddings's placement in the second spot on Territories was strategic, "because of the bugbear he has been represented" (*NYTrib*, 2/18/1856, 6). Rather than fan the flames of Southern discontent, Banks selected the ex-Democrat Grow (who was "solid" on the slavery issue) for the top spot.

[15] Relying again on past party affiliations, Silbey (1989, 12–13) argues that none of these eight committees possessed a Republican majority.

TABLE 7.2.
Composition of House standing committees, 34th Congress

Committee	Committee median	Banks voters	Banks supporters	Total members
Revisal and Unfinished Business	0.457	3	3	5
Judiciary	0.410	4	5	9
Engraving	0.401	2	2	3
Territories	0.380	6	6	9
District of Columbia	0.379	5	6	9
Public Lands	0.337	5	5	9
Patents	0.330	3	3	5
Revolutionary Claims	0.329	4	5	9
Agriculture	0.324	5	5	9
Ways and Means	0.308	5	6	9
Military Affairs	0.282	5	5	9
Elections	0.262	5	6	9
Foreign Affairs	0.241	5	5	9
Public Expenditures	0.238	5	5	9
Public Buildings and Grounds	0.223	3	3	5
Invalid Pensions	0.212	5	5	9
Indian Affairs	0.204	5	5	9
Manufactures	0.150	4	5	9
Post Office and Post Roads	0.145	5	6	9
Naval Affairs	0.145	3	5	9
Accounts	0.121	3	3	5
Roads and Canals	0.024	2	5	9
Claims	0.019	4	5	9
Private Land Claims	0.010	3	5	9
Commerce	0.009	5	5	9
Expenditures in the Treasury Dept.	0.007	2	3	5
Revolutionary Pensions	-0.030	4	5	9
Militia	-0.062	3	4	9
Expenditures in the War Dept.	-0.101	2	2	5
Expenditures in the Navy Dept.	-0.124	1	2	5
Expenditures in the Post Office	-0.129	1	1	5
Expenditures on the Public Bldgs.	-0.210	1	1	5
Mileage	-0.229	2	2	5
Expenditures in the State Dept.	-0.295	2	2	5

Note: "Committee median" is the median member's first dimension CSW-NOMINATE score. "Banks voters" indicates the number of members who voted for Banks on the final (133rd) ballot for Speaker. "Banks supporters" indicates the number of members ideologically closer to Banks than to Aiken.

Voting behavior

Having won the speakership, struggled to fill out the remainder of the officer corp, and secured control of all major standing committees, the Republicans now faced the task of operating as a floor voting coalition. After receiving the president's message in mid-February 1856, nearly three months after initially convening, the House began official legislative proceedings. The questions now were: (1) Did the group of Banks voters have the persistence to operate as a party? and (2) Could a one-issue coalition of politicians from an assortment of prior partisan backgrounds work together in a consistent and cohesive way?

The answer to these questions would be "yes," thanks mostly to the dominating effect that the "Kansas issue" would have on House politics for the remainder of the 34th Congress.[16] After the passage of the Kansas-Nebraska Act in 1854, the Kansas Territory was established. In the spring of 1855, a proslavery territorial legislature was selected, thanks in part to the votes of proslavery Missourians (termed "Border Ruffians"), who streamed into Kansas on Election Day and stuffed the ballot boxes. Antislavery Kansans, and newly arrived antislavery émigrés, rejected the legislative elections as fraudulent and set up their own rival territorial legislature. For the remainder of 1855 through early 1856, the situation was tense, as the "legitimate" government tried to crack down on the antislavery insurgents. As a result, pro- and antislavery militias were formed and marched across Kansas, which resulted in isolated cases of terror and violence. These images were portrayed in graphic detail under the banner of "Bleeding Kansas" by Northern antislavery newspapers, such as Horace Greeley's *New York Tribune*.

Thus, during the lengthy speakership battle, newspaper reports on the situation in Kansas helped keep the slavery extension issue front and center, which in turn kept the Republican coalition together. Moreover, after the organization of the House was completed, Kansas helped the Republicans segue into governing, as the president's message focused on law and order in Kansas, and the first issue on the legislative agenda was the contested election case involving Kansas's delegate seat. By May, three separate but related events solidified Kansas's hold on both Congress and the nation: (1) the sack of Lawrence, an antislavery stronghold, by the Border Ruffians; (2) the caning of Senator Charles Sumner (R-Mass.) on the Senate floor by Rep. Preston Brooks (D-S.C.) after Sumner's "Crime against Kansas" speech; and (3) the Pottawatomie Massacre, wherein the antislavery zealot John Brown murdered five proslavery Kansans. For the rest of the session, the slavery extension issue, symbolized by the happenings in and related to Kansas,

---

[16] For overviews of political happenings in Kansas during time, see Potter (1976, 199–224), Holt (1978, 192–97), and Etcheson (2004, 89–138).

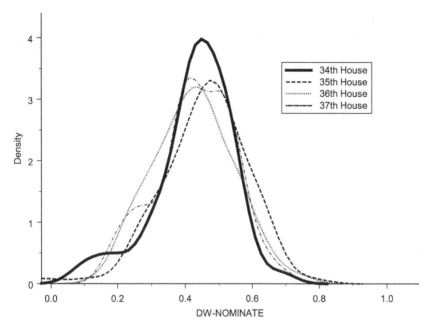

FIGURE 7.1. Kernel density plot of Banks Coalition and Republican Party.

permeated congressional debate. While many had hoped that the Kansas-Nebraska Act of 1854 would put the slavery-extension issue to rest once and for all, it in fact had the opposite effect—it established the preeminence of the issue by reorganizing partisan politics in a strictly proslavery/antislavery fashion.

Thanks to the Kansas issue, the House Republicans were able to transition from a narrowly organized ideological coalition to a partisan coalition in short order. This ideological-partisan development can be examined further by comparing the spatial location of the Banks coalition in the 34th Congress with the spatial location of House Republicans in the 35th, 36th, and 37th Congresses, using the first-dimension DW-NOMINATE score as the common metric.[17] If the Republican Party truly began as an ideological coalition organized around antislavery tenets, then the spatial location of Banks voters in the 34th Congress should correspond well to the spatial location of Republicans in succeeding Congresses. Density plots for the Banks coalition (34th Congress) and the Republican Party (35th through 37th Congresses) appear in figure 7.1. As the plots indicate, the Banks coalition and the three sets of Republicans overlap nicely on the right (antislavery) side of the first DW-NOMINATE dimension. Summary statistics, which ap-

[17] Here, we are comparing densities, as well as means and variances, across Congresses, so a dynamic measure like DW-NOMINATE is warranted.

TABLE 7.3.
Summary statistics for Banks Coalition and Republican Party

House	Number of Members	Mean DW-NOMINATE Score	Standard Deviation
34th House	103	0.427	0.117
35th House	92	0.459	0.126
36th House	118	0.425	0.121
37th House	107	0.431	0.116

Note: Figures for 34th House represent the Banks voting coalition on the last speakership ballot. Figures for the 35th through the 37th House represent the Republican Party.

pear in table 7.3, tell a similar story.[18] These results suggest that the ideological coalition that selected Banks for Speaker in the 34th Congress and the Republican Party of the 35th through 37th Congresses occupied the same space along the slavery-based dimension. Thus, what began as an ideological coalition quickly became a partisan coalition that was organized along ideological lines.

INTERLUDE: THE 35TH CONGRESS

While they made the most of their institutional rise to prominence in the 34th Congress, the Republicans still only possessed a plurality of the House, and their mass party engine was in its infancy. As a result, the Democrats took advantage of their established mass party linkages to bounce back in the 1856–57 elections and regain majority control of the House in the 35th Congress. Their electoral success bridged North and South, as the Democrats captured 56 seats in the free states and 75 in the slave states, compared to only 25 and 57, respectively, in the 1854–55 elections (Martis 1989, 108–10).[19] While a casual observer might interpret these results as evidence that the Democrats had survived and overcome the fallout from the Kansas-Nebraska Act, this was not the case. In fact, their electoral success in the North was somewhat illusory, as many of their victories were due to three-party races in which Republicans and Americans split the anti-Democratic vote. Of the 56 free state seats that the Democrats won in the 1856–57 elections, only 37 were won by outright majorities (Dubin 1998, 176–79).

[18] Results from means and variance tests (t and F tests) indicate that there are no significant differences between (a) the Banks coalition and any of the three sets of Republicans and (b) any two of the three sets of Republicans.

[19] There were 234 House seats in the 34th Congress and 237 in the 35th Congress. The 56 Democratic free state seats in the 35th Congress include two seats in Minnesota and one in Oregon, both of which had recently entered the Union.

After their initial success in the organization of the 34th House, the Republicans were faced with a dilemma—they could continue to cooperate with the Americans and work to maintain their momentum, or they could pull back, distance themselves from the nativism, and focus on emphasizing their main issue: opposition to slavery-extension. The decision would be made during the presidential convention season in 1856. The Americans met first, in February, and struggled in their attempt to organize, as the slavery issue divided party members. After lengthy and contentious politicking, the Southern wing of the party emerged victorious by passing a plank supporting the Kansas-Nebraska Act. Many Northern Americans who were keen on the growing antislavery sentiment in the free states refused to accept the plank and withdrew from the convention. The remaining American delegates selected ex-president (and ex-Whig) Millard Fillmore as their presidential nominee. Fillmore had been instrumental in the passage of the Compromise of 1850 and was considered acceptable by Southerners; as a result, he was viewed as a "doughface" by Northern antislavery advocates.

In June, the Northern Americans met shortly before the Republican convention to select their own presidential nominee. They chose Nathaniel Banks, hoping that it would lead to a fusion effort with the Republicans. However, the Republicans had other ideas. First, Banks rejected the American nomination and severed his ties to the party, thus reasserting his support of the Republican cause. Second, the Republicans chose John C. Frémont as their presidential nominee. This was a thumb in the eye to the Americans, as the ex-Democrat Frémont was an antislavery advocate with strong Catholic ties.[20] The Northern Americans then scrambled to fuse in some fashion with the Republicans and suggested American William Johnston, a former governor from Pennsylvania, as a vice presidential candidate. But they were rebuffed again by the Republicans, who selected William L. Dayton, an ex-Whig senator from New Jersey with no connections to the American Party. The Northern Americans then tried to put together their own Frémont-Johnston ticket, but Johnston refused their nomination. In the end, they were left with the decision to support either Frémont and the Republicans or Fillmore and the Southern Americans.[21] Bowing to Northern public opinion, they grudgingly supported Frémont.[22]

[20] Frémont's father was French Catholic; in addition, Frémont's marriage ceremony was presided over by a priest, and his daughter attended a Catholic school (Anbinder 1992, 224).

[21] While the Republicans made no overt entreaties to the Americans, they adopted a convention platform that was intentionally ambiguous on nativism. This was an implicit "olive branch" to the Americans and provided them with enough of a face-saving excuse to reject Fillmore and support Frémont. It was also an attempt to reach out to the mass of German Protestant immigrants, who were considered to be up for grabs in the election. See Gienapp (1987, 336).

[22] For a description of the events surrounding the American and Republican conventions, as well as the failed Republican-American fusion, see Potter (1976, 254–58), Gienapp (1987, 305–46), and Anbinder (1992, 206–19).

While Frémont would lose to James Buchanan in the November 1856 presidential election, the Republicans had clearly made inroads. Frémont won 11 Northern states, losing only the free states of California, Illinois, Indiana, New Jersey, and Pennsylvania to Buchanan, whereas Fillmore, the Southern American candidate, could only capture Maryland. Thus, the Republicans had clearly emerged as the second major party to stand alongside the Democrats. But their refusal to coordinate with the Northern Americans on a presidential ticket was costly in the short term. Specifically, the Northern Americans refused to disband their weakening organization and vowed to compete with the Republicans for the anti-Democratic vote across a number of the free states in the 1856–57 congressional elections. This meant that the Republicans would have to kill off the Northern Americans before vying directly with the Democrats for national preeminence. As a result, the Republicans had to implicitly cede control of the House in the 35th Congress to the Democrats in order to direct their attention to eradicating the Americans. As mentioned previously, the Democrats wound up winning 19 free-state seats with a simple plurality, thanks to Republican-American electoral jockeying.

Nevertheless, the Republicans viewed the 1856–57 congressional elections as a success. They captured 91 House seats in their first organized foray as a mass party—dominating their electoral battles with the Americans and sweeping them completely from the free states.[23] Moreover, Republican candidates performed quite well in head-to-head matchups with Democratic candidates. In those states in which the Americans failed to field candidates—Connecticut, Indiana, Maine, Michigan, Minnesota, New Hampshire, Rhode Island, Vermont, and Wisconsin—Republicans won 28 of 39 seats (Dubin 1998, 176–79). From the Republicans' perspective, then, refusing to fuse with the American Party while building their organization completely around the slavery issue had paid dividends; it was just a matter of time before control of the House was theirs once again.

The politics of the 35th Congress would suggest that the Republicans' time would come quickly. The slavery extension issue once again dominated the congressional proceedings and was highlighted by two events. First, the Supreme Court handed down a decision in *Dred Scott v. Sandford* (1857) that polarized the pro- and antislavery factions even more.[24] The court ruled that the Missouri Compromise of 1820 was unconstitutional, in that Congress possessed no right under the Constitution to rule on the question of slavery in the territories. Broadly interpreted, the court's ruling suggested that slavery was a constitutional right that could not be abridged short of

[23] The Americans controlled 14 House seats at the outset of the 35th Congress: two in Georgia, two in Kentucky, one in Louisiana, three in Maryland, two in Missouri, one in North Carolina, and three in Tennessee (Martis 1989, 110).
[24] A voluminous literature exists on the *Dred Scott* case. Typical surveys of the politics of the case are found in Potter (1976, 267–96) and Fehrenbacher (1978).

adopting a constitutional amendment. This enraged antislavery advocates and, as five of the six justices supporting the decision either were or had been slaveholders, elicited further cries of a Slave Power conspiracy.

Second, the situation in Kansas intensified as the proslavery Kansas legislature organized a constitutional convention (boycotted by the antislavery advocates in the territory) at Lecompton to prepare for statehood. In December 1857, after some political twists and turns, a constitution was produced, and the people of Kansas were given the option to vote for it either with or without slavery. Charging fraud throughout the electoral process, the antislavery Kansans refused to participate in the referendum, which led to a landslide for the proslavery constitution. Thus, Congress simply needed to ratify the Lecompton Constitution and Kansas would enter the Union as a slave state. This led to a major struggle in Congress between pro- and antislavery members. While the Senate approved the Lecompton Constitution, the House did not and instead adopted a substitute that would require resubmission of the constitution to the citizens of Kansas for an up-or-down vote. A joint House-Senate conference committee eventually adopted the substitute, and on August 2, 1858, Kansans rejected the Lecompton Constitution by an overwhelming margin of 11,300 to 1,788.[25] As a result, Kansas would remain a territory until 1861, when it would enter the Union as a free state.

The battle over the Lecompton Constitution was especially damaging to the House Democrats. Much like the Kansas-Nebraska proceedings four years earlier, Southern Democrats had placed enormous pressure on the party's Northern wing to support their proslavery position, and many Northern House members subsequently buckled and voted for the Lecompton Constitution. But their support was not enough to gain its passage.

Nonetheless, Northern voters were incensed, and similar to the aftermath of the Kansas-Nebraska proceedings, Northern Democrats would be punished severely in the 1858–59 congressional elections. When the electoral dust had cleared, the Democrats' seat share in the free states dropped from 56 to 26, which left them with a total of 92 seats in the upcoming 36th House.[26] The Republicans benefited considerably from this anti-Democratic backlash by capturing 113 seats,[27] yet they were short of a majority, thanks

[25] For a detailed overview of Lecompton politics, see Potter (1976, 297–327) and Etcheson (2004, 139–84).

[26] These 92 seats include seven members who Martis codes as "Independent Democrats" (1989, 112). By and large, this was an electoral label used to sidestep explicit positions on the slavery issue; however, in Congress, these members behaved as regular Democrats, and we code them as such. Another group of eight Democrats, the Anti-Lecompton Democrats, are *not* counted among the 92, as the Anti-Lecomptons behaved as an independent party in organizational politics and subsequent house proceedings.

[27] The 92 Democratic seats and 113 Republican seats represent the share at the convening of the 36th House before contested election cases would be heard and the state of Kansas would be added to the Union. See Martis (1989, 112). Note that several differences exist be-

to the electoral success of two minor parties: Americans (24 seats) and Anti-Lecompton Democrats (8 seats).[28]

As a result, by late 1859 the future of the House organization in the 36th Congress was very much in doubt. With no majority party, and several different parties vying for advantage, a number of outcomes were possible. Much would be determined by the election of a Speaker.

THE SPEAKERSHIP ELECTION OF 1859–1860

Politicking for the House speakership began well in advance of the convening of the 36th Congress on December 5, 1859.[29] Various possible combinations involving the Americans and Anti-Lecompton Democrats with either the Republicans and/or Democrats were speculated freely (*NYT*, 11/21/1859, 1; 12/3/1859, 4; 12/5/1859, 1, 4). Yet, as the party caucuses were held in the days before December 5, it appeared that each party would enter the speakership election with an eye toward surveying the political landscape before joining any coalition. The Democratic nominee was Thomas S. Bocock (Va.), a political moderate in the Jeffersonian mold who easily defeated John Phelps (Mo.) 40–17 with five votes scattering in a caucus vote on December 3 (*NYT*, 12/5/1859, 1). The Republicans caucused but made no nomination, deciding instead to coalesce around the top vote-getter on the first speakership ballot. The leading candidates would be John Sherman (Ohio), a mainstream Republican with strong business ties, and Galusha Grow (Pa.), a favorite of the Radical element of the party (*CT*, 11/21/1859, 2; *NYT*, 12/3/1859, 4; 12/5/1859, 1, 4). The Americans and Anti-Lecomptons floated

tween the major party codes in Martis and those presented in the *Congressional Globe* (36-1, 12/5/1859, 1–2). The *Globe* lists 109 Republicans, while Martis counts 113. The discrepancies are Luther Carter (N.Y.), George Briggs (N.Y.), John T. Nixon (N.J.), and John L. N. Stratton (N.J.), all of whom are listed as Americans in the *Globe*. According to Dubin (1998, 182), Carter and Briggs were elected on a Republican-American fusion ticket, while Nixon and Stratton were elected as Republicans. Finally, the *Globe* lists all Democrats as one group, 101 in total. The one-member discrepancy between the *Globe* and Martis's total of 100 (broken into three distinct groups) is Samuel H. Woodson (Mo.), who is listed as an Opposition (Southern American) member by Martis. Dubin (1998, 182) agrees with Martis in coding Woodson as an American. As a result, we incorporate Martis's party codes throughout the remainder of this analysis.

[28] Martis (1989, 35, 43) breaks these 24 American members into two groups: Americans and Opposition. The Opposition group (19 members) was located entirely in the soon-to-be Confederate states, and combined Southern Americans and former Whigs in a fusion alignment. For simplicity, and because all 24 members participated in an American caucus prior to and during the speakership battle, we label them all as Americans for the remainder of this analysis.

[29] The speakership election of 1859–60 is covered in varying levels of detail in the following works: Nixon (1872); Rhodes (1902, 418–28); Crenshaw (1942); Nichols (1948, 270–76); Nevins (1950, 116–24); Hicken (1960); Henig (1973); Potter (1976, 386–91); Bensel (1990, 47–57); Brown (2006, 152–88). The most comprehensive examination of the election, however, is an unpublished paper by Bensel (1985).

several possible nominees but left little settled, planning instead to use their numbers strategically as opportunities permitted.

After the roll of members-elect was called on December 5, the Clerk—former Democratic House member James C. Allen (Ill.)—called the House to order and proceeded to the election of a Speaker (for a breakdown of the balloting, see appendix 2).[30] The first ballot was taken without producing a winner. With 116 votes required for a majority, Bocock led with 86 votes, followed by Sherman and Grow with 66 and 43 votes, respectively. Alexander Boteler (Va.) was the chief candidate among the Americans with 14. Twenty-one additional votes were scattered among 12 different candidates (CG, 36-1, 12/5/1859, 2). Based on the aforementioned Republican caucus agreement, Sherman—the top Republican vote-getter—became the party's official nominee, as Grow bowed out, announcing that he had no wish "to retard the organization of the House" (CT, 12/6/1859, 1).

Before a second ballot was taken, John B. Clark (D-Mo.) gained the floor and remarked on the slate of candidates for Speaker. After a period of debate (which stretched into the following day) as to whether Clark's comments were in order, the House Clerk, as presiding officer, allowed him to have his say (CG, 36-1, 12/5/1859, 3).[31] Clark questioned the fitness of Sherman to lead the chamber by citing Sherman's signature (among those of 68 Republicans in total) on a document supporting the publication and distribution of a compendium by the Southern writer Hinton R. Helper.[32] Clark's concern focused specifically on a portion of Helper's compendium, an abridgment of his 1857 work, The Impending Crisis of the South: How to Meet It, which was a stinging indictment of the Southern slave economy.[33] More threatening to Southern aristocrats, however, was Helper's focus, which was to pit poor Southern whites against white slaveholders by arguing that the average Southern farmer could not compete effectively against the slave labor employed by the plantation owner. In effect, Clark argued that Helper was attempting to foment a class-based revolution among the white inhabitants of the South. For members of the Southern elite, this was akin to treason, especially at a time when they felt their way of life was under siege—John Brown's failed raid of the federal armory at Harpers Ferry, Virginia, was only months old, and his hanging occurred less than a week earlier on December 2.[34] Moreover, they believed the Republicans, especially those members who were associated with Helper, were a party to it.

[30] For the entire congressional proceedings on the speakership election, see CG, 36-1, 12/5/1859 through 2/1/1860, 1–655.

[31] Specifically, the Clerk would not rule on the point of order, deciding instead to "submit it to the House for their decision" (CG, 36-1, 12/5/1859, 3). Not having the votes either to proceed to another ballot or to adjourn, the Republicans were forced to indulge Clark.

[32] For a transcript of Clark's remarks, see CG, 36-1, 12/6/1859, 15–18.

[33] For more on Helper and the effects of his Impending Crisis book, see Brown (2006).

[34] For a description of the events of Brown's failed raid and the implications that were wrought, see Potter (1976, 356–84).

Dion (1997, 93) contends that Clark's ability to gain the floor and introduce the "Helper issue" at a time when "the Republicans were within shouting distance of a majority" was not an accident. Rather, House Clerk James C. Allen used his position as presiding officer to recognize Clark and thus steer the politics of the speakership election down a path that disadvantaged the Republicans. This would not be the only time that Allen's decisions as de facto presiding officer were questioned on partisan grounds.

Not surprisingly, Clark's remarks sparked a lengthy debate on the true intentions of the "Black" Republicans, that is, whether their organization intended not only to oppose slavery extension in the territories but also to stamp out slavery where it already existed, and, moreover, whether they would turn a blind eye to slave revolts in the South should they arise. Sherman responded to these accusations by insisting that he had not read Helper's *Impending Crisis* book; nor did he remember signing his name in support of Helper's compendium (but took responsibility, nonetheless). Regarding the more extreme accusations, he stated that he "would not trespass on a right of a single southern citizen; and I defy any man to show anywhere a word that I have uttered that would lead to a different conclusion" (*CG*, 36-1, 12/6/1859, 21).

Nevertheless, the deed was done, as the Democrats had achieved their intended goal of prolonging the speakership contest. By taking advantage of the lingering John Brown hysteria, the Democrats used the Helper affair to paint Sherman and the Republicans as radical abolitionists who were hell-bent on purifying the nation. This radicalization prevented the Anti-Lecomptons and Americans from joining a Republican-led alliance, lest they open themselves to attack in subsequent elections.[35]

The second ballot, taken on December 7, was thus a precursor to the long struggle that lay ahead. Per their caucus agreement, the Republicans began coalescing around Sherman, who received 107 votes, 9 short of a majority. Bocock was second with 88 votes, while the Americans moved their support to John A. Gilmer (N.C.), who received 22 votes. Fourteen additional votes (cast mostly by Anti-Lecomptons) scattered among 10 other candidates. This would roughly be the pattern over the next 10 days and eight ballots, as Sherman remained in the lead, increasing his total to as many as 111 votes, 4 shy of the total necessary for election, with Bocock holding firm in the mid-80s, the Americans coalescing behind Gilmer before returning to

---

[35] That the Democrats raised the Helper issue during the speakership election was not a major surprise. The Republicans' alleged support of the *Impending Crisis*, and its revolutionary message, was a hot topic in Washington nearly a week before Congress convened (see *NYT*, 12/1/1859, 1). Moreover, when Clark was just beginning to raise the issue, Republican leaders knew exactly what he intended, and Benjamin Stanton (R-Ohio) attempted to move a quick adjournment. Thaddeus Stevens (R-Pa.), however, saw the inevitable: "I hope the gentleman from Ohio will not move to adjourn. These things must come out, and they might as well come out now" (*CG*, 36-1, 12/6/1859, 3).

Boteler, and the Anti-Lecomptons (and a few major-party members) scattering their votes.[36] Without further support from outside the Republican Party, Sherman could not secure a majority.

Despite the Democrats' continued attacks on Sherman, the Republicans stuck with him as their candidate. Their strategy was to ignore the Democrats' slings and arrows and focus on maintaining their internal cohesion, until that point when additional members would come to Sherman's side. Three Anti-Lecompton members—John B. Haskin (N.Y.), John Hickman (Pa.), and John Schwartz (Pa.)—joined the Republican coalition on the fifth ballot, inching Sherman to within four votes of victory, but no additional support was immediately forthcoming.[37] The Democrats, on the other hand, were actively trying to build a cross-party coalition. They had approached the Americans about coordinating around either Bocock or Gilmer, should a sufficient number of votes be first concentrated on one or the other for a joint coalition to effect a majority, but were rebuffed (*NYT*, 12/12/1859, 1).[38] They also placed increased pressures on the Anti-Lecompton Democrats by invoking party ties and responsibilities in an attempt to bring them in line. Finally, several Democrats, led by John J. McRae (Miss.), Martin J. Crawford (Ga.), and Otho R. Singleton (Miss.), raised the possibility of disunion should a Republican of Sherman's ilk be elected.

A 12th ballot was taken on December 19, with little change in the voting. Bocock then announced his withdrawal from the contest. This left the Dem-

---

[36] Vote totals fluctuated across the various ballots, due to various members pairing.

[37] One constant frustration for the Republicans was George Briggs (N.Y.), who was elected on a joint Republican-American fusion ticket. In the speakership balloting, he proved to be more American than Republican, since he supported Gilmer and other American candidates rather than Sherman.

[38] While the Democrats were initially denied in their request to fuse around Gilmer, they would be put to the test several days later on December 16, 1859. On the first ballot that day (the seventh overall), the Republican delegations from Pennsylvania and New Jersey switched to Gilmer, which drove his vote total to 36. The *New York Times* (12/17/1859, 8) contended that this was a strategic ploy by the Republicans to embarrass the Democrats and potentially court a few Southern Americans:

Mr. Gilmer was to receive 30 votes before being dropped to enable him and his friends at home to charge the Democracy with preventing a Southern organization by refusing to unite on him when he had a sufficient vote to elect. For this purpose the loan of a few votes [from the Republicans] for one ballot was easily negotiated . . .

The Democrats, confused by the situation and wary of the motives of the Republican defectors, stuck to Bocock. On the next ballot, the Republican defectors returned to Sherman. A subset of this group of Republicans, along with most Americans, went back to Gilmer on December 22, on the 18th ballot, but the Democrats once again refused to move from the Democratic candidate (at that point, John Millson).

Later events would suggest that the Republicans who moved to Gilmer were not doing so as a ploy to embarrass the Democrats, as the *NYT* contended; rather, their actions were directed at the Republican leadership, with the message being that Sherman should be replaced with a more moderate candidate. (For a discussion of the "conspiracy theories" surrounding the Republican defectors, see Bensel 1985, 57–61.)

ocrats scattered, as no replacement had been agreed on. As a result, for the next few days, they divided their votes among several Democratic candidates, including John S. Phelps (Mo.), William Barksdale (Miss.), Miles Taylor (La.), and John A. McClernand (Ill.), as well as American Alexander Boteler (Va.). The Republicans doggedly stuck to Sherman, who still fell at least four votes short of a majority. The Democrats' last gasp before the Christmas holiday was to coordinate behind John S. Millson (Va.), but he could get no more than 95 votes. Several American members, led by Emerson Etheridge (Tenn.) and Joshua Hill (Ga.), declared that they could not vote for Millson or any other Democrat who had supported the Lecompton policy advocated by President Buchanan and the administration Democrats.

More ballots were taken after Christmas—raising the total to 24—without a decision. Republicans continued to support Sherman, who was still four votes shy of victory, while the Democrats tried out Horace Maynard (A-Tenn.) and Charles Scott (D-Calif.) with little success. The New Year began in a similar way: 10 ballots were taken between January 4 and 11, with no majority. The Republicans remained united behind Sherman, pushing him within three votes of a majority on six different occasions, while the Democrats alternated between McClernand, Clement Vallandigham (D-Ohio), and Andrew J. Hamilton (D-Tex.). And, as before, the Americans settled in behind Gilmer, while the Anti-Lecomptons scattered their votes.

At this point, the Republicans attempted to end the stalemate by using a procedural tool of the recent past: a plurality rule. In fact, a plurality rule had been raised much earlier in the session, on December 9, by Anti-Lecompton member John Hickman. At that time, Hickman's resolution, which was identical in form to the rule used to end the speakership battles in the 31st and 34th Congresses, was embroiled in a procedural quagmire involving questions of order and precedence (CG, 36-1, 12/9/1859 and 12/10/1859, 87– 90), and it was subsequently forgotten as the House continued to ballot for Speaker. On January 13, William Pennington (R-N.J.) tried to resuscitate the plurality rule but encountered the same set of difficulties that Hickman faced. Specifically, the Clerk ruled that Pennington's plurality-rule resolution was out of order, because precedence was given to the current order of business, which, until disposed of, was the election of a Speaker by the standard House rule (i.e., majority rule). To be considered, Pennington's resolution had to come up under unanimous consent, which several Democrats insisted they would not grant (CG, 36-1, 1/13/1860, 444–47). In effect, the Democrats, with the Clerk's help, were able to stonewall to prevent a plurality rule from being considered. Three additional attempts were made to alter the voting rule—a proposal for a simpler plurality rule and two proposals for a system of runoff elections—but they too were ruled out of order (CG, 36-1, 1/17/1860 and 1/25/1860, 484–93, 579–80).

Two weeks of acrimonious debate finally led to a return to voting, as four ballots were taken on January 25 and 26, 1860, once again with no result. The Republicans remained steadfastly behind Sherman, while the Democrats were divided; some returned to Bocock and others joined a coalition of Americans behind William N. H. Smith (A-N.C.). Smith was "a new member, unobtrusive and quite unknown to his fellow members; but his colleagues represented him to be a gentleman of character, intelligence and worth, firmly a whig, elected as an American, and hostile to the administration" (Nixon 1872, 213). At this point, matters started to come to a head. The Americans and Democrats began to confer in private regarding Smith's candidacy, and an informal agreement was reached wherein the Democrats would swing en masse to Smith if the Americans could first coordinate on him with their entire coalition (Nixon 1872, 214).

The drama would unfold on January 27, on the 39th ballot.[39] After the roll call had finished, it was revealed that Smith's vote total had increased— from 33 votes on the previous ballot to 63 votes on the current one, thanks to the addition of a number of Democrats as well as six Republicans: George Briggs (N.Y.), Benjamin F. Junkin (Pa.), William Millward (Pa.), Edward Joy Morris (Pa.), George W. Scranton (Pa.), and John T. Nixon (N.J.). At that point, Robert Mallory (A-Ky.) gained the floor and stated:

> I feel myself called upon, at this stage of the proceeding, to announce the fact that we have now received enough votes for our nominee for the Speaker's chair to insure his election by the aid of the vote of the Democratic party of this House. I now announce to gentlemen upon the Democratic side, to the House, and to the country, the fact that, in view of this state of the case, we will present Mr. Smith, of North Carolina, again as our candidate for the Speakership upon the next ballot. Every member of our party has voted for him. That was the condition precedent, I understand, prescribed by gentleman upon the other side of the House to obtaining their votes. Even now, if they will rise in their places before the result is announced, and change their votes, they may make Mr. Smith, of North Carolina Speaker of this House, and the Republican party will thereby be defeated. Let the country know the fact. (CG, 36-1, 1/27/1860, 611)

This opened the floodgates, as a wave of Democrats heeded Mallory's call and began changing their votes. After 51 Democrats had switched their votes to Smith, the unthinkable for Republicans had come to pass—Smith, with 114 votes, had a bare majority. This is illustrated in table 7.4, which documents three stages of voting on the 39th ballot: the first pass through the roll, the breakdown after the 51 switchers, and the final tally.

---

[39] For details, see CG, 36-1, 1/27/1860, 611–21.

Table 7.4.
Voting during the 39th speakership ballot, 36th Congress

Candidate	First pass through the roll	After wave of Democratic switchers	Final tally
John Sherman (R-Oh.)	105	105	106
William N. H. Smith (A-N.C.)	63	114	112
Thomas Bocock (D-Va.)	25	2	1
John G. Davis (AL-Ind.)	6	1	1
Thomas Florence (D-Pa.)	4	0	0
John S. Phelps (D-Mo.)	4	0	0
Charles H. Larrabee (D-Wis.)	2	0	0
John S. Millson (D-Va.)	2	0	0
Henry Burnett (D-Ky.)	1	0	0
Horace F. Clark (AL-N.Y.)	1	1	1
Thomas Corwin (R-Ohio)	1	1	4
William Howard (D-Ohio)	1	1	1
James Jackson (D-Ga.)	1	0	0
John J. McRae (D-Miss.)	1	0	0
Otho R. Singleton (D-Miss.)	1	0	0
Miles Taylor (D-La.)	1	0	0
Zebulon B. Vance (D-N.C.)	1	1	1
Warren Winslow (D-N.C.)	1	0	0
William Pennington (R-N.J.)	0	0	1
Unknown	6	1	0
Total votes	227	227	228

Source: *Congressional Globe*, 36-1, 1/27/1860, 611–21. Successful replication of Bensel (1985, table 2.4).

Note: "Unknown" category represents members who did not announce their original vote upon switching to Smith.

But Smith's bare majority was unofficial, as the Clerk had not yet calculated and announced a final tally. At that point, John Sherman, who had been abstaining on most ballots, rose and cast a vote for Thomas Corwin (R-Ohio).[40] This had the effect of increasing the number of votes to 228, which raised the bar for victory to 115. In quick succession, three Republicans who had been supporting Smith—Junkin, Scranton, and Morris—switched their votes (to Sherman, Corwin, and Corwin, respectively), leaving Smith with 111, 4 votes shy of victory. Two additional Democrats—Clement L. Val-

[40] This was just his second vote over the many weeks of balloting; Sherman had cast a vote for William Pennington (R-N.J.) on the first speakership ballot. Tradition and notions of honor dictated that nominees for Speaker abstain from voting, especially for themselves. As far as we can tell, this is the one instance when a Speaker nominee voted in order to raise the size of the necessary majority and thus deny election to an opponent.

landigham (Ohio) and Samuel S. Cox (Ohio)—then switched their votes to Smith, but an additional Republican, Nixon, who had been supporting Smith switched to Pennington. This left the final tally at Smith 112, Sherman 106, and Corwin 4, with 6 votes scattering. Smith was thus left 3 votes short of a majority.

Immediately after the Clerk read the final tally, Warren Winslow (D-N.C.) moved to proceed to another ballot. John Hickman (AL-Pa.) countered by moving to adjourn. The Democrats saw that they had the momentum and wished to finish off the Republicans. During the lengthy switching on the 39th ballot, a number of Democrats pressured several scattering members— regular Democrats William S. Holman (Ind.) and William Allen (Ohio) and Anti-Lecompton Democrats Garnett B. Adrain (N.J.) and John G. Davis (Ind.)—to support Smith (*NYT*, 1/28/1860, 1; Nixon 1872, 215–16).[41] They felt that they could gain their support on another ballot. The Republicans, on the other hand, were stunned by the proceedings and sought to regroup. As Samuel Curtis (R-Iowa) remarked, "I wish to say, Mr. Clerk, that our ranks are a little confused just at this time [laughter]; and we are disposed to insist on an adjournment ... we ought to have a little time to consult together" (*CG*, 36-1, 1/27/1860, 621).

After some heated discussion, the House considered a full weekend adjournment, offered by Thaddeus Stevens (R-Pa.), and a roll call was taken. The result was 114–111 in favor of the extended adjournment (*CG*, 36-1, 1/27/1860, 621). The roll call broke down substantially along party lines, with Republicans voting 109–1 in favor, Democrats and Americans voting 0–85 and 1–23, respectively, in opposition, and Anti-Lecomptons split 4–2. Joining the Republicans (except for George Briggs of New York) in support of adjournment were Henry Winter Davis (A-Md.), Garnett Adrain (AL-N.J.), John Haskin (AL-N.Y.), John Hickman (AL-Pa.), and John Schwartz (AL-Pa.). The House would therefore reconvene on January 30, with the weekend provided for each side to firm up their troops.

To what degree did members' preferences on the issue of slavery extension explain this adjournment vote? Similar to previous analyses, we use CSW-NOMINATE scores to examine this question. A simple probit model (not reported) that incorporates just the first CSW-NOMINATE dimension, which taps slavery-extension preferences, explains 213 of the 215 individual vote choices, or 99.1 percent.[42] (Adding a second dimension provides no additional explanatory power.) This represents a proportional reduction in

---

[41] Also, after Nixon's vote switch, and prior to the final tally being announced, a short discussion of the voting dynamics around Smith began, led by Lawrence M. Keitt (D-S.C.). William M. Dunn (R-Ind.) angrily raised a point of order, charging "that these gentlemen are purposely delaying the declaration of this vote that they may have time to *manipulate* the tender-footed Democrats on the other side" (*CG*, 36-1, 1/27/1860, 619).

[42] The two errors were Garnett Adrain (AL-N.J.), who voted "yea" but was predicted to vote "nay," and Edward Bouligny (A-La.), who voted "nay" but was predicted to vote "yea."

error (PRE) of 0.982 over the standard naive-unanimity model and 0.5 over a basic partisan model, wherein Democrats and Americans are predicted to oppose Republicans and Anti-Lecomptons.[43]

How did Smith's near-victory come about? The evidence points to a ruse perpetrated by a small band of conservative Republicans from the Mid-Atlantic states.[44] These members, five in all—Benjamin F. Junkin (Pa.), William Millward (Pa.), Edward Joy Morris (Pa.), George W. Scranton (Pa.), and John T. Nixon (N.J.)—took advantage of the brewing deal between the Democrats and Americans to drive Sherman, whom they believed could not win, from the speakership race. As Nixon recounts:

> The friends of Pennington felt that at length their time had come and prompt action was taken. Those Republicans who persisted in adhering to Sherman were formally notified that, unless he were withdrawn, in accordance with his express wishes, in favor of either Pennington or Corwin, enough votes would be given to Smith on the next ballot, from Pennsylvania and New Jersey, added to the American and Democratic vote to elect him Speaker, and upon them must rest the responsibility of allowing the organization upon any other than a Republican basis. The notice was received by some of these gentleman as a harmless ménage rather than a faithful warning. (1872, 214)

These five Republicans made good on their promise on the 39th ballot by voting for Smith. This provided the cushion necessary for the Democrats to believe that they could organize the House by switching their support to Smith. As Smith's vote total inched up steadily, Republican floor leaders grew concerned. Eventually, they became frantic and pleaded with the five Republican mavericks to switch away from Smith; after some negotiation, they agreed that Sherman would step down as the party nominee. This agreement was alluded to by Edward Joy Morris on the House floor during his subsequent switch away from Smith:

> Understanding, sir, that there is a disposition on the part of the Republican party to change front, and to present another candidate, one of two gentlemen equally distinguished for their eminent services to the country, for their nationality of opinion, and for their soundness upon the great issues which divide the country, in my opinion, I will, for the present, withhold my vote from Mr. Smith, of North Carolina, and cast it for Mr. Corwin. (CG, 36-1, 1/27/1860, 618)[45]

[43] The partisan model explains 211 of the 215 individual vote choices, or 98.1 percent. The errors were George Briggs (R-N.Y.), Horace F. Clark (AL-N.Y.), and John G. Davis (AL-Ind.), who voted "nay" but were predicted to vote "yea," and Henry Winter Davis (A-Md.), who voted "yea" but was predicted to vote "nay."

[44] The term "conservative Republican" here refers to those members with more Whiggish backgrounds who were moderate on the slavery-extension question.

[45] Nixon states that when confronted by Republican members to change his vote, he replied that "the vote will stand as recorded until Smith's election, unless Sherman was withdrawn as

Prior to the House adjournment on January 27, Sherman announced that a conference of all those who had been supporting him would meet at noon on the following day. The conference was cordial, but a number of members expressed anger toward the "cabal of five" that placed the Republicans so close to disaster. Some felt that Sherman was still electable and only required the Republicans to wait out their opposition. But, in the end, Sherman urged harmony, and a persuasive argument was made for realigning behind William Pennington (N.J.), who would likely attract five additional members— Anti-Lecomptons Garnett B. Adrain (N.J.), Jeter R. Riggs (N.J.), and John H. Reynolds (N.Y.); Republican maverick George Briggs (N.Y.); and American Henry Winter Davis (Md.)—all of whom had refused to support Sherman in the prior balloting (*NYT*, 1/30/1860, 1; *CT*, 2/2/1860, 2; Nixon 1872, 216–17).

Pennington, former governor of New Jersey, was in his first House term.[46] An ex-Whig, he was moderate on the slavery question—opposing the Lecompton Constitution and slavery extension—but also supported adherence to the laws of the land, like the Fugitive Slave Act. And, perhaps most important for securing the remaining necessary votes, Pennington was not a

---

the Republican candidate" (1872, 215). He goes on to recount the dynamics of Sherman's eventual withdrawal (215–16):

Owen Lovejoy, of Illinois, a genial and upright gentleman of strong convictions, and who had heretofore been most tenacious in adhering to Sherman, came to the writer's seat, pale with excitement and trembling with emotion, and made the appeal, "For God's and the Country's sake change that vote."

"Never, Sir," was the reply, "except upon one condition."

"What is the condition?"

"That Sherman is withdrawn as a Candidate."

"It shall be done."

"You answer for yourself, and that is not satisfactory."

"What would be satisfactory?"

"John Sherman's pledge of personal honor from his own lips that his name shall not be voted for, after today, for Speaker."

Lovejoy hastened to find Mr. Sherman, and shortly returned exclaiming, "Sherman gives the pledge."

It is unclear whether Nixon made these statements on his own, or as a representative of the group in which he acted. His account suggests the former, placing his actions and his subsequent vote switch at the very heart of the emerging drama. However, this does not square with the evidence. First, Junkin, Scranton, and Morris all switched from Smith before Nixon did, and Morris alluded to the agreement regarding Sherman's withdrawal during his switch. Second, Nixon suggests that his vote switch was pivotal to Smith coming up short—claiming that had he not changed his vote, John G. Davis was prepared to switch to Smith, which would have provided Smith with a bare majority. The proceedings in the *Congressional Globe* suggest otherwise: prior to Nixon's switch, Smith had 113 out of 228 votes cast. Even if Nixon had stuck with Smith *and* Davis had proceeded to switch his vote to Smith, Smith would still have needed one more vote to reach 115 (a bare majority). While the broad strokes in Nixon's account largely ring true, it seems that he exaggerated his individual role in the highly charged episode.

[46] Recall that Pennington, as governor of New Jersey, played a significant role in the Broad Seal War that affected the state's representation in the 26th House (see chapter 5).

signatory of the Helper compendium. While a distinct conference nomination was not made, there was an understanding that Republicans would coalesce around Pennington on the first ballot.

Reconvening on January 30, the House proceeded to ballot for Speaker. Before the voting began, Sherman officially withdrew, asking each of his partisans to "cast his vote in favor of any one of our number who can command the highest vote, or who can be elected Speaker of this House" (CG, 36-1, 1/30/1860, 634). That person would be William Pennington, who came within 3 votes of winning the speakership on the 40th ballot and received 115 votes to William N. H. Smith's 113, with 6 votes scattering. Two additional Anti-Lecomptons—Garnett B. Adrain (N.J.) and John H. Reynolds (N.Y.)—voted for Pennington, while three other members who had been courted by Pennington's friends, Jeter R. Riggs (AL-N.J.), George Briggs (R-N.Y.), and Henry Winter Davis (A-Md.), held back, casting their votes for John G. Davis, Smith, and Smith, respectively. In addition, regular Democrats William S. Holman (Ind.) and William Allen (Ohio), along with Anti-Lecompton Democrat John G. Davis (Ind.), were pressured to support Smith but decided instead to continue scattering their votes (NYT, 1/31/1860, 1). Pennington and Smith also cast ballots, scattering their votes.

The House proceeded immediately to a 41st ballot, with nearly the same result, except that Pennington and Smith abstained from voting. This left Pennington again with 115 votes, but now only two votes short of a majority. A third ballot was then taken (the 42nd overall), with much the same result: Pennington and Smith again finished with 115 and 113 votes, respectively. However, on this ballot, Pennington had reached 116 votes at one point, as Jeter Riggs had initially supported him. Yet when neither Henry Winter Davis nor George Briggs would come around to Pennington, Riggs switched and scattered his vote before the results were announced (CG, 36-1, 1/30/1860, 635–36). The House then adjourned for the day.

That evening, the Democrats met in caucus and decided to drop Smith as their nominee in favor of John McClernand (Ill.), a regular Democrat who had opposed the Lecompton Constitution. In selecting McClernand, the Democrats explicitly chose a party member from the Northwest who was sympathetic to the Anti-Lecompton position in hopes of keeping Riggs, and perhaps Adrain and Reynolds, from voting with the Republicans (NYT, 1/31/1860, 4). While McClernand was able to hold Riggs in the Democratic fold the next day, January 31—as well as pull in the wayward scatterers Allen, Holman, and John G. Davis—he could not command the former Smith coalition to hold firm. The 43rd ballot saw McClernand manage only 91 votes, as the Americans, angry at the abandonment of Smith, and the South Carolina Democrats, angry over the choice of a Lecompton opponent as the new Democratic nominee, scattered their votes. Moreover, Pennington, finally securing the vote of Henry Winter Davis, raised his total to 116 (CG, 36-1, 1/31/1860, 641). George Briggs, however, did not support Pennington, but promised to vote for him the following day should Davis remain firm in his convictions (*NYT*, 2/1/1860, 1).

The next day, February 1, a 44th ballot was taken, and Briggs was true to his word—Henry Winter Davis maintained his vote for Pennington, and Briggs in turn swung over his vote. This gave Pennington 117 votes, a bare majority with 233 votes being cast (*CG*, 36-1, 2/1/1860, 650). Thus, nearly two months after it began, the speakership battle finally came to an end.

To what extent did the speakership endgame come down to a choice over preferences on the question of slavery extension? To answer this question, we focus on the contest between Pennington and Smith, which was the climax of the lengthy speakership battle, as well as the closest thing to a two-person race. Examining the 228 members who supported either Pennington or Smith on the 40th–42nd ballots, we find that a simple spatial model incorporating only members' first-dimension CSW-NOMINATE scores performs quite well, correctly classifying 220 of the 228 individual votes, or 96.5 percent. The eight errors are all of the same type—cases of predicted-Pennington voters in fact voting for Smith.[47] Six of these eight were Americans who chose to vote for their copartisan and thus forego their sincere preferences.

In addition, the spatial model allows us to examine a counterfactual by isolating those eight members who were courted so heavily during the final days of the contest—Garnett B. Adrain (AL-N.J.), John H. Reynolds (AL-N.Y.), Jeter R. Riggs (AL-N.J.), George Briggs (R-N.Y.), Henry Winter Davis (A-Md.), William S. Holman (D-Ind.), John G. Davis (AL-Ind.), and William Allen (D-Ohio)—to determine whether their actions were in fact pivotal to the outcome. Actual and predicted votes for these eight members are presented in table 7.5. Recall that Adrain and Reynolds voted for Pennington; Briggs and H. W. Davis voted for Smith; and Riggs, Holman, J. G. Davis, and Allen scattered their votes. This produced a 115–113 advantage for Pennington and prolonged the speakership race. However, if each of these eight members would have voted for *either* Pennington or Smith based on their sincere preferences, all else equal, this would have produced a 116–116 tie. Further, if all members voted their sincere preferences, but H. W. Davis continued to support Smith due to party loyalty (as both were Americans), then Smith would have squeaked by with 117 votes, a bare majority. Thus, what these members chose to do (and not to do) clearly affected the outcome.

Finally, we can examine the motivations of the "cabal of five"—Benjamin F. Junkin (Pa.), William Millward (Pa.), Edward Joy Morris (Pa.), George W. Scranton (Pa.), and John T. Nixon (N.J.)—who forced Sherman out of the race. When switching from Sherman to Smith, did they behave sincerely?

[47] Pennington's CSW-NOMINATE score ideal point was 0.146, while Smith's was -0.282. Pennington's moderate stance on slavery placed him at the left-most end (i.e., nearest to the Democrats) of the Republican distribution—of the 113 Republicans, he was the fourth from the left.

Table 7.5.
Examining the swing voters in the speakership contest, 36th Congress

	Actual vote	Predicted vote
Garnett B. Adrain (AL-N.J)	Pennington	Pennington
John H. Reynolds (AL-N.Y.)	Pennington	Pennington
Jeter R. Riggs (AL-N.J.)	<scatter>	Smith
George Briggs (R-N.Y.)	Smith	Smith
Henry Winter Davis (A-Md.)	Smith	Pennington
William S. Holman (D-Ind.)	<scatter>	Smith
John G. Davis (AL-Ind.)	<scatter>	Smith
William Allen (D-Ohio)	<scatter>	Smith

Note: "Predicted vote" indicates each member's sincere spatial preference (using CSW-NOMINATE scores) between William Pennington and William N. H. Smith.

The spatial breakdown in figure 7.2 illustrates the situation. When confronted with the choice of Smith (-0.282) or Sherman (0.336), the five Republican switchers were not behaving sincerely, as Millward (0.145), Nixon (0.177), Morris (0.213), Scranton (0.226), and Junkin (0.240) were all closer spatially to Sherman than to Smith. Their act, then, was strategic; in effect, they were playing a game of "chicken" with the rest of the Republican Party by demanding that a more moderate Republican candidate be chosen, lest they vote for Smith and generate an anti-Republican House organization.[48] As Smith's vote total increased steadily, thanks to a wave of Democratic switching, Sherman and the rest of the Republicans blinked; Sherman subsequently withdrew, and Pennington (0.146) emerged as the new party candidate. From the five Republican switchers' perspective, Pennington was more to their liking—each sincerely preferred him to Sherman—and was also better positioned to attract the remaining Anti-Lecompton votes necessary for a Republican victory.

The Remaining Organization

While a majority of Republicans did not get their first preference, with Sherman dropping out of the race, they managed to avoid a calamity by electing Pennington. Thus, on the whole, their first goal—electing a Republican speaker—was achieved. Once the speakership was resolved, the Republicans then turned their attention to organizing the remainder of the House.

[48] This group of five, along with some others, attempted a similar game of chicken earlier in the balloting, twice moving their votes to John Gilmer (on the 7th and 18th ballots), but both times the Democrats stuck to their party candidate. See footnote 38 for more details.

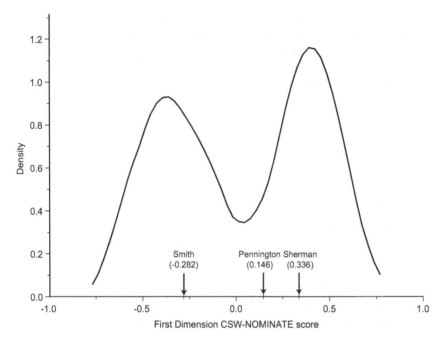

FIGURE 7.2. Distribution of House members and select speakership candidates, 36th Congress.

After adopting the rules of the previous House, the chamber adjourned until February 3. First up would be the election of the residual officers.

The election of House officers

On the evening of February 2, the Republicans met in caucus to discuss their candidates for the remaining House officers. While no official nominations would be made, members quickly agreed that John W. Forney (Pa.) and Henry W. Hoffman (Md.) would serve well as Clerk and Sergeant at Arms, respectively.[49] Forney was a former Democratic regular who had served as House Clerk in the 32nd and 33rd Congresses (and had overseen the organization of the 34th Congress). Having recently (and acrimoniously) split with the Buchanan administration on the slavery issue, he now presented

[49] Forney had been in the running for the clerkship even before the House convened, as his slavery positions, and his ability to deliver the votes of Anti-Lecompton members in the speakership contest, were considered attractive by the Republican Party (NYT, 12/3/1859, 4; 12/5/1859, 4). Moreover, it was believed that the movement of Anti-Lecompton members John B. Haskin (N.Y.), John Hickman (Pa.), and John Schwartz (Pa.) to Sherman on the fifth ballot was done at Forney's behest.

himself as an Anti-Lecompton Democrat by opposing slavery extension in
the territories while maintaining moderate views on slavery more generally,
such as adherence to the Fugitive Slave Act (*NYT*, 2/10/1860, 1; *Saturday
Evening Post*, 2/11/1860, 6; *National Era*, 2/16/1860, 1). Hoffman, an
American former House member with close ties to Henry Winter Davis, was
a strict supporter of the Union. While serving in the 34th Congress, he was
the only slave state member to support the expulsion of Preston Brooks for
his attack on Charles Sumner. For this, he was viewed warmly by many Republicans (*NYT*, 2/3/1860, 1; *CT*, 2/13/1860, 2). No firm opinions emerged
regarding candidates for the other officer positions.

Upon reconvening on February 3, the House turned to the election of the
Clerk. To oppose Forney, the Democrats nominated James C. Allen, the
House Clerk in the 35th Congress who (many claimed) had worked to prevent the Republicans' speakership victory, while the Americans nominated
Nathaniel G. Taylor. Forney emerged victorious on the first ballot, receiving
112 of the 221 votes cast, while Allen captured 77, Taylor 23, and 9 votes
scattered (*CG*, 36-1, 2/3/1860, 662–63). Every Republican who participated
in the ballot voted for Forney, along with seven Anti-Lecompton members,
five of whom had supported Pennington (Adrain, Haskin, Hickman, Reynolds, and Schwartz) and two (Clark and Riggs) who had not.[50] With Forney's many business and publishing ties in Philadelphia, New York, and
Washington, the Anti-Lecompton members were confident that they would
benefit greatly from a friend in the Clerk's office. Given Forney's antipathy
toward Buchanan and his allies, any administration ties to the Clerk's office,
either through positions or contracts, would likely be terminated.[51]

The House then moved to the election of a Sergeant at Arms. In addition
to Hoffman, the Democrats nominated Adam J. Glossbrenner, the incumbent
Sergeant at Arms. Again, only one ballot was necessary, as Hoffman emerged
victorious with 114 of 213 votes cast (*CG*, 36-1, 2/3/1860, 663). Glossbrenner could only muster 92 votes, as all participating Republicans voted
for Hoffman, along with a majority of Americans and Anti-Lecomptons.[52]
Hoffman's Republican support was an explicit courtesy to the Americans,
especially to Henry Winter Davis, whose vote for Pennington was critical to
his subsequent victory.[53] Moreover, defeating Glossbrenner was a symbolic

[50] The eighth Anti-Lecompton member in the House, John G. Davis (Ind.), voted for Allen.

[51] The *Chicago Tribune* reported, "Forney will be obliged to retain four or five of the oldest
clerks, but all the others, some twenty in number, will have to walk the plank" (2/13/1860, 2).
Moreover, the *New York Times* reported, "Mr. Buchanan declares his purpose to provide for
every man Col. Forney discharges from office. The war between these gentlemen will be to the
knife" (2/6/1860, 8).

[52] A second American candidate, a Mr. Underwood, tallied seven votes, mostly from Americans from the Deep South.

[53] Davis had initially wanted Hoffman to be made House Clerk, and had met with Horace
Greeley on the matter before the speakership balloting had convened (Henig 1973, 8). How-

victory for the Republicans, as they failed to prevent his reelection in the 34th Congress when they ostensibly controlled the House organization. It was an indication of their maturity as a party.

The Republican caucus met again on February 5, and two additional nominations were made: George Marston (N.H.) for Doorkeeper and Josiah M. Lucas (Ill.) for Postmaster. The caucus agreed that the Speaker, Clerk, and Sergeant at Arms had all come from the Mid-Atlantic states (New Jersey, Pennsylvania, and Maryland), and that a wider geographic reach was needed to fill the remaining two positions. Thus, New England (New Hampshire) and the Northwest (Illinois) would be rewarded (*NYT*, 2/6/1860, 4, 8). The next day, February 6, both Marston and Lucas would be elected on the first ballot—the former winning 110 of 207 votes cast and the latter 108 of 210—thanks, once again, to unified Republican support, along with a majority of Anti-Lecomptons and a smattering of Americans (*CG*, 36-1, 2/6/1860, 685–86).

The Printer would be a tougher nut to crack. Given its substantial patronage potential, the Democrats made it clear that they would fight doggedly before giving it up. Moreover, there were also obstacles in the form of Republicans, principally Benjamin Stanton (Ohio), who wished to cut ties with the sorts of corruption that surrounded the Buchanan administration. As Stanton stated on the House floor:

I have . . . talked a great deal about [corruption in the public printing] upon the stump, and have attributed it as one of the instances of the political corruption of this Administration which the Republican party called up the country to condemn. I am not prepared to place myself in a position of having that thing rolled back upon me when I go upon the stump during the coming summer. (*CG*, 36-1, 2/9/1860, 725)

As a result, John Sherman, who had moved that the House proceed to the election of the Printer, changed course and suggested a week's postponement—amid cries of "Agreed!" and "No!"—which passed narrowly on a teller vote (*CG*, 36-1, 2/9/1860, 726). Having won the speakership after a grueling battle, and having swept four other officer positions in one-ballot affairs, the Republicans did not wish to press their luck by assuming that party unity would continue to hold. The potential division in the party's ranks, even if only minor, could be deadly. Republican leaders were content to put off the Printer election until lingering problems could be ironed out. Moreover, another protracted election would postpone the remaining feature of the House's organization—the composition of the standing committees.

ever, given the larger role that the Anti-Lecomptons played in Pennington's election, Davis was satisfied with the subsequent offer of Sergeant at Arms.

The appointment of the standing committees

Having postponed the election of the Printer, the House proceeded immediately to the Speaker's announcement of the standing committees for the 36th Congress. Since Pennington was a congressional newcomer, his rise to the speakership presented a bit of a problem vis-à-vis the distribution of committee positions, as he was not well versed in the strengths, talents, and expertise of the various House members. With those issues in mind, John Sherman stepped in and provided assistance. Being on the verge of election for nearly two months, Sherman had given the House's organization considerable thought. As he stated in his memoirs:

> I had, during the struggle, full opportunity to estimate the capacity and qualifications of different Members for committee positions, and had the committees substantially framed, when Pennington was elected. I handed the list to him, for which he thanked me kindly, saying that he had but little knowledge of the personal qualifications of the Members. With some modifications, made necessary by my defeat and his election as speaker, he adopted the list as his own. (1896, 145–46)

One modification "made necessary by [his] defeat" was Sherman's appointment as chair of Ways and Means. Thus, while he fell short of the speakership, Sherman still managed to secure a position of significant power.

In total, Pennington appointed Republicans to chair 25 of the House's 34 standing committees (see table 7.6 for a full list). More important, he selected Republicans to chair seven of the eight major policy committees: Commerce (Elihu Washburne [Ill.]), Public Lands (Eli Thayer [Mass.]), Manufactures (Charles Francis Adams [Mass.]), Territories (Galusha Grow [Pa.]), Agriculture (Martin Butterfield [N.Y.]), Foreign Affairs (Thomas Corwin [Ohio]), and, as mentioned, Ways and Means (Sherman). The one major policy committee not given to a Republican was Judiciary, for which Anti-Lecompton John Hickman (Pa.), who had actively supported both Sherman and Pennington throughout the balloting, was selected. Overall, Pennington voters—Republicans and Anti-Lecomptons—were appointed to chair 28 of the 34 standing committees. The remaining six chairs were distributed among four Americans and two Democrats.

A number of these committee chairs would be involved in interesting story lines during the 36th Congress. Galusha Grow, a fervent free-soiler, would chair Territories at a time when Northerners would attempt to bring Kansas into the Union as a free state. Anti-Lecomptons John Hickman and John Haskin, who were close politically to John Forney, would chair Judiciary and Public Expenditures at a time when accusations were rampant regarding corruption in the Buchanan administration. Finally, American John Gilmer, who was spurned by the Democrats after a Democratic-American coalition had organized in good faith around his speakership can-

TABLE 7.6.
House committee chairmen, 36th Congress

Committee	Chairman (state)	CSW-NOMINATE score	Party	Speaker vote
Claims	Mason Tappan (N.H.)	0.493	Republican	Pennington
Expenditures in the State Dept.	James McKean (N.Y.)	0.487	Republican	Pennington
Expenditures on Public Bldgs.	William Brayton (R.I.)	0.487	Republican	Pennington
Private Land Claims	Cadwallader Washburn (Wis.)	0.455	Republican	Pennington
Invalid Pensions	Reuben Fenton (N.Y.)	0.424	Republican	Pennington
Expenditures in the Post Office	George Palmer (N.Y.)	0.420	Republican	Pennington
Commerce	Eli Washburne (Ill.)	0.410	Republican	Pennington
Revolutionary Pensions	John Potter (Wis.)	0.410	Republican	Pennington
Militia	Cydnor Tompkins (Ohio)	0.407	Republican	Pennington
Naval Affairs	Freeman Morse (Maine)	0.397	Republican	Pennington
Post Office and Post Roads	Schuyler Colfax (Ind.)	0.393	Republican	Pennington
Territories	Galusha Grow (Pa.)	0.380	Republican	Pennington
Expenditures in the Treasury Dept.	Dwight Loomis (Conn.)	0.379	Republican	Pennington
Foreign Affairs	Thomas Corwin (Ohio)	0.374	Republican	Pennington
Agriculture	Martin Butterfield (N.Y.)	0.371	Republican	Pennington
Expenditures in the War Dept.	William Stewart (Pa.)	0.343	Republican	Pennington
Ways and Means	John Sherman (Ohio)	0.336	Republican	Pennington
District of Columbia	Luther Carter (N.Y.)	0.317	Republican	Pennington
Military Affairs	Benjamin Stanton (Ohio)	0.282	Republican	Pennington

TABLE 7.6. (*Cont.*)

Committee	Chairman (state)	CSW-NOMINATE score	Party	Speaker vote
Public Buildings and Grounds	Charles Train (Mass.)	0.270	Republican	Pennington
Accounts	Francis Spinner (N.Y.)	0.262	Republican	Pennington
Manufactures	Charles Adams (Mass.)	0.252	Republican	Pennington
Public Lands	Eli Thayer (Mass.)	0.240	Republican	Pennington
Public Expenditures	John Haskin (N.Y.)	0.182	Anti-Lecompton	Pennington
Judiciary	John Hickman (Pa.)	0.173	Anti-Lecompton	Pennington
Patents	William Millward (Pa.)	0.145	Republican	Pennington
Indian Affairs	Emerson Etheridge (Tenn.)	0.010	American	Gilmer
Engraving	Garnett Adrain (N.J.)	-0.053	Anti-Lecompton	Pennington
Revolutionary Claims	George Briggs (N.Y.)	-0.069	Republican	Pennington
Elections	John Gilmer (N.C.)	-0.069	American	Etheridge
Expenditures in the Navy Dept.	Robert Hatton (Tenn.)	-0.193	American	Gilmer
Roads and Canals	Robert Mallory (Ky.)	-0.282	American	Gilmer
Revisal and Unfinished Business	John Logan (Ill.)	-0.330	Democrat	McClernand
Mileage	John Ashmore (S.C.)	-0.414	Democrat	McClernand

Note: "Speaker vote" indicates the member's vote on the final (44th) ballot for Speaker.

didacy, would chair Elections when several Democrats would have their seats challenged by Republicans.

In terms of general committee composition, Pennington made efficient use of his party's chamber plurality. As table 7.7 documents, the Republicans, despite commanding only 48 percent of the House (113 of 237 seats), constituted majorities on 56 percent (19 of 34) of the House's standing committees. In addition, seven of the eight major policy committees were constructed with Republican majorities. The one exception was Judiciary, but in this case the committee was clearly under "friendly" control, as two Anti-Lecomptons who voted for Pennington (John Hickman, the committee chair, and John Reynolds) joined four Republicans on the nine-man committee. All told, 23 of the 34 standing committees were controlled by Pennington's supporters. Of the remaining 11 committees, seven were chaired by a Republican who could maintain some control over the committee's agenda. That left four committees—Mileage, Expenditures in the Navy Department, Revisal and Unfinished Business, and Roads and Canals—with only Roads and Canals considered somewhat important in a policy-based sense. And Robert Mallory (Ky.), an old-line Whig now serving as an American, chaired that committee; this was not likely an accident, as his Whiggish tastes on internal improvements meshed well with those of most Republicans.

Pennington's committee assignments were not universally admired. The *New York Times* suggested that they "provoked a great clamor of hostility" among some members (2/10/1860, 4). Chief among those with an ax to grind were two Texas Democrats, John Reagan and Andrew Hamilton, who complained that their assignments (Private Land Claims and Revolutionary Pensions, respectively), "could be of no earthly service to their constituents." Democratic grumblings of this sort aside, the *Times* determined that "on the whole, we do not see that there is any reason for denying to Mr. Pennington the praise of a more than ordinary impartiality in the distribution of legislative honors and duties."

Election of a Printer

Before returning to the election of the Printer, on February 13, the House first passed two resolutions proposed by John Sherman, which would (1) provide the House with the right to modify the existing law on the public printing subsequent to the election and (2) stipulate that a seven-person House committee be appointed to examine the House printing and the various costs attached to it (CG, 36-1, 2/13/1860, 750). The Senate was at that time investigating allegations of corruption in the Senate printing, and many House members, in line with Benjamin Stanton's earlier statement, were unwilling to be attached to such corruption. Thus, Sherman's resolutions were an attempt to address the printing issue head-on, thereby signaling the

TABLE 7.7.
Composition of House standing committees, 36th Congress

Committee	Committee median	Republicans	Pennington voters	Total members
Territories	0.376	6	6	9
Expenditures in the War Dept.	0.339	3	3	5
Indian Affairs	0.333	5	5	9
Ways and Means	0.328	5	6	9
Post Office and Post Roads	0.306	5	5	9
Agriculture	0.304	5	5	9
Military Affairs	0.282	5	5	9
Expenditures in the Treasury Dept.	0.270	3	3	5
Accounts	0.262	3	3	5
District of Columbia	0.251	5	5	9
Public Lands	0.240	6	7	9
Public Buildings and Grounds	0.233	3	3	5
Claims	0.221	6	6	9
Foreign Affairs	0.213	5	5	9
Revolutionary Pensions	0.208	5	6	9
Elections	0.178	5	5	9
Commerce	0.177	5	5	9
Judiciary	0.173	4	6	9
Manufactures	0.159	5	5	9
Patents	0.145	3	3	5
Private Land Claims	0.140	4	3	9
Naval Affairs	0.096	4	5	9
Public Expenditures	0.083	4	5	9
Engraving	-0.053	1	2	3
Roads and Canals	-0.073	4	4	9
Expenditures on the Public Bldgs.	-0.088	2	2	5
Invalid Pensions	-0.101	4	4	9
Expenditures in the Post Office	-0.143	2	2	5
Revisal and Unfinished Business	-0.158	2	2	5
Expenditures in the State Dept.	-0.168	2	2	5
Militia	-0.189	4	4	9
Expenditures in the Navy Dept.	-0.193	2	2	5
Revolutionary Claims	-0.226	4	4	9
Mileage	-0.326	2	2	5

Note: "Committee median" is the median member's first-dimension CSW-NOMINATE score. "Pennington voters" indicates the number of members to vote for Pennington on the final (44th) ballot for Speaker.

House's active oversight of a potential problem, and the resolutions were quickly adopted.

The Printer election now at hand, the two major-party nominees were Republican John D. Defrees, editor of the *Indianapolis Atlas*, who was a candidate for Printer in the 34th Congress, and Democrat Adam J. Glossbrenner, editor of the *York* (Pennsylvania) *Gazette* and Sergeant at Arms in the 35th Congress, who had just been defeated for reelection to the post.[54] A first ballot was taken with Defrees and Glossbrenner garnering 89 and 88 votes, respectively, with 92 votes necessary for a choice.[55] (See appendix 4 for a breakdown of the balloting.) Glossbrenner received all of the Democrats' votes and most of the Americans' votes, while Defrees captured nearly all of the Republicans' votes and most of the Anti-Lecomptons' votes. However, four Republicans—Charles Francis Adams (Mass.), John Wood (Pa.), Edward Joy Morris (Pa.), and Benjamin Stanton (Pa.)—broke ranks and scattered their votes, which denied Defrees a majority. Americans Emerson Etheridge (Tenn.) and William B. Stokes (Tenn.) also resisted supporting Glossbrenner and instead voted for the ex-Whig printing duo of Gales and Seaton. A second ballot was then taken with a similar result: Defrees and Glossbrenner each gained one vote to 90 and 89, respectively, with 92 votes still necessary for victory. Defrees was able to attract the votes of Wood and Morris, but Adams still scattered his vote, while Stanton abstained. Moreover, John Carey (R-Ohio), who had supported Defrees on the first ballot, now scattered his vote.[56] Further balloting was then postponed, as the House moved on to other matters.

The election was picked up again on February 15, with three additional ballots taken. On each, Defrees came within one vote of a majority. While Carey returned to the Republican fold and Stanton paired off for the series of votes, Adams chose instead to abstain. The election was then dropped until February 23, when four additional ballots were taken. On the first bal-

---

[54] Reports suggested that the Republican caucus was internally divided over the choice for Printer. The *New York Times* (2/8/1860, 1) reported that three ballots were taken on February 5, without a choice, as three candidates split the vote: Defrees, Abram M. Mitchell (editor of the *St. Louis News*), and Joseph M. Coombs (of the *Washington Republic*). At the end of those three votes, Mitchell was reported to be in the lead. But, on February 9, the *Times* reported that Defrees had been chosen as the party's nominee (1, 4). Smith (1977, 223) states that Defrees had promised that if elected Printer, he would distribute half of his profits toward achieving Republican party goals—specifically, printing and distributing political documents in the key swing states of Pennsylvania, New Jersey, Illinois, and Indiana—prior to the 1860 elections.

[55] The proceedings and balloting in the Printer election can be found in the *Congressional Globe*, 36-1, 750–51, 768–70, 790–92, 809, 830, 872–73, 877–79, 897–99, 908, 922–24, 957–58, and 975.

[56] Carey's flip, along with Stanton's lack of support, could have stemmed in part from the Printer election in the 34th Congress, when the Indiana Republican delegation refused to support Ohioan Oran Follett for Printer. Stanton referred to some of these dynamics in his floor speech on February 9 (*CG*, 36-1, 2/9/1860, 725; *NYT*, 2/10/1860, 1).

lot of the day (the sixth overall), Glossbrenner was the top candidate with 86, 4 short of a majority. Defrees slipped to 83 votes, as Adams and Stanton once again scattered their votes. This pattern continued on the next vote, with Glossbrenner leading the way with 84 votes, 5 short of a majority, and Defrees dropping to 77 votes. Now, additional Republicans, like John Carey, John Sherman, John Hutchins, and Cydnor Tompkins (all Ohio), and John Verree (Pa.), had moved from Defrees, which left him little choice but to withdraw from the race (*CG*, 36-1, 2/23/1860, 872).

Thus, a new Republican candidate was needed. On the following ballot, the eighth overall, the Republicans began sorting themselves out, with a number of candidates receiving votes. Edward Ball, a former House member from Ohio and editor of the *Zanesville* (Ohio) *Courier*, emerged as the chief Republican vote-getter with 57, while Glossbrenner continued in the lead with 84 votes, 5 short of a majority.[57] Ball surged into the lead on the next ballot (the ninth overall), as he drew all Republican voters to his candidacy and captured 87 votes, only one short of victory. The Republicans pushed hard for one additional ballot, believing Ball would pass the post, but were stymied by a Democratic-led adjournment.

Three more ballots were taken on the following day (February 24). The first ballot, and the 10th overall, saw Ball slip back, rather than coast to victory. He received 81 votes, down from 87 on the previous ballot, amid heightened member participation (96 votes were now necessary for election). Rather than support Ball, a number of Republicans instead threw their support to Abram S. Mitchell, editor of the *St. Louis News*.[58] Ball's vote total continued to drop on the next two ballots, while the Democratic-American alliance also broke down. The Americans, sensing they could be pivotal and perhaps advance a "compromise candidate," dropped Glossbrenner and threw their support behind old-line Whig William Seaton, editor of the *National Intelligencer*. Amid this partisan free-for-all, the House adjourned.

Internal Republican divisions had clearly burst out onto the floor. Party leaders called a caucus on Saturday the 25th in an attempt to get everyone back on track. However, turnout was low, with only around 60 members attending. Moreover, divisions could not be overcome, so a new caucus nominee was not selected. Instead, party leaders negotiated an arrangement whereby members could vote independently on the next ballot for Printer, with the understanding that they would coalesce around the top vote-getter on subsequent ballots (*NYT*, 2/27/1860, 4).

[57] Ball served in the 33rd and 34th Congresses, first as a Whig then as a Republican.
[58] These Republicans were John B. Alley (Mass.), James Buffinton (Mass.), Anson Burlingame (Mass.), Henry L. Dawes (Mass.), Thomas D. Eliot (Mass.), John F. Farnsworth (Ill.), Daniel W. Gooch (Mass.), James H. Graham (N.Y.), William Kellogg (Ill.), William Millward (Pa.), Edward Joy Morris (Pa.), Alexander H. Rice (Mass.), Daniel E. Somes (Maine), and Charles Van Wyck (N.Y.).

After some initial business was conducted on Monday, February 27, the House returned to the election of the Printer. Four additional ballots would be taken. On the first ballot (13th overall), a new Republican candidate emerged: Thomas H. Ford, former lieutenant governor of Ohio, who garnered 65 votes to Ball's 31.[59] In line with the caucus agreement, the Republican dissidents began moving to Ford. His vote total rose, and he drew within eight and seven votes of victory, respectively, on the next two ballots. On the fourth ballot of the day (16th overall), Ford collected 93 votes, a bare majority, after which Speaker Pennington declared him the duly elected House Printer for the 36th Congress (CG, 36-1, 2/27/1860, 899).

That was not the end of the story. The following day, February 28, Thomas Ruffin (D-N.C.) stated that the Journal had failed to record his vote for Printer. This produced some confusion, which carried over into the following day, when a number of Democratic members confirmed that Ruffin did indeed cast a vote (for Glossbrenner) on the 16th ballot for Printer. Republicans acceded to the oversight and agreed to the correction (CG, 36-1, 2/28/1860 and 2/29/1860, 908, 922–23). However, Ruffin's vote had the effect of raising the necessary vote total on the 16th ballot to 94, which meant that Ford, with his 93 votes, was not in fact elected. Thus, further ballots would be required. One additional ballot (the 17th overall) would be taken on February 29, with Ford falling four votes short of a majority.[60] Rather than continuing to ballot, the House adjourned.

After a postponement on March 1, the election of Printer would be revisited on March 2, and Ford would be elected on the first ballot of the day (the 18th overall), collecting 96 of 187 votes cast. Once again, Speaker Pennington declared Ford the duly elected House Printer for the 36th Congress. This time the result would hold (CG, 36-1, 3/2/1860, 975).

---

[59] Smith contends that Ford emerged as the new Republican front-runner by promising to "give favors to the party, including help to the National Era of Washington" (1977, 223). Interestingly, two earlier Republican candidates for Printer, John Defrees and Abram Mitchell, had also been rumored at different times to be in league with Gamaliel Bailey, the editor of the National Era (NYT, 2/8/1860, 1; 2/9/1860, 1). This politicking for the printership patronage represented a change of course for the National Era. In 1856, when the National Era was mentioned as a possible recipient of the House printership by some members of Congress, its editor wrote:

> For Heaven's sake, gentlemen, never name us as an applicant for any patronage, to be bestowed by Congress or the Executive. We do not need it; we do not want it; could not get it if we did; would not have it if we could. There is no possible relation that the Era could sustain to Congress which could make it desirable, beneficial, or tolerable, for either to be patronized by the other. An attitude of absolute independence we regard as beyond all price. (National Era, 2/7/1856, 22)

[60] The New York Times reported that Ford's election failed on the 17th ballot due to an "improper division of the spoils," and that "a new man will be started tomorrow" (3/1/1860, 1). It appears that this "division" was ironed out over the next two days, as Ford continued to be the party's candidate and was elected on the first ballot on March 2.

Thus, more than three months after the convening of the House, the Republicans had organized the chamber. They were successful in every endeavor, electing Republican-backed candidates for each House office, as well as assembling Republican (and antislavery, more generally) majorities on all important committees, despite commanding only a plurality of the chamber.

One final point deserves mention here, as it deals specifically with House organizational politics: this would be the last time the House elected a Printer.[61] During the 36th Congress, investigatory committees in both the House and Senate uncovered massive corruption involving the public printing. A star witness was Cornelius Wendell, the House Printer in the 34th Congress, who provided testimony before the Committee on Public Expenditures in late February 1860. Among other remarks, Wendell admitted that roughly half the funds appropriated for the public printing were pure profit, most of which (based on informal arrangements) were meant to be funneled into party coffers for the basis of mass party patronage (*NYT*, 2/25/1860, 1). Rumors such as these had also dogged several of the Republican Printer candidates during the House balloting (see footnote 59). As a result, a reform movement emerged that was led by Republicans like Benjamin Stanton (Ohio), who had been suspicious of congressional printing for some time, and Congress proceeded to "nationalize" the institution by creating a Government Printing Office.[62] The first superintendent of the GPO would be John Defrees.

Winning on the Floor

This chapter and chapter 6 have covered the six Congresses—just over a decade—preceding the Civil War. Together they show that although the speakership was a coveted prize among the parties and their regional factions, winning the speakership was no guarantee of controlling the House floor for the next two years.

This is illustrated generally in figure 7.3, which displays the win-rate analysis—the percentage of times that each House member was on the prevailing side of roll call votes against his spatial (ideological) location, mea-

[61] For a more extensive overview, see Smith (1977, 224–30).

[62] The House voted 120–56 to create a Government Printing Office (*CG*, 36-1, 5/31/1860, 2512), while the Senate voted 31–14 (*CG*, 36-1, 6/16/1860, 3062). Almost a decade later, the Senate Committee on Printing did an audit of the GPO and evaluated its performance. The committee came away impressed with the GPO's efficiency, and reported (among other things) that "in comparison with the cost under the previous system the savings for the wartime period of March, 1861, to September, 1865, had amounted to over a million dollars" (Smith 1977, 230).

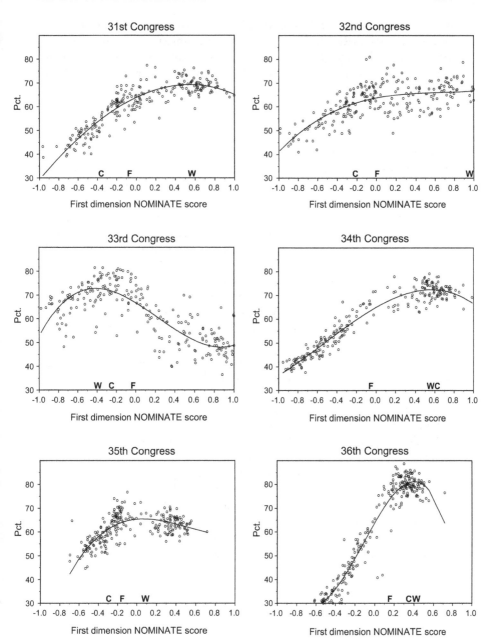

FIGURE 7.3. Winning percentage as a function of W-NOMINATE scores, 31st–36th Congresses. F = floor median; C = median of coalition that voted for winning Speaker candidate; W = estimated location of member most frequently on winning side of roll call votes.

sured by first-dimension W-NOMINATE scores—for the 31st through the 36th Congresses. (Recall that we conducted a similar set of win-rate analyses for the 26th through 30th Congresses in chapter 5.) Also indicated are the location of the floor median and the median of the organizing coalition. As before, a third-degree polynomial has been fit through the data in each graph, using least squares regression, to help in identifying where the most frequent roll call winners are located in each Congress.

In half of these Congresses—the 31st, 32nd, and 35th—Democratic coalitions claimed the speakership, but did not claim the floor. The 33rd, 34th, and 36th Congresses—especially the 36th—were more in keeping with what we would expect in the modern era, with the party that controlled the speakership controlling the floor.

The bookend Congresses of figure 7.3 are particularly instructive. The 31st Congress is an interesting case because, of course, it was the Congress that passed the Compromise of 1850. Of the five bills that constituted the compromise, three tended to garner support from Whigs (California admission, abolition of slave trade in D.C., and the Texas border bill) and two from Democrats (the organization of the Utah and New Mexico Territories and the Fugitive Slave Act). Lost to history, but just as important from the perspective of partisan control of the floor, the two civil and diplomatic appropriations bills considered by the 31st Congress, which were subjected to interminable proceedings, were overwhelmingly supported by the Whigs, with the Democrats split. For instance, H.R. 461, making appropriations for FY 1852, passed on a 127–55 vote, with all 84 Whigs voting in favor and Democrats split 36–52 in opposition. Democrats organized the chamber, but did not control policy making.

While the politics of the 31st Congress seem to have been determined largely outside of the coalition that organized the chamber, this was not true of the 36th Congress, despite the fact that the Speaker and Printer fights were protracted. Republicans both organized the chamber and controlled its politics. Pennington's committee assignments helped cement the antislavery coalition that elected him, which provided evidence to Southern political leaders that the Republican Party was both a durable and effective force in national politics. This no doubt was a factor in Southern leaders' secession calculus later in the Congress.

CONCLUSION

After Nathaniel Banks's speakership victory in 1855–56, a still-uncertain political environment lay ahead for his Republican coalition. Their first objective—organizing the remainder of the House—was only partially realized. Because the Republicans had only a plurality of the chamber, they needed to coordinate their officer nominees with the Americans. These efforts were successful in electing the Clerk, Doorkeeper, and Postmaster. But the Republicans were rolled by the Democrats in the election of the Sergeant at Arms and the Printer. The latter was a critical loss, as the Republicans were unwilling to share control of the public printing with the Americans, and as a result they did not enjoy the significant patronage that the Printer provided. The Republicans were successful, however, in the distribution of committee assignments to antislavery loyalists. Speaker Banks did an especially good job of populating the most important policy committees in the House with strong-willed, well-known Republicans. In effect, these assignments provided the "stars" of the party with a platform to communicate the party's positions.

Their successes (and failures) aside, this emerging Republican coalition was still tenuous. While hopes for a true mass party were strong, they were still a narrow ideological coalition, a slapdash group of ex-Democrats, Whigs, Americans, and Free-Soilers who happened to share one thing: antipathy toward slavery extension. While this singular policy preference brought them the speakership, the Republicans were now faced with the task of behaving like a coherent legislative coalition. This could prove to be difficult, as any number of issue-based fissures could open up during the 34th Congress and expose the coalition's narrow underpinnings.

Fortuitously, the Republicans were rarely placed in such a situation. The slavery issue—in particular, the issue of slavery in the Kansas Territory—continued to be the predominant issue in congressional politics. Indeed, it became the issue that could no longer be avoided or resolved, and it monopolized the congressional and national agendas. As a result, this one-issue ideological coalition was able to survive without broadening substantially, and proceeded to build a mass party following strictly on the issue of slavery extension. Thus, the Republicans overcame losing the House to the Democrats in the 35th Congress and used their time out of the majority to eliminate the Americans as a viable electoral competitor.

The question of Kansas statehood (along with the *Dred Scott* decision) dominated political discussion in the late 1850s, which allowed the Republicans to regain plurality control of the House in the 1858–59 elections. On this occasion, they would be more successful in consolidating their organization. This was due largely to the coalition's maturation, as the Republicans now held "party" over "ideology." For example, when it became clear that the party's first preference for Speaker, the staunchly antislavery John Sherman (Ohio), could not be elected—amid the very real possibility that a Democratic-American compromise candidate could emerge to win the speakership—party members were pragmatic in dropping Sherman in favor of William Pennington (N.J.), a Republican who was more liberal on slavery generally, but who was also sufficiently strong on the more immediate issue of slavery extension. This allowed them to attract the additional Anti-Lecompton votes necessary to produce a majority. Thus, the Republicans kept their focus on winning the speakership and did not allow ideological goals, like electing an extreme antislavery member, to override party goals that would have cost them the prize.

With the speakership in hand, the Republicans filled out the rest of the organization by joining with the Anti-Lecomptons to select solid antislavery officers, committee chairs, and committee slates. The organization was completed with the election of a Printer, which showed how far the Republicans had come as a party. When their first candidate faltered because of internal party divisions, they did not crumble as in the 34th Congress; rather, they tried various other Republican candidates until one could achieve a majority. This ability to adjust with the political climate signified an important organizational coming of age.

Thus, the speakership played a major role in the development of the Republican Party. In the 34th Congress, winning the speakership showed that a narrow ideological coalition that was centered on the issue of slavery extension could achieve political power. However, the Republicans were only partially successful in organizing the chamber, which indicated that further coalitional development and coordination was necessary. By the time the Republicans won the speakership in the 36th Congress, it was clear that a mass party built around slavery extension had become a reality. The goals of the coalition had broadened, extending beyond simple ideology to that of general partisanship. As a result, the Republicans were able to organize all aspects of the chamber by compromising with the Anti-Lecomptons and changing party nominees midstream when necessary. Simply put, by the 36th Congress, the Republicans had become both flexible and pragmatic, requiring a basic goal—opposition to slavery extension—while allowing considerable policy freedom in other areas as a way of building a majority party organization.

CHAPTER 8

Caucus Governance and the Emergence
of the Organizational Cartel, 1861–1891

As the nation entered the Civil War, the antebellum pattern of protracted House speakership battles appeared poised to continue. Despite the secession of 11 Southern states, and the fact that they possessed a large House majority, the Republicans did not settle on a Speaker nominee prior to the convening of the 37th Congress (1861–63). Unlike many previous speakership contests, however, once balloting began, the Republican majority quickly coalesced; indeed, before the official first-ballot tally was even announced, a number of dissident Republicans switched their votes to Galusha Grow (Pa.), the party front-runner, so as to elect him and forego a second ballot. This rapid turnaround in speakership voting was an important break from the recent past, and, more important, was a portent for the future. The quick election of Grow ushered in a new era in organizational politics: in all but one instance over the next century and a half, speakership contests would be straightforward affairs on the House floor, determined by a single ballot.[1]

The disappearance of protracted speakership battles did not indicate, of course, that intraparty divisions over speakership candidates had vanished. Indeed, well into the twentieth century, both major parties remained heterogeneous coalitions, and thus were often rent by ideological divisions. Nevertheless, beginning with the Civil War era, the majority party began settling intraparty disagreements over speakership candidates (and all officer candidates, generally) in caucus prior to the House's convening. The decision on the floor has thus become the public realization of the semiprivate negotiation in the majority party caucus.

Few who gathered for the first Civil War Congress would have predicted that the House would go on to enjoy relative stability in the partisan organization of the chamber during and after the war. Yet expectations changed rapidly in the years of war and Reconstruction, to the point that, in a very real sense, Martin Van Buren's plan, developed a quarter century earlier to

---

[1] The sole exception was in the 68th Congress, which we discuss in detail in chapter 9, when the speakership contest stretched nine ballots over three days (12/3–5/1923).

create a consistently secure partisan organization based on caucus decision making, finally came to fruition.

This caucus-induced, organizational arrangement solved the lingering instability that had often plagued speakership decisions during the antebellum era. Moreover, the binding party caucus on organizational matters quickly institutionalized and evolved into an *equilibrium institution* (Shepsle 1986, 1989), as both parties embraced the practice of keeping the organization of the chamber "in the family" rather than risking potential complications on the House floor. In short, the majority party had finally become an organizational cartel.

The stability of the caucus-organizing system—and emergence of the organizational cartel—was also a necessary condition for the subsequent development of party institutions in the House. That is, the majority party took steps to enhance its procedural power in the House, through firmer control of the legislative agenda, only *after* leaders and the rank and file felt secure that a reliable system was in place to settle key organizational matters (i.e., selecting the Speaker, staffing the committees) that were vital to such a procedural undertaking. More specifically, the transition to the Reed Rules in the early 1890s was only possible because of the existence of a mechanism (the organizational cartel) that ensured that key positions (Speaker, committee chairs)—which could be bestowed with *agenda power*—were controlled by the majority party at the start of a new session. This is an especially important point, as a post–Reed Rules institutional structure lies at the heart of all contemporary theories of party power in the House.

That the majority party was able to contain every speakership dispute within the family since 1861 and organize the House on one ballot, with the exception of the 68th Congress, is the subject of this chapter and chapter 9. Since the 39th Congress (1865–67), both major parties have met in caucus and settled on a single nominee for Speaker before the House first convenes. We consider this to be the beginning of the current regime of organizational politics, in which the party caucus is the unchallenged forum for the nomination of House officers. Appendix 5 summarizes the most basic information about these caucus nominations. (Appendix 6 provides more detailed accounts of the nominations, including citations to newspaper accounts of the caucus meetings.) The column labeled "margin percentage" records the relative size of the seat advantage enjoyed by the larger of the two major parties over the smaller party. Over the half century, starting in 1863 (38th Congress), the size of the party margin was less than 10 percent eight times, and the largest party held only a plurality of the chamber twice. In *none* of these cases was the minority party, or one of the minor third parties, able to leverage the margin into a protracted speakership election battle.

We consider four periods to be especially important in setting expectations about the selection of Speakers. These are (1) the Civil War and early Reconstruction years, when the Republicans exhibited great discipline to permanently establish the tactic of a binding party caucus for Speaker; (2) the mid- to late 1870s when the Democrats returned to power in the House and embraced the binding caucus, thus erasing doubt about whether this was an institution that would be embraced by both parties; (3) the decade from the early 1880s to the early 1890s, when regional and ideological tensions pervaded both parties and threatened, but did not destroy, the stability of the organizational arrangement; and (4) the 1920s, when the progressive Republican insurgency provided a momentary threat of a return to antebellum-style speakership politics. Periods 1, 2, and part of 3 are covered in this chapter; the remaining part of period 3 and period 4 are covered in chapter 9.

The Civil War and the Establishment of Party Discipline

The 37th Congress convened on July 4, 1861, in the midst of the greatest crisis the nation has ever faced. In the few short months after Abraham Lincoln's election and subsequent inauguration, 11 Southern (slave) states— South Carolina, Alabama, Florida, Georgia, Louisiana, Mississippi, Texas, Virginia, North Carolina, Tennessee, and Arkansas—had seceded from the Union, and had organized to form a separate nation, the Confederate States of America. In his role as commander in chief, Lincoln acted swiftly to preserve the Union, while the infant Confederacy actively resisted. The Civil War began.

There was one major political beneficiary among this national chaos: the Republican Party in Congress. Thanks to the Southern exodus, the Republicans were the majority party in the House for the first time in their short history, controlling 102 of the 174 seats at the opening of the 37th Congress (Dubin 1998, 191). Thus, the Republicans were in a position to organize the chamber completely on their own without having to rely on third parties for assistance. Yet they made no attempt to caucus prior to Congress convening, deciding instead to downplay overt partisanship during a time of war and allow members to vote their consciences (Bogue 1981, 122). Still, the norm from the 36th Congress would be followed, whereby the top Republican vote-getter on the first speakership ballot would subsequently command united party support (Curry 1968, 26). As Illisevich (1988, 202) notes, "the Republicans had agreed not to tolerate any protracted conflict over the speakership. There was too much to be done."

As members of Congress began arriving in Washington, three leading candidates for Speaker were regularly mentioned in the press: Galusha Grow (Pa.), a devoted Radical who had been an early speakership candidate in the 36th Congress; Frank Blair (Mo.), a moderate ex-Democrat and close associate of Lincoln's who had worked effectively to keep his home state in the Union;[2] and Schuyler Colfax (Ind.), an amiable former Whig and American with solid antislavery credentials.[3] While press accounts had the election up for grabs, the wartime mood and strong anti-Southern feelings permeating the capitol made Grow the favorite. Sensing this, Colfax withdrew from consideration just as the speakership balloting was to begin in the opening moments of Congress (CG, 37-1, 7/4/1861, 3).

When the ballot was complete, Grow led with 71 of 159 votes cast, 9 short of a majority. Blair, his closest competitor, could only muster 40 votes, with the remaining votes scattering among 12 other candidates. Before the official tally could be announced, however, Blair was recognized and (like Colfax earlier) removed himself from further consideration as a candidate. He then urged his supporters to switch their votes and back Grow immediately rather than wait for a second ballot. Twenty-six of them did, which resulted in Grow's election (CG, 37-1, 7/4/1861, 4).[4] In the spirit of downplaying partisanship, the House then quickly elected Emerson Etheridge, a Unionist from Tennessee, as Clerk; in doing so, the Republicans turned out the incumbent, John Forney, whom they had supported in the previous Congress.[5] Etheridge's candidacy was promoted by Lincoln as a direct appeal to the antisecession forces in the Union-controlled slave states of Maryland, Missouri, and Kentucky.

Upon accepting the speakership, Grow set out to complete the organization of the House. Here, he followed the path set out by Banks and Pennington before him, using committee assignments, and especially chairmanships, to allocate power within the chamber and placate different regional and ideological groups within the party (Curry 1968, 26–29; Bogue 1981, 114–15). He offered Blair, his major competitor, the chairmanship of Ways and Means, but Blair refused the assignment, choosing instead the chairmanship of Military Affairs. Grow then offered Colfax the chairmanship of Ways and Means, but he preferred to maintain his chairmanship of Post Office and Post Roads, a prime engine for pork and patronage. Grow then handed out chairmanships to prominent members of his own Radical group, with Ways and Means finally going to Thaddeus Stevens (Pa.), Judiciary to John Bingham (Ohio), Public Expenditures to John Covode (Pa.), Public Lands to John Potter (Wis.), Manufactures to John Hutchins (Ohio), and Commerce to Elihu Washburne (Ill.) (CG, 37-1, 7/8/1861, 21–22).

[2] Frank Blair was the son of Francis Preston Blair, the former House Printer.
[3] See NYT, 6/30/1861, 4; 7/1/1861, 4; 7/3/1861, 4; 7/4/1861, 1; CT, 7/6/1861, 2; and NY-Trib, 7/4/1861, 4–5.
[4] Follett (1896, 51) mistakenly reports that Grow's election required a second ballot.
[5] Forney was not a favorite of the Radical Republicans. Despite his recent conversion to antislavery politics, Forney, a former heavyweight in the Pennsylvania Democratic machine before his falling out with the Buchanan forces, remained close with many leading members of the moderate wing of the Democratic Party. Still, Forney had been useful to the Republicans in the 36th Congress, and he remained on good personal terms with Lincoln. He was compensated by being selected as Secretary of the Senate in the 37th Congress.

Thus, as the Republicans became the majority party in the House, they managed to avoid internal strife in their organization of the chamber by distributing power, via the Speaker, in the form of committee chairmanships and assignments. Grow played his part by rewarding rivals after they (and many of their supporters) conformed with the agreement to rally behind whoever the top vote-getter was on the opening speakership ballot. This tacit equilibrium allowed the Republicans to maintain their solidarity while respecting intraparty differences, which helped the party avoid the messy public spectacle of a prolonged speakership battle.

This Republican solidarity would be tested soon enough. The war went poorly for the Union throughout 1861 and 1862, which proved disheartening for both the party and the nation. This led to a significant backlash against the Republicans in the midterm elections of 1862–63. As a result, when the 38th Congress convened in December 1863, the Republicans could only manage plurality control of the House with 85 of 184 seats (Martis 1989, 116–17). Needing assistance to organize the House, they sought help from border-state Unionists, notably those who supported nationwide abolition and a vigorous prosecution of the war.[6] Rather than attempt to coordinate with Unionists on the floor, which would introduce uncertainty into the organizational process, Republican leaders called for a caucus to meet prior to Congress convening. This "Union caucus" would allow for a discussion of officers and the potential nomination of a slate of coalition candidates.

In addition to basic coordination issues, Republican leaders pushed for a caucus to head off a potential crisis of a different sort. Rumors had spread that Emerson Etheridge, the House Clerk, was plotting an organizational coup. Etheridge had been a loyal administration supporter through the end of 1862, until the war's theme broadened to include emancipation. Like many Tennessee loyalists, Etheridge opposed freedom and civil equality for slaves, and thus felt betrayed by the Republican Party (Maness 1989). As a result, a realigning of allegiances began. As Belz (1970, 555) states, "The Emancipation Proclamation portended revolution and impelled many border Unionists to cooperate with Democrats in the conservative opposition."

After some scheming, Etheridge hatched a plan to overturn Republican control of the House by tilting the roll of members-elect toward a conservative coalition of Democrats and Unionists. He intended to take advantage of the stipulations in a recently passed 1863 law that provided the Clerk with the ability to certify the credentials of members-elect.[7] The intention of the

---

[6] Martis refers to such pro-emancipation, pro-war Unionists as "Unconditional Unionists" (1989, 38).

[7] *Statutes at Large*, 37-3, 804. The law stated that the Clerk, in making his roll, "would place thereon the names of all persons and such persons only, whose credentials show that they were regularly elected in accordance with their states respectively, or the laws of the United States."

law was to enhance Republican strength in the succeeding Congress by providing the Clerk with discretion to count loyalists from portions of the
South under Union military control. Etheridge, however, planned to apply a
strict reading of the law, thereby requiring that very particular credentials be
presented in order to receive certification. He then contacted Democratic
House leaders and shared his plan, describing the exact form of credentials
necessary and urging them to disseminate the information to their partisans
and Unionists as well (Belz 1970, 555–56).

Unfortunately for Etheridge, the details of his scheme leaked out. Republican leaders, including President Lincoln, quickly countermobilized. The
caucus was an essential element in the strategy to meet Etheridge, both of-
fensively (by coordinating on a single speakership candidate) and defen-
sively (by organizing to counter Etheridge's roll call scheme).

In late November 1863, informal canvassing for the speakership was well
under way. With Speaker Grow defeated in the midterm elections, Schuyler
Colfax emerged as the near-unanimous Republican candidate. As members
began arriving in Washington, forecasts of Colfax's strength were widely
reported, with estimates of his having 85 votes already pledged.[8] These estimates proved to be accurate, as Colfax's nomination "was agreed to without
dissent and by acclamation" when the Union caucus met on December 5,
1863, two days prior to the opening of the 38th Congress (*NYT*, 12/6/1863,
1; cf. *NYTrib*, 12/7/1863, 4).[9] A long discussion also took place regarding
Etheridge's potential scheme, during which caucus members' election credentials were certified. Before adjourning, caucus leaders urged all attendees
to be present at the opening of the session.

The proceedings on the opening day of Congress, December 7, 1863,
demonstrated the value of the Union caucus just days before. Once Etheridge had finished his initial call of the House roll, 16 members from five
states (Maryland, Missouri, West Virginia, Kansas, and Oregon) had been
excluded, while three members from Louisiana had been added under Etheridge's interpretation of the Act of March 3, 1863 (*CG*, 38-1, 12/7/1863, 4).
After some heated discussion, Henry Dawes (R-Mass.) offered a resolution
that the Maryland members be added to the Clerk's roll. James C. Allen (D-
Ill.), who had served as the House Clerk in the 35th Congress, responded by
moving to table Dawes's resolution and demanded the yeas and nays.

Here, then, was the showdown. The question on Allen's tabling motion
was taken, and it failed by a vote of 74–94 (*CG*, 38-1, 12/7/1863, 5). The
Republicans unanimously opposed the tabling motion. The conservative
forces were divided, however, with five Democrats and six Unionists voting
against tabling—that is, in opposition to Etheridge's scheme to deny the

[8] *NYT*, 12/5/1863, 3; for an earlier estimate, see *NYT*, 12/2/1863, 4. Also see *NYTrib*,
12/3/1863, 1; 12/5/1863, 6.
[9] Elihu Washburne (Ill.) and Reuben Fenton (N.Y.) were entered into nomination, but both
asked to withdraw their names after the nominating speeches were made (*NYTrib*, 12/7/1863,
4).

Republicans the opportunity to organize the chamber. Had a unified coalition of Democrats and Unionists emerged in support of Etheridge, his scheme would have prevailed by a margin of two votes (Belz 1970, 562).[10]

Victorious in the procedural standoff, the Republicans then moved to add the Maryland members to the roll, followed in quick succession by the Missouri, West Virginia, Kansas, and Oregon delegations. Once accomplished, they turned their attention to organizing the chamber. Colfax was elected Speaker on the first ballot, capturing 101 of 180 votes (CG, 38-1, 12/7/1863, 6–7).[11] He received all 85 Republican votes cast, along with 16 votes from Unionists.

The Union caucus met again that evening to nominate the remaining House officers. Ballots were held and the majority winners for four positions—Edward McPherson (Pa.) for Clerk, Nehemiah Ordway (N.H.) for Sergeant at Arms, Ira Goodenow (N.Y.) for Doorkeeper, and William S. King (Minn.) for Postmaster—were announced, after which the nominations were declared unanimous (NYT, 12/8/1863, 1).[12]

The following day, December 8, the House proceeded to the rest of the organization, turning first to the election of a Clerk. James Moorhead (R-Pa.), per the guidelines of the Union caucus, nominated Edward McPherson, a protégé of Thaddeus Stevens and a former Republican House member in the 37th and 38th Congresses who had lost his reelection bid; Robert Mallory (U-Ky.) nominated Emerson Etheridge, this time as the conservative candidate rather than the administration choice. The latter action was viewed by many Republicans as unseemly. Owen Lovejoy (R-Ill.) stated that the nomination of Etheridge, after his nefarious procedural maneuver, "required a good deal of brass" (CG, 38-1, 12/8/1863, 11).

When the roll was called, McPherson emerged victorious, capturing 102 of 171 votes cast. He received all Republican votes and most Unionists',

[10] The partisan breakdown on the roll call was 0–83 for Republicans, 67–5 for Democrats, and 7–6 for Unionists. Party labels were taken from Martis (1989), but the following adjustments were made: Unionists are a combined category (Conditional and Unconditional Unionists) and one member's party code was switched (Rufus Spalding of Ohio, whom Martis classifies as a Republican while other sources code him as a Democrat).

[11] Although the House Journal reports a total of 182 votes, the roll call record only accounts for 180 votes. In addition to Colfax, Samuel S. Cox (Ohio), the chief Democratic candidate, received 42 votes, with the other 39 scattering among six other candidates: John Dawson ([Pa.], 12), Robert Mallory ([Ky.], 10), Henry G. Stebbins ([N.Y.], 8), Austin A. King ([Mo.], 6), Frank Blair ([Mo.], 2), and John D. Stiles ([Pa.], 1). Among Democrats, opposition to Cox came primarily from New York and Pennsylvania. In terms of W-NOMINATE scores, Cox's support was strongest on the left side of the space, that is, among Democrats who were most opposed to Republican political-economic policies.

[12] McPherson captured 57 votes against 44 votes for James Buffinton (Mass.) on the sixth caucus ballot for Clerk. The first ballot pitted four Republican ex-House members against each other: McPherson (32 votes), Buffinton (32 votes), Samuel C. Fessenden ([Maine], 21 votes), and Green Adams ([Ky.], 14 votes). Ordway received 51 of 92 votes cast for Sergeant at Arms; Goodenow, 55 of 99 for Doorkeeper; and King, 66 of 96 for Postmaster. See NYT, 12/8/1863, 1; CT, 12/8/1863, 1.

with Etheridge polling all Democratic votes and a smattering of Unionists.[13] The elections of the caucus nominees for Sergeant at Arms, Postmaster, and Doorkeeper quickly followed suit (*CG*, 38-1, 12/8/1863, 11–12).

The full slate of officers having been elected, Speaker Colfax worked on staffing the various standing committees. In doing so, he took seriously the necessity of sharing power across interests within the party. After consulting with party leaders and cabinet members, Colfax sequestered himself for two full days and produced more than 20 different standing committee configurations before settling on a satisfactory set of assignments (Bogue 1981, 116–17). First, he made sure to reward his chief precaucus rival for the speakership, Elihu Washburne (Ill.), by reappointing him to chair the Commerce Committee. Colfax's other rival, Reuben Fenton (N.Y.), was awarded with a coveted position on Ways and Means after a House career that had featured memberships on committees like Private Land Claims and Invalid Pensions. Colfax also placated the moderate wing of his party by distributing the chairmanships of Elections and Judiciary to Henry Dawes (Mass.) and James F. Wilson (Iowa), respectively. His Radical wing received the lion's share of chairmanships, with Ways and Means going to Thaddeus Stevens (Pa.), Public Lands to George W. Julian (Ind.), and Public Expenditures to Calvin T. Hulburd (N.Y.). Finally, he acknowledged the support of the Unionist bloc that made his election possible by appointing Henry Winter Davis (Md.) to chair Foreign Affairs and Brutus J. Clay (Ky.) to chair Agriculture.

Thus, Colfax followed Grow in his dutiful fulfillment of the caucus-directed House organization. To secure smooth and seamless decision making in the set of officer elections on the House floor, ideological divisions and conflicts were dealt with at the prefloor stage within the majority party caucus. To ensure that caucus decisions would translate into party members' votes on the floor, rewards were needed—in this case, the Speaker was the key central agent who distributed committee assignments and chairmanships to all factions within the party. And because the party was a continuing institution, the equilibrium was self-enforcing. That is, party leaders sought to ensure a steady stream of organizational outcomes into the future; thus, the Speaker, as the agent of the caucus and servant of the party, had no incentive to defect from the caucus-induced equilibrium.

Moreover, events in the 38th Congress, specifically the Etheridge conspiracy, provided Republican House leaders with an additional reason to

---

[13] After his defeat, Etheridge became an even more vociferous critic of the Republican administration. He led a group of conservatives in nominating George McClellan for the presidency. He then ran unsuccessfully for election as a conservative to the House from his former Ninth District in 1865 and to the governorship of Tennessee in 1867. He finally regained political office with his election to the Tennessee General Assembly in 1869. In time, much to his chagrin, the Conservative movement in Tennessee was subsumed by the Democratic Party. As a result, Etheridge returned to the Republican fold—supporting Rutherford Hayes's presidential bid in 1876—and he remained a loyal party member until his death in 1902.

emphasize the need for prefloor organization. Apart from the collective benefits of organization generally, Etheridge's failed coup underscored the uncertainty and potential high costs of allowing majority party factions to sort themselves out on the House floor. The lesson was clear: any individual position-taking benefits that majority party members might accrue from unconstrained balloting for Speaker were far outweighed by the inherent risks of such an arrangement for the party and nation as a whole.

The Republicans' electoral setback in the midterm elections of 1862–63 was erased by the turnaround in Union military fortunes in late 1864 and 1865. Consequently, Lincoln was reelected in November 1864, and Republican candidates swept the 1864–65 congressional elections throughout the North. The Republicans would operate in a position of dominance, without serious competition, for the next decade. As a result, Republican organization of the House, with the party caucus serving as the focal point, was relatively straightforward. Colfax remained the unanimous caucus choice for Speaker in the 39th and 40th Congresses and was reelected by wide margins on the floor, 139–36 and 127–30, respectively (CG, 39-1, 12/4/1865, 5; 40-1, 12/4/1867, 4). In each case, Republican unity was firm. Moreover, Colfax continued to distribute power within the party in an evenhanded way through his committee chairmanships and assignments. After each speakership election, a set of caucus-nominated candidates for Clerk, Sergeant at Arms, Postmaster, and Doorkeeper was elected by resolution (CG, 39-1, 12/4/1865, 5; 40-1, 12/4/1867, 5, 7).[14] This became the norm for electing the minor House officers, even though the House rules continued to provide for their election by ballot.

When Colfax left the House at the convening of the 41st Congress (March 1869), having been elected vice president, the Republicans chose James G. Blaine (Maine) as their candidate for Speaker without evidence of a serious campaign by Blaine or any other pretender for the office. After Blaine was nominated by acclamation, he won an easy victory on the floor over the Democratic nominee, Michael Kerr (D-Ind.), on a 135–57 vote that reflected perfect party unity on both sides (NYT, 3/3/1869, 1; NYTrib, 3/3/1869, 1; CG, 41-1, 3/4/1869, 4–5). Similar victories were had by the set of Republican caucus nominees for the other officer positions.[15]

---

[14] The results were 138–35 and without opposition, respectively. In the 39th Congress, McPherson, Ordway, and Goodenow were renominated for Clerk, Sergeant at Arms, and Doorkeeper, respectively, while Joshua Given (Ohio) was nominated for Postmaster. McPherson and Ordway were nominated by acclamation; Goodenow received 66 of 123 votes on a first caucus ballot; and Given received 71 of 119 votes on a second caucus ballot after no majority winner emerged on the first ballot (NYT, 12/4/1865, 1). In the 40th Congress, McPherson and Ordway were renominated (unanimously) for Clerk and Sergeant at Arms, while Charles E. Lippincott (Ill.) defeated Goodenow for Doorkeeper 64–57 and William S. King (Minn.) defeated Given for Postmaster 61–60, both on a first caucus ballot (NYT, 3/5/1867, 1).

[15] Although Blaine won nomination by acclamation, the minor offices were all contested in caucus. McPherson, Ordway, and King were renominated for Clerk, Sergeant at Arms, and Postmaster, respectively, while Otis S. Buxton (N.Y.) was nominated for Doorkeeper (CG, 41-1,

Despite Blaine's moderate predispositions, he took special pains to treat the Radical element of the party favorably. He distributed important committee chairmanships to several prominent Radicals, assigning Ways and Means to Robert C. Schenck (Ohio), Judiciary to John Bingham (Ohio), Public Lands to George Julian (Ind.), and Reconstruction to Benjamin Butler (Mass.). He balanced these Radical appointments with a string of important committee chairmanships to influential Republican moderates, with Henry Dawes (Mass.) atop Appropriations, James Garfield (Ohio) leading Banking and Currency, and Nathan Dixon (R.I.) guiding Commerce (*CG*, 41-1, 3/15/1869, 75–77). Blaine organized the House to allow each wing of the party to follow its major agenda: the Radicals were placed in positions to guide social policy, while the moderates were placed in positions to design economic/financial policies. Blaine's Solomon-like strategy was met with much approval, and he was rewarded with unanimous caucus renominations and subsequent floor reelections in the 42nd and 43rd Congresses.[16]

Thus, less than a decade after the Civil War, a clear binding caucus on organizational matters had developed in the House, at least as far as the Republicans were concerned. Majority party members were expected to support caucus nominations, so that the election of House officers, and the subsequent distribution of patronage and power (via committee assignments), could be accomplished in a smooth and timely manner. The binding party caucus thus solved the instability problem in speakership elections that surfaced in the last two decades of the antebellum era. The caucus effected a *structure-induced equilibrium* (Shepsle 1979; Shepsle and Weingast 1981) by providing an institutional solution to the organizational difficulties that had often spilled out onto the House floor at the convening of a new Congress.

The caucus was *binding* because of the very real sanctions that could be imposed on defectors. As Washington correspondent for the *Chicago Tribune*, George Alfred Townsend, stated in his portrait of political life in the nation's capital, *Washington, Outside and Inside*:

> Whoever goes into caucus must abide by its verdict or be dishonored, like the man who gambles and then must pay up, though it be plucking bread from the mouths of his wife and children. He must obey the

---

3/5/1869, 19). McPherson was challenged in caucus by Ephraim R. Eckley (Ohio) and Samuel McKee (Ky.). McPherson received 83 votes to Eckley's 26 and McKee's 20. Ordway defeated H. W. Washburn (Ind.) on a 75–57 ballot. Buxton defeated W. T. Collins (Minn.) 98–29. King required more than one ballot to narrowly defeat Joshua Given. See *NYT*, 3/3/1869, 1; *NYTrib*, 3/3/1869, 1.

[16] Blaine defeated George W. Morgan (D-Ohio) and Fernando Wood (D-N.Y.) 126–92 and 189–76 (with four votes scattering), respectively (*CG*, 42-1, 3/4/1871, 6; *CR*, 43-1, 12/1/1873, 6). McPherson, Ordway, and Buxton would also be renominated (and reelected) Clerk, Sergeant at Arms, and Doorkeeper, respectively, in these two Congresses, while Henry Sherwood (Mich.) would replace William S. King as Chaplain in the 43rd Congress.

party behest, conscience or no conscience. . . . Suppose a member . . .
bolts caucus; what are the consequences? He forfeits his right to meet
in private sessions of his party again, and one might as well be in limbo
now-a-days as in no party. (1873, 505–6)

This theme was echoed a decade later by political scientist Woodrow
Wilson in his academic treatise *Congressional Government*:

There is no place in congressional jousts for the free lance. The man
who disobeys his party caucus is understood to disavow party allegiance altogether, and to assume that dangerous neutrality which is so
apt to degenerate into mere caprice, and which is almost sure to destroy his influence by bringing him under the suspicion of being unre-
liable—a suspicion always conclusively damning in practical life. An
individual, or any minority of weak numbers of small influence, who
has the temerity to neglect the decisions of the caucus is sure . . . to be
read out of the party, almost without chance of reinstatement. ([1885]
1973, 213)

Thus, the conventional wisdom of the time was that caucus violators, or
"bolters," could expect swift reprisals from party leaders. In addition to penalties like having their committee assignments stripped (or their seniority on
committees eliminated) and their share of policy spoils taken away, bolters
were potentially putting their entire political futures on the line. In short, in
the new caucus-driven organizational arrangement, the possibility of being
cast out of the party, for all practical purposes, was a credible outcome.

That said, this binding caucus arrangement was limited to organizational
matters. Efforts to expand the caucus's role into the realm of policy—and
thus create a legislative structure more similar to a parliamentary system—
was attempted but failed. This possibility seemed far from remote at first. In
the Republican caucus prior to the convening of the 39th Congress, after a
slate of officer nominations was determined, a motion was offered by Thaddeus Stevens to appoint a joint congressional committee to examine and
report on the former rebel states, specifically to determine if they should
receive representation in Congress (*NYT*, 12/5/1865, 4; *NYH*, 12/5/1865).
The motion was considered and unanimously agreed upon. The next day,
following the election of House officers, the motion to create a Joint Committee of Fifteen (six members from the Senate and nine from the House)
was then considered on the House floor and passed 133–36, with all Republicans voting in support (*CG*, 39-1, 12/4/1865, 6). Just over a week later, the
Senate concurred.[17] As a result, Congress, led by the Radicals, was given
procedural control of Southern Reconstruction.

---

[17] The Senate vote was 33–11, with Republicans voting 33–3 and Democrats voting 0–8
(*CG*, 39-1, 12/12/1865, 30).

A crucial part of this Radical initiative depended on Edward McPherson, the House Clerk. If a congressional committee was to take charge of Southern Reconstruction, it was imperative that the Clerk not recognize Southern representatives in his roll of members-elect prior to the organization of the 39th Congress; otherwise, a precedent for readmission would be set. McPherson, a loyal Republican and advocate of the Radical cause, played his part in the drama by failing to recognize members-elect from Tennessee, Virginia, and Louisiana, states that were reorganized along the lines of President Johnson's Reconstruction plan, while allowing no interference or interruption during his call of the roll (Trefousse 1997, 174–76; Jenkins and Stewart 2004).[18]

Although the Radicals believed the creation of the Joint Committee of Fifteen was merely the first step in a caucus-driven set of Reconstruction policies, many Republican House members viewed this simply as an organizational decision not unlike those associated with officer elections. As a result, Radical and moderate Republicans continued to lock horns on the true role of the caucus; the former would push to make *all* caucus decisions—organizational *and* policy-related—binding on all members, while the latter would hold fast to the notion that members were only bound to caucus decisions on matters of organization. Blaine, the leader of the moderate wing, articulated a clear view on the issue:

> The caucus is a convenience of party organization to determine the course to be pursued in matters of expediency which do not involve question[s] of moral obligation or personal justice. Rightfully employed, the caucus is not only useful but necessary in the conduct and government of party interests. Wrongfully applied, it is a weakness, an offense, a stumbling-block in the way of party prosperity. (1886, 504)

While Radical leaders routinely threatened moderates when divisions on Reconstruction-related policies emerged in caucus, they were unable to bind members on policy. The Radicals simply were not a large enough faction within the party to employ effective coercion, certainly not without risking the health and future well-being of the party as a whole. Moreover, public opinion was against them; mainstream media outlets, like the *New York*

[18] As McPherson had remained loyal at a crucial time, Stevens tapped him for a larger role in the Radical agenda. On March 2, 1867, the penultimate day of the 39th Congress, the House passed a sundry appropriations bill (*Statutes at Large*, 39-2, 466–67). Tucked away in the bill was a provision transferring authority for the selection of newspapers to publish the nation's laws in the former Confederate states from the secretary of state, who had possessed this authority since 1787, to the House Clerk. This provision provided McPherson with a prime patronage tool, as the compensation paid to selected newspapers was substantial (C. Smith 1977, 238). Moreover, per Stevens's wishes, McPherson could use this patronage to select newspapers sympathetic to the Radicals' point of view. In Stevens's view, the current secretary of state, William Seward, was not reliable, as he would likely pursue a more moderate course.

Times, echoed Blaine's perspective by framing caucus-imposed constraints on questions of policy as inherently undemocratic:

> The party caucus which may be usefully employed to promote a private citizen to the rank of Sergeant-at-Arms is hardly the sort of thing by which to operate upon men's convictions in concerns of national import. (*NYT*, 1/18/1866, 4)
>
> The obvious use of a caucus is for consultation and exchange of views. A vote of a legislative caucus is not binding upon its members, but decides how many of those present are in favor of a certain outcome. . . . when a caucus . . . takes away a man's right of private judgment, it becomes an instrument of oppression; it cannot long live. (*NYT*, 3/11/1875, 6)

Thus, Republican divisions on issues like the impeachment of President Johnson and the granting of amnesty to former Confederate soldiers created disagreements in caucus that inevitably spilled out onto the House floor. While the Radicals won some policy victories, like the creation of the Freedmen's Bureau and the drafting of the Reconstruction amendments, they were reined in by the lack of a binding caucus on policy. Thus, the course of Southern Reconstruction was not as extreme as the ideal Radical blueprint would have prescribed.

THE DEMOCRATS EMBRACE THE BINDING CAUCUS ON ORGANIZATIONAL MATTERS

The Republicans were not alone in recognizing the importance of the binding party caucus on organizational matters. During their time as the minority party, the Democrats had striven to present themselves as a unified opposition. While the Republicans' sizable numerical advantage made this coordination hopelessly in vain, Democratic leaders viewed the effort as an investment that would yield dividends when the party regained the majority.

Throughout the 1860s, the Democrats labored in the shadows of the Republicans. As far as we can tell, leadership of the party throughout the decade was uncontested in caucus, as a series of sacrificial lambs were given the dubious honor of being named the party's choice for Speaker: James Brooks (N.Y., 39th Cong.), Samuel Marshall (Ill., 40th Cong.), Michael Kerr (Ind., 41st Cong.), and George W. Morgan (Ohio, 42nd Cong.).

The election of 1872, in which Democrats experienced their best showing in any presidential year since 1860, changed the party's approach toward leadership selection as the opening of the 43rd Congress (1873–75) approached. Even though they remained in the minority, the Democrats could sense majority power returning, as the readmitted Southern states were sending more and more Democratic members to Washington. Thus, the Democratic leadership was now valuable, and it would be seriously contested.

The Democratic caucus that preceded the opening of the 43rd Congress was a trial run for later caucuses when the Democrats held the majority. Three candidates presented themselves for the honor of being given the party's nomination for Speaker: Fernando Wood (N.Y.), James C. Robinson (Ill.), and Samuel S. Cox (N.Y.).[19] Wood led on the first ballot with 30 votes against 20 for Cox and 19 for Robinson. On the second ballot Robinson's supporters united behind Wood, giving him 44 votes to 22 for Cox and 4 votes scattered among four other candidates (*NYT*, 11/30/1873, 1). Reflecting deep divisions over Wood's prominent role in the congressional salary increase—the so-called Salary Grab—in the 42nd Congress, the caucus broke up rancorously, with several Democrats threatening to bolt and support Blaine. The next day when the House organized, one Democrat (Harry B. Banning [Ohio]) did in fact support Blaine, and three others cast their votes for Democrats other than Wood—Richard Bland ([Mo.], who voted for Alexander H. Stephens [Ga.]), Thomas J. Creamer ([N.Y.], who voted for Heister Clymer [Pa.]), and William S. Holman ([Ind.], who voted for Cox). The rest, however, suppressed their disappointment and supported Wood.

The Democrats largely stayed unified on organizational votes through the 43rd Congress, even though these votes were largely symbolic. Coordinating would be more consequential at the start of the 44th Congress (1875–77), which followed on the heels of the Democratic landslide in the midterm elections of 1874–75. The organization of the House was theirs to lose, as they controlled 176 of 292 seats at the outset (Dubin 1998, 235). Yet, the Democrats struggled for an identity, as they were comprised of a heterogeneous group of members—protectionists and free traders, inflationists and hard-money advocates, and reformers and machine politicians, among others. Democratic leaders looked to the caucus to produce the framework for an organization. Thus, by the mid-1870s, the caucus had become an *equilibrium institution*—the institution *chosen* by leaders of *both* parties to solve problems of chamber organization.

As members began arriving in Washington, and as the caucus meeting approached, politicking on possible speakership candidates was prevalent.[20] Three candidates eventually emerged: Michael Kerr (Ind.), a hard-money, antitariff intellectual; Samuel Randall (Pa.), a protariff, pro-South machine politician; and Samuel S. Cox (N.Y.), the Tammany-backed spoilsman and political opportunist—with none a clear favorite. Fernando Wood originally

---

[19] Cox had served previously in the House as a member from Ohio and had run unsuccessfully for Speaker in the 38th Congress. After losing his reelection bid in 1864, he moved to New York, where he curried favor with the Tammany politicians. Eventually, he earned their trust and received their backing in his return to Congress (Lindsey 1959).

[20] See *NYT*, 11/26/1875, 1; 12/1/1875, 1; 12/2/1875, 1; 12/3/1875, 1; 12/4/1875, 1.

campaigned for the nomination but withdrew on the eve of the caucus, instead devoting his energies to the canvass for Randall (*NYT*, 11/26/1875, 1; *Boston Globe* [hereafter abbreviated as *BG*], 12/1/1875, 1).

On Saturday, December 4, 1875, the Democratic caucus convened. The first ballot read Kerr 71, Randall 59, and Cox 31. A second ballot was then held, with Kerr receiving 77 votes to Randall's 63 and Cox's 21. Finally, on the third ballot, Kerr emerged victorious, garnering 90 votes to Randall's 63 and Cox's 7. Randall was then recognized and urged the Democrats to coalesce in harmony; to that end, he moved that Kerr's nomination be made unanimous, which carried amid applause (*NYT*, 12/5/1875, 1; *NYTrib*, 12/6/1875, 2).[21]

When the 44th Congress convened two days later, the speakership balloting went according to plans—Kerr was elected on the first ballot, besting Blaine 173–106 on a strict party-line vote (*Congressional Record* [hereafter abbreviated as *CR*], 44-1, 12/6/1875, 167).[22] Kerr would then play his part in promoting party harmony and maintaining the caucus-induced House organization by appointing Randall to chair Appropriations and Cox to chair Banking and Currency. To round out the major "money" committees, Kerr appointed William H. Morrison (Ill.), a midwestern colleague who shared his own policy views, to chair Ways and Means. Power was thus parceled out among the Democratic factions, with no one faction gaining an exclusive advantage on tariff and currency legislation as the House opened for business.

Kerr died shortly after the completion of the first session of the 44th Congress, leaving the speakership vacant. The choice of Speaker in this instance helped provide a footnote to the disputed Hayes-Tilden presidential race, since the winner would be responsible for protecting Tilden's interests in the outcome of the affair. The race was similar to the earlier contest, with Kerr removed and a couple of dark horses (William R. Morrison [Ill.] and Milton Sayler [Ohio]) added to the mix in the event the caucus deadlocked. Tilden's interest in the speakership contest led him to announce a preference for Randall. As the caucus convened, Morrison withdrew in deference to Randall and Sayler withdrew in favor of Cox. Randall narrowly prevailed against Cox, 73–63 (*BG*, 12/1/1876, 1; *NYT*, 12/3/1876, 7), and would go on to defeat James Garfield (R-Ohio) for the speakership, 162–82 (*CR*, 44-2, 12/4/1876, 6).

Randall would be reelected Speaker in the next two Congresses. In both instances, he was challenged in caucus but survived with first-ballot victories to win the nomination. And, each time, Democrats rallied around him on the floor once the caucus had settled the matter.

---

[21] For an extensive analysis of the speakership election of 1875, especially the Democrats' precaucus and caucus politicking, see House (1965).

[22] The three scattering votes were cast by members who had caucused with neither major party.

While it is perhaps not surprising that Randall held his party together on the floor at the start of the 45th Congress (1877–79) when the Democrats maintained a slim majority, the same cannot be said about the start of the 46th (1879–81), when the Democrats held only a plurality of House seats. Overall, the 1878 midterm elections had been a mixed bag for the party nationally, as Democrats lost seats in the House, moving from a majority of 19 to a plurality of 9, but gained seats in the Senate, moving from a minority of 5 to a majority of 9 (Martis 1989, 130–33). The balance in the House was held by 13 members of the Greenback Party, a third party built on an anti-monopoly ideology.[23] Greenbackers had presented problems for both Democrats and Republicans, as the lingering effects of the Panic of 1873 persisted and the implementation of the Specie Resumption Act loomed.[24]

Democrats from the South and West argued that Greenback gains were a signal for Democrats to embrace soft money and tariff reduction as a way to regain the presidency in 1880. Practically speaking, with the election of 13 Greenbackers to the 46th Congress, considerable Greenback sympathy among Southern and midwestern Democrats, and a small numerical Democratic advantage over the Republicans, the ingredients were in place for a return to antebellum patterns in the organization of the House. Randall's hold on the speakership was immediately cast in doubt once the midterm results were known.

Adding to the complications of organizing the 46th Congress was the deadlock that emerged at the end of the 45th Congress over the appropriations bills, particularly the army bill, which Democratic House members were intent upon using to bar federal poll watchers from Southern elections (Stewart 1989). The 45th Congress adjourned without the army bill passing, which prompted President Hayes to call Congress into a special session on March 18, 1879, to deal with it, along with other unpassed appropriations bills and ambassadorial nominations.[25] Therefore, unlike most years, when speakership contests could unfold across a full calendar year and take advantage of the summer/fall recess for the canvassing of support, the speakership contest of 1879 was compressed into a very short time window.

Three speakership campaigns emerged.[26] On the Democratic side, sup-

---

[23] For additional background on the Greenback Party, see Ritter (1997) and Hild (2007).

[24] This act, passed on January 14, 1875, provided for the redemption of paper currency (or "greenbacks") in gold, beginning on January 1, 1879. See *Statutes at Large*, 43-2, 296.

[25] Presidential Proclamation of March 4, 1879.

[26] The following account is generally taken from the following newspaper articles: *BG* 2/11/1879, 1; 2/13/1879, 1; 3/5/1879, 1; 3/7/1879, 1; 3/8/1879, 1; 3/10/1879, 1; 3/13/1879, 1; 3/17/1879, 1, 3; 3/18/1879, 1; 3/19/1879, 1; 3/24/1879, 2; *WP* 11/15/1878, 1; 11/11/1878, 2; 2/14/1879, 1; 2/15/1879, 1; 3/7/1879, 1; 3/11/1879, 1; 3/14/1879, 2; 3/15/1879, 2; 3/17/1879, 2; 3/17/1879, 1; 3/18/1879, 1; 3/21/1879, 1; 3/22/1879, 2; 3/26/1879, 1; *NYT* 3/7/1879, 1; 3/8/1879, 1; 3/10/1879, 1; 3/16/1879, 1; 3/17/1879, 1; 3/18/1879, 1; 3/19/1879, 1; 3/20/1879, 1.

porters of Joseph J. Blackburn (Ky.) organized quickly and actively, making explicit appeals to substance (i.e., soft money) and to region; on this latter point, the realization that Southerners now constituted a majority of the Democratic caucus and that Blackburn had been an officer in the Confederate army was lost on no one. Randall, preoccupied with House business, was slower to act, but his supporters likewise set up shop. Not to be outdone, the Greenback central committee also established a campaign operation that was headed by James B. Weaver (Iowa). Interestingly, not only was there little evidence of overt Republican organization for the speakership campaign, but the one mention of Republican efforts came in a reported telegram from James Garfield (Ohio) to Randall offering Republican help should he need it on the House floor (*Washington Post* [hereafter abbreviated as *WP*], 3/11/1879, 1).

Under past practices, the party caucuses would have convened the night before the formal opening of Congress to decide on their nominations. In this case, however, senior Democratic leaders were uncertain enough about Greenback strength and tactics that they allowed extra time to organize if the caucus did not evolve smoothly. Therefore, the Democrats called their caucus to meet on Saturday, March 15, three days before the House's convening.

Going into the caucus meeting, both the Randall and Blackburn forces claimed substantial support—Randall maintaining that 93 votes were locked up and Blackburn 69 (*NYT*, 3/17/1879, 1). If Blackburn's numbers were solid, then it spelled danger for Randall, and perhaps the whole party, since it portended the possibility of a multiballot affair in caucus that might spill out onto the House floor.

As the caucus was forming, a significant arrival was that of Samuel S. Cox (N.Y.), who had been identified as a possible nominee of the Greenbacks. Cox left the chamber when his name was placed in nomination, according to custom, but his appearance and willingness to contest within the Democratic caucus was taken as evidence that the Democrats would be able to confine the conflict within the caucus itself.

A motion to vote in caucus by secret ballot passed; this was seen as a test of strength between the two candidates, which Randall won.[27] Balloting took an hour and a half to complete. In the end, the precaucus support of each candidate had proven to be overstated, but more so for Blackburn: Randall received the support of 75 caucus members, compared to 57 for Blackburn, and 9 other votes scattered among Cox, John McMahon (Ohio), and William Morrison (Ill.).

[27] Why Randall would have supported a secret ballot was never made clear in newspaper accounts, but he presumably relied on Southern support, some of which would have melted under public scrutiny. Thus, it appears that Randall had learned the long-run lesson of the antebellum viva voce reform, which was that interregional partisan alliances were more stable when cloaked in secrecy.

Immediately upon the announcement of the tally, Blackburn entered the chamber and asked recognition from the chair. At the end of a "manly speech," Blackburn made the following appeal:

> I am a party man. I am a partisan, not for the sake of a party, but because I honestly believe the best interests of my country are to be subserved by the triumph of my party's principles. I have this to say: The edict of this caucus is to be final and conclusive, and if there be one among the 57 gentlemen whose partial friendship has given me their votes that hesitates or doubts, to him I now appeal to make the verdict of this caucus effective when to-morrow's roll is called. (*BG*, 3/18/1879, 1; *NYT*, 3/18/1879, 1)

Blackburn then continued, "I move you Sir, that the nomination of the gentleman from Pennsylvania [Mr. Randall] for Speakership of the House of Representatives of the Forty-sixth Congress be made unanimous."

Whether the Democrats would in fact close ranks around Randall would only be known the next day. Since only four Democrats (excluding the nominated candidates) had been absent from the caucus meeting, any defection from Randall would be a sign of the caucus's weakness as an organizing tool.[28]

Once the roll had been called and the House turned to the business of organizing, Randall and Garfield were placed in nomination, as expected, by their respective parties. Gilbert De La Matyr (G-Ind.), a Methodist preacher whose one term of service was in the 46th Congress, caused a stir by rising and placing in nomination Hendrick B. Wright, a Democrat from Pennsylvania. This development caused a physical reaction from Randall and a ripple of worry among Democratic leaders. In the end, the worry was unfounded. The Democrats remained solidly behind Randall, as he collected 143 votes to 125 for Garfield, 13 for Wright, and 1 scattered (*CR*, 46-1, 3/18/1879, 5). Only one Democrat, Adlai Stevenson (Ill.), voted for Wright.[29] The rest of Wright's support came from Republicans and Greenbackers.

In the end, the only true drama came when it was realized that Randall had received a majority of all votes cast, but not a majority of all *members elected*.[30] As Omar Conger (R-Mich.) appealed to the Clerk to declare that

[28] Other than the nominated speakership candidates, the absent Democrats were identified as Hendrick B. Wright (Pa.), Alfred M. Lay (Mo.), Daniel O'Reilly (N.Y.), and David B. Culberson (Tex.). In the end only Wright abandoned Randall.

[29] Wright, himself, did not vote. Martis classifies Wright as a Greenbacker during the 46th Congress, but all the press accounts, and his subsequent behavior in attending Democratic caucuses, lead us to classify him as a Democrat.

[30] There were 293 House seats in the 46th Congress, but at the time of the speakership election, two were vacant (12th District seat in New York and 6th District seat in Texas) and California had yet to hold its elections for four seats (see Dubin 1998, 249). Thus, there were 287

a majority of all elected members was necessary for the selection of a Speaker, Democrats filibustered long enough to allow for the arrival of Daniel O'Reilly (D-N.Y.) from the train depot, who demanded to have his vote (no. 144) counted for Randall—this gave Randall a bare majority of members elected and made Conger's point moot (*NYT*, 3/19/1879, 7).[31]

For his part, Randall smoothed over the factional rift in his party through his committee appointments. He rewarded Blackburn by appointing him to Appropriations (after first offering him the chair of Banking and Currency) and to Rules (*BG*, 4/6/1879, 1).[32] Since the most important piece of business for the special session was the negotiation over the army appropriations bill, with its restriction on Southern poll workers the sticking point, Randall's appointment of Blackburn to Appropriations and his continued chairmanship of the Expenditure in the War Department Committee was more than symbolic—it was a strong signal that the national Democratic Party was committed to dismantling Reconstruction.

Overall, Randall's committee assignments were viewed as equitably balancing the regional interests of his party (*BG*, 4/12/1879, 1; *NYT*, 4/12/1879, 5; *WP*, 4/12/1879, 2). Of the 52 committees, 26 were chaired by Northerners and an equal number by Southerners. The *Boston Globe* correspondent reported that "the anti-Randall element among the Democrats has been treated much better than it was two years ago—as well, perhaps, as could be expected, or as [John] Atkins [D-Tenn.] put it today, 'as well as was possible, under the circumstances; that is, as well as the speaker could do without reflecting upon his own friends'" (4/12/1879, 1).

The Democratic desire to court those with soft-money sentiments was acknowledged with committee assignments that caused the Greenback members to be "highly pleased" (*WP*, 4/12/1879, 1). Gilbert De La Matyr (Ind.), who had acted as the leader of the Greenbacks when he nominated Wright, was placed on Coinage, and remarked that he felt his party had been treated handsomely.

The same was not the case for the nominal Democrats who had dallied with the Greenbacks on the vote for Speaker. Wright himself, who had chaired Manufactures in the 45th Congress, was removed from the committee altogether, allowed to retain his seat on Public Lands, and given the chair of a select committee to investigate "the depression of labor." This last committee was viewed as a platform for Wright and accorded little weight as far

---

members elected, which meant that a successful speakership candidate had to win 144 votes for a majority.

[31] In his response to Conger, the Clerk, George M. "Green" Adams, stated that his opinion was that "it requires a majority of those voting to elect a Speaker" (*CR*, 46-1, 3/18/1879, 5). Thus, it appears that if O'Reilly had not made a last-minute appearance, Adams was prepared to push forward and announce that Randall had been duly elected with 143 votes.

[32] A preliminary account that Randall had named Blackburn to chair Appropriations was in error. See *BG*, 3/18/1879, 1.

nfluence in the chamber went.[33] On the other hand, Stevenson was appointed to chair the Mines and Mining Committee and given a seat on Private Land Claims.

Thus, Randall, like Kerr and the Republican Speakers before him, put party interests ahead of his personal preferences by preserving the organizational equilibrium that had developed around caucus decision making and the distribution of power (via committee assignments) in the chamber. Most important, through their actions the Democrats demonstrated that they too had added the binding party caucus on organizational matters to their repertoire.

FACTIONAL DIVISIONS AND THREATS
TO THE CAUCUS ORGANIZATION

While the congressional party caucuses would emerge to be critical organizational instruments in House politics between the 38th and 46th Congresses (1863–81), the equilibrium nature of their design would be directly challenged during the Gilded Age. Specifically, the binding commitment attached to the party caucus on organizational matters would be tested by several intraparty speakership battles within a span of a decade. What is most important is that the caucus held steady in the face of being tested.

The first case to challenge the binding party caucus would be in the 47th Congress (1881–83), after the Republicans rode the coattails of presidential nominee James Garfield in the national election of 1880 and regained control of Congress. The world had changed considerably since their last period of unified majority control in 1875—the Reconstruction of the South had ended, the protective tariff and currency issues had come to dominate the national agenda, and clear factions within the Republican Party had developed. This new context would frame the battle within the Republican caucus over officer selection, specifically the choice of Speaker.

Nearly a month before the convening of the 47th Congress, in December 1881, the jockeying over the speakership was already in full swing. Several contenders had emerged and descended on Washington to set up their campaign operations in anticipation of the arrival of the Republican House members. These Republican speakership hopefuls were Frank Hiscock (N.Y.), J. Warren Keifer (Ohio), Thomas B. Reed (Maine), Julius Burrows (Mich.), Mark Dunnel (Minn.), and John Kasson (Iowa) (*NYT*, 11/17/1881, 1). A seventh contender, Godlove Orth (Ind.), emerged shortly thereafter.

For the next three weeks, the Republican speakership jockeying would be covered extensively in the national press. Of the seven candidates, three

---

[33] The *New York Times* correspondent that analyzed the composition of the committee referred to Wright as a "lunatic" (4/12/1879, 4).

received the lion's share of the news coverage: Hiscock, who was perceived to be the leading eastern candidate and overall front-runner going into the caucus; Keifer, who had sizable support in the Midwest; and Kasson, who was the leading candidate of the West.[34] All of the others were viewed mostly as "favorite sons." Nevertheless, there was a general belief that a first-ballot winner would not emerge; thus, the supporters of these minor candidates would be critical in the eventual nomination of one of the major candidates. As a result, newspaper stories were rife with rumors of various "combinations."

On December 2, 1881, one day before the convening of the Republican caucus, the mood shifted decidedly in the speakership campaign. As party bosses began cutting deals behind the scenes, Keifer suddenly vaulted into front-runner status. To that point, press accounts had emphasized regional divisions within the party, describing the thinking of the various players in decidedly geographical terms. Now, the campaign shifted to an emphasis on policy and party-building strategy. Specifically, leaders of the party's two major factions, the Stalwarts and Half-Breeds, began to view the speakership as a chit in their tug-of-war for party control.

The Stalwarts represented the conservative wing of the party; they were machine politicians who survived on patronage politics and thus opposed the reform efforts (such as civil service reform) that had arisen in the late 1870s. They had been major supporters of the Grant administration and Reconstruction, and had opposed President Hayes's decision to forego the continued maintenance of a Southern wing of the party. The Half-Breeds represented the moderate wing of the party; they were less dependent on patronage politics and worked to design a more pragmatic party, especially one tied to the interests of the business community. They were open to moderate reform efforts, supported the end of Reconstruction, and favored Hayes's approach of courting white Southern Democrats.[35]

Keifer's sudden rise was connected to a deal struck between two Stalwart leaders—former senator Roscoe Conkling, the New York party boss, and Senator J. Donald Cameron, the Pennsylvania party boss. Conkling considered Hiscock, his fellow New Yorker, to be closer to Blaine and the Half-Breeds, while he viewed Keifer, a former Civil War general, proponent of Reconstruction, and supporter of Grant, as more of a Stalwart.[36] To main-

[34] See *NYT*, 11/17/1881, 1; 11/25/1881, 1; 11/27/1881, 1; 11/28/1881, 1, 4; 11/29/1881, 1; 12/1/1881, 1; 12/2/1881, 1; and *CT*, 11/27/1881, 3; 11/28/1881, 1; 11/29/1881, 2; 11/30/1881, 2; 12/1/1881, 4; 12/2/1881, 2.

[35] For a more extensive description of the Stalwarts and Half-Breeds, see Morgan (1969), Doenecke (1981), and Peskin (1984–85).

[36] Conkling did not view Keifer as a "prime" Stalwart, however, as Keifer had supported John Sherman (Ohio) and then James Garfield (Ohio) rather than backing Grant in the Republican National Convention of 1880. Still, Keifer was a loyal Grant supporter during Grant's presidency, while Hiscock had been a vocal Grant opponent in 1872. Thus, Keifer, in Conkling's mind, was the best option among the "eligible" candidates. See *NYT*, 12/3/1881, 3.

tain congressional patronage, and control of committees to which potential reform legislation would be assigned, Conkling and Cameron agreed to throw their influence behind Keifer. Cameron, in particular, was able to convince all but one of the 18 members of the Pennsylvania delegation to support Keifer, after many of them had previously pledged their support to Hiscock. These efforts were supplemented by the influence of President Chester Arthur, a Stalwart and former Conkling lieutenant, who ascended to the presidency after Garfield's assassination. Arthur's control of executive patronage was a useful tool in assembling a Stalwart House organization, especially in acquiring the support of the 10 Republican members from the South.[37]

When the Republican caucus met on December 3, 1881, the speakership divisions were apparent. On the first ballot, thanks to the Stalwart efforts on his behalf, Keifer led the crowded field with 52 votes, followed by Hiscock with 44, and 50 votes scattering among Kasson, Reed, Burrows, Orth, and Dunnell. A second ballot was then taken, with very little change. It was apparent that a protracted contest was under way.

Six hours and 16 ballots would eventually be needed to settle the nomination battle. (The individual ballot results appear in appendix 6.) Keifer maintained his lead throughout, Hiscock steadfastly held on to second place, while the minor candidates persevered and remained in the race. Eventually, Burrows relinquished his voters following the 15th ballot, and Hiscock and Kasson immediately followed suit. Many of their supporters swung their support to Keifer on the 16th ballot, which provided him with enough votes for victory. Each of the minor candidates hoped that by staying in the race he might emerge as the compromise candidate. Yet, Keifer's vote total remained strong, and Burrows, Hiscock, and Kasson finally acquiesced and allowed Keifer to take the nomination. In doing so, they hoped to be rewarded later in the committee assignment process.

The drama then continued with the nomination for Clerk. Edward McPherson (Pa.), the former House Clerk in the 39th–43rd Congresses, was the clear front-runner in the preballoting period. However, McPherson had run afoul of Cameron and his Pennsylvania cronies during the 1880 Republican National Convention, and Cameron wished to exact revenge by denying him the clerkship nomination. Unfortunately for Cameron, McPherson was well liked by Republican House members and won an easy victory on the first caucus ballot, collecting 92 votes to 42 for Joseph H. Rainey, a former House member from South Carolina, with 7 votes scattering (*CT*, 12/4/1881, 9). Two members of the Pennsylvania delegation—Samuel F. Barr and Russell Errett—refused to accept McPherson's nomination, how-

---

[37] For a detailed account of the Stalwart intrigue and the roles played by Conkling, Cameron, and Arthur, see *CT*, 12/3/1881, 3; 12/9/1881, 4, 9; and *NYT*, 12/3/1881, 1, 4; 12/4/1881, 1, 8.

ever, and vowed to oppose him on the House floor. Three other Pennsylvania members also threatened to follow suit. A possible caucus bolt was in the offing (*NYT*, 12/5/1881, 1, 4).

The stage now shifted to the House floor and the opening of the 47th Congress on December 5, 1881. As the Republicans controlled only 146 of 293 House seats, one short of a bare majority,[38] the party's caucus nominations seemed quite precarious on their face.[39] Despite receiving voting assurances from three minor party members—Independent Republican J. Hyatt Smith (N.Y.) and Readjusters John Paul and Abram Fulkerson (both Va.)—a successful Republican organization was susceptible to any number of possible calamities. Several disgruntled Half-Breeds could hold out to challenge the Stalwart organizational plan; a sectional alliance could form to extract additional benefits; the Pennsylvanians could try to deny McPherson the clerkship; and so on.

None of these disastrous scenarios transpired. Keifer was elected Speaker on the first House ballot, receiving 148 votes—*all* of the 145 Republicans (he himself abstained) plus the three pledged minor party members—to 129 for Samuel Randall (Pa.) and 8 for Nicholas Ford (Mo.), the Greenback candidate (*CR*, 47-1, 12/5/1881, 8–9). McPherson was also elected on the first House ballot, receiving the *same* set of 148 votes—which, of course, included the full Pennsylvania delegation (*CR*, 47-1, 12/5/1881, 16). Thus, with little margin for error, the Republicans maintained perfect unity and successfully elected their caucus nominees.

What of the threatened bolt by the Pennsylvania members on the clerkship election of McPherson? As noted, the bolt did not occur, in large part due to the actions of J. Donald Cameron in leading his state delegation. As the *New York Times* reported, "Senator Cameron bitterly opposed McPherson's nomination, but this opposition will not be maintained against the action of [the] caucus. . . . [h]is prompt disavowal of sympathy with the action of the threatening Pennsylvanians is undoubtedly prompted by a sincere desire to preserve intact the caucus as a direct means of grace" (12/5/1881, 1, 4). Thus, Cameron accepted the caucus decision and turned the partisan thumbscrew to ensure its success. As a result, Barr, Errett, and all other Pennsylvanians who had considered a bolt "had been led to perceive the folly of the course they had marked out for themselves and their votes were found recorded for [McPherson]" (*NYT*, 12/6/1881, 1).

Cementing the party unity on the floor, and the maintenance of the caucus-induced equilibrium, was the distribution of standing committee as-

[38] The Republicans would add five seats via election contests in the 47th Congress, which brought their total to 151 seats. See Jenkins (2004).

[39] Third-party House members—Greenbackers, Readjusters, and Independents—numbered between 11 and 14 in the 47th Congress (depending on the party codes of Dubin and Martis).

signments, especially the committee chairmanships. Keifer took his time putting together his committee slates, amid almost constant speculation in the press, and finally released the results more than two weeks after the conclusion of the speakership contest. The list was balanced to maintain harmony across the various geographic and ideological interests in the party, while still structured to reward his caucus supporters. Keifer appointed Hiscock, his chief rival, to chair Appropriations. He also took care of his other speakership rivals by appointing Burrows chair of Territories, Reed chair of Judiciary, and Kasson and Dunnell to prime positions: the second and third spots on Ways and Means. In sum, Pennsylvania received seven chairmanships, Ohio four, and New York and Wisconsin three each, which reflected Keifer's winning coalition. The western states received a number of prime committee positions and chairmanships, and were provided with a stacked Coinage Committee, which would be open to a liberal silver policy. Ways and Means was largely protectionist, but there was also widespread sentiment within the committee that a slight downward revision in tariff schedules was necessary.

In sum, the caucus-Speaker-committees institutional arrangement held fast and preserved a seamless House organization by the Republicans. While the organizational efficiency of this institutional arrangement was impressive, its normative aspects drew criticism. At a time when the press had jumped on the government-reform bandwagon, the institutional equilibrium inherent in the House's organization reeked of corruption. The following editorial from the *Chicago Tribune* captures this sentiment well:

> The case of Mr. Speaker McKeever, *alias* Keifer, promises to become a leading case, so to speak, on the subject of abuses in the appointment of House Committees. Doubtless no Speaker of the National House of Representatives has, for many years, reached the dignity of the gavel without having "traded" more or less in committee assignments. It is part and parcel of the spoils system which is the shame of American politics. "You tickle me and I'll tickle you," insinuatingly remarks the candidate for the Speakership to this and that member of the House. Precisely as the candidate for Congress offers a post-office, or a Deputy-Marshalship for a vote in convention, so the candidate for the Speakership offers this or that place or this or that committee for a vote in caucus. . . . What could be more monstrous than the act of the Speaker of the House of Representatives in converting the committee assignments at his disposal into a certain kind of patronage to be distributed among those who howled the loudest for his election? . . . Exactly when trading in committeeships began it is not necessary to inquire. It began a long time ago, and has been continued down to the present time. Mr. Speaker Keifer is charged with having reduced committeeship trading to a science. (1/11/1882, 4)

Arguments such as these aside, the institutional arrangement was securely in place, and from the vantage point of congressional party leaders, it was doing the job.

The very next Congress (the 48th) was another instance of party control of the chamber giving way to a contentious battle over the nomination, followed by a unified front on the House floor. On the surface, the Democratic speakership contest in 1883 resembled the one in 1879, as the two major protagonists were Samuel Randall and a leading antiprotectionist from Kentucky, this time John G. Carlisle.[40]

But party politics had changed in the ensuing decade, setting the stage for the triumph of a border-state Southerner. The end of Reconstruction had diffused regional issues per se. The issue of the protective tariff had risen to preeminence in national politics, with the great majority of Democrats favoring a "tariff for revenue only." This turn of events put Randall's protectionist stance significantly out of the party mainstream; nevertheless, his allies fought hard for his election, and a spirited speakership campaign arose and extended over much of the year (Barnes 1931). Finally, on December 1, 1883, the Democratic caucus met and Carlisle emerged victorious, garnering 106 votes to 52 for Randall and 30 for Samuel S. Cox (NYT, 12/3/1883, 1). One distinctive feature of the caucus was that the vote was taken viva voce—a decision that was regarded as a test of strength for Randall, which he lost badly.[41] While the individual votes appear to have been lost to the dustbin of history, the state-by-state tallies have not; they are reported in table 8.1 and reveal the strong regional structuring of the vote.[42]

Once elected Speaker, Carlisle maintained past practice by treating his chief caucus opponent well, appointing Randall chair of Appropriations and assigning him the third-ranked position on Rules (behind himself and his Kentucky ally, Joseph Blackburn). This maintained harmony between the pro- and antitariff factions in the party. Carlisle would be unanimously renominated in the Democratic caucus in both the 49th and 50th Congresses, and go on to win an easy victory on the House floor each time.

---

[40] Indeed, it could have seemed *exactly* like 1879, since Blackburn was initially a candidate for Speaker. Eventually, Blackburn and Carlisle worked out a deal in which Blackburn would contest the reelection of John Williams to the Senate in February 1884, with Carlisle's assistance (NYT, 8/30/1883, 1). Carlisle publicly denied the tit for tat (NYT, 9/3/1883, 1), but following the *Times* report, Blackburn was never mentioned in any press accounts as an active speakership candidate again, and his efforts on behalf of Carlisle were regularly noted. Blackburn eventually defeated Williams for a Senate seat in a 19-ballot contest. Although Carlisle's name was consistently mentioned as the logical compromise Senate candidate, he never consented to having his name put forward.

[41] As in the speakership nomination contest of 1879, Randall's only hope rested on his ability to gain support from Southerners whose constituents regarded Randall's protectionist stance an anathema. Without a secret ballot in place, there was no "cover" to cut deals.

[42] Further statistical analysis, not reported here, reveals that as much as region, the state delegations that stood the firmest behind Carlisle were also the least protectionist.

TABLE 8.1.
Caucus support for Democratic Speaker candidates, 48th Congress

State	Carlisle	Randall	Cox
Alabama	3	4	1
Arkansas	5	0	0
California	2	1	3
Connecticut	0	3	0
Delaware	1	0	0
Florida	1	0	0
Georgia	8	1	0
Illinois	7	0	1
Indiana	7	1	1
Iowa	3	0	1
Kentucky	8	0	0
Louisiana	4	1	0
Maryland	0	4	0
Massachusetts	1	0	2
Michigan	6	0	0
Mississippi	5	0	0
Missouri	11	0	2
Nevada	1	0	0
New Jersey	0	3	0
New York	0	7	13
North Carolina	4	2	0
Ohio	2	6	5
Pennsylvania	0	11	0
South Carolina	4	2	0
Tennessee	5	2	1
Texas	10	0	0
Virginia	1	3	0
West Virginia	2	1	0
Wisconsin	5	0	0
Total	106	52	30

Sources: Boston Globe, 12/2/1883, 1; *New York Times,* 12/2/1883, 1; *Washington Post,* 12/3/1883, 1.

When the Republicans returned to power in the 51st Congress (1889–91), an intense struggle for the speakership nomination ensued. Thomas B. Reed (Maine) eventually emerged victorious on the second caucus ballot. As with the Democrats in the 48th Congress, the Republican canvass in the 51st centered on the major ideological division in the party, which also had a strong regional structuring. The issue in this instance was not the tariff but industrial development, which included matters like currency (bimetallism) and Mississippi River improvements. Republicans tended to sort on these issues depending on how far their districts were from East Coast money centers. As a consequence, the candidates who emerged were readily identified along an East-West divide. The eastern pole was anchored by Reed; the primary western candidate was William McKinley Jr. (Ohio).

The westerners together received a bare majority of the votes on the first ballot, but a shift of seven votes toward Reed on the second ballot was sufficient to ensure his victory (*CT*, 12/1/1889, 1). Table 8.2 reports the distribution of candidates' vote totals on the first ballot by state. Three minor candidates—Joseph Cannon (Ill.), David Henderson (Iowa), and Julius Caesar Burrows (Mich.)—were essentially favorite sons who were available should the balloting become protracted. Reed likewise showed his greatest strength in his home region but also drew support outside his base as well; this was also true of McKinley's support to a lesser degree.

Reed moved quickly to mend fences via his committee assignments. He elevated McKinley to the chairmanship of Ways and Means and placed him in the second spot on Rules—making him the de facto chair of that committee, too.[43] Cannon was allowed to claim the chair of Appropriations (he had been the ranking minority member for two Congresses), though he was demoted to third on Rules to make way for Reed. Reed then split the pork barrel between Henderson and Burrows. Henderson was given the chair of Rivers and Harbors (he had been the ranking minority member on the committee since the 48th Congress), while Burrows was provided with the chair of Levees and Improvement of the Mississippi River.

An odd coda ended the organization of the 51st Congress. On the whole, the caucus actions were ratified on the House floor when it convened to organize. Reed defeated Carlisle for Speaker, 166–154, and then the Republican nominees for Clerk, Sergeant at Arms, and Doorkeeper were elected "in a bunch" and without opposition (*NYT*, 12/3/1889, 1).

Then came the election of the chaplain. When the resolution was presented to elect Charles B. Ramsdell, the Republican caucus nominee, Joseph B. Cheadle (R-Ind.) moved to substitute the name of William H. Milburn, the incumbent (Democratic) chaplain.[44] The substitute passed, first on a teller vote and then on a roll call vote of 160–155, with four Republicans bolting and supporting the Democratic nominee (*CR*, 51-1, 12/2/1889, 82–83). The roll call revealed the bolters to be Cheadle (Ind.), Hamilton G. Ewart (N.C.), Orren C. Moore (N.H.), and Herman Lehlbach (N.J.). Eight other Republicans absented themselves from the vote,[45] which allowed the Democrats to prevail with only four Republican bolters actually voting.

[43] The Speaker was the chair of the Rules Committee at the time. However, news accounts during this period make it clear that the Speaker often did not take an active role in the deliberations of Rules, leaving it to the second-ranked member to run its day-to-day business.

[44] Why the bolt would be about the chaplain is a bit of a mystery. The incumbent Milburn was a hardy partisan Democrat—it is said he was driven out of Connecticut for his Democratic sermons—but was well liked in the chamber and appreciated for his "brevity and originality." *NYT*, 1/1/1889, 1; *NYT*, 1/3/1889, 1.

[45] These were Thomas H. B. Browne (Va.), Benjamin Butterworth (Ohio), Alfred C. Harmer (Pa.), Myron H. McCord (Wis.), James O'Donnell (Mich.), William D. Owen (Ind.), Lewis E.

TABLE 8.2.
First-ballot caucus support for Republican Speaker candidates, 51st Congress

State	Burrows	Cannon	Henderson	McKinley	Reed	Total
California	0	1	0	1	1	3
Colorado	0	0	0	1	0	1
Connecticut	0	0	0	0	3	3
Illinois	0	13	0	0	0	13
Indiana	0	1	0	1	1	3
Iowa	0	0	9	0	0	9
Kansas	0	3	0	0	4	7
Kentucky	0	0	1	1	0	2
Louisiana	0	0	0	0	1	1
Maine	0	0	0	0	4	4
Maryland	0	0	1	1	0	2
Massachusetts	0	0	0	0	10	10
Michigan	9	0	0	0	0	9
Minnesota	0	2	0	1	2	5
Missouri	0	0	0	3	1	4
Montana	0	0	0	0	1	1
Nebraska	0	0	1	0	2	3
Nevada	0	1	0	0	0	1
New Hampshire	0	0	0	0	2	2
New Jersey	0	0	1	1	1	4
New York	0	0	1	0	18	19
North Carolina	0	0	0	1	2	3
North Dakota	0	0	1	0	0	1
Ohio	0	0	0	16	0	16
Pennsylvania	0	0	0	6	15	21
Rhode Island	0	0	0	0	2	2
South Dakota	0	1	1	0	0	2
Tennessee	0	0	0	2	0	2
Vermont	0	0	0	0	2	2
Virginia	1	0	0	1	0	2
Washington	0	0	0	1	0	1
Wisconsin	0	0	0	1	6	7
Total	10	22	16	39	78	165

Source: *Chicago Tribune*, 12/1/1889, 1.

Though the office was minor, this turn of events alarmed Reed, who had tried mightily to convince the bolters to stay loyal.[46] This disloyalty de-

Payson (Ill.), and Jacob J. Pugsley (Ohio). Only one Democrat, William H. Forney (Ala.) was absent on the chaplaincy vote.

[46] To indicate the perceived seriousness of this action, the headline in the *New York Times* was "The Caucus Whip Broken," with subheadlines "Republicans in Dire Dismay from a Bolt" and "Party Discipline Endangered on the First Day of the Session" (12/3/1889, 1).

manded action, which Reed took in making out the committee assignments. Cheadle, the ringleader, was in line to chair the Claims Committee, but Reed denied it to him, demoting him instead to the third-ranking Republican on the committee, and gave him no other committee assignment. Embarrassed and angry, Cheadle refused even this one assignment (*NYT*, 12/23/1889, 1), and went without a committee assignment until he was appointed to fill a vacancy on the Post Office Committee at the end of the session.

From Organizational Control to Procedural Control

Once in the Speaker's chair, Reed initiated a set of changes that would revolutionize the way business was conducted in the House. This story is well known, so we will only briefly describe his actions and their consequences for House business. We will discuss in more detail, however, how the caucus system was critical for Reed's decision making and the subsequent Reed Rules that were adopted.

After the Civil War, the House's workload increased substantially—thanks to a number of factors, such as the political-economic growth of the nation; the increase in the size of the chamber due to new western states entering the Union; and the escalating need for more particularistic legislation, like military pensions, in keeping with the development of an individual-based electoral connection—while the rules and procedures for handling legislative business were still designed to meet antebellum-era demands. This increased workload led to bills piling up on House calendars, where they were to be taken by "regular order," one at a time in order of placement (Cox and McCubbins 2005). The only rules that would allow a bill to jump the queue and be considered out of order were supermajoritarian in nature (suspension of the rules, which required a two-thirds majority, or unanimous consent), and just a few committees, such as Appropriations, were privileged to preempt the House floor at a moment's notice. Furthermore, minority rights were numerous, as a range of dilatory tactics were employed to ground the majority's agenda to a halt (Galloway 1961, 131–32). As a result, obstruction and delay characterized House politics in the 1870s and 1880s, and the only way any business got done in this "dual veto system"—wherein both the minority and majority controlled various procedural levers to effectively shut down the agenda process—was by Senate-style, cross-party compromises.[47]

Reed had long been an advocate of procedural reform in the House. His preference for this type of reform centered on granting the majority party

[47] See Den Hartog (2004) and Cox and McCubbins (2005, 56) for a discussion of this "dual veto" concept.

clear agenda power. As a second-term House member in 1880, Reed announced his position during a House debate: "The best system is to have one party govern and the other party watch; and on general principles I think it would be better for us [the Republicans] to govern and for the Democrats to watch" (*CR*, 46-2, 4/22/1880, 2661). (It should be noted that the *Congressional Record* reports that Reed's statement elicited "laughter," as the Democrats were the majority party in the 46th Congress.) During the 47th Congress (1881–83), Reed first tried his hand at procedural reform; as a member of the Republican-controlled Rules Committee, he initiated a successful rules change that limited dilatory motions during consideration of election cases and, more important, authored the first "special order," which allowed an individual bill to be considered outside of the "regular order" by a simple majority vote (Binder 1997, 122–25; Roberts and Smith 2007). Later in the decade, once again as a member of the House minority, he began to publically articulate his position of majority rule over minority rights by writing pointed essays for periodicals like the *Century Magazine* (Reed 1889a) and the *North American Review* (Reed 1889b).

Upon his elevation to Speaker in December 1889 at the beginning of the 51st Congress, Reed was finally in a position to make his vision of procedural reform in the House a reality. Within a few months, he oversaw a significant alteration to the House rules that would strengthen the hand of the majority by severely weakening the minority's ability to obstruct. Chief among the Republican-led changes were rules that: (1) allowed the Speaker to count nonresponding members during roll call votes as "present," thereby eliminating the "disappearing quorum" as a dilatory tactic; (2) allowed the Speaker to deny recognition to members who sought to propose dilatory motions; (3) reduced the quorum requirement in the Committee of the Whole (COW) to 100 members; (4) allowed the Speaker discretion to refer legislation to committees without debate; and (5) enhanced the majority's ability to control the agenda in the House by increasing the Rules Committee's procedural authority and allowing the COW greater flexibility in choosing bills on the calendars out of order.[48]

The Reed Rules were virulently opposed by the minority Democrats, who attempted to eliminate them via a series of amendments on the floor. Reed relied on House Republicans to support his initiatives, and the GOP rank and file fell in line and defeated each of the Democrats' amendments before ratifying the entire set of rules changes. Such Republican support was *unanimous* (or nearly so) on all the key votes.[49] The importance of these events for

[48] The stipulations of the Reed Rules, and politicking in the House surrounding them, are described in detail in Galloway (1961, 52–53), Binder (1997, 125–29), Schickler (2001, 32–43), Cox and McCubbins (2005, 55–58), and Strahan (2007, 102–12).

[49] On three of the five amendment votes, 100 percent of Republicans voted in opposition, while on the other two amendment votes, 99 percent of Republicans voted in opposition. On the final-passage vote, 100 percent of Republicans voted in support. See Binder (1997, 112).

House development is stressed by Binder, who argues that "Reed's contributions ... arguably were the capstones of a nearly century-long struggle between majority and minority party rights" (1997, 125–26).

More important to our discussion here is the role the party caucus played in Reed's revolution. In the brave new world of the Reed Rules, the House would be dominated by a majority party procedural cartel led by the Speaker, the Rules Committee, and the standing committee chairs. Under Reed's speakership, the Rules Committee would evolve into a critical gatekeeper and agenda-setter in the chamber's legislative process; specifically, Rules went from being able to issue special orders, which would determine when bills would be considered, to also being able to issue special *rules*, which would determine when and *how* bills would be considered. Such special rules were often restrictive and limited the time for debate or the number and kind of amendments that would be allowed; an especially restrictive rule, a closed rule, barred amendments entirely. Such restrictive rules could be granted to bills controlled by the various committees, which ensured that their work would be protected against amending activity on the House floor.[50] As a result, committee chairs who managed the agenda process within their committees would possess significant positive-agenda control in the new post–Reed Rules House environment. The Speaker, who chaired Rules, designated all committee chairs, and assembled the various committees, was the central agent in the cartel arrangement.

Reed's willingness to place the speakership, the Rules Committee, and the standing committee chairs at the heart of his new procedural cartel system spoke to his confidence in being able to control each of these positions *with certainty* at the convening of a new Congress. This certainty rested on what we have called the organizational cartel, which is the willingness of the majority to use practices such as the binding caucus, distribution of committee assignments, and sanctions for defectors to ensure that the party can ultimately control the organizational makeup of the chamber. By 1890, Reed and other House GOP leaders had nearly three decades worth of experience in dealing with the binding party caucus on organizational matters, and thus could observe its success in dictating nominations and seeing those nominations fulfilled on the House floor.

Only by assuming that key House positions were reliably controlled by the majority party would it have made sense for Reed to embed agenda-setting power in those positions. Organizational control of the chamber by

---

[50] Roberts and Smith (2007) note that seven special rules were offered by the Rules Committee in the 47th Congress. Two of these seven were closed rules (the first in House history). Moreover, with the emergence of special rules came a demand by party leaders that the rank and file fall in line behind the Rules Committee's decisions; this was a critical part of the procedural cartel that Reed had devised. As Alexander notes, the conventional wisdom of the day was that "one must support whatever the Rules Committee brought forward or become irregular" (1916, 210).

the majority, therefore, was a *necessary condition* for the development of procedural control by the majority. While theories of party government often assume the existence of procedural control (unconditionally in cartel theory, and conditionally in conditional party government theory), such procedural control was not preordained. In short, the evolution of party government in the House occurred in steps; one critical step, often ignored, was the emergence of the party caucus and its ability to consistently organize the chamber. From this step, other steps followed, such as the emergence of the majority's procedural dominance in House affairs.

CONCLUSION

Recent rational-choice-based historical accounts are flush with examples of political actors searching for ways to control the uncertainties of political life and the world around them. Many such accounts involve party leaders in Congress who attempt to manipulate rules and structures for distinctly partisan gains (Stewart and Weingast 1992; Aldrich 1995; Binder 1997; Dion 1997; Jenkins 2004). The emergence of the binding party caucus on organizational matters in the House was another such partisan attempt. The final decade and a half of the antebellum era witnessed serious organizational problems in the House, as speakership battles were becoming more common and extending over weeks and sometimes months. Difficulties in electing the other officer positions (i.e., the Clerk, the Printer, etc.) only extended the organizational time line. And after all was said and done, the dominant party in the House was sometimes "rolled" on its choices, especially on some of the lesser officer positions.

As the nation entered the Civil War era, Republican leaders sought an end to this organizational instability. This was made all the more pressing after a failed coup by the House Clerk at the beginning of the 38th Congress. The solution Republican House leaders settled on was to pull organizational decisions off the floor and embed them in a party caucus, which would meet before the new Congress convened.

This strategy, of course, was not new. As we documented in chapters 4 and 5, the Van Burenites attempted to develop a party-nominating caucus in the late 1830s and 1840s, but the slavery-extension issue cut across the interregional coalitions at the heart of the Second Party System. In the end, party gave way to section (and constituency) and the organizational battles in the 1850s reversed any caucus-based momentum that the Van Burenites had attempted to build up.

Now, with the slavery issue off the agenda, and a fairly homogenous Republican Party holding a comfortable majority in the House, version 2.0 of Van Buren's ambitious strategy had a real chance of success. What was different this time is that the party caucus succeeded in holding together dissident factions once the organization of the House moved to the floor. On organizational matters, at least, the party caucus was at last binding.

The logic of the caucus-based system was simple: (1) within the caucus, officer candidates would be debated and nominees would eventually be chosen; and (2) party members would then be bound by the caucus decisions. To instill and preserve party harmony, and to placate party factions that had lost out on the organizational decisions, the Speaker would disperse power liberally through committee assignments and chairmanships. The occasional bolter was punished by the withholding of valued committee assignments. Thus, the party would explicitly agree to coordinate on organizational matters so that the House could begin functioning, as long as the power to control policy areas, via committee chairmanships, was shared.

Thus, an institutional solution was created to solve the instability in organizational choice, with the caucus serving as the institutional "glue." Within this caucus-induced organizational arrangement, the Speaker was the linchpin—his was the first and most important office to be filled, as it controlled the means (committee assignments) to disperse power within the chamber and fulfill the power-sharing agreement underlying the explicit party bond in caucus. Should a Speaker renege on the agreement, he (as agent of the underlying majority) would lose his authority and put his position (at that point, and certainly in terms of possible reelection in the future) at risk.

Once it was clear that the binding party caucus on organizational matters had taken hold, and that the organizational cartel was functioning, a new generation of majority party leaders began devising additional strategies to tighten partisan control of the chamber. This culminated with Thomas B. Reed's ascension to the speakership; his Reed Rules effectively established majority rule over minority rights in the House by vesting power in a procedural cartel arrangement made up of the Speaker, the Rules Committee, and the standing committee chairmen. The majority's development of procedural control thus came only after the majority's organizational control of the relevant power nodes (the Speaker, the committees) was routinized.

While the binding party caucus on organizational matters had institutionalized by the late nineteenth century, challenges still lay ahead. More—and more divisive—nomination battles were on the horizon, and growing internal party divisions would lead in one case to an antebellum-style speakership contest on the House floor. In short, the resilience of the binding party caucus and the stability of the organizational cartel would be tested into the twentieth century. We turn now to a discussion of these events.

CHAPTER 9

The Organizational Cartel Persists, 1891–2011

The three decades after the onset of the Civil War saw the party caucus take firm hold in settling the initial organizational decisions on the House floor that were so critical to subsequent partisan success. With the certainty that caucus organization brought, a true organizational cartel emerged. In time, partisan leaders turned their attention to expanding their institutional control. This led to the Republicans' development of the procedural cartel, wherein agenda power in the chamber would be dominated by the majority party and minority rights would be greatly restricted. The two decades between 1890 and 1910 would serve as the high-water mark for partisanship in the House, based on various commonly used measures of intraparty cohesion and interparty polarization, until finally being eclipsed in the first decade of the twenty-first century.

While "regularity" in the caucus-induced House organization would characterize the post-1890 era, challenges would still emerge. Indeed, one of the most serious intraparty caucus battles in House history would transpire during this time, and an extended speakership contest of the antebellum-era variety would play out on the House floor. These cases, a 30-ballot nomination battle in the Democratic caucus in 1891 and a 9-ballot battle on the House floor in 1923, will be examined in detail. Their deviation from the norm, while interesting, only serves to underscore the running theme in this and the prior chapter: since the Civil War, the caucus bond has sometimes bent, but it has not broken. Partisan fidelity would hold on the floor after the bruising caucus battle in 1891, while loyalty to the caucus agreement would be driven home by party leaders in the years after intrapartisan disputes spilled out onto the floor in 1923. Moreover, the binding party caucus and organizational cartel would survive and flourish despite other problematic events and contexts, such as the revolt against the Republican Speaker in 1910 and severe regional divisions within the majority Democratic Party in the decades spanning the mid-twentieth century.

In discussing these various challenges to the binding caucus on organizational matters, we pick up where chapter 8 left off and cover the period from 1891 to the present day. We conclude the chapter by stepping back and examining the relationship between organizational control and agenda control using the vehicle of win-rate analysis that we employed in chapters 5 and 7. Once accomplished, and in combination with prior chapters, we will have documented more than two centuries of House organization.

FACTIONAL DIVISIONS AND FURTHER THREATS TO THE CAUCUS ORGANIZATION

As noted, Thomas Reed's term as Speaker in the 51st Congress was both notorious and revolutionary, as he expanded the scope of the Speaker's parliamentary powers to explicitly and parochially favor the majority party. But his hold on the Speaker's gavel did not last long, as the Republicans suffered significant losses in the 1890 midterm elections, losses that were attributed to voter backlash against the McKinley Tariff—an interpretation bolstered by the defeat of McKinley for reelection, along with other Republican House leaders like Thomas H. Carter (Mont.) and Joseph G. Cannon (Ill.). Thus, the Democrats, firmly in control of the House organization, looked ahead to the 52nd Congress (1891–93). What they did not anticipate was a caucus battle that would eclipse—in acrimony and intensity—the Republicans' 16-ballot affair in 1881, prior to the opening of the 47th Congress.

The Democrats' first order of business was to select a new leading man, as the party's Speaker nominee for the past four Congresses, John Carlisle (Ky.), had been elected to the Senate. The results of the 1890 elections framed the Democrats' speakership canvass and emboldened the tariff reform forces, which spurred the eastern protectionist wing into countervailing action. In the end, two major candidates for the nomination emerged: John Q. Mills (Tex.) and Charles F. Crisp (Ga.). Mills had chaired Ways and Means in the 50th Congress and was the Democrats' leading expert on the tariff. He had advocated a downward reduction of the tariff in that Congress, which passed in the House but died in the Republican-controlled Senate.[1] Crisp, on the other hand, was known for his parliamentary skills and had been at the forefront of the Democratic sparring with Reed over his use of House rules in the 51st Congress. Among the minor candidates, William K. Springer (Ill.) had built a constituency in the Great Lakes states of Illinois, Michigan, and Wisconsin, while Benton McMillin (Tenn.) carved out support in the Border South. William H. Hatch (Mo.) had a more limited following, with advocates mainly in his home state.

As the opening of the 52nd Congress neared, Mills emerged as the front-runner. He began actively campaigning in October 1891, giving speeches throughout the South, Midwest, and Mid-Atlantic, generating exposure, and building his candidacy as he traveled toward Washington. To many,

---

[1] For a detailed overview of tariff politics in the 1880s and 1890s, see Morgan (1969), Terrill (1973), Reitano (1994), and Bensel (2000). The Mills Tariff Bill, in fact, forms the major basis of Reitano's analysis.

Mills's victory seemed a foregone conclusion. A correspondent for the *New York Times*, writing in the second week of November 1891, stated, "Unless the spirit of the Democratic Party is very much misunderstood, the majority for Mr. Mills will be so large before the caucus meets that all other competitors for the prize will withdraw and permit the election to be made by acclamation" (11/10/1891, 1).

By the third week of November, however, these early predictions appeared premature. During Mills's travels, Crisp had been campaigning hard and opted to cast his lot with the eastern wing of the party, with its preferences for more moderate tariff reform. As a result, he received the support of the Tammany Hall crowd and the followers of Samuel Randall, and with them, votes in New York and Pennsylvania.[2] Crisp also broke with Mills on the currency issue, as Crisp came out in favor of bimetallism—gaining him votes in the West—while Mills remained a firm advocate of gold. Crisp was also open to a return to patronage policies of years past, which appealed to machine politicians in places like Ohio and New Jersey, while Mills stood for continued civil service reform. Thus, the choice between Mills and Crisp very quickly became a choice between the policies of former President Grover Cleveland and those of his Democratic opponents. Mills was the reform candidate—for significant tariff reduction, opposed to free silver, and anti-spoils. Crisp was the candidate of the Old Guard—for protection (or, at least, less extensive tariff reform), in favor of free silver, and pro-spoils.

Through the end of November and into early December, the race continued to heat up and grew increasingly bitter, with accusations and insults flying freely between the Mills and Crisp camps. Media coverage of the day-to-day campaign developments was extensive.[3] Springer, McMillin, and Hatch felt significant pressure to drop out of the race, but each balked. Thus, as the caucus date neared, Mills and Crisp were running roughly neck and neck, with Springer, McMillin, and Hatch seemingly commanding enough votes to prevent a first-ballot victory.

When the Democratic caucus convened on December 5, 1891, a public ballot was adopted, so individual vote choices would be known by all. The first ballot revealed several divisions, with Crisp emerging as the leading vote-getter at 84, followed by Mills with 78, Springer with 32, McMillin

---

[2] Crisp was careful not to be pinned down on the tariff during his campaign. In the past, his voting record in Congress on tariff issues mirrored that of Mills. By the fall of 1891, Crisp only made general references to tariff policy and appeared to have assured the protectionists in the East that they would be treated well under his regime as Speaker.

[3] For coverage of the speakership race up to the convening of the caucus, see, for example, *CT*, 11/13/1891, 9; 11/17/1891, 6; 11/20/1891, 9; 11/21/1891, 9; 11/25/1891, 10; 11/26/1891, 2; 11/27/1891, 10; 11/28/1891, 1, 12; 11/29/1891, 10; 11/30/1891, 5; 12/1/1891, 1; 12/2/1891, 1; 12/3/1891, 1; 12/4/1891, 1; 12/5/1891, 1; and *NYT*, 11/13/1891, 5; 11/17/1891, 5; 11/18/1891, 3; 11/19/1891, 1; 11/20/1891, 5; 11/21/1891, 1; 11/22/1891, 2; 11/27/1891, 1; 11/28/1891, 1; 11/29/1891, 1, 4; 12/1/1891, 1, 4; 12/2/1891, 1; 12/3/1891, 1; 12/4/1891, 2; 12/5/1891, 1, 2.

with 18, Hatch with 14, and Moses Stevens (Mass.) with 1. This would prove to be the first of 30 ballots that stretched over two days.[4] (The breakdown of the balloting appears in appendix 6.)

The balloting would proceed as a kind of political trench warfare. After 17 ballots and little voter movement, the caucus adjourned, with an agreement to reconvene two days later. In the interim, politicking for votes was widespread. Advocates for Crisp and Mills entered into discussions with the Springer, Hatch, and McMillin camps. But the three minor candidates and their supporters stood firm, and little was expected to change on the first ballot of the second day. The frustration of the reformist element in the Democratic Party outside the halls of Congress was summed up by an editorial in the *New York Times*:

> Ever since the people declared in 1890 by an overwhelming majority against McKinley and Reed Republicanism and in favor of a reform and reduction of the tariff, the sole reliance of the defeated party has been on the known treachery to Democracy of the leaders now backing Crisp, and on the assumed folly, stupidity, and appetite of a certain number of Democratic politicians. Messrs. Springer and McMillin and their followers have done all that they could do, so far, to justify the calculations of the Republicans. . . . The injury inflicted upon the Democratic Party by the proceedings of Saturday [Dec. 5] cannot by wholly repaired. It will be impossible to efface the impression made on the country of the power of those leaders in the party who are Democrats for spoils, and not for principle. (12/7/1891, 4)

When the caucus reconvened on December 7, the 18th ballot was not much different from the 17th, and the next three were more of the same. Between the 22nd and 24th ballots, some movement occurred, as Hatch withdrew from the race and Springer lost five votes. These erstwhile Hatch and Springer voters scattered between Crisp and Mills, but Crisp was the major beneficiary as he extended his lead over Mills from three votes to six. The next three ballots showed no change, as Springer and McMillin met with their respective supporters and held impromptu conferences with agents of Crisp and Mills. On the next two ballots, more of Springer's supporters defected, and Crisp's lead over Mills extended to 10 votes. Prior to the 30th ballot, McMillin withdrew from the race and threw his support to Mills. Springer followed moments later with his own withdrawal and threw his support to Crisp. The former Springer and McMillin votes scattered between Crisp and Mills, but Crisp won out again. When the voting on the 30th ballot was completed, Crisp had emerged victorious with 119 votes to 105 for Mills, 4 for Springer, and 1 dogged vote for Moses Stevens. Nomina-

---

[4] For coverage of the caucus nomination battle, see *CT*, 12/6/1891, 1, 12; 12/7/1891, 1, 4; 12/8/1891, 1, 4; and *NYT*, 12/6/1891, 1; 12/7/1891, 1, 2, 4, 6; 12/8/1891, 2, 4.

tions for the minor officer positions—Clerk, Sergeant at Arms, Doorkeeper, and Postmaster—were then dealt with quickly, each on one ballot.[5]

Given the contentiousness of the Crisp-Mills nomination battle, would the Mills men stand behind Crisp in the speakership vote on the floor? After the caucus had finished its work and Crisp had been nominated, Mills was asked about the result and replied, "I have nothing to say to the press" (*Los Angeles Times* [hereafter abbreviated as *LAT*], 12/8/1891, 1). Moreover, when the House convened the following day, the Mills men were clearly bitter about the previous night's outcome (*NYT*, 12/8/1891, 1).

Yet the party bond prevailed. When his place on the speakership roll call was reached, "Mills, who stood at the back of the House awaiting the call of his name, answered promptly and clearly with the name of his opponent [Crisp]" (*NYT*, 12/8/1891, 1). When the roll call was finished, Crisp was elected with the full support of the members who attended the Democratic caucus the previous night.

As with all the other highly contested party contests during this period, Crisp and Mills began their canvass with strong regional and ideological endorsements forming their base of support. But the final distribution of Crisp's support ended up more evenly spread throughout the caucus. This can be seen in table 9.1, which compares Crisp's vote totals on the first and 30th caucus ballots. By the end of the balloting, Crisp picked up considerable support in the Great Lakes states (Illinois, Indiana, and Michigan) and border states (Missouri and Tennessee), while strengthening his control in Northern states like Ohio, Pennsylvania, and New York, and in Southern states like Mississippi, South Carolina, and Virginia. As a result, Crisp would distribute committee seats broadly, to reflect all the major voices in the party.

But first he had to deal with those who had contested unsuccessfully for the speakership. The two candidates who threw their support to Crisp—Hatch and Springer—received prime assignments. Hatch received the chair of Agriculture. Springer was made chairman of Ways and Means, which put him in charge of crafting tariff policy. Springer supported only minor downward revision—and in fact would oversee the crafting of small, targeted tariff bills, the so-called popgun tariffs—which thereby met the needs of the protectionist element that had backed Crisp. Giving the chair of Ways and Means to Springer was a rebuff to Mills, who was compensated with the chair of Commerce. McMillin was not given a chairmanship but was granted the second-ranked spot on Ways and Means.

Crisp then worked to balance the key themes in the race: protection vs. tariff revision; gold vs. bimetallism; and patronage vs. civil service reform. To

[5] The minor offices elicited little interest in the caucus, except the Doorkeeper position. The New York delegation wanted to control the spoils of the office—the Doorkeeper at that point controlled more than 150 salaried positions—and they required that Crisp and his supporters fall in line behind their candidate, fellow New Yorker Charles "Iceman" Turner, before they would promise to support Crisp's speakership cause. Crisp and his supporters agreed to this condition, and Turner was easily nominated Doorkeeper.

Table 9.1.
Democratic caucus support for Charles Crisp, 52nd Congress

State	1st nomination ballot	30th nomination ballot
Alabama	8	8
Arkansas	1	2
Florida	2	2
Georgia	8	8
Illinois	0	5
Indiana	0	3
Kentucky	3	4
Louisiana	2	3
Maryland	6	6
Massachusetts	0	1
Michigan	0	5
Minnesota	1	1
Mississippi	4	5
Missouri	0	4
New Hampshire	1	1
New Jersey	5	5
New York	12	13
North Carolina	8	8
Ohio	8	10
Pennsylvania	3	7
Rhode Island	0	1
South Carolina	5	6
Tennessee	0	3
Virginia	5	6
West Virginia	2	2
Total	84	119

Source: *Chicago Tribune*, 12/6/1891, 5; *New York Times*, 12/8/1891, 2.

offset the selection of Springer as chair of Ways and Means, Crisp appointed William Holman (Ind.) to chair Appropriations; this was an acknowledgment that some tariff reform was needed, as Holman was notoriously frugal and supported a reduction in the huge surplus that had been created by the protectionist aspects of the tariff. In addition, Crisp appointed one of Mills's supporters, John Andrew (Mass.), to chair the Reform in Civil Service Committee. This was a blow to the spoilsmen in the party. Finally, Crisp selected Richard "Silver Dick" Bland (Mo.), who was the nation's leading advocate of "free silver," to chair the Coinage Committee. As a result, Bland would be in a position to push for an aggressive bimetal program.

Despite an often acrimonious speakership campaign and a lengthy caucus battle, the Democratic Party remained intact, thanks in large part to the caucus-Speaker-committees institutional arrangement. Because of Crisp's balancing of committee assignments, the losers in the caucus were allotted a degree of power, which maintained party harmony.

PROGRESSIVE INSURGENCY AND THE REPUBLICAN PARTY

A relative calm pervaded caucus nominations after the conclusion of the Crisp-Mills contest in 1891. While the two parties would continue to battle internally over tariff and currency issues, as well as over larger issues related to populism and progressivism, the sanctity of caucus decisions and unity on matters of House officer selection would be respected by all. Indeed, the Crisp-Mills battle in 1891 would be the last instance of a majority party speakership nomination in caucus extending beyond the first ballot.[6] As a result, the next significant threat to the majority party's ability to organize the House occurred outside of the caucus—on the House floor. This episode, in 1923 at the opening of the 68th Congress (1923–25), would resemble the pre–Civil War floor battles over the House organization. Before discussing the 1923 episode, however, we must first set the stage by pausing at the 1910 revolt against Speaker Cannon.

The revolt against Cannon, 1910

The brouhaha in the 68th Congress had its roots in House politics more than a decade earlier and corresponded to the growing disaffection within the majority Republican Party after the turn of the twentieth century. Young House Republicans—the so-called progressive Republicans—were increasingly unhappy with the way Speaker Joseph G. Cannon (Ill.), the heir to Reed's legacy, used his powers to favor the interests of senior Republicans.[7] As a result, reform efforts emerged in the later part of the 60th Congress (1907–9), but fell just short of being enacted. A show of opposition against Cannon was then made in the Republican caucus in March 1909, prior to the opening of the 61st Congress (1909–11). Cannon, who had received the Republican speakership nomination by acclamation three previous times, garnered 162 votes, with 25 votes scattering and 30 absences (NYT, 3/14/1909, 1).

---

[6] In fact, over the next 13 Congresses (the 53rd through 65th) the choice for Speaker in the majority party caucus would be *unanimous* on the first ballot in all but one Congress (the 61st).

[7] Reed would regain the speakership in the 54th Congress (1895–97), after four years of Democratic control of the chamber, and hold it through the 55th Congress. David B. Henderson (R-Iowa) would *officially* succeed Reed in the Speaker's chair in the 56th and 57th Congresses (1899–1903) before Cannon took over the speakership in the 58th Congress (1903–5). Henderson has typically been viewed as a weak caretaker as Speaker (Fuller 1909; Hoing 1957; cf. Finocchiaro and Rohde 2007), while Cannon would adopt Reed's more ironfisted approach.

The caucus vote on Cannon foreshadowed darker events to come. Midway through the 61st Congress in May 1910, the progressive Republicans combined with the Democrats to alter the House rules—the Speaker was removed from the Rules Committee, and its membership was expanded from 5 to 10, with committee members elected by the chamber (Holt 1967; Schickler 2001).[8] (When the Democrats took control of the House in the following [62nd] Congress, they finished the job by stripping the Speaker of his ability to make *all* standing committee assignments.) This famous episode in House history had lasting effects, as the decentralization of power from the Speaker to the committees remained the institutional status quo until the latter part of the twentieth century.[9]

More important for our story, however, is the *way* the revolt against Cannon transpired. While a previous move against Cannon occurred in the 60th Congress, and a symbolic coalition opposed him in the nominating caucus in March 1909, the progressive Republicans did not seek to topple him during the initial House organization in the 61st Congress. Despite possessing a pivotal bloc of votes, the progressive Republicans honored the caucus commitment—of the 55 Republican members who did not cast a vote for Cannon in caucus, only 12 opposed him on the floor. The other 43 backed his candidacy. This allowed Cannon to be elected with 204 of 382 votes cast (*CR*, 61-1, 3/15/1909, 18). Only shortly thereafter, on the issue of readopting the rules from the previous House, did the progressive Republicans bolt the party and work to decentralize power in the chamber (*NYT*, 3/16/1909, 1; *CT*, 3/16/1909, 1).

Thus, while disagreeing with Cannon's rule, the progressive Republicans recognized the short- and long-term importance of remaining united on the election of House officers and organizing the chamber along the lines outlined in caucus. Indeed, after stripping Cannon of some of his powers, the progressives had a chance to oust him. Viewing the revolt against him as a "vote of no confidence," Cannon proposed to allow the House to deem the Speaker's office vacant. Although the Democrats were eager to fulfill his wish, the progressives eased back and allowed Cannon to remain in the Speaker's chair.[10] They were unwilling to join the Democrats on a compromise candidate, and they were equally unwilling to force the House into an extended speakership battle. While they may have disagreed with the regu-

[8] Progressive Republicans lost their initial skirmish with Cannon in March 1909 on the adoption of the House rules, thanks to a few Democrats who backed Cannon in exchange for a minor reform concession (see Schickler 2001, 72).

[9] For a more detailed overview of progressive Republican insurgency and the revolt against Cannon, see Ripley (1967), Holt (1967, 16–28), Jones (1968), Bolling (1968, 74–85); Polsby, Gallaher, and Rundquist (1969), Peabody (1976), Shepsle (1978), Rager (1998), and Schickler (2001, 71–83); cf. Lawrence, Maltzman, and Wahlbeck (2001), Krehbiel and Wiseman (2001).

[10] Only nine progressive Republicans voted with the Democrats to remove Cannon. The roll call to declare the speakership vacant was 155–192, with perfect party unity on both sides, outside of the nine progressive defections (*CR*, 61-2, 3/19/1910, 3438–39).

lar Republican leadership, the "partisanship of most of the [progressives] were as deep-dyed as that of their constituents" (Holt 1967, 22–23).

Democratic interlude, 1911–1919

The next eight years after the revolt against Cannon were quite tranquil in terms of caucus nominations. The Democrats returned to power and controlled the House from the 62nd through 65th Congresses (1911–19), and Champ Clark (Mo.) was unanimously chosen as the Democratic caucus nominee each time. Election on the House floor followed in a straightforward manner.

Beginning in the 63rd Congress (1913–15) and extending through the 65th Congress (1917–19)—corresponding to the first six years of President Woodrow Wilson's administration—the Democrats would enjoy unified control of government for the first time since the 53rd Congress (1893–95), the first two years of Grover Cleveland's second administration. Once in power, the Democrats would turn to a new organizational tool to consolidate party authority and push a partisan agenda: the *binding policy caucus*. Part of the move to "caucus government" in the House followed on progressive changes in the wake of the Cannon revolt. For example, the caucus would now choose both the Speaker *and* majority leader (which had previously been a position selected by the Speaker).[11] The caucus would designate the majority leader to chair the Ways and Means Committee, and fill the remaining party slots on Ways and Means via election. The Democratic contingent on Ways and Means would then serve as the party's "Committee on Committees," which would determine the rest of the House's committee assignments. The Speaker thus played a more limited role in the Democrats' new policy-based caucus system, with the majority leader serving as the more important figure. The caucus would be secret in its proceedings, and a two-thirds vote would bind all members on subsequent policy-related floor action (Galloway 1961).

The best analysis of the binding policy caucus's effectiveness is provided by Matthew Green, who argues that the caucus was not as meaningful as some historians have thought. Green finds that "the caucus bound Democrats' votes on just 15 legislative measures in four Congresses" (2002, 622).

---

[11] Another part of the move to caucus government was purely pragmatic. Wilson and the Democrats believed (probably correctly) that their rise to power was directly a function of the split in the Republican Party—between the regular "Taft Republicans" and the progressive "Roosevelt Republicans." Democratic leaders in Congress, in particular, believed that party cohesion and the passage of Wilson's policy agenda (and subsequent electoral coattails) were critical to remaining in power. Wilson could thus impose his will on congressional Democrats and underscore the importance of adopting a mechanism—the binding policy caucus—that would (in theory) generate policy success.

Moreover, many of these binding caucus resolutions proved to be unnecessary, as they were linked to bills that were already supported by a sizable majority of Democrats on pure ideological grounds. When a measure *was* ideologically divisive, a binding caucus resolution could not typically compel party allegiance on the floor, as defections were often numerous. In sum, Green's research suggests that instituting parliamentary-style rules on matters other than organizational votes was a stretch—something the Radical Republicans had discovered, much to their chagrin, almost a half century earlier—especially when crosscutting or ideologically divisive issues emerged.

Besides the binding policy caucus, one additional, significant change to the House organization occurred after the Democrats regained control of the House in the 62nd Congress. As they had run collectively on a reform agenda, the Democrats examined the chamber's organizational bureaucracy and determined that nearly $200,000 could be trimmed from the budget by eliminating "superfluous" House patronage (*NYT*, 4/2/1911, 1; 4/4/1911, 10; *CT*, 4/2/1911, 6). The bulk of this savings (over $120,000) came from the elimination of 101 jobs in the House organization: 3 in the Speaker's office; 28 in the Clerk's office; 42 in the Sergeant at Arms office; and 28 in the Doorkeeper's office.[12] In addition, the Democratic caucus, on the recommendation of its Committee on Committees, took the remaining patronage positions in the offices of the Clerk, Doorkeeper, and Postmaster and placed them under the authority of a new three-man caucus committee, the Committee on Organization. This new committee was to distribute this patronage among the various state delegations by ratio of the size of the state's Democratic contingent to the Democratic membership in the chamber (*NYT*, 4/2/1911, 1; *WP*, 4/2/1911, 1).

While individual aspirants would still vie for the minor House offices, as there were still significant salaries attached to each, the Democratic reforms eliminated much of the coalitional competition. Because the patronage aspect of the officer positions was stripped, they were no longer prime repositories for spoils and thus did not attract regional/ideological interests.[13] As a result, over time, these minor officer positions professionalized, becoming much less distinctly partisan. Consequently, any subsequent jockeying in caucus over leadership positions would primarily involve the speakership, along with other emerging intraparty positions held by the members themselves (majority leader, majority whip, caucus/conference chairman, etc.).

[12] The remainder of the savings dealt with the elimination of six "useless" committees and the elimination of one month's extra pay to each employee annually.

[13] Moreover, by this time, the parties had developed other mechanisms to generate revenue for party building and maintenance. Notably, congressional campaign committees (CCCs), which first emerged in the mid- to late 1860s, worked to fund and direct their respective party's efforts to achieve (or maintain) majority party status in the House. See Kolodny (1998).

A progressive floor challenge and leadership retribution, 1923–1927

When the Republicans returned to power in the 66th Congress (1919–21), they selected Frederick Gillett (Mass.) as their Speaker nominee, as they did again in the next Congress. Gillett's speakership was similar in spirit to that of Clark's, that is, weak relative to the iron fist that characterized Cannon's reign. The decentralization after the "revolt" spread power throughout the chamber, which resulted in the majority leader, steering committee, and Committee on Committees becoming more central to House business than the Speaker.[14] Amid this decentralization, the Republican House agenda stalled, and the 1922 midterm elections reduced the Republicans' share of the chamber from 302 to 225 (out of 435) seats.

One set of Republicans that survived the electoral backlash in 1922 were the western progressives, the political heirs of members who had initiated the revolt against Cannon in 1910. They were upset at the myopia of the regular Republicans—the Old Guard—and blamed their overly conservative nature for the party's poor electoral fortunes. The progressives believed that a liberalization of House rules was required to free up legislation that languished in committees dominated by the regulars. Beginning in the lame-duck session of the 67th Congress (1921–23), the progressive Republicans began operating as free agents, cooperating with the liberal faction of the Democratic Party on House votes and signaling that they would use their pivotal status to push for rules changes in the subsequent Congress.

The progressives made their intentions formally known in caucus on December 1, 1923. Gillett was renominated Speaker easily on the first ballot, winning 190 votes, but 24 votes from the progressive Republican ranks were cast against him—15 for Henry Cooper (Wis.), 8 for Martin Madden (Ill.), and 1 for Edward Little (Kans.) (CT, 12/2/1923, 1; NYT, 12/2/1923, 1).[15] As the Republicans would count 225 House seats at the opening of the 68th Congress, compared to the 207 held by the Democrats, the progressive wing of the party, which asserted control of 20 to 25 seats, would determine the balance of power.

The progressive Republicans demanded a revision of the House rules in order to distribute power in the chamber more evenly, and announced they would vote against Gillett unless they were provided with assurances to that end (NYT, 12/3/1923, 1; LAT, 12/3/1923, 11). Nicholas Longworth (Ohio), the Republican majority leader, responded that he was unwilling to compro-

---

[14] Whereas the Democrats in the post-Cannon era centralized authority in the party contingent on the Ways and Means Committee, the Republicans split power between a Steering Committee, which dealt with administrative business and developed policy policies, and a Committee on Committees, which handled committee staffing issues (G. R. Brown 1922, 211–12).

[15] Eleven members were absent from the caucus.

mise with the "insurgents" (*LAT*, 12/3/1923, 11). Thus, an intraparty stare down occurred as the House was set to convene.

The progressives refused to blink. When the 68th Congress opened on December 3, 1923, they broke from the regular Republicans and prevented the organization of the House. Four separate speakership ballots were held, with no election. (The breakdown of the balloting is presented in appendix 2.) Twenty progressive Republicans, joined by two members of the Farmer-Labor Party, opposed Gillett; 17 votes were distributed to Henry Cooper and 5 to Martin Madden (*NYT*, 12/4/1923, 1).[16] Gillett and Finis J. Garrett (D-Tenn.) ran virtually neck and neck, each about 10 to 12 votes short of victory. Without a quick resolution in sight, Longworth moved an adjournment until the following day. The progressive Republicans reiterated their call for rules reforms that evening, but Longworth and his allies would make no concessions, and argued that public opinion would support their position and force the progressives to yield (*NYT*, 12/4/1923, 1; *CT*, 12/4/1923, 1).

Longworth underestimated the progressives' resolve. The House met again on December 4, held four additional ballots, and still no Speaker was chosen. The 20 progressive Republicans held firm behind Cooper and Madden, and Gillett made no gains. After the fourth ballot of the day (eighth overall), Longworth moved for an adjournment and reversed his position. He offered the progressives a compromise: the rules from the previous House would be adopted for one month, during which time members could debate rules changes on the floor. After such debate, the House could then adopt any rules changes favored by a majority of the members. Progressive leaders were receptive, and a deal between them and Longworth was hashed out in a conference that evening (*NYT*, 12/5/1923, 1; *CT*, 12/5/1923, 1; *LAT*, 12/5/1923, 1). The following day, Gillett was elected on the first ballot (ninth overall), with 215 votes to 197 for Garrett and 2 for Madden. Eighteen of the 20 progressive Republicans swung their support to Gillett, which provided him with the margin of victory.[17]

After completing the organization of the chamber, Longworth kept his promise and allowed debate on the House rules to proceed. Several changes were eventually adopted, the major ones being the development of a workable discharge rule (which required the support of only 150 members) by which legislation could be drawn out of committee, and the reduction in the power of committee chairmen via the elimination of the "pocket veto," which they used to stifle the will of the committee (Hasbrouck 1927, 20–22; Schickler 2001, 102–9).

[16] Madden declared himself not a candidate before the balloting began and voted for Gillett. Richard Yates (R-Ill.) swung his vote from Gillett to Madden on the second ballot, but returned to the Gillett fold on the third ballot.

[17] Only William F. James (Mich.) and Frank R. Reid (Ill.) continued to support Madden. See *NYT*, 12/6/1923, 1; *CT*, 12/6/1923, 3; *LAT*, 12/6/1923, 1.

In examining contemporary accounts of the intraparty Republican skirmish, we find no indication that progressives ever entertained joining with the Democrats to elect Garrett. Moreover, the Democrats had no illusion the progressive Republicans would reject their partisan identity and cross the aisle. As a correspondent for the *New York Times* described, "The Democrats are keeping hands off in the matter, taking the stand that it is purely a Republican affair" (12/4/1923, 1).[18] Thus, while the progressives were willing to challenge the caucus bond by refusing to unconditionally support Gillett, they were unwilling to reject the Republican label more generally. Nevertheless, they chose to go public with their grievances after failing to achieve their goals in caucus, and used their pivotal numbers to produce a deadlock and extract a deal. In the short term, they were winners, but would there be retribution?

The answer would come soon enough. The 1924 elections, with Calvin Coolidge providing strong coattails, increased the GOP's House majority from 225 to 247 seats. This gave Longworth and the regular Republicans a working majority in the 69th Congress (1925–27) without having to cooperate with the progressives. Longworth and the regulars saw this as an opportunity to tighten the party bond and force the progressives to toe the line. A first salvo was fired in advance of the Republican caucus in late February 1925, when it was announced that 13 progressives who had worked against the party's presidential ticket of Coolidge and Dawes would be excluded from attending the caucus.[19] These 13 progressives—Henry Cooper, Edward Voigt, John M. Nelson, John C. Shafer, Florian Lampert, Joseph D. Beck, Edward E. Browne, George J. Schneider, James A. Frear, and Hubert H. Peavey (all Wis.), and James H. Sinclair (N.D.), Oscar E. Keller (Minn.), and Fiorello H. La Guardia (N.Y.)[20]—had come out in support of Robert La Follette's third-party presidential bid, and had also been part of the bloc that had held up the House organization in the prior Congress.[21]

---

[18] Democratic leaders seemed content reveling in the GOP's public intraparty squabble. If anything, they communicated to the *regular* Republican leadership that no Democratic votes would be forthcoming (in support of Gillett) to end the speakership drama.

[19] Rumors of the exclusion of the progressives began almost immediately after the November elections. It was not made official, however, until January 29, 1925, when William R. Wood (R-Ind.), chairman of the Republican Congressional Campaign Committee, announced the decision. See *CT*, 1/30/1925, 1; *NYT*, 1/30/1925, 1; *LAT*, 1/30/1925, 1.

[20] La Guardia's exclusion is a bit more complicated. The regular Republicans contended that in addition to supporting La Follette, La Guardia had also become a Socialist (and won election on the Socialist ticket). La Guardia disputed this, claiming that he was still entitled to be treated as a Republican in chamber politics. His arguments were to no avail, however, and he went without a committee assignment in the 69th Congress. He would run under the Republican banner in the 1926 elections, and reassume more formal ties with the Republicans in the 70th Congress.

[21] A similar scenario played out in the Republican Senate conference, where La Follette, Edwin Ladd (N.D.), Smith Brookhart (Iowa), and Lynn Frazier (N.D.) were excluded for refusing to support the Coolidge-Dawes ticket.

With the progressives barred from the caucus, Nicholas Longworth was nominated Speaker on the first ballot, besting Martin Madden (Ill.) 145 to 85 (*NYT*, 2/28/1925, 1; *CT*, 2/28/1925, 1, 5).[22] Longworth would revitalize the speakership during his tenure,[23] and his first order of business was to devise a plan to punish the progressives. Longworth and Bertrand Snell (N.Y.), chairman of the Rules Committee, favored stripping the progressives of their prime committee assignments (*NYT*, 3/1/1925, 20). The first formal decision in this regard occurred on March 5, 1925, when the Republican Committee on Committees (RCOC) removed Frear (Wis.) from his seat on Ways and Means. The RCOC also announced that the progressives would find themselves at the end of the line when committee assignments were announced, which meant that they would receive nothing better than low rank on some very minor committees (*NYT*, 3/6/1925, 1; *CT*, 3/6/1925, 1; *LAT*, 3/6/1925, 3). Consistent with their decree, the RCOC announced early assignments to Appropriations and Commerce, with no progressives selected.

The 69th Congress would not convene until December 7, 1925, which left a good deal of time for the Republican blocs to iron out their differences. But Longworth continued to take a hard line. Declaring that he would work to return the speakership to a position of prominence in the House, he identified party unity as a critical goal in reestablishing a strong party organization. In that vein, the *New York Times* reported that he favored "vigorous warfare on all members who accept election as Republicans but refuse to work in harness with the organization" (12/1/1925, 27). To regain their status within the Republican caucus, Longworth determined that the 13 members of the progressive bloc had to support his speakership candidacy on the House floor. This would be the critical test of the progressives' party loyalty. To underscore the threat, the RCOC met on December 5, 1925, and dropped progressive John M. Nelson (Wis.) from the Rules Committee (*NYT*, 12/6/1925, 1).[24]

Rather than cave to Longworth's demands, the progressives grew defiant. Once again they rallied around Henry Cooper (Wis.), fellow progressive and elder statesman in the House, and vowed to resist Longworth and his gag rule (*NYT*, 12/7/1925, 1; *CT*, 12/7/1925, 1; *LAT*, 12/7/1925, 1). When the 69th Congress convened on December 7, 1925, the progressives were true to their word. Longworth won the speakership easily, receiving 229 votes to

[22] Gillett had been elected to the Senate in 1924, and thus was not an option for Speaker.

[23] During Longworth's speakership, a "Big Four" took control of the party, which was comprised of Longworth (Speaker), Bertrand Snell ([N.Y.], chairman of the Rules Committee), John Tilson ([Conn.], majority leader), and James Begg ([Ohio], Longworth's right-hand man, often referred to informally as the "assistant Speaker"). In doing so, the Big Four usurped power that had resided in the Steering Committee during Gillett's speakership. For more, see Kitchin (1969, 84–86).

[24] A second requirement was that the progressives support the regular Republicans in rescinding the liberalized discharge rule (which required only 150 signatures) that was passed in the 68th Congress. This requirement, however, was never made a critical test of party loyalty.

173 for Finis Garrett (Tenn.) and 13 for Cooper (*CR*, 69-1, 12/7/1925, 381). Of the 13 progressives barred from the caucus, 11 voted for Cooper, the 12th member of the excluded group.[25] Only Oscar E. Keller (Minn.) buckled and voted for Longworth.

In his acceptance speech, Longworth noted the "unanimity" of his Republican support, and spoke at length in favor of "responsible party government" and against European-style "bloc government." In doing so, Longworth "read out of the Republican councils the handful of insurgents who opposed his election" (*NYT*, 12/9/1925, 1). He then proceeded to oversee the rolling back of the progressive-led rules reforms of the previous Congress—the most notable being the increase in the number of signatures needed to discharge a committee (from 150 to 218).

In finalizing the House committee assignments over the next few days, the RCOC would perform the coup de grâce against the progressives. While the RCOC did recognize the progressives as "Republicans," and thus as members of the majority party, punishment in the form of committee demotions would nonetheless be severe.[26] The committee assignments for the 12 members who supported La Follette and subsequently refused to vote for Longworth appear in table 9.2. For comparison, their assignments in the 68th Congress are also listed.

All of the progressives were clearly worse off in the 69th Congress. In addition to Nelson and Frear losing their seats on Rules and Ways and Means, respectively, Browne was dropped from Foreign Affairs, La Guardia and Schneider lost their spots on Post Office and Post Roads, Peavey was booted from Rivers and Harbors, Sinclair and Voigt were removed from Agriculture, Shafer was dropped from Coinage, and Lampert lost his chairmanship of Patents. Members who were allowed to retain their committees of origin, such as Cooper on Foreign Affairs and Beck on Labor, were stripped of their seniority and placed at the end of the Republican contingent. In addition, many of these members were encumbered with minor committees, most of which possessed little value and dealt with mundane (but potentially time-consuming) matters. Oscar E. Keller (Minn.), the one member of the original bloc of 13 La Follette supporters who ended up voting for Longworth, was considerably more fortunate by comparison—he retained his chairmanship of Railways and Canals as well as his seats (and seniority) on Claims and District of Columbia. Keller's favorable treatment by the RCOC was an explicit thumb in the eye to his progressive brethren.

With their comfortable majority, the regular Republicans did not need to bargain with the progressive wing of the party in the 69th Congress. In re-

[25] These 11 were joined by Farmer-Labor Party members Knud Wefald (Minn.) and Ole J. Kvale (Minn.).

[26] The exception would be La Guardia, who was deemed a Socialist and treated as a third-party member for committee assignment purposes.

TABLE 9.2.
Progressive House Republicans and committee assignments, 68th and 69th Congresses

Member	68th Congress: Committee (rank)	69th Congress: Committee (rank)
Joseph D. Beck (Wis.)	Labor (2) Railways and Canals (3) Claims (5) Expenditures in Dept. of Agriculture (3)	Labor (8) Railways and Canals (6) Claims (9)
Edward E. Browne (Wis.)	Foreign Affairs (4)	Alcohol Liquor Traffic (4) Civil Service (8) Expenditures in the Dept. of State (3)
Henry A. Cooper (Wis.)	Foreign Affairs (7)	Foreign Affairs (13)
James A. Frear (Wis.)	Ways and Means (5)	Expenditures in the Dept. of Justice (4) Flood Control (9) Indian Affairs (13)
Fiorella La Guardia (N.Y.)	Post Office and Post Roads (8)	Alcohol Liquor Traffic (third-1) Public Buildings and Grounds (third-1) Public Lands (third-2) Woman Suffrage (third-1)
Florian Lampert (Wis.)	Patents (chair) Coinage, Weights, and Measures (2) District of Columbia (3) Expenditures in Dept. of Navy (2)	Patents (7) Coinage, Weights, and Measures (9) District of Columbia (13) Territories (10)
John M. Nelson (Wis.)	Rules (5) Invalid Pensions (3) Roads (3)	Expenditures in the Dept. of Interior (4) Invalid Pensions (8) Roads (13)
Hubert H. Peavey (Wis.)	Rivers and Harbors (11)	Expenditures in the Post Office Dept. (4) Mileage (4) War Claims (9)

TABLE 9.2. (*Cont.*)

Member	68th Congress: Committee (rank)	69th Congress: Committee (rank)
John C. Schafer (Wis.)	Coinage, Weights, and Measures (8)	Railways and Canals (8)
	Insular Affairs (10)	Woman Suffrage (3)
	Expenditures in the Dept. of War (4)	Expenditures in the Dept. of War (4)
George J. Schneider (Wis.)	Post Office and Post Roads (12)	Expenditures in the Dept. of Interior (3)
		Railways and Canals (7)
James H. Sinclair (N.D.)	Agriculture (8)	Alcohol and Liquor Traffic (5)
		Expenditures in the Dept. of State (4)
		War Claims (8)
Edward Voight (Wis.)	Agriculture (4)	Census (10)
		Expenditures in the Dept. of Agriculture (4)
		Pensions (8)
		Revision of Laws (8)

Source: Canon, Nelson, and Stewart (2002).

sponse, the progressives loudly and defiantly maintained their independence throughout Congress's proceedings. However, they had been marginalized; sitting outside of the caucus and inhabiting only minor committees, their ability to influence legislation was minimal. Thus, when the regular Republican leadership made a peace offering in advance of the 70th Congress—readmittance to the caucus and thus reinstatement as "regulars" in exchange for loyalty on matters of party organization—the progressives were receptive (*NYT*, 1/28/1927, 7; 2/5/1927, 7). Although only one member of the progressive bloc, John M. Nelson, attended the Republican caucus on February 21, 1927, at which Longworth was nominated by acclamation, there was a general understanding that they would fall in line behind the GOP choice for Speaker on the House floor.[27]

[27] While the Republican share of House seats fell from 247 in the 69th Congress to 238 in the 70th Congress, the regular bloc still possessed a relatively comfortable majority in the chamber. Thus, the Republican leadership did not have to bargain with the progressives. This was a case of Longworth showing leadership by meeting the progressives halfway in an attempt to mend fences and strengthen the party for the long run.

And that is what occurred. On December 5, 1927, the 70th Congress (1927–29) convened, and Longworth was elected Speaker, receiving 225 votes to 187 for Finis J. Garrett (*CR*, 70-1, 12/5/1927, 7–8). Of the 11 dissident progressives who had been reelected to the 70th Congress, 10 were present for the speakership vote.[28] All 10 voted for Longworth.

In his acceptance speech, Longworth paid special note to the progressives' "homecoming." He declared:

> I am particularly blessed to have received the votes of gentlemen who have been seated on my party's side of the aisle for the past four years but who on two previous occasions have preferred to vote for a candidate for Speaker other than the one proposed by the Republican majority. I welcome your return to the Republican Party, where you rightfully belong. I like to row in the same boat with that fine old veteran of a hundred political battles, Henry Allen Cooper, and with Nelson and Frear, and all of you. (*NYT*, 12/6/1927, 2)

Thus, just as Longworth had read the progressives out of the party two years before, he now read them back in. Moreover, through his actions, "Longworth restored to the Republican caucus a requirement that members be bound by its decisions" (Bolling 1968, 115). The tightening of the party noose, via expulsion from the caucus and sanctions in the committee assignment process, had done the trick.[29]

Were the progressives transformed into regulars? Hardly. They continued to maintain their maverick tendencies. Nevertheless, they were back in tow on matters of party organization, and the power of the binding party caucus was reestablished. Writing contemporaneously with these events, political scientist Paul Hasbrouck noted succinctly, "The vote on the caucus nominee for Speaker has come to be the critical test of party allegiance" (1927, 35).

POSTINSURGENCY AFTERMATH: LATE 1920s THROUGH THE PRESENT

Since the 70th Congress, the caucus-Speaker-committees institutional arrangement (which can be expanded to include other important partisan leadership positions, like the majority leader and seats on the Committee on Committees) has been extremely stable.[30] There have been no election con-

---

[28] Voight was the only nonreturning member, and Beck did not attend the opening of Congress.

[29] For an overview of the conflicts between progressive and regular Republicans over matters of House organization in the 68th through 70th Congresses, see Berdahl (1949a, 1949b).

[30] And while the speakership was formally weakened after the revolt against Cannon, Speakers over the next several decades still managed to exert influence in an informal sense, which often extended to the selection of majority leaders and members of the Committee on

troversies on the House floor; while caucus decisions have sometimes been contentious, no speakership nominations in the majority party's caucus have extended beyond a single ballot. Moreover, only once since the progressive revolt against Longworth in the 69th Congress has a member of the majority party supported someone other than the caucus nominee for Speaker on the House floor: in the 105th Congress (1997), when four Republican members opposed the reelection of Speaker Newt Gingrich (R-Ga.).[31]

What makes this pattern of rank-and-file fidelity to the caucus agreement striking is how the majority party in the House was constituted during much of the twentieth century. Between 1931 (72nd Congress) and 1992 (103rd Congress), except in two instances, the House was organized by the Democratic Party.[32] During these years, the Democrats were often divided by region (North vs. South) and by ideological vision for the role of government in society (liberal vs. conservative). These ideological divisions often led to conservative Southern Democrats voting *with* (conservative) Republicans *against* liberal Northern Democrats on a range of economic-based policy issues. This "Conservative Coalition" was a major force in congressional decision making,[33] to the point that Poole and Rosenthal characterize this era as a "three-party system" (1997, 44–46, 109–11).

Policy disputes aside, the House Democrats saw eye to eye on the necessity of maintaining party discipline in the initial decisions to organize the chamber at the start of a new Congress. Decisions in caucus, which could be actively contested, were to be the party's positions on the floor, and all members regardless of region were expected to fall in line. One way the Democrats were able to maintain organizational harmony during this period, despite their heterogeneity, was through regional/ideological balancing. Similar to balancing strategies from before the Civil War, the party made sure that institutional wins by one regional/ideological faction would be balanced against subsequent wins by the other faction.[34]

Committees. For example, Ripley (1967) notes that "[the Speaker] has usually operated behind the scenes to assure the election of Majority Leaders he favors" (54) and "Democratic Speakers have substantial influence over assignments to the Ways and Means Committee, which acts as the Committee on Committees" (56).

[31] The four Republicans were Thomas Campbell (Calif.) and Michael Forbes (N.Y.), who voted for James Leach (R-Iowa); Leach, who voted for former House member, Robert Michel (R-Ill.); and Linda Smith (Wash.), who voted for former House member Robert Walker (R-Pa.). Five other Republicans—John Hostettler (Ind.), Scott Klug (Wis.), Constance Morella (Md.), Mark Neumann (Wis.), and Frank Wolf (Va.)—voted "present" rather than support Gingrich.

[32] The two exceptions to Democratic rule during this period were in 1947 (80th Congress) and 1953 (83rd Congress), when the Republicans organized the chamber.

[33] For more on the Conservative Coalition, see Manley (1973) Patterson (1966, 1967), Shelley (1983), Nye (1993), and Schickler (2001).

[34] Another example of regional balancing—or, in this case, regional power sharing—in caucus occurred in 1967 (90th Congress), when House Democrats ousted the incumbent House Clerk, Ralph R. Roberts (Ind.), who had served in the office for 16 years (81st–82nd, 84th–89th Congresses). W. Pat Jennings (Va.) defeated Roberts 138–105 in the caucus vote (*CT,*

This balancing is illustrated in table 9.3, which documents the Democratic Speakers and majority leaders during this Conservative Coalition era. Almost without exception, the two Democratic leaders were split between the regional (and usually ideological) factions within the party. The one exception was in the 92nd Congress, when two Southerners controlled the top leadership positions.[35] This regional/ideological balancing was adopted across lower-level party positions as well (e.g., majority whip, caucus chairman, etc.). In addition, potential problems in committee allocations were alleviated through the use of seniority to manage career advancement. As Peters notes, "The Democratic leadership tended to use the committee appointment power to broaden its base of support, and the seniority rule was 'safe' in this respect" (1997, 96). Seniority was thus a means to avoid intraparty disputes, especially given the significant heterogeneity within the Democratic Party.[36]

Thanks to techniques like balancing and guiding principles like seniority, conflict within the Democratic caucus during much of this period was minimal. Speakership nominations, in particular, were mostly "unanimous" or "by acclamation." (See appendixes 5 and 6 for details.) On those rare occasions when a speakership nomination was contested and regional/ideological division was present, such as in 1933 (73rd Congress) and 1969 (91st Congress), the losers in caucus accepted the nomination outcome and closed ranks on the House floor.[37]

On the minority side, organization has been almost as stable. After the Republicans were pushed out of power following the 1930 midterm elections, the progressive wing of the party continued to be a hindrance throughout the decade. In 1932, at the start of the 72nd Congress, five progressive Republicans voted for George J. Schneider (R-Wis.) for Speaker, rather than the caucus nominee, Bertrand H. Snell (N.Y.). Because Snell's hold on power in the Republican caucus was precarious—he had won the speakership nomination after a grueling eight-ballot affair over John Q. Tilson (Conn.)—

1/10/1967, 3). Jennings, who had served six terms as a House member (84th–89th Congresses) from Virginia, was defeated for reelection to the 90th Congress.

[35] Oklahoma is typically considered "Southern" in orientation, and is in fact coded as "South" by the ICPSR.

[36] On the rise of the seniority rule, see also Polsby, Gallaher, and Rundquist (1969) and Hinckley (1971).

[37] One exception occurred in the 89th Congress (1965), when Albert William Watson (D-S.C.) answered "present" during the speakership vote. Watson was only a tangential Democrat by that time, as he was stripped of his seniority rights by the Democratic caucus on January 2, 1965, for supporting Republican Barry Goldwater for president in November 1964 (NYT, 1/3/1965, 1). On February 1, Watson resigned his seat; he later won a special election as a Republican, to fill the vacancy caused by his own resignation. (Another Democrat, John Bell Williams of Mississippi, was stripped of his seniority rights by the caucus for supporting Goldwater; however, Williams would vote for the Democratic speakership nominee, John McCormack [D-Mass.], on the floor.)

TABLE 9.3.
Democratic balancing in caucus, 72nd–103rd Congresses

Congress	Speaker	Majority leader
72	John N. Garner (Tex.)	Henry T. Rainey (Ill.)
73	Henry T. Rainey (Ill.)	Joseph W. Byrns (Tenn.)
74	Joseph W. Byrns (Tenn.)	William B. Bankhead (Ala.)
	William B. Bankhead (Ala.)	
75	William B. Bankhead (Ala.)	Sam Rayburn (Tex.)
76	William B. Bankhead (Ala.)	Sam Rayburn (Tex.)
	Sam Rayburn (Tex.)	John W. McCormack (Mass.)
77	Sam Rayburn (Tex.)	John W. McCormack (Mass.)
78	Sam Rayburn (Tex.)	John W. McCormack (Mass.)
79	Sam Rayburn (Tex.)	John W. McCormack (Mass.)
81	Sam Rayburn (Tex.)	John W. McCormack (Mass.)
82	Sam Rayburn (Tex.)	John W. McCormack (Mass.)
84	Sam Rayburn (Tex.)	John W. McCormack (Mass.)
85	Sam Rayburn (Tex.)	John W. McCormack (Mass.)
86	Sam Rayburn (Tex.)	John W. McCormack (Mass.)
87	Sam Rayburn (Tex.)	John W. McCormack (Mass.)
	John W. McCormack (Mass.)	Carl B. Albert (Okla.)
88	John W. McCormack (Mass.)	Carl B. Albert (Okla.)
89	John W. McCormack (Mass.)	Carl B. Albert (Okla.)
90	John W. McCormack (Mass.)	Carl B. Albert (Okla.)
91	John W. McCormack (Mass.)	Carl B. Albert (Okla.)
92	Carl B. Albert (Okla.)	Thomas Hale Boggs (La.)
93	Carl B. Albert (Okla.)	Thomas P. "Tip" O'Neill (Mass.)
94	Carl B. Albert (Okla.)	Thomas P. "Tip" O'Neill (Mass.)
95	Thomas P. "Tip" O'Neill (Mass.)	James C. Wright (Tex.)
96	Thomas P. "Tip" O'Neill (Mass.)	James C. Wright (Tex.)
97	Thomas P. "Tip" O'Neill (Mass.)	James C. Wright (Tex.)
98	Thomas P. "Tip" O'Neill (Mass.)	James C. Wright (Tex.)
99	Thomas P. "Tip" O'Neill (Mass.)	James C. Wright (Tex.)
100	James C. Wright (Tex.)	Thomas S. Foley (Wash.)
101	James C. Wright (Tex.)	Thomas S. Foley (Wash.)
	Thomas S. Foley (Wash.)	Richard A. Gephardt (Mo.)
102	Thomas S. Foley (Wash.)	Richard A. Gephardt (Mo.)
103	Thomas S. Foley (Wash.)	Richard A. Gephardt (Mo.)

Note: The Republicans were the majority party in the 80th and 83rd Congresses.

the five progressives were not disciplined. Republican Party defections also occurred on Speaker votes in 1933 (73rd Congress), 1935 (74th Congress), and 1937 (75th Congress), but Snell had by this time consolidated power and proceeded to punish the defectors—William Lemke and Usher L. Burdick (both N.D.)—by placing them at the bottom of minor committees.[38] More generally, the progressive element of the Republican Party was driven out of the party beginning in the 74th Congress, when residual members started their own Progressive Party. They continued to weaken in strength until finally disappearing after the 78th Congress (1943–45).

Two serious minority party nomination battles occurred in 1959 (86th Congress) and 1965 (89th Congress), each involving struggles for the future direction of the Republican Party. In each case, the incumbent leader of the House Republican Party was ousted: Joseph W. Martin (Mass.) by Charles A. Halleck (Ind.) on a 74–70 vote (86th Congress), and Halleck by Gerald R. Ford (Mich.) on a 73–67 vote (89th Congress). While the nomination battles and subsequent outcomes were acrimonious, the Martin and Halleck supporters in 1959 and 1965, respectively, fell in line, and the Republicans displayed a united front behind their speakership nominee on the floor.

No additional minority party caucus violations occurred until 2001, when James A. Traficant Jr. (D-Ohio) rebuffed the Democratic speakership nominee, Richard Gephardt (Mo.), and voted instead for the Republican nominee, Dennis Hastert (Ill.). As a result, Traficant was expelled from the Democratic caucus and had his committee assignments stripped (Cohn 2001).[39] The other case was Gary Eugene "Gene" Taylor (D-Miss.), who voted for John Murtha (D-Pa.) for Speaker in 2001 (107th Congress), 2003 (108th Congress), and 2005 (109th Congress).[40] In doing so, he opposed his party's nominees, Gephardt (107th Congress) and Nancy Pelosi (D-Calif.).[41] Unlike Traficant, Taylor was allowed to remain in the Democratic caucus and was not obviously sanctioned. When the Democrats regained control of

[38] Lemke would vote for Paul J. Kvale (Farmer-Labor-Minn.) in the 73rd Congress, William P. Lambertson (R-Kans.) in the 74th Congress, and Fred L. Crawford (R-Mich.) in the 75th Congress. Burdick would join Lemke in voting for Lambertson and Crawford.

[39] Traficant would later be expelled by the House after being found guilty of nine rules violations dealing with bribery, racketeering, and tax evasion. He was then convicted of similar charges in federal court and sentenced to serve eight years in prison.

[40] In 1995, Taylor and Mike Parker (D-Miss.), who supported Charlie Rose (D-N.C.) for Speaker in the Democratic caucus in the 104th Congress, voted "present" rather than support Gephardt, the Democratic caucus nominee, on the House floor. Parker would change his party affiliation to Republican later in the session. In 1997 (105th Congress) and 1999 (106th Congress), Taylor did vote for Gephardt in the speakership election on the House floor.

[41] In 2003 (108th Congress), Ralph Hall (D-Tex.), Ken Lucas (D-Ky.), and Charles Stenholm (D-Tex.) voted "present" rather than support Pelosi, the Democratic caucus nominee, on the House floor. Hall would change his party affiliation to Republican later in the session.

the House in the 110th Congress, Taylor did vote for Pelosi, both in caucus and on the floor.[42]

The most extensive set of minority party defections occurred in 2011, at the opening of the 112th Congress. Following the Democrats' "shellacking" in the 2010 midterm elections, which resulted in a loss of 63 House seats for the party, along with control of the chamber, calls for Pelosi to step down as the Democratic leader were frequent. Pelosi refused such calls and survived a challenge in caucus to the minority leader's post by Heath Shuler (D-N.C.), on a 150–43 vote (Hunter 2010b). When the issue of electing the Speaker reached the floor upon the organization of the House, Shuler maintained his challenge, garnering 11 votes for Speaker, including his own (Palmer and Hunter 2011).[43] Overall, 19 Democrats registered a public protest against Pelosi, either by voting for someone else or by voting "present," making this the most significant defection since the progressive bolts of the 1920s.[44] All of the defectors were on the conservative side of the Democratic caucus, as measured by DW-NOMINATE scores from the 111th Congress. Despite speculation that Pelosi would punish the defectors in making committee assignments, there is no evidence that she did so—at least right away.[45]

ORGANIZATIONAL CONTROL AND PROCEDURAL CONTROL

At the end of chapters 5 and 7, we tied together efforts to control the organization of the House with efforts to control the legislative agenda by undertaking an analysis of the relative win rates of members of the coalition that elected the Speaker, which we termed the "organizing coalition," compared

[42] Interestingly, Pelosi voted for *herself* for Speaker in 2003 (108th Congress), 2005 (109th Congress), 2007 (110th Congress), 2009 (111th Congress), and 2011 (111th Congress). John Boehner (R-Ohio) also voted for himself for Speaker in 2007 (110th Congress), but did not cast a speakership vote in 2009 or 2011. These appear to be the only cases of major speakership candidates voting for themselves across the history of House speakership elections.

[43] Democrats also voting for Shuler were Jason Altmire (Pa.), Dan Boren (Okla.), Jim Cooper (Tenn.), Joe Donnelly (Ind.), Tim Holden (Pa.), Larry Kissell (N.C.), Jim Matheson (Utah), Mike McIntyre (N.C.), Mike Michaud (Maine), and Mike Ross (Ark.).

[44] One other Democrat, Peter DeFazio (Ore.), skipped the organization of the House entirely to attend "a meeting on a VA medical facility" back in his district (Associated Press 2011).

[45] On the speculation, see "House Democrats Who Voted Against Pelosi Could Suffer Politically," foxnews.com, January 6, 2011, http://www.foxnews.com/politics/2011/01/06/democrats-voted-pelosi-suffer-politically. In examining the committee assignments of the defectors, comparing the 111th and 112th Congress assignments, there are no unusual patterns after we account for Democrats losing assignments because of shifting party ratios on the committees. There is no evidence that the defectors lost seniority within the committees they remained on, nor is there any indication that defectors were removed from committees other than because they requested it or the shifting party ratios mandated removing low-ranked Democrats from some committees. Indeed Shuler, the beneficiary of the largest number of non-Pelosi votes, was appointed to the critical Budget Committee. In passing, the most interesting case of a bolter is Gabrielle Giffords (Ariz.), who was the target of an assassination attempt in early 2011.

to the win rate of the median member of the chamber. If the organizing co-alition is successful in controlling the agenda-setting apparatus of the House to further the interests of its members, then the median of that coalition should be on the winning side of roll call votes at least as often as the me-dian of the chamber, and certainly no less.

In chapters 5 and 7, we examined relative win rates in the House for the 26th–36th Congresses (1839–60) in some detail. We located the spatial po-sitions of the chamber median, the median of the coalition that voted for the Speaker, and the "most frequent winner" in roll call votes. We showed that the coalition that claimed the speakership before the Civil War oftentimes could not parlay organizational control into agenda control. Although the most forward-thinking party leaders of the day could imagine the regimes that we call procedural cartels, they were unable to move from conception to implementation on a regular basis.

What about the period during and after the Civil War? We have identified 1865 as the date in which both parties began the historically unbroken prac-tice of using the party caucuses to nominate candidates for the speakership, and of expecting the rank and file to follow through on the caucus dictate or else risk punishment by party leaders. We have also shown that for the next quarter century, in the face of significant challenges, the organizational car-tel came to be institutionalized; this gave Speaker Reed and the rest of the House Republican leadership confidence in knowing that if they went the next step by demanding that the committee system be the mechanism through which the majority party manipulated the legislative agenda to its advantage, committee members would comply. But do we see evidence that the increase in post–Civil War organizational control coincided with in-creased agenda control?

Yes.

To answer this last question, we return to the roll call victory data we examined in chapters 5 and 7. Because we are now analyzing a much longer time period, from 1839 to the present, we take a slightly different tack than before in analyzing win rates. In the interest of simplicity, we focus on the average winning percentage of members of the Speaker's electoral coalition on roll call votes relative to the opposition, instead of presenting spatial lo-cations of chamber medians, party medians, and most frequent winners on a Congress-by-Congress basis. As we will see, this alternative approach pro-duces insights into the antebellum Houses that are entirely consistent with the win-rate analysis in chapters 5 and 7, which then provides a basis of comparison with the analysis related to the Civil War and beyond.

Figure 9.1 graphs the results of performing this comprehensive win-rate analysis starting with the 26th Congress.[46] To aid in legibility, we have split

---

[46] The most important difference between our analysis and that offered by Lawrence, Maltzman, and Smith (2006) and Cox and McCubbins (2005, chap. 5) is that both previous studies confined themselves to final-passage bills, while we include all roll call votes. Tests of procedural cartel models usually operate by assuming that the majority party will "open the

a. 26th-66th Congress (1839-1921)

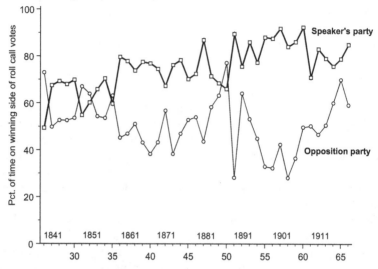

b. 67th-111th Congress (1921-2010)

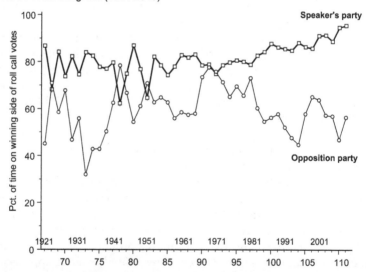

FIGURE 9.1. Percentage of time supporters of the winning Speaker candidate were on the winning side of roll call votes compared to nonsupporters, 26th–111th Congresses (1839–2010). *Source*: "Percent Voting on the Winning Side by Member— House/Senate 1–111," http://www.voteview.com/winning_side.htm.

the time series in half, plotting Congresses 26–66 (1839–1921) in the top panel and Congresses 67–111 (1921–2010) in the bottom.

Comparison of figure 9.1 with figures 5.6 and 7.3 will first confirm that this long-term analysis is consistent with the earlier Congress-by-Congress analyses. In figure 9.1, of the 11 Congresses covered in chapters 5 and 7, we see four Congresses—the 26th, 31st, 32nd, and 35th—in which the opposition coalition, measured in terms of vote for Speaker, was on the winning side of roll call votes more frequently than the coalition that elected the Speaker. These are the same four Congresses in figures 5.6 and 7.3 in which the "most frequent winner" was on the opposite side of the issue space from the organizing coalition and (usually) the chamber median. In many of these same Congresses, we previously noted that the same coalition that elected the Speaker also had difficulty claiming the subsidiary House offices and/or their fair share of committee assignments. Thus, the antebellum period is clearly one in which neither the organizational cartel *nor* the procedural cartel was generally operative.

Now, continuing our exploration from the Civil War forward, we note first that the Civil War Congresses saw a marked shift in the dominance of the majority party over the minority party on roll call votes. This shift actually occurred in the 36th Congress, immediately preceding the Civil War, and continued unabated until the 50th Congress. Recall that in the 36th Congress, the Republicans had to fight a series of battles, stretching across several months, before they could lay claim to organizational success across the complete portfolio of House offices; they built on this organizational success by fashioning themselves into a disciplined antislavery party during the same Congress. At the end of this period the majority Democrats faced significant divisions over tariff reform, with the protectionist Samuel Randall, now exiled from the speakership to the chair of the Appropriations Committee, actively opposing the leadership of the low-tariff Speaker John Carlisle (Peters 1997, 59–62; Barnes 1931).

The two parties' notable successes during this period at confining organizational infighting to the caucus illustrate the emergence of the organizational cartel before the procedural cartel. Indeed, biographers of Reed and previous historical work on this period point to Reed's contemplation of

---

gates" on a piece of legislation if it assumes that the legislation on final passage, even if amended, will be preferred by both the median of the majority party and the median of the chamber, compared to the status quo. It is reasonable to assume that the minority party will prevail more often on amendment roll call votes than on final passage roll calls. Therefore, our analysis will tend to reveal higher win rates for the minority party and lower win rates for the majority than if the analysis was conducted only on final-passage votes. Hence, our analysis provides a conservative test of procedural cartel theory. Empirically, the win rate calculated using all roll call votes is correlated with similar measures that rely only on final-passage votes. For instance, the correlation between our win-rate measure and the Cox and McCubbins (2005, table 5.1) roll-rate measure is -.39 for the majority party rate and -.77 for the minority party rate.

Carlisle's troubles in turning his procedural majority into a policy-making machine as the moment when Reed recognized the need—and opportunity—to take party government to a new level (Robinson 1930; Schickler 2001, 37–43).

The 51st Congress saw the inauguration of the Reed Rules, which is associated in figure 9.1 with the biggest one-Congress spike in the win-rate averages for both parties, each moving in the opposite direction. From this Congress until the 67th (1921–23), the winning-percentage pattern is consistent with the presence of a successful procedural cartel. This period represents the greatest degree of floor dominance enjoyed by the majority party for the entire time series.[47] This run of majority party roll call dominance also includes the 61st Congress (1909–11), which harbored the revolt against Speaker Cannon. Consistent with the conventional wisdom that the revolt dispersed power in the House and weakened the Speaker, the majority party win rate plummeted in the 61st Congress. Still, the win-rate pattern is consistent with a redistribution of power within a party-centered, agenda-setting system—movement to a different *type* of party government, perhaps, but not its complete demise. From the 61st to the 67th Congress, the majority party still dominated the minority, only by a narrower margin than before. Thus, we are comfortable with identifying the period from the 51st to the 67th Congresses as being the first in which the organizational cartel worked integrally with a robust procedural cartel.

The rest of figure 9.1 traces out a history of congressional decision making from the perspective of party government that is well known to political scientists and historians alike. From the 67th Congress forward, the majority party generally dominated the floor, but the exceptions were significant and not simply one-off affairs.

All of the exceptions beginning with the 67th Congress are associated with ideological splits within the majority party of the time. For instance, the 68th Congress, in which the emboldened progressive faction within the Republican Party balked at the renomination of Speaker Frederick Gillett—which forced a three-day, nine-ballot ordeal before the House finally organized—is one such exception. Figure 9.1 shows that the 68th Congress was bad for the Republican Old Guard in policy terms, just as it had been in organizational terms. On the other hand, the purge of the progressives in the 69th Congress led to a brief period of majority party roll call domination again, which lasted through the 1930s and the heyday of the New Deal.

The next three decades saw the greatest challenge to the majority party procedural cartel, to the point that the majority party—controlled by Democrats in all but two Congresses—could not always count on dominating

---

[47] The current period, starting with the 93rd Congress, is the longest *unbroken* period in American history of the majority party in the House winning more roll call votes than the minority. However, the average *difference* in win rates between the parties between the 51st and 67th Congresses is greater than the average difference starting with the 93rd Congress.

the House floor. Conventional accounts of the period place control of the House floor in the hands of a Conservative Coalition that was led by an often-renegade Rules Committee (Manley 1973; Schickler 2001, chap. 4). Although Cox and McCubbins (2005, 130–32) have called into question the degree to which the procedural cartel lost control of the House floor during this period, the important fact for us is that the organizational cartel held. Much to the chagrin of liberal Democrats, this illustrated that the organizational cartel—once the Speaker was elected and the committees determined—could devolve back into an arrangement among the majority party simply to rent-seek, purely for the electoral gain of its members. However, this is a pattern that Martin Van Buren, the progenitor of the organizational cartel, would have understood, and perhaps even approved of.

From the Watergate era to the present, the majority party has dominated the roll call record in an unbroken line. A significant amount of recent scholarship has documented the efforts of policy activists in both parties to reintegrate the working parts of the organizational and procedural cartels—for instance, by putting allegiance to the "majority of the majority" at the top of the list in qualities the majority party expects from committee chairs (Cox and McCubbins 2005; Rohde 2005; Sinclair 2006). We are therefore living in an era that is similar in many ways to the period of "czar rule" and its later weaker version of "caucus government." The historical record alerts us to the fact, however, that the two cartels need not always mesh so seamlessly.

CONCLUSION

As this chapter and chapter 8 document, the party caucus, which became a permanent fixture of House organization by the end of the Civil War, evolved into an equilibrium institution over time. Moreover, the binding nature of the caucus allowed the majority to become an organizational cartel, a coalition that routinely determines the institutional makeup of the chamber. While the caucus bond and organizational cartel have been challenged over time—most notably in the 1923 speakership election, which we covered at length in this chapter—they have survived all assaults and persisted, without interruption, through the present day.[48]

Yet the party caucus has not successfully broadened its authority into the realm of policy. The Radical Republicans during Reconstruction failed in this regard, and while the GOP has continued to dabble with policy-based caucus decision making at various times, it has never instituted caucus rules

[48] After the revolt against Cannon, the Speaker became less influential in House politics, with the parties' Committee on Committees playing a larger role in staffing the various standing committees. In recent decades, the Speaker has reemerged as the central player in House politics.

that were *strictly* binding on party members.[49] The Democrats did draft
strict caucus rules on policy matters—specifically, a two-thirds rule that instructed dissident party members to follow supermajority caucus decisions—and for a time, after the overthrow of Cannon, attempted to institute
a binding policy caucus (Haines 1915; Hasbrouck 1927, 29–34). But members chafed at the persistent party whip, especially in the face of constituent
pressure, and the arrangement could not be maintained (Green 2002). A
binding policy caucus has not been attempted again since.

In recent years, scholars have investigated whether congressional party
caucuses in the contemporary era are binding on *procedural* matters in the
House, specifically on rules-related votes that allow the majority party to
expedite its policy agenda. This scholarship stems from the increased role of
partisanship in congressional life since the late 1970s. Various measures of
party strength indicate that congressional voting is structured significantly
along party lines (e.g., Poole and Rosenthal 1997). Much has been written
as to *why* this is the case (see, e.g., Rohde 1991; Aldrich 1995; Cox and Mc-
Cubbins 1993, 2005), but many accounts suggest that with greater intraparty homogeneity and interparty polarization came greater delegation by
the majority party rank and file to majority party leaders. The Speaker, in
particular, has grown stronger; party reforms in the 1970s made the Speaker
the chair of the Democratic Committee on Committees (DCOC) and provided him/her with the ability (subject to caucus approval) to assign members to the Rules Committee (Sinclair 2006, 77–78).[50] When the GOP regained majority status, fidelity to the Republican conference was stressed,[51]
and "members [in both parties] are now expected to vote the party line on
procedural votes" (Sinclair 2006, 166).

Thus, many scholars now hold that the majority party in the House acts
as a procedural cartel in much the same way that the majority party did during the Reed-Cannon years.[52] The caucus (or conference, in the Republican
case), along with the Speaker and committees, appears to be at the heart of
such an arrangement, an organizational achievement that was no mean feat
in accomplishing.

[49] To underscore this, the Republicans designated their organizational apparatus a "conference" rather than a "caucus" during the period of the Wilson presidency, when the Democrats
pursued their binding policy caucus.

[50] The DCOC was a new Steering and Policy Committee, and no longer the Democratic
contingent on Ways and Means.

[51] In an interview with a Republican leadership aide, Sinclair reports the following statement: "You don't need to be beholden to the leadership so much as to the Conference at large"
(2006, 137).

[52] For research on the procedural cartel in the modern U.S. House, see Cox and McCubbins
(1993, 1994, 2002, 2005), Schickler and Rich (1997a, 1997b), Schickler (2001), Peters (2002),
Forgette (2004), and Jenkins, Crespin, and Carson (2005).

Conclusion

We have covered more than 200 years of House organizational history in the last nine chapters. In this final chapter, we bring things full circle and return to key points initially raised in our introductory chapter. We focus first on the role that the party caucus has played in hastening a consistent House organization by the majority party. We follow by offering some thoughts about how the idea of an organizational cartel would translate into other legislative settings. Changing gears, we reflect on the role of Martin Van Buren in building the American party system, and how a fuller appreciation of how Congress fit into that story might provide a richer and more accurate accounting of the development of the party system. We close with some final thoughts on parties and congressional organization.

BUILDING AN ORGANIZATIONAL CARTEL

Cox and McCubbins (2005) have proposed the procedural cartel as the principle that guides the operation of the modern House of Representatives. As previously noted, in justifying one of the key assumptions that underlies the legislative cartel model in *Setting the Agenda*, they write that in order to establish a near-monopoly on agenda-setting officers, the procedural cartel "establishes an intracartel procedure to decide on the nominee for speaker and on a slate of committee appointments" (2005, 24n9). This is essentially the story of our book—*how* the majority party finally got to the point where it could control the floor votes that ultimately determine the Speaker (and other officers) and committee appointments. This finally happened after the Civil War, and the locus of this control ("the intracartel procedure to decide on the nominee") was the party caucus.

We depart only somewhat from Cox and McCubbins by distinguishing between the arrangement that imposes near-monopoly control over the agenda—the procedural cartel—and the arrangement that establishes control over its consequential offices: the organizational cartel. The two institutions often work together, but as we have shown, not always. In the particular case of the House, the parties were able to impose monopoly control

304

over the positions of institutional leadership decades before they were able to impose agenda control.

Speaker Thomas B. Reed established the practice by which key House positions set the legislative agenda on behalf of the majority party. He would have only pursued this course if he felt confident that the majority party would control key House positions *with certainty* at the outset of a new Congress. By the time Reed was Speaker, in the 51st Congress (1889–91), he could look back on a quarter century of institutional history and conclude that the majority party, via its binding caucus on organizational matters, could count on exercising persistent control over the key power nodes in the House, starting from the opening moments of a Congress and extending through the next two years, even though some members of the majority would be tempted to defect to the minority on individual questions of organization.

Before the Civil War, the organizational cartel was an aspiration, not a reality. That it was merely aspirational is evident in two ways. First, for the most part, disgruntled House members could abandon their party's caucus with impunity. Although someone who bolted the party over the election of the Speaker (or one of the other officers) might not gain the cream of the committee assignments and influence in party circles that loyalists enjoyed, neither would he be written out of the party for his disloyalty.

Second, not only could members of the majority abandon their party on organizational matters with impunity, but the organizational coalitions that elected antebellum Speakers could not always parlay that organizational majority into an enduring agenda-setting majority. Notable were the 26th, 31st, 32nd, and 35th Congresses. These cases demonstrate that achieving an organizational majority may be a necessary condition for the creation of a procedural cartel, but it is not a sufficient condition.

Once the tenets of the organizational cartel were established during the Civil War and tested in the years thereafter, congressional leaders began to push matters further to see whether they could use the caucus to bind members on specific policy-related votes. These efforts were notable failures.

The organizational cartel that eventually emerged in the second half of the nineteenth century, and which continues today, relies on a caucus whose influence on policy making occupies a middle ground along a continuum. At one end is a caucus in which party members debate issues and informally agree on strategy but take no actions to either bind participants or manipulate the agenda to achieve the majority viewpoint; at the other end is a caucus that can bind its members on the structure and content of the floor agenda and can sanction those who are disloyal. The caucus as it currently operates in the House comes closest to exercising positive agenda control in organizational matters while relying on negative agenda control in procedural matters that underlie policy choice.

The organizational cartel has been seriously challenged three times since its presence solidified in the period from 1861 to 1891. Two divisive intra-party battles over speakership nominees, one among the majority Republicans in 1881 and the other among the majority Democrats in 1891, tested the boundaries of the caucus bond on organizational matters—but that bond held and warring factions came together on the floor without incident. The fight between progressive and regular Republicans in caucus in 1923, which *did* spill out onto the floor and delay the election of the Speaker for two days, nonetheless worked within the confines of the organizational cartel. Even the progressive Republican renegades operated under the assumption that they would eventually support the GOP nominee for Speaker. Finally, the organizational cartel survived the Conservative Coalition, the combination of conservative Southern Democrats and Republicans whose unofficial presence from 1937 until the 1980s provided the greatest challenge to the operation of the procedural cartel since its inception under Reed. As a potential threat to the organizational cartel, the Conservative Coalition was the proverbial dog that did not bark.

Had the Democrats retained their majority following the 2010 election—admittedly a big "if"—the organizational cartel undoubtedly would have faced its biggest challenge since the Roaring Twenties. Almost two dozen House Democrats announced during the fall campaign that they would refuse to vote for Nancy Pelosi as Speaker (Hunter 2010a)—a threat that held the potential of throwing the organization of the House into chaos when Congress convened on January 3, 2011. Of course, the results of the November election made these threats moot. Still, 19 Democrats, mostly the Blue Dog remnant of the Conservative Coalition, ended up throwing away their votes when it came time to stand behind Pelosi as the Democratic nominee for Speaker. The fact that this display of disloyalty had no material consequences means that it was viewed as an act of position-taking by electorally vulnerable members, not a body blow to the principle of party organization of the chamber. In other words, it was an accepted form of highly visible dissent meant for public consumption, not a serious assault on the organizational cartel itself.

Should a more serious challenge to the binding party caucus emerge, or should a caucus be threatened with deadlock over the nominee for Speaker, the danger can be averted. This is because the parties in recent years have further routinized the nomination process such that conflict over leadership might be more easily stage-managed. Most significantly, beginning with the 94th Congress, both parties stopped waiting until the last minute to nominate their speakership candidates and instead chose to hold their organizational meetings in early December, less than a month after the federal election and roughly a month before Congress next convened. (See appendix 6.) Beginning with the 105th Congress, the organizational meetings have been pushed up even earlier, to the middle of November, within days of the election.

Furthermore, the parties have adopted rules that limit the number of ballots that might be used to select party leaders. For instance, Rule 4(c) of the House Republican Conference provides that whenever three or more candidates contest any leadership position, the candidate with the fewest votes is dropped after each round of voting until one of the candidates receives a majority.[1] Thus, the confining of organizational conflict within the parties has become codified in the party rules. Such rules are certainly endogenous and could be overturned in the future. Nonetheless, the taming of the nomination process in this way is a good indicator of the degree to which the great bulk of party members now assume that conflict over leadership should stay in the caucus.

ORGANIZATIONAL CARTELS IN OTHER SETTINGS

With the exception of making reference to cross-chamber intrigue surrounding Printer elections, we have confined our focus in this book to the U.S. House of Representatives. The House shares a number of institutional details—committees, party leaders, caucuses, officers, and so on—with other legislatures. Having spent a book exploring the rise of the organizational cartel in one chamber of one national legislature, it is natural to ask whether this is a concept that helps cast light on important aspects of institutional behavior in other chambers and legislatures as well.

Answering this question will require numerous detailed studies of other settings. In the interest of spawning new lines of research, we offer comments that frame the applicability of the organizational cartel idea in the case of the U.S. Senate, American state legislatures, and other countries' legislatures, particularly the Mother of Parliaments.

The U.S. Senate

The most natural starting point for extending the idea of the organizational cartel is the U.S. Senate, since it shares so many of the same institutional details as the House, and since service in the House is the most common shared prior experience among senators. Despite organizational similarities and shared prior experience, it is also easy to imagine why the organizational cartel idea would not profitably translate into the Senate setting. Some may object that any theory that posits agenda control by political parties in the U.S. Senate will not go far because of the filibuster (and strong

[1] House Republican Conference, *Rules of the House Republican Caucus for the 112th Congress,* 9.

minority rights generally), a tradition of collegiality, and the lack of a constitutional presiding officer elected by the underlying membership.

However, some recent analyses have suggested that the majority party in the Senate can in fact exercise power and set the agenda, even if the processes for such power and agenda setting may differ in some respects from the House (Monroe, Roberts, and Rohde 2008; Den Hartog and Monroe 2011). If this is the case, it is also reasonable to suspect that the Senate possesses the raw ingredients with which to construct a party-centered organizational cartel. Furthermore, recall that the energies of the organizational cartel need not be directed solely at policy. Patronage is another prominent goal of those who seek to control a legislative chamber. There is no reason to assume a priori that senators of any generation are less driven by non-policy goals than House members. Indeed, the intrigues over the printership encountered in the early chapters of this book often had their parallels in Senate proceedings (Smith 1977). Whether the other Senate officers were equally contested and guarded for their patronage opportunities is unknown—and thus presents an opportunity for future research into early American party building.

Despite the early struggles over electing the House Printer, the most intense struggles were eventually over electing the Speaker, a constitutional officer that House rules endowed with significant discretionary authority from the earliest days. If we cast our gaze to the Senate and ask about conflict over the constitutional leader in that chamber, we are of course faced with the reality that the leader, the vice president, is imposed on the Senate from the outside. Not only is the vice president not "of" the Senate, he can readily be from the Senate's minority party. This naturally leads any majority coalition in the Senate to look elsewhere for political leadership. For reasons not entirely clear, the Senate never latched on to the obvious alternative, the president pro tempore, as the political leader. However, the inability to marry political leadership with the (pro tempore) presiding officer still presents a puzzle that is relevant to this book, since we know that legislators are driven to establish organizational advantage within the institutions they inhabit. The question is, how might a majority exercise organizational control of the Senate if not through the presiding officer?

Accounts of the Senate in the antebellum period have focused primarily on conflict that emerged over the appointment of Senate committees in the absence of a strong presiding officer that the majority party might control.[2] No doubt because of the lack of such a presiding officer, the Senate continued to ballot for committee memberships long after the House had abandoned the practice. Hoping to avoid this time-sink, in 1823 the Senate chose to vest committee appointments in the presiding officer, which seemed

---

[2] This account is based on Canon and Stewart (2002), Gamm and Smith (2002), and Canon, Nelson, and Stewart (2002).

workable when the frequently absent Daniel Tompkins was vice president. This arrangement became untenable when John C. Calhoun was elected vice president, because he had different ideas (than did the majority of the Senate) about how committees should be composed—and a willingness to occupy the chair in order to make such committee assignments. This prompted the Senate to revert back to balloting, which proved to be unsatisfactory both to those worried about the Senate's time and to members of the majority party who were often outfoxed on the floor by a concerted minority.

At a critical moment in the second session of the 29th Congress (1846), the Senate finally hit upon the idea of having the parties nominate slates of committee members, which would then be adopted via unanimous consent. With some notable exceptions—such as when Free-Soil senator John P. Hale (N.H.) objected in the 30th and 31st Congresses because he was not on either list—this moment in the 29th Congress marked the beginning of party control over appointing committees.

This was not *monopoly* control by the majority party, however, because minority party senators continued to claim some chairs and committee majorities until the great contraction of the Senate committee system in the 67th Congress. Still, it was party control of a sort. And if this form of party control over committee assignments did not give the majority party monopoly control over setting the agenda, it at least gave the majority a leg up.

The advantage held by the majority party in setting the Senate's legislative agenda has been explored by Campbell, Cox, and McCubbins (2002) by using a "roll rate" analysis that is similar in spirit to our earlier win-rate analysis.[3] Their analysis has demonstrated that traces of majority party negative agenda control emerged around the 55th Congress (1893–95).

Our own win-rate analysis, which pushes the window back to the 26th Congress, shows that the House and Senate have moved largely in parallel, as far as the policy advantage held by members of the majority party is concerned. This is illustrated in figure 10.1. It is worth noting that in the 29th Congress, no party held a roll call advantage in the Senate, despite the fact that parties took control over the appointment of committees.

Yet the important question for us is whether the majority party agenda advantage typically enjoyed in the Senate—we leave aside the question of whether it can properly be called a procedural cartel—rests on an organizational cartel. Certainly, when the parties were given the authority to present committee lists to the floor for ratification, authority over composing the list was not given to an individual. Rather, authority was retained by the caucus. Doing so merely shifted the location of the interminable balloting over committee appointments from the Senate floor to the caucus itself, at least in the antebellum period through Reconstruction (Gamm and Smith 2002, 223).

[3] See also Gailmard and Jenkins (2007), which compares House and Senate roll rates on various legislative vehicles between the 45th and 106th Congresses (1877–2000).

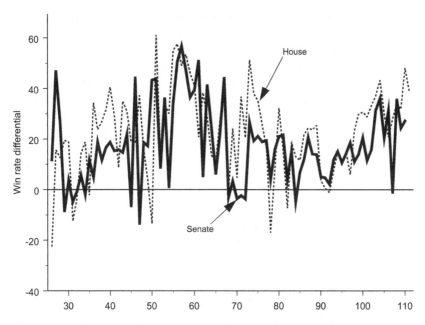

FIGURE 10.1. Win-rate differential in the House and Senate, 26th–111th Congresses, 1839–2010. *Note*: Win-rate differential is calculated by subtracting the average percentage of the time members of the majority party were on the winning wide of roll call votes from the average percentage of time members of the minority party were on the winning side.

The rise of a more formal and articulated party organization in the Senate occurred after Reconstruction in response to pressures felt by party leaders who were trying to respond to strategic challenges posed by the persistence of narrow partisan margins in the chamber—narrow margins that were echoes of hotly contested Senate elections in the state legislatures. As told by Gamm and Smith (2002), the impetus for building party organizations in the Senate was to enhance coordination among members and solve collective action problems in the face of bruising interparty conflict, both within the institution and the electorate at large.

Therefore, it seems reasonable to suspect that if a procedural cartel exists in the Senate (to whatever degree), it does not rest on an organizational cartel. At least, the case would need to be built. However, it also seems reasonable to surmise that one of the reasons why party control over agenda setting is weaker in the Senate than in the House is precisely because the Senate lacks a strong presiding officer who can be controlled by the majority party.[4] Thus, the Senate serves as an illustration that agenda control does

[4] On this point, see Roberts and Smith (2007). They also note that the Senate lacks a previous-question motion, which also limits the majority's control over the floor agenda.

not *require* an organizational cartel, but that an organizational cartel can *enhance* the effectiveness of a procedural cartel, if it does exist.

In any event, these remarks convince us that one fruitful line of research would be to examine the institutional development of the Senate from the perspective of the organizational cartel. This would be a different perspective than the one taken by previous scholars, and would more explicitly consider the coevolution of committees and party leadership organizations as potentially integrated systems. Some have focused on conflict concerning the committee appointment authority exercised by the parties, especially before the Civil War (Canon and Stewart 2002; McConachie 1898). Others, most notably Gamm and Smith (2002), have explored the rise of party organizations by focusing on how their emergence facilitated partisan coordination within and beyond the chamber. What remains to be done is a comprehensive accounting of the Senate's institutional development from the perspective of party leaders—from the founding to the present—with the idea of the organizational cartel in mind.

American state legislatures

American state legislatures would seem another field ripe to explore through the lens of organizational cartels. The large number of legislatures developing over time, sometimes in concert but often independently, provides an obvious laboratory for the exploration of how American legislators structure how they struggle over positions of authority in their chamber. Furthermore, if we regard Martin Van Buren as the progenitor of the organizational cartel, then it serves us well to remember that he first developed his theories about party building in the cauldron of New York state politics.

Assessing the widespread applicability of the organizational cartel model to the institutional development of state legislatures would seem a natural path to tread were it not for the practical barrier of assembling evidence from a set of sometimes-obscure state legislatures scattered across a continent. Furthermore, the obscurity of materials documenting the behavior of state legislatures across time has tended to drive out studies of state legislatures that take a developmental perspective.

The difficulties of studying the longitudinal development of state legislatures have spurred scholarship about these bodies to be relentlessly contemporary, tending toward a replication of congressional findings in the state context. So, for example, the extensive research by Francis (1982, 1985, 1989) in the 1980s, which touched on state legislative committees and party influence, was guided by the functionalist scholarship of the day and therefore of limited use in ascertaining whether party caucuses (or leaders) controlled committees, and whether parties exercised agenda control in general, not to mention whether party caucuses had the ability to sanction recalcitrant members.

Francis's work established that state legislatures, at least as of roughly 1980, varied considerably in how much power party leaders, party caucuses, and legislative committees held over internal decision making. Other research has subsequently applied more modern theories of party control to state legislatures, such as Aldrich and Battista (2002), Cox, Kousser, and McCubbins (2010), and Wright and Schaffner (2002).

However, none of this scholarship—nor any other scholarship of which we are aware—has taken up the topic addressed in this book, which is the use of party organizations, such as the caucus, to cement control over the valuable positions of the legislature, ranging from patronage to committee slots. Nor have these studies examined the consequences of disloyalty in organizational matters.

Just as the original research for this book was inspired by our observing the great variation throughout American history in how easily U.S. House Speakers have been elected, we hope that an observation about variation across the states will help spur similar research in state legislatures. Even a casual examination of American history, plus a reading of the news today, shows that majority party control over the reins of power in state legislatures is variable. This is evident, for instance, if we focus our attention on state legislatures during the Gilded Age. One interesting example is the election of Republican Edward Shurtleff as Speaker of the Illinois House of Representatives in 1909. Shurtleff walked out of the Republican caucus, which had been called for the nomination of a speakership candidate, due to intraparty disputes concerning alcohol regulation and meddling from the governor. Shurtleff was eventually elected Speaker with the support of Democrats—Democrats who had already endorsed one of their own for the speakership nomination. Thus, Shurtleff was able to prevail only by appealing to individual Democrats to defect from their caucus's binding choice.[5]

Even legislatures today can find themselves hamstrung by the inability of the majority party caucus to take organizational control of the chamber. The best-known recent case was the New York state senate in 2009, which started out in the hands of the Democrats, who held a narrow 32–30 majority. After ruling the chamber for five months, the Democrats lost organizational control when two of their own joined with all the Republicans to oust the chamber's leadership and install one of the disloyal Democrats, Pedro Espada Jr., as president pro tempore in an arrangement termed by the Republican leadership as a "bipartisan coalition."[6] Within days, the Democratic caucus agreed to elect a leader more to the liking of the second defec-

[5] See *CT*, 1/4/1909, 6; 1/5/1909, 1; 1/6/1909, 1.

[6] "Republicans Seize Control of State Senate," *New York Times*, http://cityroom.blogs.ny times.com/2009/06/08/revolt-could-imperil-democratic-control-of-senate. The president pro tempore is the highest position held by New York state senators, as the constitutional presiding officer is the lieutenant governor.

tor, Hiram Monserrate; with the election of the new leader, Monserrate returned to the Democratic fold. This produced an organizational tie that was unbreakable because the lieutenant governor position—whose occupant would normally cast the tiebreaking vote in the New York state senate—was vacant. The resolution of the crisis came when Governor Paterson appointed a Democratic lieutenant governor on constitutionally dubious grounds. Eventually, Espada returned to the Democratic Party.

Other contemporary examples of this sort are not unheard-of, such as the election of Thomas Finneran (D-Mass.) as Speaker of the Massachusetts House of Representatives in 1996, in an election precipitated by the resignation of Charles Flaherty, who pleaded guilty to tax evasion. Finneran lost the nomination vote in the Democratic caucus, 56–67, to House majority leader Richard Voke. Rather than rally behind his party's nominee, Finneran reached out to the Republican caucus by combining his 56 Democratic supporters with the votes of all 35 House Republicans to win the speakership on a 91–67 tally (Page 1996).[7]

While many American state legislatures certainly behave in ways that are similar to the organizational cartel, it is still a practice that varies state to state and year to year, and cannot be taken for granted in any specific legislative setting. Simply mapping out the contemporary terrain—ascertaining which legislatures are the most and least likely to be organized outside of the party caucuses—would be a useful first step in establishing the basis for party control in the various state legislatures. Mapping out how this variability has developed over time would be daunting but would move us a long way toward understanding how party control over organization interacts with party control over the agenda more generally.

The organizational cartel in a comparative setting

The empirical questions at the core of this book—when and how did the majority party in the House gain unquestioned control over the valuable positions of authority in the chamber?—has a comparative analogue as well.[8] It is often noted that parties in American legislatures are typically "weaker" than in their counterparts elsewhere. Party strength is generally measured in ways that readily map onto the two major cartels we have sought to distinguish. Strength of the procedural cartel is seen in terms of the agenda-setting powers of ministries and the power of party whips. These matters, in turn, are viewed as a consequence of factors we have ascribed to the organizational cartel, including the practice of composing the ministries

[7] In 1997, when it came to the election of a Speaker for a full term, Finneran easily received the nomination of the Democratic caucus, and then was elected speaker on a purely party-line vote.

[8] We thank Gary Cox (personal communication) for helping to provide some important guideposts in thinking about the comments that follow, while absolving him of any errors.

entirely of members of the party that won the last election—or perhaps of a coalition of parties—but the emphasis is on *parties*, not on freelancing members.

A casual assessment of international parliamentary behavior suggests that the operation of organizational and procedural cartels typically goes hand in hand, although this precise analytical distinction is not one that has been widely made in quite these terms. A more systematic survey of international legislative development notes the empirical regularity by which parties and legislative institutions tend to coevolve (Cox 2005), and that the driving force behind this coevolution is the need in busy legislatures to ration access to the floor.

Our analysis has demonstrated that at least in one prominent case, this coevolution was prompted initially by a desire to divert the organizational resources of the House toward the electoral advantage of the parties in an effort to control patronage, as much as to control the legislative agenda. Policy is not the only output of a legislature, and as a consequence, control over the legislature's valuable offices may not always have a strong policy motivation.

Thinking more concretely about the world's national legislatures, the most natural comparison is with the British Parliament, particularly the House of Commons. We could pose a question about Commons that sounds a lot like the puzzle we posed in the introduction to chapter 2. In the May 2010 British general election, it was understood that the leader of the party that won a majority of seats in Commons would be offered the opportunity to form a government. The party leaders were chosen in advance of the election so that voters knew ahead of time who the prime minister would be, depending on the outcome of the election. They also knew that each and every one of the cabinet ministers in the next government would be drawn from among the membership of the majority party. They expected that members of the majority party would be called on to support the new government's policy proposals when brought to a vote on the floor of Commons, even in the face of individual doubts. Finally, they could assume (as eventually transpired) that if no party received a majority, bargaining to form a majority would focus on party actors, not on individual members. Only then might the party portfolios of ministries be adjusted to reflect the bargain.

The choice of prime minister and other cabinet ministers was nothing like this in 1770, when Lord North was named prime minister, nor was the role of political parties in structuring the election and choice of government ministers. How did we get from the politics of Lord North to the politics of David Cameron? More generally, at what point would one say that it was pretty much guaranteed that if a party won a majority of seats in Parliament, the leader of the majority party (who was identifiable as the leader during the election period) would be offered the opportunity to form a government, that all party members would stand behind the prime minister in make-or-break votes, and that a large and stable share of the cabinet ministers would be unambiguously identified as members of that party?

A considerable body of work has documented the degree to which this transition in the U.K. occurred in the nineteenth century, roughly in parallel with the story we have told here about the U.S. House of Representatives. Much of this scholarship has grown up over the past two decades, which makes it part of the New Institutionalist approach to legislative politics, of which the current book is a part.[9] It would be tempting to glibly note the parallel institutional developments in two of the world's most important legislatures and conclude that the organizational cartel within the British Parliament (best exemplified by the monopoly control of the cabinet by the majority party) is the foundation upon which the procedural cartel (best exemplified by the principle that all important legislation originate in the cabinet) was built.

Although simple importation of our analysis to the British context would be glib, many of the same elements were in place during the nineteenth century, which makes investigations into parliamentary development using our approach a fruitful line of future research. It does appear that the organizational cartel developed in Britain before the full procedural cartel. The principle of ministerial responsibility and votes of confidence date back to the Glorious Revolution, although they were not tied to partisan politics in the way we would understand them. The political unity of the cabinet developed in the early 1800s (Cox 1993). The identification of the leader prior to the election is generally considered to date to the Tamworth Manifesto in 1834, which suggests that the routinization of leadership struggles had been settled precisely at the time that members of the U.S. House were struggling, yet failing, to do similar things. Finally, procedural changes cementing the agenda-setting power of the cabinet developed in fits and starts beginning in the late 1820s, before being firmly set in place by the 1860s (Cox 1987, chap. 6).

Thus, the internalization of struggles for leadership within the majority party, and the use of the outcomes of these struggles to form legislative agendas, reached their climax in Britain a quarter century before they did so in the U.S. However, the institutional changes that followed as a consequence appear to have been similar, if shifted forward by a similar amount of time. In particular, once party control over leadership and agenda setting was firmly in place, it became easier to generate greater party unity within Parliament, at least in part by using the promise of future cabinet membership as a reward for party unity.

---

[9] Among these works, which helped form our comments in this section, are Cox's many works on the subject (1987, 1993, 2011).

A New Take on the Legacy of Martin Van Buren

Casting our sights back to the earliest part of our narrative, we are compelled to comment further on the role that Martin Van Buren played in developing the organizational capacity of the Democratic Party. The organizational cartel that structures the election of House leaders is a direct descendant of Van Buren's thinking about partisan organization and, in fact, may be the purest expression of this strategic thinking still in use among the parties. Historians and political scientists alike have lionized the strategic prowess of Van Buren, as he generalized what he learned from New York politics to the nation. The early chapters of this book add a layer of complexity to our understanding of what Van Buren was trying to accomplish by highlighting the role of the House in his party-building plans.

Our antebellum narrative dovetails with Van Buren's better-known efforts to build an electoral machine capable of submerging regional differences among Democrats in order to win the White House. Even in the early days of the Republic, the presidency was the top political prize; any political organization that hoped to dominate national politics needed to dominate presidential elections. Yet this book shows that the presidency was not the only institution that caught Van Buren's eye. Congress, through its control of patronage in the Clerk and propaganda in the Printer, possessed resources that were critical pieces to the larger puzzle that comprised the popular side of the Van Buren system. Moreover, Democrats needed to deliver once in office; that is, they needed to *legislate* in order to continue achieving their electoral goals. Thus, the power of party needed to be felt in Congress—via the Speaker, with his powers of recognition and appointment, and the committees—in guiding and manufacturing legislation. Van Buren's focus on controlling the House through the party caucus naturally complemented his efforts to build an organization that could win presidential elections.

In emphasizing the underappreciated role of Congress in Van Buren's party-building efforts, we offer a corrective to the existing scholarly perspective. We contend that historians' near-exclusive focus on the presidency—as an office and arena of mass political struggle—has resulted in a lopsided view of party building at the national level during the Jacksonian era.[10] The Jacksonian system did not abolish the separation of powers. Indeed, the scholarly consensus is that during the nineteenth century (with notable exceptions) the real locus of national political power remained in Congress. An ascendant presidency was mostly a twentieth-century phe-

---

[10] This preoccupation with the presidency and presidential elections as the central feature in historical accounts of how national political events have unfolded across time has been termed the "presidential synthesis." See Cochran (1948) and, more recently, Zelizer (2007) for critiques. Studies that offer sweeping historical analyses of American politics but *do* provide a role for Congress include Brady (1988), Silbey (1992), and Aldrich (1995).

nomenon. Thus, any view of party building and development in antebellum America that does not incorporate a rich understanding of the machinations of Congress risks mischaracterizing that system significantly.

While Van Buren was indeed a mastermind, he was ahead of his time, at least with regard to his plans to anchor control of the House in an organizational cartel. Efforts to create such an organizational cartel from the 1830s to the 1850s proved difficult, and provide ample evidence regarding the constraints on Van Buren's grandest schemes. The biggest constraint was the messiness of House elections. In particular, congressional leaders could not control nominations to the House nor ensure that all legislators who carried the party label were as dedicated to the "party principle" as were Van Buren and his supporters. Especially vexing to Van Buren's plans was that he had precisely zero control over the behavior of minority parties for whom a spoils-based party system offered no allure. The rise of slavery as an incendiary issue in national politics always meant that the party principle could be undermined by majority party renegades who prioritized region over party. And if that did not materialize, minor parties like the Free-Soil Party and the American Party, whose attention was on what we would now call "social issues," could prove pivotal on the floor.

The history of organizational politics in the U.S. House illustrates the difficult task of bringing together elections and governing through the actions of political parties. Van Buren's activities are immediately recognized by modern students of social choice as an effort to reduce policy dimensionality, so that a majority of officeholders could extract the rents of office holding. However, no one brought the congressional electorate into the deal. A sufficient number of voters in the antebellum period insisted that politics was about something else—slavery, for instance—meaning that a significant number of their representatives also refused to go along with a game that valued patronage or distributive politics over everything else.

Since the Civil War and the disappearance of slavery as a viable national issue, other divisive issues—like bimetallism, industrialization, the tariff, and civil rights—have emerged and possessed the potential to disrupt organizational politics in the House. But none has. The Republicans' unity on organizational matters through Reconstruction while they served as the majority party was copied by the Democrats when they returned to prominence in the mid-1870s. Over time, the value of organizational fidelity became ingrained in both parties. When disruptions within caucus occurred, resources were brought to bear—usually committee assignments distributed by the Speaker—to smooth over hard feelings and maintain intraparty harmony. While real *policy* differences might persist within the majority party, all members recognize the value of coordinating to organize the chamber and capture the range of benefits that come with such a majority-controlled organization. Van Buren's vision is indeed a reality.

As American political scientists, we have been taught to act as if American political parties are by their very nature weak and inconsequential, and that fights over the control of party organs is nothing more than a tempest in a teapot. However, the perspective offered by this book helps us appreciate the degree to which the modern party caucuses in Congress, especially the caucuses in the House of Representatives, have become prime venues for the development of party government in the United States. To paraphrase Gloria Steinem, this is what party government looks like.

The importance of the organizational cartel for the general development of political parties in the United States is illustrated through the central role played by the House Democratic caucus in procedural reform efforts during the 1970s.[11] Between 1969 and 1975, the Democratic caucus, which had been moving in a liberal direction since the late 1950s, instituted a number of procedural changes to open up the legislative process in the House and make it more representative of the bulk of the Democratic membership (Rohde 1991). These changes included the elimination of the seniority system that automatically governed committee chairmanships, which was replaced by a new caucus rule that provided for a secret ballot for all chairmanships at the beginning of each Congress; a decentralization of authority from committees to subcommittees; an expansion of resources throughout the congressional ranks that gave junior members more opportunities to participate; and a strengthening of the powers of the Speaker, who was granted the ability to appoint the chair and Democratic members of the Rules Committee (once again making Rules an arm of the party leadership), given new authority to determine appointments to all other standing committees (through disproportionate influence on the new Steering and Policy Committee), and provided with the right to refer bills to more than one committee ("multiple referral") and set deadlines for reporting.

In the early years after the reforms, politics in the House became unwieldy, thanks to a proliferation of participatory efforts by members looking to make their mark and appeal to constituent sentiment. In response, the Democratic rank and file looked to the leadership for guidance and coordination. Because the Democratic Party had become increasingly homogenous by the late 1970s, as conservative Southerners began disappearing, the caucus was willing to allow leaders more discretion in setting and overseeing the legislative agenda. To control proceedings, the leadership began relying on special (restrictive) rules to structure debate and floor voting (Sinclair 2005). Leaders also took on a more active role at the prefloor stage by negotiating with committees on the content and language of legislation and generally using their authority to ensure that the party's agenda proceeded expeditiously.

---

[11] The material from this and the following paragraph is drawn from Jenkins (2011) and Stewart (2011).

By this time, the Republican minority, increasingly homogenous as a conservative group, began adopting similar conference-based rules in the hopes of better countering the Democrats.[12] When the House changed partisan hands after the 1994 elections, the Republicans under Newt Gingrich (Ga.), and then later under Dennis Hastert (Ill.), used their conference to further centralize decision-making authority in the Speaker, who took an ever more active role in committee selection and legislative policy making. When the Democrats recaptured the House following the 2006 elections, new Speaker Nancy Pelosi (D-Calif.) followed the Gingrich-Hastert plan in terms of activity and assertiveness but also relied more upon the expertise of committee chairmen to share in leadership decisions.

With the Republican return to power after the 2010 election, it was natural to expect new Speaker, John Boehner (R-Ohio), to follow the Gingrich-Hastert plan, although with a lighter hand due to his own loud protestations regarding Pelosi's centralization pursuits in the previous Congress and his efforts to placate the GOP's boisterous Tea Party faction, which grew in prominence after the midterm elections (Hooper 2010). Even though Boehner's hold over the speakership has been regarded as precarious, the early politics of the 112th Congress only underscored the degree to which the majority party caucus has become the center of attention for the politics of the House.

Because the organizational cartel is an endogenous institution, it is natural to ask where it is most vulnerable to attack. It is also natural to ask whether such an attack would be successful and thereby thrust the House back into a terra incognita of organizational politics not seen in Washington since the Civil War. In short, what are the chances that the House could find itself once again deadlocked in organizing?

The history we have explored suggests two conditions under which the House will find itself deadlocked. The first is when a faction of the majority party has sympathies with the minority, and thus finds it advantageous to hold up the election of a Speaker in order to extract centrist concessions from the leadership of the majority party. This occurred most recently in 1923 due to the demands of progressive Republicans. The second condition is when a second dimension introduces a crosscutting cleavage into both parties, which makes a cross-party organization of the House at least plausible, insofar as off-dimension members of both parties could credibly threaten to organize the House together on an alternative basis, which would cut the major party establishments out of the deal. This was the common condition for most of the protracted speakership fights before the Civil War.

In the current period, a Democratic cartel seems more vulnerable to an attack because of the first condition, with a Republican cartel more susceptible because of the second condition. For the Democrats, the most cohesive

[12] Recall that the Republicans call their caucus a "conference." See footnote 49 in chapter 9 for an explanation.

dissident faction is the Blue Dogs, who are more conservative than the mainstream of the party, and thus could plausibly be enticed to form coalitions with Republicans on a variety of issues, mainly economic, but sometimes social. The anti-Pelosi pledge taken by nearly two dozen House Democratic candidates in 2010 provides evidence of this type of vulnerability lurking over the horizon.

Ensuring against the breakdown of a Democratic organizational cartel due to left-right ideological tension is the now-well-worn path of disaffected Democrats defecting to the Republican Party. Since the passage of the Civil Rights Act in 1964, 23 House members have switched parties, 19 of whom were conservative Democrats who became Republicans, and some of whom were already well into Republican ideological territory prior to switching (Nokken and Poole 2004; Yoshinaka 2005; Nokken 2009).[13] Thus, any Democrat who might be tempted to bolt the party when the roll is called to elect the Speaker has probably already defected to the Republican Party.

Republicans seem considerably less vulnerable to fracturing over organizational matters due to left-right ideological divisions because their most cohesive dissidents, the Tea Party sympathizers, are on the right wing of the party, far from the center of the chamber. Thus, defection to the Democratic Party is not a credible threat. The most Tea Party sympathizers can do is withhold support for the Republican nominee and lobby for a more conservative Speaker, the alternative being the inability of the House to conduct business at all. Under this scenario, the Tea Party faction would become like the Impracticables of 1849 (see chapter 6).

Another opportunity for organizational chaos with Republicans in the majority could arise if a party like Ross Perot's Reform Party or the Libertarian Party elected enough members to be pivotal in an organization of the House, much like the 34th Congress, when the American Party kept the Republicans and Democrats from holding a majority outright. In such a situation, the Tea Party faction would be tempted to join with a Reform/Libertarian Party contingent, with the Democrats unlikely to help either set of actors (the Libertarians or traditional Republicans) organize the House for business. As with the resolution of the speakership contest in 1856, there would also be speculation about whether organization would need to be effected through a plurality vote.

Any of these scenarios is a bit of a stretch. The likelihood of organizational chaos in the next few years is low. Still, the fact that it is not hard to assign modern actors to the roles of actors in antebellum speakership fights suggests that these scenarios are not entirely constructed out of whole cloth.

As this conclusion is being written, the House Republican Party has been in the midst of two years of intense political battle with a Democratic president. The results of this battle will reverberate throughout the rest of the

---

[13] Excluded from this calculation were Joseph Moakley (D-Mass.) and Thomas M. Foglietta (D-Pa.), because the circumstances of their election cloud analysis of their party changes.

century. Should the House Republicans prove successful in taking on the Democratic president and Senate, it will be because its leaders have harnessed the organizational cartel to its advantage and overcome a numerical disadvantage in holding only one of three institutions necessary to pass legislation.

FINAL THOUGHTS

For the past two decades, students of legislatures have argued over the relevance of Mayhew's claim that "[t]he fact that no theoretical treatment of the United States Congress that posits parties as analytical units will go very far" (1974, 27).[14] The analysis offered in this book suggests that at least part of that argument has overlooked major aspects of the politics of congressional organization and what we are calling the organizational cartel. First, for nearly 200 years, the most respected and visible members of Congress have acted as if the Speaker's gavel is something of value to be fought over, and that the value comes in the ability of the winners to appoint committees and direct the agenda of the chamber for two years. If, as a general matter, parties have no meaningful role as analytical units, then the efforts of the most ambitious politicians in American history have been as deluded as those who search for the Loch Ness Monster, the Holy Grail, or perpetual motion.

At the same time, the construction and maintenance of the organizational cartel illustrates that the "easiest" task for cohesive parties to achieve—staying together to elect the Speaker and share the institutional spoils—is no easy task and is prone to destruction by the most primitive of social choice dynamics. The robustness of the organizational cartel is a variable, not a constant. Other American legislatures with otherwise identical structures do not operate by assuming that the organizational cartel will dominate—and the House itself spent its first century constructing its foundation. There is nothing in the laws of physics that mandate its appearance. There are plausible scenarios that could eventually lead to an unraveling of the precedents established by the Republican Party during the Civil War, by which all roads to the speakership went through the caucuses, which ultimately led to the historical moment that Speaker Thomas Reed grasped in 1890. Indeed, the Democrats may have dodged a test of the organizational cartel's persistence by losing the 2010 House midterms.

Still, for more than a century, the House has organized its business under the assumption that the majority party elects the Speaker, that the Speaker's power to set the agenda derives from the fact that even his sharpest partisan critics will stand behind him on the floor if he is challenged, and that he will

---

[14] Mayhew eventually backed off the claim. See Mayhew (2004, xvii).

use the agenda-setting levers at his disposal to keep his party unified on the floor. The organizational cartel was not handed to the House. Rather, the House constructed it piece by piece, and party leaders have devoted time to learning how to master it. As a result, the organizational cartel is now an indispensable part of congressional politics as we know it.

APPENDIXES

House Officer Elections and Caucus Nominations

Summary of House Organization, First–112th Congresses (1789–2011)

Cong.	Year	Majority party		Speaker			
		Name	% seats held	Name	Party	Ballots	Winning pct.
1	1789	Pro-adm.	56.9	Muhlenberg	Pro-adm.	Unk.	Unk.
2	1791	Pro-adm.	56.5	Trumbull	Pro-adm.	Unk.	Unk.
3	1793	Anti-adm.	51.4	Muhlenberg	Anti-adm.	3	Unk.
4	1795	Rep.	55.7	Dayton	Fed.	1	58.2
5	1797	Fed.	53.8	Dayton	Fed.	1	97.5
6	1799	Fed.	56.6	Sedgwick	Fed.	2	51.2
7	1801	Rep.	63.6	Macon	Rep.	1	65.4
8	1803	Rep.	72.5	Macon	Rep.	1	71
9	1805	Rep.	80.3	Macon	Rep.	3	54.7
10	1807	Rep.	81.7	Varnum	Rep.	1	50.4
11	1809	Rep.	64.8	Varnum	Rep.	2	55.1
12	1811	Rep.	74.8	Clay	Rep.	1	63
13	1813	Rep.	62.6	Clay	Rep.	1	60.1
				Cheves	Rep.	1	57
14	1815	Rep.	65	Clay	Rep.	1	71.3
15	1817	Rep.	78.9	Clay	Rep.	1	95.3
16	1819	Rep.	86	Clay	Rep.	1	94.8
				Taylor	Rep.	22	51.4
17	1821	Rep.	82.9	Barbour	Rep.	12	51.2
18	1823	A-C Rep.	33.8	Clay	A-C Rep.	1	76.8
19	1825	Adams	51.2	Taylor	Adams	2	51.3
20	1827	Jack.	53.1	Stevenson	Jack.	1	50.7
21	1829	Jack.	63.9	Stevenson	Jack.	1	79.6
22	1831	Jack.	59.1	Stevenson	Jack.	1	50.2
23	1833	Jack.	59.6	Stevenson	Jack.	1	65.1
				Bell	Jack.	10	52.3
24	1835	Jack.	59.1	Polk	Jack.	1	58.7
25	1837	Dem.	52.9	Polk	Dem.	1	51.8
26	1839	Dem.	51.7	Hunter	Whig	11	51.3

	Clerk				Printer[a]			
Name	Party	Ballots	Winning pct.		Name	Party	Ball.	Winning pct.
Beckley	Pro-adm.	2	Unk.	Printer appointed by Clerk				
Beckley	Pro-adm.	1	100					
Beckley	Pro-adm.	1	100					
Beckley	Rep.	1	61.5					
Condy	Fed.	1	50.6					
Condy	Fed.	1	54.7					
Oswald	Fed.	1	54.8					
Beckley	Rep.	1	66.3					
Beckley	Rep.	1	88.2					
Beckley	Rep.	1	82.5					
Magruder	Rep.	4	61					
Magruder	Rep.	1	51.2					
Magruder	Rep.	1	85.8					
Magruder	Rep.	1	85.4					
Dougherty	Rep.	2	51.9					
Dougherty	Rep.	1	93.4					
Dougherty	Rep.	1	100		Gales & Seaton	Rep.	1	Unk.
Dougherty	Rep.	1	100		Gales & Seaton	Rep.	1	65.4
Dougherty	Rep.	1	100		Gales & Seaton	Rep.	1	65.8
Clarke	Rep.	11	65.3					
Clarke	A-C Rep.	1	100		Gales & Seaton	A-C Rep.	1	73.8
Clarke	Adams	1	100		Gales & Seaton	Adams	1	73.2
Clarke	Jack.	1	100		Green	Jack.	1	51.4
Clarke	Jack.	1	70.3		Green	Jack.	1	52.4
Clarke	Jack.	1	100		Gales & Seaton	Anti-Jack.	14	50.3
Franklin	Jack.	3	51.5		No election	—	—	—
Franklin	Jack.	1	100		Blair & Rives	Jack.	1	60.5
Franklin	Dem.	1	72.6		Allen	Whig[c]	12	50.2
Garland	Dem.	3	50.5					
Garland	Dem.	1	50.9		Blair & Rives	Jack.	1	53.1

(Continued on next page)

(*Continued*)

Cong.	Year	Majority party Name	% seats held	Speaker Name	Party	Ballots	Winning pct.
27	1841	Whig	58.7	White	Whig	1	54.8
28	1843	Dem.	66	Jones	Dem.	1	68.1
29	1845	Dem.	62.3	Davis	Dem.	1	57.1
30	1847	Whig	50.5	Winthrop	Whig	3	50.5
31	1849	Dem.	48.5	Cobb	Dem.	63	46
32	1851	Dem.	54.5	Boyd	Dem.	1	55.1
33	1853	Dem.	67.1	Boyd	Dem.	1	65.9
34	1855	Opp.	42.7	Banks	Amer.[f]	133	48
35	1857	Dem.	55.7	Orr	Dem.	1	56.9
36	1859	Rep.	48.7	Pennington	Rep.	44	50
37	1861	Rep.	59	Grow	Rep.	1	62.3
38	1863	Rep.	46.2	Colfax	Rep.	1	55.5
39	1865	Rep.	70.5	Colfax	Rep.	1	79.4
40	1867	Rep.	76.6	Colfax	Rep.	1	80.9
				Pomeroy	Rep.	1	100
41	1869	Rep.	70.4	Blaine	Rep.	1	70.3
42	1871	Rep.	56	Blaine	Rep.	1	57.5
43	1873	Rep.	68.2	Blaine	Rep.	1	70.3
44	1875	Dem.	62.1	Kerr	Dem.	1	61.3
				Randall	Dem.	1	65.6
45	1877	Dem.	52.9	Randall	Dem.	1	53
46	1879	Dem.	48.1	Randall	Dem.	1	50.9
47	1881	Rep.	51.6	Keifer	Rep.	1	51.9
48	1883	Dem.	60.3	Carlisle	Dem.	1	61.7
49	1885	Dem.	56	Carlisle	Dem.	1	56.3
50	1887	Dem.	51.4	Carlisle	Dem.	1	52.2
51	1889	Rep.	53.9	Reed	Rep.	1	51.7
52	1891	Dem.	71.7	Crisp	Dem.	1	71.5
53	1893	Dem.	61.2	Crisp	Dem.	1	62.3
54	1895	Rep.	71.2	Reed	Rep.	1	70.2
55	1897	Rep.	57.7	Reed	Rep.	1	59.5
56	1899	Rep.	52.4	Henderson	Rep.	1	52.8
57	1901	Rep.	56	Henderson	Rep.	1	55.5
58	1903	Rep.	53.6	Cannon	Rep.	1	54.2
59	1905	Rep.	65	Cannon	Rep.	1	65.5
60	1907	Rep.	57	Cannon	Rep.	1	56.8
61	1909	Rep.	56	Cannon	Rep.	1	53.4

	Clerk				Printer[a]		
Name	Party	Ballots	Winning pct.	Name	Party	Ball.	Winning pct.
Clarke	Whig	4	58.2	Gales & Seaton	Whig	1	62.3
McNulty	Dem.	1	65.3	Blair & Rives	Dem.	1	66.3
French	Dem.	1	100				
French	Dem.	1	100	Ritchie & Heiss	Dem.	1	62.1
Campbell	Whig	1	50.2	House adopted a lowest-bid system for			
Campbell	Whig	20	50.9	Printer			
Young	Dem.	9	51.1				
Forney	Dem.	1	61.7	Armstrong	Dem.	1	57.2
Forney	Dem.	1	61	Armstrong	Dem.	1	57.8
Cullom	Whig	1	100	Wendell	Dem.	11	56.9
Allen	Dem.	1	58.7	Steedman	Dem	1	56.3
Forney	Rep.	1	50.5	Ford	Rep	18	51.3
Etheridge	Unionist[d]	1	59	House eliminated the position of Printer.			
McPherson	Rep.	1	59.4				
McPherson	Rep.	1	58.6				
McPherson	Rep.	1[c]	100				
McPherson	Rep.	1[c]	70				
McPherson	Rep.	1[c]	100				
McPherson	Rep.	1[c]	100				
Adams	Dem.	1[c]	100				
Adams	Dem.	1[c]	100				
Adams	Dem.	1[c]	100				
McPherson	Rep.	1	51.7				
Clark	Dem.	1[c]	100				
Clark	Dem.	1[c]	100				
Clark	Dem.	1[c]	100				
McPherson	Rep.	1[c]	100				
Kerr	Dem.	1[c]	100				
Kerr	Dem.	1[c]	100				
McDowell	Rep.	1[c]	100				
McDowell	Rep.	1[c]	100				
McDowell	Rep.	1[c]	100				
McDowell	Rep.	1[c]	100				
McDowell	Rep.	1[c]	100				
McDowell	Rep.	1[c]	100				
McDowell	Rep.	1[c]	100				
McDowell	Rep.	1[c]	100				

(*Continued on next page*)

(*Continued*)

Cong.	Year	Majority party		Speaker			
		Name	% seats held	Name	Party	Ballots	Winning pct.
62	1911	Dem.	58.3	Clark	Dem.	1	59.8
63	1913	Dem.	66.9	Clark	Dem.	1	67
64	1915	Dem.	52.9	Clark	Dem.	1	52.6
65	1917	Rep.[b]	49.5	Clark	Dem.	1	50.7
66	1919	Rep.	55.2	Gillett	Rep.	1	57
67	1921	Rep.	69.2	Gillett	Rep.	1	70.7
68	1923	Rep.	51.8	Gillett	Rep.	9	51.9
69	1925	Rep.	56.8	Longworth	Rep.	1	54.5
70	1927	Rep.	54.7	Longworth	Rep.	1	54
71	1929	Rep.	62.1	Longworth	Rep.	1	63.8
72	1931	Rep./Dem.	49.9	Garner	Dem.	1	50.7
73	1933	Dem.	71.9	Rainey	Dem.	1	72.2
74	1935	Dem.	74	Byrns	Dem.	1	74.4
				Bankhead	Dem.	1	100
75	1937	Dem.	76.8	Bankhead	Dem.	1	76.8
76	1939	Dem.	60.2	Bankhead	Dem.	1	59.3
				Rayburn	Dem.	1	100
77	1941	Dem.	61.4	Rayburn	Dem.	1	60.2
78	1943	Dem.	51.1	Rayburn	Dem.	1	50.9
79	1945	Dem.	55.7	Rayburn	Dem.	1	56.9
80	1947	Rep.	56.6	Martin	Rep.	1	57.3
81	1949	Dem.	60.5	Rayburn	Dem.	1	61.3
82	1951	Dem.	54	Rayburn	Dem.	1	54.2
83	1953	Rep.	50.8	Martin	Rep.	1	51.9
84	1955	Dem.	53.3	Rayburn	Dem.	1	53.5
85	1957	Dem.	53.8	Rayburn	Dem.	1	53
86	1959	Dem.	64.8	Rayburn	Dem.	1	65.2
87	1961	Dem.	60.2	Rayburn	Dem.	1	60
				McCormack	Dem.	1	59.9
88	1963	Dem.	59.5	McCormack	Dem.	1	59.1
89	1965	Dem.	67.8	McCormack	Dem.	1	67.5
90	1967	Dem.	56.8	McCormack	Dem.	1	56.9
91	1969	Dem.	55.9	McCormack	Dem.	1	56.3
92	1971	Dem.	58.6	Albert	Dem.	1	58.7
93	1973	Dem.	55.6	Albert	Dem.	1	55.7
94	1975	Dem.	66.9	Albert	Dem.	1	66.4
95	1977	Dem.	67.1	O'Neill	Dem.	1	66.8
96	1979	Dem.	63.7	O'Neill	Dem.	1	63.5
97	1981	Dem.	55.6	O'Neill	Dem.	1	60
98	1983	Dem.	61.8	O'Neill	Dem.	1	62.4

	Clerk				Printer[a]		
Name	Party	Ballots	Winning pct.	Name	Party	Ball.	Winning pct.
Trimble	Dem.	1[c]	100				
Trimble	Dem.	1[c]	100				
Trimble	Dem.	1[c]	100				
Trimble	Dem.	1	50.5				
Page	Rep.	1[c]	100				
Page	Rep.	1[c]	100				
Page	Rep.	1[c]	100				
Page	Rep.	1[c]	100				
Page	Rep.	1[c]	100				
Page	Rep.	1[c]	100				
Trimble	Dem.	1[c]	100				
Trimble	Dem.	1[c]	100				
Trimble	Dem.	1[c]	100				
Trimble	Dem.	1[c]	100				
Trimble	Dem.	1[c]	100				
Trimble	Dem.	1[c]	100				
Trimble	Dem.	1[c]	100				
Trimble	Dem.	1[c]	100				
Megill	Dem.						
Andrews	Rep.	1[c]	100				
Roberts	Dem.	1[c]	100				
Roberts	Dem.	1[c]	100				
Snader	Rep.	1[c]	100				
Roberts	Dem.	1[c]	100				
Roberts	Dem.	1[c]	100				
Roberts	Dem.	1[c]	100				
Roberts	Dem.	1[c]	100				
Roberts	Dem.	1[c]	100				
Roberts	Dem.	1[c]	100				
Jennings	Dem.	1[c]	100				
Jennings	Dem.	1[c]	100				
Jennings	Dem.	1[c]	100				
Jennings	Dem.	1[c]	100				
Jennings	Dem.	1[c]	100				
Henshaw	Dem.						
Henshaw	Dem.	1[c]	100				
Henshaw	Dem.	1[c]	100				
Henshaw	Dem.	1[c]	100				
Guthrie	Dem.	1[c]	100				

(Continued on next page)

(*Continued*)

Cong.	Year	Majority party		Speaker			
		Name	% seats held	Name	Party	Ballots	Winning pct.
99	1985	Dem.	58.2	O'Neill	Dem.	1	58.1
100	1987	Dem.	59.3	Wright	Dem.	1	59.2
101	1989	Dem.	59.8	Wright	Dem.	1	59.5
				Foley	Dem.	1	60.2
102	1991	Dem.	61.4	Foley	Dem.	1	61.1
103	1993	Dem.	59.3	Foley	Dem.	1	59.2
104	1995	Rep.	52.9	Gingrich	Rep.	1	52.5
105	1997	Rep.	52.4	Gingrich	Rep.	1	50.8
106	1999	Rep.	51.3	Hastert	Rep.	1	52
107	2001	Rep.	50.8	Hastert	Rep.	1	51.7
108	2003	Rep.	52.6	Hastert	Rep.	1	52.5
109	2005	Rep.	53.3	Hastert	Rep.	1	52.9
110	2007	Dem.	53.6	Pelosi	Dem.	1	53.6
111	2009	Dem.	59.1	Pelosi	Dem.	1	59.4
112	2011	Rep.	55.6	Boehner	Rep.	1	55.8

Note: Party seat percentages taken from the House Clerk's webpage (http://artandhistory.house.gov/ house_history/partydiv.aspx), which uses the Martis (1989) party codes from the First through 100th Congresses.

[a]From the 15th through 22nd Congress (election of Gales & Seaton), the House Printer was elected for the *following* Congress. Beginning with the 24th Congress, the House elected its Printer for the *current* Congress. Printers are listed in the Congress that elected them.

[b]The Democrats were able to organize the House with the help of three Progressives, a Prohibitionist, and a Socialist.

[c]Elected unanimously by resolution, not by ballot.

[d]Etheridge's partisanship is suspect. He is listed in various sources as "American," "Whig," "Conservative," and "Unionist." At the time of his election as Clerk, "Unionist" is probably the best characterization.

[e]Allen was elected by a coalition of conservative Democrats and Whigs. Shortly thereafter, he moved over to the states' rights wing of the Whig Party (Smith 1977, 160).

[f]Banks was elected as a member of the American Party in November 1854, but switched to the Republican Party by December 1855 when the 34th Congress convened.

Party names follow the labels assigned by Martis (1989). They are abbreviated as follows:

Pro-adm: Pro-administration
Anti-adm: Anti-administration
Rep: Republican
Fed: Federalist
A-C Rep: Adams-Clay Republican
Jack: Jacksonian
Anti-Jack: Anti-Jacksonian
Dem: Democrat
Whig: Whig
Amer: American
Unionist: Unionist

	Clerk				Printer[a]		
Name	Party	Ballots	Winning pct.	Name	Party	Ball.	Winning pct.
Guthrie	Dem.	1[c]	100				
Anderson	Dem.	1[c]	100				
Anderson	Dem.	1[c]	100				
Anderson	Dem.	1[c]	100				
Anderson	Dem.	1[c]	100				
Carle	Rep.	1[c]	100				
Carle	Rep.	1[c]	100				
Trandahl	Rep.						
Trandahl	Rep.	1[c]	100				
Trandahl	Rep.	1[c]	100				
Trandahl	Rep.	1[c]	100				
Trandahl	Rep.	1[c]	100				
Haas	Rep.	1[c]	100				
Haas	Rep.	1[c]	100				
Miller	Dem.	1[c]	100				
Miller	Dem.	1[c]	100				
Haas	Rep.	1[c]	100				

APPENDIX 2

Election of House Speaker, First–112th Congresses

FIRST CONGRESS (ELECTION DATE: APRIL 1, 1789)
> Frederick A. Muhlenberg (Pro-Adm.-Pa.) was elected by a "majority of votes," with reports of 23 votes for Muhlenberg and 7 votes split between two other candidates. Jonathan Trumbull Jr. was also nominated.
>
> *Source*: *House Journal*, 1-1, 6; *Independent Gazetteer* (Philadelphia), April 9, 1789, 3; Risjord (1992), 631.

SECOND CONGRESS (ELECTION DATE: OCTOBER 24, 1791)
> Jonathan Trumbull Jr. (Anti-Adm.-Conn.) was elected by a "majority of votes." No further details provided.
>
> *Source*: *House Journal*, 2-1, 434; *American Mercury* (Hartford, Conn.), October 31, 1791, 3.

THIRD CONGRESS (ELECTION DATE: DECEMBER 2, 1793)
> Frederick A. Muhlenberg (Anti-Adm.-Pa.) was elected on the third ballot.

Ballot:	1	2	3
Frederick Muhlenberg	21	33	37
Theodore Sedgwick	24	29	27
Abraham Baldwin	14		
Gilman	1		
Smith (sc)	3		
Boudinot	2		
Goodhue	1		
Scattering		some	a few
Total votes	66	?	?
Necessary for a choice	34	?	?

> *Source*: *General Advertiser* (Philadelphia), December 3, 1793, 3.

FOURTH CONGRESS (ELECTION DATE: DECEMBER 7, 1795)
> Jonathan Dayton (F-N.J.) was elected on the first ballot. Dayton received 46 votes to 31 for Frederick Muhlenberg and 2 votes scattering. (Total votes: 79. Necessary for a choice: 40.)
>
> *Source*: *Aurora General Advertiser* (Philadelphia), December 8, 1795, 3; *Daily Advertiser* (New York), December 10, 1795, 2.

FIFTH CONGRESS (ELECTION DATE: MAY 15, 1797)
  Jonathan Dayton (F-N.J.) was elected on the first ballot. Dayton received 78 votes to 1 for George Dent and 1 for Abraham Baldwin. (Total votes: 80. Necessary for a choice: 41.)
  Source: Federal Gazette & Baltimore Daily Advertiser, May 17, 1797, 3; *Alexandria Advertiser* (Virginia), May 19, 1797, 2.

SIXTH CONGRESS (ELECTION DATE: DECEMBER 2, 1799)
  Theodore Sedgwick (R-Mass.) was elected on the second ballot. On the first ballot, Sedgwick received 42 votes to 27 for Nathaniel Macon, 13 for George Dent, 2 for John Rutledge Jr., and 1 for Thomas Sumter. (Total votes: 85. Necessary for a choice: 43.) On the second ballot, Sedgwick received 44 votes to 38 for Macon, 3 for Dent, and 1 for Rutledge. (Total votes: 86. Necessary for a choice: 44.)
  Source: Annals of Congress, 6-1, 186.

SEVENTH CONGRESS (ELECTION DATE: DECEMBER 7, 1801)
  Nathaniel Macon (R-N.C.) was elected on the first ballot. Macon received 53 votes to 26 for James A. Bayard and 2 for Samuel Smith. (Total votes: 81. Necessary for a choice: 41.)
  Source: Commercial Advertiser (New York), December 12, 1801, 3; *New York Evening Post*, December 12, 1801, 3.

EIGHTH CONGRESS (ELECTION DATE: OCTOBER 17, 1803)
  Nathaniel Macon (R-N.C.) was elected on the first ballot. Macon received 76 votes to 30 for Joseph Varnum and 1 for John Dawson. (Total votes: 107. Necessary for a choice: 54.)
  Source: Commercial Advertiser (New York), October 21, 1803, 3.

NINTH CONGRESS (ELECTION DATE: DECEMBER 2, 1805)
  Nathaniel Macon (R-N.C.) was elected on the third ballot.

Ballot:	1	2	3
Nathaniel Macon	51	53	58
Joseph Varnum	26	26	23
John C. Smith	16	17	18
John Dawson	10	7	3
Andrew Gregg	2	3	2
Thomas Moore			1
David Holmes			1
Total votes	105	106	106
Necessary for a choice	53	54	54

Source: Aurora General Advertiser (Philadelphia), December 6, 1805, 3.
Note: Discrepancies exist regarding the vote totals of Macon, Varnum,

and Gregg on the first ballot, with different sources reporting as many as 52 votes for Macon, 27 for Varnum, and 3 for Gregg.

10TH CONGRESS (ELECTION DATE: OCTOBER 26, 1807)
Joseph B. Varnum (R-Mass.) was elected on the first ballot. Varnum received 59 votes to 17 for Charles Goldsborough, 17 for Burwell Bassett, 8 for Josiah Masters, 7 for Thomas Blount, 4 for John Dawson, 2 for John Smilie, 1 for Benjamin Tallmadge, 1 for Timothy Pitkin, and 1 for R. Nelson. (Total votes: 117. Necessary for a choice: 59.)
Source: Annals of Congress, 10-1, 782.

11TH CONGRESS (ELECTION DATE: MAY 22, 1809)
Joseph B. Varnum (R-Mass.) was elected on the second ballot. On the first ballot, Varnum received 60 votes to 36 for Nathaniel Macon, 20 for Timothy Pitkin, 1 for Roger Nelson, 1 for Charles Goldsborough, and 2 blank. (Total votes: 120. Necessary for a choice: 61.) On the second ballot, Varnum received 65 votes to 45 for Macon, 6 for Pitkin, 1 for Benjamin Howard, 1 for Nelson, and 1 for Goldsborough. (Total votes: 118. Necessary for a choice: 60.)
Source: Annals of Congress, 11-1, 54–56.

12TH CONGRESS (ELECTION DATE: NOVEMBER 4, 1811)
Henry Clay (R-Ky.) was elected on the first ballot. Clay received 75 votes to 38 for Bibb, 3 for Macon, 2 for Nelson, and 1 for Bassett. (Total votes: 119. Necessary for a choice: 60.)
Source: National Intelligencer (Washington, D.C.), November 6, 1811, 1; *Balance and State Journal* (Albany), November 12, 1811, 362.

13TH CONGRESS (ELECTION DATE: MAY 24, 1813)
Henry Clay (R-Ky.) was elected on the first ballot. Clay received 89 votes to 54 for Timothy Pitkin, 2 for Nathaniel Macon, 1 for Breckenridge, 1 for Nelson, and 1 for Bibb. (Total votes: 148. Necessary for a choice: 75.)
Source: Annals of Congress, 13-1, 106; *Boston Daily Advertiser*, May 31, 1813, 2.
Note: Clay resigned the speakership in order to attend the peace talks in Europe.

13TH CONGRESS—REPLACEMENT ELECTION (ELECTION DATE: JANUARY 19, 1814)
Langdon Cheves (R-S.C.) was elected on the first ballot. Cheves received 94 votes to 59 for Felix Grundy and 12 scattering. (Total votes: 165. Necessary for a choice: 83.)

Source: *Annals of Congress*, 13-2, 1057; *Repertory* (Boston), January 27, 1814, 1.

14TH CONGRESS (ELECTION DATE: DECEMBER 4, 1815)
   Henry Clay (R-Ky.) was elected on the first ballot. Clay received 87 votes to 13 for Hugh Nelson, 9 for Timothy Pitkin, 7 for Nathaniel Macon, 2 for Joseph Lewis, 1 for T. Pickering, and 3 blanks. (Total votes: 122. Necessary for a choice: 62.)
   Source: *Niles' Weekly Register*, December 9, 1815, 254.

15TH CONGRESS (ELECTION DATE: DECEMBER 1, 1817)
   Henry Clay (R-Ky.) was elected on the first ballot. Clay received 143 votes to 6 for Samuel Smith and 1 blank. (Total votes: 150. Necessary for a choice: 76.)
   Source: *Annals of Congress*, 15-1, 398.

16TH CONGRESS (ELECTION DATE: DECEMBER 6, 1819)
   Henry Clay (R-Ky.) was elected on the first ballot. Clay received 147 votes with 8 scattering. (Total votes: 155. Necessary for a choice: 78.)
   Source: *Annals of Congress*, 16-1, 702; *New York Gazette & Daily Advertiser*, December 9, 1819, 2.
   Note: Clay resigned after the first session to return home to take care of some financial matters.

16TH CONGRESS—REPLACEMENT ELECTION (ELECTION DATE: NOVEMBER 15, 1820)
   John W. Taylor (R-N.Y.) was elected on the 22nd ballot.

Date:	November 13, 1820							November 14			
Ballot:	1	2	3	4	5	6	7	8	9	10	11
John W. Taylor	40	49	50	60	65	67	62	64	66	64	61
William Lowndes	34	44	56	61	63	61	57	54	47	25	31
Samuel Smith	27	25	16	11	8	7	15	33	33	50	50
John Sergeant	18	13	11	—	—	—	—	—	—	—	5
Hugh Nelson	10	—	—	—	—	—	—	—	—	—	—
Scattering	3	1	1	3	2	1	1	1	1	1	1
Total votes	132	132	134	135	138	136	135	152	147	140	148
Necessary for a choice	67	67	68	68	70	69	68	77	74	71	75

Date:	November 14								November 15		
Ballot:	12	13	14	15	16	17	18	19	20	21	22
John W. Taylor	47	32	27	26	30	44	55	66	67	73	76
William Lowndes	23	30	37	55	68	72	66	65	65	42	44
Samuel Smith	53	48	42	27	23	17	21	14	8	32	27
John Sergeant	19	32	35	32	24	11	2	—	—	—	—
Gideon Tomlinson	3	–	—	—	—	—	—	—	—	—	—
Scattering	3	3	3	6	—	—	—	—	1	—	1
Total votes	148	145	144	146	145	144	144	145	141	147	148
Necessary for a choice	75	73	73	74	73	73	73	73	71	74	75

Source: Annals of Congress, 16-2, 435–38; Niles' Weekly Register, November 18, 1820, 186.

Note: Eleven additional members arrived and took their seats prior to the Nov. 14 balloting; another five appeared and were seated prior to the Nov. 15 balloting.

Note: Lowndes is credited with 32 votes on the 10th ballot by the account provided in Niles' Weekly Register.

17TH CONGRESS (ELECTION DATE: DECEMBER 4, 1821)
Philip P. Barbour (R-Va.) elected on the 12th ballot.

Date:	December 3, 1821							December 4				
Ballot:	1	2	3	4	5	6	7	8	9	10	11	12
John W. Taylor	60	58	61	60	67	72	77	64	69	70	68	67
Caesar A. Rodney	45	60	61	69	72	65	59	36	15	4	5	3
Louis McLane	29	31	30	23	16	8	—	—	—	2	—	—
Samuel Smith	20	10	5	8	10	19	26	25	18	10	6	4
Hugh Nelson	5	—	2	—	—	—	—	—	—	—	—	—
Scattering	2	2	—	—	—	—	—	12	3	2	5	4
Philip P. Barbour	—	—	—	—	—	—	—	35	64	83	85	88
Henry Baldwin	—	—	—	—	—	—	—	—	4	3	4	6
Total votes	161	161	159	160	165	164	162	172	173	174	173	172
Necessary for a choice	81	81	80	81	83	83	82	87	87	88	87	87

Source: Annals of Congress, 17-1, 514–17; Niles' Weekly Register, December 8, 1821, 233–34.

Note: Seven additional members arrived and took their seats prior to the Dec. 4 balloting.

Note: Nelson is credited with zero votes on the first ballot by the account provided in Niles'.

18TH CONGRESS (ELECTION DATE: DECEMBER 1, 1823)
Henry Clay (R-Ky.) was elected on the first ballot. Clay received 139 votes to 42 for Philip P. Barbour. (Total votes: 181. Necessary for a choice: 91.)
Source: *Annals of Congress*, 18-1, 795.

19TH CONGRESS (ELECTION DATE: DECEMBER 5, 1825)
John W. Taylor (Adams-N.Y.) was elected on the second ballot. On the first ballot, Taylor received 89 votes to 41 for John W. Campbell, 36 for Louis McLane, 17 for Andrew Stevenson, 6 for Lewis Condict, and 5 scattering. (Total votes: 194. Necessary to a choice: 98.) On the second ballot, Taylor received 99 votes to 44 for McLane, 42 for Campbell, 5 for Stevenson, and 3 scattering. (Total votes: 193. Necessary for a choice: 97.)
Source: *Register of Debates*, 19-1, 795–96.

20TH CONGRESS (ELECTION DATE: DECEMBER 3, 1827)
Andrew Stevenson (Jacksonian-Va.) was elected on the first ballot. Stevenson received 104 votes to 94 for John W. Taylor, 4 for Philip P. Barbour, and 3 scattering. (Total votes: 205. Necessary for a choice: 103.)
Source: *Register of Debates*, 20-1, 811.

21ST CONGRESS (ELECTION DATE: DECEMBER 7, 1829)
Andrew Stevenson (Jacksonian-Va.) was elected on the first ballot. Stevenson received 152 votes to 21 for William D. Martin, 4 for Joel B. Sutherland, 4 for Henry R. Storrs, 3 for John W. Taylor, with 7 votes scattering. (Total votes: 191. Necessary for a choice: 96.)
Source: *Republican Star & General Advertiser* (Easton, Md.), December 15, 1829, 3; *Boston Patriot*, December 9, 1829, 2.

22ND CONGRESS (ELECTION DATE: DECEMBER 5, 1831)
Andrew Stevenson (Jacksonian-Va.) was elected on the first ballot. Stevenson received 98 votes to 54 for Joel B. Sutherland (Pa.), 15 for C. A. Wickliffe (Ky.), 18 for John W. Taylor (N.Y.), 4 for Lewis Condict (N.J.), and 6 scattering. (Total votes: 195. Necessary for a choice: 98.)
Source: *Register of Debates*, 22-1, 1420.

23RD CONGRESS (ELECTION DATE: DECEMBER 2, 1833)
Andrew Stevenson (Jacksonian-Va.) was elected on the first ballot. Stevenson received 142 votes to 39 for Lewis Williams, 15 for Edward Everett, 4 for John Bell, 2 for Richard Coulter, 2 for R. H. Wilde, 2 for C. F. Mercer, 1 for John Davis, 1 for Samuel A. Foot, 1 for John

Vance, 1 for James K. Polk, and 8 blank. (Total votes: 218. Necessary for a choice: 110.)

Source: *Congressional Globe*, 23-1, 3; *Register of Debates*, 23-1, 2136.

Note: Stevenson resigned the speakership to become American minister to London.

Note: Both the *Register* and the *Globe* indicate that there were 218 votes cast in the election, making 110 the number necessary for a choice. But both sources only report candidate totals that add up to 217 votes.

23RD CONGRESS—REPLACEMENT ELECTION
(ELECTION DATE: JUNE 2, 1834)

John Bell (Jacksonian-Tenn.) was elected on the 10th ballot.

Ballot:	1	2	3	4	5	6	7	8	9	10
R. H. Wilde (Ga.)	64	64	59	49	37	24	16	11	11	11
James K. Polk (Tenn.)	42	53	57	59	67	67	73	78	76	78
Joel B. Sutherland (Pa.)	34	30	26	25	16	16	10	9	4	2
John Bell (Tenn.)	30	39	47	49	57	65	76	97	104	114
Jesse Speight (N.C.)	18	16	8	4	3	1	3	3	2	1
James M. Wayne (Ga.)	15	13	15	25	30	36	26	13	8	6
Lewis Williams (N.C.)	4	—	—	—	—	—	—	—	—	—
Edward Everett (Mass.)	3	1	—	—	—	—	—	—	—	—
Thomas Chilton (Ky.)	2	—	—	—	—	—	—	—	—	—
Henry Hubbard (N.H.)	2	1	1	2	1	—	—	—	—	—
Roger L. Gamble (Ga.)	1	1	—	—	—	—	—	—	—	—
G. R. Gilmer (Ga.)	1	1	—	—	—	—	—	—	—	—
Benjamin Hardin	—	1	—	—	—	—	—	—	—	—
Amos Lane	—	1	—	—	—	—	—	—	—	—
William S. Archer	—	—	1	—	—	—	—	—	—	—
David Crockett	—	—	1	—	—	—	—	—	—	—
Thomas Marshall	—	—	—	1	—	—	—	—	—	—
John Q. Adams	—	—	—	—	2	—	—	—	—	—
Richard Coulter	—	—	—	—	1	—	1	—	—	—
Horace Binney	—	—	—	—	—	—	—	1	—	—
Blank	4	2	4	7	5	5	10	7	6	6
Total votes	220	223	219	221	219	214	215	219	211	218
Necessary for a choice	111	112	110	111	110	108	108	110	106	110

Source: *Register of Debates*, 23-1, 4371–73; *Congressional Globe*, 23-1, 421.

Note: On the third ballot, the tellers discovered two votes folded together (in the same handwriting), both for John Bell. These votes were not counted. See *Register*.

Note: Wayne is credited with zero votes on the 10th ballot by the account provided in the *Register*. The *Globe* account of 6 votes is likely correct, as the *Register*'s individual vote total falls 6 votes short of the announced total.

Note: *Register* reports zero blanks on the seventh ballot.

24TH CONGRESS (ELECTION DATE: DECEMBER 7, 1835)
James K. Polk (Jacksonian-Tenn.) was elected on the first ballot. Polk received 132 votes to 84 for John Bell, 3 for Charles F. Mercer, 2 for John Quincy Adams, 1 for Francis Granger, and 3 blanks. (Total votes: 225. Necessary for a choice: 113.)
Source: *Congressional Globe*, 24-1, 3.

25TH CONGRESS (ELECTION DATE: SEPTEMBER 4, 1837)
James K. Polk (D-Tenn.) was elected on the first ballot. Polk received 116 votes to 103 for John Bell and 5 scattering. (Total votes: 224. Necessary for a choice: 113.)
Source: *Congressional Globe*, 25-1, 3.

26TH CONGRESS (ELECTION DATE: DECEMBER 16, 1839)
Robert M. T. Hunter (W-Va.) was elected on the 11th ballot.

Date:	December 14, 1839						December 16				
Ballot:	1	2	3	4	5	6	7	8	9	10	11
John W. Jones (Va.)	113	113	110	101	71	39	2	—	—	14	55
John Bell (Tenn.)	102	99	1	2	22	21	64	80	33	12	—
William C. Dawson (Ga.)	11	11	103	77	4	1	5	5	6	3	—
Francis W. Pickens (S.C.)	5	5	7	8	6	4	—	1	1	5	9
Dixon H. Lewis (Ala.)	3	5	6	14	49	79	110	113	110	73	1
George W. Hopkins (Va.)	1	1	—	—	1	1	1	1	1	1	—
Robert M. T. Hunter (Va.)	—	1	5	29	68	63	22	16	59	85	119
John Q. Adams (Mass.)	—	—	1	1	1	—	—	1	1	1	—
John C. Clark (N.Y.)	—	—	1	—	1	—	—	—	—	—	—
Henry A. Wise (Va.)	—	—	—	1	—	—	—	—	—	—	—
Waddy Thompson (S.C.)	—	—	—	1	—	—	—	—	—	—	—
Levi Lincoln (Mass.)	—	—	—	—	4	11	—	—	—	2	—
Francis Granger (N.Y.)	—	—	—	—	2	1	12	—	—	2	—
George Evans (Maine)	—	—	—	—	2	—	1	—	—	—	—
Thomas Corwin (Ohio)	—	—	—	—	2	1	—	—	—	1	—
Zadok Casey (Ill.)	—	—	—	—	1	3	3	5	5	8	10
Linn Banks (Va.)	—	—	—	—	—	1	—	—	—	—	—
George Dromgoole (Va.)	—	—	—	—	—	1	1	1	1	1	—
R. Barnwell Rhett (S.C.)	—	—	—	—	—	1	—	—	—	—	—
David Petrikin (Pa.)	—	—	—	—	—	1	—	—	—	—	—
Francis Thomas (Md.)	—	—	—	—	—	—	4	7	11	10	3
John Sergeant (Pa.)	—	—	—	—	—	—	1	—	—	—	—
Joseph Underwood (Ky.)	—	—	—	—	—	—	1	—	—	—	—

(*Continued on next page*)

(*Continued*)

Date:	December 14, 1839						December 16				
Ballot:	1	2	3	4	5	6	7	8	9	10	11
Cave Johnson (Tenn.)	—	—	—	—	—	—	1	1	—	—	—
Henry W. Connor (N.C.)	—	—	—	—	—	—	1	—	—	—	—
Lewis Williams (N.C.)	—	—	—	—	—	—	—	1	—	—	—
John Campbell (S.C.)	—	—	—	—	—	—	—	—	2	—	—
Edward Curtis (N.Y.)	—	—	—	—	—	—	—	—	1	—	—
George M. Keim (Pa.)	—	—	—	—	—	—	—	—	—	12	24
William Medill (Ohio)	—	—	—	—	—	—	—	—	—	2	—
Charles Atherton (N.H.)	—	—	—	—	—	—	—	—	—	—	4
Thomas Davee (Maine)	—	—	—	—	—	—	—	—	—	—	3
David Starkweather (Ohio)	—	—	—	—	—	—	—	—	—	—	1
Nathan Clifford (Maine)	—	—	—	—	—	—	—	—	—	—	1
Tilghman Howard (Ind.)	—	—	—	—	—	—	—	—	—	—	1
Linn Boyd (Ky.)	—	—	—	—	—	—	—	—	—	—	1
Total votes	235	235	234	234	234	228	229	232	231	232	232
Necessary for a choice	118	118	118	118	118	115	115	117	116	117	117

Source: *House Journal*, 26-1, 57–79.

Note: This election was the first using the viva voce voting rule. All subsequent speakership elections were determined by viva voce, unless otherwise noted.

27TH CONGRESS (ELECTION DATE: MAY 31, 1841)
John White (W-Ky.) was elected on the first ballot. White received 121 votes to 84 for John W. Jones, 8 for Henry A. Wise, 5 for Joseph Lawrence, 1 for William Cost Johnson, 1 for Nathan Clifford, and 1 for George N. Briggs. (Total votes: 221. Necessary for a choice: 111.)
Source: *House Journal*, 27-1, 10–11.

28TH CONGRESS (ELECTION DATE: DECEMBER 4, 1843)
John W. Jones (D-Va.) was elected on the first ballot. Jones received 128 votes to 59 for John White (Ky.) and 1 for William Wilkins (Pa.). (Total votes: 188. Necessary for a choice: 95.)
Source: *House Journal*, 28-1, 7–8.

29TH CONGRESS (ELECTION DATE: DECEMBER 1, 1845)
John W. Davis (D-Ind.) was elected on the first ballot. Davis received 120 votes to 71 for Samuel F. Vinton, 9 for Moses Norris, 5 for William S. Miller, 1 for Robert C. Winthrop, 1 for Daniel M. Barringer, 1 for John G. Chapman, 1 for John H. Campbell, and 1 for Andrew Stewart. (Total votes: 210. Necessary for a choice: 106.)
Source: *House Journal*, 29-1, 7–9.

30TH CONGRESS (ELECTION DATE: DECEMBER 6, 1847)
Robert C. Winthrop (W-Mass.) was elected on the third ballot.

	1	2	3
Robert C. Winthrop (W–Mass.)	108	109	110
Linn Boyd (D–Ky.)	61	82	64
Robert McClelland (D–Mich.)	23	13	14
John A. McClernand	11	5	8
James J. McKay	5	—	—
Howell Cobb	3	2	4
James Wilson	2	3	2
Henry C. Murphy	1	—	—
Charles J. Ingersoll	1	—	—
John P. Gaines	1	—	—
Joseph R. Ingersoll	1	1	—
Timothy Jenkins	1	—	—
Charles Hudson	1	1	1
John Gayle	1	—	—
Armistead Burt	—	1	4
R. Barnwell Rhett	—	1	7
John J. Hermanson	—	1	—
Jacob Thompson	—	—	1
Isaac E. Holmes	—	—	1
Joseph A. Woodward	—	—	1
Richard French	—	—	1
Total votes	220	219	218
Necessary for a choice	111	110	110

Source: *House Journal*, 30–1, 8–14.

31ST CONGRESS (ELECTION DATE: DECEMBER 22, 1849)
Howell Cobb (D-Ga.) was elected on the 61st ballot.

Date:	12/3/1849				12/4					
Ballot:	1	2	3	4	5	6	7	8	9	10
Robert C. Winthrop	96	96	96	96	96	97	97	97	97	97
Howell Cobb	103	102	102	102	102	101	100	99	100	99
David Wilmot	8	8	7	7	10	9	9	9	8	9
Meredith P. Gentry	6	6	6	6	6	6	6	6	6	6
Emery D. Potter	—	—	1	1	1	3	3	4	4	4
Horace Mann	2	2	2	2	2	2	2	2	2	2
William A. Richardson	—	—	—	—	2	2	3	2	2	3
Chauncey F. Cleveland	1	1	2	2	1	1	1	1	1	1
Frederick P. Stanton	—	1	1	1	1	1	1	1	1	2
James A. Seddon	1	1	1	2	—	—	—	—	—	—

(Continued on next page)

(*Continued*)

Date:	12/3/1849				12/4					
Ballot:	1	2	3	4	5	6	7	8	9	10
Scattering	4	4	3	2	3	2	2	3	3	1
Total votes	221	221	221	221	224	224	224	224	224	224
Necessary for a choice	111	111	111	111	113	113	113	113	113	113

Date:	12/5				12/6				12/7	
Ballot:	11	12	13	14	15	16	17	18	19	20
Robert C. Winthrop	97	97	98	99	101	100	100	99	102	102
Howell Cobb	98	97	93	89	89	73	66	63	63	62
William A. Richardson	4	4	6	8	9	19	25	27	29	28
Emery D. Potter	4	5	9	10	10	16	17	18	15	18
Meredith P. Gentry	5	5	5	5	5	5	5	5	5	5
Amos Tuck	—	—	—	—	7	8	8	9	—	—
Joseph M. Root	7	7	7	7	—	1	—	—	—	—
David Wilmot	—	—	—	—	—	—	—	—	8	7
Chauncey F. Cleveland	2	2	2	3	2	2	1	1	—	—
Horace Mann	2	2	1	—	—	—	—	—	—	—
Scattering	4	4	2	2	2	1	3	3	3	3
Total votes	223	223	223	223	225	225	225	225	225	225
Necessary for a choice	112	112	112	111	113	113	113	113	113	113

Date:	12/7		12/8						12/10	
Ballot:	21	22	23	24	25	26	27	28	29	30
Robert C. Winthrop	101	102	102	102	102	102	102	101	102	102
Emery D. Potter	19	18	29	40	48	61	70	76	76	77
Howell Cobb	66	65	31	16	9	7	6	5	5	5
William Richardson	23	23	23	16	12	6	5	4	1	1
Linn Boyd	—	—	3	14	22	22	17	14	5	4
David Wilmot	7	7	7	7	8	7	7	7	6	6
Meredith P. Gentry	5	5	4	5	5	5	5	5	5	5
James S. Green	—	—	—	1	—	—	—	1	10	12
Daniel F. Miller	—	—	5	8	8	—	—	—	—	—
John K. Miller	—	—	—	—	—	6	5	3	3	4
Thomas H. Bayly	—	—	2	3	2	2	2	2	1	1
William Strong	—	2	5	5	—	—	—	—	—	—
Richard K. Meade	—	—	2	2	1	1	1	1	1	1
John A. McClernand	1	1	2	1	2	1	—	1	—	—
James McDowell	—	—	3	2	1	—	—	—	—	—
William J. Brown	—	—	—	—	1	—	—	—	2	2
David T. Disney	—	—	2	1	—	—	—	—	—	—
Scattering	3	2	4	2	4	5	5	4	7	4
Total votes	225	225	224	225	225	225	225	224	224	224
Necessary for a choice	113	113	113	113	113	113	113	113	113	113

Date:	12/10		12/11							12/12
Ballot:	31	32	33	34	35	36	37	38	39	40
Robert C. Winthrop	101	101	101	101	101	101	100	100	101	17
William J. Brown	2	53	80	84	88	97	107	109	109	112
Emery D. Potter	78	1	—	—	—	—	—	—	—	—
Linn Boyd	5	15	15	12	12	7	1	1	1	3
David Wilmot	6	6	5	5	5	5	6	6	7	—
Charles S. Morehead	—	—	—	—	5	5	5	5	5	17
Howell Cobb	5	10	5	5	5	4	—	—	—	—
David T. Disney	—	13	8	7	4	—	—	—	—	—
William Duer	—	—	—	—	—	—	—	—	—	26
Meredith P. Gentry	5	5	5	5	—	—	—	—	—	—
Edward Stanly	—	—	—	—	—	—	—	—	—	18
James S. Green	10	5	—	—	—	—	—	—	—	—
Edward McGaughey	—	—	—	—	—	—	—	—	—	13
Horace Mann	—	1	1	1	1	1	1	1	—	5
John K. Miller	3	3	—	—	—	—	—	—	—	—
Samuel F. Vinton	—	—	—	—	—	—	—	1	1	2
Thomas H. Bayly	2	—	1	1	—	—	—	—	—	—
George W. Julian	—	—	—	—	—	—	—	—	—	3
James Thompson	—	3	—	—	—	—	—	—	—	—
William Strong	—	3	—	—	—	—	—	—	—	—
Joseph R. Chandler	—	—	—	—	—	—	—	—	—	2
Thaddeus Stevens	—	—	—	—	—	—	—	—	—	2
Scattering	7	5	3	3	3	4	3	2	2	6
Total votes	224	224	224	224	224	224	223	225	226	226
Necessary for a choice	113	113	113	113	113	113	112	113	114	114

Date:	12/13		12/14		12/15			12/17		
Ballot:	41	42	43	44	45	46	47	48	49	50
Linn Boyd	26	51	68	82	82	85	85	86	87	87
Robert C. Winthrop	59	36	25	27	20	14	10	70	72	75
Edward Stanly	21	30	40	49	55	67	66	3	1	1
Emery D. Potter	24	24	24	22	22	17	18	17	14	15
Thaddeus Stevens	4	11	13	12	24	23	27	18	11	9
Charles S. Morehead	11	9	10	6	8	5	4	16	22	18
Howell Cobb	40	18	6	1	1	1	1	1	1	1
William Strong	1	—	—	2	3	5	2	3	4	3
David Wilmot	4	6	6	6	—	—	—	—	—	—
David T. Disney	1	2	—	—	1	3	3	4	5	3
Robert M. McLane	2	8	7	—	—	—	—	—	—	1
William Duer	—	5	5	3	1	1	1	—	—	—
David Outlaw	1	2	3	2	1	1	1	2	1	2
Charles M. Conrad	1	—	3	—	—	—	1	1	2	2
George W. Julian	2	2	2	2	—	—	—	—	1	1
Edward McGaughey	3	3	1	1	—	—	—	—	—	—

(Continued on next page)

(*Continued*)

Date:	12/13	12/14			12/15			12/17		
Ballot:	41	42	43	44	45	46	47	48	49	50
Henry W. Hilliard	2	3	2	1	—	—	—	—	—	—
Thomas H. Bayly	6	—	—	—	—	—	—	—	—	—
John A. McClernand	2	1	1	1	1	—	—	—	—	—
Edward D. Baker	—	1	2	1	1	—	—	—	—	—
James McDowell	2	2	1	—	—	—	—	—	—	—
Humphrey Marshall	1	2	1	—	—	—	—	—	—	—
Robert C. Schenck	2	—	—	1	1	—	—	—	—	—
Samuel F. Vinton	—	2	1	—	—	—	—	—	—	1
Willis A. Gorman	2	1	—	—	—	—	—	—	—	—
Scattering	8	6	4	4	5	4	5	2	2	2
Total votes	225	225	225	223	226	226	224	223	223	221
Necessary for a choice	113	113	113	112	114	114	113	112	112	111

Date:	12/17	12/18				12/19			12/20	12/22
Ballot:	51	52	53	54	55	56	57	58	59	60
Robert C. Winthrop	57	95	97	97	97	84	88	86	13	90
Linn Boyd	87	66	59	51	47	37	33	32	28	3
John A. McClernand	—	13	18	23	26	35	40	46	50	—
Howell Cobb	1	7	8	11	16	15	13	10	2	95
William Strong	4	—	—	4	16	17	17	17	15	4
Edward Stanly	2	—	—	—	—	1	—	—	75	—
Charles S. Morehead	14	4	4	5	5	4	4	4	1	4
Emery D. Potter	13	11	10	8	—	—	—	—	1	3
George W. Julian	2	7	7	4	3	4	4	5	—	—
David T. Disney	4	9	9	8	4	—	—	—	—	—
Thaddeus Stevens	6	3	2	2	2	2	2	2	2	—
David Wilmot	—	—	—	—	—	1	1	1	7	9
James G. King	5	—	—	—	—	5	5	4	—	—
Hugh White	16	—	—	—	—	—	—	—	—	—
James McDowell	—	—	—	—	—	4	5	5	2	—
Edward C. Cabell	—	1	1	—	—	1	—	1	6	4
John L. Robinson	1	2	3	3	2	1	—	—	—	—
John K. Miller	—	—	—	1	—	1	1	1	6	—
Charles M. Conrad	4	—	—	—	—	2	2	1	1	—
Henry W. Hilliard	1	—	—	1	2	1	2	1	—	—
Edward McGaughey	—	—	—	—	—	1	1	1	1	3
Robert C. Schenck	3	—	—	—	—	—	—	—	3	—
Robert M. McLane	1	1	2	1	—	—	—	—	1	—
Edward D. Baker	—	1	1	—	—	3	—	—	—	—
Christopher Williams	—	—	—	—	—	—	—	2	—	—
William H. Bissell	—	—	—	—	—	2	2	1	—	—
Scattering	1	3	2	3	2	3	3	4	4	2
Total votes	222	223	223	222	222	224	223	224	218	217
Necessary for a choice	112	112	112	112	112	113	112	113	110	109

Date:		12/22	
Ballot:	61	62	63
Howell Cobb	96	97	102
Robert C. Winthrop	92	97	100
David Wilmot	9	9	8
Charles S. Morehead	4	4	4
William Strong	4	4	3
Emery D. Potter	3	3	1
Linn Boyd	3	3	1
Edward C. Cabell	2	2	—
Edward McGaughey	3	—	—
Scattering	4	2	3
Total votes	220	221	221
Necessary for a choice	111	111	—

Source: *House Journal*, 31-1, 8–163.

Note: William Hebard is recorded as having voted for both Winthrop and Cobb on the 21st ballot. Hebard, a Whig, voted for Winthrop on every other ballot for Speaker. Cobb was elected Speaker on the 63rd ballot under a plurality rule resolution adopted by the House. Immediately following the 63rd ballot, Edward Stanly offered the resolution that "Howell Cobb, a representative from the State of Georgia, be declared duly elected Speaker of the House of Representatives for the thirty-first Congress," which passed on a 149–35 vote (*House Journal*, 31-1, 163–64).

32ND CONGRESS (ELECTION DATE: DECEMBER 1, 1851)

Linn Boyd (D-Ky.) was elected on the first ballot. Boyd received 118 votes to 22 for Edward Stanly, 21 for Joseph R. Chandler, 15 for Thaddeus Stephens, 9 for Thomas Bayly, 6 for John L. Taylor, 4 for Alexander Evans, 4 for Thomas S. Bocock, 3 for Meredith P. Gentry, 2 for Junius Hillyer, 1 for John W. Howe, 1 for Willis A. Gorman, 1 for Richard I. Bowie, 1 for David Outlaw, 1 for John Allison, 1 for William S. Ashe, 1 for E. Carrington Cabell, 1 for James Meacham, 1 for Preston King, and 1 for George W. Jones. (Total votes: 214. Necessary for a choice: 108.)

Source: *House Journal*, 32-1, 8–10.

33RD CONGRESS (ELECTION DATE: DECEMBER 5, 1853)

Linn Boyd (D-Ky.) was elected on the first ballot. Boyd received 143 votes to 35 for Joseph R. Chandler, 11 for Lewis D. Campbell, 7 for Presley Ewing, 6 for Solomon Haven, 4 for James L. Orr, 3 for John G. Miller, 3 for William Preston, 2 for Thomas M. Howe, 1 for William S. Ashe, 1 for John S. Millson, and 1 for John C. Breckinridge. (Total votes: 217. Necessary for a choice: 109.)

Source: *House Journal*, 33-1, 8–10.

34TH CONGRESS (ELECTION DATE: FEBRUARY 2, 1856)
Nathaniel Banks (R-Mass.) was elected on the 133rd ballot.

Date:	12/3				12/4				
Ballot:	1	2	3	4	5	6	7	8	9
Richardson (D-Ill.)	74	74	74	72	78	75	75	75	75
Campbell (R-Ohio)	53	55	55	56	58	57	54	51	51
Marshall (A-Ky.)	30	30	30	30	19	18	20	18	16
Banks (R-Mass.)	21	22	23	22	23	25	28	32	31
Fuller (A-Pa.)	17	18	18	17	20	22	20	20	21
Pennington (R-N.J.)	7	7	8	8	8	9	10	9	10
Scattering	23	18	16	17	18	17	17	17	19
Total Votes	225	224	224	222	224	223	224	222	223
Necessary for a Choice	113	113	113	112	111	112	113	112	112

Date:	12/5					
Ballot:	10	11	12	13	14	15
Richardson (D-Ill.)	72	74	73	74	74	74
Campbell (R-Ohio)	48	47	75	79	81	80
Marshall (A-Ky.)	25	26	21	22	13	6
Banks (R-Mass.)	32	37	12	9	8	8
Fuller (A-Pa.)	21	19	19	21	21	19
Pennington (R-N.J.)	9	9	6	7	5	7
Scattering	13	11	13	10	21	25
Total Votes	220	223	219	222	223	219
Necessary for a Choice	111	112	110	112	112	110

Date:	12/6					
Ballot:	16	17	18	19	20	21
Richardson (D-Ill.)	72	73	72	71	71	71
Campbell (R-Ohio)	79	69	62	57	48	46
Banks (R-Mass.)	6	14	18	18	23	21
Fuller (A-Pa.)	20	21	21	23	22	21
Pennington (R-N.J.)	9	10	11	14	19	20
Scattering	36	31	33	31	33	32
Total Votes	222	218	217	214	216	211
Necessary for a Choice	112	110	109	108	109	106

Date:	12/7						12/8		
Ballot:	22	23	24	25	26	27	28	29	30
Richardson (D-Ill.)	73	73	74	72	72	73	73	73	73
Campbell (R-Ohio)	74	75	1	1	1	1	0	0	0
Banks (R-Mass.)	11	10	41	44	46	49	86	97	98
Fuller (A-Pa.)	20	16	19	22	27	28	26	18	28
Pennington (R-N.J.)	9	9	18	18	17	17	8	6	5
Scattering	34	38	67	62	58	47	26	27	15
Total Votes	221	221	220	219	221	215	219	221	219
Necessary for a Choice	111	111	111	110	111	108	110	111	110

Date:	12/8			12/10					
Ballot:	31	32	33	34	35	36	37	38	39
Richardson (D-Ill.)	72	72	73	74	76	76	76	75	76
Banks (R-Mass.)	99	100	100	100	105	106	106	107	107
Fuller (A-Pa.)	29	30	30	31	29	29	28	28	28
Scattering	21	19	19	16	15	15	14	15	15
Total Votes	221	221	222	221	225	226	224	225	226
Necessary for a Choice	111	111	112	111	113	114	113	113	114

Date:	12/11					
Ballot:	40	41	42	43	44	45
Richardson (D-Ill.)	74	74	75	75	74	74
Banks (R-Mass.)	107	107	106	107	107	106
Fuller (A-Pa.)	27	28	27	28	28	27
Scattering	16	16	17	16	16	16
Total Votes	224	225	225	226	225	223
Necessary for a Choice	113	113	113	114	113	112

Date:	12/12					12/13				
Ballot:	46	47	48	49	50	51	52	53	54	55
Richardson (D-Ill.)	74	74	74	75	75	75	75	74	74	73
Banks (R-Mass.)	106	106	105	105	105	105	104	104	104	104
Fuller (A-Pa.)	33	32	32	35	33	33	32	34	35	38
Scattering	11	11	12	9	11	11	11	10	9	7
Total Votes	224	223	223	224	224	224	222	222	222	222
Necessary for a Choice	113	112	112	113	113	113	112	112	112	112

(Continued on next page)

348

(*Continued*)

Date:		12/14			12/15
Ballot:	56	57	58	59	60
Richardson (D-Ill.)	73	74	73	74	74
Banks (R-Mass.)	106	106	106	105	105
Fuller (A-Pa.)	40	41	41	41	40
Scattering	5	5	5	4	5
Total Votes	224	226	225	224	224
Necessary for a Choice	113	114	113	113	113

Date:	12/15		12/17			12/19		12/20	12/24
Ballot:	61	62	63	64	65	66	67	68
Richardson (D-Ill.)	74	73	73	73	73	75	73	72
Banks (R-Mass.)	105	106	105	106	102	106	103	101
Fuller (A-Pa.)	40	37	38	38	38	34	34	31
Scattering	7	7	7	6	6	9	11	11
Total Votes	226	223	223	223	219	224	221	215
Necessary for a Choice	114	112	112	112	110	113	111	108

Date:		12/27			12/28		
Ballot:	69	70	71	72	73	74	75
Richardson (D-Ill.)	66	67	67	67	68	68	68
Banks (R-Mass.)	100	103	103	103	101	100	101
Fuller (A-Pa.)	30	31	31	31	30	31	31
Scattering	9	10	10	10	8	8	8
Total Votes	205	211	211	211	207	207	208
Necessary for a Choice	103	106	106	106	104	104	105

Date:	12/28				12/29				
Ballot:	76	77	78	79	80	81	82	83	84
Richardson (D-Ill.)	67	68	68	68	68	68	68	67	66
Banks (R-Mass.)	101	101	103	102	101	102	100	99	98
Fuller (A-Pa.)	31	32	32	31	30	30	30	29	29
Scattering	9	8	8	8	9	9	10	10	10
Total Votes	208	209	211	209	208	209	208	205	203
Necessary for a Choice	105	105	106	105	105	105	105	103	102

Date:	1/2		1/3						
Ballot:	85	86	87	88	89	90			
Richardson (D-Ill.)	72	71	73	73	73	72			
Banks (R-Mass.)	103	101	102	102	102	101			
Fuller (A-Pa.)	32	30	33	33	33	30			
Scattering	11	11	11	11	11	11			
Total Votes	218	213	219	219	219	214			
Necessary for a Choice	110	107	110	110	110	108			

Date:	1/4		1/5		1/7				
Ballot:	91	92	93	94	95	96	97	98	
Richardson (D-Ill.)	73	73	72	72	73	73	73	72	
Banks (R-Mass.)	104	104	105	98	101	99	97	99	
Fuller (A-Pa.)	34	34	32	29	29	30	30	30	
Scattering	10	10	10	11	11	12	14	15	
Total Votes	221	221	219	210	214	214	214	216	
Necessary for a Choice	111	111	110	106	108	108	108	109	

Date:	1/9								
Ballot:	99	100	101	102	103	104	105		
Richardson (D-Ill.)	72	68	65	68	67	67	63		
Banks (R-Mass.)	97	90	88	92	92	92	88		
Fuller (A-Pa.)	33	32	28	28	26	29	28		
Scattering	12	10	11	11	11	11	9		
Total Votes	214	200	192	199	196	199	188		
Necessary for a Choice	108	101	97	100	99	100	95		

Date:	1/9	1/11	1/13	1/14			1/15		
Ballot:	106	107	108	109	110	111	112	113	114
Richardson (D-Ill.)	62	70	69	66	65	64	65	65	66
Banks (R-Mass.)	88	98	94	95	95	95	92	92	93
Fuller (A-Pa.)	27	32	34	34	33	33	34	33	33
Scattering	10	12	10	16	16	16	16	16	17
Total Votes	187	212	207	211	209	208	207	206	209
Necessary for a Choice	94	107	104	106	105	105	104	104	105

(*Continued* on next page)

(*Continued*)

Date:	1/16	1/18	1/19	1/21		
Ballot:	115	116	117	118	119	120
Richardson (D-Ill.)	65	68	69	66	67	67
Banks (R-Mass.)	88	94	94	92	91	91
Fuller (A-Pa.)	29	32	31	31	29	28
Scattering	13	9	8	8	8	8
Total Votes	195	203	202	197	195	194
Necessary for a Choice	98	102	102	99	98	98

Date:	1/21	1/23	1/24		1/25		
Ballot:	121	122	123	124	125	126	127
Richardson (D-Ill.)	67	65	0	0	0	0	0
Banks (R-Mass.)	91	90	96	95	94	94	94
Fuller (A-Pa.)	29	30	12	25	28	29	25
Orr (D-S.C.)	0	0	68	68	66	65	64
Aiken (D-S.C.)	0	0	0	0	0	0	0
Scattering	8	9	27	13	12	11	12
Total Votes	195	194	203	201	200	199	195
Necessary for a Choice	98	98	102	101	101	100	98

Date:	1/28	1/29	2/2			
Ballot:	128	129	130	131	132	133
Richardson (D-Ill.)	0	0	0	0	0	0
Banks (R-Mass.)	97	99	102	102	102	103
Fuller (A-Pa.)	35	34	14	13	13	6
Orr (D-S.C.)	67	69	0	0	0	0
Aiken (D-S.C.)	0	0	93	93	92	100
Scattering	7	8	6	6	6	5
Total Votes	206	210	215	214	213	214
Necessary for a Choice	104	106	108	108	107	--

Source: *House Journal*, 34-1, 8–444.

35TH CONGRESS (ELECTION DATE: DECEMBER 7, 1857)
James L. Orr (D-S.C.) was elected on the first ballot. Orr received 128 votes to 84 for Galusha A. Grow, 3 for Lewis D. Campbell, 3 for Felix K. Zollicoffer, 2 for Henry Winter Davis, 2 for James B. Ricaud, 1 for Valentine B. Horton, 1 for Francis P. Blair Jr., and 1 for Humphrey Marshall. (Total votes: 225. Necessary for a choice: 113.)
Source: *House Journal*, 35-1, 8–10.

36TH CONGRESS (ELECTION DATE: FEBRUARY 1, 1860)
William Pennington (R-N.J.) was elected on the 44th ballot.

Date:	12/5	12/7	12/9	12/14	12/15	
Ballot:	1	2	3	4	5	6
Thomas S. Bocock (D-Va.)	86	88	88	86	85	85
John Sherman (R-Ohio)	66	107	110	108	110	110
Galusha A. Grow (R-Pa.)	43	0	0	0	0	0
Alexander R. Boteler (A-Va.)	14	1	2	1	1	5
John A. Gilmer (A-N.C.)	3	22	20	22	22	18
Scattering	18	13	11	10	8	8
Total Votes	230	231	231	227	226	226
Necessary for a Choice	116	116	116	114	114	114

Date:	12/16		12/17		12/19
Ballot:	7	8	9	10	11
Thomas S. Bocock (D-Va.)	86	83	85	84	85
John Sherman (R-Ohio)	96	111	111	111	112
Galusha A. Grow (R-Pa.)	0	0	0	0	0
Alexander R. Boteler (A-Va.)	1	25	23	15	21
John A. Gilmer (A-N.C.)	36	1	1	1	1
Scattering	8	8	8	17	11
Total Votes	227	228	228	228	230
Necessary for a Choice	114	115	115	115	116

Date:	12/19		12/20			12/21
Ballot:	12	13	14	15	16	17
Thomas S. Bocock (D-Va.)	19	12	8	7	6	0
John Sherman (R-Ohio)	112	110	111	110	109	106
Alexander R. Boteler (A-Va.)	29	31	39	43	38	0
John A. Gilmer (A-N.C.)	1	1	3	2	2	6
John G. Davis (AL-Ind.)	7	13	8	14	7	4
John S. Phelps (D-Mo.)	16	6	0	2	1	0
John McQueen (D-S.C.)	3	2	3	3	1	3
William Barksdale (D-Miss.)	5	20	15	10	5	0
William Maclay (D-N.Y.)	5	1	0	0	4	0
Miles Taylor (D-La.)	12	7	6	2	2	0
George Houston (D-Ala.)	2	1	3	1	7	0
John McClernand (D-Ill.)	2	4	21	25	28	1
John S. Millson (D-Va.)	0	0	0	0	0	95
Charles Scott (D-Calif.)	0	0	0	0	0	0
Scattering	17	18	12	7	13	10
Total Votes	230	226	229	226	223	225
Necessary for a Choice	116	114	115	114	112	114

(*Continued on next page*)

(*Continued*)

Date:	12/22		12/23	12/24	12/27
Ballot:	18	19	20	21	22
Thomas S. Bocock (D-Va.)	0	1	10	20	14
John Sherman (R-Ohio)	95	108	103	100	101
Alexander R. Boteler (A-Va.)	0	0	0	0	0
John A. Gilmer (A-N.C.)	36	21	19	17	14
John G. Davis (AL-Ind.)	4	5	7	11	5
John S. Phelps (D-Mo.)	1	1	1	1	1
John McQueen (D-S.C.)	1	1	3	1	1
William Barksdale (D-Miss.)	0	0	2	1	2
William Maclay (D-N.Y.)	1	0	1	9	12
Miles Taylor (D-La.)	0	0	2	0	0
George Houston (D-Ala.)	1	3	8	17	15
John McClernand (D-Ill.)	0	0	1	3	0
John S. Millson (D-Va.)	79	69	27	2	0
Charles Scott (D-Calif.)	0	0	0	3	17
Scattering	5	13	28	21	26
Total Votes	223	222	212	206	208
Necessary for a Choice	112	112	107	104	105

Date:	12/28	12/29	1/4	1/5		1/6
Ballot:	23	24	25	26	27	28
Thomas S. Bocock (D-Va.)	7	0	7	2	56	32
John Sherman (R-Oh.)	101	102	101	104	103	109
John A. Gilmer (KN-N.C.)	2	14	14	17	9	4
John G. Davis (AL-Ind.)	4	3	9	3	6	9
John McClernand (D-Ill.)	5	0	33	2	9	37
Horace Maynard (O-Tenn.)	65	0	0	0	0	0
Clement Vallandingham (D-Ohio)	2	0	12	69	2	0
Charles Scott (D-Calif.)	3	83	0	0	0	0
Andrew J. Hamilton (ID-Tex.)	1	0	0	0	1	0
Scattering	18	8	31	16	25	32
Total Votes	208	210	207	213	211	223
Necessary for a Choice	105	106	104	107	106	112

Date:	1/7	1/9			1/11
Ballot:	29	30	31	32	33
Thomas S. Bocock (D-Va.)	0	0	0	0	0
John Sherman (R-Oh.)	103	105	105	105	108
John A. Gilmer (KN-N.C.)	14	22	19	18	19
John G. Davis (AL-Ind.)	0	0	1	1	4
John McClernand (D-Ill.)	0	0	0	0	0
Horace Maynard (O-Tenn.)	0	0	0	0	0

Date:	1/7	1/9			1/11	
Ballot:	29	30	31	32	33	
Clement Vallandingham (D-Ohio)	0	0	0	0	0	
Charles Scott (D-Calif.)	0	0	0	0	0	
Andrew J. Hamilton (ID-Tex.)	89	88	88	88	81	
Scattering	5	4	6	7	9	
Total Votes	211	219	219	219	221	
Necessary for a Choice	106	110	110	110	111	

Date:	1/11	1/25	1/26			1/27
Ballot:	34	35	36	37	38	39
Thomas S. Bocock (D-Va.)	1	51	58	55	51	1
John Sherman (R-Oh.)	106	105	109	110	109	106
John A. Gilmer (KN-N.C.)	25	3	2	1	4	0
John G. Davis (AL-Ind.)	8	6	5	7	7	1
William Pennington (R-N.J.)	0	0	0	0	1	1
John McClernand (D-Ill.)	0	0	3	3	2	0
William N. H. Smith (O-N.C.)	1	26	37	36	33	112
Andrew J. Hamilton (ID-Tex.)	75	4	0	0	0	0
Scattering	5	20	12	14	19	7
Total Votes	221	215	226	226	226	228
Necessary for a Choice	111	108	114	114	114	115

Date:	1/30			1/31	2/1
Ballot:	40	41	42	43	44
Thomas S. Bocock (D-Va.)	1	1	0	1	0
John Sherman (R-Oh.)	0	0	0	0	0
John A. Gilmer (KN-N.C.)	0	0	0	5	16
John G. Davis (AL-Ind.)	2	2	1	0	0
William Pennington (R-N.J.)	115	115	115	116	117
John McClernand (D-Ill.)	0	0	2	91	85
William N. H. Smith (O-N.C.)	113	113	113	1	4
Andrew J. Hamilton (ID-Tex.)	0	0	0	0	0
Scattering	3	1	2	19	11
Total Votes	234	232	233	233	233
Necessary for a Choice	118	117	117	117	117

Source: *House Journal*, 36-1, 8–164.

37TH CONGRESS (ELECTION DATE: JULY 4, 1861)
  Galusha A. Grow (R-Pa.) was elected on the first ballot. Grow received
  99 votes to 12 for John J. Crittenden, 11 for Francis P. Blair Jr., 7 for
  John S. Phelps, 7 for Clement L. Vallandingham, 7 for Erastus Corn-
  ing, 6 for Samuel S. Cox, 3 for William A. Richardson, 2 for John A.

McClernand, 1 for John W. Crisfield, 1 for Charles B. Calvert, 1 for Hendrick B. Wright, 1 for John W. Noell, and 1 for George H. Pendleton. (Total votes: 159. Necessary for a choice: 80).
Source: *House Journal*, 37-1, 8–9; *Congressional Globe*, 37-1, 4.

38TH CONGRESS (ELECTION DATE: DECEMBER 7, 1863)

Schuyler Colfax (R-Ind.) was elected on the first ballot. Colfax received 101 votes to 42 for Samuel S. Cox, 12 for John L. Dawson, 10 for Robert Mallory, 8 for Henry G. Stebbins, 6 for Austin A. King, 2 for Francis P. Blair Jr., and 1 for John D. Stiles. (Total votes: 182. Necessary for a choice: 92.)
Source: *House Journal*, 38-1, 9–11; *Congressional Globe*, 38-1, 6–7.
Note: *Congressional Globe* miscounts total votes as 181.

39TH CONGRESS (ELECTION DATE: DECEMBER 4, 1865)

Schuyler Colfax (R-Ind.) was elected on the first ballot. Colfax received 139 votes to 36 for James Brooks. (Total votes: 175. Necessary for a choice: 88.)
Source: *House Journal*, 39-1, 7–8; *Congressional Globe*, 39-1, 5.

40TH CONGRESS (ELECTION DATE: MARCH 4, 1867)

Schuyler Colfax (R-Ind.) was elected on the first ballot. Colfax received 127 votes to 30 for Samuel S. Marshall. (Total votes: 157. Necessary for a choice: 79)
Source: *House Journal*, 40-1, 6–7; *Congressional Globe*, 40-1, 4.
Note: Colfax resigned the speakership on March 3, 1869. *Congressional Globe*, 40-3, 1867–68.

40TH CONGRESS—REPLACEMENT ELECTION (ELECTION DATE: MARCH 3, 1869)

Theodore M. Pomeroy (R-N.Y.) was elected unanimously via resolution moved by Henry L. Dawes (R-Mass.).
Source: *House Journal*, 40-3, 513; *Congressional Globe*, 40-3, 1868.
Note: Pomeroy served a single day as Speaker.

41ST CONGRESS (ELECTION DATE: MARCH 4, 1869)

James G. Blaine (R-Maine) was elected on the first ballot. Blaine received 135 votes to 57 for Michael C. Kerr. (Total votes: 192. Necessary for a choice: 97.)
Source: *House Journal*, 41-1, 8–9; *Congressional Globe*, 41-1, 4–5.

42ND CONGRESS (ELECTION DATE: MARCH 4, 1871)

James G. Blaine (R-Maine) was elected on the first ballot. Blaine received 126 votes to 93 for George W. Morgan. (Total votes: 219. Necessary to a choice: 110.)

Source: *House Journal*, 42-1, 7–9; *Congressional Globe*, 42-1, 6.
Note: *Congressional Globe* reports 92 votes for Morgan.

43RD CONGRESS (ELECTION DATE: DECEMBER 1, 1873)
James G. Blaine (R-Maine) was elected on the first ballot. Blaine received 189 votes to 76 for Fernando Wood, 2 for Samuel S. Cox, 1 for Hester Clymer, and 1 for Alexander A. Stephens. (Total votes: 269. Necessary for a choice: 135.)
Source: *House Journal*, 43-1, 9–10; *Congressional Record*, 43-1, 6.

44TH CONGRESS (ELECTION DATE: DECEMBER 6, 1875)
Michael C. Kerr (D-Ind.) was elected on the first ballot. Kerr received 173 votes to 106 for James G. Blaine, 1 for Alexander Campbell, 1 for William B. Anderson, and 1 for Alpheus S. Williams. (Total votes: 282. Necessary for a choice: 142.)
Source: *Congressional Record*, 44-1, 167.
Note: Kerr died between sessions of the 44th Congress.

44TH CONGRESS—REPLACEMENT ELECTION (ELECTION DATE: DECEMBER 4, 1876)
Samuel J. Randall (D-Pa.) was elected on the first ballot. Randall received 162 votes to 82 for James A. Garfield, 1 for Charles G. Williams, 1 for W. R. Morrison, and 1 for George F. Hoar. (Total votes: 247. Necessary for a choice: 124.)
Source: *Congressional Record*, 44-2, 6.
Note: *Congressional Record* miscounts total votes as 246 and necessary to a choice as 114.

45TH CONGRESS (ELECTION DATE: OCTOBER 15, 1877)
Samuel J. Randall (D-Pa.) was elected on the first ballot. Randall received 149 votes to 132 for James A. Garfield. (Total votes: 281. Necessary for a choice: 141.)
Source: *Congressional Record*, 45-1, 53.

46TH CONGRESS (ELECTION DATE: MARCH 18, 1879)
Samuel J. Randall (D-Pa.) was elected on the first ballot. Randall received 144 votes to 125 for James A. Garfield, 13 for Hendrick B. Wright, and 1 for William D. Kelley (Total votes: 283. Necessary to a choice: 142.)
Source: *Congressional Record*, 46-1, 5.

47TH CONGRESS (ELECTION DATE: DECEMBER 5, 1881)
J. Warren Keifer (R-Ohio) was elected on the first ballot. Keifer received 148 votes to 129 for Samuel J. Randall and 8 for Nicholas Ford (Total votes: 285. Necessary for a choice: 143.)

Source: Congressional Record, 47-1, 8–9.
Note: Congressional Record notes 8 members not voting.

48TH CONGRESS (ELECTION DATE: DECEMBER 3, 1883)
John G. Carlisle (D-Ky.) was elected on the first ballot. Carlisle received 190 votes to 113 for J. Warren Keifer, 2 for George D. Robinson, 1 for E. S. Lacey, 1 for J. W. Wasdworth, and 1 for John S. Wise (Total votes: 308. Necessary for a choice: 155.)
Source: Congressional Record, 48-1, 4–5.
Note: Congressional Record notes 13 members not voting.

49TH CONGRESS (ELECTION DATE: DECEMBER 7, 1885)
John G. Carlisle (D-Ky.) was elected on the first ballot. Carlisle received 178 votes to 138 for Thomas B. Reed (Total votes: 316. Necessary for a choice: 159.)
Source: Congressional Record, 49-1, 106–7.
Note: Congressional Record notes 9 members not voting.

50TH CONGRESS (ELECTION DATE: DECEMBER 5, 1887)
John G. Carlisle (D-Ky.) was elected on the first ballot. Carlisle received 163 votes to 147 for Thomas B. Reed and 2 for Charles N. Brumm. (Total votes: 312. Necessary for a choice: 157.)
Source: Congressional Record, 50-1, 6.
Note: Congressional Record notes 13 members not voting.

51ST CONGRESS (ELECTION DATE: DECEMBER 2, 1889)
Thomas B. Reed (R-Maine) was elected on the first ballot. Reed received 166 votes to 154 for John G. Carlisle and 1 for Amos J. Cummings. (Total votes: 321. Necessary for a choice: 161.)
Source: Congressional Record, 51-1, 80–81.

52ND CONGRESS (ELECTION DATE: DECEMBER 8, 1891)
Charles F. Crisp (D-Ga.) was elected on the first ballot. Crisp received 228 votes to 83 for Thomas B. Reed and 8 for Thomas E. Watson. (Total votes: 319. Necessary for a choice: 160.)
Source: Congressional Record, 52-1, 7–8.
Note: Congressional Record notes 12 members not voting.

53RD CONGRESS (ELECTION DATE: AUGUST 7, 1893)
Charles F. Crisp (D-Ga.) was elected on the first ballot. Crisp received 213 votes to 121 for Thomas B. Reed and 8 for Jerry Simpson. (Total votes: 342. Necessary for a choice: 122.)
Source: Congressional Record, 53-1, 201.
Note: Congressional Record reports that 343 votes were cast. It also

lists eight names under Simpson's column while reporting a vote total of seven. The *New York Times* (August 8, 1893, 2) reports 343 votes cast, with Crisp receiving 214, Reed 122, and Simpson 7, but provides no individual votes.

54TH CONGRESS (ELECTION DATE: DECEMBER 2, 1895)
Thomas B. Reed (R-Maine) was elected on the first ballot. Reed received 240 votes to 95 for Charles F. Crisp, 6 for John C. Bell, and 1 for David B. Culberson. (Total votes: 342. Necessary for a choice: 172.)
Source: *Congressional Record*, 54-1, 3–4.

55TH CONGRESS (ELECTION DATE: MARCH 15, 1897)
Thomas B. Reed (R-Maine) was elected on the first ballot. Reed received 200 votes to 114 for Joseph W. Bailey, 21 for John C. Bell, and 1 for Francis G. Newlands. (Total votes: 336. Necessary for a choice: 169.)
Source: *Congressional Record*, 55-1, 15.

56TH CONGRESS (ELECTION DATE: DECEMBER 4, 1899)
David B. Henderson (R-Iowa) was elected on the first ballot. Henderson received 181 votes to 156 for James D. Richardson, 4 for John C. Bell, and 2 for Francis G. Newlands. (Total votes: 343. Necessary for a choice: 172.)
Source: *Congressional Record*, 56-1, 4–5.
Note: *Congressional Record* notes 12 members not voting.
Note: The House Clerk in the *Congressional Record* reports that tellers announced the following tally: Henderson 177, Richardson 153, Bell 4, and Newlands 2. The individual accounting, however, corresponds to the 181 (Henderson) and 156 (Richardson) reported above.

57TH CONGRESS (ELECTION DATE: DECEMBER 2, 1901)
David B. Henderson (R-Iowa) was elected on the first ballot. Henderson received 192 votes to 152 for James D. Richardson, 1 for William L. Stark, and 1 for Amos J. Cummings. (Total votes: 346. Necessary for a choice: 174.)
Source: *Congressional Record*, 57-1, 44.
Note: *Congressional Record* notes 9 members not voting.

58TH CONGRESS (ELECTION DATE: NOVEMBER 9, 1903)
Joseph G. Cannon (R-Ill.) was elected on the first ballot. Cannon received 198 votes to 167 for John Sharp Williams. (Total votes: 365. Necessary for a choice: 183.)
Source: *Congressional Record*, 58-1, 147–48.
Note: *Congressional Record* notes 19 members not voting.

59TH CONGRESS (ELECTION DATE: DECEMBER 4, 1905)
Joseph G. Cannon (R-Ill.) was elected on the first ballot. Cannon received 243 votes to 128 for John Sharp Williams. (Total votes: 371. Necessary for a choice: 186.)
Source: *Congressional Record*, 59-1, 40–41.
Note: *Congressional Record* notes 15 members not voting.

60TH CONGRESS (ELECTION DATE: DECEMBER 2, 1907)
Joseph G. Cannon (R-Ill.) was elected on the first ballot. Cannon received 213 votes to 162 for John Sharp Williams. (Total votes: 375. Necessary to a choice: 188.)
Source: *Congressional Record*, 60-1, 4–5.
Note: *Congressional Record* notes 13 members not voting.

61ST CONGRESS (ELECTION DATE: MARCH 15, 1909)
Joseph G. Cannon (R-Ill.) was elected on the first ballot. Cannon received 204 votes to 166 for Champ Clark, 8 for Henry A. Cooper, 2 for George W. Norris, 1 for John J. Esch, and 1 for William P. Hepburn. (Total votes: 382. Necessary for a choice: 192.)
Source: *Congressional Record*, 61-1, 18.
Note: *Congressional Record* notes 7 members not voting.

62ND CONGRESS (ELECTION DATE: APRIL 4, 1911)
Champ Clark (D-Mo.) was elected on the first ballot. Clark received 220 votes to 131 for James A. Mann, 16 for Henry A. Cooper, and 1 for George W. Norris. (Total votes: 368. Necessary for a choice: 185.)
Source: *Congressional Record*, 62-1, 6–7.
Note: *Congressional Record* notes 1 member voting "present." This was not included in the total number of votes cast, as it would be later (beginning in 1915).

63RD CONGRESS (ELECTION DATE: APRIL 7, 1913)
Champ Clark (D-Mo.) was elected on the first ballot. Clark received 272 votes to 111 for James A. Mann, 18 for Victor Murdock, 4 for Henry A. Cooper, and 1 for John M. Nelson. (Total votes: 406. Necessary for a choice: 204.)
Source: *Congressional Record*, 63-1, 63–64.

64TH CONGRESS (ELECTION DATE: DECEMBER 6, 1915)
Champ Clark (D-Mo.) was elected on the first ballot. Clark received 222 votes to 195 for James A. Mann and 5 answering "present." (Total votes: 422. Necessary for a choice: 212.)
Source: *Congressional Record*, 64-1, 5–6.
Note: Assertions of being "present" were counted as votes by the tellers.

65TH CONGRESS (ELECTION DATE: APRIL 2, 1917)
Champ Clark (D-Mo.) was elected on the first ballot. Clark received 217 votes to 205 for James A. Mann, 2 for Frederick H. Gillett, 2 for Irvine L. Enroot, and 2 answering "present." (Total votes: 428. Necessary for a choice: 215.)
Source: Congressional Record, 65-1, 107–8.
Note: Assertions of being "present" were counted as votes by the tellers.

66TH CONGRESS (ELECTION DATE: MAY 19, 1919)
Frederick H. Gillett (R-Mass.) was elected on the first ballot. Gillett received 228 votes to 172 for Champ Clark. (Total votes: 400. Necessary for a choice: 201.)
Source: Congressional Record, 66-1, 7–8.

67TH CONGRESS (ELECTION DATE: APRIL 11, 1921)
Frederick H. Gillett (R-Mass.) was elected on the first ballot. Gillett received 297 votes to 122 for Claude Kitchin and 1 answering "present." (Total votes: 420. Necessary for a choice: 221.)
Source: Congressional Record, 67-1, 79–80.
Note: Assertion of being "present" was counted as a vote by the tellers.

68TH CONGRESS (DECEMBER 5, 1923)
Frederick H. Gillett (R-Mass.) was elected on the ninth ballot.
Source: Congressional Record, 68-1, 8–13, 15–16.
Note: Congressional Record notes 4, 3, 3, 3, 3, 3, 3, 3, and 4 members answering "present" on ballots 1 through 9, respectively. Unlike the speakership elections in the 64th, 65th, and 67th Congresses, however, these assertions of being "present" were not counted as votes by the tellers (or the Clerk).

	December 3, 1923				Dec. 4				Dec. 5
Ballot:	1	2	3	4	5	6	7	8	9
Frederick H. Gillett	197	194	195	197	197	195	196	197	215
Finis J. Garrett	195	194	196	196	197	197	198	198	197
Henry A. Cooper	17	17	17	17	17	17	17	17	—
Martin B. Madden	5	6	5	5	5	5	5	5	2
Total votes	414	411	413	415	416	414	416	417	414
Necessary for a choice	208	206	207	208	209	208	209	209	208

69TH CONGRESS (ELECTION DATE: DECEMBER 7, 1925)
Nicholas Longworth (R-Ohio) was elected on the first ballot. Longworth received 229 votes to 173 for Finis J. Garrett, and 13 for

Henry A. Cooper, and 5 answering "present." (Total votes: 420. Necessary for a choice: 221.)

Source: *Congressional Record*, 69-1, 381.

Note: Unlike the speakership election in the 68th Congress, but like the speakership elections in the 64th, 65th, and 67th Congresses, the assertions of being "present" (by 5 members) were counted as votes by the tellers.

70TH CONGRESS (ELECTION DATE: DECEMBER 5, 1927)

Nicholas Longworth (R-Ohio) was elected on the first ballot. Longworth received 225 votes to 187 for Finis J. Garrett, and 5 answering "present." (Total votes: 417. Necessary for a choice: 209.)

Source: *Congressional Record*, 70-1, 7–8.

Note: Assertions of being "present" were counted as votes by the tellers.

71ST CONGRESS (ELECTION DATE: APRIL 15, 1929)

Nicholas Longworth (R-Ohio) was elected on the first ballot. Longworth received 254 votes to 143 for John N. Garner, and 1 answering "present." (Total votes: 398. Necessary for a choice: 200.)

Source: *Congressional Record*, 71-1, 23–24.

Note: Assertion of being "present" was counted as a vote by the tellers.

72ND CONGRESS (ELECTION DATE: DECEMBER 7, 1931)

John N. Garner (D-Tex.) was elected on the first ballot. Garner received 218 votes to 207 for Bertrand H. Snell, 5 for George J. Schneider, and 3 answering "present." (Total votes: 430. Necessary for a choice: 216.)

Source: *Congressional Record*, 72-1, 8.

Note: Like the speakership election in the 68th Congress but *unlike* the speakership elections in the 64th, 65th, 67th, and 69th–71st Congresses, the assertions of being "present" were not counted as votes by the tellers.

73RD CONGRESS (ELECTION DATE: MARCH 9, 1933)

Henry T. Rainey (D-Ill.) was elected on the first ballot. Rainey received 302 votes to 110 for Bertrand H. Snell, 5 for Paul J. Kvale, and 1 answering "present." (Total votes: 418. Necessary for a choice: 210.)

Source: *Congressional Record*, 73-1, 69–70.

Note: Assertion of being "present" was counted as a vote by the tellers.

Note: Rainey died on August 19, 1934, two months after the conclusion of the 73rd Congress.

74TH CONGRESS (ELECTION DATE: JANUARY 3, 1935)

Joseph W. Byrns (D-Tenn.) was elected on the first ballot. Byrns received

317 votes to 95 for Bertrand H. Snell, 9 for George J. Schneider, 2 for
H. P. Lambertson, and 3 answering "present." (Total votes: 426. Necessary for a choice: 214.)

Source: *Congressional Record*, 74-1, 11.

Note: Assertions of being "present" were counted as votes by the tellers.

Note: Byrns died on June 4, 1936, during the second session of the 74th
Congress.

74TH CONGRESS—REPLACEMENT ELECTION (ELECTION DATE: JUNE 4,
1936)

William B. Bankhead (D-Ala.) was elected via resolution moved by John
J. O'Connor (D-N.Y.).

Source: *Congressional Record*, 74-2, 9016.

75TH CONGRESS (ELECTION DATE: JANUARY 5, 1937)

William B. Bankhead (D-Ala.) was elected on the first ballot. Bankhead
received 324 votes to 83 for Bertrand H. Snell, 10 for George J. Schneider, 2 for Fred L. Crawford, and 3 answering "present." (Total
votes: 422. Necessary for a choice: 212.)

Source: *Congressional Record*, 75-1, 11.

Note: *Congressional Record* notes the individual vote tallies above, but
reports that 421 votes were cast.

Note: Assertions of being "present" were counted as votes by the tellers.

76TH CONGRESS (ELECTION DATE: JANUARY 3, 1939)

William B. Bankhead (D-Ala.) was elected on the first ballot. Bankhead
received 249 votes to 168 for Joseph W. Martin Jr., 1 for Bernard J.
Gehrmann, 1 for Merlin Hull, and 1 answering "present." (Total
votes: 420. Necessary for a choice: 211.)

Source: *Congressional Record*, 76-1, 10–11.

Note: Assertion of being "present" was counted as a vote by the tellers.

Note: Bankhead died on September 15, 1940, during the third session
of the 76th Congress.

76TH CONGRESS—REPLACEMENT ELECTION (ELECTION DATE: SEPTEMBER
16, 1940)

Sam Rayburn (D-Tex.) was elected via resolution moved by John W.
McCormack (D-Mass.).

Source: *Congressional Record*, 76-3, 12231.

77TH CONGRESS (ELECTION DATE: JANUARY 3, 1941)

Sam Rayburn (D-Tex.) was elected on the first ballot. Rayburn received
247 votes, to 159 for Joseph W. Martin Jr., 2 for Merlin Hull, 1 for
Bernard J. Gehrmann, and 1 answering "present." (Total votes: 410.
Necessary for a choice: 206.)

Source: *Congressional Record*, 77-1, 6–7.
Note: Assertion of being "present" was counted as a vote by the tellers.

78TH CONGRESS (ELECTION DATE: JANUARY 6, 1943)
   Sam Rayburn (D-Tex.) was elected on the first ballot. Rayburn received
      217 votes to 206 for Joseph W. Martin Jr., Harry Sauthoff, 1 for
      Merlin Hull, and 1 answering "present." (Total votes: 426. Necessary
      for a choice: 214.)
   Source: *Congressional Record*, 78-1, 6.
   Note: Assertion of being "present" was counted as a vote by the tellers.

79TH CONGRESS (ELECTION DATE: JANUARY 3, 1945)
   Sam Rayburn (D-Tex.) was elected on the first ballot. Rayburn received
      224 votes to 168 for Joseph W. Martin Jr., and 2 answering "pres-
      ent." (Total votes: 394. Necessary for a choice: 198.)
   Source: *Congressional Record*, 79-1, 8.
   Note: Assertions of being "present" were counted as votes by the tellers.

80TH CONGRESS (ELECTION DATE: JANUARY 3, 1947)
   Joseph W. Martin Jr. (R-Mass.) was elected on the first ballot. Martin re-
      ceived 244 votes to 182 for Sam Rayburn. (Total votes: 426. Neces-
      sary for a choice: 214.)
   Source: *Congressional Record*, 80-1, 35.

81ST CONGRESS (ELECTION DATE: JANUARY 3, 1949)
   Sam Rayburn (D-Tex.) was elected on the first ballot. Rayburn received
      255 votes to 160 for Joseph W. Martin Jr. and 1 answering "present."
      (Total votes: 416. Necessary for a choice: 209.)
   Source: *Congressional Record*, 81-1, 8–9.
   Note: Assertion of being "present" was counted as a vote by the tellers.
   Note: *Congressional Record* notes 16 members not voting.

82ND CONGRESS (ELECTION DATE: JANUARY 3, 1951)
   Sam Rayburn (D-Tex.) was elected on the first ballot. Rayburn received
      231 votes to 192 for Joseph W. Martin Jr. and 3 answering "present."
      (Total votes: 426. Necessary for a choice: 214.)
   Source: *Congressional Record*, 82-1, 7.
   Note: Assertions of being "present" were counted as votes by the tellers.
   Note: *Congressional Record* notes 8 members not voting.

83RD CONGRESS (ELECTION DATE: JANUARY 3, 1953)
   Joseph W. Martin Jr. (R-Mass.) was elected on the first ballot. Martin re-
      ceived 220 votes to 201 for Sam Rayburn and 3 answering "present."
      (Total votes: 424. Necessary for a choice: 213.)

Source: *Congressional Record*, 83-1, 13.
Note: Assertions of being "present" were counted as votes by the tellers.
Note: *Congressional Record* notes 9 members not voting.

84TH CONGRESS (ELECTION DATE: JANUARY 5, 1955)
   Sam Rayburn (D-Tex.) was elected on the first ballot. Rayburn received
      228 votes to 198 for Joseph W. Martin Jr. and 2 answering "present."
      (Total votes: 426. Necessary for a choice: 214.)
   Source: *Congressional Record*, 84-1, 8–9.
   Note: Assertions of being "present" were *not* counted as votes by the
      tellers (similar to 68th and 72nd Congresses).
   Note: *Congressional Record* notes 6 members not voting.

85TH CONGRESS (ELECTION DATE: JANUARY 3, 1957)
   Sam Rayburn (D-Tex.) was elected on the first ballot. Rayburn received
      227 votes to 199 for Joseph W. Martin Jr. and 2 answering "present."
      (Total votes: 428. Necessary for a choice: 215.)
   Source: *Congressional Record*, 85-1, 45–46.
   Note: Assertions of being "present" were counted as votes by the tellers.
   Note: *Congressional Record* notes 5 members not voting.

86TH CONGRESS (ELECTION DATE: JANUARY 7, 1959)
   Sam Rayburn (D-Tex.) was elected on the first ballot. Rayburn received
      281 votes to 148 for Charles A. Halleck and 2 answering "present."
      (Total votes: 431. Necessary for a choice: 216.)
   Source: *Congressional Record*, 86-1, 13.
   Note: Assertions of being "present" were counted as votes by the tellers.
   Note: *Congressional Record* notes the individual vote tallies above but
      (mistakenly) reports that the tellers attributed 149 votes to Halleck.
   Note: *Congressional Record* notes 5 members not voting.

87TH CONGRESS (ELECTION DATE: JANUARY 3, 1961)
   Sam Rayburn (D-Tex.) was elected on the first ballot. Rayburn received
      258 votes to 170 for Charles A. Halleck and 2 answering "present."
      (Total votes: 430. Necessary for a choice: 216.)
   Source: *Congressional Record*, 87-1, 22–23.
   Note: Assertions of being "present" were counted as votes by the tellers.
   Note: Rayburn died on November 16, 1961, between the first and sec-
      ond sessions of the 87th Congress.

87TH CONGRESS—REPLACEMENT ELECTION (ELECTION DATE: JANUARY 10,
1962)
   John W. McCormack (D-Mass.) was elected on the first ballot. McCor-

mack received 248 votes to 166 for Charles A. Halleck and 2 answering "present." (Total votes: 414. Necessary for a choice: 208.)
Source: *Congressional Record*, 87-2, 5.
Note: Assertions of being "present" were *not* counted as votes by the tellers.
Note: *Congressional Record* notes 13 members not voting.

88TH CONGRESS (ELECTION DATE: JANUARY 9, 1963)
    John W. McCormack (D-Mass.) was elected on the first ballot. McCormack received 256 votes to 175 for Charles A. Halleck and 2 answering "present." (Total votes: 433. Necessary for a choice: 217.)
    Source: *Congressional Record*, 88-1, 11–12.
    Note: Assertions of being "present" were counted as votes by the tellers.

89TH CONGRESS (ELECTION DATE: JANUARY 4, 1965)
    John W. McCormack (D-Mass.) was elected on the first ballot. McCormack received 289 votes to 139 for Gerald R. Ford, and 3 answering "present." (Total votes: 428. Necessary for a choice: 215.)
    Source: *Congressional Record*, 89-1, 17.
    Note: Assertions of being "present" were *not* counted as votes by the tellers.

90TH CONGRESS (ELECTION DATE: JANUARY 10, 1967)
    John W. McCormack (D-Mass.) was elected on the first ballot. McCormack received 246 votes to 186 for Gerald R. Ford and 2 answering "present." (Total votes: 432. Necessary for a choice: 217.)
    Source: *Congressional Record*, 90-1, 12–13.
    Note: Assertions of being "present" were *not* counted as votes by the tellers.

91ST CONGRESS (ELECTION DATE: JANUARY 3, 1969)
    John W. McCormack (D-Mass.) was elected on the first ballot. McCormack received 241 votes to 187 for Gerald R. Ford and 2 answering "present." (Total votes: 428. Necessary for a choice: 216.)
    Source: *Congressional Record*, 91-1, 13–14.
    Note: Assertions of being "present" were *not* counted as votes by the tellers.

92ND CONGRESS (ELECTION DATE: JANUARY 21, 1971)
    Carl Albert (D-Okla.) was elected on the first ballot. Albert received 250 votes to 176 for Gerald R. Ford. (Total votes: 426. Necessary for a choice: 214.)
    Source: *Congressional Record*, 92-1, 10–11.

93RD CONGRESS (ELECTION DATE: JANUARY 3, 1973)

Carl Albert (D-Okla.) was elected on the first ballot. Albert received 236 votes to 188 for Gerald R. Ford. (Total votes: 424. Necessary for a choice: 213.)

Source: *Congressional Record*, 93-1, 13.

94TH CONGRESS (ELECTION DATE: JANUARY 14, 1975)

Carl Albert (D-Okla.) was elected on the first ballot. Albert received 287 votes to 143 for John J. Rhodes and 2 answering "present." (Total votes: 432. Necessary for a choice: 217.)

Source: *Congressional Record*, 94-1, 17.

Note: Assertions of being "present" were counted as votes by the tellers.

95TH CONGRESS (ELECTION DATE: JANUARY 4, 1977)

Thomas P. O'Neill Jr. (D-Mass.) was elected on the first ballot. O'Neill received 290 votes to 142 for John J. Rhodes and 2 answering "present." (Total votes: 434. Necessary for a choice: 218.)

Source: *Congressional Record*, 95-1, 50–51.

Note: Assertions of being "present" were counted as votes by the tellers.

96TH CONGRESS (ELECTION DATE: JANUARY 15, 1979)

Thomas P. O'Neill Jr. (D-Mass.) was elected on the first ballot. O'Neill received 268 votes to 152 for John J. Rhodes and 2 answering "present." (Total votes: 422. Necessary for a choice: 212.)

Source: *Congressional Record*, 96-1, 4–5.

Note: Assertions of being "present" were counted as votes by the tellers.

97TH CONGRESS (ELECTION DATE: JANUARY 5, 1981)

Thomas P. O'Neill Jr. (D-Mass.) was elected on the first ballot. O'Neill received 234 votes to 182 for Robert M. Michel and 2 answering "present." (Total votes: 418. Necessary for a choice: 210.)

Source: *Congressional Record*, 97-1, 94–95.

Note: *Congressional Record* notes the individual vote tallies above but reports that the tellers counted 419 total votes.

Note: Assertions of being "present" were counted as votes by the tellers.

Note: *Congressional Record* also notes 2 members not voting.

98TH CONGRESS (ELECTION DATE: JANUARY 3, 1983)

Thomas P. O'Neill Jr. (D-Mass.) was elected on the first ballot. O'Neill received 260 votes to 155 for Robert M. Michel and 2 answering "present." (Total votes: 417. Necessary for a choice: 209.)

Source: *Congressional Record*, 98-1, 30–31.

Note: *Congressional Record* notes the individual vote tally for O'Neill was 259, different from the 260 reported by the tellers.

Note: Assertions of being "present" were counted as votes by the tellers.
Note: *Congressional Record* also notes 2 members not voting.

99TH CONGRESS (ELECTION DATE: JANUARY 3, 1985)
   Thomas P. O'Neill Jr. (D-Mass.) was elected on the first ballot. O'Neill received 247 votes to 175 for Robert M. Michel and 3 answering "present." (Total votes: 425. Necessary for a choice: 213.)
   Source: *Congressional Record*, 99-1, 378–79.
   Note: Assertions of being "present" were counted as votes by the tellers.

100TH CONGRESS (ELECTION DATE: JANUARY 6, 1987)
   Jim Wright (D-Tex.) was elected on the first ballot. Wright received 254 votes to 173 for Robert M. Michel and 2 answering "present." (Total votes: 429. Necessary for a choice: 215.)
   Source: *Congressional Record*, 100-1, 2–3.
   Note: Assertions of being "present" were counted as votes by the tellers.

101ST CONGRESS (ELECTION DATE: JANUARY 3, 1989)
   Jim Wright (D-Tex.) was elected on the first ballot. Wright received 253 votes to 170 for Robert M. Michel and 2 answering "present." (Total votes: 425. Necessary for a choice: 213.)
   Source: *Congressional Record*, 101-1, 68.
   Note: Assertions of being "present" were counted as votes by the tellers.
   Note: *Congressional Record* notes 1 member not voting.
   Note: Wright resigned from the House of Representatives on June 6, 1989, during the first session of the 101st Congress.

101ST CONGRESS—REPLACEMENT ELECTION (ELECTION DATE: JUNE 6, 1989)
   Thomas S. Foley (D-Wash.) was elected on the first ballot. Foley received 251 votes to 164 for Robert M. Michel and 2 answering "present." (Total votes: 417. Necessary for a choice: 209.)
   Source: *Congressional Record*, 101-1, 10800–801.
   Note: Assertions of being "present" were counted as votes by the tellers.
   Note: *Congressional Record* notes 17 members not voting.

102ND CONGRESS (ELECTION DATE: JANUARY 3, 1991)
   Thomas S. Foley (D-Wash.) was elected on the first ballot. Foley received 262 votes to 165 for Robert M. Michel and 2 answering "present." (Total votes: 429. Necessary for a choice: 215.)
   Source: *Congressional Record*, 102-1, pp. 36–37.
   Note: Assertions of being "present" were counted as votes by the tellers.
   Note: *Congressional Record* notes 1 member not voting.

103RD CONGRESS (ELECTION DATE: JANUARY 5, 1993)

Thomas S. Foley (D-Wash.) was elected on the first ballot. Foley received 255 votes to 172 for Robert M. Michel and 2 answering "present." (Total votes: 431. Necessary for a choice: 216.)

Source: Congressional Record, 103-1, 46–47.

Note: Assertions of being "present" were counted as votes by the tellers.

Note: Congressional Record notes 1 member not voting.

104TH CONGRESS (ELECTION DATE: JANUARY 4, 1995)

Newt Gingrich (R-Ga.) was elected on the first ballot. Gingrich received 228 votes to 202 for Richard A. Gephardt and 4 answering "present." (Total votes: 434. Necessary for a choice: 218.)

Source: Congressional Record, 104-1, 441–42.

Note: Assertions of being "present" were counted as votes by the tellers.

105TH CONGRESS (ELECTION DATE: JANUARY 7, 1997)

Newt Gingrich (R-Ga.) was elected on the first ballot. Gingrich received 216 votes to 205 for Richard A. Gephardt, 2 for James Leach, 1 for Robert M. Michel, 1 for Robert Walker, and 6 answering "present." (Total votes: 425. Necessary for a choice: 213.)

Source: Congressional Record, 105-1, 117.

Note: Assertions of being "present" were *not* counted as votes by the tellers. Tally was based explicitly on "votes cast for a person by name."

Note: Congressional Record notes 1 member not voting.

Note: An issue was raised about Gingrich not receiving a majority of all members-elect. The House Clerk used the 1923 (68th House) case as a precedent—explicitly citing Cannon's Precedents, vol. 6, section 24—stating that a majority of members-elect present and voting by surname was the principle.

106TH CONGRESS (ELECTION DATE: JANUARY 6, 1999)

J. Dennis Hastert (R-Ill.) was elected on the first ballot. Hastert received 222 votes to 205 for Richard A. Gephardt and 2 answering "present." (Total votes: 427. Necessary for a choice: 214.)

Source: Congressional Record, 106-1, 43.

Note: Congressional Record notes mistakenly report the individual vote tallies for Hastert as 220 but accurately record the tellers' tally as 222.

Note: Assertions of being "present" were *not* counted as votes by the tellers.

Note: Congressional Record notes 7 members not voting.

107TH CONGRESS (ELECTION DATE: JANUARY 3, 2001)

J. Dennis Hastert (R-Ill.) was elected on the first ballot. Hastert received 222 votes to 206 for Richard A. Gephardt, 1 for John P. Murtha, and 2 answering "present." (Total votes: 429. Necessary for a choice: 215.)

Source: Congressional Record, 107-1, 21.

Note: Assertions of being "present" were not counted as votes by the tellers. Tally was based explicitly on "votes cast for a person by name."

Note: Congressional Record notes 3 members not voting.

108TH CONGRESS (ELECTION DATE: JANUARY 7, 2003)

J. Dennis Hastert (R-Ill.) was elected on the first ballot. Hastert received 228 votes to 201 for Nancy Pelosi, 1 for John P. Murtha, and 4 answering "present." (Total votes: 434. Necessary for a choice: 218.)

Source: Congressional Record, 108-1, 3–4.

Note: Assertions of being "present" were counted as votes by the tellers.

Note: Congressional Record notes 1 member not voting.

109TH CONGRESS (ELECTION DATE: JANUARY 4, 2005)

J. Dennis Hastert (R-Ill.) was elected on the first ballot. Hastert received 226 votes to 199 for Nancy Pelosi, 1 for John P. Murtha, and 1 answering "present." (Total votes: 427. Necessary for a choice: 214.)

Source: Congressional Record, 109-1, 37–38.

Note: Assertion of being "present" was counted as a vote by the tellers.

Note: Congressional Record notes 7 members not voting.

110TH CONGRESS (ELECTION DATE: JANUARY 4, 2007)

Nancy Pelosi (D-Calif.) was elected on the first ballot. Pelosi received 233 votes to 202 for John A. Boehner. (Total votes: 435. Necessary for a choice: 218.)

Source: Congressional Record, 110-1, 3.

111TH CONGRESS (ELECTION DATE: JANUARY 6, 2009)

Nancy Pelosi (D-Calif.) was elected on the first ballot. Pelosi received 255 votes to 174 for John A. Boehner. (Total votes: 429. Necessary for a choice: 215.)

Source: Congressional Record Daily, 111-1, H3–4.

Note: Congressional Record notes 5 members not voting.

112TH CONGRESS (ELECTION DATE: JANUARY 5, 2011)

John A. Boeher (R-Ohio) was elected on the first ballot. Boehner received 241 votes to 173 for Nancy Pelosi, 11 for Heath Shuler, 2 for John Lewis, 1 for Jim Costa, 1 for Dennis Cardoza, 1 for Jim Cooper,

1 for Marcy Kaptur, 1 for Steny Hoyer, and 1 answering "present." (Total votes: 432. Necessary for a choice: 217.)

Source: *Congressional Record Daily*, 112-1, H3.

Note: Assertion of being "present" was *not* counted as a vote by the tellers. Tally was based explicitly on "votes cast for a person by name."

Note: *Congressional Record* notes 2 members not voting.

Election of House Clerk, First–112th Congresses

1ST CONGRESS (ELECTION DATE: APRIL 1, 1789)
John Beckley (Va.) was elected on the second ballot. Samuel Stockton was also nominated (and presumably received some votes), but no further details were provided.
Source: *House Journal*, 1-1, 6; *Independent Gazetteer* (Philadelphia), April 9, 1789, 3.

2ND CONGRESS (ELECTION DATE: OCTOBER 24, 1791)
John Beckley (Va.) was elected unanimously on the first ballot.
Source: *Annals of Congress*, 2-1, 142.

3RD CONGRESS (ELECTION DATE: DECEMBER 2, 1793)
John Beckley (Va.) was elected unanimously on the first ballot.
Source: *General Advertiser* (Philadelphia), December 3, 1793, 3; *Daily Advertiser* (New York), December 5, 1793, 3.

4TH CONGRESS (ELECTION DATE: DECEMBER 7, 1795)
John Beckley (Va.) was elected on the first ballot. Beckley received 48 votes to 30 for Peter Baynton. (Total votes: 78. Necessary for a choice: 40.)
Source: *Aurora General Advertiser* (Philadelphia), December 8, 1795, 3; *Daily Advertiser* (New York), December 10, 1795, 2.

5TH CONGRESS (ELECTION DATE: MAY 15, 1797)
Jonathan W. Condy (Pa.) was elected on the first ballot. Condy received 41 votes to 40 for John Beckley. (Total votes: 81. Necessary to a choice: 41.)
Source: *Annals of Congress*, 5-1, 52; *Federal Gazette & Baltimore Daily Advertiser*, May 17, 1797, 3.

6TH CONGRESS (ELECTION DATE: DECEMBER 2, 1799)
Jonathan W. Condy (Pa.) was elected on the first ballot. Condy received 47 votes to 39 for John Beckley. (Total votes: 86. Necessary for a choice: 44.)
Source: *Annals of Congress*, 6-1, 186.

Note: Condy resigned on December 9, 1800, due to ill health.

6TH CONGRESS—REPLACEMENT ELECTION (ELECTION DATE: DECEMBER 9, 1800)
    John Holt Oswald (Pa.) was elected on the first ballot. Oswald received 51 votes to 42 for John Beckley. (Total votes: 93. Necessary for a choice: 47.)
    Source: *Alexandria Advertiser and Commercial Intelligencer* (Virginia), December 11, 1800, 3; *Gazette of the United States* (Philadelphia), December 13, 1800, 3; *House Journal*, 6-2, 736.
    Note: Newspapers report Oswald's middle initial as "C."

7TH CONGRESS (ELECTION DATE: DECEMBER 7, 1801)
    John Beckley (Va.) was elected on the first ballot. Beckley received 57 votes to 29 for John Holt Oswald. (Total votes: 86. Necessary for a choice: 44.)
    Source: *Commercial Advertiser* (New York), December 12, 1801, 3; *New York Evening Post*, December 12, 1801, 3.

8TH CONGRESS (ELECTION DATE: OCTOBER 17, 1803)
    John Beckley (Va.) was elected on the first ballot. Macon received 93 votes to 4 for E. B. Caldwell and 1 each for two or three others (not heard). (Total votes: 99 or 100. Necessary for a choice: 50 or 51.)
    Source: *Commercial Advertiser* (New York), October 21, 1803, 3.

9TH CONGRESS (ELECTION DATE: DECEMBER 2, 1805)
    John Beckley (Va.) was elected on the first ballot. Beckley received 85 votes to 18 for Thomas Lambert. (Total votes: 103. Necessary for a choice: 52.)
    Source: *Aurora General Advertiser* (Philadelphia), December 6, 1805, 3.

10TH CONGRESS (ELECTION DATE: OCTOBER 26, 1807)
    Patrick Magruder (Md.) was elected on the fourth ballot.

Ballot:	1	2	3	4
Nicholas B. Vanzandt	37	52	16	
Patrick Magruder	26	28	52	72
James Elliot	16	15	27	
J. W. King	16	10	9	
(Unknown candidate 1)	14	—	—	
(Unknown candidate 2)	14	—	—	
(Unknown candidate 3)	5	—	—	

(*Continued on next page*)

(*Continued*)

Ballot:	1	2	3	4
(Unknown candidate 4)	1	—	—	
William Lambert	—	7	8	
Theodosius Hansford	—	4	5	
C. Minifie	—	1	—	
Total votes	129	117	117	?
Necessary for a choice	65	59	59	59

Source: *Annals of Congress*, 10-1, 783–85.

Note: The details of the last ballot were not provided, only Magruder's total and the number of votes necessary to a choice.

Note: Before the third ballot, Randolph took the floor and accused Vanzandt of leaking comments he had made in an executive session of the House. Vanzandt denied this. While some called for a postponement of the balloting for Clerk, the House refused and balloting continued.

11TH CONGRESS (ELECTION DATE: MAY 22, 1809)

Patrick Magruder (Va.) was elected on the first ballot. Magruder received 63 votes to 38 for Daniel Brent, 14 for Nicholas B. Vanzandt, 7 for William Lambert, and 1 for Mr. Scott. (Total votes: 123. Necessary for a choice: 62.)

Source: *Annals of Congress*, 11-1, 56.

12TH CONGRESS (ELECTION DATE: NOVEMBER 4, 1811)

Patrick Magruder (Va.) was elected on the first ballot. Magruder received 97 votes to 16 for William Lambert. (Total votes: 113. Necessary for a choice: 57.)

Source: *National Intelligencer* (Washington, D.C.), November 6, 1811, 1; *Balance and State Journal* (Albany), November 12, 1811, 362.

13TH CONGRESS (ELECTION DATE: MAY 24, 1813)

Patrick Magruder (Va.) was elected on the first ballot. Magruder received 111 votes to 19 for George Richards. (Total votes: 130. Necessary for a choice: 66.)

Source: *Annals of Congress*, 13-1, 107; *Columbian* (New York), May 27, 1813, 3; *Boston Daily Advertiser*, May 31, 1813, 2.

Note: Magruder fell under controversy concerning his evacuation from the Capitol during the British invasion of Washington. Facing a resolution to remove him office, Magruder resigned on January 28, 1815.

13TH CONGRESS—REPLACEMENT ELECTION (ELECTION DATE: JANUARY 30, 1815)

Patrick Dougherty (Ky.) was elected on the second ballot. On the first ballot, Dougherty received 80 votes to 35 for Thomas L. McKenney, 19 for Samuel Burch, 13 for O. B. Brown, 4 for Nicholas B. Vanzandt, and 6 scattering. (Total votes: 157. Necessary for a choice: 79.) On the second ballot, Dougherty received 83 votes, to 73 for McKenney, and 4 scattering. (Total votes: 160. Necessary for a choice: 81.)

Source: Annals of Congress, 13-3, 1114.

Note: It appears that Dougherty received a majority on the first ballot, but that fact was not noted in the Annals of Congress.

14TH CONGRESS (ELECTION DATE: DECEMBER 4, 1815)

Patrick Dougherty (Ky.) was elected on the first ballot. Dougherty received 114 votes with 8 scattering. (Total votes: 122. Necessary for a choice: 62.)

Source: Annals of Congress 14-1, 375; Niles' Weekly Register, December 9, 1815, 254.

15TH CONGRESS (ELECTION DATE: DECEMBER 1, 1817)

Patrick Dougherty (Ky.) was elected unanimously (144 votes) on the first ballot. (Total votes: 144. Necessary for a choice: 73.)

Source: Annals of Congress, 15-1, 398.

16TH CONGRESS (ELECTION DATE: DECEMBER 6, 1819)

Thomas Dougherty (Ky.) was elected "without opposition" via resolution.

Source: Annals of Congress, 16-1, 703.

17TH CONGRESS (DECEMBER 4, 1821)

Thomas Dougherty (Ky.) was elected "without opposition" via resolution.

Source: Annals of Congress, 17-1, 517.

Note: Dougherty died during the recess between the first and second sessions.

17TH CONGRESS—REPLACEMENT ELECTION (ELECTION DATE: DECEMBER 3, 1822)

Matthew St. Clair Clarke (D.C.) was elected on the 11th ballot.

Date:	December 2						December 3				
Ballot:	1	2	3	4	5	6	7	8	9	10	11
William Milnor	14	12	9	7	—	—	11	9	—	—	—
Samuel Burch	10	6	—	—	—	—	—	—	—	—	—
Levi H. Clarke	19	22	24	26	21	12	19	5	—	—	—
B. S. Chambers	17	20	20	25	28	29	26	25	23	7	—
S. D. Franks	15	13	13	8	10	9	16	20	15	2	—
Tobias Watkins	12	10	12	6	—	—	3	—	—	—	—
Robert Temple	13	15	23	28	46	54	46	47	50	55	48
Edward W. DuVal	5	—	—	—	—	—	—	—	—	—	—
S. A. Foot	9	9	8	6	—	—	13	16	16	13	—
James H. Pleasants	13	13	15	17	8	17	12	3	—	—	—
Mr. Briggs	5	—	—	—	—	—	—	—	—	—	—
J. S. Williams	4	—	—	—	—	—	—	—	—	—	—
Matthew St. Clair Clarke	9	12	14	17	21	24	5	29	15	71	98
Mr. Goldsborough	—	4	—	7	—	—	—	—	—	—	—
Scattering	9	4	11	—	9	3	—	—	—	—	4
Total votes	154	140	149	147	143	148	151	154	119	148	150
Necessary for a choice	78	71	75	74	72	75	76	78	60	75	76

Source: Annals of Congress, 17-2, 327–29.

Note: Tellers made a mistake in crediting a number of votes to Levi H. Clarke on the seventh ballot that rightfully belong to Matthew St. Clair Clarke. This error was reported in the Annals.

Note: Matthew St. Clair Clarke is sometimes listed as hailing from Pennsylvania, as he was born in Greencastle (Franklin County). He moved to D.C. sometime after being admitted to the bar in 1811. Most newspaper stories that discuss clerkship elections of which he was a part classify him as a resident of the District of Columbia. We thus follow this convention.

18TH CONGRESS (ELECTION DATE: DECEMBER 1, 1823)

Matthew St. Clair Clarke (D.C.) was elected unanimously via a resolution moved by John Campbell (Jacksonian Rep.-Ohio).

Source: Annals of Congress, 18-1, 796.

19TH CONGRESS (ELECTION DATE: DECEMBER 5, 1825)

Matthew St. Clair Clarke was elected via a resolution moved by Samuel Lathrop (Adams-Mass.).

Source: Register of Debates, 19-1, 796; Niles' Weekly Register, December 10, 1825, 233.

20TH CONGRESS (ELECTION DATE: DECEMBER 3, 1827)
Matthew St. Clair Clarke (D.C.) was elected unanimously via a resolution moved by Lemuel Sawyer (Jacksonian-N.C.).
Source: Register of Debates, 20-1, 812; *Niles' Weekly Register*, December 8, 1827, 239.

21ST CONGRESS (ELECTION DATE: DECEMBER 7, 1829)
Matthew St. Clair Clarke (D.C. was elected on the first ballot. Clarke received 135 votes to 54 for Virgil Maxcy and 3 scattering. (Total votes: 192. Necessary for a choice: 97.)
Source: Niles' Weekly Register, December 12, 1829, 254; Charleston *Courier*, December 7, 1829, 2; *Daily National Intelligencer*, December 8, 1829, 3.

22ND CONGRESS (ELECTION DATE: DECEMBER 5, 1831)
Matthew St. Clair Clarke (D.C.) was elected unanimously by resolution moved by Jesse Speight (Jacksonian-N.C.).
Source: Register of Debates, 22-1, 1421.

23RD CONGRESS (ELECTION DATE: DECEMBER 2, 1833)
Walter S. Franklin (Pa.) was elected on the third ballot.

Ballot:	1	2	3
Matthew St. Clair Clarke	113	112	110
Walter S. Franklin	107	114	117
Eleezer Early	2	—	—
Walter F. Clarke	1	—	—
Thomas C. Love	5	—	—
Blank	3	2	2
Total votes	231	228	229
Necessary for a choice	116	115	115

Source: Register of Debates, 23-1, 2137; *Congressional Globe*, 23-1, 3.

24TH CONGRESS (ELECTION DATE: DECEMBER 7, 1835)
Walter S. Franklin (Pa.) was elected "without objection" via a resolution moved by Samuel Beardsley (Jacksonian-N.Y.).
Source: Congressional Globe, 24-1, 3; *Register of Debates*, 24-1, 1946; *Niles' Weekly Register*, December 12, 1835, 248.

25TH CONGRESS (ELECTION DATE: SEPTEMBER 4, 1837)
Walter S. Franklin (Pa.) was elected on the first ballot. Franklin received 146 votes to 48 for Samuel Shock, 7 for Matthew St. Clair Clarke, and 8 blanks. (Total votes: 209. Necessary for a choice: 105.)

Source: *Congressional Globe*, 25-1, 3.
Note: Franklin died on September 20, 1838, between the second and
    third sessions in Lancaster, Pennsylvania.

25TH CONGRESS—REPLACEMENT ELECTION (DECEMBER 3, 1838)
    Hugh A. Garland (Va.) was elected on the third ballot.

Ballot:	1	2	3
Matthew St. Clair Clarke	55	88	104
Hugh A. Garland	48	59	106
Edward Livingston	31	26	
Samuel Shoch	21	13	—
Arnold Naudain	20	4	—
Henry Buehler	16	13	—
James H. Birch	9	—	—
John Bigler	8	6	—
Reuben M. Whitney	2	—	—
Total votes	210	209	210
Necessary for a choice	106	105	106

Source: *House Journal*, 25-3, 10–14.
Note: This election was the first using the viva voce voting rule. All sub-
    sequent clerkship elections were determined by viva voce, unless oth-
    erwise noted.

26TH CONGRESS (ELECTION DATE: DECEMBER 21, 1839)
    Hugh A. Garland (Va.) was elected on the first ballot. Garland received
    118 votes to 105 for Matthew St. Clair Clarke and 8 for Richard C.
    Mason. (Total votes: 231. Necessary for a choice: 116.)
    Source: *House Journal*, 26-1, 97–99.

27TH CONGRESS (ELECTION DATE: MAY 31, 1841)
    Matthew St. Clair Clarke (D.C.) was elected on the fourth ballot.

Ballot:	1	2	3	4
Francis O. J. Smith	90	90	80	67
Hugh A. Garland	81	61	15	6
Matthew St. Clair Clarke	38	51	91	128
Richard C. Mason	13	17	32	19
Total votes	222	219	218	220
Necessary for a choice	112	110	110	111

Source: *House Journal*, 27-1, 13–18.

28TH CONGRESS (ELECTION DATE: DECEMBER 6, 1843)

Caleb J. McNulty (Ohio) was elected on the first ballot. McNulty received 124 votes to 66 for Matthew St. Clair Clarke. (Total votes: 190. Necessary for a choice: 96.)

Source: *House Journal*, 28-1, 28–29.

Note: McNulty was suspected of embezzlement and dismissed as Clerk by unanimous vote on January 18, 1845. See *House Journal*, 28-1, 230, 233.

28TH CONGRESS—REPLACEMENT ELECTION (JANUARY 18, 1845)

Benjamin B. French (N.H.) was elected unanimously via a resolution moved by George W. Hopkins (D-Va.).

Source: *House Journal*, 28-2 233.

29TH CONGRESS (DECEMBER 2, 1845)

Benjamin B. French (N.H.) was elected unanimously via a resolution moved by Howell Cobb (D-Ga.).

Source: *House Journal*, 29-1, 13.

30TH CONGRESS (DECEMBER 7, 1847)

Thomas J. Campbell (Tenn.) was elected on the first ballot. Campbell received 113 votes to 109 for Benjamin B. French, 1 for Samuel L. Gouverneur, 1 for Nathan Sargent, and 1 for George Kent. (Total votes: 225. Necessary for a choice: 113.)

Source: *House Journal*, 30-1, 15–17.

31ST CONGRESS (JANUARY 11, 1850)

Thomas J. Campbell (Tenn.) was elected on the 20th ballot.

Date:	January 3		January 7					January 8		
Ballot:	1	2	3	4	5	6	7	8	9	10
John W. Forney	98	103	107	107	106	106	107	106	105	105
Thomas J. Campbell	77	81	94	95	102	72	13	13	13	13
Calvin W. Pilleo	8	6	6	6	4	4	4	4	5	4
John H. C. Mudd	7	5	2	—	—	—	—	—	—	—
Samuel L. Gouverneur	5	1	—	—	1	—	1	1	1	1
Philander B. Prindle	4	4	1	—	2	6	1	1	—	—
Nathan Sargent	3	3	3	3	2	2	—	—	—	—
De Witt C. Clarke	2	2	2	1	1	—	—	1	1	1
Samuel P. Benson	2	—	—	—	—	—	—	—	—	—
Solomon Foot	2	3	3	5	—	25	92	94	93	93
Benjamin B. French	—	1	2	2	2	4	2	1	1	—
Total votes	208	209	220	219	220	219	220	221	219	217
Necessary for a choice	105	105	111	110	111	110	111	111	110	109

(*Continued on next page*)

(*Continued*)

Date:		January 9				January 10			January 11	
Ballot:	11	12	13	14	15	16	17	18	19	20
John W. Forney	106	105	105	103	102	96	93	93	97	96
Thomas J. Campbell	—	—	—	—	—	32	28	96	103	112
Calvin W. Pilleo	4	4	4	4	4	4	3	—	—	—
Samuel L. Gouverneur	1	—	—	—	—	—	1	1	—	—
Philander B. Prindle	—	—	—	1	—	63	63	2	2	1
De Witt C. Clarke	3	5	—	—	—	—	—	—	—	—
Solomon Foot	104	103	103	98	103	2	2	3	3	2
Benjamin B. French	1	3	4	4	3	11	18	18	13	9
Matthew St. Clair Clarke	—	—	5	7	3	—	—	—	—	—
George P. Fisher	—	—	—	—	—	7	9	—	—	—
John Smith	—	—	—	—	—	1	—	—	—	—
Total votes	218	220	221	217	215	216	217	213	208	220
Necessary for a choice	110	111	111	109	108	109	109	107	110	111

Source: *House Journal*, 31-1, 216–20, 237–51, 259–65, 267–68, 277–83, 286–91.

Note: Campbell died on April 13, 1850.

31ST CONGRESS—REPLACEMENT ELECTION (ELECTION DATE: APRIL 17, 1850)

Richard M. Young (Ill.) was elected on the ninth ballot.

Date:			April 16					April 17	
Ballot:	1	2	3	4	5	6	7	8	9
Philander B. Prindle	48	47	44	45	32	30	26	16	5
Richard M. Young	22	35	44	55	63	72	73	70	96
Hiram Walbridge	17	19	18	15	11	5	4	2	—
John W. Forney	17	13	12	9	6	5	3	3	—
James C. Walker	17	19	29	33	51	47	49	55	82
Albert Smith	15	15	12	9	8	3	—	—	—
Adam J. Glossbrenner	12	12	9	5	3	4	3	2	—
Matthew St. Clair Clarke	12	11	10	8	5	6	8	13	1
James H. Forsyth	10	—	—	—	—	—	—	—	—
James W. Moorhead	10	10	8	3	—	—	—	—	—
J. H. Clay Mudd	6	4	2	—	—	—	—	—	—
Edmund Burke	1	—	—	—	—	—	—	—	—
Ethan A. Stansbury	—	—	—	—	—	7	8	6	—
Jesse E. Dow	—	—	—	—	—	1	—	—	—
Albert Smith	—	—	—	—	—	—	1	1	—
Charles B. Flood	—	—	—	—	—	—	—	4	—
Ethan A. Stansbury	—	—	—	—	—	—	—	—	4
Total votes	187	185	188	182	178	180	175	172	188
Necessary for a choice	94	93	95	92	90	91	88	87	95

Source: *House Journal*, 31-1, 789–805.

32ND CONGRESS (ELECTION DATE: DECEMBER 1, 1851)

John W. Forney (Pa.) was elected on the first ballot. Forney received 128 votes to 72 for James C. Walker, 3 for E. A. Stansbury, 2 for George Darsey, and 2 for Richard M. Young. (Total votes: 207. Necessary for a choice: 104.)

Source: *House Journal*, 32-1, 11–13.

33RD CONGRESS (ELECTION DATE: DECEMBER 5, 1853)

John W. Forney (Pa.) was elected on the first ballot. Forney received 122 votes to 27 for Richard M. Young, 18 for Philander B. Prindle, 12 for Ebenezer Hutchinson, 10 for E. P. Smith, 6 for James C. Walker, 2 for W. H. Bogart, 1 for Charles Brown, 1 for G. W. Mumford, and 1 for John M. Barclay. (Total votes: 200. Necessary for a choice: 101.)

Source: *House Journal*, 33-1, 12–14.

34TH CONGRESS (ELECTION DATE: FEBRUARY 4, 1856)

William Cullom (Tenn.) was elected via a resolution moved by Russell Sage (Opposition-N.Y.), 126–89.

Source: *House Journal*, 34-1, 449–52.

35TH CONGRESS (ELECTION DATE: DECEMBER 7, 1857)

James C. Allen (Ill.) was elected on the first ballot. Allen received 128 votes to 85 for B. Gratz Brown, 4 for William Cullom, and 2 for John M. Sullivan. (Total votes: 219. Necessary for a choice: 110.)

Source: *House Journal*, 35-1, 11–13; *Congressional Globe*, 35-1, 3.

36TH CONGRESS (ELECTION DATE: FEBRUARY 3, 1860)

John W. Forney (Pa.) was elected on the first ballot. Forney received 112 votes to 77 for James C. Allen, 23 for Nathaniel G. Taylor, 8 for D. L. Dalton, and 1 for Z. W. McKnew. (Total votes: 221. Necessary for a choice: 111.)

Source: *House Journal*, 36-1, 172–74; *Congressional Globe*, 36-1, 662–63.

37TH CONGRESS (ELECTION DATE: JULY 4, 1861)

Emerson Etheridge (Tenn.) was elected on the first ballot. Etheridge received 92 votes to 41 for John W. Forney, 21 for John E. Dietrich, and 2 for Thomas B. Florence. (Total votes: 156. Necessary for a choice: 79).

Source: *House Journal*, 37-1, 14–16; *Congressional Globe*, 37-1, 10.

38TH CONGRESS (ELECTION DATE: DECEMBER 8, 1863)

Edward McPherson (Pa.) was elected on the first ballot. McPherson received 101 votes to 69 for Emerson Etheridge. (Total votes: 170. Necessary for a choice: 86.)

Source: *House Journal*, 38-1, 14–16; *Congressional Globe*, 38-1, 11.
Note: *Congressional Globe* reports McPherson's vote total as 102.

39TH CONGRESS (ELECTION DATE: DECEMBER 4, 1865)
   Edward McPherson (Pa.) was elected via a resolution moved by James
   F. Wilson (R-Iowa), 138–35.
   Source: *House Journal*, 39-1, 8–9; *Congressional Globe*, 39-1, 5.

40TH CONGRESS (ELECTION DATE: MARCH 4, 1867)
   Edward McPherson (Pa.) was elected via a resolution moved by Henry
   L. Dawes (R-Mass.).
   Source: *House Journal*, 40-1, 9; *Congressional Globe*, 40-1, 5.

41ST CONGRESS (ELECTION DATE: MARCH 5, 1869)
   Edward McPherson (Pa.) was elected on the first ballot. McPherson re-
   ceived 128 votes to 55 for Charles C. Carrigan. (Total votes: 183.
   Necessary for a choice: 92.)
   Source: *House Journal*, 41-1, 15–16; *Congressional Globe*, 41-1, 19.

42ND CONGRESS (ELECTION DATE: MARCH 4, 1871)
   Edward McPherson (Pa.) was elected via a resolution moved by Henry
   L. Dawes (R-Mass.). A substitute amendment, which replaced
   McPherson with James G. Berrett (D.C.) was defeated, 87–126.
   Source: *House Journal*, 42-1, 11–12; *Congressional Globe*, 42-1,
   10–11.

43RD CONGRESS (ELECTION DATE: DECEMBER 1, 1873)
   Edward McPherson (Pa.) was elected via a resolution moved by Horace
   Maynard (R-Tenn.). A substitute amendment, which replaced
   McPherson with George C. Weddeburn (Va.) was defeated, 86–178.
   Source: *House Journal*, 43-1, 11–12; *Congressional Record*, 43-1, 6–7.

44TH CONGRESS (ELECTION DATE: DECEMBER 6, 1875)
   George M. Adams (Ky.) was elected via a resolution moved by Lucius
   Q. C. Lamar (D-Miss.). A substitute amendment, which replaced
   Adams with Edward McPherson (Pa.), was defeated.
   Source: *Congressional Record*, 44-1, 173.

45TH CONGRESS (ELECTION DATE: OCTOBER 15, 1877)
   George M. Adams (Ky.) was elected via a resolution moved by Hiester
   Clymer (D-Pa.). A substitute amendment, which replaced Adams with
   Jeremiah Rusk (Wis.), was defeated.
   Source: *Congressional Record*, 45-1, 54.

46TH CONGRESS (ELECTION DATE: MARCH 18, 1879)

George M. Adams (Ky.) was elected via a resolution moved by Hiester Clymer. A substitute amendment, which replaced Adams with a Joseph H. Rainey (S.C.), was defeated, 119–145. A second substitute amendment, which replaced Adams with Lee Crandall (Ala.), a Greenbacker, was also defeated with seven yeas and nays not counted.

Source: Congressional Record, 46-1, 9–10.

47TH CONGRESS (ELECTION DATE: DECEMBER 5, 1881)

Edward McPherson (Pa.) was elected on the first ballot. McPherson received 148 votes to 129 for George M. Adams and 9 for Gilbert De La Matyr. (Total votes: 286. Necessary for a choice: 144.)

Source: Congressional Record, 47-1, 16.

48TH CONGRESS (ELECTION DATE: DECEMBER 4, 1883)

John B. Clark Jr. (Mo.) was elected via a resolution moved by George W. Geddes (D-Ohio). A substitute amendment, which replaced Clark with Edward McPherson (Pa.), was defeated.

Source: Congressional Record, 48-1, 26–27.

49TH CONGRESS (ELECTION DATE: DECEMBER 7, 1885)

John B. Clark Jr. (Mo.) was elected via a resolution moved by John Randolph Tucker (D-Va.). A substitute amendment, which replaced Clark with W. O. Crosby (Iowa), was defeated.

Source: Congressional Record, 49-1, 107–8.

50TH CONGRESS (ELECTION DATE: DECEMBER 5, 1887)

John B. Clark Jr. (Mo.) was elected via a resolution moved by Samuel S. Cox (D-N.Y.). A substitute amendment, which replaced Clark with Edward McPherson (Pa.), was defeated. A second substitute amendment, which replaced Clark with Robert Shilling (Wis.), was also defeated.

Source: Congressional Record, 50-1, 7.

51ST CONGRESS (ELECTION DATE: DECEMBER 2, 1889)

Edward McPherson (Pa.) was elected via a resolution moved by Thomas J. Henderson (R-Ill.). A substitute amendment, which replaced McPherson with John B. Clark (Mo.), was defeated.

Source: Congressional Record, 51-1, 81–82.

52ND CONGRESS (ELECTION DATE: DECEMBER 8, 1891)

James Kerr (Pa.) was elected via a resolution moved by William S. Hol-

man (D-Ind.). A substitute amendment, which replaced Kerr with Edward McPherson (Pa.), was defeated.
Source: *Congressional Record*, 52-1, 9.

53RD CONGRESS (ELECTION DATE: AUGUST 7, 1893)
James Kerr (Pa.) was elected via a resolution moved by William S. Holman (D-Ind.). A substitute amendment, which replaced Kerr with Edward McPherson (Pa.), was defeated.
Source: *Congressional Record*, 53-1, 202.

54TH CONGRESS (ELECTION DATE: DECEMBER 2, 1895)
Alexander McDowell (Pa.) was elected via a resolution moved by Charles H. Grosvenor (R-Ohio). A substitute amendment, which replaced McDowell with James Kerr (Pa.), was defeated.
Source: *Congressional Record*, 54-1, 5.

55TH CONGRESS (ELECTION DATE: MARCH 15, 1897)
Alexander McDowell (Pa.) was elected via a resolution moved by Charles H. Grosvenor (R-Ohio). A substitute amendment, which replaced McDowell with James Kerr (Pa.), was defeated. A second substitute amendment, which replaced McDowell with J. A. Edgerton (Neb.), was also defeated.
Source: *Congressional Record*, 55-1, 16.

56TH CONGRESS (ELECTION DATE: DECEMBER 4, 1899)
Alexander McDowell (Pa.) was elected via resolution moved by Charles H. Grosvenor (R-Ohio). A substitute amendment, which replaced McDowell with James Kerr (Pa.), was defeated.
Source: *Congressional Record*, 56-1, 6.

57TH CONGRESS (ELECTION DATE: DECEMBER 2, 1901)
Alexander McDowell (Pa.) was elected via a resolution moved by Joseph G. Cannon (R-Ill.). A substitute amendment, which replaced McDowell with James Kerr (Pa.), was defeated.
Source: *Congressional Record*, 57-1, 45.

58TH CONGRESS (ELECTION DATE: NOVEMBER 9, 1903)
Alexander McDowell (Pa.) was elected via a resolution moved by William P. Hepburn (R-Iowa). A substitute amendment, which replaced McDowell with Charles A. Edwards (Tex.), was defeated.
Source: *Congressional Record*, 58-1, 148.

59TH CONGRESS (ELECTION DATE: DECEMBER 4, 1905)
Alexander McDowell (Pa.) was elected via a resolution moved by Wil-

liam P. Hepburn (R-Iowa). A substitute amendment, which replaced McDowell with W. S. Cowherd (Mo.), was defeated.
Source: *Congressional Record*, 59-1, 41.

60TH CONGRESS (ELECTION DATE: DECEMBER 2, 1907)
Alexander McDowell (Pa.) was elected via a resolution moved by William P. Hepburn (R-Iowa). A substitute amendment, which replaced McDowell with Charles A. Edwards (Tex.), was defeated.
Source: *Congressional Record*, 60-1, 5.

61ST CONGRESS (ELECTION DATE: MARCH 15, 1909)
Alexander McDowell (Pa.) was elected via a resolution moved by Frank D. Currier (R-N.H.). A substitute amendment, which replaced McDowell with W. P. Kimball (Ky.), was defeated.
Source: *Congressional Record*, 61-1, 19.

62ND CONGRESS (ELECTION DATE: APRIL 4, 1911)
South Trimble (Ky.) was elected via a resolution moved by Albert S. Burleson (D-Tex.). A substitute amendment, which replaced Trimble with Alexander McDowell (Pa.), was defeated.
Source: *Congressional Record*, 62-1, 8.

63RD CONGRESS (ELECTION DATE: APRIL 7, 1913)
South Trimble (Ky.) was elected via a resolution moved by Palmer (D-Pa.). A substitute amendment, which replaced Trimble with Alexander McDowell (Pa.), was defeated. A second substitute amendment, which replaced Trimble with Nevin Detrich (Pa.), was also defeated.
Source: *Congressional Record*, 63-1, 67–68.

64TH CONGRESS (ELECTION DATE: DECEMBER 6, 1915)
South Trimble (Ky.) was elected via a resolution moved by Edward W. Saunders (D-Va.). A substitute amendment, which replaced Trimble with Clarence N. Price (Kans.), was defeated.
Source: *Congressional Record*, 64-1, 6.

65TH CONGRESS (ELECTION DATE: APRIL 2, 1917)
South Trimble (Ky.) was elected on the first ballot. Trimble received 217 votes to 213 for William Tyler Page (Md.). (Total votes: 430. Necessary for a choice: 216.)
Source: *Congressional Record*, 65-1, 108–9.

66TH CONGRESS (ELECTION DATE: MAY 19, 1919)
William Tyler Page (Md.) was elected via a resolution moved by Horace

M. Towner (R-Iowa). A substitute amendment, which replaced Page
with South Trimble (Ky.), was defeated.
Source: Congressional Record, 66-1, 8.

67TH CONGRESS (ELECTION DATE: APRIL 11, 1921)
William Tyler Page (Md.) was elected via a resolution moved by Frank
W. Mondell (R-Wyo.). A substitute amendment, which replaced Page
with South Trimble (Ky.), was defeated.
Source: Congressional Record, 67-1, 82–83.

68TH CONGRESS (ELECTION DATE: DECEMBER 5, 1923)
William Tyler Page (Md.) was elected via a resolution moved by Sydney
Anderson (R-Minn.). A substitute amendment, which replaced Page
with South Trimble (Ky.), was defeated.
Source: Congressional Record, 68-1, 18–19.

69TH CONGRESS (ELECTION DATE: DECEMBER 7, 1925)
William Tyler Page (Md.) was elected via a resolution moved by Willis
C. Hawley (R-Ore.). A substitute amendment, which replaced Page
with South Trimble (Ky.), was defeated.
Source: Congressional Record, 69-1, 382.

70TH CONGRESS (ELECTION DATE: DECEMBER 5, 1927)
William Tyler Page (Md.) was elected via a resolution moved by Willis
C. Hawley (R-Ore.). A substitute amendment, which replaced Page
with South Trimble (Ky.), was defeated.
Source: Congressional Record, 70-1, 10–11.

71ST CONGRESS (ELECTION DATE: APRIL 15, 1929)
William Tyler Page (Md.) was elected via a resolution moved by Willis
C. Hawley (R-Ore.). A substitute amendment, which replaced Page
with South Trimble (Ky.), was defeated.
Source: Congressional Record, 71-1, 25.

72ND CONGRESS (ELECTION DATE: DECEMBER 7, 1931)
South Trimble (Ky.) was elected via a resolution moved by William W.
Arnold (D-Ill.). A substitute amendment, which replaced Trimble
with William Tyler Page (Md.), was defeated.
Source: Congressional Record, 72-1, 9.

73RD CONGRESS (ELECTION DATE: MARCH 9, 1933)
South Trimble (Ky.) was elected via a resolution moved by Clarence F.
Lea (D-Calif.). A substitute amendment, which replaced Trimble with
William Tyler Page (Md.), was defeated.
Source: Congressional Record, 73-1, 74–75.

74TH CONGRESS (ELECTION DATE: JANUARY 3, 1935)
South Trimble (Ky.) was elected via a resolution moved by Edward T.
Taylor (D-Colo.). A substitute amendment, which replaced Trimble
with William Tyler Page (Md.), was defeated.
Source: *Congressional Record*, 74-1, 12–13.

75TH CONGRESS (ELECTION DATE: JANUARY 5, 1937)
South Trimble (Ky.) was elected via resolution moved by Robert L.
Doughton (D-N.C.). A substitute amendment, which replaced Trim-
ble with William Tyler Page (Md.), was defeated.
Source: *Congressional Record*, 75-1, 13.

76TH CONGRESS (ELECTION DATE: JANUARY 3, 1939)
South Trimble (Ky.) was elected via a resolution moved by John W. Mc-
Cormack (D-Mass.). A substitute amendment, which replaced Trim-
ble with William Tyler Page (Md.), was defeated.
Source: *Congressional Record*, 76-1, 12.

77TH CONGRESS (ELECTION DATE: JANUARY 3, 1941)
South Trimble (Ky.) was elected via a resolution moved by Richard M.
Duncan (D-Mo.). A substitute amendment, which replaced Trimble
with William Tyler Page (Md.), was defeated.
Source: *Congressional Record*, 77-1, 7–8.

78TH CONGRESS (ELECTION DATE: JANUARY 6, 1943)
South Trimble (Ky.) was elected via a resolution moved by Harry R.
Sheppard (D-Calif.). A substitute amendment, which replaced Trim-
ble with John Andrews (Mass.), was defeated.
Source: *Congressional Record*, 78-1, 12.

79TH CONGRESS (ELECTION DATE: JANUARY 3, 1945)
South Trimble (Ky.) was elected via a resolution moved by Jere Cooper
(D-Tenn.). A substitute amendment, which replaced Trimble with
John Andrews (Mass.), was defeated.
Source: *Congressional Record*, 79-1, 9–10.
Note: Harry Newlin Megill was appointed acting Clerk effective August
2, 1946. See *Congressional Record*, 79-1, 10768, 10781. Megill was
empowered earlier in the session on May 23, 1946, to act on Trim-
ble's behalf, while Trimble was temporarily absent from the House.
Congressional Record, 79-1, 5527. Trimble died on November 23,
1946.

80TH CONGRESS (ELECTION DATE: JANUARY 3, 1947)
John Andrews (Mass.) was elected via resolution moved by Roy O.

Woodruff (R-Mich.). A substitute amendment, which replaced Andrews with Ralph R. Roberts (Ind.), was defeated.
Source: *Congressional Record*, 80-1, 37.

81ST CONGRESS (ELECTION DATE: JANUARY 3, 1949)
Ralph R. Roberts (Ind.) was elected via a resolution moved by Francis E. Walter (D-Pa.). A substitute amendment, which replaced Roberts with John Andrews (Mass.), was defeated.
Source: *Congressional Record*, 81-1, 10.

82ND CONGRESS (ELECTION DATE: JANUARY 3, 1951)
Ralph R. Roberts (Ind.) was elected via a resolution moved by Jere Cooper (D-Tenn.). A substitute amendment, which replaced Roberts with Irving Swanson (Wis.), was defeated.
Source: *Congressional Record*, 82-1, 8–9.

83RD CONGRESS (ELECTION DATE: JANUARY 3, 1953)
Lyle O. Snader (Ill.) was elected via a resolution moved by Clifford R. Hope (R-Kans.). A substitute amendment, which replaced Snader with Ralph R. Roberts (Ind.), was defeated.
Source: *Congressional Record*, 83-1, 14–15.

84TH CONGRESS (ELECTION DATE: JANUARY 5, 1955)
Ralph R. Roberts (Ind.) was elected via a resolution moved by John J. Rooney (D-N.Y.). A substitute amendment, which replaced Roberts with Lyle O. Snader (Ill.), was defeated.
Source: *Congressional Record*, 84-1, 10.

85TH CONGRESS (ELECTION DATE: JANUARY 3, 1957)
Ralph R. Roberts (Ind.) was elected via a resolution moved by Charles M. Price (D-Ill.). A substitute amendment, which replaced Roberts with Lyle O. Snader (Ill.), was defeated.
Source: *Congressional Record*, 85-1, 47.

86TH CONGRESS (ELECTION DATE: JANUARY 7, 1959)
Ralph R. Roberts (Ind.) was elected via a resolution moved by Charles M. Price (D-Ill.). A substitute amendment, which replaced Roberts with Harry L. Brookshire (Ohio), was defeated.
Source: *Congressional Record*, 86-1, 14.

87TH CONGRESS (ELECTION DATE: JANUARY 3, 1961)
Ralph R. Roberts (Ind.) was elected via a resolution moved by Francis E. Walter (D-Pa.). A substitute amendment, which replaced Roberts with Harry L. Brookshire (Ohio), was defeated.
Source: *Congressional Record*, 87-1, 25.

88TH CONGRESS (ELECTION DATE: JANUARY 9, 1963)

    Ralph R. Roberts (Ind.) was elected via a resolution moved by Francis
      E. Walter (D-Pa.). A substitute amendment, which replaced Roberts
      with Harry L. Brookshire (Ohio), was defeated.
    Source: *Congressional Record*, 88-1, 13.

89TH CONGRESS (ELECTION DATE: JANUARY 4, 1965)

    Ralph R. Roberts (Ind.) was elected via a resolution moved by Eugene J.
      Keogh (D-N.Y.).
    Source: *Congressional Record*, 89-1, 20.

90TH CONGRESS (ELECTION DATE: JANUARY 10, 1967)

    W. Pat Jennings (Va.) was elected via a resolution moved by Daniel D.
      Rostenkowski (D-Ill.). A substitute amendment, which replaced Jen-
      nings with Harry L. Brookshire (Ohio), was defeated.
    Source: *Congressional Record*, 90-1, 27.

91ST CONGRESS (ELECTION DATE: JANUARY 3, 1969)

    W. Pat Jennings (Va.) was elected via a resolution moved by Daniel D.
      Rostenkowski (D-Ill.). A substitute amendment, which replaced Jen-
      nings with Harry L. Brookshire (Ohio), was defeated.
    Source: *Congressional Record*, 91-1, 34.

92ND CONGRESS (ELECTION DATE: JANUARY 21, 1971)

    W. Pat Jennings (Va.) was elected via a resolution moved by Olin E.
      Teague (D-Tex.). A substitute amendment, which replaced Jennings
      with Joe Bartlett (Ohio), was defeated.
    Source: *Congressional Record*, 92-1, 13.

93RD CONGRESS (ELECTION DATE: JANUARY 3, 1973)

    W. Pat Jennings (Va.) was elected via a resolution moved by Olin E.
      Teague (D-Tex.). A substitute amendment, which replaced Jennings
      with Joe Bartlett (Ohio), was defeated.
    Source: *Congressional Record*, 93-1, 16–17.

94TH CONGRESS (ELECTION DATE: JANUARY 14, 1975)

    W. Pat Jennings (Va.) was elected via a resolution moved by Phillip Bur-
      ton (D-Calif.). A substitute amendment, which replaced Jennings
      with Joe Bartlett (Ohio), was defeated.
    Source: *Congressional Record*, 94-1, 19–20.
    Note: Jennings resigned on November 15, 1975, during the first session
      of the 94th Congress. Edmund L. Henshaw Jr. (Va.) was appointed
      acting Clerk effective at the close of business on November 15, 1975
      (and reported on November 17, 1975). See *Congressional Record*,
      94-1, 36901.

95TH CONGRESS (ELECTION DATE: JANUARY 4, 1977)
   Edmund L. Henshaw Jr. (Va.) was elected via resolution moved by
      Thomas S. Foley (D-Wash.). A substitute amendment, which replaced
      Henshaw with Joe Bartlett (Ohio), was defeated.
   Source: Congressional Record, 95-1, 52.

96TH CONGRESS (ELECTION DATE: JANUARY 15, 1979)
   Edmund L. Henshaw Jr. (Va.) was elected via a resolution moved by
      Thomas S. Foley (D-Wash.). A substitute amendment, which replaced
      Henshaw with Joe Bartlett (Ohio), was defeated.
   Source: Congressional Record, 96-1, 6–7.

97TH CONGRESS (ELECTION DATE: JANUARY 5, 1981)
   Edmund L. Henshaw Jr. (Va.) was elected via a resolution moved by
      Gillis W. Long (D-La.). A substitute amendment, which replaced
      Henshaw with Hyde H. Murray (Md.), was defeated.
   Source: Congressional Record, 97-1, 97.

98TH CONGRESS (ELECTION DATE: JANUARY 3, 1983)
   Benjamin J. Guthrie (Va.) was elected via a resolution moved by Gillis
      W. Long (D-La.). A substitute amendment, which replaced Guthrie
      with Hyde H. Murray (Md.), was defeated.
   Source: Congressional Record, 98-1, 33.

99TH CONGRESS (ELECTION DATE: JANUARY 3, 1985)
   Benjamin J. Guthrie (Va.) was elected via a resolution moved by Rich-
      ard Gephardt (D-Mo.). A substitute amendment, which replaced
      Guthrie with Hyde H. Murray (Md.), was defeated.
   Source: Congressional Record, 99-1, 392.

100TH CONGRESS (ELECTION DATE: JANUARY 6, 1987)
   Donnald K. Anderson (Calif.) was elected via a resolution moved by
      Richard Gephardt (D-Mo.). A substitute amendment, which replaced
      Anderson with Hyde H. Murray (Md.), was defeated.
   Source: Congressional Record, 100-1, 5–6.

101ST CONGRESS (ELECTION DATE: JANUARY 3, 1989)
   Donnald K. Anderson (Calif.) was elected via a resolution moved by
      William H. Gray (D-Pa.).
   Source: Congressional Record, 101-1, 71.

102ND CONGRESS (ELECTION DATE: JANUARY 3, 1991)
   Donnald K. Anderson (Calif.) was elected via a resolution moved by

Steny H. Hoyer (D-Md.). A substitute amendment, which replaced Anderson with William R. Pitts Jr. (Va.), was defeated.
Source: *Congressional Record*, 102-1, 39.

103RD CONGRESS (ELECTION DATE: JANUARY 5, 1993)
Donnald K. Anderson (Calif.) was elected via a resolution moved by Steny H. Hoyer (D-Md.). A substitute amendment, which replaced Anderson with William R. Pitts Jr. (Va.), was defeated.
Source: *Congressional Record*, 103-1, 48–49.

104TH CONGRESS (ELECTION DATE: JANUARY 4, 1995)
Robin H. Carle (Va.) was elected via a resolution moved by John A. Boehner (R-Ohio). A substitute amendment, which replaced Carle with Thomas O'Donnell (Md.), was defeated.
Source: *Congressional Record*, 104-1, 447.

105TH CONGRESS (ELECTION DATE: JANUARY 7, 1997)
Robin H. Carle (Va.) was elected via a resolution moved by John A. Boehner (R-Ohio). A substitute amendment, which replaced Carle with Marti Thomas (D.C.), was defeated.
Source: *Congressional Record*, 105-1, 120.
Note: Carle announced on December 21, 1998, that she would be resigning her post effective January 1, 1999. Jeffrey J. Trandahl was appointed Clerk effective January 1, 1999.
Source: *Congressional Record Daily*, 106-1, H228.

106TH CONGRESS (ELECTION DATE: JANUARY 6, 1999)
Jeffrey J. Trandahl (Va.) was elected via a resolution moved by J. C. Watts (R-Okla.). A substitute amendment, which replaced Trandahl with Dan Turton (Va.), was defeated.
Source: *Congressional Record*, 106-1, 46.

107TH CONGRESS (ELECTION DATE: JANUARY 3, 2001)
Jeffrey J. Trandahl (S.D.) was elected via a resolution moved by J. C. Watts (R-Okla.). A substitute amendment, which replaced Trandahl with Dan Turton (Va.), was defeated.
Source: *Congressional Record*, 107-1, 24.

108TH CONGRESS (ELECTION DATE: JANUARY 7, 2003)
Jeffrey J. Trandahl (S.D.) was elected via a resolution moved by Deborah D. Pryce (R-Ohio). A substitute amendment, which replaced Trandahl with George Crawford (Calif.), was defeated.
Source: *Congressional Record*, 108-1, 6–7.

109TH CONGRESS (ELECTION DATE: JANUARY 4, 2005)
> Jeffrey J. Trandahl (S.D.) was elected via a resolution moved by Deborah D. Pryce (R-Ohio). A substitute amendment, which replaced Trandahl with Jerry Hartz (Iowa), was defeated.
> Source: Congressional Record, 109-1, 41–42.
> Note: Trandahl resigned on November 18, 2005, during the first session of the 109th Congress. Karen L. Haas was appointed Clerk effective November 18, 2005. Congressional Record, 109-1, 27489.

109TH CONGRESS—REPLACEMENT ELECTION (ELECTION DATE: DECEMBER 6, 2005)
> Karen L. Haas (Md.) was elected via a resolution moved by Deborah D. Pryce (R-Ohio). A motion to reconsider was laid on the table.
> Source: Congressional Record, 109-1, 27569.

110TH CONGRESS (ELECTION DATE: JANUARY 4, 2007)
> Karen L. Haas (Md.) was elected via a resolution moved by John B. Larson (D-Conn.). A substitute amendment, which replaced Haas with Paula Nowakowski (Mich.), was defeated.
> Source: Congressional Record, 110-1, 6.
> Note: Haas announced on February 6, 2007, that she would be resigning her post effective February 14, 2007. Congressional Record, 110-1, 3156.

110TH CONGRESS—REPLACEMENT ELECTION (ELECTION DATE: FEBRUARY 6, 2007)
> Lorraine C. Miller (Tex.) was elected via a resolution moved by Steny H. Hoyer (D-Md.). A motion to reconsider was laid on the table.
> Source: Congressional Record, 110-1, 3156–60.
> Note: Miller's term as Clerk took effect on February 15, 2007. Congressional Record, 110-1, 4242.

111TH CONGRESS (ELECTION DATE: JANUARY 6, 2009)
> Lorraine C. Miller (Tex.) was elected via a resolution moved by Xavier Becerra (D-Calif.). A substitute amendment, which replaced Miller with Paula Nowakowski (Mich.), was defeated.
> Source: Congressional Record Daily, 111-1, H6.

112TH CONGRESS (ELECTION DATE: JANUARY 5, 2011)
> Karen L. Haas (Md.) was elected via a resolution moved by Jeb Hensarling (R-Tex.). A substitute amendment, which replaced Haas with John Lawrence (N.J.), was defeated.
> Source: Congressional Record Daily, 112-1, H6.

APPENDIX 4

Election of House Printer, 15th–36th Congresses

15TH CONGRESS (ELECTION DATE: MARCH 3, 1819)
  Joseph Gales Jr. and William W. Seaton were elected on the first ballot.
  No details on the vote.
  Source: *Annals of Congress*, 15-2, 1441; *House Journal*, 15-2, 354.

16TH CONGRESS (ELECTION DATE: MARCH 3, 1821)
  Joseph Gales Jr. and William W. Seaton were elected on the first ballot.
  Gales and Seaton received 87 votes to 31 for Elliott and Irvine, 9 for
  Davis and Force, and 6 for E. De Krafft. (Total votes: 133. Necessary
  for a choice: 67.)
  Source: *Annals of Congress*, 16-2, 1291–92.

17TH CONGRESS (ELECTION DATE: FEBRUARY 25, 1823)
  Joseph Gales Jr. and William W. Seaton were elected on the first ballot.
  Gales and Seaton received 102 votes to 43 for Andrew Way Jr. and
  10 scattering. (Total votes: 155. Necessary for a choice: 78.)
  Source: *Annals of Congress*, 17-2, 1097.
  Note: *Annals of Congress* mistakenly reports that 79 votes were neces-
  sary to a choice.

18TH CONGRESS (ELECTION DATE: FEBRUARY 21, 1825)
  Joseph Gales Jr. and William W. Seaton were elected on the first ballot.
  Gales and Seaton received 141 votes to 40 for Hezekiah Niles, 8 for
  Davis and Force, and 2 for Jonathan Elliot. (Total votes: 191. Neces-
  sary for a choice: 96.)
  Source: *Niles' Weekly Register*, February 26, 1825, 414.

19TH CONGRESS (ELECTION DATE: FEBRUARY 29, 1827)
  Joseph Gales Jr. and William W. Seaton were elected on the first ballot.
  Gales and Seaton received 134 votes, to 25 for Rowland and Greer, 8
  for Duff Green, 1 for M. M. Noah, 1 illegible, and 14 blank. (Total
  votes: 183. Necessary for a choice: 92.)
  Source: *House Journal*, 19-2, 1266–67.

20TH CONGRESS (ELECTION DATE: FEBRUARY 10, 1829)
> Duff Green was elected on the first ballot. Green received 107 votes to 95 for Joseph Gales Jr. and William W. Seaton, 2 for Edward De Krafft, 1 for Amos Kendall, 1 for D. S. Carr, and 2 blanks. (Total votes: 208. Necessary for a choice: 105.)
>
> *Source*: *House Journal*, 20-2, 270–71.

21ST CONGRESS (ELECTION DATE: FEBRUARY 2, 1831)
> Duff Green was elected on the first ballot. Green received 108 votes to 76 for Joseph Gales Jr. and William W. Seaton, 16 for William Greer, 1 for Way and Gideon, 3 scattering, and 2 blanks. (Total votes: 206. Necessary for a choice: 104.)
>
> *Source*: *Niles' Weekly Register*, February 5, 1831, 408.

22ND CONGRESS (ELECTION DATE: FEBRUARY 15, 1833)
> Joseph Gales Jr. and William W. Seated were elected on the 14th ballot.

	February 14, 1833									
	1	2	3	4	5	6	7	8	9	10
Gales & Seaton	60	69	77	78	80	79	78	78	83	84
Francis P. Blair	88	93	96	95	93	97	96	98	97	95
Duff Green	25	25	20	16	14	14	14	12	14	11
Thurlow Weed	12	7	—	1	—	1	1	—	1	2
William Greer & Son	8	3	—	—	—	—	—	—	—	—
Condy Raguet	5	4	5	10	8	7	5	4	6	5
Scattering	1	—	—	—	—	1	—	—	—	—
Blank	4	—	3	4	—	6	9	4	4	5
Total votes	203	201	201	204	195	205	203	196	205	202
Necessary for a choice	102	101	101	103	98	103	102	99	103	102

	February 15			
	11	12	13	14
Gales & Seaton	91	94	93	99
Francis P. Blair	90	91	90	94
Duff Green	7	3	2	1
Thurlow Weed	—	—	—	—
William Greer & Son	—	—	—	—
Condy Raguet	7	5	2	1
Scattering	—	—	—	—
Blank	4	3	2	2
Total votes	199	196	189	197
Necessary for a choice	100	99	95	99

Source: *Register of Debates*, 22-2, 1725–26.

23RD CONGRESS
No election.

24TH CONGRESS (ELECTION DATE: DECEMBER 7, 1835)
Francis P. Blair and John C. Rives were elected on the first ballot. Blair and Rives received 138 votes to 59 for Joseph Gales Jr. and William W. Seaton, 26 for Bradford and Learned, 2 for Duff Green, 1 for Thurlow Weed, and 2 blanks. (Total votes: 228. Necessary for a choice: 115.)
Source: Congressional Globe, 24-1, 3.
Note: Congressional Globe reports the aforementioned vote break-down, but announces
an aggregate vote of 223 and votes necessary for a choice of 112.

25TH CONGRESS (ELECTION DATE: SEPTEMBER 7, 1837)
Thomas Allen was elected on the 12th ballot.

	September 5, 1837				
	1	2	3	4	5
Gales & Seaton	100	102	101	103	100
Blair & Rives	103	103	103	100	104
Thomas Allen	22	22	23	22	23
Scattering	1	1	1	2	—
Blank	4	2	—	—	1
Total votes	230	230	228	227	228
Necessary for a choice	116	116	115	114	115

	September 6			September 7			
	6	7	8	9	10	11	12
Gales & Seaton	93	81	68	48	21	8	9
Blair & Rives	107	101	101	104	105	102	101
Thomas Allen	27	42	53	70	99	111	113
Scattering	—	—	—	3	2	2	1
Blank	3	4	5	3	2	2	1
Total votes	230	228	227	228	229	225	225
Necessary for a choice	116	115	114	115	115	113	113

Source: Congressional Globe, 25-1, 11, 13, 15–16.

26TH CONGRESS (ELECTION DATE: JANUARY 30, 1840)
Francis P. Blair and John C. Rives were elected on the first ballot. Blair and Rives received 110 votes to 92 for Joseph Gales Jr. and William W. Seaton, 2 for Thomas W. White, 1 for Jacob Gideon, 1 for S. St-

ambaugh, and 1 for Duff Green. (Total votes: 207. Necessary for a choice: 104.)
Source: *House Journal*, 26-1, 261–63.

27TH CONGRESS (ELECTION DATE: JUNE 11, 1841)
Joseph Gales Jr. and William W. Seaton were elected on the first ballot. Gales and Seaton received 134 votes to 75 for Francis P. Blair and John C. Rives and 6 for Peter Force. (Total votes: 215. Necessary for a choice: 108.)
Source: *House Journal*, 27-1, 88–89.

28TH CONGRESS (ELECTION DATE: DECEMBER 7, 1843)
Francis P. Blair and John C. Rives were elected on the first ballot. Blair and Rives received 124 votes to 62 for Joseph Gales Jr. and William W. Seaton, and 1 for Jacob Gideon. (Total votes: 187. Necessary for a choice: 94.)
Source: *House Journal*, 28-1, 35–37.

29TH CONGRESS (ELECTION DATE: DECEMBER 3, 1845)
Thomas Ritchie and John P. Heiss elected on the first ballot. Ritchie and Heiss received 123 votes to 69 for Fisk & Dow, 4 for Joseph Gales Jr. and William W. Seaton, and 2 for Jefferson and Co. (Total votes: 198. Necessary for a choice: 100.)
Source: *Congressional Globe*, 29-1, 18–19.

30TH AND 31ST CONGRESSES
No election. Printers were selected by the House Clerk in accordance with lowest-bid law.

32ND CONGRESS (ELECTION DATE: AUGUST 27, 1852)
Robert Armstrong was elected on the first ballot. Armstrong received 107 votes to 28 for John T. Towers, 20 for Joseph Gales Jr. and William W. Seaton, 9 for George S. Gideon, 6 for G. Bailey, 4 for William C. Bryant, 3 for Horace Greeley, 3 for John C. Rives, 2 for J. M. Daniel, 2 for W. G. Brownlow, 2 for H. J. Raymond, and 1 for John Forsyth. (Total votes: 187. Necessary for a choice: 94.)
Source: *House Journal*, 32-1, 1096–97.

33RD CONGRESS (ELECTION DATE: DECEMBER 7, 1853)
Robert Armstrong was elected on the first ballot. Armstrong received 126 votes to 64 for Joseph Gales, 20 for Beverley Tucker, 3 for Gamaliel Bailey, 1 for Lemuel Towers, 1 for Gideon and Co., 1 for Horace Greeley, 1 for Roger Pryor, and 1 for John C. Rives. (Total votes: 218. Necessary for a choice: 110.)
Source: *House Journal*, 33-1, 41–43.

34TH CONGRESS (ELECTION DATE: FEBRUARY 13, 1856)
Cornelius Wendell was elected on the 11th ballot.

	February 6, 1856			February 11			February 12			Feb. 13	
	1	2	3	4	5	6	7	8	9	10	11
Oran Follett	80	77	74	68	68	65	65	63	54	36	26
Cornelius Wendell	68	68	66	66	74	71	69	65	62	73	91
Robert Farnham	18	22	25	16	15	9	9	10	11	8	3
Nathan Sargent	11	10	10	9	6	6	6	6	6	8	8
John T. Towers	7	4	—	1	—	—	1	—	—	—	—
John D. Defrees	4	5	7	3	3	4	6	7	12	12	15
Francis P. Blair Jr.	2	1	1	—	—	—	—	—	—	—	—
William W. Seaton	1	—	—	—	—	—	—	—	—	—	—
Jared V. Peck	1	1	1	—	—	—	—	—	—	—	—
Beverly Tucker	1	1	1	1	1	1	—	—	—	—	—
R. Ridgway	1	1	3	—	—	—	—	—	—	—	—
J. Watson Webb	1	1	1	—	1	—	—	—	—	5	7
Edward Morris	—	—	—	4	4	3	1	3	3	4	—
Joseph Gales	—	—	—	2	1	—	—	—	—	—	—
Charles Sentelle	—	—	—	1	1	1	1	1	1	—	—
_____ Jones	—	—	—	1	—	—	—	—	—	—	—
R. W. Hughes	—	—	—	1	1	1	—	—	—	—	—
George Knapp	—	—	—	—	—	5	—	—	3	1	1
J. Thompson	—	—	—	—	—	1	—	—	—	—	—
George D. Prentice	—	—	—	—	—	—	3	3	3	—	1
A. D. Banks	—	—	—	—	—	—	3	5	5	2	—
John B. Norman	—	—	—	—	—	—	—	—	2	—	—
Joseph M. Coombs	—	—	—	—	—	—	—	—	—	9	8
A. McIntosh	—	—	—	—	—	—	—	—	—	2	—
Total votes	195	191	189	173	175	167	164	163	162	160	160
Necessary for a choice	98	96	95	87	88	84	83	82	82	81	81

Source: *Congressional Globe*, 34-1, 373–74, 389–90, 396–97, 409–10.

35TH CONGRESS (ELECTION DATE: DECEMBER 9, 1857)
James B. Steedman was elected on the first ballot. Steedman received 121 votes to 89 for George M. Weston, 3 for Joseph Gales Jr. and William W. Seaton, and 1 for Robert Cawthon. (Total votes: 215. Necessary for a choice: 108.)

Source: *House Journal*, 35-1, 51–53.

36TH CONGRESS (ELECTION DATE: MARCH 2, 1860)
Thomas H. Ford was elected on the 18th ballot.

	2/13		2/15			2/23			
	1	2	3	4	5	6	7	8	9
John D. Defrees	89	90	90	90	91	83	77	2	—
Adam J. Glossbrenner	88	89	89	89	90	86	87	84	82
Mr. Blanchard	2	1	—	—	—	—	—	1	—
Gales & Seaton	2	2	2	1	1	5	2	2	—
Mr. Flanagan	1	—	—	—	—	—	—	—	—
A. S. Mitchell	1	—	—	—	—	—	—	9	1
Mr. Coombs	—	1	—	—	—	1	—	—	—
Mr. Beaumont	—	—	—	—	—	3	4	3	3
Mr. Winton	—	—	—	—	—	1	1	1	1
Edward Ball	—	—	—	—	—	—	9	57	87
Ellis H. Roberts	—	—	—	—	—	—	—	4	—
Henry Barnes	—	—	—	—	—	—	—	4	—
Mr. Sulgrove	—	—	—	—	—	—	—	3	—
Samuel Bowles	—	—	—	—	—	—	—	1	—
W. S. King	—	—	—	—	—	—	—	1	—
Robert G. Harper	—	—	—	—	—	—	—	1	—
M. C. Garber	—	—	—	—	—	—	—	1	—
James Barker	—	—	—	—	—	—	—	1	—
N. C. Geer	—	—	—	—	—	—	—	1	—
Joseph Gales	—	—	—	—	—	—	—	—	1
Harvey Watterston	—	—	—	—	—	—	—	—	—
Mr. Pangbore	—	—	—	—	—	—	—	—	—
William W. Seaton	—	—	—	—	—	—	—	—	—
Mr. Howell	—	—	—	—	—	—	—	—	—
Mr. Barksdale	—	—	—	—	—	—	—	—	—
Thomas H. Ford	—	—	—	—	—	—	—	—	—
Mr. Holloway	—	—	—	—	—	—	—	—	—
Mr. Ritchie	—	—	—	—	—	—	—	—	—
Mr. Roland	—	—	—	—	—	—	—	—	—
John F. Zimmerman	—	—	—	—	—	—	—	—	—
Total votes	183	183	181	180	182	179	180	176	175
Necessary for a choice	92	92	91	91	92	90	91	89	88

	2/24			2/27				2/29	3/2
	10	11	12	13	14	15	16	17	18
John D. Defrees	—	—	—	2	—	—	—	—	—
Adam J. Glossbrenner	92	89	75	81	81	74	72	78	73
Mr. Blanchard	—	—	—	—	—	—	—	—	—
Gales & Seaton	—	2	—	—	—	—	—	—	—
Mr. Flanagan	—	—	—	—	—	—	—	—	—
A. S. Mitchell	15	17	16	—	—	—	—	—	—

	2/24			2/27				2/29	3/2
	10	11	12	13	14	15	16	17	18
Mr. Coombs	—	—	—	1	1	1	—	—	—
Mr. Beaumont	—	—	—	—	—	—	—	—	—
Mr. Winton	1	1	1	2	1	1	1	2	1
Edward Ball	81	78	75	31	8	7	2	3	3
Ellis H. Roberts	—	—	—	—	—	—	—	—	—
Henry Barnes	—	—	—	—	—	—	—	—	—
Mr. Sulgrove	—	—	—	—	—	—	—	—	—
Samuel Bowles	—	—	—	—	—	—	—	—	—
W. S. King	—	—	—	—	—	—	—	—	—
Robert G. Harper	—	—	—	—	—	—	—	—	—
M. C. Garber	—	—	—	—	—	—	—	—	—
James Barker	—	—	—	—	—	—	—	—	—
N. C. Geer	—	—	—	—	—	—	—	—	—
Joseph Gales	—	—	—	—	—	—	—	—	—
Harvey Watterston	1	1	—	—	—	—	—	—	—
Mr. Pangbore	1	—	—	—	—	—	—	—	—
William W. Seaton	—	—	16	14	14	17	18	9	9
Mr. Howell	—	—	1	—	—	—	—	—	—
Mr. Barksdale	—	—	1	—	—	—	—	—	—
Thomas H. Ford	—	—	—	65	91	88	93	87	96
Mr. Holloway	—	—	—	1	1	1	—	—	—
Mr. Ritchie	—	—	—	—	—	—	—	1	2
Mr. Roland	—	—	—	—	—	—	—	—	2
John F. Zimmerman	—	—	—	—	—	—	—	—	1
Total votes	191	188	185	197	197	189	186	180	187
Necessary for a choice	96	95	93	99	99	95	94	91	94

Source: *House Journal*, 36-1, 262–65, 286–90, 359–65, 372–76, 383–88, 390–91, 408–9, 425–27.

APPENDIX 5

Summary of Democratic and Republican Caucus Nominations for Speaker,
38th–112th Congresses

						Democrats		
Cong.	Year	D	R	Oth.	Margin pct.	Nominee	Ballots	Effective no. of candidates
38	1863	72	86	27	7.6*	No choice		No report
39	1865	38	**136**	19	50.8	James Brooks (N.Y.)	Unknown	
40	1867	47	**173**	4	56.3	Samuel S. Marshall (Ill.)	1	1.8
41	1869	67	**171**	5	42.8	Michael C. Kerr (Ind.)	Unknown	No report
42	1871	104	**136**	3	13.2	George W. Morgan (Ohio)	1	1.9
43	1873	88	**199**	5	38.0	Fernando Wood (N.Y.)	2	3.0
44	1875	**182**	103	8	27.0	**Michael C. Kerr (Ind.)**	3	2.7
						Samuel Randall (Pa.)	1	2.0
45	1877	**155**	136	8	6.4	**Samuel Randall (Pa.)**	1	1.7
46	1879	**141**	132	20	3.1*	**Samuel Randall (Pa.)**	1	2.2
47	1881	128	**151**	14	7.8	Samuel Randall (Pa.)	1	1
48	1883	**196**	117	12	24.3	**John Carlisle (Ky.)**	1	2.4
49	1885	**182**	141	2	12.6	**John Carlisle (Ky.)**	1	1
50	1887	**167**	152	6	4.6	**John Carlisle (Ky.)**	1	1
51	1889	152	**179**	1	8.1	John Carlisle (Ky.)	1	No report
52	1891	**238**	86	8	45.8	**Charles F. Crisp (Ga.)**	30	3.5
53	1893	**218**	124	14	26.4	**Charles F. Crisp (Ga.)**	1	1
54	1895	93	**254**	10	45.1	Charles F. Crisp (Ga.)	1	1
55	1897	124	**206**	27	23.0	Joseph W. Bailey (Tex.)	1	2.6
56	1899	161	**187**	9	7.3	James D. Richardson (Tenn.)	6	3.9
57	1901	151	**200**	6	13.7	James D. Richardson (Tenn.)	1	1
58	1903	176	**207**	3	8.0	John B. Williams (Miss.)	1	1
59	1905	135	**251**	0	30.1	John B. Williams (Miss.)	1	1
60	1907	167	**223**	1	14.3	John B. Williams (Miss.)	1	1
61	1909	172	**219**	0	12.0	Champ Clark (Mo.)	1	1
62	1911	**230**	162	2	17.3	**Champ Clark (Mo.)**	1	1
63	1913	**291**	134	10	36.1	**Champ Clark (Mo.)**	1	1
64	1915	**230**	196	9	7.8	**Champ Clark (Mo.)**	1	1
65	1917	214	215	6	0.2*	**Champ Clark (Mo.)**	1	1
66	1919	192	**240**	2	11.1	Champ Clark (Mo.)	1	1
67	1921	131	**302**	2	39.3	Claude Kitchin (N.C.)	1	No report
68	1923	207	**225**	3	4.1	Finis J. Garrett (Tenn.)	1	1
69	1925	183	**247**	5	14.7	Finis J. Garrett (Tenn.)	1	1
70	1927	194	**238**	3	10.1	Finis J. Garrett (Tenn.)	1	No report
71	1929	164	**270**	1	24.4	John Garner (Tex.)	1	1
72	1931[a]	216	218	1	0.5	**John Garner (Tex.)**	1	1
73	1933	**313**	117	5	45.1	**Henry T. Rainey (Ill.)**	1	1.3

						Democrats		
						---	---	---
Cong.	Year	D	R	Oth.	Margin pct.	Nominee	Ballots	Effective no. of candidates
74	1935	**322**	103	10	50.3	Joseph W. Byrns (Tenn.)	1	1
						William B. Bankhead (Ala.)	No caucus	
75	1937	**334**	88	13	56.6	William B. Bankhead (Ala.)	1	1
76	1939	**262**	169	4	21.4	William B. Bankhead (Ala.)	1	1
						Samuel Rayburn (Tex.)	No caucus	
77	1941	**267**	162	6	24.1	Samuel Rayburn (Tex.)	1	1
78	1943	**222**	209	4	3.0	Samuel Rayburn (Tex.)	1	1
79	1945	**242**	191	2	11.7	Samuel Rayburn (Tex.)	1	No report
80	1947	188	**246**	1	13.3	Samuel Rayburn (Tex.)	1	No report
81	1949	**263**	171	1	21.1	Samuel Rayburn (Tex.)	1	1
82	1951	**235**	199	1	8.3	Samuel Rayburn (Tex.)	1	1
83	1953	213	**221**	1	1.8	Samuel Rayburn (Tex.)	1	1
84	1955	**232**	203	0	6.7	Samuel Rayburn (Tex.)	1	1
85	1957	**234**	201	0	7.6	Samuel Rayburn (Tex.)	1	No report
86	1959	**283**	153	1	29.7	Samuel Rayburn (Tex.)	1	1
87	1961	**263**	174	0	20.4	Samuel Rayburn (Tex.)	1	No report
						John W. McCormack (Mass.)	1	1
88	1963	**259**	176	0	19.1	John W. McCormack (Mass.)	1	1
89	1965	**295**	140	0	35.6	John W. McCormack (Mass.)	1	No report
90	1967	**247**	187	0	13.8	John W. McCormack (Mass.)	1	1
91	1969	**243**	192	0	11.7	John W. McCormack (Mass.)	1	1.6
92	1971	**255**	180	0	17.2	Carl Albert (Okla.)	1	1.2
93	1973	**242**	192	1	11.5	Carl Albert (Okla.)	1	1.2
94	1975	**291**	144	0	33.8	Carl Albert (Okla.)	1	1
95	1977	**292**	143	0	34.3	Thomas P. "Tip" O'Neill (Mass.)	1	1
96	1979	**277**	158	0	27.4	Thomas P. "Tip" O'Neill (Mass.)	1	1
97	1981	**242**	192	1	11.5	Thomas P. "Tip" O'Neill (Mass.)	1	1
98	1983	**269**	166	0	23.7	Thomas P. "Tip" O'Neill (Mass.)	1	1
99	1985	**253**	182	0	16.3	Thomas P. "Tip" O'Neill (Mass.)	1	1
100	1987	**258**	177	0	18.6	James Wright (Tex.)	1	1
101	1989	**260**	175	0	19.5	James Wright (Tex.)	1	1
						Thomas Foley (Wash.)	1	No report
102	1991	**267**	167	1	23.0	Thomas Foley (Wash.)	1	1

(Continued on next page)

(Continued)

						Democrats		
Cong.	Year	D	R	Oth.	Margin pct.	Nominee	Ballots	Effective no. of candidates
103	1993	258	176	1	18.9	Thomas Foley (Wash.)	1	1
104	1995	204	230	1	6.0	Richard A. Gephardt (Mo.)	1	1.7
105	1997	206	228	1	5.1	Richard A. Gephardt (Mo.)	1	1
106	1999	211	223	1	2.8	Richard A. Gephardt (Mo.)	1	1
107	2001	212	221	2	2.1	Richard A. Gephardt (Mo.)	1	1
108	2003	204	229	1	5.8	Nancy Pelosi (Calif.)	1	1.3
109	2005	202	232	1	6.9	Nancy Pelosi (Calif.)	1	1
110	2007	233	202	0	7.1	Nancy Pelosi (Calif.)	1	1
111	2009	257	178	0	18.2	Nancy Pelosi (Calif.)	1	1
112	2011	193	242	0	11.3	Nancy Pelosi (Calif.)	1	1.5

						Republicans		
Cong.	Year	D	R	Oth.	Margin pct.	Nominee	Ballots	Effective no. of candidates
38	1863	72	86	27	7.6*	Schuyler Colfax (Ind.)	1	1
39	1865	38	136	19	50.8	Schuyler Colfax (Ind.)	1	1
40	1867	47	173	4	56.3	Schuyler Colfax (Ind.)	Unknown	No report
41	1869	67	171	5	42.8	James G. Blaine (Maine)	1	1
42	1871	104	136	3	13.2	James G. Blaine (Maine)	1	1
43	1873	88	199	5	38.0	James G. Blaine (Maine)	1	1
44	1875	182	103	8	27.0	James G. Blaine (Me.)	Unknown	No report
						James Garfield (Ohio)	1	1
45	1877	155	136	8	6.4	James Garfield (Ohio)	1	1
46	1879	141	132	20	3.1*	James Garfield (Ohio)	1	1
47	1881	128	151	14	7.8	J. Warren Keifer (Ohio)	16	4.1
48	1883	196	117	12	24.3	J. Warren Keifer (Ohio)	1	1.6
49	1885	182	141	2	12.6	Thomas B. Reed (Maine)	1	2.0
50	1887	167	152	6	4.6	Thomas B. Reed (Maine)	1	1
51	1889	152	179	1	8.1	Thomas B. Reed (Maine)	2	3.2
52	1891	238	86	8	45.8	Thomas B. Reed (Maine)	1	1
53	1893	218	124	14	26.4	Thomas B. Reed (Maine)	1	1
54	1895	93	254	10	45.1	Thomas B. Reed (Maine)	1	1
55	1897	124	206	27	23.0	Thomas B. Reed (Maine)	1	1
56	1899	161	187	9	7.3	David B. Henderson (Iowa)	1	1
57	1901	151	200	6	13.7	David B. Henderson (Iowa)	1	1
58	1903	176	207	3	8.0	Joseph G. Cannon (Ill.)	1	1

						Republicans		
Cong.	Year	D	R	Oth.	Margin pct.	Nominee	Ballots	Effective no. of candidates
59	1905	135	**251**	0	30.1	**Joseph G. Cannon (Ill.)**	1	1
60	1907	167	**223**	1	14.3	**Joseph G. Cannon (Ill.)**	1	1
61	1909	172	**219**	0	12.0	**Joseph G. Cannon (Ill.)**	1	1.3
62	1911	**230**	162	2	17.3	James R. Mann (Ill.)	1	1
63	1913	**291**	134	10	36.1	James R. Mann (Ill.)	1	1
64	1915	**230**	196	9	7.8	James R. Mann (Ill.)	1	1
65	1917	214	215	6	0.2*	James R. Mann (Ill.)	1	1
66	1919	192	**240**	2	11.1	**Frederick H. Gillett (Mass.)**	1	2.1
67	1921	131	**302**	2	39.3	**Frederick H. Gillett (Mass.)**	1	1
68	1923	207	**225**	3	4.1	**Frederick H. Gillett (Mass.)**	1	1.3
69	1925	183	**247**	5	14.7	**Nicholas Longworth (Ohio)**	1	1.9
70	1927	194	**238**	3	10.1	**Nicholas Longworth (Ohio)**	1	1
71	1929	164	**270**	1	24.4	**Nicholas Longworth (Ohio)**	1	1
72	1931[a]	216	218	1	0.5	Bertrand L. Snell (N.Y.)	8	2.0
73	1933	**313**	117	5	45.1	Bertrand L. Snell (N.Y.)	1	1
74	1935	**322**	103	10	50.3	Bertrand L. Snell (N.Y.)	1	1
75	1937	**334**	88	13	56.6	Bertrand L. Snell (N.Y.)	1	1
76	1939	**262**	169	4	21.4	Joseph W. Martin (Mass.)	1	1
77	1941	**267**	162	6	24.1	Joseph W. Martin (Mass.)	1	No report
78	1943	**222**	209	4	3.0	Joseph W. Martin (Mass.)	1	No report
79	1945	**242**	191	2	11.7	Joseph W. Martin (Mass.)	1	No report
80	1947	188	**246**	1	13.3	**Joseph W. Martin (Mass.)**	1	1
81	1949	**263**	171	1	21.1	Joseph W. Martin (Mass.)	1	1
82	1951	**235**	199	1	8.3	Joseph W. Martin (Mass.)	1	No report
83	1953	213	**221**	1	1.8	**Joseph W. Martin (Mass.)**	1	1
84	1955	**232**	203	0	6.7	Joseph W. Martin (Mass.)	1	1
85	1957	**234**	201	0	7.6	Joseph W. Martin (Mass.)	1	1
86	1959	**283**	153	1	29.7	Charles S. Halleck (Ind.)	2	2.0
87	1961	**263**	174	0	20.4	Charles S. Halleck (Ind.)	1	No report
						Charles S. Halleck (Ind.)	1	No report
88	1963	**259**	176	0	19.1	Charles S. Halleck (Ind.)	1	No report
89	1965	**295**	140	0	35.6	Gerald R. Ford (Mich.)	1	2.0
90	1967	**247**	187	0	13.8	Gerald R. Ford (Mich.)	1	No report
91	1969	**243**	192	0	11.7	Gerald R. Ford (Mich.)	1	1
92	1971	**255**	180	0	17.2	Gerald R. Ford (Mich.)	1	1
93	1973	**242**	192	1	11.5	Gerald R. Ford (Mich.)	1	1
94	1975	**291**	144	0	33.8	John Rhodes (Ariz.)	1	1
95	1977	**292**	143	0	34.3	John Rhodes (Ariz.)	1	1

(*Continued on next page*)

(*Continued*)

						Republicans		
Cong.	Year	D	R	Oth.	Margin pct.	Nominee	Ballots	Effective no. of candidates
96	1979	277	158	0	27.4	John Rhodes (Ariz.)	1	1
97	1981	242	192	1	11.5	Robert H. Michel (Ill.)	1	2.0
98	1983	269	166	0	23.7	Robert H. Michel (Ill.)	1	1
99	1985	253	182	0	16.3	Robert H. Michel (Ill.)	1	1
100	1987	258	177	0	18.6	Robert H. Michel (Ill.)	1	1
101	1989	260	175	0	19.5	Robert H. Michel (Ill.)	1	1
						Robert H. Michel (Ill.)	1	No report
102	1991	267	167	1	23.0	Robert H. Michel (Ill.)	1	1
103	1993	258	176	1	18.9	Robert H. Michel (Ill.)	1	1
104	1995	204	230	1	6.0	**Newt Gingrich (Ga.)**	1	1
105	1997	206	228	1	5.1	**Newt Gingrich (Ga.)**	1	1
106	1999	211	223	1	2.8	**Robert Livingston (La.)**	1	1
						Dennis Hastert (Ill.)	1	1
107	2001	212	221	2	2.1	**Dennis Hastert (Ill.)**	1	1
108	2003	204	229	1	5.8	**Dennis Hastert (Ill.)**	1	1
109	2005	202	232	1	6.9	**Dennis Hastert (Ill.)**	1	1
110	2007	233	202	0	7.1	**John A. Boehner (Ohio)**	1	1.3
111	2009	257	178	0	18.2	John A. Boehner (Ohio)	1	No report
112	2011	193	242	0	11.3	**John A. Boehner (Ohio)**	1	1

*Plurality

[a]Between Election Day and the first day of Congress, 14 members-elect died. In the subsequent special elections, enough Democrats won to switch the majority in favor of the Democrats.

Note: Names in **bold** indicate the eventual House choice for Speaker.

The measure of the effective number of candidates is similar to Rae's (1967, chap. 3) measures of the fractionalization of the seat and vote shares of parliamentary parties and is the reciprocal of the economists' "Hyrfendahl index," which measures the concentration of firms in an industry. It is constructed this way. Let f_i be the fraction of votes received by candidate i on a ballot and c be the total number of candidates receiving votes. Then the measure of the effective number of candidates on that ballot is simply

$$e = \left(\sum_{i=1}^{c} f_i^2 \right)^{-1}$$

Whenever there is more than one ballot for Speaker, the effective number of candidates is calculated using the first ballot vote.

APPENDIX 6

Democratic and Republican Caucus Nominations for Speaker,

38th–112th Congresses

Note: Boldface text in this section indicates the majority party in the particular Congress.

38TH CONGRESS
   Republicans chose Schuyler Colfax (Ind.) on first ballot "by acclamation."
   Source: *New York Times*, December 6, 1863, 1.
   Democrats did not make a caucus nomination. A caucus did meet to select other officers, but a rift occurred when trying to choose a speakership candidate.
   Source: *Chicago Tribune*, December 8, 1863, 1.

39TH CONGRESS
   Republicans chose Schuyler Colfax (Ind.) on first ballot "by acclamation."
   Source: *New York Times*, Dec. 4, 1865, 1; *Chicago Tribune*, Dec. 4, 1865, 1.
   Democrats chose James Brooks (N.Y.). No details on the caucus vote.
   Source: *New York Times*, December 5, 1865, 4.

40TH CONGRESS
   Republicans chose Schuyler Colfax (Ind.). No details on the caucus vote.
   Source: *New York Times*, March 5, 1867, 5.
   Democrats chose Samuel S. Marshall (Ill.) on first ballot. Marshall received 11 votes to 6 for James Brooks (N.Y.). No details on the caucus vote.
   Source: *Daily Cleveland Herald*, March 5, 1867, 1.

41ST CONGRESS
   Republicans chose James G. Blaine (Maine) on first ballot "by unanimous vote."
   Source: *Chicago Tribune*, March 3, 1869, 1; *New York Times*, Mar. 3, 1869, 1.

Democrats chose Michael C. Kerr (Ind.). No details regarding caucus vote.

Source: *Chicago Tribune*, March 3, 1869, 1.

42ND CONGRESS

Republicans chose James G. Blaine (Maine) on first ballot "by acclamation."

Source: *New York Times*, March 3, 1871, 1.

Democrats chose George W. Morgan (Ohio) on first ballot. Morgan received 45 votes to 28 for Samuel S. Cox (N.Y.).

Source: *Bangor Daily Whig and Courier*, March 4, 1871, 2.

43RD CONGRESS

Republicans chose James G. Blaine (Maine) on first ballot "by acclamation."

Source: *New York Times*, November 30, 1873, 1; *Chicago Tribune*, November 30, 1873, 4.

Democrats chose Fernando Wood (N.Y.) on second ballot. On the first ballot, Wood received 30 votes to 20 for Samuel S. Cox (N.Y.), 19 for James C. Robinson (Ill.), 1 for Alexander Stephens (Ga.), and 1 for Lucius Lamar (Miss.). On the second ballot, Wood received 44 votes to 22 for Cox, 1 for Robinson, 1 for Stephens, 1 for Lamar, and 1 for William E. Niblack (Ind.).

Source: *Chicago Tribune*, November 30, 1873, 4.

44TH CONGRESS

Republicans chose James Garfield (Ohio) on first ballot, "unanimously."

Source: *Bangor Daily Whig and Courier*, December 5, 1876, 3.

Democrats chose Michael C. Kerr (Ind.) on third ballot.

	1	2	3
Michael C. Kerr (Ind.)	77	77	90
Samuel Randall (Pa.)	59	63	63
Samuel S. Cox (N.Y)	31	21	7
Milton Saylor (Ind.)	1	1	—

Kerr was then made the unanimous choice of the caucus.

Source: *Chicago Tribune*, December 5, 1875, 9.

44TH CONGRESS, 2ND SESSION (TO FILL SPEAKERSHIP AFTER KERR'S DEATH)

Republicans chose James Garfield (Ohio) "unanimously."

Source: *Bangor Daily Whig and Courier*, December 5, 1876, 3.

Democrats chose Samuel Randall (Pa.) on first ballot. Randall received
73 votes to 63 for Samuel S. Cox (N.Y.).
Source: New York Times, December 3, 1876, 7.

45TH CONGRESS

Republicans chose James Garfield (Ohio) on first ballot "by
acclamation."
Source: Wheeling (West Virginia) *Daily Register*, October 16, 1877, 1.
Democrats chose Samuel Randall (Pa.) on first ballot. Randall received
107 votes to 27 for John Goode (Va.) and 12 for Milton Sayler
(Ohio).
Source: New York Times, October 14, 1877, 1.

46TH CONGRESS

Republicans chose James Garfield (Ohio) on first ballot, "unanimously."
Source: New York Times, March 18, 1879, 1.
Democrats chose Samuel Randall (Pa.) on first ballot. Randall received
75 votes to 57 for Joseph Blackburn (Ky.), and 9 scattering. Blackburn then moved that Randall's nomination be made unanimous,
which "was adopted without a dissenting vote."
Source: New York Times, March 18, 1879, 1.

47TH CONGRESS

Republicans chose J. Warren Keifer (Ohio) on 16th ballot.
Source: New York Times, December 4, 1881, 1.

	December 3, 1881							
	1	2	3	4	5	6	7	8
J. Warren Keifer (Ohio)	52	55	55	55	56	54	51	51
Frank Hiscock (N.Y.)	44	41	38	35	32	34	34	34
John Kasson (Iowa)	15	16	19	20	19	18	16	17
Thomas Reed (Maine)	13	12	12	15	18	18	20	18
Julius C. Burrows (Mich.)	10	10	10	10	10	10	11	10
Godlove S. Orth (Ind.)	8	8	8	8	8	8	10	8
Mark H. Dunnell (Minn.)	4	3	3	3	3	3	3	4
Total	146	145	145	146	146	145	145	142
	9	10	11	12	13	14	15	16
J. Warren Keifer (Ohio)	56	56	55	56	59	58	61	93
Frank Hiscock (N.Y.)	35	38	40	39	37	35	34	18
John Kasson (Iowa)	19	17	16	16	16	17	16	10
Thomas Reed (Maine)	13	14	14	11	13	13	13	11
Julius C. Burrows (Mich.)	10	10	10	9	10	10	11	1
Godlove S. Orth (Ind.)	9	8	8	8	8	8	7	8
Mark H. Dunnell (Minn.)	4	3	3	3	4	4	3	3
Total	146	146	146	142	147	145	145	144

Democrats choose Samuel Randall (Pa.) on first ballot, by "viva voce without dissent."
Source: *New York Times*, December 4, 1881, 1.

48TH CONGRESS
Republicans chose J. Warren Keifer (Ohio) on first ballot. Keifer defeated George D. Robinson (Mass.) 44 to 15. Less than half of the Republican membership participated.
Source: *New York Times*, December 2, 1883, 1.
Democrats chose John G. Carlisle (Ky.) on first ballot. Carlisle received 106 votes to 52 for Samuel Randall (Pa.) and 30 for Samuel S. Cox (N.Y.). Carlisle's nomination was then made unanimous.
Source: *New York Times*, December 3, 1883, 1. Correction of totals reported in the *New York Times*, December 2, 1883, 1.

49TH CONGRESS
Republicans chose Thomas B. Reed (Maine) on first ballot. Reed received 63 votes to 42 for Frank Hiscock (N.Y.) and 3 for Thomas Ryan (Kans.). Hiscock then moved that Reed's nomination be made unanimous, "and this was done."
Source: *New York Times*, December 6, 1885, 1.
Democrats chose John G. Carlisle (Ky.) on first ballot "by acclamation."
Source: *New York Times*, December 6, 1885, 1.

50TH CONGRESS
Republicans chose Thomas B. Reed (Maine) on first ballot "without opposition."
Source: *Chicago Tribune*, December 4, 1887, 12.
Democrats chose John G. Carlisle on first ballot "by acclamation."
Source: *New York Times*, December 4, 1887, 5.

51ST CONGRESS
Republicans chose Thomas B. Reed (Maine) on the second ballot. On the first ballot, Reed received 78 votes to 39 for William McKinley (Ohio), 22 for Joseph Cannon (Ill.), 16 for David Henderson (Iowa), and 10 for Julius Burrows (Mich.). On the second ballot, Reed received 85, McKinley 38, Cannon 19, Burrows 14, and Henderson 10. On McKinley's motion, Reed's nomination was then made unanimous.
Source: *New York Times*, December 1, 1889, 1.
Democrats chose John G. Carlisle (Ky.). No details on the caucus vote.
Source: *Dallas Morning News*, December 3, 1889, 1.

52ND CONGRESS

Republicans chose Thomas B. Reed (Maine) on first ballot "by acclamation."

Source: *New York Times*, December 6, 1891, 2.

Democrats chose Charles F. Crisp (Ga.) on the 30th ballot.

Source: *New York Times*, December 8, 1891, 2.

	December 5, 1891								
	1	*2*	*3*	*4*	*5*	*6*	*7*	*8*	*9*
Charles F. Crisp (Ga.)	84	89	91	93	95	95	94	94	95
Roger Q. Mills (Tex.)	78	80	82	87	89	89	91	91	91
William Springer (Ill.)	32	28	24	20	20	20	18	17	16
Benton McMillin (Tenn.)	18	18	18	18	18	18	18	19	19
William Hatch (Mo.)	14	11	11	8	4	4	5	5	5
Moses Stevens (Mass.)	1	1	1	1	1	1	1	1	1
	227	227	227	227	227	227	227	227	227

	10	*11*	*12*	*13*	*14*	*15*	*16*	*17*
Charles F. Crisp (Ga.)	94	93	92	94	93	92	94	94
Roger Q. Mills (Tex.)	90	89	89	91	89	89	91	91
William Springer (Ill.)	17	16	19	16	17	19	17	19
Benton McMillin (Tenn.)	19	20	19	20	19	17	19	17
William Hatch (Mo.)	5	5	5	5	5	5	5	5
Moses Stevens (Mass.)	—	1	1	1	1	1	1	1
	225	224	225	227	224	223	227	227

	December 7, 1891						
	18	*19*	*20*	*21*	*22*	*23*	*24*
Charles F. Crisp (Ga.)	94	94	92	94	95	100	101
Roger Q. Mills (Tex.)	90	91	90	91	93	95	95
William Springer (Ill.)	17	17	17	17	15	13	12
Benton McMillin (Tenn.)	19	19	17	19	19	19	19
William Hatch (Mo.)	5	5	5	5	4	—	—
Moses Stevens (Mass.)	1	1	1	1	1	1	1
	226	227	222	227	227	228	228

	25	*26*	*27*	*28*	*29*	*30*
Charles F. Crisp (Ga.)	101	101	101	103	104	119
Roger Q. Mills (Tex.)	95	95	95	96	94	105
William Springer (Ill.)	12	12	12	8	9	4
Benton McMillin (Tenn.)	19	19	19	19	19	—
William Hatch (Mo.)	—	—	—	—	—	—
Moses Stevens (Mass.)	1	1	1	1	1	1
	228	228	228	227	227	229

53RD CONGRESS

Republicans chose Thomas B. Reed (Maine) on first ballot "by
    acclamation."
Source: *New York Times*, August 6, 1893, 1.
Democrats chose Charles F. Crisp (Ga.) on first ballot "by acclamation."
Source: *New York Times*, August 6, 1893, 1.

54TH CONGRESS

Republicans chose Thomas B. Reed (Maine) on first ballot "by
    acclamation."
Source: *New York Times*, December 1, 1895, 1.
Democrats chose Charles F. Crisp (Ga.) on first ballot "unanimously."
Source: *New York Times*, December 1, 1895, 2.

55TH CONGRESS

Republicans chose Thomas B. Reed (Maine) on first ballot
    "unanimously."
Source: *New York Times*, March 14, 1897, 1.
Democrats chose Joseph W. Bailey (Tex.) on first ballot. Bailey received
    56 votes to 30 for Benton McMillin (Tenn.) and 22 for Richard "Sil-
    ver Dick" Bland (Mo.).
Source: *New York Times*, March 14, 1897, 2.

56TH CONGRESS

Republicans chose David B. Henderson (Iowa) on first ballot "by
    acclamation."
Source: *New York Times*, December 3, 1899, 2.
Democrats chose James D. Richardson (Tenn.) on sixth ballot. The con-
    test began as a four-man race. After the sixth ballot, William Sulzer
    withdrew and "asked friends to vote for Richardson." A second roll
    call was then taken (the second on the sixth ballot), and Richardson
    was victorious.

	1	2	3	4	5	6-1	6-2
James Richardson (Tenn.)	43	These four ballots "showed little change"				65	90
David De Armond (Mo.)	39					45	47
John H. Bankhead (Ala.)	34					—	—
William Sulzer (N.Y.)	32					20	2

Source: *New York Times*, December 3, 1899, 2; *Chicago Tribune*, De-
    cember 3, 1899, 2.

57TH CONGRESS

Republicans chose David B. Henderson (Iowa) on first ballot
    "unanimously."
Source: *New York Times*, December 1, 1901, 1.

Democrats chose James D. Richardson (Tenn.) on first ballot "by unanimous vote."

Source: *New York Times*, December 1, 1901, 2.

58TH CONGRESS

Republicans chose Joseph G. Cannon (Ill.) on first ballot "unanimously."

Source: *Chicago Tribune*, November 8, 1903, 5.

Democrats chose John Sharp Williams (Miss.) on first ballot "unanimously."

Source: *Chicago Tribune*, November 8, 1903, 5; *New York Times*, November 8, 1903, 1.

59TH CONGRESS

Republicans chose Joseph G. Cannon (Ill.) on first ballot "by unanimous vote."

Source: *New York Times*, December 3, 1905, 3.

Democrats chose John Sharp Williams (Miss.) on first ballot "by unanimous vote."

Source: *New York Times*, December 3, 1905, 3.

60TH CONGRESS

Republicans chose Joseph G. Cannon (Ill.) on first ballot "with a harrah."

Source: *New York Times*, December 1, 1907, 1; *Chicago Tribune*, December 1, 1907, 4.

Democrats chose John Sharp Williams (Miss.) on first ballot with "no opposition."

Source: *New York Times*, December 1, 1907, 1; *Chicago Tribune*, December 1, 1907, 4.

61ST CONGRESS

Republicans chose Joseph G. Cannon (Ill.) on first ballot. Cannon received 162 votes to 10 for Walter Smith (Iowa), 7 for James Tawney (Minn.), 5 for Joseph Keifer (Ohio), 1 for Charles Townsend (Mich.), 1 for Edgar Crumpacker (Ind.), and 1 for Bird McGuire (Okla.).

Source: *New York Times*, March 14, 1909, 1.

Democrats chose James Beauchamp "Champ" Clark (Mo.) on first ballot, by "unanimous" vote.

Source: *Washington Post*, December 6, 1908, 1.

62ND CONGRESS

Republicans chose James R. Mann (Ill.) on first ballot "unanimously."

Source: *Chicago Tribune*, April 4, 1911, 1.

Democrats chose James Beauchamp "Champ" Clark (Mo.) on first ballot "unanimously."
Source: *New York Times*, January 20, 1911, 1.

63RD CONGRESS

Republicans chose James R. Mann (Ill). No details on caucus vote.
Source: *New York Times*, April 6, 1913, 2; *Los Angeles Times*, April 6, 1913, 12.
Democrats chose James Beauchamp "Champ" Clark (Mo.) on first ballot by "unanimous" vote.
Source: *New York Times*, March 6, 1913, 2.

64TH CONGRESS

Republicans chose James R. Mann (Ill.) on first ballot "unanimously."
Source: *Chicago Tribune*, December 3, 1915, 6.
Democrats chose James Beauchamp "Champ" Clark (Mo.) on first ballot "unanimously."
Source: *Los Angeles Times*, February 5, 1915, 13.

65TH CONGRESS

Republicans chose James R. Mann (Ill.) on first ballot by "unanimous vote."
Source: *New York Times*, April 1, 1917, 6.
Democrats chose James Beauchamp "Champ" Clark (Mo.) on first ballot "unanimously."
Source: *New York Times*, March 31, 1917, 4.

66TH CONGRESS

Republicans chose Frederick H. Gillett (Mass.) on first ballot. Gillett received 138 votes to 69 for James R. Mann (Ill.), 13 for Philip P. Campbell (Kans.), 4 for John Esch (Wis.), and 1 for Franklin Mondell (Wyo.). On Mann's motion, Gillett's nomination was then made unanimous.
Source: *Chicago Tribune*, February 28, 1919, 1.
Democrats chose James Beauchamp "Champ" Clark (Mo.) on first ballot "by acclamation."
Source: *Chicago Tribune*, May 18, 1919, 7.

67TH CONGRESS

Republicans chose Frederick H. Gillett (Mass.) on first ballot "without opposition."
Source: *New York Times*, March 1, 1921, 15.
Democrats chose Claude Kitchin (N.C.). No details of the caucus voting provided.
Source: *Chicago Tribune*, April 10, 1921, 6.

68TH CONGRESS

Republicans chose Frederick H. Gillett (Mass.) on first ballot. Gillett received 190 votes to 15 for Henry Cooper (Wis.), 8 for Martin B. Madden (Ill.), and 1 for Edward Little (Kans.).

Source: Chicago Tribune, December 2, 1923, 1; Los Angeles Times, December 3, 1923, 11. Democrats chose Finis J. Garrett (Tenn.) on first ballot, which was "unanimous."

Source: Los Angeles Times, December 3, 1923, 11.

69TH CONGRESS

Republicans chose Nicholas Longworth (Ohio) on first ballot. Longworth received 140 votes to 85 for Martin B. Madden (Ill.). Thirteen Republicans who opposed the Coolidge-Dawes ticket were excluded from the caucus.

Source: New York Times, February 28, 1925, 1; Chicago Tribune, February 28, 1925, 1.

Democrats chose Finis J. Garrett on first ballot "by acclamation."
Source: Chicago Tribune, March 1, 1925, 15.

70TH CONGRESS

Republicans chose Nicholas Longworth (Ohio) on first ballot "by acclamation."
Source: New York Times, February 22, 1927, 21.

Democrats chose Finis J. Garrett (Tenn.). No details on the caucus vote.
Source: New York Times, December 6, 1927, 2.

71ST CONGRESS

Republicans chose Nicholas Longworth (Ohio) on first ballot "without opposition."
Source: New York Times, March 3, 1929, 3.

Democrats chose John Garner (Tex.) on first ballot "unanimously."
Source: Los Angeles Times, March 2, 1929, 3.

72ND CONGRESS

Republicans chose Bertrand L. Snell (N.Y.) on eighth ballot.

	1	2	3	4	5	6	7
Bertrand Snell (N.Y.)	55	63	70	80	84	87	96
John Tilson (Conn.)	59	64	65	69	67	66	64

Note: Eleven different "favorite son" candidates were in the running at different points in the balloting. On the seventh ballot, Snell fell one vote short of a majority. Tilson then bowed out and asked that Snell's election be unanimous on the eighth ballot, which was done.

Source: *New York Times*, December 1, 1931, 1; *Los Angeles Times*, December 1, 1931, 1; *Chicago Tribune*, December 1, 1931, 16; *Washington Post*, December 1, 1931, 1.

Democrats chose John Garner on first ballot "unanimously."

Source: *New York Times*, December 6, 1931, 2; *Wall Street Journal*, December 7, 1931, 1.

73RD CONGRESS

Republicans chose Bertrand L. Snell (N.Y.) on first ballot "unanimously."

Source: *New York Times*, March 1, 1933, 2.

Democrats chose Henry T. Rainey (Ill.) on first ballot. Rainey received 166 votes to 112 for John McDuffie (Ala.), 20 for John E. Rankin (Miss.), and 1 for William B. Bankhead (Ala.).

Source: *Chicago Tribune*, March 3, 1933, 3.

74TH CONGRESS

Republicans chose Bertrand L. Snell (N.Y.) on first ballot. Snell received 85 votes to 1 for Carl Mapes (Mich.).

Source: *Los Angeles Times*, January 3, 1935, 7.

Democrats chose Joseph W. Byrns (Tenn.) on first ballot "by acclamation."

Source: *New York Times*, January 3, 1935, 16; *Los Angeles Times*, January 3, 1935, 1.

Note: Byrns died in office, and William B. Bankhead (Ala.) was elected unanimously as speaker on June 4, 1936, shortly before the conclusion of the Congress. There did not appear to be caucuses on either side prior to the replacement speakership election.

Source: *Chicago Tribune*, June 5, 1936, 7.

75TH CONGRESS

Republicans chose Bertrand L. Snell (N.Y.). There are no details on the caucus vote.

Source: *New York Times*, January 5, 1937, 1.

Democrats chose William B. Bankhead (Ala.) on first ballot "by acclamation."

Source: *New York Times*, January 5, 1937, 1.

76TH CONGRESS

Republicans chose Joseph W. Martin (Mass.) on first ballot, "by acclamation."

Source: *Chicago Tribune*, January 3, 1939, 1; *New York Times*, January 3, 1939, 1.

Democrats chose William B. Bankhead (Ala.) on the first ballot, "without opposition."

Source: *The Oregonian*, January 3, 1939, 1.

Note: Bankhead died in office, and Samuel T. Rayburn (Tex.) was elected "by acclamation" as Speaker on September 16, 1940, shortly before the conclusion of the Congress. There were no caucuses on either side prior to the replacement speakership election.

Source: *New York Times*, September 17, 1940, 19.

77TH CONGRESS

Republicans chose Joseph W. Martin (Mass.). There are no details on the caucus vote.

Source: *Los Angeles Times*, January 3, 1941, 2.

Democrats chose Samuel T. Rayburn (Tex.) on first ballot "unanimously."

Source: *Washington Post*, January 3, 1941, 1.

78TH CONGRESS

Republicans chose Joseph W. Martin (Mass.). There are no details on the caucus vote.

Source: *Los Angeles Times*, January 6, 1943, 1.

Democrats chose Samuel T. Rayburn (Tex.) on first ballot "unanimously."

Source: *Los Angeles Times*, January 6, 1943, 1.

79TH CONGRESS

Republicans chose Joseph W. Martin (Mass.). There are no details on the caucus vote.

Source: *New York Times*, January 3, 1945, 34.

Democrats chose Samuel T. Rayburn (Tex.). There are no details on the caucus vote.

Source: *New York Times*, January 3, 1945, 34.

80TH CONGRESS

Republicans chose Joseph W. Martin (Mass.) on first ballot "by acclamation."

Source: *Chicago Tribune*, January 3, 1947, 1.

Democrats chose Samuel T. Rayburn (Tex.). There are no details on the caucus vote.

Source: *Chicago Tribune*, January 3, 1947, 1.

81ST CONGRESS

Republicans chose Joseph W. Martin (Mass.) on first ballot "by acclamation."

Source: *Washington Post*, January 1, 1949, 1.

Democrats chose Samuel T. Rayburn (Tex.) on the first ballot, "without opposition."
Source: *Washington Post*, January 2, 1949, M1.

82ND CONGRESS

Republicans chose Joseph W. Martin (Mass.). There are no details on the caucus vote.
Source: *Chicago Tribune*, January 3, 1951, 1.
Democrats chose Samuel T. Rayburn (Tex.) on first ballot "unanimously."
Source: *Chicago Tribune*, January 3, 1951, 1.

83RD CONGRESS

Republicans chose Joseph W. Martin (Mass.) on first ballot; voting was "unanimous."
Source: *New York Times*, January 3, 1953, 8.
Democrats chose Samuel T. Rayburn (Tex.) on first ballot; voting was "unanimous."
Source: *Washington Post*, January 3, 1953, 1.

84TH CONGRESS

Republicans chose Joseph W. Martin (Mass.) "unanimously."
Source: *The Oregonian*, January 5, 1955, 1.
Democrats chose Samuel T. Rayburn (Tex.) on first ballot "unanimously."
Source: *Chicago Tribune*, January 5, 1955, 1.

85TH CONGRESS

Republicans chose Joseph W. Martin (Mass.) "unanimously."
Source: *Washington Post*, January 3, 1957, A1.
Democrats chose Samuel T. Rayburn (Tex.). There are no details on the caucus vote.
Source: *New York Times*, January 3, 1957, 1; *Los Angeles Times*, January 3, 1957, 18.

86TH CONGRESS

Republicans chose Charles A. Halleck (Ind.) on the second ballot. On the first ballot, Halleck received 73 votes to 72 for Joseph W. Martin (Mass.), with one illegible ballot. On the second ballot, Halleck received 74 votes to 70 for Martin.
Source: *Chicago Tribune*, January 7, 1959, 1; *New York Times*, January 7, 1959, 1.

Democrats chose Samuel T. Rayburn (Tex.) on first ballot "unanimously."
Source: *Chicago Tribune*, January 7, 1959, 1.

87TH CONGRESS
Republicans chose Charles A. Halleck (Ind.). There are no details on the caucus vote.
Source: *Chicago Tribune*, January 4, 1961, 3.
Democrats chose Samuel T. Rayburn (Tex.). There are no details on the caucus vote.
Source: *Chicago Tribune*, January 4, 1961, 3.

87TH CONGRESS, 2ND SESSION (TO FILL SPEAKERSHIP AFTER RAYBURN'S RETIREMENT AND DEATH)
Republicans chose Charles A. Halleck (Ind.). There are no details on the caucus vote.
Source: *Chicago Tribune*, January 11, 1962, 3.
Democrats chose John W. McCormack (Mass.) on first ballot "unanimously."
Source: *New York Times*, January 10, 1962, 1.

88TH CONGRESS
Republicans chose Charles A. Halleck (Ind.). There are no details on the caucus vote.
Source: *Chicago Tribune*, January 10, 1963, 2.
Democrats chose John W. McCormack (Mass.) on first ballot "without dissent."
Source: *Los Angeles Times*, January 9, 1963, 1.

89TH CONGRESS
Republicans chose Gerald R. Ford (Mich.) on first ballot. Ford received 73 votes to 67 for Charles A. Halleck (Ind.).
Source: *Chicago Tribune*, January 5, 1965, 1.
Democrats chose John W. McCormack (Mass.). There are no details on caucus vote.
Source: *Chicago Tribune*, January 5, 1965, 1.

90TH CONGRESS
Republicans chose Gerald R. Ford (Mich.). There are no details on caucus vote.
Source: *Chicago Tribune*, January 10, 1967, 3.
Democrats chose John W. McCormack (Mass.) on first ballot "without opposition."
Source: *New York Times*, January 10, 1967, 1.

91ST CONGRESS

Republicans chose Gerald R. Ford (Mich.) on first ballot "without opposition."

Source: *Chicago Tribune*, January 3, 1969, 9.

Democrats chose John W. McCormack (Mass.) on first ballot. McCormack received 178 votes to 58 for Morris K. Udall (Ariz.).

Source: *New York Times*, January 3, 1969, 1.

92ND CONGRESS

Republicans chose Gerald R. Ford (Mich.) on first ballot "without opposition."

Source: *Los Angeles Times*, January 21, 1971, 6.

Democrats chose Carl B. Albert (Okla.) on first ballot. Albert received 220 votes to 20 for John Conyers Jr. (Mich.).

Source: *New York Times*, January 20, 1971, 1; *Los Angeles Times*, January 20, 1971, A4.

93RD CONGRESS

Republicans chose Gerald. R. Ford (Mich.) on first ballot "without opposition."

Source: *Los Angeles Times*, January 4, 1973, A1.

Democrats chose Carl B. Albert (Okla.) on first ballot. Albert received 202 votes to 25 for John Conyers Jr. (Mich.).

Source: *Los Angeles Times*, January 2, 1973, 2; *New York Times*, January 3, 1973, 1.

94TH CONGRESS

Republicans chose John J. Rhodes (Ariz.) on first ballot "unanimously."

Source: *Los Angeles Times*, December 2, 1974, 1; *Chicago Tribune*, December 3, 1974, 12.

Democrats chose Carl B. Albert on first ballot "without opposition."

Source: *Los Angeles Times*, December 2, 1974, 1; *Chicago Tribune*, December 3, 1974, 12.

95TH CONGRESS

Republicans chose John J. Rhodes (Ariz.) on first ballot "unopposed."

Source: *Chicago Tribune*, December 9, 1976, 2.

Democrats chose Thomas P. "Tip" O'Neill (Mass.) on first ballot "without opposition."

Source: *Los Angeles Times*, December 6, 1976, A1; *Chicago Tribune*, December 7, 1976, 2.

96TH CONGRESS
Republicans chose John J. Rhodes (Ariz.) on first ballot "without opposition."
Source: *New York Times*, December 5, 1978, A20.
Democrats chose Thomas P. "Tip" O'Neill (Mass.) on first ballot "without opposition."
Source: *New York Times*, December 5, 1978, A20.

97TH CONGRESS
Republicans chose Robert H. Michel (Ill.) on first ballot. Michel received 103 votes to 87 for Guy Vander Jagt (Mich.).
Source: *New York Times*, December 9, 1980, B19.
Democrats chose Thomas P. "Tip" O'Neill (Mass.) on first ballot "without opposition."
Source: *Los Angeles Times*, December 9, 1980, B7.

98TH CONGRESS
Republicans chose Robert H. Michel (Ill.) on first ballot "without opposition."
Source: CRS Report, RL30607
Democrats chose Thomas P. "Tip" O'Neill (Mass.) on first ballot "unanimously."
Source: *Los Angeles Times*, December 7, 1982, A2.

99TH CONGRESS
Republicans chose Robert H. Michel (Ill.) on first ballot "without opposition."
Source: *Los Angeles Times*, December 3, 1984, A2; *New York Times*, December 4, 1984, A28.
Democrats chose Thomas P. "Tip" O'Neill (Mass.) on first ballot "by acclamation."
Source: *Los Angeles Times*, December 3, 1984, A2.

100TH CONGRESS
Republicans chose Robert H. Michel (Ill.) on first ballot "without opposition."
Source: CRS Report, RL30607.
Democrats chose James C. Wright Jr. (Tex.) on first ballot "without opposition."
Source: *New York Times*, December 9, 1986, A1.

101ST CONGRESS
Republicans chose Robert H. Michel (Ill.) on first ballot "without opposition."

Source: CRS Report, RL30607

Democrats chose James C. Wright Jr. (Tex.) on first ballot "unanimously."

Source: *New York Times*, December 6, 1988, B13.

Note: Wright left office amid a scandal, and Thomas S. Foley (Wash.) was elected Speaker on a pure party-line vote, 251–164, over Robert Michel. The two party caucuses met on the morning of the House vote (June 6, 1989) and selected Michel and Foley as nominees. No specific details of the caucus votes were announced.

Source: *New York Times*, June 7, 1989, A1.

102ND CONGRESS

Republicans chose Robert H. Michel (Ill.) on first ballot "without opposition."

Source: *New York Times*, December 4, 1990, B14.

Democrats chose Thomas S. Foley (Wash.) on first ballot "by acclamation."

Source: *New York Times*, December 4, 1990, B14.

103RD CONGRESS

Republicans chose Robert H. Michel (Ill.) on first ballot "without opposition."

Source: *New York Times*, December 8, 1992, B12.

Democrats chose Thomas S. Foley (Wash.) on first ballot "unopposed."

Source: *New York Times*, December 8, 1992, B12.

104TH CONGRESS

Republicans chose Newton L. Gingrich (Ga.) on first ballot "unanimously."

Source: *New York Times*, December 6, 1994, A1.

Democrats chose Richard A. Gephardt (Mo.) on first ballot. Gephardt received 150 votes, to 58 for Charlie Rose (N.C.).

Source: *New York Times*, December 1, 1994, A28.

105TH CONGRESS

Republicans chose Newton L. Gingrich (Ga.) on first ballot "without dissent."

Source: *New York Times*, November 21, 1996, A1.

Democrats chose Richard A. Gephardt (Mo.) on first ballot "without opposition."

Source: *New York Times*, November 19, 1996, A20.

106TH CONGRESS

Republicans chose Robert L. Livingston Jr. (La.) on first ballot "unanimously."

Source: New York Times, November 19, 1998, A1.

Democrats chose Richard A. Gephardt (Mo.) on first ballot "unopposed."

Source: New York Times, November 17, 1998, A17.

Note: Livingston resigned due to scandal, prior to the speakership election. The Republicans then selected J. Dennis Hastert (Ill.) as their new speakership nominee. Hastert was chosen on the first ballot "unanimously."

Source: Los Angeles Times, January 6, 1999, 9.

107TH CONGRESS

Republicans chose J. Dennis Hastert (Ill.) on first ballot "without opposition."

Source: St. Louis Post-Dispatch, November 15, 2000, A4.

Democrats chose Richard A. Gephardt (Mo.) on first ballot "without opposition."

Source: St. Louis Post-Dispatch, November 15, 2000, A4.

108TH CONGRESS

Republicans chose J. Dennis Hastert (Ill.) on first ballot "unopposed."
Source: CQ Weekly, November 16, 2002, 3009.

Democrats chose Nancy Pelosi (Calif.) on first ballot. Pelosi received 177 votes to 29 for Harold E. Ford Jr. (Tenn).

Source: New York Times, November 15, 2002, A28.

109TH CONGRESS

Republicans chose J. Dennis Hastert (Ill.) on first ballot by "unanimous voice vote."

Source: Houston Chronicle, November 17, 2004, 4.

Democrats chose Nancy Pelosi (Calif.) on first ballot "without opposition."

Source: CRS Report, RL30607.

110TH CONGRESS

Republicans chose John Boehner (Ohio) on first ballot. Boehner received 168 votes to 27 for Mike Pence (Ind.) and 1 for Joe Barton (Tex.).

Source: New York Times, November 18, 2006, A15.

Democrats chose Nancy Pelosi (Calif.) on first ballot "unanimously."
Source: New York Times, November 17, 2006, A1.

111TH CONGRESS

Republicans chose John Boehner (Ohio) on first ballot. Boehner received a majority against Dan Lungren (Calif.).

Source: *New York Times*, November 20, 2008, A30; *CQ Weekly*, November 24, 2008, 3154.

Democrats chose Nancy Pelosi (Calif.) on first ballot "without opposition."

Source: *CQ Weekly*, November 24, 2008, 3154.

112TH CONGRESS

Republicans chose John Boehner (Ohio) on first ballot "without opposition."

Source: *CQ Weekly*, November 22, 2010, 2712.

Democrats chose Nancy Pelosi (Calif.) on first ballot. Pelosi received 150 votes to 43 for Heath Shuler (N.C.).

Source: *New York Times*, November 18, 2010, A22.

REFERENCES

❦

Adams, John Quincy. 1876. *Memoirs of John Quincy Adams, Comprising Portions of His Diary from 1795–1848.* Vol. 9, ed. Charles Francis Adams. Philadelphia: Lippincott.

Adams, John Quincy. 1876. *Memoirs of John Quincy Adams, Comprising Portions of His Diary from 1795–1848.* Vol. 10, ed. Charles Francis Adams. Philadelphia: Lippincott.

Aldrich, John H. 1995. *Why Parties? The Origin and Transformation of Political Parties in America.* Chicago: University of Chicago Press.

Aldrich, John H., and James S. Coleman Battista. 2002. "Conditional Party Government in the States." *American Journal of Political Science* 46: 164–72.

Aldrich, John H., and David W. Rohde. 2005. "Congressional Committees in a Partisan Era." In Lawrence C. Dodd and Bruce I. Oppenheimer, eds., *Congress Reconsidered.* 8th ed. Washington, D.C.: Congressional Quarterly Press.

Alexander, De Alva. 1916. *History and Procedure of the House of Representatives.* Boston: Houghton Mifflin.

Allen, William C. 2001. *History of the United States Capitol: A Chronicle of Design, Construction, and Politics.* Honolulu, Hawaii: University Press of the Pacific.

Altman, O. R. 1937. "First Session of the Seventy–fifth Congress, January 5, 1937, to August 21, 1937." *American Political Science Review* 31: 1071–93.

Ambler, Charles Henry. 1913. *Thomas Ritchie: A Study in Virginia Politics.* Richmond: Bell Book & Stationary Co.

Ames, William E. 1972. *A History of the* National Intelligencer. Chapel Hill: University of North Carolina Press.

Anbinder, Tyler. 1992. *Nativism and Slavery: The Northern Know Nothings and the Politics of the 1850s.* New York: Oxford University Press.

Anderson, James L., and W. Edwin Hemphill. 1972. "The 1843 Biography of John C. Calhoun: Was R.M.T. Hunter Its Author?" *Journal of Southern History* 38: 469–74.

Associated Press. 2011. "19 Democrats Don't Back Pelosi in Speaker Vote." http://cnsnews.com/news/article/19-democrats-dont-back-pelosi-speaker-vote.

Axelrod, Robert M. 1970. *Conflict of Interest: A Theory of Divergent Goals with Applications to Politics.* Chicago: Markham Publishing.

Barnes, James A. 1931. *John G. Carlisle: Financial Statesman.* New York: Dodd, Mead & Co.

Belz, Herman. 1970. "The Etheridge Conspiracy of 1863: A Projected Conservative Coup." *Journal of Southern History* 36: 549–67.

Bensel, Richard Franklin. 1985. "The Antebellum Political Economy and the Speaker's Contest of 1859." Paper presented at the Annual Meeting of the American Political Science Association, New Orleans, Louisiana.

Bensel, Richard Franklin. 1990. *Yankee Leviathan: The Origins of Central State Authority in America, 1859–1877*. Cambridge: Cambridge University Press.

Bensel, Richard Franklin. 2000. *The Political Economy of American Industrialization, 1877–1900*. Cambridge: Cambridge University Press.

Benton, Thomas Hart. 1856. *Thirty Years' View*. Vol. 2. New York: D. Appleton and Company.

Berdahl, Clarence A. 1949a. "Some Notes on Party Membership in Congress, I." *American Political Science Review* 43: 309–21.

Berdahl, Clarence A. 1949b. "Some Notes on Party Membership in Congress, II." *American Political Science Review* 43: 492–508.

Berkeley, Edmund, and Dorothy S. Berkeley. 1962. "'The Ablest Clerk in the U.S.': John James Beckley." *Virginia Magazine of History and Biography* 70: 434–46.

Berkeley, Edmund, and Dorothy S. Berkeley. 1973. *John Beckley: Zealous Partisan in a Nation Divided*. Philadelphia: American Philosophical Society.

Berkeley, Edmund, and Dorothy S. Berkeley. 1975. "The First Librarian of Congress: John Beckley." *Quarterly Journal of the Library of Congress* 32: 83–117.

Bianco, William T. 1994. *Trust: Representatives and Constituents*. Ann Arbor: University of Michigan Press.

Billington, Roy A. 1938. *The Protestant Crusade, 1800–1860: A Study of the Origins of American Nativism*. Chicago: Quadrangle Books.

Binder, Sarah A. 1997. *Majority Rights, Minority Rule: Partisanship and the Development of Congress*. New York: Cambridge University Press.

Blaine, James G. 1886. *Twenty Years of Congress: From Lincoln to Garfield*. Vol. 2. Norwich, Conn.: Henry Bill.

Bogue, Allan G. 1981. *The Congressman's Civil War*. New York: Cambridge University Press.

Bolling, Richard. 1968. *Power in the House: A History of the Leadership of the House of Representatives*. New York: Dutton.

Borome, Joseph. 1951. "Two Letters of Robert Charles Winthrop." *Mississippi Valley Historical Review* 38: 289–96.

Brady, David W. 1988. *Critical Elections and Congressional Policy Making*. Stanford, Calif.: Stanford University Press.

Brauer, Kinley J. 1967. *Cotton versus Conscience: Massachusetts Whig Politics and Southwestern Expansion, 1843–1848*. Lexington: University of Kentucky Press.

Brown, David. 2006. *Southern Outcast: Hinton Rowan Helper and the Impending Crisis of the South*. Baton Rouge: Louisiana State University Press.

Brown, Everett S., ed. 1926. *The Missouri Compromises and Presidential Politics, 1820–1825*. St. Louis, Mo.: St. Louis Historical Society.

Brown, George Rothwell. 1922. *The Leadership of Congress*. Indianapolis: Bobbs-Merrill.

Bruns, Roger A. 1975. "The Covode Committee, 1860." In Arthur M. Schlesinger Jr. and Roger Bruns, eds., *Congress Investigates: A Documented History, 1792–1974*. Vol. 2. New York: Chelsea House Publishers.

Campbell, Andrea C., Gary W. Cox, and Mathew D. McCubbins. 2002. "Agenda Power in the U.S. Senate, 1877–1986." In David W. Brady and Mathew D. McCubbins, eds., *Party, Process, and Political Change in Congress*. Stanford, Calif.: Stanford University Press.

Canon, David T., Garrison Nelson, and Charles Stewart III. 2002. *Committees in the*

U.S. Congress, 1789–1946. Vols. 1–4. Washington, D.C.: Congressional Quarterly Press.

Canon, David T., and Charles Stewart III. 1995. "Taking Care of Business: The Revolution of the House Committee System before the Civil War." Paper presented at the annual meeting of the American Political Science Association.

Canon, David T., and Charles Stewart III. 2001. "The Evolution of the Committee System in Congress." In Lawrence C. Dodd and Bruce I. Oppenheimer, eds., *Congress Reconsidered.* 7th ed. Washington, D.C.: Congressional Quarterly Press.

Canon, David T., and Charles Stewart III. 2002. "Parties and Hierarchies in Senate Committees, 1789–1946." In Bruce I. Oppenheimer, ed., *U.S. Senate Exceptionalism.* Columbus: Ohio State University Press.

Carson, David A. 1986. "The Ground Called Quiddism: John Randolph's War with the Jefferson Administration." *Journal of American Studies* 20: 71–92.

Chambers, William N., and Phillip C. Davis. 1978. "Party, Competition, and Mass Participation: The Case of the Democratizing Party System, 1824–1852." In Joel H. Silbey, Allan G. Bogue, and William H. Flanigan, eds., *The History of American Electoral Behavior.* Princeton: Princeton University Press.

Charles, Joseph. 1955. "The Jay Treaty: The Origins of the American Party System." *William and Mary Quarterly* 12: 581–630.

Cochran, Thomas C. 1948. "The 'Presidential Synthesis' in American History." *American Historical Review* 53: 748–59.

Cohn, Peter. 2001. "Traficant Thumbs a Ride with Republicans." *CQ Weekly Report*, January 6: 6.

Cook, Timothy E. 1989. *Making Laws and Making News.* Washington, D.C.: Brookings Institution.

Cook, Timothy E. 1998. *Governing with the News: The News Media as a Political Institution.* Chicago: University of Chicago Press.

Cooper, Joseph. (1960) 1988. *Congress and Its Committees.* New York: Garland.

Cooper, Joseph. 1970. *The Origins of the Standing Committees and the Development of the Modern House.* Houston: Rice University Studies.

Cooper, Joseph, and Cheryl D. Young. 1989. "Bill Introduction in the Nineteenth Century: A Study of Institutional Change." *Legislative Studies Quarterly* 14: 67–105.

Cox, Gary W. 1987. *The Efficient Secret.* Cambridge: Cambridge University Press.

Cox, Gary W. 1993. "The Development of Collective Responsibility in the U.K." *Parliamentary History* 13: 32–47.

Cox, Gary W. 2005. "The Organization of Democratic Legislatures." In Barry R. Weingast and Donald Wittman, eds., *The Oxford Handbook of Political Economy.* Oxford: Oxford University Press.

Cox, Gary W. 2011. "War, Moral Hazard, and Ministerial Responsibility: England after the Glorious Revolution." *Journal of Economic History* 71: 133–61.

Cox, Gary W., Thad Kousser, and Mathew D. McCubbins. 2010. "Party Power or Preferences? Quasi-Experimental Evidence from American State Legislatures." *Journal of Politics* 72: 799–811.

Cox, Gary W., and Mathew D. McCubbins. 1993. *Legislative Leviathan: Party Government in the House.* Berkeley: University of California Press.

Cox, Gary W., and Mathew D. McCubbins. 1994. "Bonding, Structure, and the Stability of Political Parties: Party Government in the House." *Legislative Studies Quarterly* 19: 215–31.

Cox, Gary W., and Mathew D. McCubbins. 1997. "Toward a Theory of Legislative Rules Changes: Assessing Schickler and Rich's Evidence." *American Journal of Political Science* 41: 1376–86.

Cox, Gary W., and Mathew D. McCubbins. 2002. "Agenda Power in the U.S. House of Representatives, 1877 to 1986." In David W. Brady and Mathew D. McCubbins, eds., *Party, Process, and Political Change in Congress: New Perspectives on the History of Congress*. Stanford, Calif.: Stanford University Press.

Cox, Gary W., and Mathew D. McCubbins. 2005. *Setting the Agenda: Responsible Party Government in the U.S. House of Representatives*. Cambridge: Cambridge University Press.

Crenshaw, Ollinger. 1942. "The Speakership Contest of 1859–1860: John Sherman's Election a Cause of Disruption?" *Mississippi Valley Historical Review* 29: 323–38.

Cunningham, Noble E. 1956. "John Beckley: An Early American Party Manager." *William and Mary Quarterly* 13: 40–52.

Cunningham, Noble E. 1957. *The Jeffersonian Republicans: The Formation of Party Organization, 1789–1801*. Chapel Hill: University of North Carolina Press.

Cunningham, Noble E. 1978. *The Process of Government under Jefferson*. Princeton: Princeton University Press.

Curry, Leonard P. 1968. *Blueprint for Modern America: Nonmilitary Legislation of the First Civil War Congress*. Nashville, Tenn.: Vanderbilt University Press.

Cushing, Luther Stearns. 1856. *Elements of the Law and Practice of Legislative Assemblies in the United States of America*. Boston: Little, Brown and Company.

Dauer, Manning J. 1953. *The Adams Federalists*. Baltimore: Johns Hopkins University Press.

Dempsey, John T. 1956. "Control by Congress over the Seating and Disciplining of Members." Ph.D. dissertation, University of Michigan.

Den Hartog, Christopher F. 2004. "Limited Party Government and the Majority Party Revolution in the Nineteenth-Century House." Ph.D. dissertation, University of California, San Diego.

Den Hartog, Chris, and Nathan W. Monroe. 2011. *Agenda Setting in the U.S. Senate: Costly Consideration and Majority Party Advantage*. Cambridge: Cambridge University Press.

Denzau, Arthur, William Riker, and Kenneth Shepsle. 1985. "Farquharson and Fenno: Sophisticated Voting and Home Style." *American Political Science Review* 79: 1117–34.

Dion, Douglas. 1997. *Turning the Legislative Thumbscrew: Minority Rights and Procedural Change in Congress*. Ann Arbor: University of Michigan Press.

Dodd, Lawrence C., and Bruce I. Oppenheimer. 2001. "A House Divided: The Struggle for Partisan Control, 1994–2000." In Lawrence C. Dodd and Bruce I. Oppenheimer, eds., *Congress Reconsidered*. 7th ed. Washington, D.C.: Congressional Quarterly Press.

Doenecke, Justus D. 1981. *The Presidencies of James A. Garfield and Chester A. Arthur*. Lawrence: University Press of Kansas.

Dubin, Michael J. 1998. *United States Congressional Elections, 1788–1997*. Jefferson, N.C.: McFarland and Co.

Enelow, James. 1981. "Saving Amendments, Killer Amendments, and an Expected Utility Theory of Sophisticated Voting." *Journal of Politics* 43: 1062–89.

Enelow, James, and David Koehler. 1980. "The Amendment in Legislative Strategy: Sophisticated Voting in the U.S. Congress." *Journal of Politics* 42: 396–413.

Engstrom, Erik J., and Samuel Kernell. 2005. "Manufactured Responsiveness: The Impact of State Electoral Laws on Unified Party Control of the Presidency and House of Representatives, 1840–1940." *American Journal of Political Science* 49: 531–49.

Etcheson, Nicole. 2004. *Bleeding Kansas: Contested Liberty in the Civil War Era.* Lawrence: University Press of Kansas.

Farquharson, Robin. 1969. *The Theory of Voting.* New Haven: Yale University Press.

Fehrenbacher, Don E. 1978. *The Dred Scott Case: Its Significance in American Law and Politics.* Oxford: Oxford University Press.

Ferguson, Thomas. 1983. "Party Realignment and American Industrial Structures: The Investment Theory of Political Parties in Historical Perspective." In Paul Zarambka, ed., *Research in Political Economy.* Vol. 6. Greenwich, Conn.: JAI Press.

Ferraro, Thomas. 2011. "ANALYSIS-Cantor upstaging Boehner in US debt talks?" *Reuters News Service*, July 15, 2011, http://www.trust.org/alertnet/news/analysis-cantor-upstaging-boehner-in-us-debt-talks.

Finocchiaro, Charles J., and David W. Rohde. 2007. "Speaker David Henderson and the Partisan Era of the U.S. House." In David W. Brady and Mathew D. McCubbins, eds., *Party, Process, and Political Change in Congress, Volume 2: Further New Perspectives on the History of Congress.* Stanford, Calif.: Stanford University Press.

Fiorina, Morris P., David W. Rohde, and Peter Wissel. 1975. "Historical Change in House Turnover." In Norman J. Ornstein, ed., *Congress in Change: Evolution and Reform.* New York: Praeger.

Fisher, John Eugene. 1968. "Statesman of a Lost Cause: R.M.T. Hunter and the Sectional Controversy, 1847–1887." Ph.D. dissertation, University of Virginia.

Fisher, John Eugene. 1973. "The Dilemma of a States' Rights Whig: The Congressional Career of R.M.T. Hunter, 1837–1841." *Virginia Magazine of History and Biography* 81: 387–404.

Follett, Mary Parker. 1896. *The Speaker of the House of Representatives.* New York: Longmans, Green, and Co.

Foner, Eric. 1970. *Free Soil, Free Labor, Free Men: The Ideology of the Republican Party before the Civil War.* New York: Oxford University Press.

Forgette, Richard. 2004. "Party Caucuses and Coordination: Assessing Caucus Activity and Party Effects." *Legislative Studies Quarterly* 29: 407–30.

Fowler, Dorothy Ganfield. 1943. *The Cabinet Politician: The Postmasters General, 1829–1909.* New York: Columbia University Press.

Francis, Wayne L. 1982. "U.S. State Legislative Committees: Structure, Procedural Efficiency, and Party Control." *Legislative Studies Quarterly* 7: 435–71.

Francis, Wayne L. 1985. "Leadership, Party Caucuses, and Committees in U.S. State Legislatures." *Legislative Studies Quarterly* 10: 243–57.

Francis, Wayne L. 1989. *The Legislative Committee Game: A Comparative Analysis of Fifty States.* Columbus: Ohio State University Press.

Freehling, William W. 1990. *The Road to Disunion: Secessionists at Bay, 1776–1854.* New York: Oxford University Press.

French, Benjamin Brown. 1989. *Witness to the Young Republic: A Yankee's Journal, 1828–1870*. Donald B. Cole and John J. McDonough, eds. Hanover, N.H.: University Press of New England.

Fuller, Hubert Bruce. 1909. *The Speakers of the House*. Boston: Little, Brown and Company.

Furlong, Patrick J. 1967. "John Rutledge, Jr., and the Election of the Speaker of the House in 1799." *William and Mary Quarterly* 24: 432–36.

Gailmard, Sean, and Jeffery A. Jenkins. 2007. "Negative Agenda Control in the Senate and House: Fingerprints of Majority Party Power." *Journal of Politics* 69: 689–700.

Galloway, George B. 1961. *History of the House of Representatives*. New York: Thomas Y. Crowell Company.

Gamm, Gerald, and Kenneth Shepsle. 1989. "Emergence of Legislative Institutions: Standing Committees in the House and Senate, 1810–1825." *Legislative Studies Quarterly* 14: 39–66.

Gamm, Gerald, and Steven S. Smith. 2002. "Emergence of Senate Party Leadership." In Bruce I. Oppenheimer, ed., *U.S. Senate Exceptionalism*. Columbus: Ohio State University Press.

Gatell, Frank Otto. 1958. "Palfrey's Vote, the Conscience Whigs, and the Election of Speaker Winthrop." *New England Quarterly* 31: 218–31.

Gawalt, Gerard W., ed. 1995. *Justifying Jefferson: The Political Writing of John James Beckley*. Washington, D.C.: Library of Congress.

Gerring, John. 1998. *Party Ideologies in America, 1828–1996*. Cambridge: Cambridge University Press.

Giddings, Joshua R. 1864. *History of the Rebellion: Its Authors and Causes*. New York: Follett, Foster & Co.

Gienapp, William E. 1987. *The Origins of the Republican Party, 1852–1856*. New York: Oxford University Press.

Gordon, Martin K. 1975. "Patrick Magruder: Citizen, Congressman, Librarian of Congress." *Quarterly Journal of the Library of Congress* 32: 154–71.

Green, Donald, Bradley Palmquist, and Eric Schickler. 2002. *Partisan Hearts and Minds: Political Parties and the Social Identities of Voters*. New Haven: Yale University Press.

Green, Matthew N. 2002. "Institutional Change, Party Discipline, and the House Democratic Caucus: 1911–19." *Legislative Studies Quarterly* 27: 601–34.

Green, Matthew N. 2010. *The Speaker of the House: A Study of Leadership*. New Haven: Yale University Press.

Groseclose, Tim, and Charles Stewart III. 1998. "The Value of Committee Seats in the House, 1947–1991." *American Journal of Political Science* 42: 453–74.

Haines, Wilder H. 1915. "The Democratic Caucus of Today." *American Political Science Review* 9: 696–706.

Hamilton, Holman. 1951. *Zachary Taylor: Soldier in the White House*. Indianapolis: Bobbs-Merrill.

Hamilton, Holman. 1957. "Kentucky's Linn Boyd and the Dramatic Days of 1850." *Register of the Kentucky Historical Society* 55: 185–95.

Hammond, Jabez D. 1850. *The History of Political Parties in the State of New York*. 4th ed. Vol. 1. Buffalo: Phinney & Co.

Harlow, Ralph V. 1917. *The History of Legislative Methods in the Period before 1825*. New Haven: Yale University Press.

Harrington, Fred Harvey. 1939. "The First Northern Victory." *Journal of Southern History* 5: 186–205.

Harris, Douglas. 1998. "The Rise of the Public Speakership." *Political Science Quarterly* 113: 193–212.

Hasbrouck, Paul DeWitt. 1927. *Party Government in the House of Representatives.* New York: Macmillan.

Henig, Gerald S. 1973. "Henry Winter Davis and the Speakership Contest of 1859–1860." *Maryland Historical Magazine* 68: 1–19.

Hennessy, M. E. 1935. *Four Decades of Massachusetts Politics, 1890–1935.* Norwood, Mass.: Norwood Press.

Hicken, Victor. 1960. "John A. McClernand and the House Speakership Struggle of 1859." *Journal of the Illinois State Historical Society* 53: 163–78.

Hild, Matthew. 2007. *Greenbackers, Knights of Labor, and Populists: Farmer-Labor Insurgency in the Late-Nineteenth Century South.* Athens: University of Georgia Press.

Hildreth, Richard. 1856. *The History of the United States of America.* Vol. 4. New York: Harper.

Hinckley, Barbara. 1971. *The Seniority System in Congress.* Bloomington: Indiana University Press.

Hinds, Asher C. 1909. "The Speaker of the House of Representatives." *American Political Science Review* 3: 155–66.

Hofstadter, Richard. 1969. *The Idea of a Party System: The Rise of Legitimate Opposition in the United States, 1789–1840.* Berkeley: University of California Press.

Hoing, Willard L. 1957. "David B. Henderson: Speaker of the House." *Iowa Journal of History* 55: 1–34.

Hollandsworth, James G. 1998. *Pretense of Glory: The Life of General Nathaniel P. Banks.* Baton Rouge: Louisiana State University Press.

Hollcroft, Temple R. 1956. "A Congressman's Letters on the Speaker Election in the Thirty-Fourth Congress." *Mississippi Valley Historical Review* 43: 444–58.

Holt, James. 1967. *Congressional Insurgents and the Party System, 1909–1916.* Cambridge, Mass.: Harvard University Press.

Holt, Michael F. 1978. *The Political Crisis of the 1850s.* New York: Wiley.

Holt, Michael F. 1985. "The Election of 1840, Voter Mobilization, and the Emergence of the Second American Party System: A Reappraisal of Jacksonian Voting Behavior." In William J. Cooper Jr., Michael F. Holt, and John McCardell, eds., *A Master's Due: Essays in Honor of David Herbert Donald.* Baton Rouge: Louisiana State University Press.

Holt, Michael F. 1999. *The Rise and Fall of the American Whig Party: Jacksonian Politics and the Onset of the Civil War.* New York: Oxford University Press.

Hooper, Molly K. 2010. "Boehner Won't Resurrect Hastert's 'Majority of the Majority.'" *The Hill,* December 17, 2010.

House, Albert V. 1965. "The Speakership Contest of 1875: Democratic Response to Power." *Journal of American History* 52: 252–74.

Howe, Daniel Walker. 2007. *What Hath God Wrought: The Transformation of America, 1815–1848.* Oxford: Oxford University Press.

Hunter, Kathleen. 2010a. "Blue Dog Childers Likes Shuler for Speaker." *Roll Call,* October 30, 2010.

Hunter, Kathleen. 2010b. "Pelosi Wins Bid for Leader Despite 43 Defections." *Roll Call*, November 17, 2010.

Hunter, Martha T. 1903. *A Memoir of Robert M. T. Hunter*. Washington, D.C.: Neale Publishing Co.

Ilisevich, Robert D. 1988. *Galusha A. Grow: The People's Candidate*. Pittsburgh: University of Pittsburgh Press.

Jahoda, Gloria. 1960. "John Beckley: Jefferson's Campaign Manager." *Bulletin of the New York Public Library* 64: 247–60.

Jameson, J. Franklin, ed. 1900. "Correspondence of John C. Calhoun." In *Annual Report of the American Historical Association for the Year 1899*. Vol. 2. Washington, D.C.: Government Printing Office.

Jenkins, Jeffery A. 1998. "Property Rights and the Emergence of Standing Committee Dominance in the Nineteenth-Century House." *Legislative Studies Quarterly* 23: 493–519.

Jenkins, Jeffery A. 2004. "Partisanship and Contested Election Cases in the House of Representatives, 1789–2002." *Studies in American Political Development* 18: 113–35.

Jenkins, Jeffery A. 2011. "The Evolution of Party Leadership." In Eric Schickler and Frances Lee, eds., *The Oxford Handbook of the American Congress*. Oxford: Oxford University Press.

Jenkins, Jeffery A., Michael H. Crespin, and Jamie L. Carson. 2005. "Parties as Procedural Coalitions in Congress: An Examination of Differing Career Tracks." *Legislative Studies Quarterly* 30: 365–89.

Jenkins, Jeffery A., and Timothy P. Nokken. 1997. "The Institutional Emergence of the Republican Party: A Spatial Voting Analysis of the House Speakership Election of 1855–56." Paper presented at the Annual Meeting of the Southern Political Science Association.

Jenkins, Jeffery A., and Timothy P. Nokken. 2000. "The Institutional Origins of the Republican Party: Spatial Voting and the House Speakership Election of 1855–56." *Legislative Studies Quarterly* 25: 101–30.

Jenkins, Jeffery A., and Brian R. Sala. 1998. "The Spatial Theory of Voting and the Presidential Election of 1824." *American Journal of Political Science* 42: 1157–79.

Jenkins, Jeffery A., and Charles Stewart III. 1997. "Order from Chaos: The Transformation of the Committee System in the House, 1810–1822." Paper presented at the annual meeting of the American Political Science Association.

Jenkins, Jeffery A., and Charles Stewart III. 2001. "Out in the Open: The Emergence of *Viva Voce* Voting in House Speakership Elections." Presented at the annual meeting of the American Political Science Association.

Jenkins, Jeffery A., and Charles Stewart III. 2002. "Order from Chaos: The Transformation of the Committee System in the House, 1816–1822." In David W. Brady and Mathew D. McCubbins, eds., *Party, Process, and Political Change in Congress: New Perspectives on the History of Congress*. Stanford, Calif.: Stanford University Press.

Jenkins, Jeffery A., and Charles Stewart III. 2003a. "The Gag Rule, Congressional Politics, and the Growth of Anti-Slavery Popular Politics." Paper presented at the annual meeting of the Midwest Political Science Association.

Jenkins, Jeffery A., and Charles Stewart III. 2003b. "Out in the Open: The Emergence of *Viva Voce* Voting in House Speakership Elections." *Legislative Studies Quarterly* 28: 481–508.

Jenkins, Jeffery A., and Charles Stewart III. 2004. "More than Just a Mouthpiece: The House Clerk as Party Operative, 1789–1870." Paper presented at the annual meeting of the American Political Science Association.

Jillson, Calvin, and Rick K. Wilson. 1994. *Congressional Dynamics: Structure, Coordination, and Choice in the First American Congress, 1774–1789.* Stanford, Calif.: Stanford University Press.

Johnston, Richard Malcolm, and William Hand Browne. 1878. *Life of Alexander Stephens.* Philadelphia: J. B. Lippincott & Co.

Jones, Charles O. 1968. "Joseph G. Cannon and Howard W. Smith: An Essay on the Limits of Leadership in the House of Representatives." *Journal of Politics* 30: 617–46.

Kennon, Donald R., ed. 1986. *The Speakers of the U.S. House of Representatives: A Bibliography, 1789–1984.* Baltimore: Johns Hopkins University Press.

Kernell, Samuel, and Erik Engstrom. 2005. "Manufactured Responsiveness: The Impact of State Electoral Laws on Unified Party Control of the President and House of Representatives." *American Journal of Political Science* 49: 547–65.

Key, V. O. 1964. *Politics, Parties, and Pressure Groups.* 5th ed. New York: Crowell.

Kitchin, William Irwin. 1969. "The Speaker of the United States House of Representatives, 1910–1940." M.A. thesis, University of Virginia.

Kolodny, Robin. 1998. *Pursuing Majorities: Congressional Campaign Committees in American Politics.* Norman: University of Oklahoma Press.

Krehbiel, Keith. 1991. *Information and Legislative Organization.* Ann Arbor: University of Michigan Press.

Krehbiel, Keith. 1993. "Where's the Party?" *British Journal of Political Science* 23: 235–66.

Krehbiel, Keith. 1998. *Pivotal Politics: A Theory of U.S. Lawmaking.* Chicago: University of Chicago Press.

Krehbiel, Keith, and Alan Wiseman. 2001. "Joseph G. Cannon: Majoritarian from Illinois." *Legislative Studies Quarterly* 26: 357–90.

Laver, Michael, and Kenneth A. Shepsle. 1990. "Coalitions and Cabinet Government." *American Political Science Review* 84: 873–90.

Laver, Michael, and Kenneth A. Shepsle, eds. 1994. *Cabinet Ministers and Parliamentary Government.* New York: Cambridge University Press.

Laver, Michael, and Kenneth A. Shepsle. 1996. *Making and Breaking Governments: Cabinets and Legislatures in Parliamentary Democracies.* Cambridge: Cambridge University Press.

Lawrence, Eric D., Forrest Maltzman, and Steven S. Smith. 2006. "Who Wins? Party Effects in Legislative Voting." *Legislative Studies Quarterly* 31: 33–70.

Lawrence, Eric D., Forrest Maltzman, and Paul J. Wahlbeck. 2001. "The Politics of Speaker Cannon's Committee Assignments." *American Journal of Political Science* 45: 551–62.

Levine, Michael, and Charles Plott. 1977. "Agenda Influence and Its Implications." *Virginia Law Review* 63: 561–604.

Levine, Peter D. 1977. *The Behavior of State Legislative Parties in the Jacksonian Era: New Jersey, 1829–1844.* Rutherford, N.J.: Fairleigh Dickinson University Press.

Library of Congress Manuscript Division. 1910. *Calendar of the Papers of Martin Van Buren.* Washington, D.C.: Government Printing Office.

Lientz, Gerald R. 1974. House Speaker Elections and Congressional Parties, 1789–1860. Master's thesis, University of Virginia.

Lientz, Gerald R. 1978. "House Speaker Elections and Congressional Parties, 1789–1860." *Capitol Studies* 6: 62–89.

Lippmann, Walter. (1885) 1973. Introduction to *Congressional Government: A Study in American Politics,* by Woodrow Wilson. Gloucester, Mass.: Peter Smith.

Lindsey, David. 1959. *"Sunset Cox": Irrepressible Democrat.* Detroit: Wayne State University Press.

Maness, Lonnie E. 1989. "Emerson Etheridge and the Union." *Tennessee Historical Quarterly* 48: 97–110.

Manley, John F. 1973. "The Conservative Coalition in Congress." *American Behavioral Scientist* 17: 223–47.

Marsh, Philip M. 1948. "John Beckley: Mystery Man of the Early Jeffersonians." *Pennsylvania Magazine of History and Biography* 72: 54–69.

Martin, Raymond V., Jr. 1949–50. "Eminent Virginian: A Study of John Beckley." *West Virginia History* 11: 44–61.

Martis, Kenneth C. 1989. *Historical Atlas of Political Parties in the United States Congress, 1789–1989.* New York: Macmillan.

Mayer, George H. 1967. *The Republican Party, 1854–1966.* 2nd ed. New York: Oxford University Press.

Mayhew, David R. 1974. *Congress: The Electoral Connection.* New Haven: Yale University Press.

Mayhew, David R. 2000. *America's Congress: Actions in the Public Sphere, James Madison through Newt Gingrich.* New Haven: Yale University Press.

Mayhew, David R. 2004. *Congress: The Electoral Connection.* 2nd ed. New Haven: Yale University Press.

McConachie, Lauros G. 1898. *Congressional Committees: A Study of the Origins and Development of Our National and Local Legislative Methods.* Boston: Crowell.

McCormick, Richard P. 1953. *The History of Voting in New Jersey: A Study of the Development of Election Machinery, 1664–1911.* New Brunswick: Rutgers University Press.

McCormick, Richard P. 1960. "New Perspectives on Jacksonian Politics." *American Historical Review* 65: 288–301.

McCormick, Richard P. 1966. *The Second American Party System: Party Formation in the Jacksonian Era.* Chapel Hill: University of North Carolina Press.

Miller, William Lee. 1996. *Arguing about Slavery: The Great Battle in the United States Congress.* New York: Knopf.

Monroe, Nathan W., Jason M. Roberts, and David W. Rohde, eds. 2008. *Why Not Parties? Party Effects in the U.S. Senate.* Chicago: University of Chicago Press.

Moore, Glover. 1953. *The Missouri Controversy, 1819–1821.* Lexington: University of Kentucky Press.

Morgan, H. Wayne. 1969. *From Hayes to McKinley: National Party Politics, 1877–1896.* Syracuse: Syracuse University Press.

Morgan, William G. 1969. "The Origin and Development of the Congressional

Nominating Caucus." *Proceedings of the American Philosophical Society* 113: 184–96.

Morrison, Michael A. 1997. *Slavery and the American West: The Eclipse of Manifest Destiny and the Coming of the Civil War.* Chapel Hill: University of North Carolina Press.

Mott, Frank Luther. 1941. *American Journalism: A History of Newspapers in the United States through 250 Years, 1690 to 1940.* New York: Macmillan.

Nelson, Garrison. 1994. *Committees in the U.S. Congress, 1947–1992.* 2 vols. Washington, D.C.: CQ Press.

Nelson, Garrison, and Charles Stewart III. 2010. *Committees in the U.S. Congress, 1993–2010.* Washington, D.C.: CQ Press.

Nevins, Allan. 1950. *The Emergence of Lincoln.* Vol. 2. New York: Charles Scribner's Sons.

Nichols, Roy Franklin. 1948. *The Disruption of American Democracy.* New York: Macmillan.

Nichols, Roy Franklin. 1967. *The Invention of the American Political Parties.* New York: Macmillan.

Niven, John. 1983. *Martin Van Buren: The Romantic Age of Popular Politics.* New York: Oxford University Press.

Niven, John. 1988. *John C. Calhoun and the Price of Union.* Baton Rouge: Louisiana State University Press.

Nixon, John T. 1872. "The Circumstances Attending the Election of William Pennington of New Jersey, as Speaker of the Thirty–Sixth Congress." *Proceedings of the New Jersey Historical Society* 2: 205–20.

Nokken, Timothy P. 2009. "Party Switching and the Procedural Party Agenda in the U.S. House of Representatives." In William B. Heller and Carol Mershon, eds. *Political Parties and Legislative Party Switching.* New York: Palgrave Macmillan.

Nokken, Timothy P., and Keith T. Poole. 2004. "Congressional Party Defection in American History." *Legislative Studies Quarterly* 29: 545–68.

Nye, Mary Alice. 1993. "Conservative Coalition Support in the House of Representatives, 1963–1988." *Legislative Studies Quarterly* 18: 255–70.

Ordeshook, Peter C. 1986. *Game Theory and Political Theory.* Cambridge: Cambridge University Press.

Ostrogorski, M. 1899. "The Rise and Fall of the Nominating Caucus, Legislative and Congressional." *American Historical Review* 5: 253–83.

Overdyke, W. D. 1968. *The Know-Nothing Party in the South.* Gloucester, Mass.: Peter Smith.

Page, Connie. 1996. "Finneran Wins Battle for House Speaker." *Boston Herald,* April 10, 1996.

Palmer, Anna, and Kathleen Hunter. 2011. "Pelosi's Splintered Support Goes on Display." *Roll Call,* January 5, 2011.

Palmer, Beverly Wilson. 1990. *The Selected Letters of Charles Sumner.* Vol. 1. Boston: Northeastern University Press.

Parks, Joseph H. 1950. *John Bell of Tennessee.* Baton Rouge: Louisiana State University Press.

Pasley, Jeffrey L. 1996. "'A Journeyman, Either in Law or Politics': John Beckley and the Social Origins of Political Campaigning." *Journal of the Early Republic* 16: 531–69.

Pasley, Jeffrey L. 2001. *"The Tyranny of the Printers": Newspaper Politics in the Early American Republic*. Charlottesville: University of Virginia Press.

Patterson, James T. 1966. "A Conservative Coalition Forms in Congress, 1933–1939." *Journal of American History* 52: 757–72.

Patterson, James T. 1967. *Congressional Conservatism and the New Deal: The Growth of the Conservative Coalition in Congress, 1933–39*. Lexington: University of Kentucky Press.

Peabody, Robert L. 1976. *Leadership in Congress*. Boston: Little, Brown and Company.

Peskin, Allan. 1984–85. "Who Were the Stalwarts? Who Were Their Rivals? Republican Factions in the Gilded Age." *Political Science Quarterly* 99: 703–16.

Peters, Ronald M., Jr. 1997. *The American Speakership: The Office in Historical Perspective*. 2nd ed. Baltimore: Johns Hopkins University Press.

Peters, Ronald M., Jr. 2002. "Caucus and Conference: Party Organization in the U.S. House of Representatives." Paper presented at the annual meeting of the Midwest Political Science Association.

Peterson, Merrill D. 1987. *The Great Triumvirate: Webster, Clay, and Calhoun*. New York: Oxford University Press.

Polsby, Nelson W., Miriam Gallaher, and Barry Spencer Rundquist. 1969. "The Growth of the Seniority System in the U.S. House of Representatives." *American Political Science Review* 63: 787–807.

Poole, Keith T. 1998. "Recovering a Basic Space from a Set of Issue Scales." *American Journal of Political Science* 42: 954–93.

Poole, Keith T. 2005. *Spatial Models of Parliamentary Voting*. Cambridge: Cambridge University Press.

Poole, Keith T., and Howard Rosenthal. 1991. "Patterns of Congressional Voting." *American Journal of Political Science* 35: 228–78.

Poole, Keith T., and Howard Rosenthal. 1993. "Spatial Realignment and the Mapping of Issues in U.S. History: The Evidence from Roll Call Voting." In *Agenda Formation*, ed. William H. Riker. Ann Arbor: University of Michigan Press.

Poole, Keith T., and Howard Rosenthal. 1997. *Congress: A Political-Economic History of Roll Call Voting*. New York: Oxford University Press.

Poole, Keith T., and Howard Rosenthal. 2001. "D–NOMINATE after 10 Years: A Comparative Update to *Congress: A Political-Economic History of Roll Call Voting*." *Legislative Studies Quarterly* 26: 5–26.

Poole, Keith T., and Howard Rosenthal. 2007. *Ideology and Congress*. Piscataway, N.J.: Transaction.

Potter, David T. 1976. *The Impending Crisis, 1848–1861*. New York: HarperPerennial.

Rager, Scott William. 1998. "Uncle Joe Cannon: The Brakeman of the House of Representatives, 1903–1911." In Roger H. Davidson, Susan Webb Hammond, and Raymond M. Smock, eds., *Masters of the House*. Boulder, Colo.: Westview Press.

Rae, Douglas W. 1967. *The Political Consequences of Electoral Laws*. New Haven: Yale University Press.

Reed, Thomas B. 1889a. "Rules of the House of Representatives." *Century Magazine* 37: 792–95.

Reed, Thomas B. 1889b. "Obstruction in the National House." *North American Review* 149: 421–28.

Reitano, JoAnne R. 1994. *The Tariff Question in the Gilded Age: The Great Debate of 1888*. University Park: Pennsylvania State University Press.

Remini, Robert V. 1959. *Martin Van Buren and the Making of the Democratic Party*. New York: Columbia University Press.

Remini, Robert V. 1963. The Election of Andrew Jackson. Philadelphia: Lippincott.

Remini, Robert V., ed. 1972. *The Age of Jackson*. Columbia: University of South Carolina Press.

Rhodes, James Ford. 1902. *History of the United States from the Compromise of 1850*. Vol. 2. New York: Macmillan.

Richards, Leonard L. 2000. *The Slave Power: The Free North and Southern Domination, 1780–1860*. Baton Rouge: Louisiana State University Press.

Riker, William H. 1962. *The Theory of Political Coalitions*. New Haven: Yale University Press.

Riker, William H. 1980. "Implications from the Disequilibrium of Majority Rule for the Study of Institutions." *American Political Science Review* 74: 432–46.

Riker, William H. 1986. *The Art of Political Manipulation*. New Haven: Yale University Press.

Ripley, Randall B. 1967. *Party Leaders in the House of Representatives*. Washington, D.C.: Brookings Institution.

Risjord, Norman K. 1992. "Partisanship and Power: House Committees and the Powers of the Speaker, 1789–1801." *William and Mary Quarterly* 49: 628–51.

Ritter, Gretchen. 1997. *Goldbugs and Greenbacks: The Antimonopoly Tradition and the Politics of Finance in America, 1865–1896*. Cambridge: Cambridge University Press.

Roberts, Jason M., and Steven S. Smith. 2007. "The Evolution of Agenda-Setting Institutions in Congress: Path Dependency in House and Senate Institutional Development." In David W. Brady and Mathew D. McCubbins, eds., *Party, Process, and Political Change in Congress, Volume 2: Further New Perspectives on the History of Congress*. Stanford, Calif.: Stanford University Press.

Robinson, William A. 1930. *Thomas B. Reed: Parliamentarian*. New York: Dodd, Mead.

Rohde, David W. 1989. "'Something's Happening Here: What It Is Ain't Exactly Clear': Southern Democrats in the House of Representatives." In Morris P. Fiorina and David W. Rohde, eds., *Home Style and Washington Work: Studies of Congressional Politics*. Ann Arbor: University of Michigan Press.

Rohde, David W. 1991. *Parties and Leaders in the Postreform Congress*. Chicago: University of Chicago Press.

Rohde, David W. 2005. "Committees and Policy Formulation." In Paul J. Quirk and Sarah A. Binder, eds. *The Legislative Branch*. New York: Oxford University Press.

Rowell, Chester H. 1901. *A Historical and Legal Digest of All the Contested Election Cases in the House of Representatives from the First to the Fifty-Sixth Congress, 1789–1901*. House Document 510, 56th Congress, 2nd Session. Washington, D.C.: U.S. Government Printing Office.

Rusk, Jerrold G. 2001. *A Statistical History of the American Electorate*. Washington, D.C.: CQ Press.

Schickler, Eric. 2001. *Disjointed Pluralism: Institutional Innovation and the Development of the U.S. Congress*. Princeton: Princeton University Press.

Schickler, Eric, and Andrew Rich. 1997a. "Controlling the Floor: Parties as Procedural Coalitions in the House." *American Journal of Political Science* 41: 1340–75.

Schickler, Eric, and Andrew Rich. 1997b. "Party Government in the House Reconsidered: A Response to Cox and McCubbins." *American Journal of Political Science* 41: 1387–94.

Schlesinger, Arthur M., Jr. 1947. *The Age of Jackson*. Boston: Little, Brown and Company.

Schlesinger, Joseph A. 1985. "The New American Political Party." *American Political Science Review* 79: 1152–69.

Schmeckebier, Laurence F. 1925. *The Government Printing Office: Its History, Activities, and Organization*. Institute for Government Research, *Service Monographs of the United States*, no. 36. Baltimore: Johns Hopkins University Press.

Schroeder, John H. 1973. *Mr. Polk's War: American Opposition and Dissent, 1846–1848*. Madison: University of Wisconsin Press.

Sellers, Charles. 1991. *The Market Revolution: Jacksonian America, 1815–1846*. New York: Oxford University Press.

Sellers, Charles G., Jr. 1957. *James K. Polk: Jacksonian*. Princeton: Princeton University Press.

Sewell, Richard. 1976. *Ballots for Freedom: Antislavery Politics in the United States, 1837–1860*. New York: Norton.

Shelley, Mack C., II. 1983. *The Permanent Majority: The Conservative Coalition in the United States Congress*. Tuscaloosa: University of Alabama Press.

Shepsle, Kenneth A. 1978. *The Giant Jigsaw Puzzle: Democratic Committee Assignments in the Modern House*. Chicago: University of Chicago Press.

Shepsle, Kenneth A. 1979. "Institutional Arrangements and Equilibrium in Multidimensional Voting." *American Journal of Political Science* 23: 27–60.

Shepsle, Kenneth A. 1986. "Institutional Equilibrium and Equilibrium Institutions." In Herbert Weisberg, ed., *Political Science: The Science of Politics*. New York: Agathon.

Shepsle, Kenneth A. 1989. "Studying Institutions: Some Lessons from the Rational Choice Approach." *Journal of Theoretical Politics* 1: 131–47.

Shepsle, Kenneth A., and Barry R. Weingast. 1981. "Structure-Induced Equilibrium and Legislative Choice." *Public Choice* 36: 221–37.

Shepsle, Kenneth A., and Barry R. Weingast. 1987. "The Institutional Foundations of Committee Power." *American Political Science Review* 81: 85–104.

Sherman, John. 1896. *Recollections of Forty Years in the House, Senate and Cabinet: An Autobiography*. Chicago: Werner Company.

Silbey, Joel H. 1989. "After 'The First Northern Victory': The Republican Party Comes to Congress, 1855–1856." *Journal of Interdisciplinary History* 10: 1–24.

Silbey, Joel H. 1992. *The American Political Nation, 1838–1893*. Stanford, Calif.: Stanford University Press.

Silbey, Joel H. 2002. *Martin Van Buren and the Emergence of American Popular Politics*. Lanham, Md.: Rowman and Littlefield.

Silbey, Joel H. 2005. *Storm over Texas: The Annexation Controversy and the Road to Civil War*. New York: Oxford University Press.

Silbey, Joel H. 2009. *Party Over Section: The Rough and Ready Presidential Election of 1848*. Lawrence: University Press of Kansas.

Simms, Henry Harrison. 1935. *Life of Robert M. T. Hunter: A Study in Sectionalism and Secession*. Richmond, Va.: William Byrd Press.

Simpson, John Eddins. 1973. *Howell Cobb: The Politics of Ambition*. Chicago: Adams Press.

Simpson, John Eddins. 1974. "Prelude to Compromise: Howell Cobb and the House Speakership Election of 1849." *Georgia Historical Quarterly* 58: 389–99.

Sinclair, Barbara. 2005. "Parties and Leadership in the House." In Paul J. Quirk and Sarah A. Binder, eds. *The Legislative Branch*. New York: Oxford University Press.

Sinclair, Barbara. 2006. *Party Wars: Polarization and the Politics of National Policy Making*. Norman: University of Oklahoma Press.

Smith, Culver H. 1977. *The Press, Politics, and Patronage: The American Government's Use of Newspapers, 1789–1875*. Athens: University of Georgia Press.

Smith, Elbert B. 1980. *Francis Preston Blair*. New York: Free Press.

Smith, Elbert B. 1988. *The Presidencies of Zachary Taylor and Millard Filmore*. Lawrence: University of Kansas Press.

Smith, Steven S. 2007. *Party Influence in Congress*. New York: Cambridge University Press.

Spann, Edward K. 1957. "John W. Taylor: The Reluctant Partisan, 1784–1854." Ph.D. dissertation, New York University.

Spann, Edward K. 1960. "The Souring of Good Feelings: John W. Taylor and the Speakership Election of 1821." *New York History* 41: 379–99.

Stagg, J.C.A. 1989. *The Papers of James Madison*. Vol. 16. Charlottesville: University of Virginia Press.

Stanton, John. 2011. "Boehner's Style Weakened Hand in Negotiations," *Roll Call*, July 20, 2011, http://www.rollcall.com/issues/57_10/John-Boehner-Weakened-Hand-Negotiations-207474-1.html?pos=hftxt.

Stewart, Charles, III. 1989. *Budget Reform Politics*. New York: Cambridge University Press.

Stewart, Charles III. 1998. "Architect or Tactician? Henry Clay and the Institutional Development of the U.S. House of Representatives." Paper presented at the annual meeting of the American Political Science Association.

Stewart, Charles, III. 1999. "The Inefficient Secret: Organizing for Business in the U.S. House of Representatives, 1789–1861." Paper presented at the annual meeting of the American Political Science Association.

Stewart, Charles, III. 2005. "Congress and the Constitutional System." In Paul J. Quirk and Sarah A. Binder, eds., *The Legislative Branch*. New York: Oxford University Press.

Stewart, Charles, III. 2007. "Architect or Tactician? Henry Clay and the Institutional Development of the U.S. House of Representatives." In David W. Brady and Mathew D. McCubbins, eds., *Party, Process, and Political Change in Congress, Volume 2: Further New Perspectives on the History of Congress*. Stanford, Calif.: Stanford University Press.

Stewart, Charles, III. 2011. "Congressional Committees in a Partisan Era." In Jamie L. Carson, ed., *New Directions in Congressional Politics*. New York: Routledge.

Stewart, Charles, III, and Tim Groseclose. 1999. "The Value of Committee Seats in the United States Senate, 1947–91." *American Journal of Political Science* 43: 963–73.

Stewart, Charles, III, and Barry R. Weingast. 1992. "Stacking the Senate, Changing the Nation: Republican Rotten Boroughs, Statehood Politics, and American Political Development." *Studies in American Political Development* 6: 223–71.

Stewart, Charles, III, and Jonathan Woon. 2009. Congressional Committee Assignments, 103rd to 111th Congresses, 1993–2009: House, June 21.

Strahan, Randall. 2007. *Leading Representatives: The Agency of Leaders in the Politics of the U.S. House.* Baltimore: Johns Hopkins University Press.

Strahan, Randall, Matthew Gunning, and Richard L. Vining Jr. 2006. "From Moderator to Leader: Floor Participation by U.S. House Speakers, 1789–1841." *Social Science History* 30: 51–74.

Strahan, Randall, Vincent Moscardelli, Moshe Haspel, and Richard Wike. 2000. "The Clay Speakership Revisited." *Polity* 32: 561–93.

Terrill, Tom E. 1973. *The Tariff, Politics, and American Foreign Policy, 1874–1901.* Westport, Conn.: Greenwood Press.

Townsend, George Alfred. 1873. *Washington, Outside and Inside.* Hartford, Conn.: James Betts.

Trefousse, Hans L. 1997. *Thaddeus Stevens: Nineteenth–Century Egalitarian.* Chapel Hill: University of North Carolina Press.

Tyrell, Ian R. 1979. *Sobering Up: Temperance to Prohibition in Antebellum America, 1800–1860.* Westport, Conn.: Greenwood Press.

Van Horne, William E. 1967. "Lewis D. Campbell and the Know-Nothing Party in Ohio." *Ohio History* 76: 202–21.

Wallace, Michael. 1968. "Changing Concepts of Party in the United States: New York, 1815–1828." *American Historical Review* 74: 453–91.

Watson, Harry L. 2006. *Liberty and Power: The Politics of Jacksonian America.* Rev. ed. New York: Hill and Wang.

Wayland, Francis Fry. 1949. *Andrew Stevenson, Democrat and Diplomat, 1785–1857.* Philadelphia: University of Pennsylvania Press.

Weingast, Barry R. 1996. "Institutions and Political Commitment: A New Political Economy of the American Civil War Era." Unpublished manuscript, Hoover Institution, Stanford University.

Weingast, Barry R. 1998. "Political Stability and Civil War: Institutions, Commitment, and American Democracy." In Robert Bates et al., eds. *Analytic Narratives.* Princeton: Princeton University Press.

Weingast, Barry R., and William Marshall. 1988. "The Industrial Organization of Congress." *Journal of Political Economy* 96: 132–63.

Weisman, Jonathan. 2006. "In an Upset, Boehner Is Elected House GOP Leader." *Washington Post*, February 3.

Welch, Theodore E., Jr. 1965. *Theodore Sedgwick, Federalist: A Political Portrait.* Middletown, Conn.: Wesleyan University Press.

White, Leonard D. 1948. *The Federalists: A Study in Administrative History.* New York: Macmillan.

White, Leonard D. 1954. *The Jacksonians: A Study in Administrative History, 1829–1861.* New York: Macmillan.

Wilentz, Sean. 2005. *The Rise of American Democracy: Jefferson to Lincoln.* New York: Norton.

Wilson, Clyde N., ed. 1959. *The Papers of John C. Calhoun.* Vol. 13. Columbia: University of South Carolina Press.

Wilson, Woodrow. (1885) 1973. *Congressional Government: A Study in American Politics.* Gloucester, Mass.: Peter Smith.

Wiltse, Charles M. 1949. *John C. Calhoun: Nullifier, 1829–1939.* Indianapolis: Bobbs-Merrill Company.

Winthrop, Robert C., Jr. 1897. *A Memoir of Robert C. Winthrop.* Boston: Little, Brown and Company.

Wright, Gerald C., and Brian F. Schaffner. 2002. "The Influence of Party: Evidence from the State Legislatures." *American Political Science Review* 96: 367–79.

Yoshinaka, Antoine. 2005. "House Party Switchers and Committee Assignments: Who Gets 'What, When, How?'" *Legislative Studies Quarterly* 30: 391–406.

Young, James Sterling. 1966. *The Washington Community, 1800–1828.* New York: Columbia University Press.

Zelizer, Julian E. 2007. "Beyond the Presidential Synthesis: Reordering Political Time." In Jean-Christophe Agnew and Roy Rosenzweig, eds., *A Companion to Post-1945 America.* Oxford: Blackwell Publishing.

INDEX

❦

Accounts Committee: in 26th Congress, 127t; in 30th Congress, 141, 142; in 31st Congress, 169; in 34th Congress, 203, 205; in 36th Congress, 230, 232; dismissal of McNulty as Clerk, 133n52

Adams, Charles Francis: as committee chair, 228, 230; and Printer election for 36th Congress, 233, 234

Adams, George M. "Green": and clerkship election for 38th Congress, 247n12; on speakership election, 259n31

Adams, John: administration of, 13; election of, 64

Adams, John Quincy: antislavery petitions of, 115; as "chairman" of the House, 115; on Clarke's ouster, 70n21; and clerkship election for 30th Congress, 140; House rules introduced by, 39, 40; on Hunter's committee appointments, 126n34; as Library of Congress Committee chair, 142; on Manufactures Committee, 127t; as National Republican, 71; on New Jersey election dispute, 114n10, 115, 115n12; and speakership election for 26th Congress, 119, 123; and speakership election for 27th Congress, 130n44; and speakership election for 30th Congress, 139; Taylor's relationship with, 69; ties to Gales and Seaton, 82; on viva voce resolution, 83; on Whig Party, 99–100

ad hoc proceeding, election of Speaker as, xiii

Adrain, Garnett B.: and clerkship election of 36th Congress, 226; as committee chair, 230; and speakership election for 36th Congress, 219, 219n42, 221, 222, 223, 224

agenda-setting, 274–75; cartelizing the agenda, 12–13; by committees, 32, 39, 61, 271; conditional party government in, 13; by Democratic Party, 317; influencing, 3, 5, 6; by majority party, 307–8; negative agenda control, 32, 33; organizational cartel in, 242; in organizational matters, 304; positive agenda control, 32, 36; by procedural cartel, 145–46; in procedural matters, 304; during Second and Third Party Systems, 9–10; in Senate, 307; sophisticated agenda setting, 153, 154; and third parties, 154; under two-party government, 153

Agriculture Committee: in 26th Congress, 127t; in 28th Congress, 134n57; in 30th Congress, 141, 142, 143; in 31st Congress, 169; in 34th Congress, 202, 204, 205; in 36th Congress, 228, 232; in 38th Congress, 248; in 52nd Congress, 278; in 68th Congress, 290; in 69th Congress, 288

Aiken, William: and speakership election for 34th Congress, 186–88, 189, 190; and standing committees of 34th Congress, 201n13

Alabama, secession of, 243

Albany Argus, 113n8; on speakership election for 1849, 164, 165, 168n21

Albany Regency, 101, 102

Albert, Carl B., as Speaker, 294

Alcohol and Liquor Traffic Committee, in 69th Congress, 289, 290

Alexander, De Alva: on important committees, 141n73; on Rules Committee's decisions, 271n

Alford, Julius C.: and speakership election for 27th Congress, 130n44; on viva voce voting, 95

Alien and Sedition Act, 59, 60

Allen, Charles: committee assignment in 31st Congress, 169n; pledge to oppose slavery extension, 157n9; and speakership election for 31st Congress, 162

Allen, James C.: and certification of members-elect by Etheridge, 246; as Clerk, 213, 214, 226; and clerkship election of 36th Congress, 226

Allen, Thomas, 51t, 72; elected Printer, 87–90; printing contract secured by, 89n21

New York Evening Post, 113–14; on clerk-ship elections, 130; on speakership election for 1849, 158n9, 158n10, 164

New York Express, on Toombs motion, 158n12

New York Herald: on House committees of 34th Congress, 204; on Printer election for 34th Congress, 199, 200n9

New York Journal of Commerce: on speak-ership election for 31st Congress, 173; on William J. Brown, 161

New York State: organizational control of legislature, 311–12; party nominating caucuses in, 101; political divisions in, 68; postmaster appointments in, 162; and speakership election for 52nd Congress, 276, 278

New York Times: on binding party caucus, 252–53; on chaplain nomination for 51st Congress, 268n46; on Clerk election in 32nd Congress, 175n31; on Clerk election in 34th Congress, 194; on Clerk election in 36th Congress, 226n51; on Fuller's candidacy for speakership, 180n50; on Longworth's speakership, 287; on officer elections in 33rd Congress, 176; on Printer election in 34th Congress, 197, 199; on Printer election in 36th Congress, 233n54, 235n60; on Sergeant at Arms election for 34th Congress, 195; on speak-ership election in 34th Congress, 181, 182n56; on speakership election in 52nd Congress, 276, 277, 278; on speakership election in 68th Congress, 286; on stand-ing committee appointments in 36th Con-gress, 231; on Wright as "lunatic," 260n

New York Tribune: on "Bleeding Kansas," 206; on Fuller's candidacy for speaker-ship, 189

Nicholas, Mathias, and Sergeant at Arms election for 34th Congress, 195

Nicholson, A. O. P., 51t

Nisbet, Eugenius A., and speakership elec-tion for 26th Congress, 123n

Niven, John, on Van Buren and Polk speak-ership, 90n23

Nixon, John T.: and congressional elections of 36th Congress, 212n27; and speaker-ship election for 36th Congress, 217, 219, 220, 220n45, 223–24

NOMINATE scores, 18–21

nominating caucus. *See* caucus nominations

nomination politics, post-Civil War, xv

North American and United States Gazette, on Democratic caucus activity, 175n31

North Carolina: and congressional elections of 1856–57, 210n23; secession of, 243

Northern Democrats. *See* regionalism

nullification theories: and voting on viva voce resolution, 84–85, 92–93, 95–99. *See also* states' rights

Nullifiers, and viva voce voting resolution, 83–86, 92

O'Donnell, James, and chaplain nomination for 51st Congress, 267n45

officers, election of, 272, 273; of 39th Con-gress, 249; in 40th Congress, 249; in 52nd Congress, 278; elimination of patronage positions in 62nd Congress, 283; and re-volt against Speaker Cannon, 281. *See also* patronage

officers, selection of, 78; for 37th Congress, 244; for 38th Congress, 247–48; binding party caucus in, 242–43; effect of viva voce voting on, 100–102; and majority party caucus, 248; organizational cartel controlling, 3; party caucus role in, 242–43; post-Reconstruction era, 243; and re-gionalism, 243

Ogle, Charles: as committee chair, 127t; and speakership election for 26th Congress, 119

Ohio, and speakership election for 52nd Congress, 276, 278

Oklahoma, as "Southern" state, 293n35

Oliver, Andrew, as committee chair, 203

O'Neill, Thomas P. "Tip," as Speaker, 294

Ordway, Nehemiah: and Sergeant at Arms election for 38th Congress, 247, 247n12; and Sergeant at Arms election for 39th Congress, 249n14; and Sergeant at Arms election for 40th Congress, 249n14; and Sergeant at Arms election for 41st Con-gress, 249n15; and Sergeant at Arms elec-tion for 42nd & 43rd Congresses, 250n16

Oregon: certification of members-elect by Etheridge, 246, 247; entrance into Union, 208n19

Oregon border question, British position on, 135

O'Reilly, Daniel, 77n4; and speakership elec-tion for 46th Congress, 258n28, 259, 259n31

organizational cartel, 16, 102, 150, 271, 273, 320–21, xv; in agenda-setting, 242; break-

Ruffin, Thomas, and Printer election for 36th
Congress, 235
Rules Committee, 36, 273; in 31st Congress,
169; in 47th Congress, 270; in 48th Congress, 265; in 68th Congress, 289; of 69th
Congress, 287, 287n23, 288; appointments to all other steering committees,
317; assignment of members to, 302;
committee assignments of, 267; and Conservative Coalition, 301; expansion of
membership of, 281; procedural authority
of, 270, 271; Speaker as chair of, 267n43,
281; support of committee decisions,
271n
rules governing House proceedings, 38–39
runoff elections for Speaker, in 36th Congress, 216

Sabin, Alvah, as committee chair, 202
Saltonstall, Leverett: as committee chair,
127t; on viva voce voting, 95
Sargent, Nathan, 140; and Printer elections
for 34th Congress, 197
Saturday Evening Post, 117
Sawtelle, Cullen, as committee chair, 169
Sayler, Milton, and presidential election of
1876, 255
Schafer, John C., committee assignment of,
290
Schenck, Robert C.: committee assignment
in 30th Congress, 142; as committee
chair, 250; Toombs motion opposed by,
158n12
Schneider, George J.: committee assignment
of, 288, 290; and Republican caucus of
1925, 286; and speakership election of
72nd Congress, 293
Schwartz, John: and clerkship election for
36th Congress, 226; and speakership election for 36th Congress, 215, 219, 225n
Scott, Charles, and speakership election for
36th Congress, 216
Scott, Harvey D., and speakership election
for 34th Congress, 182n56
Scranton, George W., and speakership election for 36th Congress, 217, 218, 220,
221n45, 223–24
Seaton, William Winston, 48n24, 51t, 52; as
Printer, 53, 67, 71, 72, 82; and Printer
election for 22nd Congress, 82; and
Printer election for 25th Congress, 88, 89;
and Printer election for 26th Congress,

128; and Printer election for 27th Congress, 131–32; and Printer election for
28th Congress, 133; and Printer election
for 36th Congress, 233, 234; Whig Party
supported by, 82n11
secession of Southern states, 109, 241, 243;
and amnesty for former Confederate soldiers, 253; slavery issue tied to, 78
Second Party System, 3, 53, 81, 272, xiii; and
Compromise of 1850, 174; and Congressional elections, 191–92; efficiency of election process under, 153–54; evolution of,
9; interregional coalitions underlying, 102;
and Kansas-Nebraska Act, 177; party development during, 9–10; and party nominating caucus, 171; and slavery, 152; slavery issue during, 154; and speakership
election for 31st Congress, 171
Secretary of the Senate, Forney as, 244n5
secret ballot, 4, 14, 21, 73, 76–77, xiii; attempts to reinstate, 97–100; defections
within party ranks, 77, 78; evidence of,
17; and majority party strength, 73–75;
for Massachusetts Speaker, 76n3; and
party-building, 83; Printer elected by, 67;
recording of, 56; and regionalism, 104;
and speakership election for 46th Congress, 257n
sectionalism, and speakership election in
26th Congress, 124–25
Seddon, James A.: and speakership election
for 29th Congress, 134n54; and speakership election for 31st Congress, 159, 160,
162
Sedgwick, Theodore, 13, 59; balloting for,
57–58; as partisan leader, 60n, 61; speakership of, 60, 61, 64
Senate: agenda-setting in, 307; committee
appointments in, 307–8; majority party's
role in, 307–8; minority rights in, 306–7;
organizational cartel in, 306–10; patronage opportunities, 307; president pro tempore of, 307; previous-question motion
in, 309n; vice president as presiding officer of, 307, 308
Senate Committee on Printing, audit of GPO
by, 236n62
Senate Conference of 1925, 286n21
Senate Printer: of 33rd Congress, 176n37;
allegations of corruption in 36th Congress, 231; bidding system for, 135; return
to elective position, 135

<small>Princeton Studies in American Politics</small>
HISTORICAL, INTERNATIONAL, AND COMPARATIVE PERSPECTIVES
Ira Katznelson, Martin Shefter, and Theda Skocpol, Series Editors

Fighting for the Speakership: The House and the Rise of Party Government
by Jeffery A. Jenkins and Charles Stewart III

*Three Worlds of Relief: Race, Immigration, and the American Welfare State from
the Progressive Era to the New Deal* by Cybelle Fox

Building the Judiciary: Law, Courts, and the Politics of Institutional Development
by Justin Crowe

Still a House Divided: Race and Politics in Obama's America
by Desmond S. King and Rogers M. Smith

The Litigation State: Public Regulations and Private Lawsuits in the United States
by Sean Farhang

*Reputation and Power: Organizational Image and Pharmaceutical Regulation at
the FDA* by Daniel Carpenter

Presidential Party Building: Dwight D. Eisenhower to George W. Bush
by Daniel J. Galvin

*Fighting for Democracy: Black Veterans and the Struggle against
White Supremacy in the Postwar South* by Christopher S. Parker

The Fifth Freedom: Jobs, Politics, and Civil Rights in the United States, 1941–1972
by Anthony Chen

Reforms at Risk: What Happens after Major Policy Changes Are Enacted
by Eric Patashnik

*The Rise of the Conservative Legal Movement: The Long Battle for
Control of the Law* by Steven M. Teles

Why Is There No Labor Party in the United States? by Robin Archer

*Black and Blue: African Americans, the Labor Movement,
and the Decline of the Democratic Party* by Paul Frymer

*Political Foundations of Judicial Supremacy: The Presidency, the Supreme Court,
and Constitutional Leadership in U. S. History* by Keith E. Whittington

*The Transformation of American Politics: Activist Government and the Rise of
Conservatism* edited by Paul Pierson and Theda Skocpol

Disarmed: The Missing Movement for Gun Control in America by Kristin A. Goss

Printed in the USA
CPSIA information can be obtained
at www.ICGtesting.com
JSHW021803160724
66513JS00005B/50